Police Psychology

Police Psychology
New Trends in Forensic Psychological Science

Edited by

Paulo Barbosa Marques

Inspector
Immigration and Borders Service (SEF)
Porto, Portugal

Mauro Paulino

Mind, Institute of Clinical and Forensic Psychology
Lisbon, Portugal

ACADEMIC PRESS
An imprint of Elsevier

ELSEVIER

Academic Press is an imprint of Elsevier
125 London Wall, London EC2Y 5AS, United Kingdom
525 B Street, Suite 1650, San Diego, CA 92101, United States
50 Hampshire Street, 5th Floor, Cambridge, MA 02139, United States
The Boulevard, Langford Lane, Kidlington, Oxford OX5 1GB, United Kingdom

Police Psychology

Notices

Practitioners and researchers must always rely on their own experience and knowledge in evaluating and using any information, methods, compounds or experiments described herein. Because of rapid advances in the medical sciences, in particular, independent verification of diagnoses and drug dosages should be made. To the fullest extent of the law, no responsibility is assumed by Elsevier, authors, editors or contributors for any injury and/or damage to persons or property as a matter of products liability, negligence or otherwise, or from any use or operation of any methods, products, instructions, or ideas contained in the material herein.

ISBN: 978-0-12-816544-7

Publisher: Stacy Masucci
Acquisition Editor: Elizabeth Brown
Editorial Project Manager: Fernanda A. Oliveira
Production Project Manager: Sreejith Viswanathan
Cover Designer: Matthew Limbert

Working together to grow libraries in developing countries

www.elsevier.com • www.bookaid.org

The Editors would like to dedicate this book to their families.

Contents

PART I Psychology in police culture and law enforcement agencies

PART II Psychology applied to policing issues

Notes on editors

Paulo Barbosa Marques

Paulo Barbosa Marques is a chartered clinical and forensic psychologist and a law enforcement officer. He began his law enforcement career serving as a frontline police officer in the Polícia de Segurança Pública (PSP) and later as a criminal investigator at the Criminal Investigation Department - Organized Crime Brigade. Paulo is now an inspector at the Serviço de Estrangeiros e Fronteiras (SEF), the Portuguese Immigration and Borders Service. He holds a Master's in Law and Security from the Faculty of Law - NOVA University of Lisbon, a postgraduate diploma in Internal Security, and specialized training in forensic psychological assessment and criminal investigation. Over the past years, his research has focused on the police officers, prosecutors and judges perceptions of investigative interviewing operational practices and training needs in Portugal. Paulo is a founding member and a former Secretary-General of the Portuguese Society of Psychiatry and Psychology of Justice and an International Investigative Interviewing Research Group (iIIRG) Regional Champion for Portugal. Paulo regularly presents at conferences to both academics and practitioners. He is a co-editor of *Psychopathy and Criminal Behavior: Current Trends and Challenges*.

Mauro Paulino

Mauro Paulino is currently a coordinator at Mind, Institute of Clinical and Forensic Psychology (Lisbon, Portugal). He is also a forensic psychologist consultant at the Instituto Nacional de Medicina Legal e Ciências Forenses, I.P. (Gabinete Médico-Legal e Forense Península Setúbal). Mauro received his Master's degree in Legal Medicine and Forensic Sciences at the University of Lisbon, Faculty of Medicine, completing his research in the field of spousal violence. He is a PhD student of Forensic Psychology at the Faculty of Psychology and Education Sciences, University of Coimbra (Portugal). He is also a member of the Center for Research in Neuropsychology and Cognitive Behavioral Intervention (CINEICC) and the Psychological Assessment and Psychometrics Laboratory (PsyAssessmentLab). He is an author and coordinator of several books and is a guest lecturer at various national and international universities.

About the contributors

Michael G. Aamodt

Dr. Mike Aamodt is a Principal Consultant for DCI Consulting Group, Inc. Prior to working for DCI, Mike spent 26 years as a professor of Industrial/Organizational Psychology at Radford University. He received his BA in psychology from Pepperdine University in Malibu, California, and both his MA and PhD from the University of Arkansas. Mike has published several books in the human resources area, published over 60 research articles and book chapters, and presented over 140 papers at professional conferences.

Bruce A. Arrigo

Bruce A. Arrigo, PhD, is a Professor of Criminology, Law and Society, and of Public Policy at the University of North Carolina—Charlotte. He is a Fellow of the American Psychological Association and the Academy of Criminal Justice Sciences. He is the recipient of Lifetime Achievement Awards from divisions of both the American Society of Criminology and from the Society for the Study of Social Problems. He began his professional career in community service, advocating for the homeless mentally ill.

Eric Beauregard

Eric Beauregard is a Professor in the School of Criminology at Simon Fraser University (Canada). While completing his PhD in criminology at the University of Montreal, Dr. Beauregard worked for Correctional Service of Canada where he was responsible for the assessment of individuals convicted for sexual crimes. Dr. Beauregard has published more than 150 articles and/or book chapters in the field of sexual violence and policing. His main research interests focus on sexual homicide, the crime-commission process, typologies, and the criminal investigation. Dr. Beauregard has also provided training on sexual crimes to law enforcement agencies around the world.

Lynne Bibeau

Lynne Bibeau is a forensic psychologist with the Sûreté du Québec—Quebec Provincial Police. From Intelligence Service to Behavioral Sciences Unit which includes support to investigations and police interviews; she is on the Crisis/Hostage Negotiation Team. She is teaching at the Quebec National Police Academy. Threat Assessment specialist—on the Board of Directors of the Canadian Association of Threat Assessment Professionals (CATAP). Lynne Bibeau is an author of a few articles, chapters, and a French book on threat and risk assessment in different contexts of violence.

Daniel M. Blumberg

Daniel M. Blumberg, Ph.D. is a licensed clinical psychologist who has spent more than three decades providing all facets of clinical and consulting psychological services to numerous local, state, and federal law enforcement agencies. He is the director of The POWER Project (policepowerproject.org). In addition to his expertise in workplace stress prevention and trauma recovery, Dr. Blumberg is an authority on the selection, training, and clinical supervision of undercover operatives. His research interests include police integrity, the moral risks of policing, and programs to improve relations between the police and the community.

Susan E. Brandon

Susan E. Brandon, PhD, is a consultant to industry and the US government on science-based investigative interview techniques. She served for 8 years as the Research Program Manager for the US government's High-Value Detainee Interrogation Group (HIG), where she was instrumental in setting up a science-based training program on interviewing techniques. She also was Chief for Research of the Behavioral Science Research Program at DIA, Program Chief in Affect and Bio-behavioral Regulation at the National Institutes of Health, and Assistant Director at the White House Office of Science and Technology Policy (OSTP). She served as Visiting Scientist at the American Psychological Association after 15 years as a faculty member in the Behavioral Neuroscience Division of the Department of Psychology at Yale University.

JoAnne Brewster

JoAnne Brewster, PhD, ABPP (Police and Public Safety Psychology), is a professor of Psychology at James Madison University. She has served as president, secretary, and membership chair of the Society for Police and Criminal Psychology (SPCP). She is a member of the Psychological Services Section of the International Association of Chiefs of Police (IACP-PPSS), a founding Board Member of the American Board of Police and Public Safety Psychology (ABPPSP), past President of the American Academy of Police and Public Safety Psychology (AAPPSP), and a member of the Council of Organizations in Police Psychology (COPP).

Julien Chopin

Julien Chopin, PhD, is a researcher at the International Centre for Comparative Criminology at the University of Montréal and an associate member of the Terrorism, Violence and Security Institute Research Centre at Simon Fraser University. His research focuses on victimological and criminological analysis of sexual offending. Some of his most recent work has appeared in Child Abuse and Neglect, Journal of Criminal Justice, Sexual Abuse, Journal of Interpersonal Violence, and Criminal Justice & Behavior.

Anna Corbo Crehan

Anna Corbo Crehan, PhD, is a Senior Lecturer at Charles Sturt University's Australian Graduate School of Policing and Security and former Presiding Officer of that University's Human Research Ethics Committee. She is a philosopher who teaches and researches in the areas of police ethics, professional ethics more generally, and research ethics. She has published papers on topics including obedience to authority, policing vulnerable people, policing domestic violence and procedural justice, professional boundaries, and ethics in policing.

Sarah Creighton

Sarah Creighton retired from the San Diego Police Department in February 2017 as an assistant chief. In 2011, she developed the Department's first wellness unit and center, providing leadership and a vision for employee help resources. Sarah holds a bachelor's degree in Liberal Studies and a master's degree in Human Behavior. She is a certified hypnotherapist, officer wellness technical advisor, management training coordinator, and currently volunteers for COPLINE—a 24-hour national crisis hotline for law enforcement.

Gary Dalton

Gary Dalton is a lecturer in Criminal Psychology at the Institute of Criminal Justice Studies at the University of Portsmouth. The main focus of his work is frontline communication with the emergency services and the use of body worn video. In addition, he has collaborated on research projects focusing on, eyewitness memory, face recognition, and lie detection. He is also a member of the Centre of Forensic Interviewing.

Ask Elklit

Ask Elklit, MPsych, is Professor of clinical psychology at the Institute of Psychology at the Southern Danish University and director of the National Centre for Psychotraumatology. He is a licensed psychologist and psychotherapist. Professor Elklit was the cofounder of the first Danish center for rape victims and has conducted research on many trauma types and populations (maltreated children, victims of violence, disasters, workplace violence, serious illnesses, and war). He also studied trauma rehabilitation and trauma in various cultures.

Ivar A. Fahsing

Dr. Ivar A. Fahsing is a Detective Chief Superintendent and Associate Professor at the Norwegian Police University College. He has published widely in the field of investigative management and decision-making, investigative interviewing, eyewitness testimony, forensic psychology, detective skills, expert performance, knowledge management and organised crime. He is used as expert-witness in courts and has for many years conducted training of law-enforcement personnel, intelligence officers, and civilian partners in Scandinavia, Europe, Africa, Asia, United Nations, etc. He has 15 years of experience as a homicide detective in the Oslo Police department and at the National Criminal Investigation Service of Norway.

David P. Farrington

David P. Farrington, O.B.E., is Emeritus Professor of Psychological Criminology at Cambridge University. He has been President of the American Society of Criminology, President of the European Association of Psychology and Law, and President of the British Society of Criminology. He has received many prizes and awards, including the Stockholm Prize in Criminology. His major research interest is in developmental criminology, and he is Director of the Cambridge Study in Delinquent Development, which is a prospective longitudinal survey of over 400 London males from age 8 to age 61. In addition to 866 published journal articles and book chapters on criminological and psychological topics, he has published 117 books, monographs and government publications, and 163 shorter publications (total = 1,146). According to GoogleScholar on March 10, 2021, his publications have been cited a total of 113,271 times, and 750 of his works have been cited at least 10 times each.

Bryanna Fox

Dr. Bryanna Fox is an Associate Professor of Criminology at the University of South Florida. Dr. Fox earned her PhD from Cambridge University and is a former FBI Special Agent. Dr. Fox's research on psychological risk factors for criminal behavior and evidence-based policing has been recognized with the 2014 Excellence in Law Enforcement Research Award from the International Association of Chiefs of Police and 2017 Early Career Award from the ASC Division of Developmental and Life-Course Criminology.

Naomi Glover

Dr Naomi Glover is a Clinical Psychologist who completed her Doctorate in Clinical Psychology at University College London. As part of her thesis, she worked with Dr David Turgoose and Dr Lucy Maddox to develop training for the London Metropolitan Police which focused on the recognition of posttraumatic stress disorder (PTSD) and trauma in people who have been sexually assaulted as well as the impact of burnout, secondary trauma, and compassion fatigue on police officers. Naomi is currently working for the United Kingdom's National Health Service in a service for people experiencing psychosis.

Jane Goodman-Delahunty

Jane Goodman-Delahunty, JD, PhD, is a Professor at Newcastle Law School, University of Newcastle and a Member of the NSW Civil and Administrative Tribunal.

Her empirical legal studies promote evidence-based practices to enhance justice. She is a Fellow of the American Psychological Association, past president of the American Psychology-Law Society and the Australian and New Zealand Association of Psychiatry, Psychology and Law, a former editor of *Psychology, Public Policy, & Law*, and was a NSW Law Reform Commissioner for 11 years.

Ilvy Goossens

Ilvy Goossens is a doctoral student in the forensic psychology-law program at Simon Fraser University (Canada) and a graduate research assistant with the Provincial Health Services Authority. Her overarching research interests focus on the intersection between mental health and the criminal justice system (e.g., complex concurrent disorders, trauma-informed care, risk assessment, postdischarge patient well-being). Her doctoral work focuses on risk, health and social justice issues around individuals in the correctional system. She is also a coauthor of the DIARI (Decision-making in Abusive Relationships Interview: Nicholls, Hilterman, & Goossens, 2016), an interview guide to collaborate on safety planning with women in abusive relationships.

Lea Katrine Jørgensen

Lea Katrine Jørgensen is a graduate student at the Institute of Psychology at the University of Southern Denmark. She has been working at the National Centre of Psychotraumatology in Denmark for three years and has worked on multiple research projects including a mapping of resources at the Nordic centers for rape victims. She is currently working on a project mapping psychological sequalae among Danish stalking victims with a special focus on Posttraumatic Stress Disorder and Complex Posttraumatic Stress Disorder.

Chuck Kaye

Chuck Kaye is currently the Chief of Police for the city of Coronado, California. Chief Kaye has more than 30 years of public safety experience serving in both large and small police departments. He first joined the San Diego Police Department in 1986. He worked various assignments in patrol, administration, and investigations. He retired as an assistant chief. He worked as a captain with the San Diego State University Police Department for less than a year before joining the Coronado Police Department. Chief Kaye earned his undergraduate degree from San Diego State University and later obtained a master's degree in Public Administration from National University.

Mark Kebbell

Mark Kebbell is Professor of Forensic Psychology at the School of Applied Psychology. He is a Registered Psychologist in Australia and a Chartered Forensic Psychologist in the United Kingdom. He is the Queensland President of the Australian New Zealand Association of Psychology, Psychiatry and Law. His research and practice concerns risk assessment and investigations.

Caroline Logan

Caroline Logan is Lead Consultant Forensic Clinical Psychologist in Greater Manchester Mental Health NHS Foundation Trust and also an Honorary Senior Lecturer at University of Manchester, England. She has worked as a researcher and as a clinician in forensic mental health and criminal justice services for over 20 years. Dr Logan has on-going research and practice interests in the areas of risk and threat assessment and management and violent extremism.

Lucy Maddox

Dr Lucy Maddox is a consultant clinical psychologist and writer. After working for 13 years in the United Kingdom's National Health Service, mostly with children, young people, and their families, she now works in a mix of third sector organisations. She is currently undertaking further study in organisational psychology and has a particular interest in compassion fatigue and ways to prevent and reduce it. Lucy has researched compassion fatigue in UK police settings.

Becky Milne

Becky Milne is a Professor of Forensic Psychology at the Institute of Criminal Justice Studies at the University of Portsmouth. The main focus of her work over the past 20 years concerns the examination of police interviewing and investigation. Jointly with practitioners, she has helped to develop procedures that improve the quality of interviews of witnesses, victims, intelligence sources, and suspects of crime across many countries. She is also the Director of the Centre of Forensic Interviewing, which is an internationally recognized centre of excellence for investigative interviewing that brings together research, teaching, and innovation activities.

Stephen J. Morewitz

Stephen Morewitz is a Lecturer at the Department of Justice Studies, San Jose State University. Among others, his teaching and research focuses on the delivery of health care and violence research. He is President of the consulting firm, Stephen J. Morewitz, PhD, and Associates. He is the President of Forensic Social Sciences Association, past Chair of the Society for the Study of Social Problems, Crime and Delinquency Division, and an award-winning researcher and author of more than 100 publications. He is the author of the award-winning book *Kidnapping and Violence: New Research and Clinical Perspectives*.

Konstantinos Papazoglou

Dr. Konstantinos Papazoglou, PhD, CPsych is a licensed psychologist (clinical, police, & forensic) and researcher. He is the founder and director of the ProWellness Inc., a division of his psychology professional corporation, in Toronto, Canada primarily aimed to provide mental health services to first responders. In addition, he is also the director of the POWER Institute and the principal founder and vice-president of the POWER Project: A non-profit public benefit corporation in San Diego, California. He recently completed his appointment as a postdoctoral scholar at Yale University School of Medicine. He earned his doctoral degree (PhD) in psychology (clinical - forensic area) as Vanier Scholar at the University of Toronto (UofT). He is a former police captain of the Hellenic Police Force and European Police College and he holds a master's degree in applied psychology from New York University (NYU) as Onassis Scholar. In addition, he is affiliated researcher with the Loss, Trauma, and Emotion Lab at Teachers College, Columbia University of New York. His research work focuses on performance, wellness, and resilience promotion among law enforcement officers. He presented to many major conferences and he published numerous articles to scholarly journals and book chapters.

Karl Roberts

Karl Roberts is a forensic psychologist and is a Consultant in policing for the World Health Organization and Professor and Chair of Policing and Criminal Justice at Western Sydney University, Australia. His areas of expertise are within the field of violence prevention and police processes with a focus upon violence risk assessment and risk management, health security, police investigative strategies, and police suicide. He spends much of his time advising and training police and other agencies on these issues.

Miguel Oliveira Rodrigues

Miguel Oliveira Rodrigues holds a PhD in Education. He is an Invited Teacher at the Social Service Institute (ISS) of the Lusophone University of Humanities and Technologies (ULHT), Lisbon, Portugal, and a Collaborating Researcher of the Center for Interdisciplinary Studies in Education and Development (CEIED) of the Lusophone University of Humanities and Technologies (ULHT), Lisbon, Portugal. He is a Sergeant of the Public Security Police (PSP), in the Proximity Policing Prevention Section of the Lisbon Metropolitan Command, Portugal, and Social Director of the Independent Union of Police Officers (SIAP/PSP), Portugal.

Ronald Roesch

Ronald Roesch is a Professor of Psychology and Director of the Mental Health, Law, and Policy Institute at Simon Fraser University. His research focuses on competency assessment of adults and youth, jail/prison mental health programs, and assessment and treatment of young offenders. He has published over 160 journal articles and chapters and 15 books. He has served as president of the American Psychology–Law Society (AP-LS) and the International Association of Forensic Mental Health Services

Nathan Ryan

Dr Nathan Ryan is a lecturer of Criminology at the Australian College of Applied Psychology, Melbourne, Australia. He has conducted research in forensic areas such as jury decision-making processes, investigative interviewing, and spatial memory in the context of homicide and rape cases. His current research examines ways of improving the Investigative Interviewing methods used in missing body homicide cases by combining the practical knowledge of Homicide investigators with the research knowledge of academics.

Michel Saint-Yves

Michel St-Yves is a forensic psychologist working with the Behavioural Analysis Unit at the Sûreté du Québec (Quebec Provincial Police). This unit is specialised in offering support in criminal investigations, both by profiling suspects and preparing investigative interviewing. He also teaches the psychology of investigative interviews and crisis negotiation at the École nationale de police du Québec (Quebec Police Academy) and is a lecturer at the Department of Criminology of the University of Montreal. He is the author of several scientific articles and books, including *Investigative Interviewing: The Essentials* (2014), *The Psychology of Crisis Intervention: for Law Enforcement Officers* (2012), and *The Psychology of Criminal Investigations: The Search for the Truth* (2008), Carswell (Thomson), Toronto.

Detlef Schröder

The Executive Director of CEPOL, Dr. h.c. Detlef Schröder was appointed in this position on 16 February 2018. Before, he was the Deputy Director of CEPOL since August 2009. Prior to joining CEPOL, he was a Senior lecturer at the German Police University in Muenster, with over 100 publications in national and international police and science journals and six book publications. Before taking up this position, he had a career within the Police of the Federal State of North Rhine-Westphalia up to senior police management positions, starting 1980. Dr. h.c. Schröder has a master's degree in Social Science, Law and Psychology, a master's degree in Police Management, and a BA in Public Administration.

Brian G. Sellers

Dr. Brian Sellers is an Associate Professor of Criminology at Eastern Michigan University. His research interests include juvenile justice policy, juvenile homicide, psychology and law, justice studies, restorative justice, school violence, and surveillance studies. He is the coauthor of *Ethics of Total Confinement: A Critique of Madness, Citizenship, and Social Justice*, and he is the coeditor of *The Pre-Crime Society: Crime, Culture, and Control in the Ultramodern Age*. He has also recently published in *Criminal Justice and Behavior, Behavioral Sciences and the Law, Contemporary Justice Review, Youth Violence and Juvenile Justice*, and *Children and Youth Services Review*. Dr. Sellers is a trained civil mediator, victim-offender conference facilitator, and peacemaking circle keeper.

Clifford Stott

Clifford Stott is a Professor of Social Psychology, the Director of the Keele Policing Academic Collaboration (KPAC), and the Dean for Research in the Faculty of Natural Sciences at Keele University in Staffordshire, United Kingdom. His work revolves around crowd psychology, collective conflict, and public order policing. Reflecting the influence of his work, he was awarded the 2014 First Prize for "Outstanding Impact on Public Policy" by the Economic and Social Research Council (ESRC). In 2015, the ESRC also acknowledged his work as one of its top 50 "Landmark Research" achievements of its 50-year history.

Jeff Thompson

Jeff Thompson, PhD, is an Adjunct Associate Research Scientist at the Molecular Imaging and Neuropathology Division of the New York State Psychiatric Institute at Columbia University Medical Center. He is a 16-year law enforcement veteran detective with the New York City Police Department (NYPD) and a former hostage negotiator. In his current role at the NYPD, Detective Thompson is currently the first-ever Mental Health and Wellness Coordinator. He is also a professor at Lipscomb University and New York University, researcher, and trainer.

David Turgoose

Dr David Turgoose is a clinical psychologist who trained at University College London. His doctoral thesis concerned compassion fatigue, burnout, and empathy in specialist police officers working with victims of sexual assault. His research interests include complex PTSD and developmental trauma, as well as burnout and compassion fatigue in helping professionals. In his clinical work, David provides specialist assessment and psychological therapy to children with a history of trauma through abuse and neglect at Great Ormond Street Hospital, London. David is also a lecturer in clinical psychology at the University of Leeds.

Dave Walsh

Dave Walsh is a Professor of Criminal Investigation at De Montfort University, Leicester. Prior to joining academia, he was (for over 20 years) an investigator in various UK government departments. He successfully defended his PhD in 2010 concerning the investigative interviewing of suspects. He has authored, coauthored, and edited over 70 peer-reviewed journal articles, book chapters, and books. He continues to engage with practitioners around the world in efforts to both help improve their practice as well as identify areas requiring further research.

Neil Williams

At the time of publishing, Neil Williams had recently completed writing his PhD thesis in Social Psychology at Keele University in England under the supervision of Professor Clifford Stott, Dr Sammyh Khan and Dr Masi Noor. Neil spent 8 years teaching English around the world before he returned to the United Kingdom to complete a master's degree in Criminal Justice at Durham University. While abroad, he taught in China, Syria, and Turkey and was heavily influenced by his experiences during the early stages of the Syrian Civil War and the Gezi Park Protests in Turkey. His current research looks at how the intergroup dynamics of conflict situations can affect intragroup behavioural norms and thus influence either the escalation or deescalation of conflict.

Foreword

Since the 1960s, police services seek support of psychologists on a variety of matters in policing and law enforcement, especially on the selection and well-being of their staff (Yuille, 1992).

Psychology as a science and the profession of psychologists went through very dynamic developments over the past decades. It is also clear every year that psychology is becoming increasingly more relevant for the police services and law enforcement in Europe. Over this time span the relationship between police services and psychologists has seen dynamic fluctuations. The progress of cooperation was by far not linear, and it took efforts from both professional sides so that today psychological know-how is not only fully accepted within police services but also seen as an important element in the landscape of police science.

This development required to a certain degree a change in the cultures of policing. Some stereotypes of old-fashioned "tough cop cultures" have been almost hostile against psychologists discussing their emotions.

Through many years of practical experience and professional successes, police services have changed their attitudes toward the science of psychology and value its potential for the improvement of various areas of police operations and structures.

Without a doubt, the above applies to the area of human resources management and education and training. As Executive Director of the European Agency for Law Enforcement Training (CEPOL), I frequently experience that questions related to psychological matters and the support provided to law enforcement services by psychologists are nowadays most relevant when it comes to the definition of training needs or the design and development of training services.

To understand the current relationship between law enforcement and psychology, knowledge of the contemporary context of policing and law enforcement in Europe is necessary. Only by valuing this context and perspective can we look ahead and estimate the potential of an even stronger engagement of psychological competence and knowledge in law enforcement organizations.

What are the current challenges of law enforcement services in Europe? What will be the main security threats in Europe that will become priorities of European services?

The Special Eurobarometer 464b from 2017 provides an interesting overview about the attitudes of citizens in the European Union regarding the security situation in Europe (see European Commission, 2017). While according to the results of this survey, around nine in ten respondents say that their neighborhood or their city are secure places to live in (91% and 90%, respectively), only 68% of the citizens regard the whole of Europe as a secure area. In 2017, 95% of the respondents considered terrorism as the biggest threat of the security, followed by organized crime (93%), while 87% considered cybercrime as important. Concerning the reaction of national authorities to tackle these threats, the replies in the survey have not been very positive. Only 63% have been of the opinion that their national authorities do enough in the fight against terrorism. In the field of cybercrime, only 49% of the respondents rated the response of their national authorities as sufficient. 92% of the respondents agree to a stronger cross-border cooperation by sharing information and data. From this survey, we can assume that while EU citizens feel safe in their close environment, to a certain degree, they feel unsafe when it comes to Europe. I would like to put the results of this survey in the contemporary context. In 2017, we had a peak of terrorist attacks across the EU Member States. Law enforcement services in the Member States had to deal with 33 terrorist attacks and arrested 705 suspects (Europol, 2018). It can be assumed that this context had a relevant impact on the attitudes of the mentioned survey. At the same time, Europe has been facing the continuous and considerable challenge of illegal migration.

When we look at the crime statistics across Europe, for the last few years we can find some quite positive facts, contrary to the attitudes of the citizens. The highlights from the Eurostat Crime Statistics (Eurostat, 2018) from July 2018 deliver examples of very positive developments. For instance, the figure of car thefts dropped by 36% in Europe between 2008 and 2016, while the number of reported robberies decreased by 24% between 2012 and 2016. Furthermore, the very sensitive area of home burglaries shows a 10% reduction as well from 2012 to 2016.

However, what can we conclude out of these figures? Can we be relaxed and reduce our efforts of ensuring the security of our citizens?

Unfortunately not at all. There are no concrete signs that the threat of terrorism is over for the European Member States. Home-grown terrorism, plus so called "lone wolf" actors and threats by foreign terrorist fighters returning from war zones to Europe, keep us fully alerted.

Illegal migration accommodated by organized criminal groups is one of the current major concerns of EU citizens and often dominates political debates in our countries.

The more traditional forms of serious and organized crime across borders bloom more in the shadow of public debates. However, the threats posed by these criminal groups should not be underestimated. These groups are constantly exploiting the weaknesses of the systems of cross-border cooperation. The criminal structures are using the huge profits from illegal activities to gain a more and more hybrid status by establishing "normal" companies. In some countries, these groups are able to build up their contacts in a very sophisticated way by using governance structures of cities and regions and in some cases by operating even at a state level.

Beside these rather old phenomena, law enforcement needs to be prepared for the reality of digital transformation. It is already clear by now that life in our societies has already been transformed to some extend by the new digital age. In addition, there is much more to come: Dark web, Internet of Things, driverless cars, big data analysis, artificial intelligence, relevance of social media are only some examples of the upcoming challenges. The huge real threats can already be seen, e.g., dark web as market place for drugs and weapons. However, there are also plenty of new opportunities for law enforcement, such as the full information provided to officers on the beat by interoperable data systems accessible via handheld devices like smartphones. These developments are expected to bring massive changes also into the day-to-day life of our services. What are our future competence profiles for recruitments? How will a basic qualification in the profession look like? How can we utilize fully the electronic means to provide learning opportunities to individual officers? How will the individuals be impacted by all these changes? Moreover, what should be done while these rapid changes take place with our officers already in service? It is clear that there are already many open and urgent questions regarding the digital future of law enforcement services.

Therefore, there is no valid argument to step back from our joint efforts in Europe to ensure as best as possible a safe future for our citizens.

Unquestionably, these future perspectives require a very strong support to law enforcement services by academics from different perspectives. Psychology is already in a very prominent position to support law enforcement communities and will certainly be even more so in the future.

Therefore, it is a great honor for me to introduce this important book that collects very valuable and prevailing contributions regarding the interaction between psychology and law enforcement, especially police services.

I would also like to provide an overview of the topics and different perspectives covered by the contributions.

The first contribution by Jane Goodman-Delahunty, Anna Corbo Crehan, and Susan Brandon is focused on the ethical practice of police psychology. They describe very precise the potential role conflicts for psychologist engaged into police services stemming from various factors, e.g., national security priorities and strong result-oriented pressure in investigations. Starting from the key principles of psychologists, they further elaborate on examples that went above the limitations of these ethical standards. They describe as one example the engagement of psychologists in the abusive interviews performed by the Central Intelligence Agency of the United States in Iraq. In their conclusions, they present concrete recommendations on how to reduce such role conflicts to ensure that the ethical standards are fully maintained.

In the second chapter, Michael G. Aamodt and JoAnne Brewster provide a detailed overview on the role of psychologists in the screening and selection of law enforcement applicants, covering different contemporary tools and instruments and how they are applied by psychologists in scenarios for "selecting in" or "screening out" applicants. Undoubtedly, using the best available instruments is of utmost importance for the selection of the right candidates for police services. At the same time, there is an important need to identify individuals with possible symptoms of psychopathology.

Daniel M. Blumberg, Konstantinos Papazoglou, Sarah Creighton, and Chuck Kaye elaborate on the incorporation of psychological skills in police training. The text demonstrates that in the complex environment of modern police training activities, essential psychological skills should play a vital role. They describe the key categories of well-being and community relations to be embedded into the training.

This approach gives a very valuable perspective for the critical evaluation and further development of training curricula.

The chapter of David Turgoose, Naomi Glover and Lucy Maddox describes the impact of professional stress on the social and psychological well-being of police officers. The specific profile of risks and challenges in the police profession also entails significant risks for the health of the officers. The authors elaborate how this can be counterbalanced by effective coping strategies and also describe the suitable preventive approaches from the perspective of law enforcement organizations.

In the next chapter, Lea Katrine Jørgensen and Ask Eklit bring stress into focus and highlight the effects of long-term exposure to critical incidents and trauma. The nature of police operations involves a variety of scenarios in which the officers engaged are exposed to multiple traumatic experiences and high stress levels. This chapter provides an overview of current research activities on this topic and describes alternative options for interventions at an organizational or individual level. Clinical interventions provide a wide variety of perspectives for further analysis and consideration.

While earlier chapters paid attention to the critical risk profile of the police profession, Karl Roberts in his contribution moves the discussion a step further to include the topic of suicides of police officers. This is unquestionably a real problem of many police services in Europe. The author provides a comprehensive overview of the factors leading to the ideation of suicide by officers and its fatal execution. Work-related problems and aspects of poor management could be the most relevant factors in this area. Karl Roberts also presents strategies to prevent suicides and explains how they can be applied in practice.

In the next chapter, Bruce Arrigo and Brian Sellers change the focus to psychological jurisprudence and its relevance for community psychology. After introducing the theory and methods of psychological jurisprudence, they elaborate on how psychological jurisprudence can bridge the gap between the science of police psychology and community psychology in practice.

In the next chapter, Neil Williams and Clifford Stott elaborate on the role of police psychology for public order policing. Public order policing in the environment of modern Western European Democracies is one of the biggest challenges for modern policing. As a neutral institution, Police always has to intervene between different parties on the turbulent edge of disputes in societies. After reflecting on the traditional concepts of repressive forms of crowd control inspired by the old term of mindless mob, the authors present the model of crowd management, based on current scientific results and refer in their analysis to actual examples from different European countries.

The contribution by Ronald Roesch and Ilvy Goossens includes valuable recommendations on how the interaction between police services and mentally ill persons can be improved. When officers have to find solutions to situations where mentally ill persons are involved, they are often overstrained and fail to respond appropriately. This could potentially have fatal consequences. Roesch and Goossens provide a good overview on the current research and literature on this issue, as well as concrete recommendations on how to improve the training for police staff.

The importance of good communications strategies to solve crisis and hostage situations is underlined in the contribution Michel St-Yves, Jeff Thompson, and Lynne Bibeau. They highlight how communication can be used as an excellent tool in extreme police operations. The intervention model that they explain includes risk assessment analysis and offers guidance for practical applications.

Interventions in cases of domestic violence are unfortunately one of the regular tasks of police services. Although over the last 20 years we have seen numerous very positive developments in the police services in Europe, there is still space for significant improvements. Mauro Paulino, Paulo Barbosa Marques, Miguel Rodrigues, and Stephen Morewitz discuss this important topic in their contribution. By illustrating this issue with figures and examples from Portugal, they provide a good overview on the current situation of police services in this field.

In the next chapter, Julien Chopin and Eric Beauregard elaborate on the contribution of psychology concerning the police reaction to sexual assaults. Regardless of the intensive academic research, in general on the topic of sexual assaults, it is still very difficult for the police to deal with such cases. Especially regarding the important formal requirement to provide evidence on the consent/nonconsent, excellent communication skills are necessary for the interaction with the victim and the perpetrator. The authors review some of the existing misconceptions and provide a very good orientation on indicators for false allegations and/or false statements. Finally, Chopin and Beauregard also explore how risk assessments can be best applied for the surveillance of sex offenders in communities.

At the opening of the third part of the book, Ivar Fahsing brings in the important perspective of continuous decision-making by the detectives involved in investigations. At numerous points throughout an investigation, the detectives have to make decisions on the next steps and course of action. They will use, as human beings, their repertoire of decision-making habits based on their experiences so far. Although in some cases this might be sufficient, it can be critical and misleading in others. Based on the theoretical and empirical background of scientists like Gollwitzer and Daniel Kahnemann, Fahsing provides an excellent insight into such decision-making processes and how they can be structured successfully within investigations.

In their contribution, Nathan Ryan and Mark Kebbell outline a model of how practitioners and academics in the field of police psychology can best work together. While we can still find situations where both parties, academics, and police practitioners, maintain their mutual stereotypes, these examples give a concrete perspective on how both parties can work very successfully together.

Caroline Logan focuses on how threat assessments are applied in police services. She provides an overview on the variety of concepts for threat assessment and their practical results. Police services apply threat assessments nowadays in numerous areas of policing, especially to identify the risks of violence. The author concludes her chapter with a review of some of the challenges faced in implementing best practice in threat assessment and management in law enforcement settings and by recommending multidisciplinary teamwork in this arena.

In the next chapter, Gary Dalton and Rebecca Milne focus on the important question of contamination of witness memories. The statements based on witness memories are often key to police investigations. For many years, studies have proven that these memories are vulnerable to contamination by a variety of factors. The authors focus on the role of first-line police officers and their interaction with the victims and present concrete recommendations on how contaminations of the witness memories can be prevented at this level.

How do police officers interview suspects? Are they only trying to bring the suspect to the point of confession? These are key questions in the contribution of Dave Walsh and Paulo Barbosa Marques. In Europe, Police services have recognized some models of interviewing techniques, such as PEACE, as a kind of standard. However, regardless of these models, police officers often have the attitude and aim to bring the suspect to the point of confession. Obviously, this approach can lead to false confessions and should be described as malpractice. The authors strongly advocate for an ethical interviewing style. Such an approach ensures the integrity and trustworthiness of Police services.

The final contribution in the book by Bryanna Fox deals with the current situation of offender profiling in police services and psychology. Profiling and policing is one of the most frequent topics in popular movies on TV. The author avoids this popular TV stereotype and offers an alternative solid view on the current situation, based on her professional experience. She elaborates based on the excellent meta-analysis from Fox and Farrington (2018) on what we learned out of 40 years offender profiling. By this analysis, this chapter provides a very profound overview on the results on research on the application and success of offender profiling in and for police services.

All the authors provide their contributions excellent and in-depth descriptions and analyses of the different aspects of police psychology, entailing a lot of food for thought. Regardless of this good and comprehensive overview, it is equally important to recognize that many aspects touched upon by the authors will require even more research efforts in the future. When we look back to the early start of police psychology in the 1960s it seems that this was, so far, a very impressive development. Taking into account the currently dynamic landscape of challenges for the future of the law enforcement services in Europe, it is clear that we need to be ready for even more efforts to bring police psychology in the interest of the services further.

I would like to express my gratitude and appreciation to the two editors of this important book, Paulo Barbosa Marques and Mauro Paulino. We are all well aware that the project of initiating, developing, and enabling such a comprehensive publication has been a challenge for both of you. I can imagine how busy you have been for several years until the publication of this book, and I would like to take this opportunity to congratulate you for your excellent contribution to improve the relation between law enforcement services and psychology and provide a clearer understanding of its importance in our daily work.

By bringing together this excellent group of authors, you have prepared a publication that provides readers with important knowledge on many aspects of the current situation of police and law enforcement psychology.

Detlef Schröder

References

European Commission. (2017). *Special Eurobarometer 464b: Europeans' attitudes towards security. June 2017. TNS opinion & social*. Brussels: European Commission. https://doi.org/10.2837/889432.

Europol. (2018). TE-SAT 2018: European Union Terrorism Situation and Trend Report 2018. *The Hague: Europol*. https://doi.org/10.2813/00041.

Eurostat. (2018). *Crime statistics*. Retrieved from: https://ec.europa.eu/eurostat/statistics-explained/index.php?title=Crime_statistics.

Fox, B., & Farrington, D. P. (2018). What have we learned from offender profiling? A systematic review and meta-analysis of 40 years of research. *Psychological Bulletin, 144*(12), 1247.

Yuille, J. C. (1992). Psychologists and the police. In F. Lösel, D. Bender, & T. Bliesener (Eds.), *Psychology and law: International perspectives* (pp. 205–211). Berlin: Walter de Gruyter.

Introduction
Police Psychology and the Impact of Psychological Science on Policing

Paulo Barbosa Marques and Mauro Paulino

Police psychology can broadly be defined as the application of the principles and methods of psychological science to assist law enforcement agencies, their professionals, and the relationship between the police and the communities they "protect and serve." This specialty area, where psychology is applied to policing, includes topics such as recruitment and selection of police applicants, fitness-for-duty evaluations, postshooting interventions, hostage negotiation, supporting criminal investigations (e.g., criminal profiling, investigative interviewing, threat assessment), police management development, among others. According to Aumiller et al. (2007), police and public safety psychology (PPSP) comprises four core domains (assessment, intervention, operational support, and organizational consultation) and more than 50 specific distinct proficiencies or specific professional activities.

We subscribe to the position that although police psychology is often regarded as part of forensic psychology, this is a reductive vision of such a broad and emerging specialty. Police psychology is a compilation of different types of psychology practice (Kitaeff, 2011). While accepting that the contribution of psychological services to the activity of a law enforcement agency may in some circumstances prove to be forensic in nature, many aspects of police psychology practice such as the psychological screening of police recruits are derived from industrial/organizational psychology and clinical psychology. Furthermore, interventions like a critical incident debriefing and psychological first aid or providing psychotherapy are more clinical in nature.

The definition of the core domains and proficiencies in the field of police psychology was a milestone in the development of the specialty; nevertheless, we advocate a perspective where police psychology should be viewed more by its scope than by the duties of the police psychologists in police organizations. In adopting this point of view, we do not run the risk of limiting such a rich and vast area to just a few aspects that are not representative of all the facets of police psychology.

For example, in a research conducted by Delprino and Bahn (1988), 336 police departments in the United States were invited to provide information on their use of 25 psychological services and found that more than half of the 232 departments that responded used some sort of psychological service, usually for assessing recruits and counseling (e.g., personal and family problems, job-related stress).

Moreover, the findings reported in Bartol's study of police psychologists' monthly work activities (1996) also show that these professionals spent most of their time in preemployment screening and counseling/treatment of personnel and their families.

This introduction aims to present police psychology not as a specialty that is reduced to the practices of psychologists in police organizations, but much more than that it intends to open the spectrum and to include the contributions that different specialties in Psychology lend to Policing. In this line of reasoning, we consider that the focus should be placed more on the manifestations of the psychological science in the day-to-day activities of law enforcement personnel and how this domain of knowledge can contribute to the effectiveness of police and public safety organizations in the essential function of the State to guarantee the security of the citizens.

Recent strategies designed to improve the law enforcement presence in various urban, rural, and suburban neighborhoods have relied upon community-oriented policing techniques (Arrigo & Shipley, 2005). Police psychologists can advance police-community relations by improving culturally competence community police training.

Additionally, law enforcement agencies find that communication skills and conflict resolution training are integral dimensions to effective police-citizen encounters. The benefits of involving police psychologists in police academy training are even more important when preparing cadets to better respond to people with mental disorders.

Thus, we considered the core domains already mentioned in the literature and included the communities as being one of the actors in interaction to present the following model (Fig. 1).

Provision of police psychological services stems back to psychological tests used in police selection in 1916 (Dietz & Reese, 1986), and then it picked up momentum in the 1950s (Zelig, 1987) and took a *quantum leap* forward in the 1980s, when police psychology started to be recognized as a distinct field and area of practice (Scrivner, 1994).

While the National Advisory Commission on Criminal Justice Standards and Goals report, in 1973, emphasized only one particular aspect of police psychology (the psychological assessment of all law enforcement applicants), within the next 10 years, police psychology continued to grow and other services followed (e.g., crisis/hostage negotiation, field consultation, critical incident intervention, etc.). Helping to maintain the effective functioning of police professionals through clinical intervention, training, research, and organizational consulting emerged as other aspects of PPSP.

Delprino and Bahn (1988) found that, in 1979, only 20% of agencies surveyed utilized these services, compared to over 50% of the departments queried in 1988.

It is impossible to determine precisely how many psychologists provide services to law enforcement professionals and agencies due to considerable overlap in membership in the professional organizations and an unknown number of police

FIGURE 1

Police psychology core domains and subpopulations served.

and public safety psychologists who have not joined one of the professional organizations. It has been estimated that as many as 4,500 psychologists conduct police and public safety preemployment evaluations in the United States (Corey, Cuttler, & Moss, 2009).

Forty years after the National Advisory Commission on Criminal Justice Standards and Goals report, Corey and Borum (2013) noted that 38 states had established preemployment or precertification requirements for the emotional, mental, or psychological health, functioning, fitness, or suitability of peace officers, and most agencies in the remaining 12 states conducted such evaluations in compliance with standards of the Commission on Accreditation for Law Enforcement Agencies.

Police psychology has assumed itself as a fully developed specialty, with its own literature, journals, and professional organizations whose scope of intervention ranges from the recruiting and screening of applicants to the retirement problems of police employees and all of the points in between (Kurke & Scrivner, 1995; Reiser, 1995; Trompetter, 2017).

According to Reiser (1995, p. xii):

The advent of police psychology has created a vital new area of theory and practice within the purview of applied psychology. Because it deals with the everyday stresses and strains, and with the life and death conflicts affecting the police and the larger community, police psychology operates on the cutting edge of what is happening in the community.

Scrivner and Kurke (1995), as well as Reese (1995), describe "three traditions of police psychology." The "first tradition" of police psychology was created by the applied research spurred by the 1968 Law Enforcement Assistance Administration (LEAA) and its predecessor, the Department of Justice's Office of Justice Programs, particularly two of its affiliated agencies, the National Institute of Justice and the Bureau of Justice Assistance.

According to Scrivner and Kurke (1995), the funding through LEAA grants allowed conducting the early research regarding the selection of law enforcement personnel. Many applied experimental and engineering psychologists contributed research, development, and operational analytic results to the LEAA program.

The roots of the first tradition originated from Lewis Terman's use in 1916 of the Stanford revision of the Binet-Simon scale that became known as the Stanford-Binet IQ Test for measuring intelligence with children (Terman et al., 1917). Louis Terman, using an abbreviated form of the Stanford-Binet Intelligence Scale, tested San Jose (CA) Police Department officers to assess their intelligence as a step toward instituting job-related criteria for police selection. Terman published his results in 1917 concluding that police positions apparently attracted individuals of below-average intelligence and that the education level of applicants for police officers positions was limited. As a result of Terman's research, police administrators became aware that intelligence testing could be potentially valuable as a selection tool (Bartol, 1996; Weiss & Inwald, 2010).

A contemporary of Terman, psychologist Louis Thurstone, soon followed his interest in the value of mental testing in the screening and selection of law enforcement personnel. Thurstone (1922) administered the Army Alpha Intelligence Test to assess 358 variously ranking officers in the Detroit Police Department and found that the police officers at all ranks scored below average on the scale. In fact, the more experienced the police officer was, the lower was his intelligence, since that patrolmen scored higher (mean IQ = 71.44) than their lieutenants (mean IQ = 57.80). Like Terman, Thurstone concluded that law enforcement agencies simply did not attract intelligent individuals and, on the other hand, police organizations were unable to keep the more intelligent individuals in their ranks as they eventually moved to other occupations, where their skills and intelligence were presumably better recognized (Bartol, 1996).

The recognition of the potential of psychological assessment in the screening and selection of police officers is evidenced by the increasingly recurrent adherence to this recruitment method by other departments. Another example of this trend is provided by the Los Angeles (CA) Police Department in 1954 when they administered an Minnesota Multiphasic Personality Inventory (MMPI), group Rorschach, projective drawing, and a clinical interview to police officer applicants (Weiss & Inwald, 2010).

Blau (1994) reported that before 1950 there were some early attempts to use "personality instruments" in the selection of police officers. These efforts for the first half of the century were important but generally reflected the efforts of academic or experimental psychologists venturing into the police psychology world, where they applied developing methodologies and assessment tools.

There was an increase in demand for psychological assessment in police selection due to societal and cultural shifts in the 1960s. For the past decades, the crime rate in the United States skyrocketed. In conjunction with the civil rights movement and other protests against the war with Vietnam, President Lyndon B. Johnson formed the Commission on Law Enforcement and Administration of Justice in 1965. The members of the commission were charged to determine the causes of criminal activity and advise on how and what society could do to reduce it. The Presidential Commission on Law Enforcement and the Administration of Justice report (1967) made it clear that it was imperative to implement reforms in personnel structure, officer selection and training, community relations, and overall management practices. The importance of assessing emotional stability in police officer candidates as well as the Commission's stress on selection and training was a milestone event for police psychology. As such, in 1973, the National Advisory Commission on Criminal Justice Standards and Goals published its recommendations on how to improve the task forces with specific recommendations for upgrading the quality of police personnel, including the recommendation that police agencies employ a psychological evaluation in the hiring process.

The focus on federally funded research and program development led to the "second tradition" in police psychology: the delivery of direct psychological services to police agencies (Reese, 1995; Srivner & Kurke, 1995). In the wake of the 1967 Presidential Commission on Law Enforcement and the Administration of Justice recommendations, several psychologists were drawn to provide comprehensive psychological services to law enforcement.

In December of 1968, Martin Reiser was selected by the Los Angeles Police Department (LAPD) as the first full-time, in-house police psychologist (Reiser, 1972). Reiser became what most consider being the "father of police psychology" because of his pioneering work in the specialty (Kurke & Scrivner, 1995; Reese, 1988; Trompetter, 2017).

Since that time, many psychologists and other mental health professionals have been employed by federal, state, and local law enforcement agencies or have been contracted to provide for full- or part-time psychological services to police organizations.

The first registered internship in police psychology took place in the LAPD in 1972. This was considered a training site for police psychologists and resulted in much sought after staff resources. Crime-related consultation was one of the growing activities that were mostly requested by detectives. This included the psychological profiling of suspects in major homicide and rape cases. Police psychologists also performed evaluations of threats against celebrities, politicians, and other notable public figures, as well as the assessment of the suitability of emotionally disturbed suspects for polygraph examination (Reiser, 1972, 1982).

The "third tradition" of police psychology arose in the late 1970s but blossomed in the 1980s with the largest influx of new specialists in the history of specialty. The "third tradition" had its origins in federal law enforcement agencies, where psychologists were engaged in behavioral science research or policy matters related to their agencies missions. Their activities included further development of selection testing and assessment; career development; program planning; and practical application of psychological knowledge to police operations such as hostage negotiations, criminal profiling, and methods to improve witness recall, to name but a few. While police selection had matured significantly by the 1980s with increasing acceptance of psychologists by law enforcement, agencies started asking for additional services including employee assistance for their officers, critical incident interventions following officer-involved shootings, field consultation for crisis negotiators team callouts, and other forms of operational and organizational consultation.

The beginning of specialty-specific professional groups and conferences for specialty-specific continuing education was accompanied by the growth of the specialty practice. Since graduate training in police psychology was unfortunately not available for the early adopters, the newly developed organizations and their events (e.g., conferences, seminars) provided the bulk of their specialty training.

In September 1984, the first and most important gathering of police psychologists ever assembled was hosted by the FBI Jim Reese, with the assistance of Harvey Goldstein (Reese, 1995). Never before had there been such an organized and concerted effort to highlight the specialty and bring together most of the professionals who were currently providing psychological services to law enforcement agencies across the United States.

While there have long been efforts to define the roles and scope of practice of police psychologists (Aamodt, 2000; Blau, 1994; Dietz, 2000; Kurke & Scrivner, 1995), only by the fall of 2007, it was possible to witness what was probably the most valuable endeavor toward providing the first comprehensive definition and description of the specialty, which was defined by the Police Psychology Core Domains and Proficiencies Joint Committee on Police Psychology Competencies. This committee was a joint effort between members of the International Association of Chiefs of Police, Police Psychological Services Section (IACP-PPSS); members of the Society for Police and Criminal Psychology (SPCP); and members of the American Psychological Association (APA), Division 18, Police & Public Safety Section. They identified 57 distinct tasks and proficiencies of police psychologists that were then separated into four core domains: assessment, intervention, operational support, and organizational consultation (Aumiller et al., 2007). In 2008, the Council of Organizations in Police Psychology (COPP) was formed as the specialty council to advance the interests of PPSP through the collaboration of the three main national police psychology organizations. The COPP successfully established PPSP as the 14th specialty board in the American Board of Professional Psychology on October 21, 2011, and prepared and submitted an application to APA that resulted in the official recognition of police psychology on July 31, 2013, as a specialty (it had been approved as a proficiency on August 13, 2008). This application, which was presented to APA in 2011, provided a comprehensive definition of police psychology (COPP, 2011, p.2):

> *Police and Public Safety Psychology is concerned with assisting law enforcement and other public safety personnel and agencies in carrying out their missions and societal functions with optimal effectiveness, safety, health, and conformity to laws and ethics. It consists of the application of the science and profession of psychology in four primary domains of practice: assessment, clinical intervention, operational support, and organizational consulting.*

The *assessment* domain comprises activities associated with the development, implementation, and appraisal of procedures for evaluating individuals, police officer candidates, officers, and administrators. The assessment procedures include methods as self-report questionnaires, interviews, performance tests, and case history reviews; they are used to make decisions about such things as recruitment, selection, and promotion. The *intervention* domain encompasses activities linked with the provision of clinical services to law enforcement personnel. These clinical services are intended to increase and promote the health and well-being of officers. The *operational* domain includes actions associated with supporting and advancing the work of police officers, including investigation and incident management. Finally, the *consulting* domain consists of procedures related to supporting and improving the administration of police organizations (Aumiller et al., 2007; Roesch, Zapf, & Hart, 2010). Table 1 presents some examples of different proficiencies within each of these four domains.

Police psychology has been given a bigger focus as a professional practice and as a research branch. The establishment of professional societies specialized in specific matters and conferences, specialized journals, peer-reviewed research and books dedicated to police psychology, and the study of the nature of psychological services in law enforcement agencies (e.g. Bartol, 1996; Delprino & Bahn, 1988) support the assumption of an ever-increasing focus in the different spheres of police psychology.

Although the contribution of psychological science is critical to the mission of law enforcement agencies and is now established to a degree where police organizations worldwide now employ psychologists as part of their available manpower, we can agree that the field would likely benefit from a better alignment between scientific research and the needs of those who practice it (Snook, Doan, Cullen, Kavanagh, & Eastwood, 2009).

In our view, law enforcement agencies can benefit from a more comprehensive and effective application of psychology to policing by adopting a collaborative insight where academics and practitioners cooperate (Sherman, 2013).

When we decided to bring this book into existence, our primary purpose was to gather a panel of experts in order to show how the different realms of police psychology incorporated scientific evidence—based knowledge and give the reader a genuine perspective of the impact of psychological research on policing.

Table 1 Core Domains and Specific Proficiencies of Police Psychology

Core Domain	Specific Proficiencies	
	Example	Description
Assessment Domain	Psychological fitness-for-duty evaluations of incumbents	Involves the psychological evaluation of an incumbent police officer's ability to safely and effectively carry out the essential functions of his or her position.
	Evaluations (medical) for high-risk, high-demand assignments	Psychological evaluations for police special assignments (e.g., SWAT, hostage negotiatior, undercover officer, etc.) to ensure that they meet minimum requirements for emotional stability or other standards.
	Test development	Development of psychologically-based tests or assessment instruments involves the conceptualization, design, construction and validation of psychometric assessment instruments, which typically are used for selection and/or assessment of individual strengths and weaknesses.
Intervention Domain	Individual therapy or counseling	In the law enforcement setting, this includes providing treatment or advice concerning a wide range of possible concerns related to the individual's goals, needs, values, attitudes, conflicts, personal and interpersonal styles, education and career choice, academic and work functions, and developmental and social challenges unique to law enforcement personnel.
	Critical incident early intervention	Critical incident early intervention—including debriefing, "psychological first aid", defusing, etc.—encompasses initial, immediate efforts to meet the needs of law enforcement officers impacted by a critical incident.
	Substance abuse treatment	Substance abuse treatment is an umbrella term used to refer to the processes of medical and/or psychotherapeutic treatment for dependency on psychoactive substances such as alcohol, prescription drugs, and illegal drugs of abuse, such as cocaine, heroin or methamphetamines.
Operational Domain	Psychological intelligence	Psychological intelligence encompasses a broad range of activities and involves the application of psychological knowledge, principles, and methods to aid police in criminal investigations. These activities can include gathering, organizing, integrating, or interpreting case information; advising or participating in witness, informant or suspect interviews; and specialized operational support.
	Criminal profiling	Criminal profiling involves the identification of personality, behavioral, and demographic factors characteristic of the perpetrators of particular crimes or criminal patterns.
	Threat assessments	Threat assessment is employed to evaluate and manage persons who are identified as possibly posing a risk of substantial harm to the assets or mission of the police agency. Threat assessment concerns itself with the factors that increase (risk factors) and decrease (protective factors) the likelihood of harm, as well as methods for minimizing or managing risk.
Consulting Domain	Organizational development	Organizational development program components frequently include, but are not limited to, leadership development training, employee problem-solving groups, content-based training programs, specialized training programs (e.g., management decision making, ethics, communication, field training/performance coaching, relationship/diversity training, etc.), evaluation of policies and procedures, and strategic planning.
	Executive consultation	Psychologists engage in consultation with agency executives for a variety of purposes including, but not limited to, personnel-related issues (selection, individual performance issues, interpersonal problems, etc.), leadership-related issues (style, impact, relationships, team building), organizational issues (agency mission and strategy, values, culture) general performance issues (coaching) and/or personal issues.
	Consulting-related education & training	Consulting psychologists provide education and training to assist agency personnel in optimizing their leadership, management, and supervisory effectiveness. The broad array of consulting psychology topics amenable to education and training efforts include organizational change, leadership transformation, ethical decision making, managing in a multicultural workforce, etc.

Source: Aumiller et al. (2007)

As Editors, we owe our contributors a very personal debt; each chapter has been developed systematically by the combined effort of skilled practitioners and researchers worldwide, focused on our main goal and designed to give the reader a pragmatic appraisal of where police psychology has impacted practice.

References

Aamodt, M. G. (2000). The role of the I/O psychologist in police psychology. *Journal of Police and Criminal Psychology, 15*(2), 8−10. https://doi.org/10.1007/BF02802660.

Arrigo, B. A., & Shipley, S. L. (2005). Family/community issues in policing. In B. A. Arrigo, & S. L. Shipley (Eds.), *Introduction to forensic psychology. Issues and controversies in crime and justice*. San Diego: Elsevier.

Aumiller, G. S., Corey, D., Allen, S., Brewster, J., Cuttler, M., Gupton, H., & Honig, A. (2007). Defining the field of police psychology: Core domains and proficiencies. *Journal of Police and Criminal Psychology, 22*, 65−76. https://doi.org/10.1007/s11896-008-9020-0.

Bartol, C. R. (1996). Police psychology: Then, now, and beyond. *Criminal Justice and Behavior, 23*(1), 70−89. https://doi.org/10.1177/0093854896023001006.

Blau, T. H. (1994). *Psychological services for law enforcement*. New York: John Wiley.

Corey, D. M., & Borum, R. (2013). Forensic assessment for high-risk occupations. In R. K. Otto, & I. B. Weiner (Eds.), *Handbook of Psychology: Forensic Psychology* (pp. 246−270). New Jersey: John Wiley & Sons.

Corey, D. M., Cuttler, M. J., & Moss, J. A. (2009, December). Pre-application discussion with the ABPP Board of Trustees regarding a proposed Specialty Board in police and public safety psychology. In *Presentation made to the Board of Trustees*. Chapel Hill, NC: American Board of Professional Psychology.

Council of Organizations in Police Psychology. (2011). *Petition to the American Psychological Association Commission on Recognition of Specialties and Proficiencies in Professional Psychology (CRSPPP) for the recognition of police and public safety psychology as a specialty in professional psychology*. Unpublished manuscript.

Delprino, R. P., & Bahn, C. (1988). National survey of the extent and nature of psychological services in police departments. *Professional Psychology: Research and Practice, 19*(4), 421−425. https://doi.org/10.1037/0735-7028.19.4.421.

Dietz, A. S. (2000). Toward the development of a roles framework for police psychology. *Journal of Police and Criminal Psychology, 15*(2), 1−7. https://doi.org/10.1007/BF02802659.

Dietz, P. E., & Reese, J. T. (1986). The perils of police psychology: 10 strategies for minimizing role conflicts when providing mental health service and consultation to law enforcement agencies. *Behavioral Sciences & the Law, 4*(4), 385−400. https://doi.org/10.1002/bsl.2370040404.

Kitaeff, J. (2011). History of police psychology. In J. Kitaeff (Ed.), *Handbook of police psychology* (pp. 1−59). New York: Routledge/Taylor & Francis Group.

Kurke, M. I., & Scrivner, E. M. (1995). *Police psychology into the 21st century*. Hillsdale, NJ: Lawrence Erlbaum.

National Advisory Commission on Criminal Justice Standards and Goals. (1973). *Report on Police*. Washington, DC: US Government Printing Office.

President's Commission on Law Enforcement and Administration of Justice. (1967). *The challenge of crime in a free society*. Washington, DC: US Government Printing Office.

Reese, J. T. (1988). Psychological aspects of policing violence. In J. T. Reese, & J. M. Horn (Eds.), *Police Psychology: Operational Assistance* (pp. 347—361). Washington, D.C: National Institute of Justice. Retrieved from https://www.ncjrs.gov/pdffiles1/Digitization/130933NCJRS.pdf.

Reese, J. T. (1995). A history of police psychological services. In M. I. Kurke, & E. M. Scrivner (Eds.), *Police psychology into the 21st century* (pp. 31—44). Hillsdale, NJ: Lawrence Erlbaum.

Reiser, M. (1972). *The police department psychologist*. Springfield, IL: Charles C. Thomas.

Reiser, M. (1982). *Crime-specific consultation* (pp. 53—56). The Police Chief.

Reiser, M. (1995). Foreword. In M. I. Kurke, & E. M. Scrivner (Eds.), *Police psychology into the 21st century*. Hillsdale, NJ: Lawrence Erlbaum.

Roesch, R., Zapf, P. A., & Hart, S. D. (2010). Police Psychology. In R. Roesch, P. A. Zapf, & S. D. Hart (Eds.), *Forensic Psychology and Law* (pp. 239—267). New Jersey: John Wiley & Sons.

Scrivner, E. M. (1994). *The role of the police psychology in controlling excessive force*. Washington, D.C: National Institute of Justice. Retrieved from https://www.ncjrs.gov/pdffiles1/Digitization/146206NCJRS.pdf.

Scrivner, E. M., & Kurke, M. I. (1995). Police psychology at the dawn of the 21st century. In M. I. Kurke, & E. M. Scrivner (Eds.), *Police psychology into the 21st century* (pp. 3—29). Hillsdale, NJ: Lawrence Erlbaum.

Sherman, L. W. (2013). The rise of evidence-based policing: Targeting, testing, and tracking. *Crime and Justice, 42*, 377—451. https://doi.org/10.1086/670819.

Snook, B., Doan, B., Cullen, R. M., Kavanagh, J. M., & Eastwood, J. (2009). Publication and research trends in police psychology: A review of five forensic psychology journals. *Journal of Police and Criminal Psychology, 24*(1), 45—50. https://doi.org/10.1007/s11896-008-9032-9.

Terman, L. M., Otis, A. S., Dickson, V., Hubbard, O. S., Norton, J. K., Howard, L., & Cassingham, C. C. (1917). A trial of mental and pedagogical tests in a civil service examination for policemen and firemen. *Journal of Applied Psychology, 1*(1), 17—29. https://doi.org/10.1037/h0073841.

Thurstone, L. L. (1922). The intelligence of policemen. *Journal of Personnel Research, 1*, 64—74.

Trompetter, P. (2017). A history of police psychology. In C. L. Mitchell, & E. H. Dorian (Eds.), *Police psychology and its growing impact on modern law enforcement*. Hershey, PA: IGI Global.

Weiss, P. A., & Inwald, R. (2010). A brief history of personality assessment in police psychology. In P. A. Weiss (Ed.), *Personality assessment in police psychology: A 21st century perspective* (pp. 5—28). Springfield, IL: Charles C. Thomas.

Zelig, M. (1987). Clinical services and demographic characteristics of police psychologists. *Professional Psychology Research and Practice, 18*(3), 269—275. https://doi.org/10.1037/0735-7028.18.3.269.

Psychology in police culture and law enforcement agencies

The ethical practice of police psychology

Jane Goodman-Delahunty, Anna Corbo Crehan and Susan Brandon

Introduction

This chapter reviews psychological research and demonstrates how policing practices informed by the tenets of procedural justice (PJ), a leading theory of contemporary policing, are consistent with psychologists' ethical principles. The global shift to evidence-based policing (EBP) has increased police reliance on psychological research on interrogation and interviews,[1] thereby engaging more psychologists in work with or for policing organizations. This topic is the focus of this chapter because in recent years, intelligence and investigative interviews have been "hot spots" for the role conflicts faced by psychologists working with military and policing agencies and have engendered controversy.

This chapter begins by reviewing issues raised about role conflicts when psychologists assist law enforcement with interviews. Recent history demonstrated that responses to national security priorities, result-oriented pressures, and cost sensitivity can lead to police practices which increase the risk that psychologists' collaboration will compromise their professional ethics. Analyses of the connections between these research findings and psychologists' ethical codes demonstrate the effectiveness of these strategies per se. They also provide a robust ethical vocabulary and literacy that can be extended beyond interviewing to psychologists' collaborative practice with police in other contexts. By mapping these links, the aim of this chapter is to offer a potential framework for behavioral scientists in policing contexts to develop their ethical literacy and so articulate and evaluate potential ethical issues in their practice.

Professional ethics codes and demands on police psychologists

As psychological services diversified, more psychologists were hired as consultants or employees by government agencies to provide services affecting the lives of many people (Koocher, 2009). Opportunities for police psychologists and police officers to

---

[1] The term "interrogation" is more commonly used in North American and some East Asian jurisdictions, whereas "interview" is more commonly used in Australian, British, European, and New Zealand practice. We use "interview" as a neutral umbrella term to avoid connotations of an accusatory or coercive procedure.

Police Psychology, Edited by Marques and Paulino. https://doi.org/10.1016/B978-0-12-816544-7.00001-2

work together increased. Indeed, some might argue that professionals from these two groups ought to work together, given the synergies between their areas of expertise. For instance, four key areas where behavioral scientists' contributions to national security counterintelligence operations expanded in the past decade were identified as (1) psychological risk assessment, (2) help in recruiting and training human sources, (3) help in managing the relationship between a case officer and his or her intelligence sources, and (4) consultation on the interrogation of an uncooperative source (Shumate & Borum, 2006).

Many police psychologists face difficult challenges as a result of the demands imposed by their employers. These have clearly been an aspect of police psychologists' work for some time. Over 30 years ago, 56 police psychologists were asked (among other things) "What ethical dilemmas have you experienced, if any, in providing psychological services to law enforcement agencies?" (Zelig, 1988, p. 336). Respondents identified: "confidentiality" (41%), "conflicts between the psychologists' professional standards and the needs of the organization" (13%), "dual relationships" (9%), "concerns about the use and administration of psychological tests" (4%), and "problems with the organization's overruling the recommendations of the psychologist" (4%) (p. 336). Importantly, these issues were conceptualized by Zelig as manageable by psychologists. The only specific recommendation was for psychologists to make "agreements" with their law enforcement colleagues "clarify[ing] the nature and direction of their loyalties and responsibilities and keep[ing] all parties informed of their commitments" to "neutralize many conflicts before they arise" (1988, p. 338).

Later, a more nuanced approach was advocated. Rather than focus on management of the challenges encountered, Ewing and Gelles, for instance, reasoned that since police psychologists are not acting in a "traditional" clinical role they therefore should not be held to "traditional" ethical standards:

> When serving as consultants to the military, an intelligence agency or law enforcement … psychologists and psychiatrists generally are not functioning in a traditional clinical role, do not have ultimate authority and responsibility for case management, and are not acting in the best interest of the individual being assessed. Indeed, in many instances, the professional acts with the knowledge that his or her input will likely have negative consequences for the individual in question (e.g., arrest, detention, prosecution, physical injury or even death)
>
> **Ewing & Gelles (2003), p. 96.**

Moreover, Ewing and Gelles argued that the ethical issues faced by clinical psychologists in these consultant roles were "peculiar" to those roles, arising out of the specific contexts in which those roles were undertaken (2003, p. 97). They identified these contexts as ones where psychologists might have no access to the individual on whom their input would impact, where they did interact with an individual but for purposes that were not (fully, or partially) disclosed to that individual, and/or where "certain aspects of the consultant's role are dictated in part by legal parameters outside the consultant's control" (2003, p. 97). On this view, psychologists undertaking these law enforcement roles and the like face a set of ethical issues different not only from those of their "traditional" clinical colleagues but also from those of colleagues engaged in other forms of nonclinical practice.

The ethical principles and standards of practice pertaining to this growing area of forensic consultation received little public discussion until the human rights abuses and interrogations conducted by the US military post-9/11 at Abu Ghraib and other American prisons in Iraq were publicized in 2003−04. Individuals who were suspected terrorists were transferred to CIA "black sites" (secret prisons) outside of US borders and subjected to enhanced interrogation techniques (EITs) authorized by President Bush (e.g., waterboarding; short-shackling; isolation; deprivation of sleep, light, and sound), based on "ticking time bomb scenarios". The infliction on detainees of individual abuse and torture was justified for the potential safety of greater numbers of innocent persons and national security.

Psychologists' contributions to these abuses shocked a great number of psychologists worldwide, including those working with law enforcement and similar organizations.[2] In 2005, the American Psychological Association (APA) convened a Presidential Task Force on Psychological Ethics and National Security to provide the sort of guidance that Ewing and Gelles contended was unavailable. The Task Force affirmed that "when psychologists serve in any position by virtue of their training, experience, and expertise as psychologists, the APA Ethics Code applies, … [and] was unambiguous that psychologists do not engage in, direct, support, facilitate, or offer training in torture or other cruel, inhuman, or degrading treatment" and emphasized psychologists' "unique position to assist in ensuring that these processes are safe and ethical for all participants" (APA Presidential Task Force, 2005, p. 1). The report clarified psychologists' roles in light of the APA Code of Ethics in effect at the time, offered a human rights framework and explicit guidance on 12 common sources of ethical confusion and conflict, and made recommendations to increase support in the future for psychologists working in national security-related settings, acknowledging that they often worked closely with other professionals from various disciplines.

One provision on resolving conflicts between ethical obligations and the law referred to APA Ethical Standard 1.02 (implemented in 2002), stating that psychologists "may adhere to the requirements of the law" and went on to advise that an ethical reason not to follow the law was adherence to international principles and

---

[2] There were military psychologists who pushed back against the abusive interrogation methods (e.g., James, 2008). Unfortunately, the fact that psychologists continued to provide counsel to interrogators appears to have overshadowed their efforts to train and support the use of alternative, non-abusive interrogation methods.

covenants of human rights (APA Presidential Task Force, 2005, p. 5). This Ethical Standard in the APA Code of Ethics, and consequently, the entire Task Force Report, became the source of controversy because it

> … *rejected the historic Nuremberg Ethic, [instead] stating that when facing an irreconcilable conflict between their "ethical responsibilities" and the state's authority, "psychologists may adhere to the requirements of the law, regulations, or other governing legal authority" (Section 1.02)*

Pope (2011), p. 153.

This standard was particularly vexing because the US had adopted more permissive definitions of torture than those applied in the international human rights treaties and legislation to which the Task Force Report referred. But even had that not been the case, the Code provision setting aside the Nuremberg standards constituted a significant departure from accepted ethical standards, especially for health-related professionals.

In light of this "cover" provided by the APA Code, that provision of the Ethics Code was amended as were policies on psychologists working in national security settings (APA, 2013), further clarifying that psychologists may not engage in either deception or coercion. Accordingly, the position endorsed by some psychologists that interrogation practices with which psychologists had been involved with the US military were not unethical and indeed were obligatory in some circumstances struck a particularly discordant note: "*It is not clear … that EITs ['enhanced interrogation techniques'] are in fact unethical. Indeed, arguments have been presented that show under certain conditions EITs may be ethically obligatory*" (O'Donohue et al., 2014, p. 121). Moreover, extending this conclusion led to their assertion that "Psychologists, in order to behave consistently with their moral obligations to the community, to their ethical duties, in order to minimize harm, and to act virtuously may, in certain circumstances, need to participate in torture" (2014, p. 121).

These contentions by O'Donohue et al. were rejected by other psychologists (Arrigo, DeBatto, Rockwood, & Mawe, 2015) on a number of grounds, but not one that seems most in need of attention—namely, that if it is sometimes obligatory for EITs to be used, psychologists are required to participate in them. Indeed, the same question can be put more generally: even if some of the practices in which psychologists might engage with law enforcement, the military, or intelligence agencies are morally acceptable, or even morally obligatory, for some practitioners, are they so for psychologists? This question was tackled by Eisenhower (2017) who submitted that participation in EITs is never morally right (much less obligatory) for psychologists, based on the nature of the psychologist's role, and the importance of public trust in the performance of that role:

> *For a psychologist to be thought of as trustworthy enough to have authority over someone—ever—requires that all psychologists show themselves to be trustworthy. In this, there are no excuses, or rather, if excuses are allowed, anywhere,*

> *for any reason, the trustworthiness of the entire profession is liable to suffer because the commitment of the entire profession qua profession has been compromised*
>
> **Eisenhower (2017), p. 433.**

One of the many things demonstrated by this debate, and the various confusions and disagreements it encompassed, was what we will call a lack of moral literacy, a failure to demonstrate a shared understanding of ethical concepts, terminology and theory, both per se, in terms of their normative power, and the application of these concepts in logically consistent and defensible ways. In the remainder of this chapter, through the prism of research on the application of PJ tenets to interviewing, we expose existing connections between core ethical principles and evidence-based psychological policies and practices. In this way, we demonstrate that significant levels of moral literacy currently exist, which can be brought to bear in situations of role conflict. Since such conflicts typically involve tensions between moral values, moral literacy increases psychologists' confidence to articulate and defend their professional ethical values.

Evidence-based policing and ethical practice

EBP is rapidly becoming the global standard in contemporary policing practice (Knutsson & Tompson, 2017; Lum & Koper, 2017; Mitchell, 2019). EBP is "the use of best research evidence on 'what works' as a guide to police decisions" (Sherman, 2013, p. 383). Essential to this development is the ethical responsibility of police to use practices that are demonstrably the most effective available and that cause the least harm (Mitchell, 2019, p. 12). This, however, is not to put too onerous a burden of ethical responsibility on police officers—something may cause less harm than the likely alternatives, but still be unethical. Perhaps less expected is the impact that choices made by practitioners and governments about what counts as robust evidence can have on ethical practice.

EBP has uncovered a bias by police and governments favoring physical or "hard" evidence. Consequently, practices reliant on police practitioners' relational skills have been denigrated. This curious development runs counter to increased support for community policing paradigms (Wisler & Onwudiwe, 2009) and thus increased priority to police relational expertise, undermining the importance of ethical practice intrinsic to EBP. Concomitant with these developments, pressures on police due to national security priorities, result-oriented demands, and cost sensitivity have challenged police psychologists' (perceived) ability to comply with their professional code of ethics.

Soft science, hard science, and relational skills in policing

Starting in the 1970s, theories of community policing and community engagement by law enforcement agencies steadily gained traction, with a focus on interpersonal relational values (e.g., Giwa, James, Anucha, & Schwartz, 2014; Kearns, 2017;

Stronks, 2015). Research supporting policies and practices that incorporate relational values, such as procedural fairness, has aggregated. These approaches demonstrate that the manner in which police communicate with the public and with suspects affects police legitimacy (Bottoms & Tankebe, 2012; Mazerolle, Bennett, Davis, Sargeant, & Manning, 2013; Tyler, 2004). The uptake of policies based on interpersonal police-community relations in the context of increased sensitivity to possible terrorist attacks has been impaired by heightened security concerns, risk averse legislation, and criminal justice policies that have privileged seemingly more objective, hard evidence and the "hard" sciences.

Areas of the most extensive growth in EBP have been a panoply of forensic scientific "trace" evidence, such as forensic ballistics, fingerprint matching, DNA profiling, etymology, pathology, podiatry, and toxicology. Paradoxically, widespread critique of many "hard" scientific forensic investigative procedures (e.g., arson chromatography, microscopic hair analysis, fingerprint matching, and DNA profiling) in the past decade centered on the absence of robust, rigorous quality control measures to ensure reliable results (National Research Council, 2009). Yet, incriminating prosecutorial forensic evidence that lacks a scientific foundation (bite marks, facial mapping, photographic images, voice identification) is rarely excluded at trial (Edmond, Cole, Cunliffe, & Roberts, 2013). These commentators called prosecutors and police "unethical" for using apparently objective or hard evidence that is unreliable, noting the counterproductive and costly consequences, such as wrongful convictions. EBP is premised on understanding "what works" and also "what makes it work" (Bennett, Mazerolle, Antrobus, Martin, & Hine, 2019, p. 158). Theory testing is critical in understanding what makes something work. In evaluating the deficiencies of several types of "hard" forensic scientific evidence, the US National Research Council noted that those technologies were unsupported by theories (2009, pp. 99, 102, 112, 128, 174).

When forensic scientific evidence is unavailable, policing agencies often rely on covert wiretaps and digital surveillance (GPS monitors, CCTV, drones) in major investigations (Fraser, 2018) in preference to information elicited in interviews with suspects whom police often incorrectly anticipate will invoke their right to silence and refuse to cooperate (Dixon, 2007). However, the suspect is the most direct source of information (Geurts, Ask, Granhag, & Vrij, 2018). In many high impact crimes such as terrorism, organized crime, child exploitation and abuse, and human trafficking, human sources are essential. Thus, while developments in policing continue to build a strong evidence base emphasizing the need to be people-centered, pervasive skepticism about the effectiveness of "soft science" approaches persists, including whether reliable information can be secured from human sources in investigative interviews using noncoercive "soft science" approaches.

EBP that neglects the value of psychological relational skills runs the risk of failure and may be unethical. For example, in other areas of psychological practice, critics noted that evidence-based psychological therapeutic patient interventions that neglected practitioners' relational skills resulted in saturation of the field with short-term models based on limited laboratory research, many of which were inappropriate, counterproductive, and unethical (e.g., Gnaulati, 2018).

The same caveat can be extended to EBP that overlooks police practitioners' interpersonal relational skills, specifically in relation to investigative interviewing practices with a short-term focus based on no or limited laboratory research. According to Guiora, "the interrogation measures we adopt define who we are as a society" (2008, p. ix). Consider then President Trump's announcement that torture works and his commitment to intensify treatment of detainees in American custody (ABC News, 2017). Over 250 years ago, Cesare Beccaria berated this inconvenient "pretended test of truth worthy only of a cannibal" and repudiated the popular notion "that pain should be the test of truth, as if truth resided in the muscles and fibres of a wretch in torture. By this method, the robust will escape, and the feeble be condemned" (1794/1872, p. 15). Torture is not theoretically supported or evidence-based and produces unreliable information (Vrij et al., 2017). Nonetheless, more than 140 countries continue to endorse torture (Amnesty International, 2014), and many jurisdictions aside from North America continue to use investigative methods that are not compliant with EBP.

Evidence-based interviewing, procedural fairness, and ethical practice

The discipline of psychology has made substantial contributions to EBP. The development of a body of specialized knowledge on effective communication skills to gather intelligence and oral evidence from suspects, sources, and witnesses is a prime example (Meissner, Surmon-Bohr, Oleszkiewizc, & Alison, 2017). Much of this research focuses on assessments of the mind-set and counter-interrogation techniques used by guilty, deceptive suspects to aid in deception detection, consistently demonstrating the effectiveness of noncoercive relational practices with high-value interviewees (Meissner, Kelly, & Woestehoff, 2015). Torture and other harsh and accusatory interrogation methods which rely on psychological manipulation and control were shown to be ineffective in (1) securing cooperation and overcoming resistance; (2) eliciting useful information; and (3) assessing credibility (Vrij et al., 2017).

A paradigm shift (Kuhn, 1970) from accusatory, guilt-presumptive, confession-based approaches to direct, information-gathering, and strategic approaches is well documented (Geurts et al., 2018; Hartwig, Granhag, & Vrij, 2005). The latter focus on interpersonal relations to develop rapport and elicit an account (Abbe & Brandon, 2014). As many as 71 strategies comprising six key domains used in interviewing (rapport and relationship building, context manipulation, emotion provocation, confrontation/competition, collaboration, and presentation of evidence) were identified (Kelly, Redlich, & Miller, 2015; Sivasubramaniam & Goodman-Delahunty, 2019).

Continuum of ethical compliance in interview practice

The foregoing interviewing practices have been classified by type and degree of coercion applied, producing a continuum of ethical compliance. For instance, four levels from high to low compliance were ranked by Skerker (2018): (1) information gathering; (2) strategic techniques; (3) confession-focused techniques; and (4) torture. Along this continuum, some methods, such as certain confession-focused techniques, might be abusive, but not torturous. Another way to conceptualize the ethical continuum of interview practices is by strategy type (social relational, cognitive, legalistic, and physical), each of which can be applied more or less coercively (Goodman-Delahunty, 2016; Goodman-Delahunty, Dhami, & Martschuk, 2014).

The manipulative nature of certain interview approaches such as the Strategic Use of Evidence (Brimbal, Kleinman, Oleszkiewicz, & Meissner, 2019) was rated less ethical than open-ended, information-gathering approaches by Hartwig, Luke, and Skerker (2016), although both may draw on rapport building and social relational strategies. Whether they are deemed coercive may depend on the precise manner of their application, the vulnerability of the interviewee, and other contextual features. When psychologists use their training in an effort to strip interviewees of their autonomy, this is dehumanizing, and per Lauritzen (2013), crosses the ethical line. Pretending to have incriminating evidence, faking it, allowing a suspect to think you know more than you do in reality, and deliberately failing to correct a suspect's mistaken assumptions (deception by omission rather than commission) may overstep that boundary, as they are deceptive practices, thus more coercive and ethically questionable. By comparison, manipulative strategies that have an unconscious influence, such as priming and social persuasion, may be "a morally and legally acceptable form of interrogation" (Lauritzen, 2013, p. 181). Here, the philosophical literature on ethical implications of the distinction between doing harm and allowing harm to happen (most often discussed in the context of euthanasia and debates on killing vs. letting die) may be helpful for unraveling where on the spectrum specific strategies fall (e.g., Frowe, 2010). While it has been argued that the distinction between killing and letting die is morally unimportant (e.g., Bennett, 1995), it does seem to capture an important moral intuition (meaning, perhaps, that we have not yet properly discerned the nature of the distinction).

Alignment of procedural justice theory with ethical principles

A leading social psychological theory that has been applied since the 1990s to police practitioners' relational skills is PJ theory, based on the Group Value Relational Model (Tyler, 1989). PJ theory has been applied internationally (Jackson, 2018) to a variety of topics where police interact with the public, the community, victims, and suspects, and where interpersonal police-citizen contact is crucial (Mazerolle et al., 2013), such as domestic violence (Goodman-Delahunty & Corbo Crehan, 2016), routine traffic stops for random breath testing (Bennett et al., 2019), complaints against police (Corbo Crehan & Goodman-Delahunty, 2019), and organizational justice within policing agencies (Roberts & Herrington, 2013).

Procedural justice research since 1990 has sought to refine the relationship of procedural justice to legitimacy and the various outcomes of trust, satisfaction, compliance, and cooperation. Through this scholarship, procedural justice theory is now perceived to have two distinct, but linked, components. The first is referred to as the quality of decision-making procedures, where a power holder (such as a police officer, court official, or prison officer) intervenes in a situation (which is not necessarily an illegal situation) and gives citizens the "voice" to express their point of view, behaves in a professional and unbiased manner, and is perceived to be competent in the way he or she resolves the situation. The second component focuses on the quality of treatment, where assessments are made as to whether the power holder (i.e., the decision maker) has treated a person with dignity and respect. Both components need to be exercised for procedural justice to be delivered

Bennett et al. (2018), p. 1.

PJ legitimacy theory and research are especially relevant to an examination of ethical issues in interview strategies because they explore causal relationships between PJ and citizen cooperation and compliance with the law. They are further relevant in contexts where police psychologists experience tension between their professional codes of ethics and the support they are requested to provide to police agencies because of obvious synergies between the four key tenets of PJ and the four principles of the *Universal Declaration of Ethical Principles for Psychologists* (a distillation of numerous psychologists' codes of ethics). While a careful unpacking of each element and each principle (see Gauthier, 2018) would allow specific commonalities to be identified, for current purposes, Table 1.1 simply associates each PJ element with the ethical principle with which it has most in common, overall. "Dignity" encompasses autonomy, thus "voice" as it includes "the ability to make informed choices and to reason prudentially in relation to those choices" (Lauritzen, 2013, p. 185). The fourth principle, "Professional and scientific responsibilities to society", is linked to the PJ element "legitimacy" which ensues when the other four PJ tenets are present.

Table 1.1 Ethical underpinnings of procedural justice.

Universal ethical principles of psychologists[a]	Procedural justice tenets[b]
Respect for the dignity of persons and peoples	Respect, voice
Competent caring for the well-being of persons and peoples	Trustworthiness
Integrity, transparency	Neutrality, absence of bias
Professional and scientific responsibilities to society	Legitimacy, accountability

[a] *http://www.iupsys.net/about/governance/universal-declaration-of-ethical-principles-for-psychologists.html.*
[b] *Goodman-Delahunty (2010); Tyler (2004).*

By exploring the overlap between tenets of PJ and the professional ethics of psychologists and linking them to contemporary research findings that focus on interpersonal relations, with effective EBP interview practices as examples, the integral and salient link between PJ and ethical interviewing is more apparent.

Interviewing research incorporating procedural justice tenets

Due to its focus on interpersonal relations, communication is central to PJ research (Bennet et al., 2019, p. 146). As discussed above, some research with high-value detainees emphasizes the social relational features of the interview interactions to a greater degree than studies which emphasize cognitive, legalistic, and physical interview features. Research with extremists has revealed that their needs and drives appeared undifferentiated from those of the rest of the population (i.e., missing loved ones, longing for a normal life, feelings of guilt, burnout, Dalgaard-Nielsen, 2013). This finding indicates that attending to basic PJ tenets in an interview with a high-risk detainee, such as showing a genuine interest in their well-being, may be effective. Results confirming this have emerged in interviewing research that tested social psychological relational constructs.

With a handful of notable exceptions such as recent research on trust (e.g., Brimbal et al., 2019) and research on PJ tenets (e.g., Sivasubramaniam & Goodman-Delahunty, 2019, 2021), relatively few investigative interviewing studies have directly tested the effects of procedural fairness interventions in police interviews on key study outcomes such as the extent to which specific PJ interview tenets increase interviewee cooperation and yield diagnostic or reliable information. Thus, most evidence gathered to date on the effectiveness of PJ tenets is indirect, through examination of studies where other research constructs incorporated PJ tenets. Most notably, in the field of psychological counseling, a series of constructs that reflect PJ tenets comprise the core interpersonal relational skills of motivational interviewing (Miller & Rollnick, 2013), e.g., allowing the interviewee to give a complete account and responding with active or reflective listening skills incorporates the PJ element of voice. Counselors are trained to show strong respect for the interviewee, and to establish trust through empathy, positive support, rapport building, sincerity, and honesty. Finally, interviewers are advised to avoid judgmental comments and to be transparent in their communications—the PJ element neutrality. For these reasons, programs of policing research that have applied motivational interviewing constructs are useful in assessing the effectiveness of PJ features in investigative interviews.

Studies applying PJ have been undertaken using an array of research methods. A relatively small number of researchers have been granted access to archival data in the form of actual video and audio recordings of police interviews with high-value detainees. By retrospectively coding the association between questioning strategies used in these interviews, responses of detainees, and interview outcomes, these researchers validated the application of PJ principles in practice in the field. Other research methods testing PJ theory in investigative interviews include case studies, controlled laboratory studies, field surveys, and field experiments. Illustrative examples are provided below of each method, showing the connections between PJ tenets and interview outcomes.

Archival interview studies of procedural justice

"Ticking time bomb" case

The application and effectiveness of fair interview procedures with a high-value detainee was demonstrated in the field by Norwegian police psychologists who interviewed Anders Breivik after he killed 77 persons by bomb and gunshot near Oslo, and then generated a "ticking time bomb" scenario by declaring that cells two and three would soon be activated. In all 31 interviews, conducted nonconfrontationally in the presence of his lawyer in a comfortable room with armchairs, curtains and carpets, and ample drinking water, the detainee was informed of and reminded of his human rights. Ethical interviewing was put to the test: the detainee was fully cooperative in response to evidence-based questioning using only rapport building, interpersonal communication theories, respect for human rights, and cognitive and strategic interviewing. The Norwegian police achieved their objectives without coercion or manipulation. They emphasized that it is in exigent cases that adherence to fair information-seeking noncoercive procedures is most vital (Rachlew, 2017).

Quantitative analyses of interviews with high-value detainees

Rapport and relationship building strategies were most frequently used multinationally and had a positive effect on suspect cooperation (Alison et al., 2014a, 2014b; Kelly, Miller, & Redlich, 2016). Findings gathered from both suspects and interviewers converged on this point. For example, field studies of reports of interviews by convicted murderers and sex offenders (Holmberg & Christianson, 2002) and suspected sex offenders (Kebbell, Hurren, & Mazerolle, 2006) demonstrated that admissions were more likely in response to interviews conducted fairly, with empathy, and humanely, compared with accusatory and authoritarian approaches.

An analysis of interviewer behaviors observed in field interviews with 48 convicted terrorists explored the association between their social relational skills and interview outcomes. Interviewers with greater interpersonal competence and versatility were more successful at engaging detainees, securing their cooperation, and adducing information (Christiansen, Alison, & Alison, 2018). Similarly, another field study of 181 recorded interviews showed that noncoercive interview techniques that incorporated both rapport building and PJ tenets (treatment of suspects with respect, dignity, and integrity) were associated with a significant reduction in the likelihood of counter-interrogation strategies, i.e., resistance from the 49 convicted terrorism suspects diminished (Alison et al., 2014a). Analyses of a sample of 408 video interviews of convicted terrorists conducted by 58 different interviewers were coded to assess the effectiveness of rapport-based motivational interviewing skills (autonomy, acceptance, adaptation, empathy, and evocation) (Alison, Alison, Noone, Elntib, & Christiansen, 2013). The result confirmed the sensitivity of suspects to relationally based skills as even minor maladaptive interpersonal conduct by interviewers increased counter-interrogation responses in suspects and reduced the amount of information disclosed of evidential value. The same pattern was found via analyses of 29 interrogations conducted by the Robbery Homicide Division of the Los Angeles Police Department. Investigators who used rapport and relationship building were significantly more likely to elicit critical information from their subjects (Kelly et al., 2016).

Laboratory experiments related to procedural justice

Comparisons of three communication styles used by police in a simulated traffic stop showed that incorporating PJ relational tenets outstripped neutral (standard direct questioning) and overly accommodating styles in the perceived professionalism and authority attributed to police (Lowrey-Kinberg, 2018). In related work in experimental simulations of police interviews, Duke, Wood, Bolin, Scullin, and Labianca (2017) found six discrete rapport factors reflecting PJ to be effective: Attentiveness, Trust/Respect, Expertise, Cultural Similarity, Connected Flow and Commitment to Communication. Similarly, rapport has repeatedly been demonstrated as vital to successful information elicitation in mock police and military interviews (Collins, Lincoln, & Frank, 2002; Evans et al., 2014; Kieckhaefer, Vallano, & Schreiber-Compo, 2014; Vallano & Schreiber Compo, 2011, 2015; cf. Geurts et al., 2018).

A program of research that specifically tests ways to establish and strengthen the PJ tenet of trust as a critical component of rapport building (Brimbal et al., 2019) has been undertaken. It has distinguished the contributions of four discrete relational elements (reciprocity, empathy, genuineness, and independence) and explored tactics that interviewers can use to demonstrate their trustworthiness and willingness to trust.

Field studies of procedural justice

Survey research

Survey research has been instrumental in examining the application of PJ tenets globally. For instance, cross-cultural surveys demonstrated that when interacting, people focus on the interpersonal relational dimensions of warmth and competence to assess the extent to which others are friendly and trustworthy (Fiske & Durante, 2016). These attributes are related to PJ and ethical principles, as shown in Table 1.1. Two large-scale survey studies of multinational samples of criminal investigators and intelligence operators about six broad strategy types and their perceived effectiveness were conducted in different jurisdictions and cultures, such as North America, Europe, Australasia, and several Southeast Asian countries (Kelly et al., 2015; Sivasubramaniam & Goodman-Delahunty, 2019). Results confirmed practitioners' use in the field of PJ tenets to build rapport, and of widespread consensus favoring PJ rapport-based over coercive strategies.

Interviews with practitioners and detainees

The majority of 123 interviewing practitioners in the Asia Pacific who described their experience of effective interviewing practices gave most emphasis to the PJ tenets of respect and trust. They endorsed strategies respectful of suspect rights, genuine attention to their well-being, and the importance of avoiding behaviors that diminish police trustworthiness (Goodman-Delahunty & Howes, 2016; Goodman-Delahunty, O'Brien, & Gumbert-Jourjon, 2013). Strong practitioner support emerged for the effectiveness of noncoercive social relational strategies in high-stakes interviews, especially sincere mutual liking and reciprocity (Goodman-Delahunty & Howes, 2016). Interviews with a sample of 34 terrorist interviewers and 30 terrorist detainees disclosed faster, more complete disclosures and an increase in reliable incriminating admissions in response to noncoercive neutral and respectful methods that allowed detainees the opportunity to express their viewpoints (voice) (Goodman-Delahunty & Martschuk, 2018; Goodman-Delahunty, Martschuk, & Dhami, 2014).

A "ticking time bomb" field experiment

An experimental study conducted with a multinational sample of 404 seasoned, professional investigative interviewers in 15 Asian Pacific and European countries explored their responses to a "ticking time bomb" dilemma in which crime severity was either high (many innocent persons injured and 15 killed) or low (property damage and minor injuries) (Sivasubramaniam & Goodman-Delahunty, 2021). Participants were randomly assigned to one of the three interviewing conditions, in which the questioning was either noncoercive and procedurally fair, coercive and harsh or mixed (started noncoercively, but after the suspect was uncooperative, switched to coercive and harsh). The results unequivocally refuted perceptions of widespread support for harsh interrogation techniques as a last resort in exigent circumstances when a detainee is uncooperative and consequences for the community are severe. Key drivers were concerns by interviewers that the interview procedures were respectful of the detainee and effective in gathering useful information.

Table 1.2 summarizes the relationships observed between the foregoing research constructs and study outcomes, as they pertain to each of the four PJ tenets and corresponding psychological ethical principles.

Conclusions

In this chapter, through the prism of contemporary evidence-based research on the application of social psychological PJ tenets to police interviewing, we exposed existing connections between the four core ethical principles of psychologists and constructs incorporating all four relational tenets of PJ. Space permitted only a few illustrative examples; however, the enumerated studies, conducted by diverse research teams in many different countries, using a wide variety of research methods, revealed a picture of convergent findings. While some of the relevant

Table 1.2 Relationship between procedural justice tenets, research constructs, and study outcomes.

PJ element	Research constructs	Study outcomes
Respect	Respect	Information gain
Voice	Voice, active listening Dignity Autonomy	Rapid disclosure Greater cooperation Reliable admissions
Trustworthiness	Trust, empathy, warmth Positive emotions Attentiveness, reciprocity	Information gain Greater cooperation
Neutrality	Acceptance Integrity Transparency	Information gain Greater cooperation Reliable admissions
Legitimacy	Competence	Compliance with the law

research was prompted by practices in military settings, the fundamental issues are undifferentiated from those arising in civilian policing.

This research review, albeit limited, amply demonstrated the significant extent of currently existing moral literacy among psychologists, which can be brought to bear in situations of role conflict. Since role conflicts typically involve tensions between moral values, moral literacy increases psychologists' confidence to articulate and defend their professional ethical values. It also allows practitioners to avoid making morally hazardous claims that may, if left unchallenged, lead to injustice. The latter is particularly important in collaborative situations where different levels of moral literacy exist among collaborators, the collaborative practices are not synergistic and integrated, and there are power disparities between collaborators. In sum, more optimism is justified about EBP that relies on "soft" social psychological behavioral science to give priority to police interviewers' relational skills.

References

Abbe, A., & Brandon, S. E. (2014). Building and maintaining rapport in investigative interviews. *Police Practice and Research, 15*, 207–220.

ABC News. (January 25, 2017). *Trump says torture works as his government readies a review.* Retrieved from https://www.ctvnews.ca/world/trump-says-torture-works-as-his-government-readies-a-review-1.3256819.

Alison, L., Alison, E., Noone, G., Elntib, S., & Christiansen, P. (2013). Why tough tactics fail and rapport gets results: Observing Rapport-Based Interpersonal Techniques (ORBIT) to generate useful information from terrorists. *Psychology, Public Policy, and Law, 19*, 411–431.

Alison, L., Alison, E., Noone, G., Elntib, S., Waring, S., & Christiansen, P. (2014a). Whatever you say, say nothing: Individual differences in counter interrogation tactics amongst a field sample of right wing, AQ inspired and paramilitary terrorists. *Personality and Individual Differences, 68*, 170–175.

Alison, L., Alison, E., Noone, G., Elntib, S., Waring, S., & Christiansen, P. (2014b). The efficacy of rapport-based techniques for minimizing counter-interrogation tactics amongst a field sample of terrorists. *Psychology, Public Policy, and Law, 20*, 421–430.

American Psychological Association. (2013). *Policy related to psychologists' work in national security settings and reaffirmation of the APA position against torture and other cruel, inhuman, or degrading treatment or punishment.* Washington, DC: Author. Retrieved from https://www.apa.org/about/policy/national-security.aspx.

American Psychological Association Presidential Task Force. (2005). *Psychological ethics and national security.* Washington, D.C: Author.

Amnesty International. (2014). *Torture in 2014: 30 years of broken promises.* Retrieved from: https://www.amnesty.org/download/Documents/4000/act400042014en.pdf.

Arrigo, J. M., DeBatto, D., Rockwood, L., & Mawe, T. G. (2014). The "good" psychologist, "good" torture, and "good" reputation—response to O'Donohue, Snipes, Dalto, Soto, Maragakis, and Im (2014) "The ethics of enhanced interrogations and torture". *Ethics & Behavior, 25*(5), 1–12.

Beccaria, C. (1764). *An essay on crimes and punishments, by the Marquis Beccaria of Milan, with a commentary by M. de Voltaire: A new edition corrected.* Albany: Little & Co. Retrieved from https://oll.libertyfund.org/titles/beccaria-an-essay-on-crimes-and-punishments.

Bennett, J. (1995). *The act itself.* Oxford: Clarendon Press.

Bennett, S., Hine, L., & Mazerolle, L. (2018). Procedural justice. In *Oxford bibliographies.* New York: Oxford University Press. https://doi.org/10.1093/OBO/9780195396607-0241.

Bennett, S., Mazerolle, L., Antrobus, E., Martin, P., & Hine, L. (2019). The trials and tribulations of evidence based procedural justice. In R. J. Mitchell, & L. Huey (Eds.), *Evidence-based policing: An introduction* (pp. 145–160). Bristol, UK: Policy Press.

Bottoms, A., & Tankebe, J. (2012). Beyond procedural justice: A dialogic approach to legitimacy in criminal justice. *Journal of Criminal Law and Criminology, 102*(1), 119–170.

Brimbal, L., Kleinman, S. M., Oleszkiewicz, S., & Meissner, C. A. (2019). Developing rapport and trust in the interrogative context. In S. Barela, et al. (Eds.), *Interrogation and torture: Research on efficacy and its integration with morality and legality.* New York: Oxford University Press.

Christiansen, P., Alison, L., & Alison, E. (2018). Well begun is half done: Interpersonal behaviours in distinct field interrogations with high-value detainees. *Legal and Criminological Psychology, 23*, 68–84.

Collins, R., Lincoln, R., & Frank, M. G. (2002). The effect of rapport in forensic interviewing. *Psychiatry, Psychology and Law, 9*, 69–78.

Corbo Crehan, A., & Goodman-Delahunty, J. (2019). Procedural justice and complaints about police. *Salus, 7*(1), 58–87.

Dalgaard-Nielsen, A. (2013). Promoting exit from violent extremism: Themes and approaches. *Studies in Conflict and Terrorism, 36*, 99–115.

Dixon, D. (2007). *Interrogating images: Audio-visually recorded police questioning of suspects.* Sydney, Australia: Sydney Institute of Criminology.

Duke, M. C., Wood, J. M., Bolin, B., Scullin, M., & Labianca, J. (2017). Development of the rapport scales for investigative interviews and interrogations (RS3i), interviewee version. Psychology. *Public Policy & Law, 24*(1), 64–79. https://doi.org/10.1037/law0000147.

Edmond, G., Cole, S., Cunliffe, E., & Roberts, A. (2013). *Admissibility compared: The reception of incriminating expert evidence (i.e., forensic science) in four adversarial jurisdictions* (Vol. 3, pp. 31–109). University of Denver Criminal Law Review.

Evans, J. R., Houston, K. A., Meissner, C. A., Ross, A. B., LaBianca, J. R., Woestehoff, S. A., et al. (2014). An empirical evaluation of intelligence gathering interrogation techniques from the United States Army Field Manual. *Applied Cognitive Psychology, 28*, 867–875.

Eisenhower, W. D. (2017). Torture in the naked public square. *Ethics & Behavior, 27*(5), 423–435. https://doi.org/10.1080/10508422.2016.1172313.

Ewing, C. P., & Gelles, M. G. (2003). Ethical concerns in forensic consultation regarding national safety and security. *Journal of Threat Assessment, 2*(3), 95–107.

Fiske, S. T., & Durante, F. (2016). Stereotype content across cultures: Variations on a few themes. In M. J. Gelfand, C.-Y. Chiu, & Y.-Y. Hong (Eds.), *Advances in culture and psychology* (Vol. 6, pp. 209–258). New York: Oxford University Press.

Fraser, H. (2018). Thirty years is long enough: It is time to create a process that ensures covert recordings used as evidence in court are interpreted reliably. *Journal of Judicial Administration, 27*(30), 95–104.

Frowe, H. (2010). Killing John to save Mary: A defense of the moral distinction between killing and letting die. In J. K. Campbell, M. O'Rourke, & H. S. Silverstein (Eds.), *Action, ethics, and responsibility* (pp. 47–66). Cambridge, MA: MIT.

Gauthier, J. (2018). References to human rights in codes of ethics for psychologists: Critical issues and recommendation. Part II. *RUDN Journal of Psychology and Pedagocics, 15*(2), 131–146.

Geurts, R., Ask, K., Granhag, P. A., & Vrij, A. (2018). Interviewing to manage threats: Exploring the effects of interview style on information gain and threateners' counter-interview strategies. *Journal of Threat Assessment and Management, 5*(4), 189–204.

Giwa, S., James, C. E., Anucha, U., & Schwartz, K. (2014). Community policing—a shared responsibility: A voice-centered relational method analysis of a police/youth-of-color dialogue. *Journal of Ethnicity in Criminal Justice, 12*(3), 218–245. https://doi.org/10.1080/15377938.2013.837856.

Gnaulati, E. (2018, Sep). Overlooked ethical problems associated with the research and practice of evidence-based treatments. *Journal of Humanistic Psychology*, 1–16.

Goodman-Delahunty, J. (2010). Four ingredients: New recipes for procedural justice in Australian policing. *Policing: A Journal of Policing and Practice, 4*, 403–410.

Goodman-Delahunty, J. (2016). Insights on investigative interviewing from practitioners and suspects in Indonesia, the Philippines and Sri Lanka. In D. Walsh, G. E. Oxburgh, A. D. Redlich, & T. Myklebust (Eds.), *International developments and practices in investigative interviewing and interrogation: Volume II Suspects* (pp. 18–33). Abingdon, UK: Routledge Press.

Goodman-Delahunty, J., & Corbo Crehan, A. (2016). Enhancing police responses to domestic violence incidents: Reports from client advocates in New South Wales. *Violence Against Women, 22*(8), 1007–1026. doi: 077801215613854.

Goodman-Delahunty, J., & Howes, L. M. (2016). Social persuasion to develop rapport in high stakes interviews: A qualitative analysis of Asian-Pacific policing practices. *Policing and Society: An International Journal of Research and Practice, 26*(3), 270–290.

Goodman-Delahunty, J., & Martschuk, N. (2018). Securing reliable information in investigative interviews: Coercive and noncoercive strategies preceding turning points. *Police Practice and Research*. https://doi.org/10.1080/15614263.2018.1531752.

Goodman-Delahunty, J., Martschuk, N., & Dhami, M. K. (2014). Interviewing high value detainees: Securing cooperation and disclosures. *Applied Cognitive Psychology, 28*(6), 883−897. https://doi.org/10.1002/acp.3087.

Goodman-Delahunty, J., O'Brien, K., & Gumbert-Jourjon, T. (2013). Police professionalism in interviews with high value detainees: Cross-cultural endorsement of procedural justice. *The Journal of the Institute of Justice & International Studies, 13*, 65−82.

Guiora, A. N. (2008). *Constitutional limits on coercive interrogation*. New York: Oxford University Press.

Hartwig, M., Granhag, P. A., & Vrij, A. (2005). Police interrogation from a social psychology perspective. *Policing and Society, 15*(4), 379−399.

Hartwig, M., Luke, T., & Skerker, M. (2016). Ethical perspectives on interrogation: An analysis of contemporary techniques. In J. Jacobs, & J. Jackson (Eds.), *Handbook of criminal justice ethics* (pp. 326−347). New York: Routledge.

Holmberg, U., & Christianson, S. A. (2002). Murderers' and sexual offenders' experiences of police interviews and their inclination to admit or deny crimes. *Behavioral Sciences & the Law, 20*, 31−45.

Jackson, J. (2018). Norms, normativity, and the legitimacy of justice institutions: International perspectives. *Annual Review of Law and Social Science, 14*(17), 1−17.

James, L. A. (2008). *Fixing hell: An army psychologist confronts Abu Ghraib*. New York, NY: Grand Central Publishing.

Kearns, M. A. (2017). Why are some officers more supportive of community policing with minorities than others? *Justice Quarterly, 34*(7), 1213−1245. https://doi.org/10.1080/07418825.2017.1380837.

Kebbell, M., Hurren, E., & Mazerolle, P. (2006). An investigation into the effective and ethical interviewing of suspected sex offenders. *Trends & Issues in Crime and Criminal Justice, 327*, 1−6.

Kelly, C. E., Miller, J. C., & Redlich, A. D. (2016). The dynamic nature of interrogation. *Law and Human Behavior, 40*, 295−309. https://doi.org/10.1037/lhb0000172.

Kelly, C. E., Redlich, A. D., & Miller, J. C. (2015). Examining the meso-level domains of the interrogation taxonomy. *Psychology, Public Policy, and Law, 21*, 179−191. https://doi.org/10.1037/law0000034.

Kieckhaefer, J. M., Vallano, J. P., & Schreiber-Compo, N. S. (2014). Examining the positive effects of rapport building: When and why does rapport building benefit adult eyewitness memory? *Memory, 22*, 1010−1023.

Knutsson, J., & Tompson, L. (2017). *Advances in evidence-based policing*. London, UK: Routledge.

Koocher, G. P. (2009). Ethics and the invisible psychologist. *Psychological Services, 6*(2), 97−107.

Kuhn, T. (1970). *The structure of scientific revolutions*. Chicago, IL: University of Chicago Press.

Lauritzen, P. (2013). *The ethics of interrogation: Professional responsibility in an age of terror*. Washington, D.C.: Georgetown University Press.

Lowrey-Kinberg, B. V. (2018). Procedural justice, over accommodation, and police authority and professionalism: Results from a randomized experiment. *Police Practice and Research, 19*(2), 111−124. https://doi.org/10.1080/15614263.2018.1418167.

Lum, C., & Koper, C. S. (2017). *Evidence-based policing: Translating research into practice*. New York: Oxford University Press.

Mazerolle, L., Bennett, S., Davis, J., Sargeant, E., & Manning, M. (2013). Legitimacy in policing: A systematic review. *The Campbell Collaboration Library of Systematic Reviews, 9*(1), 1−147.

Meissner, C. A., Kelly, C. E., & Woestehoff, S. A. (2015). Improving the effectiveness of suspect interrogations. *Annual Review of Law & Social Sciences, 11*, 211−233. https://doi.org/10.1146/annurev-lawsocsci-120814- 121657.

Meissner, C. A., Surmon-Bohr, F., Oleszkiewizc, S., & Alison, L. J. (2017). Developing an evidence-based perspective on interrogation: A review of the US government's high value detainee interrogation group research program. *Psychology, Public Policy, and Law, 23*, 438−457. https://doi.org/10.1037/law0000136.

Miller, W. R., & Rollnick, S. (2013). *Motivational interviewing: Helping people change* (3rd ed.). New York: Guildford Press.

Mitchell, R. J. (2019). A light introduction to evidencebased policing. In R. J. Mitchell, & L. Huey (Eds.), *Evidence-based policing: An introduction* (pp. 3−14). Bristol, UK: Policy Press.

National Research Council. (2009). *Strengthening forensic science in the United States: A path forward*. Washington, D.C.: National Academy of Science.

O'Donohue, W., Snipes, C., Dalto, G., Soto, C., Maragakis, A., & Im, S. (2014). The ethics of enhanced interrogations and torture: A reappraisal of the argument. *Ethics & Behavior, 24*(2), 109−125. https://doi.org/10.1080/10508422.2013.814088.

Pope, K. S. (2011). Psychologists and detainee interrogations: Key decisions, opportunities lost, and lessons learned. *Annual Review of Clinical Psychology, 7*, 459−481.

Rachlew, A. (2017). *From interrogating to interviewing suspects of terror: Towards a new mindset*. Retrieved from https://www.penalreform.org/blog/interrogating-interviewing-suspects-terror-towards-new-mindset/.

Roberts, K., & Herrington, V. (2013). Organisational and procedural justice: A review of the literature and its implications for policing. *Journal of Policing, Intelligence and Counter Terrorism, 8*(2), 115−130.

Sherman, L. (2013). The rise of evidence-based policing: Targeting, testing, and tracking. *Crime & Justice, 42*, 377−384.

Shumate, S., & Borum, R. (2006). Psychological support to defense counterintelligence operations. *Military Psychology, 18*(4), 283−296.

Sivasubramaniam, D., & Goodman-Delahunty, J. (2019a). International consensus on effective and ineffective interviewing strategies: A survey of experienced interviewing practitioners. *Police Practice and Research*. https://doi.org/10.1080/15614263.2019.1628756.

Sivasubramaniam, D., & Goodman-Delahunty, J. (2021). Interrogators' evaluations of procedural justice: What drives support for coercive procedures. *Manuscript in preparation*.

Skerker, M. (2018). *Interrogation: Efficacy and ethics*. Retrieved from http://counterterrorismethics.com/interrogation-efficacy-and-ethics/.

Stronks, S. (2015). Community police officers and self-involved conflict: An explorative study on reconciliation with citizens. *Policing, 10*(3), 206−221. https://doi.org/10.1093/police/pav032.

Tyler, T. R. (1989). The psychology of procedural justice: A test of the group-value model. *Journal of Personality and Social Psychology, 57*(5), 830−838. https://doi.org/10.1037//0022-3514.57.5.830.

Tyler, T. R. (2004). Enhancing police legitimacy. *The Annals of the American Academy of Political and Social Science, 593*(1), 84−99.

Vallano, J. P., & Schreiber Compo, N. (2011). A comfortable witness is a good witness: Rapport-building and susceptibility to misinformation in an investigative mock-crime interview. *Applied Cognitive Psychology, 25*, 960–970.

Vallano, J. P., & Schreiber Compo, N. (2015). Rapport-building with cooperative witnesses and criminal suspects: A theoretical and empirical review. *Psychology, Public Policy, and Law, 21*(1), 85–99.

Vrij, A. J., Meissner, C. A., Fisher, R. P., Kassin, S. M., Morgan, C. A., III, & Kleinman, S. M. (2017). Psychological perspectives on interrogation. *Perspectives on Psychological Science, 12*(6), 927–955. https://doi.org/10.1177/1745691617706515.

Wisler, D., & Onwudiwe, I. D. (2009). *Community policing: International perspectives and comparative perspectives*. Boca Raton, FLA: CRC Press.

Zelig, M. (1988). Ethical dilemmas in police psychology. *Professional Psychology: Research and Practice, 19*(3), 336–338.

The role of the psychologist in the screening and selection of law enforcement applicants

Michael G. Aamodt and JoAnne Brewster

Introduction

It is common for psychologists to work with law enforcement agencies in the selection and promotion of law enforcement personnel. Typically, these psychologists have a background either in industrial-organizational psychology (I-O psychology) or in clinical psychology. I-O psychologists are involved in developing, selecting, and administering tests to determine whether applicants have the competencies necessary to perform the job. Clinical psychologists administer tests and conduct clinical interviews to determine whether applicants who possess the competencies needed to perform law enforcement duties are psychologically suited to perform these duties. Typically, law enforcement agencies will contract with external psychologists to assess candidates, but in large agencies the psychologist might actually be an employee of the agency.

In this chapter, we will describe the processes used by psychologists to select law enforcement personnel. The first half of the chapter will focus on the work performed by I-O psychologists to "select in" applicants and the second half will focus on the work performed by clinical psychologists to "screen out" applicants.

Although we realize that the readership for this book includes professionals from many countries, our primary focus will be the selection process in the United States, as that is our area of expertise. With that said, we are confident that most of what we say in this chapter will generalize to police psychologists in other countries.

Selecting in applicants
Conducting a job analysis

The first step in the selection process is to conduct a job analysis to determine the tasks that must be performed, the conditions under which the tasks are performed, and the competencies needed to perform the tasks under the identified conditions.

Police Psychology, Edited by Marques and Paulino. https://doi.org/10.1016/B978-0-12-816544-7.00002-4

This information is obtained in a variety of ways including observations, interviews, and task inventories. The end result of a job analysis is a report that lists:

* Each task and the frequency with which it is performed, as well as ratings of the importance of that task in performing the job.
* The conditions under which each task is performed.
* The competencies (knowledge, skills, abilities, and other characteristics) needed to perform each task. These competencies are often very detailed. For example, if the job analysis indicates that math skills are needed, information should be obtained regarding the type of math to be performed (e.g., addition, subtraction), the unit of analysis (e.g., decimals, whole numbers, fractions), how it is performed (e.g., by hand, using a calculator, using a computer program), and the speed with which the mathematical calculations must be performed. Such information is used to create/select an appropriate math test and to determine whether applicants can use calculators to complete the test and whether the test will be timed.

As part of the job analysis, the agency will develop a profile of the ideal employee. For example, a law enforcement agency might determine that it wants:

* Cadets who will do well in the academy
* Officers with a high level of on-the-job performance, as indicated by:
    * Supervisor ratings
    * Activity (citations, arrests)
    * Attendance
    * Tenure
    * Safety
* Officers who do not cause trouble, as indicated by:
    * Citizen complaints
    * Department discipline
    * Unnecessary use of force
    * Law suits
* Officers who engage in organizational citizenship behaviors
    * People who "play nice"
    * People who do the "extras"

Identifying the best way to tap each competency

Once the necessary competencies have been identified, the next step is to identify the best way to tap each competency. Potential methods might include cognitive ability tests, background checks, simulations and work samples, physical ability tests, personality inventories, structured interviews, and biographical information (e.g., education, military history, work history). In choosing the nature and type of assessment, psychologists must consider the extent to which the assessment is valid, minimizes legal challenges, and is cost and time effective.

Valid

For a selection test to have value, it must predict a relevant aspect of employee performance (i.e., the test must be valid). In the next several pages, we will discuss what the research literature has found about the validity of commonly used predictors of law enforcement performance. The correlations and conclusions we report in this chapter are based on a prior meta-analysis[1] conducted by the first author (Aamodt, 2004) as well as an update to that meta-analysis that is still in progress. The correlations reported in this chapter have *not* been corrected for such study artifacts as reliability and range restriction.

Minimizes legal challenges

In the United States, law suits are often the result of an applicant's perception that the tests used in the selection process unfairly disadvantage applicants based on their sex, race, ethnicity, disability status, or age. This disadvantage can either be the result of intentional discrimination (disparate treatment) or of unintentional discrimination (disparate/adverse impact). Disparate impact occurs when a neutral practice, such as a physical ability test, results in a lower percentage of one group (e.g., women) being hired than another group (e.g., men). In the United States, the defense to disparate impact is to demonstrate that the test is job related or consistent with business necessity.

Tests that reduce the chance of a legal challenge have lower disparate impact than similar tests and are "face valid." A test is face valid if it "appears" to the applicant to be related to the job. For example, consider the following two math questions.

> An officer writes five tickets on Monday, seven tickets on Tuesday, and three tickets on Wednesday. How many tickets did the officer write during the week?
> Bob baked five pizzas on Monday, seven pizzas on Tuesday, and three pizzas on Wednesday. How many pizzas did Bob bake during the week?

Although both questions require the same mathematical ability, the first question would, on the face of it, appear to a law enforcement applicant to be more job-related than the second. Likewise, a physical agility test in which an applicant runs an obstacle course might appear to be more job-related than an agility test involving sit-ups, push-ups, and a mile-long run.

Cost and time effective

Given limited public agency budgets, it is important that the assessment tool be cost-effective to create or purchase, administer, and score. Take, for example, a

---

[1] A meta-analysis is a statistical review of the literature in which the results of all studies on a topic are statistically combined resulting in an average correlation between a selection technique and employee performance across all studies.

large public agency that averages 2000 applicants per year and wants to assess their cognitive ability. Although such tests as the Wechsler Adult Intelligence Scale or the Stanford Binet are excellent measures of cognitive ability, their cost per applicant would not make either an efficient choice for initial screening due to the time needed to administer and score each test.[2] Instead, an agency might select a measure of cognitive ability that can be administered in a group setting and can be machine scored.

Assessments that predict law enforcement performance
Cognitive ability

Cognitive ability tests used in law enforcement selection can take many forms, ranging from a test of a single construct (e.g., reading) to tests of general cognitive ability. The cognitive ability tests found in the law enforcement selection literature can be placed in one of three general categories.

Publisher developed tests

Although tests in this category were designed to measure cognitive ability in the general population, they have frequently been used in law enforcement selection. Examples of these tests include the Nelson-Denny Reading Test, Watson-Glaser Critical Thinking Appraisal, Wechsler Adult Intelligence Scale (WAIS), Wonderlic Personnel Test, and Shipley Institute of Living Scale.

Nationally developed law enforcement tests

Tests in this category have been developed by trade organizations or consulting firms specifically for use in law enforcement selection. Examples of such tests include the National Police Officer Selection Test (POST) by Stanard and Associates, Police Selection Test (PST) by PSI, and the SIGMA Survey for Police Officers (SSPO) by SIGMA Assessment Systems. Some tests, such as the Law Enforcement Selection Tool (LST) published by Industrial/Organizational Solutions, the Law Enforcement Aptitude Battery (LEAB) by PSI, and the Police Officer Entry-level (PO-EL) published by IPMA-HR, have both cognitive and noncognitive components.

Locally developed civil service exams

Tests in this category were developed by law enforcement agencies or civil service commissions for use by the agency itself, often with the help of I-O psychologists.

Meta-analysis results across a wide variety of occupations indicate that cognitive ability tests are the best predictor of work performance (Schmidt & Hunter, 1998)

---

[2] Although use of tests such as the WAIS are impractical at the initial screening stage, they can be useful during the clinical evaluation process described later in this chapter.

and performance in training (Hunter & Hunter, 1984), but will result in high levels of adverse impact (Roth, BeVier, Bobko, Switzer, & Tyler, 2001).

Our meta-analysis of law enforcement studies indicates that officers with higher cognitive ability perform better in the academy ($r = 0.34$), get higher on-the-job supervisor ratings ($r = 0.15$), have higher levels of activity (e.g., arrests, citations; $r = 0.19$), and are terminated less frequently ($r = -0.09$) than applicants scoring lower on cognitive ability tests.

Education

Between 15% and 20% of law enforcement agencies require education above a high school degree, with only 1% requiring a bachelor's degree (Gardiner, 2017; Reaves, 2015). These low educational requirements are driven by concerns that requiring a bachelor's degree will reduce the applicant pool, as well as result in an increase in the salary needed to entice college graduates to apply (Gardiner, 2017). Although higher education is seldom required, most agencies provide incentives for officers who have college degrees or want to pursue a college degree (Gardiner, 2017).

Are officers with college degrees better cops? Our meta-analysis results suggest that they are. Education is related to higher academy grades ($r = 0.27$), higher on-the-job supervisor ratings ($r = 0.16$), fewer disciplinary problems ($r = -0.08$), lower absenteeism ($r = -0.12$), fewer vehicle accidents ($r = -0.09$), fewer times assaulted ($r = -0.11$), and fewer use of force incidents (-0.09).

Interestingly, both education and cognitive ability tests have higher correlations with academy grades in shorter academies (<20 weeks) than in longer academies (20 or more weeks). Presumably, this difference is because a college background and higher cognitive ability allow a cadet to learn the material in a shorter period of time.

Our results also suggest that the advantage of a college degree kicks in after 2 years of experience (Aamodt, 2004). This type of finding is called the "Honeymoon Effect" and refers to the fact that what predicts performance of newly hired employees may be different from what predicts performance of more seasoned employees (Helmreich, Sawin, & Carsud, 1986).

Background information

In law enforcement selection, background information comes from a variety of sources, such as application blanks, criminal history checks, psychological interviews, polygraphs, and background investigations. The rationale for collecting this information is that a history of legal, work, or life problems increases the odds of future problems as a police officer.

Although there have not been a lot of studies investigating the relationship between prior problems and future law enforcement performance, our meta-analyses have found:

- A negative correlation between applicant traffic citations and future supervisor ratings of performance ($r = -0.12$) and a positive correlation between applicant traffic citations and future disciplinary problems ($r = 0.03$).

- A negative correlation between applicant arrests and future supervisor ratings ($r = -0.25$) and a positive correlation between applicant arrests and future discipline problems ($r = 0.08$).
- A negative correlation between prior job problems and future supervisor ratings ($r = -0.21$) and a positive correlation between prior job problems and future discipline problems ($r = 0.07$).
- A positive correlation between the overall background rating and future supervisor ratings of job performance ($r = 0.19$)

It is important to note that although all of these correlations are statistically significant, some of them are very low. Although counterintuitive, a history of legal and work problems seems to be a better predictor of supervisor ratings than it is of future law enforcement discipline problems. This finding is consistent with meta-analysis results of both law enforcement and nonlaw enforcement occupations (Aamodt, 2014).

Interviews

Interviews are a common component of the law enforcement selection process, as they are with most occupational areas. The interviews used by law enforcement agencies vary on two main factors: the number and type of interviewers and the degree of structure of the interview.

Although many occupations use combinations of individual and panel interviews, a rather unique characteristic of some law enforcement agencies is the use of external members in the interview panel. For example, several agencies we have worked with have members of a Civil Service Board conduct an interview in addition to that conducted by the law enforcement agency. Other agencies that we are familiar with include representatives from agencies such as women's resource center or a local university.

Law enforcement interviews also vary in their degree of structure. A fully structured interview is one in which all applicants are asked the same questions; the questions are based on a job analysis and thus are job-related, and there is a standard scoring system for responses to each of the questions. A fully unstructured interview is one in which applicants are not asked the same questions, the questions may or may not be job related (e.g., What was your favorite class in school?), and what is considered a "good answer" varies across interviewers. Most law enforcement interviews fall somewhere between a fully structured and a fully unstructured interview.

Meta-analysis results across a variety of occupations indicate that validity of highly structured interviews ($r = 0.34$) is higher than that of less structured interviews ($r = 0.11$, Huffcutt & Arthur, 1994). Additionally, structured interviews have relatively low levels of potential adverse impact (Huffcutt & Roth, 1998).

Given the extensive use of interviews by law enforcement agencies, there have been surprisingly few studies investigating the validity of interviews in a law enforcement context. Our meta-analysis results indicate that, based on a small number of studies, interviews correlate 0.10 with academy grades and 0.08 with supervisor ratings of performance.

Personality inventories

Personality inventories are commonly used in law enforcement selection (Weiss, 2010a). Although there are hundreds of personality inventories available, they generally fall into one of the two broad categories based on their intended purpose: measures of psychopathology and measures of normal personality.

Measures of psychopathology

Measures of psychopathology (abnormal behavior or mental disorder) determine whether individuals have serious psychological problems, such as depression, bipolar disorder, or schizophrenia. Tests of psychopathology are used to "screen out" applicants who have psychological problems that would cause performance or discipline problems on the job. Measures of psychopathology are not designed to "select in" applicants and are seldom predictive of job performance (Aamodt, 2004; 2010). These tests will be discussed in the second half of the chapter.

Measures of normal personality

Tests of normal personality measure the traits exhibited by normal individuals in everyday life. Examples of such traits are extraversion, shyness, assertiveness, and friendliness. Although there is some disagreement, psychologists generally agree that there are five main personality dimensions. Known as the "Big Five," these dimensions are openness to experience (bright, adaptable, inquisitive), conscientiousness (reliable, dependable, rule oriented), extraversion (outgoing, friendly, talkative), agreeableness (works well with others, loyal), and emotional stability (calm, not anxious or tense). Commonly used measures of normal personality in law enforcement selection include the California Psychological Inventory (CPI), M-PULSE, 16PF, NEO PI-R, and the Law Enforcement Work Styles Test (LEWST). In contrast to measures of psychopathology, measures of normal personality are used to "select in" rather than "screen out" applicants.

As shown in Table 2.1, our meta-analysis results indicate that openness ($r = 0.09$) and conscientiousness ($r = 0.09$) are the best personality predictors of academy performance, conscientiousness is the best predictor of supervisor ratings of performance ($r = 0.09$), and emotional stability is the best predictor of on-the-job problems ($r = -0.08$).

Table 2.1 Uncorrected correlations between Big Five personality dimensions and law enforcement performance.

Big 5 Dimension	Academy	Performance	On-the-job problems
Openness	0.09[a]	0.04[a]	-0.03
Conscientiousness	0.09[a]	0.09[a]	-0.06[a]
Extraversion	0.08[a]	0.05[a]	0.00
Agreeableness	0.02	0.05[a]	-0.04[a]
Emotional stability	0.04[a]	0.07[a]	-0.08[a]

[a] *Correlation is statistically significant.*

Important Statutory requirements in the United States

Police psychologists in the United States must be thoroughly familiar with the laws related to preemployment psychological evaluations. In addition, many states have additional statutes and regulations that describe minimum requirements for police officer candidates. Although a brief review of critical requirements follows, it is beyond the scope of this chapter to provide a thorough discussion of federal and state statutes, regulations, and case law, and of course these requirements may not apply outside of the United States. Additional information regarding the foundational legal knowledge required to properly conduct these evaluations in the United States can be found on the website of the American Board of Police and Public Safety Psychology (ABPPSP, 2018).

As noted earlier in this chapter, in the United States, discrimination on the basis of a variety of characteristics is not permitted in employment contexts. In order to prevent employers from discriminating against persons with disabilities who can perform the essential functions of the job, the Americans with Disabilities Act (ADA, 1990) requires that all medical exams, including psychological exams that might identify the presence of mental illness or other psychological or emotional problems, may not be administered until after a bona fide conditional offer of employment has been extended to otherwise acceptable job candidates.

Many psychological test instruments are specifically designed to identify psychopathology or may otherwise reveal a psychological disability and so are considered to be medical examination instruments under the ADA. This generally means that the portion of the psychological evaluation that would allow the examiner to identify disqualifying psychopathology is one of the final steps in the employment process, performed after a wide variety of other procedures designed to identify general suitability for employment (discussed in the first part of this chapter) has resulted in a conditional offer of employment contingent upon acceptable results on the medical and psychological evaluations. In addition to the requirement that the psychological evaluation must be done "postconditional offer," the evaluations must be required of all candidates, must be performed by qualified professionals, and must focus on whether or not the candidate can perform the essential functions of the job.

Screening out applicants: postconditional offer psychological evaluations

The purpose of the postconditional offer psychological evaluation is to "screen out" otherwise acceptable candidates who may be at risk for engaging in deleterious behaviors on the job due to psychological factors. Passing the evaluation does not ensure that the candidate will be a superior officer, but simply that he or she meets minimum standards required by the state and the hiring agency, and is not at high risk for performance difficulty because of psychopathology.

Ensuring the proper screening out of police officer candidates who are psychologically unfit for the job is a demanding responsibility both for police administrators and for the psychologists who perform the evaluations. Hiring even a few undesirable officers has the potential for causing damage to the agency and its employees, to the population that the agency serves, and to the psychologist who conducts the evaluation. Looking only at the financial consequences, there are enormous costs lost in selection, training, and equipment if an officer must leave the agency due to misconduct or for any other reason (Annell, Lindfors, & Sverte, 2015; Cochrane, Tett, & Vandcreek, 2003). In addition, there are the potential costs of litigation because of an officer's mistakes. It is impossible to quantify the other types of harm that might be done to individuals in the agency and the community by an unsuitable officer. Any employer might potentially be charged with negligence following the hiring or retention of an individual who has some attribute that would create an undue risk of harm to others when carrying out his or her employment responsibilities (Gregory, 1988; Jansen, 1994; Rostow & Davis, 2002; Seitzinger, Steffel, & Rossi, 1983, pp. 130—135).

In spite of the risks involved in failing to evaluate the psychological suitability of police officer candidates, not all states require such evaluations, and as a result not all police agencies employ them, but the vast majority of departments in larger cities do use them (Cochrane, Tett, & Vandecreek, 2003). Corey and Borum reported in 2013 that 38 states mandated preemployment psychological evaluations for law enforcement, and most of those states have standards that describe the acceptable candidate. For obvious reasons, the risk for police executives in not ensuring the psychological suitability of their employees is much greater than for the average employer. As a result, there are many things that police administrators and police psychologists need to know about the psychological evaluation of police officer candidates.

Ethical standards

Professional psychologists in the United States are expected to adhere to the ethical standards described by the American Psychological Association (Ethical Principles for Psychologists and Code of Conduct, 2017a). Of the 89 standards listed in the Ethical Principles, some have particular relevance to preemployment screening of law enforcement candidates; those are enumerated by Spilberg and Corey (2017). Certain ethical dilemmas are also common to police psychology (see Dietz & Reese, 1986; McCutcheon, 2011; Zelig, 1988), particularly those related to dual relationships, the limits of confidentiality, and conflicts between the Ethical Principles and the requests of the hiring agency.

Who is qualified to perform the postconditional offer evaluation?

Beginning in the 1960s and 1970s, when police departments began more systematically incorporating psychological evaluations into their hiring procedures (Trompetter, 2017; Weiss & Inwald, 2010), selection of the examining psychologist was somewhat haphazard, and the psychologists selected often had no specific training or credentials that prepared them to work with law enforcement. For example, in 1981, the second author, who was at that time employed by a mental health agency to work with children and families, and who had little prior experience working with law enforcement, was simply informed by her agency that she would be doing the psychological evaluations of police officer candidates for a local police department. Although things have come a very long way since then, the authors are also familiar with a police department that recently contracted with a local hospital to provide a psychologist to do their preemployment evaluations. The Chief of Police did not know which of several psychologists would be doing the evaluations or what their qualifications were. In fact, most locally available psychologists will not be adequately qualified to conduct preemployment screenings of law enforcement candidates based solely on their general knowledge of psychological evaluation and their general clinical competence. In the past, law enforcement administrators had few guidelines to assist them in choosing a consulting psychologist who possessed the specialized skills necessary to evaluate police officer candidates. Today, however, such guidelines exist.

Police administrators can obtain a comprehensive understanding of the specialty of police psychology by reviewing a description of its four distinct domains of practice, including assessment-related activities (Aumiller et al., 2007). In states that mandate the evaluations, there is often a specification as to who can conduct the psychological screening evaluation. Although different states may accept licensed psychiatrists, psychologists, or social workers as qualified examiners, most preemployment screenings for law enforcement are conducted by psychologists (Spilberg & Corey, 2018).

Specific guidelines for police psychologists conducting these evaluations have been published by the International Association of Chiefs of Police—Police Psychological Services Section (IACP-PPSS, 2014). The guidelines include a description of examiner qualifications; specific training and experience required; and required knowledge of applicable research, employment law, and ethical principles (including the limits of confidentiality in these situations).

What should the agency provide to the psychologist?

The law enforcement agency should provide the psychologist with a job analysis (described in the first half of this chapter) that outlines the duties and responsibilities of the job that the candidate is seeking, as well as any agency-specific requirements not covered in the job analysis (Ostrov, 2010). In addition, ideally the agency will also provide to the psychologist the background investigation, polygraph results (if used), and any other documentation that has been collected regarding the candidate's application.

What methods should the psychologist use?

A psychologist who has no specialized training in police psychology may make recommendations based on "clinical impressions" derived from test scores, observations, and interview material. Unfortunately, error rates for such clinical recommendations can be quite high, and two psychologists working from different theoretical orientations might come to different conclusions about the same applicant. In addition, if the decision is subsequently challenged, it may be difficult to defend in court. Instead, the psychologist should use actuarial-type methods similar to those used by life insurance companies, which look at the statistical relationship between the presence of behavioral or other indicators and a later event(s) (Cuttler, 2011; Rostow & Davis, 2002). For the purposes of police selection, this means that any procedures or tests used should have been shown to be related to later performance as a police officer (IACP-PPSS, 2014). Even if a test was originally designed for another purpose, as most tests of psychopathology were, the psychologist should be prepared to demonstrate how the test is connected to performance as a police officer.

Unfortunately, there is no recognized consensus as to exactly what evaluation protocol should be used for screening out police officer candidates (Daniel, 2001; Dantzker, 2011). In fact, some psychologists assert that law enforcement selection should not be standardized because, for a variety of reasons, no one has identified the "best way" to perform the evaluations (Daniel, 2001). Selection of evaluation procedures is also influenced by the fact that some jurisdictions specify particular tests that must be used for preemployment psychological evaluations of police candidates (Aamodt, 2010; Herndon, 2010).

A survey by Cochrane et al. (2003) of 155 municipal police agencies revealed that almost 92% of agencies included a psychological evaluation as part of their selection procedures. In that survey, the most frequently used test was the MMPI-2, but a variety of other tests and procedures were used quite regularly. An informal survey of approximately 20 practicing police psychologists conducted by the authors while this chapter was being written revealed that no two psychologists used exactly the same protocol, although there were underlying similarities in procedures. For example, each of the psychologists surveyed used at least one test of abnormal personality or behavior and a clinical interview, along with other procedures that might include personal history questionnaires; tests of cognitive abilities; and specific tests to identify signs of addiction, anxiety, or PTSD, among others. Unfortunately, the lack of standardization does occasionally result in hasty evaluation processes that are quite superficial and not compliant with professional guidelines, such as using a single personality inventory and a short "interview" that consists of a very small number of questions.

It is generally accepted that the police psychologist should use a variety of different procedures during the evaluation, including a review of available background and other nonmedical information, standardized tests, and an interview (Ostrov, 2010; Spilberg & Corey, 2018). Other information may be obtained when relevant to a particular applicant. Using multiple sources of data allows the information obtained through one procedure to be compared with information obtained through a different procedure. Once all of the information has been reviewed and integrated, a report should be written that summarizes the evaluation and contains a determination of the applicant's suitability for employment. Each of these steps will be described below. Ideally the psychologist will also maintain an ongoing research program to collect performance data on the candidates who were hired, in order to validate and refine the evaluation procedures.

Review of background information and other data

The IACP-PPSS Guidelines (2014) stipulate that relevant life history information should be collected and integrated with all other data before making a recommendation. Even if a review of background information was conducted by an evaluator conducting the preoffer portion of a candidate's evaluation, the psychologist conducting the postoffer screening-out portion of the evaluation should review and incorporate that information into the latter evaluation. Such information could be obtained from a variety of sources, including the background investigation; personal history questionnaires; and educational, vocational, medical, or mental health records.

As previously noted, a number of life history variables have been shown to be related to police officer performance, both in training and on the job. For example, work history, drug use history, and criminal history have been used to differentiate between officers who were involved in formal disciplinary actions and officers who had not exhibited any dysfunctional job behaviors (Sarchione, Cuttler, Muchinsky, & Nelson-Gray, 1998), although not all investigations have found consistent results (Cuttler & Muchinsky, 2006). Other authors have confirmed that candidates who have histories that include records of arrest, traffic violations, and failure in other jobs are more likely to engage in behavior that results in loss of employment (Fyfe & Kane, 2006).

Psychological testing

Often, the first face-to-face meeting between the candidate and the examining psychologist is for the administration of the psychological tests. Before any test administration actually takes place, the psychologist should clarify for the candidate the unusually complex nature of the relationship between the candidate, the psychologist, and the law enforcement agency, as mandated by the ethical principles of the American Psychological Association (APA) regarding third-party requests for services (APA, 2017). This should include explaining that the psychologist is serving as a consultant to the law enforcement agency and is not engaged in a confidential relationship with the candidate, lest the candidate mistakenly assume (as some candidates in our experience have) that any statements made to a psychologist are by definition confidential. All parties should understand that the agency, not the candidate, is the psychologist's client. It should be made clear to the candidate that a report will be sent to the hiring agency with recommendations. The candidate should also be informed as to whether he or she will receive any feedback regarding the report and recommendations from the psychologist; some psychologists and agencies permit feedback to be given to the candidate, but most do not. It should also be made clear that the agency will own the report, and the candidate will not be entitled to obtain a copy of it from the psychologist.

All of this information (and any other information relevant to the specific circumstances) should be given to the candidate both verbally and in writing, affording an opportunity for the candidate to ask questions. The candidate should sign the "Informed Consent Form" that contains these details to indicate that he or she has received the information. For the purposes of preemployment evaluations, some police psychologists prefer to call this document the "Statement of Understanding," given that the candidate has not requested the testing for personal reasons (Serafino, 2010).

Many of the tests used in the psychological evaluation of police officer candidates were designed for purposes other than personnel selection, but if a test is being used for the purposes of screening police officer candidates, it should have demonstrated reliability and validity for that purpose. Tests of cognitive ability are often used as part of the selection process and may be administered preconditional offer, as already discussed in an earlier section of this chapter. Tests of normal personality characteristics may also be administered preconditional offer, as already discussed. Those personality tests that are designed to identify psychopathology may only be administered postconditional offer.

There are numerous studies that report correlations between scores on individual scales or composite scores on such tests with a variety of performance items. Some state statutes even dictate the use of specific tests of psychopathology. Unfortunately, meta-analysis results do not support the idea that tests designed to be measures of psychopathology are good overall predictors of police performance (Aamodt, 2004, 2010), but they continue to be widely used, so we will describe them here. The following list is not exhaustive, but it describes some of the more commonly used postoffer instruments in the United States.

Test instruments

Clinical Analysis Questionnaire This instrument consists of two parts, the first part consisting of the 16 PF, and a second part that assesses 12 types of psychopathology. Some research on the relationship between clinical analysis questionnaire (CAQ) profiles and police personality and selection is available (Forero, Gallardo-Pujol, Maydeu-Olivares, & Andres-Pueyo, 2009; Hart, 1981; Lorr & Strack, 1994).

Inwald Personality Inventory (IPI and IPI-2) The IPI was perhaps the first instrument specifically designed to assess behavioral and personality characteristics that could be used to screen out police officer candidates (Inwald, 2010). Like many other inventories, it uses a true/false, self-report format. It provides one validity scale and 25 clinical scales (IPAT, 2011a, 2011b). There is literature that supports the use of the IPI and IPI-2 for evaluation of police officer candidates (Lowmaster & Morey, 2012; Weiss, 2010a). The IPI is often used in combination with other instruments originally developed by Hilson Research, including the Hilson Personnel Profile/Success Quotient (HPP/SQ), focusing on emotional intelligence; the Inwald Survey 5 (IS5), focusing on integrity issues and antisocial attitudes and behaviors; the Hilson Safety/Security Risk Inventory (HSRI), focusing on risk taking attitudes and behaviors; the Inwald Survey 2 (IS2), focusing on violent behavior; the Hilson

Life Adjustment Profile (HLAP), focusing on psychopathology; and the Hilson Background Investigation Inventory-Revised (HBI-R) (Inwald, 2008; 2010). The IPI-2 and additional Hilson tests are currently offered by PSI Services (see below).

Millon Clinical Multiaxial Inventory The Millon Clinical Multiaxial Inventory (MCMI) is another standardized self-report inventory that was designed to measure psychopathology, both long-standing personality patterns and clinical symptomatology. Although it was designed for use with psychiatric patients, it has been used with police applicants (McQuilkin, Russell, Frost, & Faust, 1990).

Minnesota Multiphasic Personality Inventory-2 and RF (MMPI-2 and MMPI-2-RF) The MMPI is arguably the test most frequently used in the postoffer psychological evaluation of police officers (Aamodt, 2004; Cochrane et al., 2003; Corey, 2016), the most current versions being the MMPI-3 and MMPI-2-RF. The MMPI is a self-report personality inventory consisting of statements that the test taker indicates are either true or false. It was originally designed for use in medical and mental health settings to identify various types of psychopathology, but it has been widely adopted for use in law enforcement preemployment evaluations, with norms available for police officer candidates. There is a substantial literature documenting the relationship between scales on the various versions of the MMPI and a wide variety of posthire outcomes in police officer candidates (see Corey & Ben-Porath, 2018, for a discussion). A relatively recent addition to the use of the MMPI-2-RF with police candidates is the Police Candidate Interpretive Report (PCIR), which uses scores from a comparison group of over 2000 police officer candidates from geographic regions all over North America (see Corey & Ben-Porath, 2018, for a complete description of its use and a review of its utility in selection with this population).

Personality Assessment Inventory The Personality Assessment Inventory (PAI) is a self-report personality inventory that asks test takers to rate themselves on 344 items representing validity, clinical, interpersonal, and treatment scales (Morey, 2007; 2014). Many examiners consider the PAI to be an alternative to the MMPI for assessing psychopathology. The PAI has been found to be useful in predicting job performance in police officers (Hargrave & Hiatt, 1989; Lowmaster & Morey, 2012; Weiss, Hitchcock, Weiss, Rostow, & Davis, 2008; Weiss, 2010b; Weiss & Weiss, 2010). A PAI Police and Public Safety Selection Report Module is available from Law Enforcement Psychological Services (LEPS, see description below).

Commercially available test batteries

Institute for forensic psychology The Candidate and Officer Personnel Survey-Revised (COPS-R) is a self-report inventory developed to predict job performance in public safety candidates, consisting of 240 true/false items, with some items pertaining to personality and some pertaining to biographical information. The scored test currently generates 31 scales in four groups: Risk Level, Potential Validity Concerns, Positive Descriptors, and Negative Descriptors (see McGrath & Guller, 2014). It is used as part of a battery developed by the Institute for Forensic Psychology, which may include the PAI, the MMPI2-RF, the CPI, the Wonderlic Personnel Test, and the Shipley. The COPS-R is also marketed to individual psychologists who use it with other tests of their choosing. Several studies have focused on the use of this instrument and battery in police selection (Guller, 2003, 2018; Hewgley, 2013; Lough, Wald, Byrne, & Walker, 2007; Lough & Ryan, 2004, 2005; McGrath & Guller, 2009).

Law Enforcement Psychological Services, Inc. (LEPS) LEPS was formed in the 1970s to deliver preemployment psychological screening services to police and public safety agencies. This group has developed a variety of life history and psychological test reports for the evaluation of applicants for law enforcement and other public safety positions, generated by software that includes a database allowing test data to be used for research. These reports include the Personal History Questionnaire (PHQ) (used preconditional offer), the California Psychological Inventory (CPI) Police and Public Safety Selection Report (used preconditional offer), the Psychological History Questionnaire (PsyQ), the PAI Police and Public Safety Selection Report, the Rotter Incomplete Sentences Blank (Rotter ISB), the Wonderlic Personnel Test, and the State-Trait Anger Expression Inventory (STAXI) Police and Public Safety Selection Report. Literature exists supporting the use of several of the instruments in this battery for the purposes of selection (see descriptions of individual tests above).

Law Enforcement Services, Inc. (LESI) This organization also uses a bifurcated process, consisting of pre- and postoffer procedures. In the preoffer phase, they use an Internet-based personal history questionnaire (onlinePHQ), to organize and analyze background information, and the Multi Domain Screening Report (Cuttler, 2000), which actuarially combines measures of cognitive/educational and personality variables (derived from the Wonderlic Personnel Test, the CPI, and a proprietary instrument) with the PHQ information into a single prediction of suitability. LESI has identified various combinations of data from three domains (life history events, cognitive skills, and interpersonal effectiveness) that predict specific job outcomes (Cuttler, 2011; Cuttler & Muchinsky, 2006; Sarchione et al., 1998). In the postoffer phase, candidates complete either the MMPI2- RF or the IPI-2 and an interview, which generates a Comprehensive Psychological Evaluation report.

Matrix-Psychological Uniform Law Enforcement Selection Evaluation (M-PULSE) The M-PULSE was developed specifically for evaluating police officer candidates. The M-PULSE Inventory itself consists of items specifically related to attitudes, values, and beliefs about law enforcement and items related to general attitudes. The M-PULSE Inventory was designed to be administered either pre- or postconditional offer (Davis & Rostow, 2010). However, the M-PULSE is typically used as part of the postconditional offer Matrix M-PULSE Methodology (Davis & Rostow, 2002), which currently combines data in an actuarial manner from the MMPI-2, M-PULSE, background history, and interview into scaled scores on 18 liabilities and an overall rating. All hired candidates are enrolled in a 5-year follow-up program, with feedback data received at 9, 18, 36, and 60 months (Gouvier & Hill, 2016; Gouvier, Hill, & Musso, 2017).

PSI Services This organization (formerly the Institute for Personality and Ability Testing, IPAT) offers both pre- and postoffer test instruments and reports. Those that are meant to be used postoffer include the 16 PF Protective Services Report Plus (PSR+), the IPI-2, the Hilson Life Adjustment Profile (HLAP), and the Hilson Career Satisfaction Index (HCSI). The PSR+ was developed specifically for use with public safety and protective services personnel; it combines information about mental and emotional functioning with information about normal personality functioning (IPAT, 2007; 2009). The PSR+ features four criterion-validity prediction scores referred to as the PSR dimensions, which include emotional adjustment, integrity/control, intellectual efficiency, and interpersonal relations. As mentioned above, the IPI-2 provides a variety of job-relevant information based on the candidate's behavioral tendencies and attitudes and can also identify candidates who may demonstrate psychopathology that could interfere with their ability to perform necessary public safety duties (IPAT, 2012). The HLAP measures specific psychological characteristics (such as depression, paranoia, anxiety, and suicidal tendencies) that may affect functioning in a high-risk occupation (IPAT, 2011a, 2011b). The HCSI measures characteristics that may affect an individual's emotional adjustment and current work satisfaction, such as stress symptoms, hostility, drug and alcohol abuse, and disciplinary history (IPAT, 2011a, 2011b).

Interview

A face-to-face interview with the examining psychologist is generally the last step in the postoffer evaluation process. According to the IACP-PPSS Guidelines (2014), the purpose of the interview is to obtain interpersonal and mental status information about the candidate and to confirm and/or clarify information obtained previously from other components of the evaluation, such as questionnaires and tests. Rather than being a free-form "clinical" interview, the interview should be structured in a similar manner for all candidates and should focus on collecting information specific to the purpose of the evaluation, including any selection criteria specific to the particular agency. The majority of such interviews take between 30 and 60 min, with only a small percentage taking more than 60 or fewer than 30 min (Corey, 2016).

Many guidelines exist regarding what topics to cover in a psychological interview, but it should be remembered that the interview conducted for preemployment reasons should be structured or semistructured, and should focus on issues relevant to the job (Corey & Borum, 2013; IACP-PPSS, 2014). The interview is an opportunity to discuss and confirm test results and information obtained from the background information, polygraph, or personal history questionnaires (Gamez & Collins, 2012); to resolve any discrepancies or inconsistencies in the data; and to explore the candidate's motivations for and understanding of the job (Mitchell, 2017). An extensive array of general areas should be covered during the interview, including family history; school history; financial history; work history (including job performance, employment problems, attendance, terminations, etc.); military service; behavioral history (including contact with the legal, mental health, and/or medical systems); and reasons for seeking the law enforcement position (Corey & Borum, 2013; Gamez & Collins, 2012).

For the purposes of a preemployment evaluation in the United States, it is also important for psychologists to be aware of information that should not be obtained in the interview or any personal history questionnaires. The Genetic Information Nondiscrimination Act (GINA, 2008) prohibits both the acquisition and disclosure of the potential employee's family medical history, including first-degree relatives and extending to all relatives between the candidate and his or her great-great grandparents and first cousins once removed. In fact, candidates should be told as part of the informed consent procedures not to provide such information. If a candidate still provides family medical information in spite of being asked not to, it cannot be disclosed to the agency or used to inform the hiring recommendation.

Interpretation of the data

The interpretation of data from a preemployment psychological evaluation of a police officer candidate requires awareness of some special considerations. Job candidates want to "pass" the psychological evaluation in order to be hired for the job, and they tend to take the testing quite seriously. For that reason, the typical police candidate rarely leaves test items blank or responds randomly or in other ways that make an item unscorable. The reasons for even a small number of unanswered or unscorable items should be explored with the candidate and taken into consideration in the interpretation of the results.

Unlike the individual who is undergoing the evaluation as part of a self-initiated mental health evaluation, the police officer candidate generally wishes to portray himself or herself as an individual who is high-functioning emotionally, psychologically, and morally, and free from psychopathology. As a result, perhaps the most common complication in interpreting evaluation results from this population is the danger of underreporting of problematic thoughts, emotions, and/or behaviors, often referred to as impression management or "faking good." This tends to result in scores on validity scales that are higher for police candidates than is typical for other populations (Corey & Ben-Porath, 2018; Gallo & Halgin, 2011) and scores on clinical scales that are lower than is typical for other populations.

Detrick and Chibnall (2014) demonstrated that the preemployment evaluation setting tended to result in higher scores on scales designed to detect underreporting than a low-demand setting, by administering a personality inventory twice to the same police candidates. The first administration took place as part of the routine preemployment psychological evaluation (a high-demand setting), while the second took place after their completion of the academy, and was described to the officers as being strictly for research purposes with no information returned to the hiring agencies (a low-demand setting). As expected, the officers' scores on scales that detect underreporting were higher in the high-demand evaluation.

To interpret validity scores of police candidates correctly, they should be compared with a police candidate reference group, to avoid disqualifying otherwise viable candidates based on validity scale scores that suggest that they are hiding psychopathology or that would otherwise invalidate the results. However, if significant underreporting has occurred, the resulting test profile will not give an accurate picture of the person's psychological adjustment and personality characteristics.

There is a second possible reason for low scores on clinical scales, aside from the problem of underreporting. Given the necessity of choosing only the most qualified individuals for police work, police officer candidates are typically scrutinized in a variety of ways before they receive a conditional offer. Candidates with obvious psychopathology or problematic behavioral characteristics are generally screened out by the hiring agency well before the psychological evaluation. As a result, candidates who reach the stage of the psychological evaluation may be genuinely better adjusted than the average individual, and lower scores on the clinical scales may reflect genuinely better functioning. Therefore, it is important, although sometimes difficult, to attempt to discriminate between candidates who are underreporting problems and candidates who are actually well adjusted. Background investigation information may be useful in this task; the genuinely well-adjusted person should have a relatively "clean" background investigation.

For these reasons, on many test instruments scores in the clinically elevated range are not routinely found in police officer candidates (Sellbom, Fischler, & Ben-Porath, 2007). The fact that police candidate populations in general tend to have lower mean scores on clinical scales than the populations typically used to develop test norms is another reason to use specialized law enforcement comparison groups and possibly different cutoff scores. Scores within normal limits, that would not generate concern in an individual who was being evaluated for other purposes, have been associated with performance problems in police officers (Detrick, Ben-Porath, & Sellbom, 2016; Tarascavege, Brewster, Corey, & Ben-Porath, 2015).

Report and recommendations

At the conclusion of the evaluation procedures, the psychologist will integrate all of the findings and will provide to the agency a written report summarizing those findings and the psychologist's determination of the candidate's suitability for employment. Just as there is no standardized set of procedures for the evaluation itself, there is no standardized format for exactly what should be included in the report. The contents of the report will be somewhat dependent upon the procedures used for the evaluation.

There are resources that describe what should be included in the report of the psychological evaluation of public safety candidates (Corey & Borum, 2013; Weiss, 2010a), but generally such reports will include the candidate's identifying information; the source of the referral and the purpose of the evaluation, including the position sought; a listing of the procedures and sources of information that were used; a review and synthesis of the information obtained from each of those procedures, specifically focusing on information that is relevant to the question of whether the candidate has any characteristics that would substantially impair his or her ability to carry out police work; and conclusions and recommendations.

Depending on the requirements of the state or the agency and/or the inclination of the psychologist, the conclusions and recommendations may be reported in a variety of formats. The report may contain a rating of the applicant's suitability using a scale such as A, B, C, D, F; or 1–5; or a list of categories such as qualified/unqualified, suitable/unsuitable, pass/fail; or not recommended/recommended/strongly recommended. Ratings that find the candidate suitable (in all of their various wordings) generally indicate that the evaluation did not find evidence of psychopathology or behavioral problems that would preclude the candidate's selection. Ratings that fall short of the highest rating but are not at the unsuitable level (in those systems that contain more than two ratings), generally indicate that there may be evidence of some symptoms or problems, but they are not at a level that would necessarily disqualify the applicant. Some psychologists will make use of categories such as "marginal," or "acceptable with reservations," but Weiss (2010) suggests that this creates a dilemma for the police administrator, who may be reluctant to hire a candidate who has technically been found acceptable, but about whom the psychologist has reservations. All ratings and/or recommendations should be linked to information that relates to whether or not the candidate can meet the essential job requirements (Ostrov, 2010). The psychologist should always be prepared to defend his or her conclusions using objective evidence derived from the evaluation.

Although it is ultimately the law enforcement agency that makes the decision as to whether to hire an applicant (Gamez & Collins, 2012), many, if not most, departments ask for or require a specific hiring recommendation from the psychologist. However, some psychologists believe that the examiner should avoid being the decision maker and should simply provide a general description of the applicant's relevant psychological and behavioral characteristics, leaving the police administrator to decide how to use the information (Serafino, 2010). This will not meet most agencies' desire for an evaluation that provides a clear recommendation, so most psychologists do provide a concrete recommendation using one of the above formats. Although providing solely a general description of the candidate's characteristics is not ideal for making a hiring decision, if the candidate is hired, descriptions of strengths and weaknesses can subsequently be useful for training and supervision purposes (Rostow & Davis, 2001).

Conclusions

In this chapter, we discussed the process for "selecting in" and "screening out" law enforcement applicants. The "selecting in" process begins with a thorough job analysis followed by the selection of assessments that tap the competencies identified in the job analysis. As discussed in the chapter, assessments that research has shown are statistically related to police performance include cognitive ability tests, level of education, personality inventories, background information, and structured interviews.

Once candidates have been identified who possess the basic competencies needed to be successful in law enforcement, the candidates go through a psychological screening process to determine if they possess psychological characteristics that might affect their ability to be successful in law enforcement. The psychological screening process includes such assessments as tests of psychopathology, background information, and an interview with a clinical psychologist. When used together, the "selecting in" and "screening out" processes should increase the odds of a successful hire.

References

Aamodt, M. G. (2004). *Research in law enforcement selection.* Boca Raton, FL: BrownWalker Press.

Aamodt, M. G. (2010). Predicting law enforcement officer performance with personality inventories. In P. Weiss (Ed.), Personality assessment in police psychology: A 21st century perspective (pp. 229−249). Springfield, IL: Charles C. Thomas.

Aamodt, M. G. (2014). Using background checks in the employee selection process. In C. Hanvey, & K. Sady (Eds.), *HR practitioners guide to legal issues in organizations* (pp. 85−110). New York: Springer.

American Board of Police and Public Safety Psychology (ABPPSP). (2018a). *Examination manual.* Retrieved on 4/15/19 from https://abpp.org/BlankSite/media/Police-and-Public-Safety-Psychology-Documents/ABPPSP-Examination-Manual-110717.pdf.

American Board of Police and Public Safety Psychology (ABPPSP). (2018b). *Core legal knowledge for the practice of police & public safety psychology.* Retrieved on 6/20/18 from https://abpp.org/BlankSite/media/Police-and-Public-Safety-Psychology-Documents/Core-Legal-Knowledge-in-PPSP-050915.pdf.

American Psychological Association (APA). (2017a). *Ethical principles of psychologists and Code of conduct.* Retrieved on 6/13/18 from http://www.apa.org/ethics/code/.

American Psychological Association (APA). (2017b). *Professional practice guidelines for occupationally mandated psychological evaluation.* Retrieved on 6/19/18 from http://www.apa.org/practice/guidelines/psychological-evaluations.aspx.

Americans with Disabilities Act (ADA) of 1990, 42 U.S.C.A. 12101 et seq.

Annell, S. T., Lindfors, P., & Sverke, M. (2015). Police selection - implications during training and early career. *Policing: An International Journal of Police Strategies & Management, 38*(2), 221−238.

Aumiller, G., Corey, D., Allen, S., Brewster, J., Cuttler, M., Gupton, H., et al. (2007). Defining the field of police psychology: Core domains and proficiencies. *Journal of Police and Criminal Psychology, 22*(2), 65−76.

Cochrane, R. E., Tett, R. P., & Vandecreek, L. (2003). Psychological testing and the selection of police officers. *Criminal Justice and Behavior, 30*(5), 511−537.

Corey, D. M. (2016). *Assessment protocols, procedures & pass rates for psychological evaluations of police candidates* (Presented at the annual meeting of the IACP Police Psychological Services Section, San Diego, CA).

Corey, D. M., & Ben-Porath, Y. (2018). *Assessing police and other public safety personnel using the MMPI-2 RF.* Minneapolis, MN: University of Minnesota Press, 528 pp.

Corey, D. M., & Borum, R. (2013). Forensic assessment for high-risk occupations. In R. K. Otto, & I. B. Weiner (Eds.), *Handbook of psychology, Volume 11: Forensic psychology* (pp. 246−270). Hoboken, N.J.: John Wiley & Sons, Inc.

Cuttler, M. J. (2000). *Multi domain screening report*. Greensboro, NC: Law Enforcement Services.

Cuttler, M. J. (2011). Pre-employment screening of police officers: Integrating actuarial prediction models with practice. In J. Kitaeff (Ed.), *Handbook of police psychology* (pp. 135–163). New York, N.Y.: Routledge.

Cuttler, M. J., & Muchinsky, P. M. (2006). Prediction of law enforcement training performance and dysfunctional job performance with general mental ability, personality, and life history variables. *Criminal Justice and Behavior, 33*(1), 3–25.

Daniel, C. (2001). Is there "One Best Way" to select law enforcement personnel? *Review of Public Personnel Administration, 21*(3), 237–247.

Dantzker, M. L. (2011). Psychological preemployment screening for police candidates: Seeking consistency if not standardization. *Professional Psychology: Research and Practice, 42*(3), 276–283.

Davis, R. D., & Rostow, C. D. (2002). M-PULSE. Matrix-psychological uniform law enforcement selection evaluation. *Forensic Examiner, 11/12*, 19–24.

Davis, R. D., & Rostow, C. D. (2010). The Use of the M-PULSE Inventory in law enforcement selection. In P. A. Weiss (Ed.), *Personality assessment in police psychology: A 21st century perspective* (pp. 132–158). Springfield, IL: Charles C. Thomas.

Detrick, P., Ben-Porath, Y. S., & Sellbom, M. (2016). Associations between MMPI-2-RF (Restructured Form) and Inwald Personality Inventory (IPI) scales scores in a law enforcement preemployment screening sample. *Journal of Police and Criminal Psychology, 31*(2), 81–95.

Dietz, P. E., & Reese, J. T. (1986). The perils of police psychology: 10 strategies for minimizing role conflicts when providing mental health service and consultation to law enforcement agencies. *Behavioral Sciences & the Law, 4*(4), 385–400.

Forero, C. G., Gallardo-Pujol, D., Maydeu-Olivares, A., & Andres-Pueyo, A. (2009). A longitudinal model for predicting performance of police officers using personality and behavioral data. *Criminal Justice and Behavior, 36*(6), 591–606.

Fyfe, J. J., & Kane, R. (2006). *Bad cops: A study of career-ending misconduct among New York city police officers*. Submitted to the U.S. Department of Justice, National Institute of Justice.

Gallo, F. J., & Halgin, R. P. (2011). A guide for establishing a practice in police preemployment postoffer psychological evaluations. *Professional Psychology: Research and Practice, 42*(3), 269–275.

Gamez, A. M., & Collins, G. C. (2012). Psychological evaluations of law enforcement applicants: The search for ethical officers. In B. D. Fitch (Ed.), *Law enforcement ethics: Classic and contemporary issues* (pp. 29–47). Thousand Oaks, CA: Sage Publications, Inc.

Gardiner, C. (2017). *Policing around the nation: Education, philosophy, and practice*. Washington, DC: Police Foundation.

Genetic Information Nondiscrimination Act of 2008 (GINA). Pub.L. 110-223, 122 Stat. 881 (2008).

Gouvier, W. D., & Hill, B. D. (September 2016). *Sensitivity, Specificity, and Base Rates: Getting realistic about psychological tests and measures in police psychology*. Paper presented at the 42nd annual meeting of the Society for Police and Criminal Psychology, Austin, TX.

Gouvier, W. D., Hill, B. D., & Musso, M. W. (October 2017). *Resistance to change? Start at the Top!*. Paper presented at the 43nd annual conference of the Society for Police and Criminal Psychology, San Diego, CA.

Gregory, D. L. (1988). Reducing the risk of negligence in hiring. *Employee Relations L.J., 14*, 31−40.

Guller, M. (2003). Predicting performance of law enforcement personnel using the candidate and officer personnel survey and other psychological measures. In *Submitted in partial fulfillment of the requirements of the degree of Doctor of Philosophy*. Seton Hall University.

Guller, M. (2018). *Test predictors of serious misconduct, substance abuse and/or pervasive performance problems with the COPS-R, PAI and short-form IQ*. Paper presented at the Consortium of Police and Public Safety Psychologists (COPPS), St. Augustine, FL, April 27, 2018.

Hargrave, G. E., & Hiatt, D. (1989). Use of the California Psychological Inventory in law enforcement officer selection. *Journal of Personality Assessment, 53*, 267−277.

Hart, R. (1981). *The use of the clinical analysis questionnaire in the selection of police officers: A validation study*. Unpublished doctoral dissertation. Florida State University.

Helmreich, R. L., Sawin, L. L., & Carsrud, A. L. (1986). The honeymoon effect in job performance: Temporal increases in the predictive power of achievement motivation. *Journal of Applied Psychology, 71*, 185−188.

Herndon, J. S. (2010). The politics of personality assessment in police agencies. In P. A. Weiss (Ed.), *Personality assessment in police psychology: A 21st century perspective* (pp. 362−371). Springfield, IL: Charles C. Thomas.

Hewgley, L. P. (2013). Cognitive, personality, and biodata predictors of police academy attrition. In *Thesis submitted in partial fulfillment for the Master of Arts*. Middle Tennessee State University.

Huffcutt, A. I., & Arthur, W. (1994). Hunter and Hunger (1984) revisited: Interview validity for entry-level jobs. *Journal of Applied Psychology, 79*(2), 184−190.

Huffcutt, A. I., & Roth, P. L. (1998). Racial group differences in employment interview evaluations. *Journal of Applied Psychology, 83*(2), 179−189.

Hunter, J. E., & Hunter, R. F. (1984). Validity and utility of alternative predictors of job performance. *Psychological Bulletin, 96*(1), 72−98.

Institute for Personality and Ability Testing (IPAT). (2007). *Protective services reports manual* (Champaign, IL).

Institute for Personality and Ability Testing (IPAT). (2009). *The 16PF fifth edition questionnaire manual* (Champaign, IL).

Institute for Personality and Ability Testing (IPAT). (2011a). *Hilson life adjustment profile technical manual* (Champaign, IL).

Institute for Personality and Ability Testing (IPAT). (2011b). *Hilson career satisfaction Index technical manual* (Champaign, IL).

Institute for Personality and Ability Testing (IPAT). (2012). *Inwald personality inventory-2 manual* (Champaign, IL).

International Association of Chiefs of Police-Police Psychological Services Section (IACP-PPSS). (2014). *Preemployment psychological evaluation guidelines*. Retrieved on 4/15/19 from https://www.theiacp.org/sites/default/files/all/p-r/Psych-PreemploymentPsychEval.pdf.

Inwald, R. E. (2008). The Inwald personality inventory (IPI) and Hilson research inventories: Development and rationale. *Agression & Violent Behavior, 13*(4), 298−327.

Inwald, R. E. (2010). Use of the Inwald personality inventory, Hilson tests, and Inwald surveys for selection, "Fitness-for-Duty" assessment, and relationship counseling. In P. A. Weiss

(Ed.), *Personality assessment in police psychology: A 21st century perspective* (pp. 91–131). Springfield, IL: Charles C. Thomas.

Jansen, G. T. (1994). Employer liability for negligent hiring or retention under Illinois law. *Illinois Bar Journal, 82*, 602–606.

Lorr, M., & Strack, S. (1994). Personality profiles of police candidates. *Journal of Clinical Psychology, 50*(2), 200–207.

Lough, J., & Ryan, M. (2004). Psychological profiling of Australian police officers: An examination of post-selection performance. *International Journal of Police Science and Management, 7*(1), 15–23.

Lough, J., & Ryan, M. (2005). Psychological profiling of Australian police officers: A longitudinal examination of post-selection performance. *International Journal of Police Science and Management, 8*(2), 143–152.

Lough, J., Wald, E., Byrne, K., & Walker, G. (2007). The impact of psychological profiling of Australian correctional officers. *Corrections Compendium, 32*(4), 1–6.

Lowmaster, S. E., & Morey, L. D. (2012). Predicting law enforcement officer job performance with the personality assessment inventory. *Journal of Personality Assessment, 94*(3), 254–261.

McCutcheon, J. L. (2011). Ethical issues in police psychology: Challenges and decision-making models to resolve ethical dilemmas. In J. Kitaeff (Ed.), *Handbook of police psychology* (pp. 89–108). New York, N.Y.: Routledge.

McGrath, R. E., & Guller, M. (2009). Concurrent validity of the candidate and officer personnel suvey (COPS). *International Journal of Police Science and Management, 11*(2), 150–159.

McGrath, R. E., & Guller, M. (2014). *COPS-R technical manual.* Oakland, NJ: IFP Test Services, Inc.

McQuilkin, J. I., Russell, V. L., Frost, A. G., & Faust, W. R. (1990). Psychological test validity for selecting law enforcement officers. *Journal of Police Science and Administration, 17*(4), 289–294.

Mitchell, C. L. (2017). Preemployment psychological screening of police officer applicants: Basic considerations and recent advances. In C. L. Mitchell, & E. H. Dorian (Eds.), *Police psychology and its growing impact on modern law enforcement* (pp. 28–50). Hershey, PA: IGI Global.

Morey, L. C. (2007). *Personality assessment inventory (professional Manual).* Lutz, FL: Psychological Assessment Resources.

Morey, L. C. (2014). The personality assessment inventory. In R. P. Archer & S. R. Smith (Eds.), *Personality assessment* (pp.181–228). Routledge/Taylor & Francis Group.

Ostrov, E. (2010). Using multiple sources of information when conducting mandatory or required police psychological evaluations. In P. A. Weiss (Ed.), *Personality assessment in police psychology: A 21st century perspective* (pp. 347–361). Springfield, IL: Charles C. Thomas.

Reaves, B. A. (2015). *Local police departments, 2013: Personnel, Policies, and practices (NCJ 248677).* Washington, DC: Bureau of Justice Statistics.

Rostow, C., & Davis, R. (2002). Psychological screening. *Law and Order, 50*(5), 100–106.

Roth, P. L., BeVier, C. A., Bobko, P., Switzer, F. S., & Tyler, P. (2001). Ethnic group differences in cognitive ability in employment and educational settings: A meta-analysis. *Personnel Psychology, 54*(2), 297–330.

Sarchione, C. D., Cuttler, M. J., Muchinsky, P. M., & Nelson-Gray, R. O. (1998). Prediction of dysfunctional job behaviors among law enforcement officers. *Journal of Applied Psychology, 83*, 904–912.

Schmidt, F. L., & Hunter, J. E. (1998). The validity and utility of selection methods in personnel psychology: Practical and theoretical implications of 85 years of research findings. *Psychological Bulletin, 124*(2), 262–274.

Seitzinger, J., Steffel, J., & Rossi, D. (1983 March). *Vicarious liability.* The Police Chief.

Sellbom, M., Fischler, G. L., & Ben-Porath, Y. S. (2007). Identifying MMPI-2 predictors of police officer integrity and misconduct. *Criminal Justice and Behavior, 34*(8), 985–1004.

Serafino, G. F. (2010). Fundamental issues in police psychological assessment. In P. A. Weiss (Ed.), *Personality assessment in police psychology: A 21st century perspective* (pp. 29–55). Springfield, IL: Charles C. Thomas.

Spilberg, S. W., & Corey, D. M. (2018). Peace officer psychological screening manual *(revised April, 2018).* Sacramento: California Commission on Peace Officer Standards and Training.

Tarascavege, A. M., Brewster, J., Corey, D. M., & Ben-Porath, Y. S. (2015). Use of pre-hire MMPI-2-RF police candidate scores to predict supervisor ratings of post-hire performance. *Assessment, 22*(4), 411–428.

Trompetter, P. S. (2017). A history of police psychology. In C. L. Mitchell, & E. H. Dorian (Eds.), *Police psychology and its growing impact on modern law enforcement* (pp. 1–26). IGI Global.

Weiss, P. A., Hitchcock, J. H., Weiss, W. U., Rostow, C., & Davis, R. (2008). The personality assessment inventory borderline, drug, and alcohol scales as predictors of overall performance in police officers: A series of exploratory analyses. *Policing and Society, 18*(3), 301–310.

Weiss, P. A. (2010a). *Personality assessment in police psychology.* Springfield, IL: Charles C. Thomas.

Weiss, P. A. (2010b). Use of the PAI in personnel selection. In M. A. Blais, M. R. Baity, & C. J. Hopwood (Eds.), *Clinical applications of the personality assessment inventory* (pp. 163–176). New York: Brunner-Routledge.

Weiss, P. A., & Inwald, R. (2010). A brief history of personality assessment in police psychology. In P. A. Weiss (Ed.), *Personality assessment in police psychology: A 21st century perspective* (pp. 5–28). Springfield, IL: Charles C. Thomas.

Weiss, W. U., & Weiss, P. A. (2010). Use of the Personality Assessment Inventory in police and security personnel selection. In P. A. Weiss (Ed.), *Personality assessment in police psychology: A 21st century perspective* (pp. 72–90). Springfield, IL: Charles C. Thomas.

Zelig, M. (1988). Ethical dilemmas in police psychology. *Professional Psychology: Research and Practice, 19*(3), 336–338.

Incorporating psychological skills in police academy training

3

Daniel M. Blumberg, Konstantinos Papazoglou, Sarah Creighton and Chuck Kaye

Introduction

Effective policing has always required a unique combination of physical, cognitive, emotional, and interpersonal skills. However, because of the introduction of new technology, these skills are more difficult than ever to learn and to master. Today's police officers carry more tools on their equipment belts (e.g., Tasers) and bodies (e.g., body-worn cameras), utilize more equipment in their patrol cars (e.g., computers), and face more public scrutiny of their actions due to smartphones and social media than officers from prior generations. It can be argued that the job has never been more demanding or, for that matter, more stressful. In the least, there is little dispute that contemporary policing is extremely complex and challenging. For this reason, law enforcement agencies are obligated to hire, train, and retain a cadre of the most psychologically fit police officers.

Police training is responsible for preparing new hires for this difficult career. Officers attend a relatively brief police academy, which is followed by training in the field. There are various academy formats, including full-time training for 6 months, part-time training for 12 months, and residential academies, which are quite similar to military boot camps. The content of police academy training is typically mandated by state or federal governing bodies. Successful completion of the academy certifies officers with police powers in the given jurisdiction.

Police academy training has two general aspects. The academic component takes place in classroom settings and requires recruits[1] to learn the basics of law, procedures, radio codes, penal codes, etc. In California, for example, recruits spend a minimum of 664 hours learning content from 42 separate learning domains (California Commission on Peace Officer Standards and Training (POST), 2018b). This is done in a didactic format and involves formal testing in which recruits must pass each exam with a certain minimum score. The other component of the police academy involves hands-on training and includes rehearsal and scenario-based performance appraisals in areas, which include arrest and control, defensive tactics, use of weapons, and driving. (Some of these skills, such as driving, tactical firearms, and arrest and control, are considered perishable and require incumbent officers to

---

[1] In some police academies the students are referred to as cadets.

Police Psychology, Edited by Marques and Paulino. https://doi.org/10.1016/B978-0-12-816544-7.00003-6

receive periodic refresher training throughout their careers [e.g., (California Commission on Peace Officer Standards and Training (POST), 2018a)].) Similar to the academic portion, recruits must demonstrate proficiency in these skills or fail that learning domain. Most academies allow recruits to fail a certain number of domains and to remediate. If any domain is not satisfactorily passed, the recruit is terminated from the academy.

Traditionally, police academies have been conducted in a paramilitary fashion. This means that recruits are held to a high standard of discipline, deportment, and regimentation while learning how to become a police officer. Often, academy training staff would be indistinguishable from military drill sergeants, who verbally harass and, even, demean recruits who are not measuring up. Push-ups, extra running, and writing reports are used as punishment. Although this training format builds camaraderie and a high level of *esprit de corps*, it tends to have a fairly high dropout rate, which may not trouble purists who are of the belief that "if they can't cut it here, they'd never survive on the streets." Although there is some truth to this (i.e., training should prepare recruits for the harshest conditions that they will face on the job), this format also lacks attention to individual differences in learning styles, personalities, and preexisting interpersonal skills.

This is not a new concern. For over 30 years, there has been a steady stream of criticism, which underscores deficiencies in police academy training when it comes to adequately preparing recruits for the actual demands of the job (e.g., Caro, 2011; Warren, 1999). Much of this criticism has come from officers themselves when asked to reflect on the relevance of their academy experience (e.g., Marion, 1998; Talley, 1986) and from police administrators who do not believe that police academy training is sufficient (e.g., Johnston & Cheurprakobkit, 2002). The general disconnect between academy training and job preparation tends to revolve around two interrelated issues concerning the content and the delivery of the academy curriculum. The typical paramilitary format fails to prepare recruits to work in a manner consistent with the community-oriented police services model and neglects basic principles of adult-learning theory. Essentially, in order to produce officers who are able to successfully perform community-oriented policing techniques (e.g., proactive collaboration with community members (Tillyer, 2018)), police academies must train recruits to be independent, creative problem solvers (e.g., Birzer, 2003; Chappell, 2008; Dwyer & Laufersweiler-Dwyer, 2004; Makin, 2016).

Past literature has discussed the importance for police academies to adopt an adult-learning theory model. Fundamentally, beyond the issues surrounding the best training techniques to prepare recruits to work within a community-oriented policing model, law enforcement agencies are faced with the broader question of what type of police officers are they training? Recruits who are trained in a manner that is consistent with adult-learning theory are encouraged to develop critical thinking skills, effective communication, and better emotional intelligence. However, this is generally not how police recruits are trained (e.g., Makin, 2016). Moreover, academies that embrace an adult-learning model recognize the significance of how training is delivered. Specifically, academy training staff serve as strong role models who socialize officers into the agency's culture (e.g., Flynn, 2002; Marion, 1998). Vodde (2011) stated this quite starkly: "Thus, if recruits are constantly exposed to an autocratic, prescriptive, and discipline-oriented instructor, as opposed to one that is benevolent, fair-minded, and mentoring, such behaviors will inevitably be modeled…" (p. 35). Stoughton (2015) goes even further by contending that traditional training models teach officers to be afraid, which "… inevitably affects the way that officers interact with civilians" (p. 228).

Keeping pace with the changing demands of contemporary policing, academy training has had to evolve. It is no longer sufficient for training to teach just the law or to focus only on the perishable skills mentioned above. And, it is extremely counterproductive to train recruits in an authoritarian, pedagogical format. Nevertheless, the voices calling for change in police academy practices tend to lack prescriptive details on how to accomplish this change and, more precisely, how to teach, strengthen, reinforce, and support the skills needed to graduate officers who are psychologically prepared to competently perform in the field. For example, although the Law Enforcement Foundation in Ohio identified 12 job competencies in 2001, police academies appear to have made little real progress in training recruits in many of these important skills: high moral/ethical standards; unbiased and understanding of diversity; service orientation; team orientation; good oral communication and listening skills; good written communication skills; high levels of motivation; strong decision-making and problem-solving skills; good human relations skills, self-control and discipline; good planning and organization skills; and a performance-driven attitude (in Caro, 2011, p. 360).

Similarly, in 2004, the California Commission on Peace Officer Standards and Training identified 10 psychological screening dimensions for agencies to consider when hiring police officers. In this chapter, the focus is on the ways in which police academies can infuse training with these psychological skills, which recruits need in order to meet the challenges faced by today's police officers. For convenience and clarity, these skills will be separated into four groups: cognitive, emotional, social, and moral. In addition to defining the skills, attention is paid to the ways in which specific academy experiences can teach and strengthen each skill.

Cognitive skills

Police work is mentally challenging. This has led to a somewhat long-standing debate about the extent to which law enforcement agencies should set minimum education requirements for their new hires. The research findings, however, have been somewhat mixed. The general argument is that formal education and the experience of attending college instills in future police officers a level of mental flexibility and other psychological skills, which are not found in their peers who have only completed high school (e.g., Johnston & Cheurprakobkit, 2002; Paterson, 2011). More specifically, Paoline and Terrill (2007) found that, although officers with any college experience tended to use less verbal force, it was only officers who completed 4 years of college who used less physical force than their less educated peers (p. 192). However, additional research has focused on the specific nature of officers' formal education and found that "criminal justice students demonstrated higher levels of authoritarianism than graduates of other disciplines" (Paterson, 2011, p. 289).

The discussion of formal education is contrasted with the role of experience and where that experience can be attained. For example, officers without formal education, but who have more job experience showed less use of verbal and physical force than newer officers (Paoline & Terrill, 2007, p. 193). Therefore, it appears that formal education is not the key factor associated with police officers' effectiveness. It is more likely that important skills, which are most often acquired during college, lead to officers' effectiveness and are the reason why many champion a college education for police recruits. However, not all who attend college acquire these skills, and college is not the only way for individuals to obtain them. Furthermore, leaving such important skill acquisition to chance is unnecessary when police agencies can ensure that all recruits develop these skills during academy training.

Police academies can seamlessly integrate essential cognitive skill training into current academy curricula. From POST (2014), the skills in question are:

> *Decision-making/judgment* involves common sense, "street smarts," and the ability to make sound decisions, demonstrated by the ability to size up situations quickly to determine and take appropriate action. It also involves the ability to sift through information to glean that which is important, and, once identified, to use that information effectively (p. 67).
> *Impulse control/attention to safety* involves taking proper precautions and avoiding impulsive and/or unnecessarily risky behavior to ensure the safety of oneself and others. It includes the ability and inclination to think before acting—to keep one's impetuous, knee-jerk reactions in check, and instead behave in conscious regard for the larger situation at hand (p. 59).
> *Conscientiousness/dependability* involves diligent, reliable, conscientious work patterns, and performing in a timely, logical manner in accordance with rules, regulations, and organizational policies (p. 56).
> *Adaptability/flexibility* involves the ability to change gears and easily adjust to the many different, sudden, and sometimes competing demands of the job (p. 55).

Although current practices tend to do a better job addressing these cognitive skills than, say, the emotional skills, this is usually done indirectly. That is, acquisition of these skills is often inferred from recruits' performance on various other assessments or evaluated in conjunction with another assessment. For example, during an evaluation of recruits' arrest and control skills, training staff determine recruits' ability to properly escalate use of force according to the use of force continuum (e.g., Flynn, 2002). Their performance may lead to inferred conclusions about decision-making, judgment, and impulse control. There are two problems when staff make such conclusions. First, it is possible to confuse a learning deficiency with a decision-making problem; the recruit's poor performance on the assessment may be due to a lack of understanding of or acuity with the use of force continuum rather than due to deficits in decision-making or judgment. Second, training staff members are not basing such conclusions on a direct assessment of decision-making. The importance of these cognitive skills for effective police performance dictates a need for standardized and specific measurements of the cognitive skills themselves.

Police academies need to improve the way in which they develop recruits' independent, critical thinking. To impart and strengthen the four cognitive skills, academies need to find a way to reduce the didactic, micromanagement of recruits (i.e., telling them exactly what to do all the time) and increase opportunities for recruits' autonomous decision-making. This can be done in various learning domains as a normal course of action. Specifically, recruits should, without training officers' presence or involvement, be given time in break-out groups to argue pros and cons of various actions. Then, after presenting the small groups' ideas to the whole group, the recruits are guided to examine the reasoning behind their decisions. This should be done, also, after each practical exercise where recruits are required to discuss why they chose to do what they did. By hearing the rationale of peers, rather than the wrath of instructors, they will develop better critical thinking skills and improve their impulse control and decision-making.

Conscientiousness and adaptability are not cultivated in a traditional paramilitary police academy. When the academy shifts to an adult learning model, recruits are confronted through scenarios associated with various learning domains with a requirement to be more flexible, to think on their feet, and to demonstrate conscientious work behavior. Punishment is replaced with logical consequences. For example, being late or forgetting a piece of equipment is not met with extra push-ups or having to write a report. Instead, these behaviors will result in the same outcomes as recruits will experience when such behavior happens on the job (i.e., progressive discipline). In other words, the traditional academy model does not teach recruits the importance of dependability and flexibility; it just reinforces compliance. Therefore, to build these cognitive skills, academies should mirror the supervision and discipline model of the agencies where their recruits will soon work.

Emotional skills

Police work is emotionally challenging. On many levels, police officers' emotions affect how well they do their job and how long they will be able to do their job well. In terms of longevity, much has been written about the emotional toll that police work takes on officers, which can lead to, among other consequences, debilitating levels of burnout (e.g., Griffin & Sun, 2018; Schaible & Gecas, 2010). A contributing factor, beyond the routine exposure to trauma and human suffering, was found to be the emotional exhaustion officers experience from constantly showing the public emotions other than what they actually feel, e.g., remaining calmly stoic when disgusted, or smiling when actually angry (Kenworthy, Fay, Frame, & Petree, 2014; also, Barber, Grawitch, & Trares, 2009; van Gelderen, Bakker, Konijn, & Demerouti, 2011). However, a recent study found that newer officers who had not yet been exposed to on-duty traumatic incidents were less emotionally well-adjusted than trauma-exposed senior officers (Thornton & Herndon, 2016), who have developed more resiliency. Of course, in a given moment, police officers' acute emotions significantly impact their job performance. For example, "When they were anxious, the officers had a stronger expectation of threat, which caused them to shoot earlier and make more mistakes" (Nieuwenhuys, Savelsbergh, & Oudejan, 2012, p. 832).

Emotional skills can improve the extent to which police officers successfully manage the emotional challenges of the job. One such skill, according to POST (2014), is *emotional regulation/stress tolerance*, which involves the ability to maintain composure and stay in control, particularly during time-critical emergency events and other stressful situations. It includes taking the negative aspects of the job in stride and maintaining an even temperament, as well as accepting criticism rather than becoming overly defensive or allowing it to hamper job performance (p. 64).

On a very promising and apropos note, research has demonstrated that police officers can be taught to improve their emotion regulation skills (e.g., Berking, Meier, & Wupperman, 2010). Nelis et al. (2011) demonstrated specific and lasting improvement in emotion regulation, which correlated with improvements "in psychological well-being, subjective health, quality of social relationship, and work success" (p. 361).

Another important skill is emotional intelligence (EI), which, in most definitions, also involves emotion regulation. EI (sometimes referred to as EQ) involves the extent to which individuals (1) recognize their emotions and understand how emotions impact their behavior; (2) control impulsive feelings and successfully manage their emotions; (3) identify others' emotional cues without letting one's own emotions interfere with behavior; and (4) maintain good relationships, communicate clearly, influence others, work well in a team, and manage conflict (e.g., Brackett, Mayer, & Warner, 2004). Individuals with higher EI tend to handle stress better than those with lower EI, and EI has been correlated with police performance (Ebrahim Al Ali, Garner, & Magadley, 2012). Moreover, there have been promising findings that training can improve emotional intelligence (e.g., Nelis, Quoidbach, Mikolajczak, & Hansenne, 2009; Schutte, Malouff, & Thorsteinsson, 2013; Zijlmans, Embregts, Gerits, Bosman, & Derksen, 2011) and encouraging efforts at applying this to police officers (e.g., Creighton & Blumberg, 2016).

Academy training is crucial to properly prepare recruits to successfully cope with the emotional challenges of police work. In fact, "it may be just as important for a modern day police officer to be emotionally aware as it is for them to be physically fit and knowledgeable about the law" (Brunetto, Teo, Shacklock, & Farr-Wharton, 2012, p. 436). Therefore, it is essential for recruits in the academy to learn how to regulate their emotions in the myriad situations that they are likely to encounter on the job and, more broadly, for the academy experience to increase recruits' level of emotional intelligence. Integrally linked to this, law enforcement agencies must ensure that academy training teaches recruits evidence-based techniques to successfully manage routine and traumatic stressors.

There has been growing attention to the importance of improving officer wellness, in general, which inherently addresses officers' emotion regulation and stress tolerance. A recent publication from the US Department of Justice (COPS Office, 2018) described the various contributors to officers' poor health outcomes and emphasized that "… the organization and its culture contribute to officer health and wellness" (p. 9). This has led to a commitment to provide grants, including one that trains "… officers on techniques for self-regulating their emotional and physiological responses to stress" (p. 4).

There are specific activities that police academies can introduce to improve recruits' wellness and stress tolerance. The first step is to instill a culture of wellness. This begins by structuring the academy to include regular, formal debriefings, which include recruits, veteran officers, and academy staff. The debriefings can be facilitated by a department psychologist, a peer support officer, or a member of the agency's wellness unit. The debriefings establish a pattern for recruits to talk about their reactions (i.e., thoughts and feelings) about academy performance issues, about incidents about which they heard that occurred on the department, and about any pertinent news reports from anywhere, which involve police officers. These debriefings validate and normalize recruits' reactions and provide a healthy outlet.

Academies should encourage, if not require, recruits to keep a journal. Starting this practice at the outset of recruits' careers will launch what has been found to be an important tool to help maintain psychological health. For example, in one study, nurses who wrote freely in a journal each day had less compassion fatigue and more compassion satisfaction than those who did not keep a journal (Christensen, 2018). If academies establish this as a mandatory activity, recruits would not have to share the content of their journals, but would be required to verify that they write each day. The hope is that, once the habit is established, the recruits will continue the practice of journaling (even electronically, e.g., on computer or smartphone) throughout their careers.

Fundamental to successful emotion regulation and stress tolerance is learning performance enhancement techniques, which keep recruits operating at peak performance levels. Much like athletes who have to learn to control the intensity of emotions in order to compete at their highest level, police officers need to understand the role that their emotions can play in the performance of their duties. The police academy is where this training should begin. In addition to the previously mentioned development of emotional intelligence skills, recruits should be taught skills to reduce acute levels of anxiety (e.g., breathing, mindfulness), which, if not controlled, significantly detract from optimal performance. Rather than training rote repetition of, for example, arrest and control techniques, recruits need more time rehearsing these techniques in highly stressful conditions where they can develop confidence and competence in their ability to manage their own level of internal distress. In addition to remaining calm enough to properly escalate contacts according to the use of force continuum, it is imperative for academies to train recruits how to manage their emotions in order to properly deescalate volatile situations.

Associated with efforts to improve recruits' ability to successfully manage acute stress, the academy can promote efforts designed to mitigate recruits' chronic distress levels. This chronic stress leads to many negative health outcomes (Mumford, Taylor,

& Kubu, 2015), which contribute to numerous work-related difficulties. For example, one study showed that recruits experienced less stress and reported better mood after participation in a yoga program that was given during the academy (Jeter, Cronin, & Khalsa, 2013). Fitness, nutrition, sleep hygiene, avoidance of self-medication (e.g., caffeine, alcohol), and activities such as yoga should be strongly promoted and modeled by recruits' mentors during academy training. The goal is for the recruits to establish a commitment to their personal wellness during the academy and to maintain these good health practices throughout their careers.

Social skills

Police work is socially challenging. In addition to the skills necessary to effectively navigate the difficulties often encountered when interacting with members of the community, police officers are faced with significant obstacles coping with the strain that police work places on their friendships and their relationships with loved ones. This pressure is especially difficult for female police officers and, even more so, for married female officers with children (Kurtz, 2012). Police officers often struggle to maintain a healthy work-life balance and may bring their work demeanor home with them, which can negatively impact their family members and, especially, their marriages (e.g., Miller, 2007; Stinson & Liederbach, 2013; Tuttle, Giano, & Merten, 2018). Similarly, police officers' spouses and children endure a variety of difficulties, which, in turn, lead to added stress on the officers.[2] This added stress, then, adversely affects officers' work performance. For example, after graduating the police academy and beginning patrol work (often on the weekends and on night-shift), many officers begin to hear grumblings from their spouse and children about never being home and about missing important family functions. These complaints can grow into direct pressure on officers to quit their job. Fundamentally, much of the family-related consternation stems from a lack of preparation and support.

The transactional nature and complexity of police-family stress dictates that law enforcement agencies take steps to address the needs of police families. This can be done in several ways. First, mental health resources should be readily available for officers, their spouses, and their children. Second, agencies can do a better job training their officers to prepare for this source of distress. This training should focus both on detection of early warning signs of family stress and on ways to prevent many common sources of it. Third, agencies can directly engage spouses and family members of their officers. This can be done through peer-support programs (e.g., wives auxiliary; Cook, 2016), but also should start much earlier in officers' careers.

An innovative program to address police-family stress and to directly prepare police families for what to expect when their loved one becomes a police officer, which

---

[2] Readers are referred to Kirschman (2018) for an excellent discussion of the stressors experienced by police families.

was implemented by a large, metropolitan police agency, takes place during recruits' academy training. This begins during a preacademy orientation, which is the recruits' first day of employment. Along with signing up for medical benefits, an introduction from command staff, and an orientation from the police union, recruits receive a 30-minute wellness orientation. They hear about the resources that are immediately available to the recruits and all of their family members, including access to chaplains, psychological service providers, and staff of the agency's Wellness Unit. The recruits receive a brochure to share with their loved ones, which contains direct contact information for all services and wellness benefits, including the clear authorization that accessing services does not require any approval from their command staff.

The program continues with a Family Orientation Day for recruits and all their family members to attend on the first Saturday following recruits' graduation from the academy. The orientation is facilitated by the agency's Wellness Unit staff and the Psychological Services staff. The morning is for the new graduates only and includes introductions of chaplains, psychologists, wellness staff, the senior officers in attendance, and each newly graduated officer. The officers discuss why they chose the profession and explain their current family makeup. The morning concludes with a few testimonials from senior officers who share stories about significant issues during their career, which impacted their wellness (e.g., officer-involved shootings, a personal tragedy or injury). These officers emphasize what they did to overcome obstacles and how they specifically coped with trauma.

The family members arrive at noon on Orientation Day to have lunch with their officer. After lunch, the new officers meet with the psychologist for 60–90 minutes while their family members meet with the staff of the agency's Wellness Unit. The officers are encouraged to seek regular "wellness checks" and to recognize the importance of good communication with their family members. Simultaneously in another room, the family members hear about detecting early warning signs of distress in their officer. They are given information about how to independently access resources without the need to first obtain approval from their loved one; this includes a promise of anonymity should they ever reach out for some support.

The officers and their family members are reunited for the final few hours of Family Orientation Day. First, an overview of available resources is presented by the chaplains, psychologists, Wellness Unit staff, and members of the agency's Peer Support Team. Next, for about 1 hour, a married couple discusses "Dynamics of a Law Enforcement Marriage/Family," which is followed by a question and answer period. Finally, the day ends with an open discussion of healthy communication patterns; the need to establish ground rules with each other; the toll of shift work; recognizing "red flags"; reinforcing healthy eating and sleeping habits; and, expectations on the officer and the family by the FTO (Field Training Officer) program. It is essential to have the family members' understanding, support, and active participation in their own and their officers' ongoing wellness.

Beyond the support for police families, police academies can seamlessly integrate essential social skill training into current academy curricula. From POST (2014), the skills in question are:

Social competence involves communicating with others in a tactful and respectful manner, and showing sensitivity and concern in one's daily interactions (p. 52).

Teamwork involves working effectively with others to accomplish goals, as well as subordinating personal interests for the good of the working group and the organization. It involves establishing and maintaining effective, cooperative working relationships with coworkers, supervisors, clients, representatives of other organizations, and others (p. 54).

Assertiveness/persuasiveness involves unhesitatingly taking control of situations in a calm and appropriately assertive manner, even under dangerous or adverse conditions (p. 70).

The three specific social skills can be taught and strengthened during the police academy with little disruption to current academy practices. The traditional authoritarian academy training style does not provide recruits with role models to emulate when their training officers and academy instructors demonstrate a rigid, autocratic leadership style. Instead, the academy staff can foster social competence by treating recruits "in a tactful and respectful manner" and by providing every recruit with an opportunity to practice effective leadership during training. Recruits should be treated in ways in which police agencies expect their officers to interact with members of the community. To learn how to show sensitivity and concern for others, recruits need to experience how it feels to be treated with sensitivity and concern, which in no way detracts from learning how to maintain officer safety.

When it comes to teamwork and assertiveness, academies can build in a mechanism for peer-level interventions. Staff should make it clear that recruits are expected to confront misconduct (e.g., cheating) and a lack of effort by their peers. Beyond supporting each other during fitness activities, it is crucial for the academy to prepare recruits to deal with conflict that is a natural by-product of group dynamics. This extends to the academy working to minimize recruits' us-versus-them attitudes vis-à-vis the community by reinforcing an expectation of cooperation with all stakeholders. This is consistent with procedural justice initiatives, which apply to officers' relations with community members as well as to law enforcement agencies' relations with their employees (e.g., COPS Office, 2018, p. 13). The goal is for recruits to learn to treat others as they would like to be treated, which is a point raised, but largely ignored, decades ago by Mahoney (1988).

Boosting assertiveness can occur in several ways during the academy. This occurs routinely during scenario work. Also, debriefings and self-reflection after every scenario can help recruits gain confidence and improve their respectful command presence. Some recruits will need to increase assertiveness, while others will need to be taught how to exchange an authoritarian, overbearing, or badge-heavy demeanor with an assertive manner. Academies also should provide every recruit with the experience of testifying in mock trials. Mastery of the social skills requires recruits to practice and rehearse; repetition is the key.

Moral skills

Police work is morally challenging. Officers are regularly confronted with moral dilemmas, which can lead to lapses in ethical behavior.[3] The situations are often fairly mundane, like deciding whether to give a motorist either a ticket or a warning or how to respond when offered a gratuity (e.g., a free meal). At the same time, police officers are routinely confronted with far more serious ethical temptations during the daily discharge of their duties, such as bribes from people looking to avoid arrest and easy access to money and other valuables while securing or collecting evidence at crime scenes. Another morally challenging part of police work stems from officers' commitment to public safety and crime control. This commitment has been described as the noble cause (e.g., Crank, Flaherty, & Giacomazzi, 2007). When officers find themselves justifying these honorable ends (protecting society) at the expense of legal means (e.g., breaking rules to catch offenders), they are committing noble cause corruption (Caldero & Crank, 2011).

It would be a mistake for police executives to assume that all new hires possess the moral maturity to successfully navigate the often ambiguous ethical waters of police work. Similarly, it would be wrong to think that officers either have or do not have these moral skills. The fact is that moral skills can be taught and strengthened. Specifically, one fundamental psychological skill that is required of police officers, according to POST (2014), is *integrity/ethics* which "involve maintaining high standards of personal conduct. It consists of attributes such as honesty, impartiality, trustworthiness, and abiding laws, regulations, and procedures" (p. 61).

Building integrity is not as complicated as it may seem. Most recruits enter law enforcement with self-reported integrity scores that are higher than those obtained from college students (Blumberg, Giromini, & Jacobson, 2016). The challenge is for academy staff to instill in recruits a lifelong commitment to ethical principles even though routine police work is rife with moral risks (Blumberg, Papazoglou, & Creighton, 2018). Recruits need to be exposed during the academy to these moral risks. However, rather than lecturing them to stay on the virtuous path (or else!), police academies that adopt the adult learning model will confront recruits with moral dilemmas throughout their training. At every turn, recruits should be asked: What would you do? What should you do? After every scenario, recruits should discuss their rationale as to why they chose the course of action that they did. Regular debriefings should confront the possibility of recruits' unethical decision-making and reinforce an unwavering commitment to maintain one's integrity.

Another factor associated with moral skills is spirituality. Although law enforcement agencies can support their employees' affiliation with any religion as well as those who are nonbelievers, it is important for police agencies to promote all officers' commitment to nonreligious spiritual practices. On one hand, spirituality

---

[3] Readers are referred to Blumberg et al. (2018) for a comprehensive review of the moral risks of police work.

can help officers maintain their sense of purpose and meaning, which provides some insulation from the deleterious effects of repeated exposure to human suffering (e.g., Tovar, 2011). Likewise, spirituality was found to "buffer stress affecting brain connections" in a sample of police officers (Charles, Travis, & Smith, 2014, p. 241). At the same time, although "spirituality might be associated with a slight reduction in burnout," other factors, such as officers' ethnicity and level of family support, also impact stress levels (Rogers, 2018, p. 6). And, there has been some mixed findings about the specific benefits of spiritual practices among police officers (e.g., Chopko, Facemire, Palmieri, & Schwartz, 2016).

Nevertheless, there are many reasons why police academies should encourage recruits to develop their own personalized spiritual program. Resources (e.g., books, chaplains, peer mentors) should be available to recruits. At several times during the training, recruits should be asked to reflect on their purpose and to discuss why they want to be a police officer. However, regardless of the possible health benefits and restorative effects of spiritual practices for police officers' wellness, it also was found that ethical decision-making in the workplace is related to employee spirituality (e.g., Moran, 2017). Therefore, to facilitate the training of ethical police officers, academies should consider ways to bolster recruits' spirituality.

Conclusions

Contemporary policing requires contemporary police training, which incorporates andragogical teaching principles. When academies shift from an authoritarian, paramilitary style to an adult learning model, recruits can develop and strengthen important psychological skills that are essential for today's effective police officers. However, this shift requires two significant initiatives if it is to be successful. First, academy instructors, training officers, and mentors need to support and believe in the value of this change. All of the trainers, also, need to be thoroughly trained to be able to properly train recruits with the aforementioned psychological skills. Academies can establish their own methods of standardized assessment for each skill, ensure satisfactory performance of each skill, provide opportunities for remediation, and require that minimum standards of each skill are met in order for recruits to graduate.

The second important factor required for psychological skills training to become endemic in police academy training is a culture shift at the organizational level. Police agencies must see the value of a psychologically skilled officer and demand that training academies emphasize development of these skills in their police recruits. In doing so, police executives will guide academies to focus less on testing recruits and more on assessment, which measures if recruits are able to apply what they are learning. Typically, when it comes to the application of what is learned in the academy, too much is left to FTOs when much more could be done during the academy, especially when it comes to demonstrating minimum standards of the psychological skills. In other words, police agencies should draw a clear line in the sand that no recruits will be sent to field training before they have satisfactorily demonstrated these important psychological skills.

This raises another important issue. There should be greater continuity between recruits' academy training and their field training. To accomplish this, academy staff and the FTO program staff need to do a better job collaborating with each other. This alliance shows recruits that there is not some arbitrary distinction between what is expected from them in the academy and the behavioral standards once they graduate and begin working on the streets. For that matter, along with other skills initially taught during the academy (e.g., firearms, defensive tactics, emergency vehicle operation), police executives should view psychological skills as perishable and begin to require ongoing training and requalification of these skills throughout officers' careers. The importance of demonstrating proficiency of one's psychological skills should extend beyond the training academy.

Finally, given the time limitations of police academy training and the mandated content that recruits must learn, some may contend that there is not enough time to focus on building recruits' psychological skills. The present authors argue that some innovation is warranted because the psychological skills are as important as any other facet of police work. One solution is for police agencies to develop criteria for basic certification in certain police knowledge and skills (e.g., firearms proficiency, radio codes, law, penal code, emergency driving), which applicants would have to achieve on their own prior to being hired. This parallels what many fire departments have established; applicants will only be considered for employment as a firefighter after they have acquired paramedic certification on their own. In this way, with a basic law enforcement certificate achieved on their own prior to employment, recruits have proven their commitment to the profession. Then, police academy training can focus on application of those skills, development of higher-order police techniques, and strengthening of the psychological skills.

Short of the requirement for police applicants to independently attain some form of certification prior to employment, police agencies can do a better job preparing new hires prior to the start of the academy. There is generally quite a bit of time between the beginning of the hiring process and candidates' academy start date. Many jurisdictions already offer preacademy physical training whereby candidates train and are exposed to the academy's fitness expectations. This is where the acculturation process begins. Similarly, there should be preacademy psychological "workouts." Candidates could learn about and have an opportunity to practice in areas such as procedural justice, community relations, stress management, and the various psychological skills. It is vital for police executives to find opportunities for their recruits and officers to learn, practice, and demonstrate the psychological skills that are critical for successful police performance.

References

Barber, L. K., Grawitch, M. J., & Trares, S. T. (2009). Service-oriented and force-oriented emotion regulation in police officers. *Applied Psychology in Criminal Justice, 5,* 182–202.

Berking, M., Meier, C., & Wupperman, P. (2010). Enhancing emotion-regulation skills in police officers: Results of a pilot controlled study. *Behavior Therapy, 41,* 329–339.

Birzer, M. L. (2003). The theory of andragogy applied to police training. *Policing, 26*(1), 29–42.

Blumberg, D. M., Giromini, L., & Jacobson, L. B. (2016). Impact of police academy training on recruits' integrity. *Police Quarterly, 19*, 63–86.

Blumberg, D. M., Papazoglou, K., & Creighton, S. (2018). Bruised badges: The moral risks of police work and a call for wellness. *International Journal of Emergency Mental Health and Human Resilience, 20*(2), 1–14.

Brackett, M. A., Mayer, J. D., & Warner, R. M. (2004). Emotional intelligence and its relation to everyday behaviour. *Personality and Individual Differences, 36*(6), 1387–1402. https://doi.org/10.1016/S0191-8869(03)00236-8.

Brunetto, Y., Teo, S. T. T., Shacklock, K., & Farr-Wharton, R. (2012). Emotional intelligence, job satisfaction, well-being, and engagement: Explaining organizational commitment and turnover intentions in policing. *Human Resource Management Journal, 22*, 428–441.

Caldero, M. A., & Crank, J. P. (2011). *Police ethics: The corruption of noble cause*. Burlington, MA: Elsevier, Inc.

California Commission on Peace Officer Standards and Training. (2014). *Peace officer psychological screening manual*. CA POST.

California Commission on Peace Officer Standards and Training (POST). (2018a). *Perishable skills program*. Retrieved from https://post.ca.gov/perishable-skills-program.

California Commission on Peace Officer Standards and Training (POST). (2018b). *Regular basic course*. Retrieved from https://post.ca.gov/regular-basic-course.

Caro, C. A. (2011). Predicting state police officer performance in the field training officer program: What can we learn from the cadet's performance in the training academy? *American Journal of Criminal Justice, 36*(4), 357–370. https://doi.org/10.1007/s12103-011-9122-6.

Chappell, A. T. (2008). Police academy training: Comparing across curricula. *Policing, 31*(1), 36–56. http://0-dx.doi.org.library.alliant.edu/10.1108/13639510810852567.

Charles, G. L., Travis, F., & Smith, J. (2014). Policing and spirituality: Their impact on brain integration and consciousness. *Journal of Management, Spirituality & Religion, 11*(3), 230–244. https://doi.org/10.1080/14766086.2014.887479.

Chopko, B. A., Facemire, V. C., Palmieri, P. A., & Schwartz, R. C. (2016). Spirituality and health outcomes among police officers: Empirical evidence supporting a paradigm shift. *Criminal Justice Studies: A Critical Journal of Crime, Law & Society, 29*(4), 363–377.

Christensen, D. (2018). Writing for wellness. *ONS Voice, 33*(6), 25.

Cook, G. (2016, November 19). *Allen ladies for police wives auxiliary*. Allen American. Retrieved from http://starlocalmedia.com/allenamerican/news/allen-ladies-form-police-wives-auxiliary/article_b1035af2-adea-11e6-86e9-1302877506d2.html.

COPS Office (Office of Community Oriented Policing Services). (2018). *Officer health and organizational wellness: Emerging issues and recommendations. Officer safety and wellness group meeting summary*. Washington, DC: Office of Community Oriented Policing Services.

Crank, J., Flaherty, D., & Giacomazzi, A. (2007). The noble cause: An empirical assessment. *Journal of Criminal Justice, 35*(1), 103–116. https://doi.org/10.1016/j.jcrimjus.2006.11.019.

Creighton, S., & Blumberg, D. M. (2016). Officer wellness is fundamental to officer safety: The San Diego Model. In *Police executive research forum*, Critical issues in policing series: Guiding principles in use of force (pp. 23–24). Washington, D.C: Police Executive Research Forum.

Dwyer, R. G., & Laufersweiler-Dwyer, D. (2004). The need for change: A call for action in community oriented police training. *FBI Law Enforcement Bulletin, 73*(11), 18—24.

Ebrahim Al Ali, O., Garner, I., & Magadley, W. (2012). An exploration of the relationship between emotional intelligence and job performance in police organizations. *Journal of Police and Criminal Psychology, 27*, 1—8.

Flynn, K. W. (2002). Training & police violence. In R. G. Burns, & C. E. Crawford (Eds.), *Police and violence* (pp. 127—146). Upper Saddle River, NJ: Prentice Hall.

van Gelderen, B. R., Bakker, A. B., Konijn, E. A., & Demerouti, E. (2011). Daily suppression of discrete emotions during the work of police service workers and criminal investigation officers. *Anxiety, Stress & Coping, 24*, 515—537.

Griffin, J. D., & Sun, I. Y. (2018). Do work-family conflict and resiliency mediate police stress and burnout: A study of state police officers. *American Journal of Criminal Justice, 43*(2), 354—370. https://doi.org/10.1007/s12103-017-9401-y.

Jeter, P. E., Cronin, S., & Khalsa, S. S. (2013). Evaluation of the benefits of a Kripalu yoga program for police academy trainees: A pilot study. *International Journal of Yoga Therapy, 23*(1), 24—30.

Johnston, C. W., & Cheurprakobkit, S. (2002). Educating our police: Perceptions of police administrators regarding the utility of a college education, police academy training and preferences in courses for officers. *International Journal of Police Science and Management, 4*(3), 182—197.

Kenworthy, J., Fay, C., Frame, M., & Petree, R. (2014). A meta-analytic review of the relationship between emotional dissonance and emotional exhaustion. *Journal of Applied Social Psychology, 44*, 94—105.

Kirschman, E. (2018). *I love a cop: What police families need to know*. Guilford Publications.

Kurtz, D. L. (2012). Roll call and the second shift: The influences of gender and family on police stress. *Police Practice and Research, 13*(1), 71—86. https://doi.org/10.1080/15614263.2011.596714.

Mahoney, T., & California Commission on Peace Officer Standards and Training. (1988). *What is the future of authoritarian-based police recruit training by the year 2000?* Sacramento, CA: California Commission on Peace Officer Standards and Training.

Makin, D. A. (2016). A descriptive analysis of a problem-based learning police academy. *Interdisciplinary Journal of Problem-Based Learning, 10*(1), 18—32. https://doi.org/10.7771/1541- 5015.1544.

Marion, N. (1998). Police academy training: Are we teaching recruits what they need to know? *Policing, 21*(1), 54—79.

Miller, L. (2007). Police families: Stresses, syndromes, and solutions. *American Journal of Family Therapy, 35*(1), 21—40. https://doi.org/10.1080/01926180600698541.

Moran, R. (2017). Workplace spirituality in law enforcement: A content analysis of the literature. *Journal of Management, Spirituality & Religion, 14*(4), 343—364. https://doi.org/10.1080/14766086.2017.1376287.

Mumford, E. A., Taylor, B. G., & Kubu, B. (2015). Law enforcement officer safety and wellness. *Police Quarterly, 18*(2), 111—133.

Nelis, D., Kotsou, I., Quoidbach, J., Hansenne, M., Weytens, F., Dupuis, P., et al. (2011). Increasing emotional competence improves psychological and physical well- being, social relationships, and employability. *Emotion, 11*, 354—366.

Nelis, D., Quoidbach, J., Mikolajczak, M., & Hansenne, M. (2009). Increasing emotional intelligence: (How) is it possible? *Personality and Individual Differences, 47*, 36—41.

Nieuwenhuys, A., Savelsbergh, G. J. P., & Oudejans, R. R. D. (2012). Shoot or don't shoot? Why police officers are more inclined to shoot when they are anxious. *Emotion, 12*, 827–833.

Paoline, E. I., & Terrill, W. (2007). Police education, experience, and the use of force. *Criminal Justice and Behavior, 34*(2), 179–196. https://doi.org/10.1177/0093854806290239.

Paterson, C. (2011). Adding value? A review of the international literature on the role of higher education in police training and education. *Police Practice and Research: International Journal, 12*(4), 286–297. https://doi.org/10.1080/15614263.2011.563969.

Rogers, R. L. (2018). Minority status and spirituality among police officers: Blacks and women in a metropolitan department. *Journal of Police and Criminal Psychology*. https://doi.org/10.1007/s11896-017-9229-x.

Schaible, L. M., & Gecas, V. (2010). The impact of emotional labor and value dissonance on burnout among police officers. *Police Quarterly, 13*, 316–341.

Schutte, N. S., Malouff, J. M., & Thorsteinsson, E. B. (2013). Increasing emotional intelligence through training: Current status and future directions. *The International Journal of Emotional Education, 5*, 56–72.

Stinson, P. M., & Liederbach, J. (2013). Fox in the henhouse: A study of police officers arrested for crimes associated with domestic and/or family violence. *Criminal Justice Policy Review, 24*(5), 601–625. https://doi.org/10.1177/0887403412453837.

Stoughton, S. (2015). Law enforcement's "warrior" problem. *Harvard Law Review, 128*(6), 225–234.

Talley, R. A. (1986). A new methodology for evaluating the curricula relevancy of police academy training. *Journal of Police Science and Administration, 14*(2), 112–120.

Thornton, M. A., & Herndon, J. (2016). Emotion regulation in police officers following distress: Effects of tenure and critical incidents. *Journal of Police and Criminal Psychology, 31*(4), 304–309. https://doi.org/10.1007/s11896-015-9186-1.

Tillyer, R. (2018). Assessing the impact of community-oriented policing on arrest. *Justice Quarterly, 35*(3), 526–555. https://doi.org/10.1080/07418825.2017.1327609.

Tovar, L. A. (2011). Vicarious traumatization and spirituality in law enforcement. *FBI Law Enforcement Bulletin, 80*(7), 16–21.

Tuttle, B. M., Giano, Z., & Merten, M. J. (2018). Stress spillover in policing and negative relationship functioning for law enforcement marriages. *The Family Journal*, 1–7. doi: 1066480718775739.

Vodde, R. F. (2011). Changing paradigms in police training: Transitioning from a traditional to an andragogical model. In M. R. Haberfeld, C. A. Clarke, & D. L. Sheehan (Eds.), *Police organization and training: Innovations in research and practice* (pp. 27–44). Springer Science & Business Media.

Warren, G. A. (1999). *Police academy training for 21st century law enforcement*. Police academy training for 21St century law enforcement. Dover, DE: Delaware Law Enforcement Institute.

Zijlmans, L. J. M., Embregts, P. J. C. M., Gerits, L., Bosman, A. M. T., & Derksen, J. J. L. (2011). Training emotional intelligence related to treatment skills of staff working with clients with intellectual disabilities and challenging behavior. *Journal of Intellectual Disability Research, 55*, 219–230.

Burnout and the psychological impact of policing: trends and coping strategies

David Turgoose, Naomi Glover and Lucy Maddox

Introduction

Police officers worldwide are at risk of high levels of stress due to the nature of their work. Officers at all hierarchical levels can be exposed to traumatic events, distressed individuals, high workloads, and organizational pressures. Very high levels of stress or an accumulation of stress over time, without sufficient coping mechanisms or organizational support, can lead to burnout. In some cases, officers are at risk of developing mental health problems such as post-traumatic stress disorder (PTSD). These challenges have the potential to severely limit the police's capacity to carry out their work effectively and can have a significant impact on the well-being of the workforce.

Several research studies have highlighted that police officers are at risk of burnout, due to the unpredictable and potentially dangerous nature of the role (Adams & Buck, 2010; Anshel, 2000; Dowler, 2005; Manzoni & Eisner, 2006). The implications of burnout in police forces could be serious for officers, the service as a whole, and the public they serve. More specifically, burnout among police officers can result in increased absenteeism, health problems, more frequent complaints, heightened levels of aggression, increased use of alcohol or drugs, more strained relations with family and friends, poorer interactions with citizens, elevated feelings of helplessness, heightened risk of depression, increased turnover, more frequent suicidal thoughts, reduced life satisfaction, lower quality of work, and increases in officers' aggressive attitudes and support for the use of force (Berg, Hem, Lau, Loeb, & Ekeberg, 2003; Kop & Euwema, 2001; Kop, Euwema, & Schaufeli, 1999; Manzoni & Eisner, 2006; Martinussen, Richardsen, & Burke, 2007; Maslach, 1982, 2003; Mostert & Rothmann, 2006; Queiros, Kaiseler, & DaSilva, 2013). Additionally, reports in the United Kingdom have suggested that since 2010, there has been a 72% increase in staff taking sick leave for mental health—related reasons, with absences coming at a great cost to police forces (Dowling, Chesworth, & Goldberg, 2017; Ingram, 2014; Pugh, 2016).

The principle aim of this chapter is to present the latest understanding and research relating to the psychological impact of working in the police. The factors influencing the stresses police officers face are likely to be numerous and complex. This chapter will explore personal and interpersonal characteristics associated with psychological stress, as well as the impact of wider organizational and cultural issues. This is a developing area of research, and our understanding of these concepts will grow as awareness and research expand.

Importantly, occupational and psychological stress will not affect every person working in a highly stressful role. Recent research has investigated protective factors which mitigate against problems developing. Nevertheless, more work is needed at both an individual and organizational level to help improve the well-being of police officers and the burden of responsibility for "resilience" should not be left with individual officers alone.

Defining occupational stress: burnout, compassion fatigue, and psychological trauma

Professionals who are either exposed to the traumatic material of others or are involved in helping others in distress (e.g., police officers, nurses, therapists) are at risk of developing psychological difficulties themselves. Various terms have been used to describe the impact of this exposure, including burnout (Maslach, 1982) and compassion fatigue (Figley, 2002).

Burnout

Burnout has been described as psychological and emotional exhaustion, associated with feelings of hopelessness and difficulties in dealing with work or in doing your job effectively (Stamm, 2010). Maslach and Jackson (1981) proposed that burnout consists of three components:

1. Emotional exhaustion: the sense of being emotionally drained and exhausted, with little desire to go to work.
2. Depersonalization: the development of cynical attitudes, and a callous or impersonal manner of interacting with others. Treating others in a negative manner is thought to serve the purpose of creating distance and becoming detached from others.
3. Reduced sense of professional accomplishment: feeling ineffective at work and unable to make a positive difference (Lambert, Qureshi, Frank, Klahm, & Smith, 2018).

As opposed to more short-term, work-related stress, burnout is said to be a chronic problem, whereby an individual withdraws from the role (e.g., psychologically, socially, emotionally), usually owing to long-term exposure to negative work-related factors (Maslach, 1982).

Compassion fatigue

The term compassion fatigue was initially described as a secondary traumatic stress reaction (Figley, 1995), whereby the defining characteristics include a reduction in the capacity or interest in bearing the suffering of others (Figley, 2002). Compassion fatigue also incorporates similar elements to burnout, such as physical and emotional exhaustion and a pronounced reduction in the ability to feel empathy and compassion for others (Elwood, Mott, Lohr, & Galovski, 2011; Evces, 2015; Mathieu, 2007).

Grant, Lavery, and Decarlo (2019) have recently suggested that professionals can lose their sense of empathy and compassion toward those they are required to help, due to the work environment placing them in states of vulnerability and tension. These ideas can be extrapolated to police work, with officers regularly encountering individuals in distress, leaving them at risk of becoming discouraged, hopeless, cynical, and exhausted. Compassion fatigue is important in contexts where compassionate care is strived for, and circumstances where compassionate care has been lacking and resulted in poor care have highlighted the importance of guarding against compassion fatigue in service professions such as healthcare (Francis, 2013). Similar concerns are relevant in police settings, where officers are often caring for victims of crime or traumatic events.

Psychological trauma

Burnout and compassion fatigue capture the impact of job-related stressors that police officers face, such as helping others in distress. Police officers, by the nature of their work, are also at risk of *direct* exposure to traumatic events which can leave them susceptible to developing psychological and mental health difficulties, such as anxiety, depression, and post-traumatic stress.

Any individual who is exposed to a highly stressful or traumatic event is at risk of developing symptoms of PTSD. Symptoms of PTSD include experiencing intrusive thoughts and memories of the event; often referred to as *flashbacks*, as well as the avoidance of any reminders of what happened. Further symptoms include *hypervigilance*, whereby an individual is highly sensitive to possible threats and experiences anxiety about their safety following the event, as well as experiencing changes in their *beliefs* about themselves, other people, or the world generally following the event, e.g., believing the world is less safe.

Recent evidence from the United States suggests that police officers endorse having experienced, on average, three traumatic experiences in their work. These included witnessing a situation in which someone was seriously injured, experiencing physical assault, being seriously injured intentionally at least once in the line of duty, being present when a fellow officer was seriously injured intentionally, or witnessing someone die in the line of duty (Soomro & Yanos, 2019). The same study reported that 12% of officers have significant levels of PTSD symptoms, which is far higher than the general population (around 4%; Kilpatrick et al., 2013). For a full review of psychological trauma relating to policing, please refer to Chapter 5.

Burnout, compassion fatigue, and police: review of current evidence

Given the potential impact of burnout on policing, it is important to investigate and understand what factors might predict its onset and make it more likely to develop. Such factors are likely to be numerous and varying, but through rigorous research and synthesizing evidence from several countries, it is possible to develop hypotheses about what might place police officers at risk of burnout, and conversely what can serve to protect them.

As described above, there are many aspects of a police officer's role which may set the conditions for burnout to develop, e.g., unpredictability, high demands, and dealing with violence and distress. In recent times, however, reports on the prevalence of burnout and compassion fatigue are surprisingly rare, with many studies investigating predictors of burnout without reporting the rates of officers suffering from it. What evidence there is suggests a mixed picture, with some studies suggesting that burnout rates are actually mostly low, or in the average range (Gray & Rydon-Grange, 2019; Turgoose, Glover, Barker, & Maddox, 2017). The absence of firm evidence of officers with high levels of burnout is best explained by a dearth of research. Additionally, if officers are experiencing high levels of burnout, they may not be able to take part in such research, for example if they are on sick leave or do not have time to take part. Nevertheless, it is also possible that some protective factors exist which mitigate against the risks of developing burnout, which are explored in this chapter.

Research into potential risk factors has investigated the demographics of the workforce to determine whether any inherent factors increase the risk of burnout developing (e.g., age). A recent review completed a meta-analysis of socio-demographic characteristics (e.g., age, sex, marital status and number of children) as potential risk factors for the development of burnout in police samples (Aguayo, Vargas, Cañadas, & De la Fuente, 2017). A total of 43 studies were included, but results showed that there were no significant effects, and that sex and age could be discarded as risk factors. The authors concluded that a lack of thorough information on the matter is leading to contradictory findings in the wider literature.

Occupational versus organizational stress

When considering the stressors related to policing, it is helpful to consider them in two areas: occupational stressors and organizational stressors, both of which can contribute to the development of burnout. Occupational stressors include the inherent dangers of police work, such as directly encountering those displaying violence and aggression, unpredictable encounters with the public, witnessing distress, or the expectation of being confronted with dangerous situations in the field (Stephens & Long, 2000). Organizational stressors relate to aspects of the job which might be perceived to compromise an officer's ability to perform their role effectively, e.g., stringent regulations and procedures, staffing issues, challenging shift patterns, interpersonal challenges (Berg, Hem, Lau, & Ekeberg, 2006a; Dabney, Copes, Tewksbury, & Hawk-Tourtelot, 2013; Soomro & Yanos, 2019). This can also include bureaucratic processes, perceived lack of support from the community and leaders, and lack of promotion opportunities (Burke & Mikkelsen, 2006; Stinchcomb, 2004).

Occupational stress and burnout

As discussed above, the stressful nature of police work lends itself to burnout as an occupational risk. Job stress and high demands have been linked to emotional exhaustion and a reduced sense of accomplishment; two factors of burnout as described above (Backteman-Erlason, Padyab, & Brulin, 2013; Lambert et al., 2018; Wang, Zheng, Hu, & Zheng, 2014). These findings are also supported by research with nonpolice populations (Lindblom, Linton, Fedeli, & Bryngelsson, 2006; Norlund et al., 2010; Soares, Grossi, & Sundin, 2007). Some studies have investigated whether officers who have been in their role longer are more likely to develop burnout; hypothesizing that job stress has a cumulative effect over time. This has been supported, but only in officers working in specialist roles investigating sexual assault (Gray & Rydon-Grange, 2019; Turgoose et al., 2017). These studies found that overall experience in the police was not associated with burnout, suggesting that there is something unique to working in sexual assault teams that increases the risk. This role is likely to involve dealing with highly distressed individuals and hearing upsetting details of assaults which might explain this association.

One aspect of occupational stress concerns *role conflict*, which has also been linked with burnout in police officers (e.g., Kwak, McNeeley, & Kim, 2018). Role conflict is a catchall term for aspects of a job experienced as being frustrating or at odds with one's expectations of the role. Role conflict can also occur when police officers are required to fulfill many different roles within the job, some of which may be perceived as not constituting "traditional" policing tasks (Ayres, 1990; Huey & Ricciardelli, 2015). Role conflict is one example of how it is not just the nature of policing per se which can be highly stressful but also the interaction between the role itself and contextual factors. In the case of role conflict, it is the mismatch between the expectation and reality of the role which can be experienced as being problematic.

Organizational stress and burnout

Research has suggested that numerous organizational factors can contribute to job stress and the development of burnout. Policing is perhaps prone to organizational challenges related to wider pressures from society and policy makers, given that law enforcement is such a critical issue which often bears great societal and political significance.

In Sweden, perceived problems with the organizational climate have been found to be associated with emotional exhaustion (Backteman-Erlason et al., 2013). Similarly, in a sample of Turkish police officers, burnout levels were higher, and job satisfaction lower, when the organization was experienced as being stress inducing (Kula, 2017). A further study of police forces in India has investigated four aspects of organizational stress: perceived unfairness, inflexible work hours, work overload, and role ambiguity. Each factor was found to contribute to the development of burnout (Kumar & Kamalanabhan, 2017). It has been suggested that organizational stressors have more of an impact on job satisfaction and burnout than occupational stressors (Kula, 2017).

Role ambiguity is one example of an organizational stressor that demonstrates how decisions beyond an officer's control can contribute to perceived stress and burnout. It has been defined as a lack of clarity in one's work role concerning work goals, the scope of responsibilities, and colleagues' expectations (Abramis, 1994; Cooper & Marshall, 1976; Jackson & Schuler, 1985; Kwak et al., 2018). There are many complex elements of policing which officers are required to keep in mind simultaneously, highlighting the need for clear direction and objectives at an organizational level. When these are unknown or confusing, officers can experience frustration and reduced job satisfaction (Ingram & Lee, 2015; Kim, Wells, Vardalis, Johnson, & Lim, 2016). Recent evidence has suggested that role ambiguity in police officers is associated with higher burnout levels; a finding which is replicated in nonpolice samples such as prison officers (Armstrong & Griffin, 2004; Lambert, Hogan, Paoline, & Clarke, 2005) and social workers (Kim & Stoner, 2008).

As with any employee, a police officer's role is determined by the employer, as are the resources required to fulfill their duties. The availability and quality of such resources can influence officers' abilities to complete their work satisfactorily, and a lack of resources could be perceived as an organizational stressor. A recent study of police officers in China found that officers were more likely to report experiencing burnout if they perceived to have insufficient resources for their role (Hu, Schaufeli, & Taris, 2017). This, when coupled with an increase in the demands of the job, led to significantly higher levels of burnout and a significant decrease in motivation to work. The Job Demands-Resources model (Demerouti, Bakker, Nachreiner, & Schaufeli, 2001) suggests that occupational stress such as burnout can develop via a combination of three related processes. Firstly, *motivational processes* effect work engagement through the availability of job resources which enhance personal development. Secondly, *health impairment processes* capture the mental and physical cost of sustained physical and psychological effort at work. Finally, it is assumed that the negative effects of these processes can be buffered by *work-based resources*, which even in the face of a highly demanding role, can maintain job satisfaction and protect against burnout.

Work-home conflict

Many police officers work antisocial hours and shift patterns owing to the 24-hour nature of policing. Therefore, police officers are at higher risk of work-family conflict (WFC), as such working hours may be more likely to impinge on family rituals and roles. As such, police work can sometimes be incompatible with family life, and the challenge of balancing work and family life can be a source of stress for many (McCarty & Skogan, 2013). Indeed, past research has suggested that WFC can negatively affect the well-being of police officers (Kinman, McDowall, & Cropley, 2012; Ola & Mathur, 2016), and has been linked with other such adversities, such as poor health, reduced job performance, and reduced job and life satisfaction (Carlson, Kacmar, & Williams, 2000; Cinamon & Rich, 2002; Fu & Schaffer, 2001; Mesmer-Magnus & Viswesvaran, 2005). Recent research in the United States has extended this to investigate the role of WFC in burnout prevalence (Griffin & Sun, 2018), finding that stress and burnout were higher in officers who reported more WFC. A number of further studies have found similar associations between WFC and burnout (Burke & Mikkelsen, 2007; Hawkins, 2001; Jackson & Maslach, 1982; Martinussen et al., 2007; McCarty & Atkinson, 2012). It has been proposed that when the repeated demands placed on police officers both at work and home occur faster than they can be dealt with, burnout is more likely to develop (Conservation of Resources (COR) theory; Hobfoll & Shirom, 2000). Some authors have suggested that officers should receive specialist guidance in work to assist them in problem-solving, or that support be offered to spouses, in order to alleviate the effects of WFC (Griffin & Sun, 2018).

Personal characteristics

In addition to occupational and organizational stress, some research has investigated whether certain individual or personality-based characteristics can leave individuals more vulnerable to developing burnout. One such factor is an individual's attachment style. Attachment style refers to a set of psychological and behavioral responses that a person uses as a way of relating to others, which are most potent at times of stress. These patterns form via one's unique experience of interactions with a primary caregiver in the formative years of life (Bowlby, 1988). Different attachment styles have been identified (Ainsworth, 1978) which persist into adulthood and inform how we forge and maintain relationships and cope with life stressors. A recent study of UK police officers in specialist roles found that officers who reported an *anxious-avoidant* attachment style had higher levels of burnout (Gray & Rydon-Grange, 2019). Broadly speaking, adults with an avoidant attachment style have developed ways of coping with stress that involve outwardly denying one's emotions (even if they are experienced internally), and not seeing other people as a source of comfort, i.e., preferring to deal with problems alone. These officers may miss out on the benefits of social support and supervision, which might explain why this avoidant style can be problematic.

Individuals can differ in the way that they perceive their ability to cope with stressful situations. The *locus of control* theory (Rotter, 1966; Spector, 1988) refers to the degree to which individuals believe they can influence events affecting their lives. Having an *internal* locus of control suggests that an individual believes they have the power to influence their lives, as opposed to events in their life being controlled by powerful others or by chance. There has been much research which suggests that having an internal locus of control is helpful in reducing stress. Recently, research has suggested that police officers who report an internal locus of control actually fared badly, in that this was related to feeling disengaged from their work; one of the three components of burnout (Wang, Zheng, Hu, & Zheng, 2014). The authors hypothesized that those officers with an internal locus of control would be more likely to blame *internal* factors when things went wrong at work, such as their skill in the role.

The impact of emotions

It is clear that emotion plays an important role in the development of burnout. Emotional exhaustion is one of the three burnout characteristics as described by Maslach (1982). Research has suggested that negative emotions affect the relationship between fatigue and emotional exhaustion in police officers (Kwak et al. 2018). The authors of this study proposed that low-arousal negative emotions are associated with daily hassles of the job which lead to stresses which, over time, decrease an individual's capacity to cope (Hobfoll, 2011; McIntyre, Korn, & Matsuo, 2008).

The nature of police work requires officers to confront the spectrum of human emotion in the people they encounter and support (Bhowmick & Mulla, 2016; Grandey, 2000; Martin, 1999; Morris & Feldman, 1996; Seron, Pereira, & Kovath, 2004; van Gelderen, Bakker, Konijn, & Demerouti, 2011; van Gelderen, Konijn, & Bakker, 2017; Wharton & Erickson, 1993). For example, police officers are required to be friendly and polite to the public (Queiros et al., 2013; Schaible & Gecas, 2010), whilst simultaneously having the ability to display hostility when required in the apprehension or interrogation of suspects (Rafaeli & Sutton, 1991; Schaible & Six, 2016; van Gelderen et al., 2011). Furthermore, officers may also need to outwardly convey a sense of calm professionalism and neutrality in the face of intimidation (Seron et al., 2004; van Gelderen et al., 2011), and show sympathy and empathy toward victims (Daus & Brown, 2012; van Gelderen, Konijn, & Bakker, 2007).

Dissonance

In addition to the possible strain of experiencing and displaying numerous emotional states, police officers may also be required to display emotions as part of their job which are at odds with how they actually feel. This *emotional dissonance* refers to the discrepancy between felt emotions and the emotions that are displayed (Zapf, Seifert, Schmutte, Mertini, & Holz, 2001; Zapf, Vogt, Seifert, Mertini, & Isic, 1999). Officers may also need to manage, regulate, and suppress their own feelings while publicly expressing a different emotion (Schaible & Gecas, 2010; van Gelderen et al., 2011), leading to emotional dissonance (van Gelderen et al., 2017).

Studies have suggested that police officers who experience frequent highly emotional interactions with the public were more likely to suffer from emotional dissonance and, in turn, elements of burnout such as emotional exhaustion and cynical attitudes toward their work (Bakker & Heuven, 2006; van Gelderen et al., 2007, 2011; Zapf, 2002). It is possible that regular experience of emotional dissonance depletes energy resources and can lead to cynical attitudes developing toward the job role (Bakker & Heuven, 2006). This can have negative implications for an officer's ability to carry out their role in serving the public. Further evidence suggests that it is the suppression of negative feelings in particular, such as anger, abhorrence, and sadness, which lead to feelings of exhaustion, rather than the suppression of happiness (van Gelderen et al., 2011).

In addition to conflicts in emotion, research has also investigated ways in which police officers cope with this dissonance regarding decisions and actions they are required to take in their job role. Researchers in Sweden have found that officers report *stress of conscience* or *troubled conscience* relating to the role, and that this was related to emotional exhaustion and depersonalization (Backteman-Erlanson, Padyab, & Brulin, 2013). Stress can be created by moral situations, and organizational or role-based constraints can prevent a professional from acting in a way they would otherwise choose to. Police officers, for example, have been asked to rate how often they have done something that did not fit with what they think and feel is right (Schaible & Six, 2016). Another term, *deep acting*, has been used to describe the effort made to embrace an emotion or stance which is required in a job role, but is contrary to what is actually felt. Research has suggested that higher levels of deep acting are associated with emotional exhaustion and depersonalization in police officers (Schaible & Six, 2016). It would appear that the emotional impact of policing plays a significant role in the development of psychological stress.

Moral injury

Moral injury has been described as the emotional or psychological strain caused by perpetrating or witnessing acts which "transgress (one's) deeply held moral beliefs and expectations" (Litz et al., 2009). It is a phenomenon which has been studied in military veterans (Frankfurt & Frazier, 2016; Williamson, Greenberg, & Murphy, 2019) and has been linked with several adverse outcomes such as depression and PTSD (Williamson, Stevelink, & Greenberg, 2018). Military veterans have described ruminating about past events during their services, e.g., thinking if they could have done something differently, experiencing guilt, self-blame, and shame. Police officers may be required to take actions within their role which could lead to the harm of others, either directly (e.g., injuring a suspect to detain them), or indirectly (e.g., a colleague being injured due to one's actions). Past research suggested that a quarter of police officers reported killing or seriously injuring a suspect (Weiss et al., 2010), and this has been linked with the development of PTSD (Komarovskaya et al., 2011). Moral injury is under-researched in police officers but is worthy of further investigation as a possible contributor or precursor to the development of chronic stress and burnout (Papazoglou & Chopko, 2017).

Police culture, perceptions, and risks of the job

Beyond the individual-level factors which contribute to officers' experience of burnout and stress, there are additional systemic issues that arise within the culture of police forces and which contribute to the way in which mental health difficulties are thought about and managed.

When discussing police culture it is important to note that police services are not a homogenous group, and there will be many differences in how individual officers, managers, and teams view and deal with stress and mental health difficulties for themselves and their colleagues. Nonetheless, it is often reported that the police forces as organizations are not settings which are conducive to openness about mental health, and the way in which individuals within this system conceptualize and respond to their own and others' experiences will be shaped by this wider culture. Research literature focuses on the way in which mental health is thought about within the police, the presence of stigma, and the impact this has on help-seeking behavior.

The high levels of stigma associated with experiencing mental health difficulties is well documented within research literature, and there is an interesting interplay between these factors within the police. Whilst some evidence exists to suggest that having an experience of mental health difficulties reduces stigma, Soomro and Yanos (2019) found that police officers who have personally experienced PTSD are more likely to hold stigmatized views about mental health difficulties. Authors hypothesized that this may impact on help-seeking, meaning that those officers who have higher levels of PTSD, and thus need support, may be less likely to seek help.

Police officers' reluctance to seek support within the police service may be, in part, explained by a perception of negative workplace attitudes toward burnout, stress, and mental health difficulties. This worry about being viewed as weak or unable to cope by peers and senior staff appears to be a prevalent experience for many officers, and research suggests that staff have concerns about confidentiality and worry that reporting mental health difficulties could negatively impact their career (Bell & Palmer-Conn, 2018; Karaffa & Tochkov, 2013). In addition, police work is characterized by a strong group identity, and officers are often worried about the views of their peers. Officers tend to underestimate the willingness of their colleagues to seek mental health support (Karaffa & Koch, 2016) which could have an impact on attitudes around their own help-seeking behavior. Kirschman, Kamena, and Fay (2013) noted that a particularly common fear for officers is that they are the only ones who have struggled with stress and, consequently, what that would mean about them. These perceptions understandably impact on officers' willingness to seek help, and indeed police officers are less likely to share their experiences with other people, less likely to consult their general practitioner (GP), less likely to inform their current employer, and less likely to confide in family and friends (Bell & Palmer-Conn, 2018). The male-dominated culture, both in terms of the gender split of officers and in the values that the organization promotes, may also contribute to the stigma of experiencing mental health difficulties and seeking help for them (Wester, Arndt, Sedivy, & Arndt, 2010).

Finally, the closed nature of the Police as an organization can result in a mistrust of outsiders (Karaffa & Tochkov, 2013) which has an impact on the available support options which exist externally to the police (e.g., psychologists). Bell and Eski (2015) suggested that the impact of austerity on police forces has increased the workload demands for officers and thus reduced the availability of colleagues to provide support and debriefing opportunities to one another. With potential barriers to accessing help from nonpolice "outsiders" and a reduced ability for colleagues to informally support each other, there are questions to be answered about where help will come for officers and how this can be provided.

Organizational psychology perspectives on what makes a job less stressful and more sustainable

As referenced above, one important theory from organizational psychology is the job demand-resources model, seen in various forms since its first incarnation as the job demand-control theory (Karasek, 1979). Fig. 4.1 shows one iteration, taken from Bakker & Demerouti, 2017.

The job demands-resources model enables a weighing up of job and personal resources in the face of job demands, and involves psychological processes, such as self-undermining and motivation (as listed in Fig. 4.1), as well as more behavioral processes such as job crafting.

Job crafting is defined as "the physical or cognitive changes individuals make in the task or relational boundaries of their work" (Wrezniewski & Dutton, 2001). In

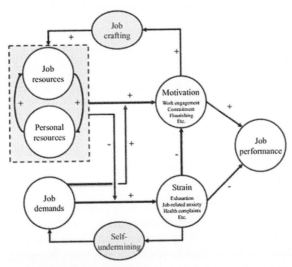

FIGURE 4.1 The job demands-resources model.

From Bakker, A.B., & Demerouti, E. (2017). Job demands–resources theory: Taking stock and looking forward. Journal of Occupational Health Psychology, *22(3), 273–285. https://doi.org/10.1037/ocp0000056. Reprinted with permission.*

other words, individuals can make their job more enjoyable and sustainable by influencing what it involves. Jobs can be shaped by individuals changing the balance of available resources and demands made on them, e.g., by making time for more satisfying elements of the job or increasing proximity to colleagues who are more nurturing and supportive.

The job demands-resources theory is particularly useful in that it involves both individual level and organizational level variables. It provides a helpful framework for approaching police well-being and burnout, and research has examined how well this model accounts for stress and burnout in police populations (e.g., Martinussen et al., 2007), what other factors should be taken into account (e.g., Hall, Dollard, Tuckey, Winefield, & Thompson, 2010), and how resources and demands should be characterized in a police setting (e.g., Frank, Lambert, & Qureshi, 2017). Hall et al. (2010) extended the model to include effects of WFC and emotional exhaustion, building on work done with police officers from Australia. This fits with the work from Kinman et al. (2012) in a UK sample which also emphasized the importance of WFC.

Brough and Biggs (2010) outline eight elements of occupational stress which contribute to the job demands-resources model in police work. They include the potential for negative working relationships, work overload, the nature of the work itself, and a lack of control over work processes and timing. Many of these aspects of work, including the potential for work-life balance, are outside an individual officer's control. Frank et al. (2017) identified role ambiguity, role conflict, and role overload as particularly influential demands in relation to officer stress. They list organizational support, formalization (e.g., creation of formal well-being policies), and increased employee input in decision-making, as particularly influential resources. Again, these factors are all more likely to be within the control of the police force which officers are working for, than to be under the control of the individuals themselves.

Interventions

The way we understand the issue of workplace well-being in general affects how we might go about trying to improve it, and affect the level on which we can approach police compassion fatigue, stress, and burnout.

Police work can be inherently stressful for a variety of reasons, and means police employees are at risk of stress and burnout. The wider literature on workplace mental health (e.g., LaMontagne et al., 2014) proposes models of intervention at different levels (Murphy, 1988), either to:

a) **Prevent harm** by working at a primary level of intervention to try to make the job less stressful or the stress better managed;
b) **Promote the positive** by working at a secondary level of intervention, usually with individuals, to try to improve resilience and ways of coping;
c) **Manage illness** by working at a tertiary level, providing access to treatment for secondary trauma, stress, and burnout.

Interventions that prevent harm

Interventions that seek to prevent the harm caused by stressful working conditions can minimize job stress by job or work environment redesign, or work to better assess the risks involved and seek to mitigate them before harm is caused.

In police settings, as in many emergency service settings, stressors include the intense and sometimes dangerous nature of the work, and can also include aspects of culture and organizational climate which may exacerbate stress (Randall, 2013).

A first step is characterizing what stresses are present and the level of risk associated with them, in order to then be able to formulate a plan to mitigate them. Risk management frameworks can be helpful for police organizations to attempt to quantify risk, especially risks associated with psychosocial hazards in the work which historically may have been overlooked (e.g., Houdmont, Kerr, & Randall, 2012).

The next step is to have practices in place which can moderate effects of work stress. Organizationally, this can include effective supervision (Brough & Williams, 2007), effective leadership (Russell, 2014), and campaigns to try to tackle potentially severe risks associated with policing (e.g., police suicide prevention campaigns; Mishara & Martin, 2012). There is still a gap in our knowledge about what is most effective for preventing post-traumatic reactions in police staff, either at an individual or organizational level, and this is an area which continues to need further research (for more on trauma see Chapter 5).

In particular, less research has been done on job redesign in police settings, likely because there are many stressful aspects of the work which are integral to the role and are hard to redesign. Literature on job crafting suggests individual-level control over work tasks can be beneficial to work stress (Tims & Bakker, 2010), and this may be an area which future research could explore further. Similar to research in other job domains where work-related stress is common, there are fewer interventions at the level of the organization and more available at an individual level.

Interventions that promote the positive

Whilst some researchers are pessimistic about the possibility of meaningful effects from secondary interventions which ignore more organizational factors (e.g., Patterson, Chung, & Swan, 2014), there is a growing body of research which suggests that there can be some beneficial effects for police officers stress from a range of secondary interventions. These include 8-week mindfulness programmes (Grupe et al., 2019), training in self-management of work-life balance (McDowall & Lindsay, 2014), training which harnesses imaginal exposure to critical incidents to promote use of helpful coping strategies (Arble, Lumley, Pole, Blessman, & Arnetz, 2017; Arnetz, Nevedal, Lumley, Backman, & Lublin, 2009), and programmes which harness peer support to encourage help-seeking post trauma (Watson & Andrews, 2018).

Research from other professions has suggested that mindfulness can help protect against the development of compassion fatigue (Turgoose & Maddox, 2017). These findings can be extended to police officers and suggest that promoting mindfulness practices in police organizations could be a useful protective measure.

The authors of this chapter were involved in trialling a secondary intervention with police sexual assault response officers (Turgoose et al., 2017), a training intervention which was divided into two parts. The first part included psychological education about stress, compassion fatigue, secondary traumatic stress, and burnout. The second focused on self-help strategies that can be used to reduce or build resistance against compassion fatigue and stress more generally.

The self-help section of the intervention was broken down into six parts, based on the literature for building resistance to compassion fatigue, secondary traumatic stress, and burnout (e.g., Figley, 2013; Flarity, Gentry, & Mesnikoff, 2013; Gentry, 2002; Mathieu, 2012; Sexton, 1999; Thieleman & Cacciatore, 2014). The six sections were: 1. Identifying physiological signs of stress; 2. Promoting self-care; 3. Anxiety and stress management, e.g., relaxation strategies; 4. Social support and debriefing (e.g., how to speak with colleagues in a helpful way after a stressful event); 5. Mindfulness; and 6. Compassion satisfaction. This training intervention was both acceptable and useful in that it seemed to boost officers' knowledge about burnout, compassion fatigue, and secondary trauma, and provided interventions which several officers continued to use (notably mindfulness).

Although some studies do show a positive reception from officers and some small to moderate effects, research from other, nonpolice-specific settings, suggests that comprehensive interventions, which tackle work-related stress at more than one level (i.e., at both the individual and organizational levels), will be more effective than interventions which focus on one level alone (Lamontagne, Keegel, Louie, Ostry, & Landsbergis, 2007). Whilst research in police settings has not looked at this in great depth, the literature from other fields suggests more comprehensive interventions which reduce organizational stressors, promote individual coping, improve access to support when needed, and are likely to be the most effective ways of impacting officer stress, burnout, and compassion fatigue.

Interventions that manage illness or significant distress

Interventions for officers at the point where significant distress has occurred and help is required need to be timely and confidential. Combinations of awareness-raising and hotline provision are one way to provide support whilst reducing stigma (Amaranto, Steinberg, Castellano, & Mitchell, 2003). Some evidence suggests that police officers are not at greater risk of developing general mental health problems than other lower risk professionals (van der Valden, 2013), but there is an increased risk of exposure to traumatic incidents, and with that an increased risk of post-traumatic stress reactions. In some countries veterans of military services are fast-tracked for access to therapy for PTSD. There are no studies of the effectiveness of this approach for police samples, although there is evidence that police officers are less likely to seek psychological or psychiatric help (Berg, Hem, Lau, & Ekeberg, 2006a,b; Fox et al., 2012), so this group is likely to need more encouragement to access talking therapies. There is some evidence of the efficacy of police cultures which have mandatory support for officers (Carlan & Nored, 2008).

Not just what but how: process as well as effect

Evaluating the effectiveness of an intervention is important, but so too is understanding the mechanisms by which an intervention is effective. Process evaluation research focuses on evaluating mechanisms of change, and combined with evaluation of effectiveness can strengthen the validity of change findings (Nielsen & Miraglia, 2017). Carrying out process evaluation as well as a robust evaluation of the effects of an intervention is more time-intensive, and it is much rarer for evaluations to include both these levels of investigation. Future research in this area concentrating on process as well as effect is needed.

Recommendations for future research

Providing interventions at the secondary or tertiary level are often easier for an organization to do than redesigning jobs to make them less stressful, but research looking at the effectiveness of different interventions in a variety of settings suggests the best approaches are more comprehensive, involving all levels if possible. There is work to do in establishing *how* the different interventions are effective, and interventions which consider process as well as effect will be an important field of research in this area in the coming years. Learning from similarly stressful fields such as healthcare could lead to cross-pollination of ideas (e.g., use of Schwartz rounds or similar; Thompson, 2013). Greater clarity over definitions of burnout, work-related stress, and compassion fatigue, as well as the measures used to assess them will also help to add clarity to the field in terms of which interventions work best for what and also for whom.

Conclusions

The stressful nature of police work means that officers are at risk of developing psychological difficulties relating to chronic stress, burnout, and compassion fatigue. These issues can have significant and wide-ranging negative effects on individuals and might explain recent figures suggesting a rise in the number of mental health–related absences in police organizations. A lack of research reporting prevalence rates for such risks leaves us unable to confidently estimate the extent or severity of these concerns in police populations.

A large amount of research has investigated a multitude of risk factors for developing such difficulties, which can be broadly broken down into occupational and organizational stressors. Most of the research points to organizational stressors as being most problematic as risk factors for burnout. However, it is the way in which police officers process the emotional, cognitive, and moral challenges relating to their role which appears to be crucial and worthy of further investigation. For example, policing requires so many variations of emotional expression and suppression, alongside performing tasks which might be at odds with an officer's hopes and expectations of their role. This dissonance is psychologically taxing and sets the scene for stress, burnout, and compassion fatigue.

As well as analyzing current research, we can use theoretical ideas from organizational psychology to help understand how the interplay between individual and organizational factors can lead to and maintain psychological distress in policing. Equally, this information can inform institutional changes to help organizations prevent and manage such problems in the workforce. By making changes to prevent harm, promote positive working, and manage difficulties when they arise, police organizations can help officers maintain well-being in their role. Further work is also required to understand and potentially change the culture around stress and mental health in the police to ensure that cultural challenges such as stigma are not contributing to the development of problems or preventing officers from accessing help.

The challenge for future research is to go beyond simple cross-sectional designs to develop a deeper understanding of these issues. Furthermore, as awareness increases, interventions should be trialled as our knowledge advances toward methods of intervening to manage and prevent psychological stress in policing. Many elements of policing cannot be changed, and they will continue to be experienced as stressful. What can be changed, however, is awareness, police culture, and how officers are supported by their institutions. The potential benefits of such changes are profound for both the workforce and the general public they serve.

References

Abramis, D. J. (1994). Work role ambiguity, job satisfaction, and job performance: Meta-analyses and review. *Psychological Reports, 75*(3), 1411–1433.

Adams, G. A., & Buck, J. (2010). Social stressors and strain among police officers: It's not just the bad guys. *Criminal Justice and Behavior, 37*(9), 1030–1040.

Aguayo, R., Vargas, C., Cañadas, G. R., & De la Fuente, E. I. (2017). Are socio-demographic factors associated to burnout syndrome in police officers? A correlational meta-analysis. *Anales de Psicología/Annals of Psychology, 33*(2), 383–392.

Ainsworth, M. D. S., Blehar, M. C., Waters, E., & Wall, S. (1978). *Patterns of attachment: A psychological study of the strange situation.* Hillsdale, NJ: Erlbaum.

Amaranto, E., Steinberg, J., Castellano, C., & Mitchell, R. (2003). Police stress interventions. *Brief Treatment and Crisis Intervention, 3*(1), 47–53.

Anshel, M. H. (2000). A conceptual model and implications for coping with stressful events in police work. *Criminal Justice and Behavior, 27*, 375–400.

Arble, E., Lumley, M. A., Pole, N., Blessman, J., & Arnetz, B. B. (2017). Refinement and preliminary testing of an imagery-based program to improve coping and performance and prevent trauma among urban police officers. *Journal of Police and Criminal Psychology, 32*(1), 1–10.

Armstrong, G. S., & Griffin, M. L. (2004). Does the job matter? Comparing correlates of stress among treatment and correctional staff in prisons. *Journal of Criminal Justice, 32*, 577–592.

References 79

Arnetz, B. B., Nevedal, D. C., Lumley, M. A., Backman, L., & Lublin, A. (2009). Trauma resilience training for police: Psychophysiological and performance effects. *Journal of Police and Criminal Psychology, 24*(1), 1–9.

Ayres, R. M. (1990). *Preventing law enforcement stress: The organization's role*. Washington DC: Bureau of Justice Assistance.

Backteman-Erlanson, S., Padyab, M., & Brulin, C. (2013). Prevalence of burnout and associations with psychosocial work environment, physical strain, and stress of conscience among Swedish female and male police personnel. *Police Practice and Research, 14*(6), 491–505.

Bakker, A. B., & Demerouti, E. (2017). Job demands—resources theory: Taking stock and looking forward. *Journal of Occupational Health Psychology, 22*(3), 273.

Bakker, A. B., & Heuven, E. (2006). Emotional dissonance, burnout, and in-role performance among nurses and police officers. *International Journal of Stress Management, 13*(4), 423.

Bell, S., & Eski, Y. (2015). 'Break a Leg—it's all in the mind': Police officers' attitudes towards colleagues with mental health issues. *Policing: A Journal of Policy and Practice, 10*(2), 95–101.

Bell, S., & Palmer-Conn, S. (2018). Suspicious minds: Police attitudes to mental ill health. *International Journal of Law and Public Administration, 1*(2), 25–40.

Berg, A. M., Hem, E., Lau, B., & Ekeberg, O. (2006a). An exploration of job stress and health in the Norwegian police service: A cross sectional study. *Journal of Occupational Medicine and Toxicology, 1*(26).

Berg, A., Hem, E., Lau, B., & Ekeberg, Ø. (2006b). Help-seeking in the Norwegian police service. *Journal of Occupational Health, 48*(3), 145–153.

Berg, A., Hem, E., Lau, B., Loeb, M., & Ekeberg, O. (2003). Suicidal ideation and attempts in Norwegian police. *Suicide and Life-Threatening Behavior, 33*, 302–312.

Bhowmick, S., & Mulla, Z. (2016). Emotional labour of policing: Does authenticity play a role? *International Journal of Police Science and Management, 18*(1), 47–60.

Bowlby, J. (1988). *A secure base: Parent-child attachment and healthy human development*. New York: Basic Books.

Brough, P., & Biggs, A. (2010). Occupational stress in police and prison staff. In E. A. Campbell (Ed.), *The cambridge handbook of forensic psychology* (pp. 707–718). Cambridge University Press.

Brough, P., & Williams, J. (2007). Managing occupational stress in a high-risk industry: Measuring the job demands of correctional officers. *Criminal Justice and Behavior, 34*(4), 555–567.

Burke, R. J., & Mikkelsen, A. (2006). Burnout among Norwegian police officers: Potential antecedents and consequences. *International Journal of Stress Management, 13*(1), 64.

Burke, R., & Mikkelsen, A. (2007). Suicidal ideation among police officers in Norway. *Policing: An International Journal of Police Strategies and Management, 30*, 228–236.

Carlan, P. E., & Nored, L. S. (2008). An examination of officer stress: Should police departments implement mandatory counseling? *Journal of Police and Criminal Psychology, 23*(1), 8–15.

Carlson, D. S., Kacmar, K. M., & Williams, L. J. (2000). Construction and initial validation of a multidimensional measure of work-family conflict. *Journal of Vocational Behavior, 56*, 249–276.

Cinamon, R. C., & Rich, Y. (2002). Gender differences in the importance of work and family roles: Implications for the work-family conflict. *Sex Roles, 47*, 531–541.

Cooper, C. L., & Marshall, J. (1976). Occupational sources of stress: A review of the literature relating to coronary heart disease and mental ill health. *Journal of Occupational and Organizational Psychology, 49*(1), 11−28.

Dabney, D. A., Copes, H., Tewksbury, R., & Hawk-Tourtelot, S. R. (2013). A qualitative assessment of stress perceptions among members of a homicide unit. *Justice Quarterly, 30*(5), 811−836.

Daus, C. S., & Brown, S. (2012). The emotion work of police. In N. M. Ashkanasy, C. E. J. Hartel, & W. J. Zerbe (Eds.), *Experiencing and managing emotions in the workplace* (pp. 305−328). Emerald Group Publishing Limited.

Demerouti, E., Bakker, A. B., Nachreiner, F., & Schaufeli, W. B. (2001). The job demands-resources model of burnout. *Journal of Applied Psychology, 86*(3), 499−512.

Dowler, K. (2005). Job satisfaction, burnout, and perceptions of unfair treatment: The relationship between race and police work. *Police Quarterly, 8*(4), 476−479.

Dowling, N., Chesworth, S., & Goldberg, A. (December 3, 2017). *Police officers talk about their battle against PTSD*. BBC News. Available at www.bbc.co.uk/news/uk-42159974. (Accessed 21 November 2019).

Elwood, L. S., Mott, J., Lohr, J. M., & Galovski, T. E. (2011). Secondary trauma symptoms in clinicians: A critical review of the construct, specificity, and implications for trauma-focused treatment. *Clinical Psychology Review, 31*(1), 25−36.

Evces, M. R. (2015). What is vicarious trauma? In G. Quitangon, & M. R. Evces (Eds.), *Vicarious trauma and disaster mental health* (pp. 9−23). New York: Routledge.

Figley, C. R. (1995). Compassion fatigue as secondary traumatic stress disorder: An overview. In C. R. Figley (Ed.), *Compassion fatigue: Coping with secondary traumatic stress disorder in those who treat the traumatized* (pp. 1−20). New York: Brunner-Routledge.

Figley, C. R. (2002). Compassion fatigue: Psychotherapists' chronic lack of self-care. *Journal of Clinical Psychology, 58*(11), 1433−1441.

Figley, C. R. (2013). ARP: The accelerated recovery program (ARP) for compassion fatigue. In C. R. Figley (Ed.), *Treating compassion fatigue* (pp. 131−146). Routledge.

Flarity, K., Gentry, J. E., & Mesnikoff, N. (2013). The effectiveness of an educational program on preventing and treating compassion fatigue in emergency nurses. *Advanced Emergency Nursing Journal, 35*(3), 247−258.

Fox, J., Desai, M. M., Britten, K., Lucas, G., Luneau, R., & Rosenthal, M. S. (2012). Mental-health conditions, barriers to care, and productivity loss among officers in an urban police department. *Connecticut Medicine, 76*(9), 525.

(chair) Francis, R. (2013). *Report of the mid Staffordshire NHS foundation trust public inquiry.* London: The Stationery Office.

Frankfurt, S., & Frazier, P. (2016). A review of research on moral injury in combat veterans. *Military Psychology, 28*(5), 318−330.

Frank, J., Lambert, E. G., & Qureshi, H. (2017). Examining police officer work stress using the job demands−resources model. *Journal of Contemporary Criminal Justice, 33*(4), 348−367.

Fu, C. K., & Shaffer, M. A. (2001). The tug of work and family: Direct and indirect domain-specific determinants of work-family conflict. *Personnel Review, 30*(5), 502−522.

van Gelderen, B. R., Bakker, A. B., Konijn, E. A., & Demerouti, E. (2011). Daily suppression of discrete emotions during the work of police service workers and criminal investigation officers. *Anxiety, Stress and Coping, 24*(5), 515−537.

van Gelderen, B. R., Heuven, E., Van Veldhoven, M., Zeelenberg, M., & Croon, M. (2007). Psychological strain and emotional labor among police-officers: A diary study. *Journal of Vocational Behavior, 71*(3), 446−459.

van Gelderen, B. R., Konijn, E. A., & Bakker, A. B. (2017). Emotional labor among police officers: A diary study relating strain, emotional labor, and service performance. *The International Journal of Human Resource Management, 28*(6), 852–879.

Gentry, J. E. (2002). Compassion fatigue: A crucible of transformation. *Journal of Trauma Practice, 1*(3–4), 37–61.

Grandey, A. A. (2000). Emotional regulation in the workplace: A new way to conceptualize emotional labor. *Journal of Occupational Health Psychology, 5*(1), 95.

Grant, H. B., Lavery, C. F., & Decarlo, J. (2019). An exploratory study of police officers: Low compassion satisfaction and compassion fatigue. *Frontiers in Psychology, 9*, 2793. https://doi.org/10.3389/fpsyg.2018.02793.

Gray, C., & Rydon-Grange, M. (2019). Individual characteristics, secondary trauma and burnout in police sexual and violent offending teams. *The Police Journal: Theory, Practice and Principles*, 0032258X19847499.

Griffin, J. D., & Sun, I. Y. (2018). Do work-family conflict and resiliency mediate police stress and burnout: A study of state police officers. *American Journal of Criminal Justice, 43*(2), 354–370.

Grupe, D. W., McGehee, C., Smith, C., Francis, A., Mumford, J. A., & Davidson, R. J. (2019). Mindfulness training reduces PTSD symptoms and other stress-related health outcomes in police officers. *Journal of Police and Criminal Psychology*, 1–14. https://doi.org/10.1007/s11896-019-09351-4. online first.

Hall, G. B., Dollard, M. F., Tuckey, M. R., Winefield, A. H., & Thompson, B. M. (2010). Job demands, work-family conflict, and emotional exhaustion in police officers: A longitudinal test of competing theories. *Journal of Occupational and Organizational Psychology, 83*(1), 237–250.

Hawkins, H. (2001). Police officer burnout: A partial replication of Maslach's burnout inventory. *Police Quarterly, 4*, 343–360.

Hobfoll, S. E. (2011). Conservation of resources theory: Its implication for stress, health, and resilience. In S. Folkman (Ed.), *The oxford handbook of stress, health, and coping* (pp. 127–147). Oxford University Press.

Hobfoll, S. E., Shirom, A., & Golembiewski, R. (2000). Conservation of resources theory. In R. T. Golembiewski (Ed.), *Handbook of organizational behavior* (pp. 57–80). New York: Marcel Dekker.

Houdmont, J., Kerr, R., & Randall, R. (2012). Organisational psychosocial hazard exposures in UK policing: Management standards indicator tool reference values. *Policing: An International Journal of Police Strategies and Management, 35*(1), 182–197.

Huey, L., & Ricciardelli, R. (2015). 'This isn't what I signed up for': When police officer role expectations conflict with the realities of general duty police work in remote communities. *International Journal of Police Science and Management, 17*(3), 194–203.

Hu, Q., Schaufeli, W. B., & Taris, T. W. (2017). How are changes in exposure to job demands and job resources related to burnout and engagement? A longitudinal study among Chinese nurses and police officers. *Stress and Health, 33*(5), 631–644.

Ingram, S. (2014). Policing and the true scale of mental health issues. *Police Oracle*. Available at www.policeoracle.com/news/StaffþAssociations/2014/Sep/04/Policing,-and-the-true-scale-of-mental-health-issues_85346.html. (Accessed 21 November 2019).

Ingram, J. R., & Lee, S. U. (2015). The effect of first-line supervision on patrol officer job satisfaction. *Police Quarterly, 18*(2), 193–219.

Jackson, S., & Maslach, C. (1982). After-effects of job-related stress: Families as victims. *Journal of Occupational Behavior, 3*, 63–77.

Jackson, S. E., & Schuler, R. S. (1985). A meta-analysis and conceptual critique of research on role ambiguity and role conflict in work settings. *Organizational Behavior and Human Decision Processes, 36*, 16–78.

Karaffa, K. M., & Koch, J. M. (2016). Stigma, pluralistic ignorance, and attitudes toward seeking mental health services among police officers. *Criminal Justice and Behavior, 43*(6), 759–777.

Karaffa, K. M., & Tochkov, K. (2013). Attitudes toward seeking mental health treatment among law enforcement officers. *Applied Psychology in Criminal Justice, 9*(2), 75–99.

Karasek, R. A., Jr. (1979). Job demands, job decision latitude, and mental strain: Implications for job redesign. *Administrative Science Quarterly*, 285–308.

Kilpatrick, D. G., Resnick, H. S., Milanak, M. E., Miller, M. W., Keyes, K. M., & Friedman, M. J. (2013). National estimates of exposure to traumatic events and PTSD prevalence using DSM-IV and DSM-5 criteria. *Journal of Traumatic Stress, 26*(5), 537–547.

Kim, H., & Stoner, M. (2008). Burnout and turnover intention among social workers: Effects of role stress, job autonomy and social support. *Administration in Social Work, 32*(3), 5–25.

Kim, J. L., Wells, W., Vardalis, J. J., Johnson, S. K., & Lim, H. (2016). Gender difference in occupational stress: A study of the South Korean National Police Agency. *International Journal of Law, Crime and Justice, 44*, 163–182.

Kinman, G., McDowall, A., & Cropley, M. (2012). Work-family conflict and job-related well-being in UK police officers: The role of recovery strategies. In *Proceedings from institute of work psychology international conference: Work, wellbeing and performance*. Sheffield, UK http://eprints.bbk.ac.uk/id/eprint/14343.

Kirschman, E., Kamena, M., & Fay, J. (2013). *Counseling cops: What clinicians need to know*. New York: Guilford Press.

Komarovskaya, I., Maguen, S., McCaslin, S. E., Metzler, T. J., Madan, A., Brown, A. D., et al. (2011). The impact of killing and injuring others on mental health symptoms among police officers. *Journal of Psychiatric Research, 45*(10), 1332–1336.

Kop, N., & Euwema, M. C. (2001). Occupational stress and the use of force by Dutch police officers. *Criminal Justice and Behavior, 28*(5), 631–652.

Kop, N., Euwema, M., & Schaufeli, W. (1999). Burnout, job stress and violent behaviour among Dutch police officers. *Work and Stress, 13*(4), 326–340.

Kula, S. (2017). Occupational stress, supervisor support, job satisfaction, and work-related burnout: Perceptions of Turkish National Police (TNP) members. *Police Practice and Research, 18*(2), 146–159.

Kumar, V., & Kamalanabhan, T. J. (2017). Moderating role of work support in stressor–burnout relationship: An empirical investigation among police personnel in India. *Psychological Studies, 62*(1), 85–97.

Kwak, H., McNeeley, S., & Kim, S. H. (2018). Emotional labor, role characteristics, and police officer burnout in South Korea: The mediating effect of emotional dissonance. *Police Quarterly, 21*(2), 223–249.

Lambert, E. G., Hogan, N. L., Paoline, E. A., III, & Clarke, A. (2005). The impact of role stressors on job stress, job satisfaction, and organizational commitment among private prison staff. *Security Journal, 18*(4), 33–50.

Lambert, E. G., Qureshi, H., Frank, J., Klahm, C., & Smith, B. (2018). Job stress, job involvement, job satisfaction, and organizational commitment and their associations with job burnout among Indian police officers: A research note. *Journal of Police and Criminal Psychology, 33*(2), 85–99.

Lamontagne, A. D., Keegel, T., Louie, A. M., Ostry, A., & Landsbergis, P. A. (2007). A systematic review of the job-stress intervention evaluation literature, 1990–2005. *International Journal of Occupational and Environmental Health, 13*(3), 268–280.

LaMontagne, A. D., Martin, A., Page, K. M., Reavley, N. J., Noblet, A. J., Milner, A. J., et al. (2014). Workplace mental health: Developing an integrated intervention approach. *BMC Psychiatry, 14*(1), 131.

Lindblom, K. M., Linton, S. J., Fedeli, C., & Bryngelsson, L. (2006). Burnout in the working population: Relations to psychosocial work factors. *International Journal of Behavioral Medicine, 13*(1), 51–59.

Litz, B. T., Stein, N., Delaney, E., Lebowitz, L., Nash, W. P., Silva, C., et al. (2009). Moral injury and moral repair in war veterans: A preliminary model and intervention strategy. *Clinical Psychology Review, 29*(8), 695–706.

Manzoni, P., & Eisner, M. (2006). Violence between the police and the public: Influences of work-related stress, job satisfaction, burnout, and situational factors. *Criminal Justice and Behavior, 33*(5), 613–645.

Martin, S. E. (1999). Police force or police service? Gender and emotional labor. *The Annals of the American Academy of Political and Social Science, 561*(1), 111–126.

Martinussen, M., Richardsen, A. M., & Burke, R. J. (2007). Job demands, job resources, and burnout among police officers. *Journal of Criminal Justice, 35*(3), 239–249.

Maslach, C. (1982). *Burnout: The cost of caring.* Englewood Cliffs: Prentice Hall.

Maslach, C. (2003). Job burnout: New directions in research and intervention. *Current Directions in Psychological Science, 12*, 189–192.

Maslach, C., & Jackson, S. (1981). The measurement of experienced burnout. *Journal of Occupational Behaviour, 2*, 99–113.

Mathieu, F. (2007). *Running on empty: Compassion fatigue in health professionals.* Retrieved from http://www.compassionfatigue.org/pages/RunningOnEmpty.pdf.

Mathieu, F. (2012). *The compassion fatigue workbook: Creative tools for transforming compassion fatigue and vicarious traumatization.* Routledge.

McCarty, R., & Atkinson, M. (2012). Resilience training program reduces physiological and psychological stress in police officers. *Global Advances in Health and Medicine, 1*(5), 44–66.

McCarty, W. P., & Skogan, W. G. (2013). Job-related burnout among civilian and sworn police personnel. *Police Quarterly, 16*(1), 66–84.

McDowall, A., & Lindsay, A. (2014). Work–life balance in the police: The development of a self-management competency framework. *Journal of Business and Psychology, 29*(3), 397–411.

McIntyre, K. P., Korn, J. H., & Matsuo, H. (2008). Sweating the small stuff: How different types of hassles result in the experience of stress. *Stress and Health: Journal of the International Society for the Investigation of Stress, 24*(5), 383–392.

Mesmer-Magnus, J., & Viswesvaran, C. (2005). Convergence between measures of work-to-family and family-to-work conflict: A meta-analytic examination. *Journal of Vocational Behavior, 67*, 215–232.

Mishara, B. L., & Martin, N. (2012). Effects of a comprehensive police suicide prevention program. *Crisis, 33*, 162–168.

Morris, J. A., & Feldman, D. C. (1996). The dimensions, antecedents, and consequences of emotional labor. *Academy of Management Review, 21*(4), 986–1010.

Mostert, K., & Rothmann, S. (2006). Work-related well-being in the South African police service. *Journal of Criminal Justice, 34*, 479–491.

Murphy, L. R. (1988). Workplace interventions for stress reduction and prevention. In C. Cooper, & R. Payne (Eds.), *Causes, coping and consequences of stress at work* (pp. 310–339). Chichester: Wiley.

Nielsen, K., & Miraglia, M. (2017). What works for whom in which circumstances? On the need to move beyond the 'what works?' question in organizational intervention research. *Human Relations, 70*(1), 40–62.

Norlund, S., Reuterwall, C., Höög, J., Lindahl, B., Janlert, U., & Birgander, L. S. (2010). Burnout, working conditions and gender-results from the northern Sweden MONICA Study. *BMC Public Health, 10*(1), 326–335.

Ola, M., & Mathur, R. (2016). The convergent and divergent impact of work environment, work-family conflict, and stress coping mechanisms on female and male police officers. *International Journal of Education and Management Studies, 6*(1), 19–24.

Papazoglou, K., & Chopko, B. (2017). The role of moral suffering (moral distress and moral injury) in police compassion fatigue and PTSD: An unexplored topic. *Frontiers in Psychology, 8*, 1999.

Patterson, G. T., Chung, I. W., & Swan, P. W. (2014). Stress management interventions for police officers and recruits: A meta-analysis. *Journal of Experimental Criminology, 10*(4), 487–513.

Pugh, R. (2016). What can mindfulness teach the police force? *The Guardian.* Available at www.theguardian.com/society/2016/jun/14/mindfulness-police-rising-stress-anxiety-depression. (Accessed 21 November 2019).

Queiros, C., Kaiseler, M., & DaSilva, A. L. (2013). Burnout as predictor of aggressivity among police officers. *European Journal of Policing Studies, 1*(2), 110–135.

Rafaeli, A., & Sutton, R. (1991). Emotional contrast strategies as means of social influence: Lessons from criminal interrogators and bill collectors. *Academy of Management Journal, 34*, 749–775.

Randall, C. (2013). Managing occupational stress injury in police services: A literature review. *International Public Health Journal, 5*(4), 413–425.

Rotter, J. B. (1966). Generalized expectancies for internal versus external control of reinforcement. *Psychological Monographs: General and Applied, 80*(1), 1–28. https://doi.org/10.1037/h0092976.

Russell, L. M. (2014). An empirical investigation of high-risk occupations: Leader influence on employee stress and burnout among police. *Management Research Review, 37*(4), 367–384.

Schaible, L. M., & Gecas, V. (2010). The impact of emotional labor and value dissonance on burnout among police officers. *Police Quarterly, 13*(3), 316–341.

Schaible, L. M., & Six, M. (2016). Emotional strategies of police and their varying consequences for burnout. *Police Quarterly, 19*(1), 3–31.

Seron, C., Pereira, J., & Kovath, J. (2004). Judging police misconduct: "Street-Level" versus professional policing. *Law and Society Review, 38*(4), 665–710.

Sexton, L. (1999). Vicarious traumatisation of counsellors and effects on their workplaces. *British Journal of Guidance and Counselling, 27*(3), 393–403.

Soares, J. J. F., Grossi, G., & Sundin, Ö. (2007). Burnout among women: Associations with demographic/socio-economic, work, life-style and health factors. *Archives of Women's Mental Health, 10*(2), 61–71.

Soomro, S., & Yanos, P. T. (2019). Predictors of mental health stigma among police officers: The role of trauma and PTSD. *Journal of Police and Criminal Psychology, 34*(2), 175–183.

Spector, P. E. (1988). Development of the work locus of control scale. *Journal of Occupational and Organizational Psychology, 61*, 335–340.

Stamm, B. H. (2010). *The ProQOL (Professional Quality of Life Scale: Compassion satisfaction and compassion fatigue)*. Pocatello, ID: ProQOL.org. Retrieved from www.proqol. org.

Stephens, C., & Long, N. (2000). Communication with police supervisors and peers as a buffer of work-related traumatic stress. *Journal of Organizational Behavior, 21*(4), 407–424.

Stinchcomb, J. B. (2004). Searching for stress in all the wrong places: Combating chronic organizational stressors in policing. *Police Practice and Research, 5*(3), 259–277.

Thieleman, K., & Cacciatore, J. (2014). Witness to suffering: Mindfulness and compassion fatigue among traumatic bereavement volunteers and professionals. *Social Work, 59*(1), 34–41.

Thompson, A. (2013). How Schwartz rounds can be used to combat compassion fatigue. *Nursing Management, 20*(4), 16–20.

Tims, M., & Bakker, A. B. (2010). Job crafting: Towards a new model of individual job redesign. *SA Journal of Industrial Psychology, 36*(2), 1–9.

Turgoose, D., Glover, N., Barker, C., & Maddox, L. (2017). Empathy, compassion fatigue, and burnout in police officers working with rape victims. *Traumatology, 23*(2), 205–213.

Turgoose, D., & Maddox, L. (2017). Predictors of compassion fatigue in mental health professionals: A narrative review. *Traumatology, 23*(2), 172–185. https://doi.org/10.1037/ trm0000116.

van der Velden, P. G., Rademaker, A. R., Vermetten, E., Portengen, M. A., Yzermans, J. C., & Grievink, L. (2013). Police officers: A high-risk group for the development of mental health disturbances? A cohort study. *BMJ Open, 3*(1), e001720.

Wang, Y., Zheng, L., Hu, T., & Zheng, Q. (2014). Stress, burnout, and job satisfaction: Case of police force in China. *Public Personnel Management, 43*(3), 325–339.

Watson, L., & Andrews, L. (2018). The effect of a Trauma Risk Management (TRiM) program on stigma and barriers to help-seeking in the police. *International Journal of Stress Management, 25*(4).

Weiss, D. S., Brunet, A., Best, S. R., Metzler, T. J., Liberman, A., Pole, N., et al. (2010). Frequency and severity approaches to indexing exposure to trauma: The Critical incident history questionnaire for police officers. *Journal of Traumatic Stress, 23*(6), 734–743.

Wester, S. R., Arndt, D., Sedivy, S. K., & Arndt, L. (2010). Male police officers and stigma associated with counseling: The role of anticipated risks, anticipated benefits and gender role conflict. *Psychology of Men and Masculinity, 11*(4), 286–302.

Wharton, A. S., & Erickson, R. I. (1993). Managing emotions on the job and at home: Understanding the consequences of multiple emotional roles. *Academy of Management Review, 18*(3), 457–486.

Williamson, V., Greenberg, N., & Murphy, D. (2019). Impact of moral injury on the lives of UK military veterans: A pilot study. *BMJ Military Health*. https://doi.org/10.1136/jramc-2019-001243. Published Online First: 21 June 2019.

Williamson, V., Stevelink, S. A., & Greenberg, N. (2018). Occupational moral injury and mental health: Systematic review and meta-analysis. *The British Journal of Psychiatry, 212*(6), 339–346.

Wrzesniewski, A., & Dutton, J. E. (2001). Crafting a job: Revisioning employees as active crafters of their work. *Academy of Management Review, 26*(2), 179–201.

Zapf, D. (2002). Emotion work and psychological well-being: A review of the literature and some conceptual considerations. *Human Resource Management Review, 12*(2), 237–268.

Zapf, D., Seifert, C., Schmutte, B., Mertini, H., & Holz, M. (2001). Emotion work and job stressors and their effects on burnout. *Psychology and Health, 16*(5), 527–545.

Zapf, D., Vogt, C., Seifert, C., Mertini, H., & Isic, A. (1999). Emotion work as a source of stress: The concept and development of an instrument. *European Journal of Work and Organizational Psychology, 8*(3), 371–400.

Trauma and critical incident exposure in law enforcement

5

Lea Katrine Jørgensen and Ask Elklit

Introduction

Policing is a profession that entails experiences and incidents which may place great psychological demands and tolls on the people who decide to work within police organizations. Police officers are faced with threatening situations that situate themselves and their colleagues at great risk. They are faced with victims of abuse and violence, children as well as adults, and with scenes of murder and suicide. These types of experiences which entail danger, threat, or harm to oneself or others are characterized as critical incidents. For most people, these experiences elicit strong reactions and for others they lead to pathological trauma symptomatology as seen in posttraumatic stress disorder (PTSD), and other accompanying negative consequences. Police officers are not only exposed to these incidents on a regular basis, but are required to intervene and react in a professional manner and to protect possible victims implicated in them. Though police officers are trained and prepared for these types of events, it does not make them entirely immune to their traumatic nature. Therefore, it is of vital importance to understand the heightened risk of pathological traumatization that the exposure to multiple critical incidents puts on police officers. This chapter will explore the extent of traumatization among police officers and the characteristics of this traumatization routed in a unique police culture. We will describe the factors that determine to which degree officers are at risk of developing persistent traumatic symptomatology and some of the interventions and treatments that can help prevent development of symptoms or treat the officers who do go on to develop them.

The nature of police traumatization

Police officers as a group are exposed to a wide range of potentially traumatic and critical incidents of a type, and in a degree, unique to this profession. The traumatic response in this particular group can therefore be expected to be of a similar nature as those characteristics shared by all first responders and some unique to the police. In this first section of the chapter, we will summarize some of the factors that characterize the unique nature of traumatization within the police force.

Police Psychology, Edited by Marques and Paulino. https://doi.org/10.1016/B978-0-12-816544-7.00005-X

Extent of traumatization

Exposure to traumatic events in general is something that most people experience at least once in their lives (Kessler et al., 2005), but for most people this does not result in traumatic stress or other harmful and debilitating symptoms. For those who are traumatized, the reaction is often conceptualized in the form of PTSD. PTSD is a psychiatric disorder that may occur after experiencing life-threatening or violent incidents. Symptoms of the disorder include avoidance behavior, reexperiencing of traumatic events, negative changes in thoughts and mood, and hypervigilance (American Psychiatric Association, 2013). About 7% of adults in the general population will develop PTSD during their life (Kessler et al., 2005). So, what is the extent of traumatization in the population of police officers?

Prevalence rates of PTSD among police officers vary widely and if we look at some of the studies that have reported prevalence rates, we see a wide range of different findings. In a longitudinal study from 1997 conducted on 262 Dutch police officers, Carlier and colleagues found that 7% of their respondents met the full diagnostic criteria for PTSD, while 34% exhibited subthreshold PTSD at some point during the study (Carlier, Lamberts, & Gersons, 1997). A study on 183 police officers from a US Midwestern state indicated that 17% had probable PTSD while 10% had clinically significant symptoms of PTSD (Chopko & Schwartz, 2012). Another study from the United States indicated that 5.8% of men and 7.1% of women met the criteria for PTSD using the clustering approach (Hartley, Sarkisian, Violanti, Andrew, & Burchfiel, 2013). A Canadian study from 2008 found that 31.9% of the Canadian officers included in the study screened positive for PTSD (Asmundson & Stapleton, 2008). Among suburban police officers a prevalence rate of 13% for PTSD was found (Robinson, Sigman, & Wilson, 1997). In a New Zealand study, the prevalence rate was established as between 7.1% and 13.6% depending on the used cutoff score (Stephens & Miller, 1998) and in a Brazilian sample, prevalence rates for full PTSD were reported as 8.9% (Maia et al., 2006). Other studies have reported prevalence rates with similar varying results (Andrew et al., 2008; Darensburg et al., 2006; Hartley et al., 2013; Martin, Marchand, Boyer, & Martin, 2009; Ménard, Arter, & Khan, 2016). In these studies, the prevalence rates range between 7% and up to 31.9%. The inconsistencies of these findings could be caused by several factors, one of which is the differing screening tools for PTSD used in the studies as well as different cutoff points for determining a full PTSD diagnosis. Furthermore, many different countries are represented in the abovementioned studies, and differences in PTSD rates between countries could represent actual differences in PTSD prevalence between the police officers who operate in different countries. Though the findings are inconsistent, the studies do indicate a considerable rate of traumatization among police officers. This could imply that police officers are an especially vulnerable group and thus highlights the need for attention and further research in the traumatization within this particular profession.

PTSD trajectories in law enforcement

The previous studies all estimate the prevalence of full PTSD among police officers, but it is also relevant to look at how these symptoms progress over a longer period of time after the experience of critical incidents. Galatazer-Levy and colleagues carried out a study of the reaction patterns following exposure to life-threatening events in 178 US police officers (Galatzer-Levy, Madan, Neylan, Henn-Haase, & Marmar, 2011). They found that most officers in their study experienced their first life-threatening and critical event within 6 months of active duty. Following this first exposure, the study found three distinct patterns of response. 88.1% of the officers followed a response pattern where they did not exhibit substantial changes in PTSD symptomatology during the 3-year course of the study. They did not seem to be affected in a substantial way by any experienced critical event. 10.7% of the officers exhibited a second pattern of response with initial high rates of PTSD symptomatology after the first exposure, which slowly decreased over time without full recovery. The final response pattern was found in the remaining 2% of the participants, and it was characterized by a consistent increase in PTSD symptoms with time. Another study of both citizens and police officers following the civil unrest in Ferguson after the shooting of Michael Brown found four response patterns among both citizens and police (Galovski, Peterson, & Fox-Galalis, 2018). In this study, 57% of participants followed a resistant pattern with constant low levels of PTSD symptoms, 23.8% followed a resilient pattern with initial increase in symptoms but quick remission and full recovery, 12.6% followed a chronically distressed pattern with constant high levels of PTSD symptoms from the offset of the study and with only a slight increase with time, while 6.1% experienced continuous increases in PTSD symptoms over time, with a small decrease before the end of the study.

Accumulation of trauma

As earlier mentioned, most people experience at least one potentially traumatizing event throughout their lifetimes, but one of the things that differentiate the general population from police officers is their repeated exposure to critical incidents at much higher frequencies than the general population. Rudofossi has suggested that police officers experience a range from 10 to more than 900 events that could be accounted as traumatic over a career (Rudofossi, 2007). This leads us to the question: How is the traumatic response to critical incidents affected by the continuing exposure to new incidents among police officers? Some research proposes that trauma accumulates, which means that every time a new critical incident is experienced, the degree of traumatization and PTSD symptomatology will also increase. In 2005, a study was carried out to test the accumulation of trauma among 277 police officers (Hammer, 2005). Using the vignette methodology, the participants were presented with a hypothetical police officer, who was described to go through a number of hypothetical and potentially traumatic events. These traumatic events were chosen based on previous research on which experiences were frequently encountered and found to be traumatic by police officers. The participants then indicated their estimates of frequency, intensity, and overall trauma experienced by the fictitious officer after each situation. The results of the study supported the hypothesis that trauma among police officers does accumulate (Hammer, 2005). This indicates that each critical incident experienced by a police officer can add to the overall degree of trauma, creating increasingly traumatized officers. The study found that a cubic model was the most fitting to present the nature of the accumulation. This means that traumatization increases after the first incident, where after following incidents do not elicit more traumatization until a certain number of critical incidents is reached, at which point traumatization starts rising exponentially (Hammer, 2005). Other studies have found similar evidence that the frequency of traumatic exposure and thereby the number of incidents experienced are correlated with a higher degree of PTSD (Asmundson & Stapleton, 2008; Green et al., 2000; Huddleston, Paton, & Stephens, 2006; Stephens & Miller, 1998). However, more recent studies have found only weak or nonexistent relationships between frequency of traumatic incidents and PTSD symptomatology, which does not support the hypothesis of accumulating trauma among police officers (Chopko & Schwartz, 2012; Weiss et al., 2010). In their study on PTSD trajectories, Galatzer-Levy and colleagues found that the officers who followed the pattern of increasing PTSD symptoms with time were the ones who were exposed to the highest frequency of critical incidents, which could indicate the effects of accumulating trauma for some officers but not for all (Galatzer-Levy, Madan, Neylan, Henn-Haase, & Marmar, 2011). As such, the research indicates that trauma can accumulate for some, but the relationship between the number of experienced critical incidents and following PTSD symptomatology is not a direct one, and many factors may mediate the relationship between the two.

Police culture

Aside from the frequency of the critical incidents that police officers are exposed to, we also must consider the special characteristics of the police culture that can contribute to the process of traumatization. The police culture is often characterized by an enormous sense of solidarity and loyalty (Andersen & Papazoglou, 2014; Henley Woody, 2005; Paoline, 2003). This loyalty can have both positive and negative effects on police traumatization. Solidarity can lead to a great feeling of support and belongingness for the individual, which works as a protective factor in the face of critical incidents. However, the great sense of loyalty contributes to a feeling of "us versus them" and can sometimes contribute to an isolation of the officers from the rest of the world including their family and friends outside the force (Henley Woody, 2005; Paoline, 2003; Steinkopf, Hakala, & Van Hasselt, 2015). This limits the support system, which is otherwise an important protective factor against traumatization, which will be explained later in this chapter. The distancing from people outside the force also contributes to a general attitude against seeking therapeutic help since therapists are part of the "outsiders" (Papazoglou & Tuttle, 2018;

Steinkopf et al., 2015). Another important consideration is that critical incidents can often be devalued and denied as traumatic by the police culture because it is seen as just "part of the job," and the police culture values bravery, heroism, and resiliency in the face of critical incidents (Andersen & Papazoglou, 2014; Papazoglou & Tuttle, 2018; Royle, Keenan, & Farrell, 2009). This leads to a general culture of repression and refusal to acknowledge symptoms of distress since it is seen as not being able to cope with the incidents and not being able to live up to the tough and resilient values. This repression and denial of symptoms can be quite taxing for the officers and wear down their mental resources (Rudofossi & Lund, 2009). The devaluation of critical incidents and expectations for bravery and resilience also contribute to a great stigmatization related to seeking help from therapists and other outsiders, leading to the idea that the possible benefits of therapy are not enough to outweigh the negative stigma (Andersen & Papazoglou, 2014; Karlsson & Christianson, 2003; Royle et al., 2009; Rudofossi & Lund, 2009; Wester, Arndt, Sedivy, & Arndt, 2010). Formality, compliance, and constant regulation can also be dominant features within the police culture, and constant scrutiny can sometimes contribute to the experience of stress and anxiety (Chae & Boyle, 2013; Henley Woody, 2005).

Many, sometimes conflicting, expectations regarding the roles of police officers in and outside their jobs are expressed in the police culture and can contribute to confusion in the formation of a work identity by young police recruits as they adopt the culture of their workplace (Rudofossi, 1996, 2007; Rudofossi & Lund, 2009). One example is the expectations for police officers to conform and be obedient and accept the hierarchical structure of the police command and the expectation of officers to be autonomous and decisive in reaction to critical incidents (Rudofossi, 1996, 2007). The prominent culture of masculinity and toughness within the police culture is also in conflict with the modern expectations of the officers to be warm, caring, and supportive fathers and husbands in their personal lives (Wester et al., 2010). Role confusions can lead to a conflicted identity formation in the role of police officer, which in turn may contribute to an increased vulnerability to traumatization (Rudofossi, 1996, 2007).

Alternative conceptions of trauma

In this chapter, we started by looking at PTSD as representing the extent of traumatization among police officers; however, since traumatization among police officers has many unique characteristics, then maybe PTSD simply does not capture the pattern of responses to traumatization in this group. This has led some researchers and clinicians to come up with other conceptions of trauma that go beyond PTSD.

Daniel Rudofossi, who started as a police officer and later became a police psychologist and therapist, has published numerous studies and two books emphasizing the characteristics of the police culture in the process of traumatization among police officers (Rudofossi, 1996, 2007; Rudofossi & Lund, 2009). Rudofossi coins the term Police and Public Safety complex trauma (PPS-CPTSD), which is a complex concept that adapts the diagnosis of complex PTSD to the unique characteristics of the police culture within an ecological and ethological perspective (Rudofossi, 2007). Complex PTSD is a disorder first described by Herman, which has been proposed to account for the repeated and prolonged exposure to trauma such as in cases of long-term child abuse or domestic violence (Hermann, 1997). Herman proposed six symptom clusters to characterize C-PTSD in addition to PTSD: (1) affect regulation, (2) amnesia and dissociation, (3) somatization, (4) self-esteem issues, (5) relational problems, and (6) loss of meaning. In the new International Classification of Diseases (ICD-11), the disorder is represented with three of these symptom clusters: affect regulation, self-esteem issues, and relational problems (World Health Organization, 2018). Rudofossi argues that the process of traumatization among police officers can be best understood through an eco-ethological framework whereby cultural characteristics interact with ethological and evolutionary influences. Cultural characteristics such as the disavowal of traumatic experiences as routine as well as conflicting role expectations contribute to a selective advantage in refraining from expression and recognition of the effects of critical incidents. Furthermore, Rudofossi emphasizes how the ongoing identity formation among many young cadets might influence their vulnerability toward experiencing traumatic events. According to Rudofossi, these interacting influences classify police officers as a particularly vulnerable group to develop a more complex form of PTSD, which he conceptualizes in PPS-CPTSD (Rudofossi, 2007; Rudofossi & Lund, 2009).

Konstantinos Papazoglou, who has also published several articles and a book exploring the traumatic experiences of police officers, proposes another concept of police trauma called police complex spiral trauma (Papazoglou, 2013). This concept symbolizes the complexities of police trauma in a spiral form, where each spiral ring represents a particular critical incident and the width of the spiral represents the tension of the traumatic experience, while the length of the spiral represents time. Papazoglou theorizes that the intensity and the number of experienced critical events will expand through time and this is symbolized in the model by a continuing expansion of width and density of the spiral as seen in Fig. 5.1. The model captures the accumulating effects of trauma in police officers and the complexities of the police trauma in a relatively simple model (Papazoglou, 2013).

Other conceptualizations include "The Theory of Cumulative Career Traumatic Stress" (CCTS) proposed by Ellen Marshal in 2006 (Marshall, 2006). She argues that police officers will experience symptoms similar to those seen in PTSD, but the symptoms will not necessarily occur all together after one specific incident and then persist for a longer period of time, as required to receive the PTSD diagnosis. Instead, different symptoms will appear sporadically throughout the career of an officer as a delayed response to the continuing experience of different critical incidents, and the symptoms may not last for longer than days or weeks (Marshall, 2006). The symptoms will not last long enough to merit a PTSD diagnosis, but they might still have a grave effect on the lives of the police officers, who may experience symptoms of various intensity throughout their career at unexpected times. All these conceptions indicate that police traumatization, in its complexity, cannot necessarily be measured or understood by the presence of PTSD rather that traumatization and

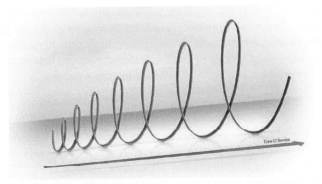

Time Of Service

FIGURE 5.1

Cumulative form of the Police Complex Spiral Trauma (PCST) through time of service

Adapted from "Conceptualizing Police Complex Spiral Trauma and its Applications in the Police Field," by K. Papazoglou, 2013

the many consequences of this can be wide-ranging and problematic, despite the lacking consensus of higher PTSD rates among police officers.

The consequences of exposure to numerous critical incidents can have many debilitating effects on the lives of police officers that go beyond the typical symptoms of PTSD or complex PTSD. The scope of this chapter does not allow us to go into detail on this subject matter, but some of the most commonly found consequences among police officers are alcohol problems (Ballenger et al., 2011; Lindsay & Shelley, 2009; Ménard & Arter, 2013; Ménard et al., 2016; Violanti, 2004), sleep disturbances (Chopko, Palmieri, & Adams, 2018; Hartley, Burchfiel, Fekedulegn, Andrew, & Violanti, 2011; Mohr et al., 2003), depression (Asmundson & Stapleton, 2008; Hartley et al., 2011) and various diseases such as cardiovascular disease (Hartley et al., 2011), and suicide or suicide ideation, though results of suicide rates among police officers are conflicted (Aamodt, 2008; Chae & Boyle, 2013; Gershon, Barocas, Canton, Li, & Vlahov, 2009; Milner, Spittal, Pirkis, & LaMontagne, 2013; Violanti, 2004).

Risk and protective factors

We have now looked at different conceptualizations of trauma reactions among police officers and how long-term exposure to critical incidents, as well as other stressors of the police job, can contribute to a unique picture of traumatization among police officers. Though all police officers are exposed to the general job conditions it is far from all who go on to develop the mental and physical health problems related to severe traumatization, as it is clear from the data on PTSD prevalence rates and response patterns. What makes the difference between those officers who come out unharmed and those who do not? Many factors contribute to this outcome;

and while some risk factors can facilitate posttraumatic symptomatology, other protective factors will prevent or protect against the development of such reactions. In this part of the chapter, we will summarize some of these individual risk and protective factors and how they operate in mediating the relationship between the stressors of the police job and the subsequent traumatic response patterns.

Gender

Among the general population, PTSD prevalence rates for women have been reported as two to three times higher than for men (Olff, 2017). However, this finding has been rarely replicated in the police population. Hartley et al. (2013) found a slightly higher prevalence for female police officers (18%) than for male police officers (15%). Several other studies have found no significant effects of gender in mediating the relationship between critical incident exposure or organizational factors and PTSD, and no significant differences in PTSD rates between female and male police officers (Andrew et al., 2008; Carlier et al., 1997; Darensburg et al., 2006; Pole et al., 2001; Prati & Pietrantoni, 2010). One explanation could be that the screening and training procedures in the police work can constitute a form of inoculation for these women, removing the increased vulnerability found among civilian women (Pole et al., 2001). Another factor could be that police work attracts a certain personality type that is more resilient than most, and that only the women who have a natural lower vulnerability to PTSD seek out police work. A study from 2008 examined the effects of the personality trait "hardiness," which refers to the manner in which someone interprets a critical incident (Andrew et al., 2008). They found that, for female police officers, the tendency to find meaning and purpose in such incidents was a protective factor against PTSD symptoms. This relationship was not found for the male police officers though the male officers actually scored higher on this aspect of hardiness than the female officers. If the police service attracts personalities particularly high in this aspect of hardiness, but it only has a protective effect for women, then maybe this is a factor in negating the gender differences in PTSD vulnerability among police officers.

Female police officers have reported less peritraumatic distress and emotional response during critical events than civilian women (Lilly, Pole, Best, Metzler, & Marmar, 2009) and since such responses are otherwise a big risk factor in the development of traumatic stress reactions, this could be an important factor in explaining the lacking gender difference. Though there seem to be no prevalence differences in PTSD for men and women, there are some factors, like the previously mentioned hardiness trait, that only work as protective or risk factors for one gender and not the other. For instance, in one study, frequency of critical incidents was only found to be a risk factor for women but not for men, while recency of the critical incident was only found to be a risk factor for male officers (Hartley et al., 2013). A study from 2004 reported that dealing with abused children have a higher impact on female officers than males (Violanti, 2004), while having more than one child was only found to be a significant risk factor for men and not women in a study from

2015 (Marchand, Nadeau, Beaulieu-Prévost, Boyer, & Martin, 2015). Identifying the risk and protective factors that differentiate the genders are very important since some intervention and prevention strategies might be more or less effective for male or female officers.

Social support

Social support is one of the most important protective factors against PTSD and the protective effects have been found in a multitude of studies (Carlier et al., 1997; Galovski et al., 2018; Martin et al., 2009; Prati & Pietrantoni, 2010; Stephens & Long, 2000; Terte, Stephens, & Huddleston, 2014). Though these results are clear, social support is a broad and multifaceted concept that can be operationalized in many different ways. To utilize the protective effects in both preventative and intervention strategies, we need to be able to distinguish the effects of different types of social support and the circumstances it is received in. First of all, there is a distinction between actual and perceived support. Perceived support is proposed to be the most effective since it has a direct relationship with reduction in PTSD symptoms, whereas actual or objectively received support might only have an effect if it is perceived as such, which is not always the case (Guilaran, de Terte, Kaniasty, & Stephens, 2018). Most studies measuring social support rely on self-report measures of perceived support. The timing of when the support is received in relation to a critical event is also important and support during or immediately after a critical event seems to be the most effective, whereas pretraumatic social support seems to be less important (Martin et al., 2009). Regarding the source of support, Martin and colleagues found that support from peers was more effective than support from a superior. They related this fact to the police culture and the emphasis on solidarity and fraternity that creates room for a good peer support network (Martin et al., 2009). The fact that police officers often do not face critical incidents alone but with one or more colleagues can contribute to a so-called "buddy experience" and serve as a strong protective factor, since they are able to provide social support for each other during the traumatic experiences.

The mechanisms of how social support can protect against trauma symptomatology are not clearly defined, but it has been proposed that talking with peers after a traumatic event can facilitate the information processing and help in integrating the information about traumatic experiences into existing cognitive schemas (Stephens & Long, 2000). In their study, Stephens and Long measured social support operationalized as the content of communication and the ease of talking about trauma in 527 working police officers. The study showed that talking about traumatic experiences with peers does ameliorate the relationship between traumatic incidents and PTSD symptoms but only at moderate levels. So social support in the form of sharing traumatic experiences can actually be harmful in high amounts (Stephens & Long, 2000). Reasons for this distinction may be that excessive talk about negative topics can be overloading to peers, which makes them subtract from the relation and diminishes the social support network. The perceived ease of talking about traumatic experiences was also an important factor in protecting against PTSD symptoms (Stephens & Long, 2000). This is an important fact that might put many police officers at risk, since the police culture values bravery and toughness and might tend to discourage talk of emotions and devaluate the severity of critical incidents. Finally, nonwork-related talk with peers was also found to be a possible risk factor in high amounts (Stephens & Long, 2000). Though this was a cross-sectional study and caution therefore must be drawn in the conclusions based upon it, the study does show the importance of specifying the types of social support as some forms might be harmful. It is not only support from peers within the police force that is helpful, better social adjustment prior to joining the force is also an important factor (Yuan et al., 2010), as well as positive relationships outside the force like marriage (Pole, Kulkarni, Bernstein, & Kaufmann, 2006).

Family psychiatric history

Mixed findings have been reported with regards to effects of family psychiatric history as a risk factor for police officers and some prospective studies have found no effect (Carlier et al., 1997; Hodgins, Creamer, & Bell, 2001). While others have reported that a psychiatric family history can cause an officer to be more vulnerable to developing PTSD symptoms after joining the force (Inslicht et al., 2009; Pole et al., 2006). A prospective study from 2009 by Inslicht and colleagues found significant effects of mood, anxiety, and substance-related disorders in the family on the development of posttraumatic stress symptoms among police officers (Inslicht et al., 2009). Interesting about this finding was that the effects of family psychiatric history were mostly mediated by the effects it had on peritraumatic distress. Police officers with a family psychiatric history had a higher degree of peritraumatic reactivity and poor emotion regulation skills, which in turn led to a higher vulnerability toward developing PTSD symptoms after a critical incident. These findings lead us to the question of how a family psychiatric history can lead to higher levels of peritraumatic distress in adult life? In the article the authors mention several different possible explanations for this effect. One explanation is that some psychiatric disorders are associated with genetic disabilities regarding emotional control and stress reactivity, which can be inherited and result in similar disabilities. Another possibility is that parents with psychiatric disorders may not be able to model the appropriate emotion regulation and coping skills to their children. A third option is that families with psychiatric disorders may not be able to provide the social support that can protect against PTSD symptoms. Finally, children of parents with psychiatric disorders or addictions are more often exposed to traumatic events in their childhoods, which can affect their later trauma response (Inslicht et al., 2009).

Prior trauma history

The experience of traumatic incidents before joining the police force might increase the possibility of developing PTSD as a result of exposure to critical incidents on the job. Hodgins and colleagues, who did not find this to be a significant risk factor, suggested that the mediating effects of trauma history were complicated, and that moderate levels of trauma exposure before entering police work might inoculate the officers toward later trauma experienced as a police officer (Hodgins et al., 2001). Though some other studies found a similar lack of effect (Maguen et al., 2009), at least two studies reported that prior experiences of trauma increased the risk of trait dissociation and peritraumatic dissociation, which in turn increases the risk of PTSD symptom development (Inslicht et al., 2009; McCaslin et al., 2008). It is possible that high levels of prior traumatic experiences can damage the general stress response leading to a higher trait dissociation which in turn can lead to high levels of peritraumatic dissociation during critical events experienced as an officer (McCaslin et al., 2008).

Peritraumatic reactions

Peritraumatic distress and peritraumatic dissociation are some of the most predictive risk factors for developing PTSD symptomatology after a traumatic experience. The mediating effects of both variables have also been well documented in the studies reporting on police populations (Carlier et al., 1997; Hodgins et al., 2001; Marchand et al., 2015; Martin et al., 2009; McCaslin et al., 2008; Prati & Pietrantoni, 2010). Peritraumatic distress includes both feelings of high emotional distress, emotional exhaustion, as well as bodily distress experienced during a critical incident (Carlier et al., 1997; Prati & Pietrantoni, 2010). This heightened distress is thought to sensitize and overload the neurobiological structures involved in emotion regulation, memory formation, and fear conditioning, which are critical in the development of pathological posttraumatic reactions like hyperarousal symptoms(Inslicht et al., 2009; Marmar et al., 2006; Prati & Pietrantoni, 2010).

Peritraumatic dissociation is a state of detachment in the face of traumatic experiences that can include a sense of emotional numbing, altered time perceptions, depersonalization, derealization, and altered body image, as well as memory impairments (Martin et al., 2009; McCaslin et al., 2008). Peritraumatic dissociation is correlated with general peritraumatic distress, which suggests that intense emotional reactivity and distress during the incident can lead to physiological hyperarousal which in turn leads to the activation of dissociative states and detachment (Marmar et al., 2006; Martin et al., 2009).

This dissociation can function as a reflexive defense mechanism against the neurobiological and emotional overload. As mentioned, many studies have reported that peritraumatic dissociation is a strong risk factor in the development of PTSD symptoms; however, McCaslin et al. (2006) reported that it may only predict hyperarousal symptoms and not intrusion or avoidance symptoms. The authors suggested that this might be explained by the fact that hyperarousal symptoms have a more biological basis in nonassociational fear conditioning related to reactions and emotional distress at the time of the incident, while avoidance and intrusion symptoms are more based on the primarily cognitive processes in associational fear conditioning

(Marmar et al., 2006; McCaslin et al., 2006). All of these results indicate that it is important to question and screen officers after experiencing critical incidents and to set in with early interventions for those who have experienced high amounts of distress or dissociation during the incident.

Type of incident

A definition of critical incidents was presented in the introduction and although there are some criteria for an event to be classified as such, many incidents that are part of police work, can be placed within this category. Not all types of incidents will elicit the same responses and many factors related to the specific type of incident can affect the later development of traumatic stress. Although all critical incidents are severe to be defined as such, there are different perceptions of which incidents are most severe and thereby most traumatizing. Generally, events that are rarer are also judged to be more severe (Chopko, Palmieri, & Adams, 2015; Weiss et al., 2010). This means that events like encountering a dead body, which to civilians might be judged to be quite severe may not be so for police officers, since it is one of the more common encounters. In a study from 2010, Weiss et al. (2010) presented a sample of 715 police officers with 34 critical incidents that might be encountered in the service as a police officer (Weiss et al., 2010). These critical incidents were rated by the officers with regard to both frequency and severity. The results showed that some of the incidents judged to be most severe were committing a mistake that would injure or kill a colleague, making a mistake that would injure or kill a bystander and to be taken hostage. Encountering a dead body was the least severe scenario.

Replicating this study in 2015, Chopko and colleagues found similar results. In a study by Violanti et al. (2016), many of the same events were identified as severe though the exposure to battered or dead children was reported as the most severe incident in this study (Violanti et al., 2016). The degree of perceived personal threat and the requirement for the use of force are other incident-related risk factors (McCaslin et al., 2006; Prati & Pietrantoni, 2010; Violanti et al., 2016). A study on South African police officers also reported that events involving poor operational planning and execution strategies like riots can also be a risk factor for PTSD (Elntib & Armstrong, 2014). In general, incidents that elicit feelings of helplessness, lack of control, or lack of meaning can be quite traumatizing and severe for police officers (Alexander & Klein, 2001; Koch, 2010). This means that incidents like suicide, which are out of the police officers' control and that are hard to make sense of, can have a greater impact on police officers (Koch, 2010). Because most police officers are action-oriented, the feelings of helplessness encountered at these events, also enhance negative reaction patterns (Koch, 2010). Though the abovementioned studies have reported general results on the general risks related to type of incident, there are differences in which incidents are experienced to be most severe for the individual officer. Personal affiliations may affect the officers, such as finding a dead or badly beaten child at the same age as your own child or dealing with suicide victims if you have a family history of suicide.

Personality factors

Research in the field of personality factors as risk factors for the development of PTSD among police officers is limited, but some studies have found certain personality traits to have either positive or negative effects. Of the big five personality traits, neuroticism is generally found to be the strongest risk factor (Haisch & Meyers, 2004; Hodgins et al., 2001; Pole et al., 2006). The negative effects of neuroticism are likely mediated by associations with poorer interpersonal functioning, leading to a decline in social support, and by a more anxious and negative mood, which could increase vulnerability to the negative emotional symptoms of PTSD. Lower agreeableness, conscientiousness, and introversion have also been reported as risk factors (Carlier et al., 1997; Haisch & Meyers, 2004; Hodgins et al., 2001). Other personality traits not included in the Big Five model have been examined as well, and in a study on German police officers, trait anger was found to be a significant risk factor, possibly due to the negative effects of this trait on emotional support systems (Meffert et al., 2008). Trait dissociation is also a very potent risk factor, since it is directly correlated with peritraumatic dissociation, which is one of the most important mediators in the relationship between critical incident exposure and PTSD (Hodgins et al., 2001; McCaslin et al., 2008). Finally, anxiety sensitivity is a trait that is characterized by a fear of anxiety symptoms caused by a belief that they are harmful and the degree of this trait has been positively associated with severity of PTSD symptoms in police officers (Asmundson & Stapleton, 2008).

Coping

After experiencing critical incidents, there are many strategies that police officers can turn to, to cope with the emotions and stress that follows. The choice of coping strategies can be a strong factor in distinguishing those officers that develop traumatic stress symptoms from those who do not. Coping styles has been categorized in many different ways in the research of coping among police officers. A new study published in 2018, looked at the difference between active and passive coping among police officers and their ability to protect against the aftereffects of work stress (Violanti et al., 2018). They found that active coping styles, which include active acceptance, positive reframing, and planning, ameliorated the relationship between exposure to physical and psychological threats and the development of PTSD symptoms. Passive coping styles in the form of self-blame, venting, denial, and behavioral disengagement had a higher risk of eliciting and maintaining PTSD symptoms after experiencing such threats (Violanti et al., 2018). Others distinguish between emotional coping, avoidance coping, and task-oriented coping styles using The Coping Inventory for Stressful Situations (CISS) to measure for these styles. Emotional coping in this scale involves self-oriented emotional reactions, task-oriented coping involves problem-solving behavior, planning and cognitive restructuring, while avoidance coping refers to activities aimed at avoiding the stressful situation (Kurokawa & Weed, 1998). Emotional coping and avoidance coping have been reported as maladaptive coping styles that can worsen the effects of critical incident exposure among police officers (LeBlanc, Regehr, Jelley, & Barath, 2008; Marchand et al., 2015). Task-oriented coping has been shown to be more beneficial and helpful in managing the stress of traumatic exposure (LeBlanc et al., 2008). In relation to the study by Violanti and colleagues on active and passive coping styles, this makes sense, since both avoidance and emotional coping are passive strategies, while task-oriented coping can be categorized as more of an active strategy. Distancing, escape, and avoidance coping styles were also reported as increasing vulnerability to developing PTSD by other studies (Pasillas, Follette, & Perumean-Chaney, 2006; Pole et al., 2006). The police subculture might encourage the use of some maladaptive coping styles, since the values of bravery and toughness as well as tendencies toward emotion suppression and critical incident devaluation might lead to more avoidance-based coping and emotion suppression, while discouraging seeking of help from others (Ménard et al., 2016). Coping is, however, a crucial element in preventing PTSD symptomatology among police officers, and it is important for police organizations to work against the cultural facilitators of maladaptive coping strategies and train the officers in using more active and task-oriented coping styles as opposed to passive and avoidance-based coping styles.

Organizational factors

Writing this chapter, we have chosen as primary focus the traumatization related to critical incident exposure among police officers. This does not mean that critical incidents are the only factors of the police job contributing to traumatic stress symptoms among police officers. Organizational or routine work stressors such as poor equipment, high workload, unsuitable partners, poor supervision, unclear roles, job insecurity, insufficient pay, and shift work have been reported to have effects on the development of traumatic stress independently of the exposure to critical incidents (Maguen et al., 2009; Violanti et al., 2018). These factors may also play a role in mediating the relationship between critical incident exposure and traumatization, as a negative work environment with many of these types of stressors may put further strain on police officers and worsen the negative effects of critical incident exposure both directly and indirectly (Maguen et al., 2009; Violanti et al., 2018).

Job type

By far most of the studies on police trauma focus on patrol/line officers, and they are likely the ones that are exposed to the widest range of different critical incidents. Compared with most special unit officers, it would also seem that they are more often exposed to direct threat on a day-to-day basis (Burruss, Holt, & Wall-Parker, 2018). The diversity of this job type entails unpredictability, which can be a risk factor in itself, since constant anticipation of threat can lead to a general hypervigilance (Papazoglou, 2013). Though it is important to acknowledge the traumatic effects of working as a patrol officer, police work can be very diverse and not all officers engage in the same tasks. While most officers work as patrol officers, others work in specialized units, and the risks associated with each of these job types have to be considered. There are many job types that could place officers at special risk, we will here only mention a few.

In 2018, Burrus and colleagues published a study on officers employed in special cybercrime and digital forensic units and identified several factors that put these officers at special risk of developing traumatic stress symptomatology (Burruss et al., 2018). Most importantly this job type includes frequent exposure to digital content involving child pornography and sexual exploitation, and viewing this content is an essential part of their work. This kind of content was found to be a strong risk factor for developing PTSD symptoms, which is also in agreement with the fact that exposure to dead or battered children is one of the most severe traumatic incidents (Violanti et al., 2016).

Officers with children of their own may be even more impacted by this content, and it might affect their family relations as well (Burruss et al., 2018). Furthermore, the officers working in special units in general may be victims of working alone, and it can be hard for them to draw support from other officers outside the units because of the specialized nature of their own work (Violanti et al., 2016). Juvenile crime investigators may also be at special risk because of their dealings with abused children and their sometimes limited options of acting or helping these children, which can lead to a more avoidant coping style (Mrevlje, 2017). Furthermore, the nature of the cases they work on can make it hard for them to share with others without burdening them. Homicide detectives are at risk because of their close contact with many bereaved relatives of homicide victims, which can increase their exposure to vicarious trauma. Their jobs often include an "on call" function, which blurs the line between office hours and free time and keep them in constant anticipation of new traumatic exposures (Mrevlje, 2017).

Another exposed job type is crime scene technicians (Mrevlje, 2016). They are more frequently exposed to dead bodies than officers in other job types, and though previous research has shown that encountering a dead body was one of the least traumatizing events for police officers (Weiss et al., 2010), the death scenes encountered by crime scene technicians can often be violent and explicit and the technicians also have to interact more with the corpses when collecting evidence (Mrevlje, 2016). They can be exposed to feelings of helplessness similar to that experienced by juvenile crime investigators, since the tragic deaths they encounter are already committed (Mrevlje, 2016).

Finally, a study from 2013 focused on traumatization among police communicators (Regehr, LeBlanc, Barath, Balch, & Birze, 2013). The communicators could be at special risk of high levels of secondary traumatization as they communicate with highly distressed callers, without the ability to directly help the callers at the scene, leaving this work to other police officers. This might lead to a feeling of powerlessness and isolation (Regehr et al., 2013). The study found a relatively high extent of PTSD among the examined communicators of 31% suggesting that this job type might also put the employees at special risk of traumatization (Regehr et al., 2013).

Other factors

In this section of this chapter, we have gone through some of the most commonly found risk and protective factors in police work. The scope of the chapter does not allow us to go through all potential factors in detail, but some other possible mediating factors are length of service (Prati & Pietrantoni, 2010), ethnicity (Pole et al., 2001, 2006), age (Darensburg et al., 2006), income (Galovski et al., 2018), and self-esteem (Prati & Pietrantoni, 2010).

Prevention and treatment

From the previous sections in this chapter, it is evident that the strain of police work can lead to some serious mental health consequences at least for some police officers. Today there are a variety of prevention and intervention strategies in place to minimize the psychological costs for the police officers, and in this section, we will look into a few possible strategies and techniques.

Although the degree of implementation and use in different countries and police organizations vary substantially, one widely implemented intervention technique is psychological debriefing and the most common model is the Critical Incident Stress Debriefing (CISD), which was developed by Jeffrey Mitchell to prevent work-related traumatic stress among high-risk occupational groups (Mitchell & Everly, 1995). The CISD should be considered as part of the more comprehensive, multicomponent Critical Incident Stress Management (CISM) program, which includes both prevention and postcrisis management efforts (Everly, Flannery, & Mitchell, 2000). Though many other components are included in this broader program, the CISD is likely the most prominent technique that has been the primary focus of the research on the subject.

CISD is a group intervention technique, where officers involved in a critical incident, as well as peer support personnel, are brought together and engage in a psychological debriefing led by a team of mental health professionals from crisis response teams (Mitchell & Everly, 1995). The debriefing is meant to be carried out as soon as possible after a critical incident. The debriefing is structured in seven phases, and it is designed to gradually probe increasingly sensitive and emotional topics concerning the incident. The first phase is an *introductory phase*, where the participants are informed about the purpose and the process of the debriefing. This has the overall effect of preparing the participants for the debriefing as well as motivating and engaging them in the process. After this introduction, the *fact phase* encourages the participants to talk about the facts of the incident, such as their own role in the incident and the proceedings of the events from their perspective. This fact phase is less personal and sensitive, and it builds the groundwork for a conversation of the more sensitive topics in the following phases. The next phase is the *thought phase*, which probes the initial and prominent thoughts of the participants during the incident, followed by the *reaction phase*, which entails a discussion of the personal reactions and emotions experienced by the participants. The reaction phase is the most emotionally powerful phase. Following the reaction phase is a *symptom phase*, which discusses the symptoms of trauma experienced by the participants during and after the incident and a *teaching phase*, where the mental health professionals provide information about the common distress symptoms experienced after a critical incident and teach the participants stress survival strategies. In the end, a *reentry phase* closes and summarizes the debriefing (Mitchell & Everly, 1995).

A shorter version of the CISD is sometimes employed called *posttrauma defusing*. This process only includes three phases, and it is designed to be flexible and possible to implement immediately after a critical incident (Mitchell & Everly, 1995).

The potential benefits of CISD build on several theoretical constructs regarding the process of traumatization. The CISD provides a safe and structured environment for verbal expression of the experiences related to the incident. It can be conducive to the cognitive structuring and reconstruction of the incident within the participants, which prevents maladaptive trauma-related conceptions and memories otherwise conducive to posttraumatic symptomatology. The group element of the intervention can also be very beneficial since it clarifies that any possible symptoms or negative emotions related to the incident is not an individual weakness but a common response (Mitchell & Everly, 1995). This might be especially important to police officers, since the police culture fosters expectations for bravery and resilience, which would differ with any experienced symptoms of distress.

Despite many theoretical benefits of the CISD, there has long been a lively debate about the utility of the CISD in practice. Many criticisms have been presented against Mitchell's model and while some studies find beneficial effects, others have found none or even harmful effects (Malcolm, Seaton, Perera, Sheehan, & Van Hasselt, 2005; Pack, 2013). Though previous research varies widely in their criticisms and findings, there are some common conditions that seem to be detrimental to the effectiveness of the CISD. First of all, it needs to be implemented as part of a wider CISM program and cannot stand as a single isolated intervention form (Malcolm et al., 2005; Pack, 2013). Furthermore, the research suggests that a single debriefing session is not enough to gain a reliable effect but several sessions must be carried out after a critical incident for the intervention to be most beneficial (Pack, 2013). Finally, it is important that the people responsible for carrying out the debriefing must be well-trained healthcare professionals, with an understanding of the police culture (Malcolm et al., 2005; Pack, 2013).

The research on the effectiveness of the model has many inconsistencies and challenges that prevent a clear picture of the effects of this form of treatment such as a lacking homogenous terminology and application of the CISD in the evaluative research as well as differing conceptions of the aims of the intervention (Malcolm et al., 2005; Pack, 2013). There is definitely a great need for future research on the subject to clarify whether CISD is an effective treatment technique and to specify more of the conditions necessary for this effect.

Police culture includes strong feelings of solidarity among the police officers and since social support has also been proven to be a prominent protective factor against the development of PTSD, it seems intuitive to draw on peer support in intervention strategies. One example of a peer-support intervention program is the Trauma Risk Management Program (TriM) (Watson & Andrews, 2017). It has been evaluated and used within military organizations, but recent studies have proven positive effects within police organizations in the UK as well. Following the TriM program, employees within the organization are taught about trauma psychology and symptomatology and trained in assessing symptoms among their peers following critical incidents. If pathological trauma symptoms are detected among individual officers, the TriM employees refer these officers to mental health professionals. In addition to assisting in early identification of police officers at risk of developing pathological posttrauma reactions, the psychoeducation and inclusion of members of the organization in this assessment can contribute in diminishing the mental health stigma and anti-help-seeking behavior otherwise found within the police culture (Watson & Andrews, 2017).

The CISD and TriM are mostly aimed at preventing the development of PTSD symptomatology after a critical incident and at identifying those officers, who are at special risk. They are not meant to treat PTSD symptoms once these have been fully developed. One such treatment developed for police officers by Berthold Gersons is Brief Eclectic Psychotherapy (Gersons & Schnyder, 2013). Gersons developed the treatment as an integration of elements from different psychological treatment schools at the time (Gersons & Schnyder, 2013). The treatment is phase oriented and consists of 16 well-defined psychotherapy sessions. The first session includes thorough psychoeducation, where partners or loved ones are invited to participate to induce a comprehensive understanding of the symptoms experienced and how the treatment can help in treating them. The following sessions include relaxation exercises and imagery exposure along with the use of certain objects connected to the trauma, called memorabilia, to elicit reexperiencing of emotions related to the trauma. The client is also instructed to write a letter to the person or the institution they deem responsible for the critical incident expressing any feelings of anger and blame.

These techniques are meant to help the patient in accessing and expressing any suppressed emotions related to the incident, which can lead to a form of catharsis and relief that can eventually alleviate PTSD symptoms. A phase of meaning and integration is also a part of the therapy sessions, where the therapist helps the client accept the fact that the critical incident has changed him, and that life is not necessarily the same as it was before the incident. It is necessary to gain an understanding of what has shaped the expectations and ideas of the client before the critical event and what shapes them now while integrating these new conceptions of the world and oneself. Finally, the sessions are concluded by a farewell ritual designed by the client to let go of the traumatic events (Gersons & Schnyder, 2013). One randomized clinical trial performed on a Dutch police office population by Gersons and colleagues showed very strong treatment effects both immediately after the treatment and 3 months later (Gersons, Carlier, Lamberts, & van der Kolk, 2000). Despite these very promising results as well as similar results found on other populations

(Lindauer et al., 2005; Schnyder, Müller, Maercker, & Wittmann, 2011), there seem to be no recent studies on the effectiveness of Brief Eclectic Psychotherapy among police officers. This calls for further research to clarify whether the strong effects found by Gersons and colleagues can be replicated in other studies on law enforcement populations.

Conclusions

Policing is a high-risk profession involving exposure to critical incidents capable of causing serious long-term consequences for both the physical and mental health of police officers. Though most police officers exhibit patterns of resilience with constant low levels of trauma symptoms, some experience patterns of consistently increasing levels of pathological trauma symptomatology. Repeated and extensive exposure to critical incidents as well as certain values and tendencies within the police culture contribute in creating a unique and complex picture of police traumatization, and several models and conceptions have been devised in the attempt to capture this picture.

Not all police officers experience the same negative effects of traumatic exposure and factors such as social support, peritraumatic reactions, coping styles, job type, and family psychiatric history can contribute in determining the outcome for the individual officer. Furthermore, not all types of critical incidents are experienced as equally traumatizing and some of the most severe experiences include making mistakes that could injure or kill colleagues and bystanders as well as encountering abused or battered children. Preventative and screening strategies, such as Critical Incident Stress Debriefing and The Trauma Risk Management Program, may be put in place to prevent the development of PTSD symptoms after exposure to critical incidents or to identify the officers in need of further treatment. Many different treatment programs and techniques are being used to treat traumatized police officers, and Brief Eclectic Psychotherapy developed by Berthold Gersons has shown very promising treatment effects in treating PTSD among police officers. However, further research is needed into the effectiveness of prevention and treatment models in order to identify and develop the best and most effective strategies. In this chapter, we hope to have conveyed the importance of contributions from the field of trauma psychology in reaching an integrative understanding of police psychology.

References

Aamodt, M. G. (2008). Reducing misconceptions and false beliefs in police and criminal psychology. *Criminal Justice and Behavior, 35*(10), 1231–1240. https://doi.org/10.1177/0093854808321527.

Alexander, D. A., & Klein, S. (2001). Ambulance personnel and critical incidents: Impact of accident and emergency work on mental health and emotional well-being. *British Journal of Psychiatry, 178*(1), 76–81.

American Psychiatric Association. (2013). *Diagnostic and statistical manual of mental disorders: DSM-5 (5. ed.)*. Arlington, Va: American Psychiatric Association.

Andersen, J. P., & Papazoglou, K. (2014). Friends under fire:Cross-cultural relationships and trauma exposure among police officers. *Traumatology, 20*(3), 182–190. https://doi.org/10.1037/h0099403.

Andrew, M. E., McCanlies, E. C., Burchfiel, C. M., Charles, L. E., Hartley, T. A., Fekedulegn, D., et al. (2008). Hardiness and psychological distress in a cohort of police officers. *International Journal of Emergency Mental Health, 10*(2), 137–147.

Asmundson, G. J. G., & Stapleton, J. A. (2008). Associations between dimensions of anxiety sensitivity and PTSD symptom clusters in active-duty police officers. *Cognitive Behaviour Therapy, 37*(2), 66–75. https://doi.org/10.1080/16506070801969005.

Ballenger, J. F., Best, S. R., Metzler, T. J., Wasserman, D. A., Mohr, D. C., Liberman, A., et al. (2011). Patterns and predictors of alcohol use in male and female urban police officers. *American Journal on Addictions, 20*(1), 21–29. https://doi.org/10.1111/j.1521-0391.2010.00092.x.

Burruss, G. W., Holt, T. J., & Wall-Parker, A. (2018). The hazards of investigating internet crimes against children: Digital evidence handlers' experiences with vicarious trauma and coping behaviors. *American Journal of Criminal Justice, 43*(3), 433–447. https://doi.org/10.1007/s12103-017-9417-3.

Carlier, I. V., Lamberts, R. D., & Gersons, B. P. (1997). Risk factors for posttraumatic stress symptomatology in police officers: A prospective analysis. *The Journal of Nervous and Mental Disease, 185*(8), 498–506. https://doi.org/10.1097/00005053-199708000-00004.

Chae, M. H., & Boyle, D. J. (2013). Police suicide: Prevalence, risk, and protective factors. *Policing: An International Journal of Police Strategies & Management, 36*(1), 91–118. https://doi.org/10.1108/13639511311302498.

Chopko, B. A., Palmieri, P. A., & Adams, R. E. (2015). Critical incident history questionnaire replication: Frequency and severity of trauma exposure among officers from small and midsize police agencies. *Journal of Traumatic Stress, 28*(2), 157–161. https://doi.org/10.1002/jts.21996.

Chopko, B. A., Palmieri, P. A., & Adams, R. E. (2018). Trauma-related sleep problems and associated health outcomes in police officers: A path analysis. *Journal of Interpersonal Violence*. https://doi.org/10.1177/0886260518767912, 88626051876791.

Chopko, B. A., & Schwartz, R. C. (2012). Correlates of career traumatization and symptomatology among active-duty police officers. *Criminal Justice Studies, 25*(1), 83–95. https://doi.org/10.1080/1478601X.2012.657905.

Darensburg, T., Andrew, M. E., Hartley, T. A., Burchfiel, C. M., Fekedulegn, D., & Violanti, J. M. (2006). Gender and age differences in posttraumatic stress disorder and depression among buffalo police officers. *Traumatology, 12*(3), 220–228. https://doi.org/10.1177/1534765606296271.

Elntib, S., & Armstrong, T. (2014). Critical incidents' impact on front-line South African police personnel in light of the current briefing and debriefing strategies. *South African Journal of Psychology, 44*(4), 416–425. https://doi.org/10.1177/0081246314529272.

Everly, G. S., Flannery, R. B., & Mitchell, J. T. (2000). Critical incident stress management (CISM): A review of the literature. *Aggression and Violent Behavior, 5*(1), 23–40. https://doi.org/10.1016/S1359-1789(98)00026-3.

Galatzer-Levy, I. R., Madan, A., Neylan, T. C., Henn-Haase, C., & Marmar, C. R. (2011). Peritraumatic and trait dissociation differentiate police officers with resilient versus symptomatic trajectories of posttraumatic stress symptoms. *Journal of Traumatic Stress, 24*(5), 557–565. https://doi.org/10.1002/jts.20684.

Galovski, T. E., Peterson, Z. D., & Fox-Galalis, A. (2018). Trajectories of posttraumatic stress and depression in police and community members following the violence during civil unrest in Ferguson, Missouri. *American Journal of Community Psychology.* https://doi.org/10.1002/ajcp.12273.

Gershon, R. R. M., Barocas, B., Canton, A. N., Li, X., & Vlahov, D. (2009). Mental, physical, and behavioral outcomes associated with perceived work stress in police officers. *Criminal Justice and Behavior, 36*(3), 275–289. https://doi.org/10.1177/0093854808330015.

Gersons, B. P., Carlier, I. V., Lamberts, R. D., & van der Kolk, B. A. (2000). Randomized clinical trial of brief eclectic psychotherapy for police officers with posttraumatic stress disorder. *Journal of Traumatic Stress, 13*(2), 333–347. https://doi.org/10.1023/A:1007793803627.

Gersons, B. P., & Schnyder, U. (2013). Learning from traumatic experiences with brief eclectic psychotherapy for PTSD. *European Journal of Psychotraumatology, 4*, 1–6. https://doi.org/10.3402/ejpt.v4i0.21369.

Green, B. L., Goodman, L. A., Krupnick, J. L., Corcoran, C. B., Petty, R. M., Stockton, P., et al. (2000). Outcomes of single versus multiple trauma exposure in a screening sample. *Journal of Traumatic Stress, 13*(2), 271–286. https://doi.org/10.1023/A:1007758711939.

Guilaran, J., de Terte, I., Kaniasty, K., & Stephens, C. (2018). Psychological outcomes in disaster responders: A systematic review and meta-analysis on the effect of social support. *International Journal of Disaster Risk Science, 9*(3), 344–358. https://doi.org/10.1007/s13753-018-0184-7.

Haisch, D. C., & Meyers, L. S. (2004). MMPI-2 assessed post-traumatic stress disorder related to job stress, coping, and personality in police agencies. *Stress and Health, 20*(4), 223–229. https://doi.org/10.1002/smi.1020.

Hammer, E. S. (2005). *Cumulative trauma in police officers* (Ph.D. Dissertation). San Diego, Ann Arbor, United States: Alliant International University. Retrieved from http://proxy1-bib.sdu.dk:2048/login?url=https://search-proquest-com.proxy3-bib.sdu.dk/docview/305374666?accountid=14211.

Hartley, T. A., Burchfiel, C. M., Fekedulegn, D., Andrew, M. E., & Violanti, J. M. (2011). Health disparities in police officers: Comparisons to the U.S. general population. *International Journal of Emergency Mental Health, 13*(4), 211–220.

Hartley, T. A., Sarkisian, K., Violanti, J. M., Andrew, M. E., & Burchfiel, C. M. (2013). PTSD symptoms among police officers: Associations with frequency, recency, and types of traumatic events. *International Journal of Emergency Mental Health, 15*(4), 241–253.

Henley Woody, R. (2005). The police culture: Research implications for psychological services. *Professional Psychology: Research and Practice, 36*(5), 525–529. https://doi.org/10.1037/0735-7028.36.5.525.

Hermann, J. L. (1997). *Trauma and recovery: The aftermath of violence - from domestic abuse to political terror.* New York: BasicBooks.

Hodgins, G. A., Creamer, M., & Bell, R. (2001). Risk factors for posttrauma reactions in police officers: A longitudinal study. *The Journal of Nervous and Mental Disease, 189*(8), 541–547. https://doi.org/10.1097/00005053-200108000-00007.

Huddleston, L. M., Paton, D., & Stephens, C. (2006). Conceptualizing traumatic stress in police officers: Preemployment, critical incident, and organizational influences. *Traumatology, 12*(3), 170–177. https://doi.org/10.1177/1534765606294911.

Inslicht, S. S., McCaslin, S. E., Metzler, T. J., Henn-Haase, C., Hart, S. L., Maguen, S., & Marmar, C. R. (2009). Family psychiatric history, peritraumatic reactivity, and posttraumatic stress symptoms: A prospective study of police. *Journal of Psychiatric Research, 44*(1), 22−31. https://doi.org/10.1016/j.jpsychires.2009.05.011.

Karlsson, I., & Christianson, S.Å. (2003). The phenomenology of traumatic experiences in police work. *Policing: An International Journal of Police Strategies & Management, 26*(3), 419−438. https://doi.org/10.1108/13639510310489476.

Kessler, R. C., Berglund, P., Demler, O., Jin, R., Merikangas, K. R., & Walters, E. E. (2005). Lifetime prevalence and age-of-onset distributions of DSM-IV disorders in the national comorbidity survey replication. *Archives of General Psychiatry, 62*(6), 593−602. https://doi.org/10.1001/archpsyc.62.6.593.

Koch, B. J. (2010). The psychological impact on police officers of being first responders to completed suicides. *Journal of Police and Criminal Psychology, 25*(2), 90−98. https://doi.org/10.1007/s11896-010-9070-y.

Kurokawa, N. K. S., & Weed, N. C. (1998). Interrater agreement on the coping inventory for stressful situations (CISS). *Assessment, 5*(1), 93−100. https://doi.org/10.1177/107319119800500111.

LeBlanc, V. R., Regehr, C., Jelley, R. B., & Barath, I. (2008). The relationship between coping styles, performance, and responses to stressful scenarios in police recruits. *International Journal of Stress Management, 15*(1), 76−93. https://doi.org/10.1037/1072-5245.15.1.76.

Lilly, M. M., Pole, N., Best, S. R., Metzler, T., & Marmar, C. R. (2009). Gender and PTSD: What can we learn from female police officers? *Journal of Anxiety Disorders, 23*(6), 767−774. https://doi.org/10.1016/j.janxdis.2009.02.015.

Lindauer, R. J. L., Gersons, B. P. R., van Meijel, E. P. M., Blom, K., Carlier, I. V. E., Vrijlandt, I., et al. (2005). Effects of Brief Eclectic Psychotherapy in patients with posttraumatic stress disorder: Randomized clinical trial. *Journal of Traumatic Stress, 18*(3), 205−212. https://doi.org/10.1002/jts.20029.

Lindsay, V., & Shelley, K. (2009). Social and stress-related influences of police officers' alcohol consumption. *Journal of Police and Criminal Psychology, 24*(2), 87−92. https://doi.org/10.1007/s11896-009-9048-9.

Maguen, S., Metzler, T. J., McCaslin, S. E., Inslicht, S. S., Henn-Haase, C., Neylan, T. C., et al. (2009). Routine work environment stress and PTSD symptoms in police officers. *The Journal of Nervous and Mental Disease, 197*(10), 754−760. https://doi.org/10.1097/NMD.0b013e3181b975f8.

Maia, D. B., Marmar, C. R., Metzler, T., Nóbrega, A., Berger, W., Mendlowicz, M. V., et al. (2006). Post-traumatic stress symptoms in an elite unit of Brazilian police officers: Prevalence and impact on psychosocial functioning and on physical and mental health. *Journal of Affective Disorders, 97*(1), 241−245. https://doi.org/10.1016/j.jad.2006.06.004.

Malcolm, A. S., Seaton, J., Perera, A., Sheehan, D. C., & Van Hasselt, V. B. (2005). Critical incident stress debriefing and law enforcement: An evaluative review. *Brief Treatment and Crisis Intervention, 5*(3), 261−278. https://doi.org/10.1093/brief-treatment/mhi019.

Marchand, A., Nadeau, C., Beaulieu-Prévost, D., Boyer, R., & Martin, M. (2015). Predictors of posttraumatic stress disorder among police officers: A prospective study. *Psychological Trauma: Theory, Research, Practice and Policy, 7*(3), 212−221. https://doi.org/10.1037/a0038780.

Marmar, C. R., McCaslin, S. E., Metzler, T. J., Best, S., Weiss, D. S., Fagan, J., et al. (2006). Predictors of posttraumatic stress in police and other first responders. *Annals of the New York Academy of Sciences, 1071*, 1−18. https://doi.org/10.1196/annals.1364.001.

Marshall, E. K. (2006). Cumulative career traumatic stress (CCTS): A pilot study of traumatic stress in law enforcement. *Journal of Police and Criminal Psychology, 21*(1), 62–71. https://doi.org/10.1007/BF02849503.

Martin, M., Marchand, A., Boyer, R., & Martin, N. (2009). Predictors of the development of posttraumatic stress disorder among police officers. *Journal of Trauma & Dissociation, 10*(4), 451–468. https://doi.org/10.1080/15299730903143626.

McCaslin, S. E., Inslicht, S. S., Metzler, T. J., Henn-Haase, C., Maguen, S., Neylan, T. C., et al. (2008). Trait dissociation predicts posttraumatic stress disorder symptoms in a prospective study of urban police officers. *The Journal of Nervous and Mental Disease, 196*(12), 912–918. https://doi.org/10.1097/NMD.0b013e31818ec95d.

McCaslin, S. E., Rogers, C. E., Metzler, T. J., Best, S. R., Weiss, D. S., Fagan, J. A., et al. (2006). The impact of personal threat on police officers' responses to critical incident stressors. *The Journal of Nervous and Mental Disease, 194*(8), 591–597. https://doi.org/10.1097/01.nmd.0000230641.43013.68.

Meffert, S. M., Metzler, T. J., Henn-Haase, C., McCaslin, S., Inslicht, S., Chemtob, C., et al. (2008). A prospective study of trait anger and PTSD symptoms in police. *Journal of Traumatic Stress, 21*(4), 410–416. https://doi.org/10.1002/jts.20350.

Ménard, K. S., & Arter, M. L. (2013). Police officer alcohol use and trauma symptoms: Associations with critical incidents, coping, and social stressors. *International Journal of Stress Management, 20*(1), 37–56. https://doi.org/10.1037/a0031434.

Ménard, K. S., Arter, M. L., & Khan, C. (2016). Critical incidents, alcohol and trauma problems, and service utilization among police officers from five countries. *International Journal of Comparative and Applied Criminal Justice, 40*(1), 25–42. https://doi.org/10.1080/01924036.2015.1028950.

Milner, A., Spittal, M. J., Pirkis, J., & LaMontagne, A. D. (2013). Suicide by occupation: Systematic review and meta-analysis. *The British Journal of Psychiatry: The Journal of Mental Science, 203*(6), 409–416. https://doi.org/10.1192/bjp.bp.113.128405.

Mitchell, J. T., & Everly, G. S., Jr. (1995). The critical incident stress debriefing (CISD) and the prevention of work-related traumatic stress among high risk occupational groups. In *Psychotraumatology: Key papers and core concepts in post-traumatic stress* (pp. 267–280). New York, NY, US: Plenum Press.

Mohr, D., Vedantham, K., Neylan, T., Metzler, T. J., Best, S., & Marmar, C. R. (2003). The mediating effects of sleep in the relationship between traumatic stress and health symptoms in urban police officers. *Psychosomatic Medicine, 65*(3), 485–489. https://doi.org/10.1097/01.PSY.0000041404.96597.38.

Mrevlje, T. P. (2016). Coping with work-related traumatic situations among crime scene technicians. *Stress and Health, 32*(4), 374–382. https://doi.org/10.1002/smi.2631.

Mrevlje, T. P. (2017). The trauma and coping in homicide and sexual offences and juvenile crime criminal investigators. *Varstvoslovje, 19*(4), 323–338.

Olff, M. (2017). Sex and gender differences in post-traumatic stress disorder: An update. *European Journal of Psychotraumatology, 8*, 1–2. https://doi.org/10.1080/20008198.2017.1351204.

Pack, M. J. (2013). Critical incident stress management: A review of the literature with implications for social work. *International Social Work, 56*(5), 608–627. https://doi.org/10.1177/0020872811435371.

Paoline, E. A. (2003). Taking stock: Toward a richer understanding of police culture. *Journal of Criminal Justice, 31*(3), 199–214. https://doi.org/10.1016/S0047-2352(03)00002-3.

Papazoglou, K. (2013). Conceptualizing police complex spiral trauma and its applications in the police field. *Traumatology: International Journal, 19*(3), 196–209. https://doi.org/10.1177/1534765612466151.

Papazoglou, K., & Tuttle, B. M. (2018). Fighting police trauma: Practical approaches to addressing psychological needs of officers. *SAGE Open, 8*(3). https://doi.org/10.1177/2158244018794794, 215824401879479.

Pasillas, R. M., Follette, V. M., & Perumean-Chaney, S. E. (2006). Occupational stress and psychological functioning in law enforcement officers. *Journal of Police and Criminal Psychology, 21*(1), 41–53. https://doi.org/10.1007/BF02849501.

Pole, N., Best, S. R., Weiss, D. S., Metzler, T., Liberman, A. M., Fagan, J., et al. (2001). Effects of gender and ethnicity on duty-related posttraumatic stress symptoms among urban police officers. *The Journal of Nervous and Mental Disease, 189*(7), 442–448. https://doi.org/10.1097/00005053-200107000-00005.

Pole, N., Kulkarni, M., Bernstein, A., & Kaufmann, G. (2006). Resilience in retired police officers. *Traumatology, 12*(3), 207–216. https://doi.org/10.1177/1534765606294993.

Prati, G., & Pietrantoni, L. (2010). Risk and resilience factors among Italian municipal police officers exposed to critical incidents. *Journal of Police and Criminal Psychology, 25*(1), 27–33. https://doi.org/10.1007/s11896-009-9052-0.

Regehr, C., LeBlanc, V. R., Barath, I., Balch, J., & Birze, A. (2013). Predictors of physiological stress and psychological distress in police communicators. *Police Practice and Research, 14*(6), 451–463. https://doi.org/10.1080/15614263.2012.736718.

Robinson, H. M., Sigman, M. R., & Wilson, J. P. (1997). Duty-related stressors and PTSD symptoms in suburban police officers. *Psychological Reports, 81*(3), 835–845. https://doi.org/10.2466/pr0.1997.81.3.835.

Royle, L., Keenan, P., & Farrell, D. (2009). Issues of stigma for first responders accessing support for post traumatic stress. *International Journal of Emergency Mental Health, 11*(2), 79–85.

Rudofossi, D. C. (1996). *The impact of trauma and loss on affective profiles of police officers* (Dissertation). Ann Arbor: New York University. Retrieved from http://proxy1-bib.sdu.dk:2048/login?url=https://search-proquest-com.proxy3-bib.sdu.dk/docview/304255311?accountid=14211.

Rudofossi, D. (2007). A brief turtorial on the nature of trauma in policing. In *Working with traumatized police officer-patients: A clinician's guide to complex PTSD syndromes in public safety professionals*. Amityville, New York: Baywood Publishing Company, Inc.

Rudofossi, D., & Lund, D. (2009). Police and public-safety complex PTSD (PPS-CPTSD): Toward an integration of the five hubs of loss. In *A Cop Doc's guide to public safety complex trauma syndrome: Using five police personality styles*. Amityville: Routledge Ltd.

Schnyder, U., Müller, J., Maercker, A., & Wittmann, L. (2011). Brief eclectic psychotherapy for PTSD: A randomized controlled trial. *Journal of Clinical Psychiatry, 72*(4), 564–566. https://doi.org/10.4088/JCP.10l06247blu.

Steinkopf, B. L., Hakala, K. A., & Van Hasselt, V. B. (2015). Motivational interviewing: Improving the delivery of psychological services to law enforcement. *Professional Psychology: Research and Practice, 46*(5), 348–354. https://doi.org/10.1037/pro0000042.

Stephens, C., & Long, N. (2000). Communication with police supervisors and peers as a buffer of work-related traumatic stress. *Journal of Organizational Behavior, 21*(4), 407–424.

Stephens, C., & Miller, I. (1998). Traumatic experiences and post-traumatic stress disorder in the New Zealand police. *Policing: An International Journal of Police Strategies & Management, 21*(1), 178–191. https://doi.org/10.1108/13639519810206664.

Terte, I., Stephens, C., & Huddleston, L. (2014). The development of a three part model of psychological resilience. *Stress and Health, 30*(5), 416–424. https://doi.org/10.1002/smi.2625.

Violanti, J. M. (2004). Predictors of police suicide ideation. *Suicide and Life-Threatening Behavior, 34*(3), 277–283. https://doi.org/10.1521/suli.34.3.277.42775.

Violanti, J. M., Fekedulegn, D., Hartley, T. A., Charles, L. E., Andrew, M. E., Ma, C. C., et al. (2016). Highly rated and most frequent stressors among police officers: Gender differences. *American Journal of Criminal Justice, 41*(4), 645–662. https://doi.org/10.1007/s12103-016-9342-x.

Violanti, J. M., Ma, C. C., Mnatsakanova, A., Fekedulegn, D., Hartley, T. A., Gu, J. K., et al. (2018). Associations between police work stressors and posttraumatic stress disorder symptoms: Examining the moderating effects of coping. *Journal of Police and Criminal Psychology, 33*(3), 271–282. https://doi.org/10.1007/s11896-018-9276-y.

Watson, L., & Andrews, L. (2017). The effect of a Trauma Risk Management (TRiM) program on stigma and barriers to help-seeking in the police. *International Journal of Stress Management.* https://doi.org/10.1037/str0000071.

Weiss, D. S., Brunet, A., Best, S. R., Metzler, T. J., Liberman, A., Pole, N., et al. (2010). Frequency and severity approaches to indexing exposure to trauma: The Critical Incident History Questionnaire for police officers. *Journal of Traumatic Stress, 23*(6), 734–743. https://doi.org/10.1002/jts.20576.

Wester, S. R., Arndt, D., Sedivy, S. K., & Arndt, L. (2010). Male police officers and stigma associated with counseling: The role of anticipated risks, anticipated benefits and gender role conflict. *Psychology of Men and Masculinity, 11*(4), 286–302. https://doi.org/10.1037/a0019108.

World Health Organization. (2018). *ICD-11 for mortality and morbidity statistics.* Retrieved from https://icd.who.int/browse11/l-m/en#/http%3a%2f%2fid.who.int%2ficd%2fentity%2f585833559.

Yuan, C., Wang, Z., Inslicht, S. S., McCaslin, S. E., Metzler, T. J., Henn-Haase, C., et al. (2010). Protective factors for posttraumatic stress disorder symptoms in a prospective study of police officers. *Psychiatry Research, 188*(1), 45–50. https://doi.org/10.1016/j.psychres.2010.10.034.

From ideation to realization: exploring the problem of police officer suicide

Karl Roberts

Introduction

Suicide is a significant social problem. In the United States, for example, it is the 10th leading cause of premature death, accounting for around 41,149 deaths per year (Center for Disease Control and Prevention (CDC), 2013). Suicide is also a significant concern for police organizations. Police officers are considered to be at particular high risk of suicide, and police officer suicides take a heavy toll both in terms of the traumatic impact upon staff and damage to morale leading to increasing stress and strain within workgroups (Violanti, 2007). It is perhaps timely then to consider the present state of knowledge about suicide in policing. This chapter will explore the extent to which police officers are at increased risk of suicide compared with other groups, the factors associated with suicidal ideation and suicide among police officers, and how this knowledge can be applied in the development of evidence-based suicide prevention strategies for police.

Are police at heightened risk of suicide? Epidemiological research

Policing is regarded as a highly stressful occupation (Coman & Evans, 1991). While around half of American adults will experience a traumatic event at some point during their lives (Hartley, Violanti, Sarkisian, Andrew, & Burchfiel, 2013; Sledjeski, Speisman, & Dierker, 2008), this is considerably higher for police officers (Kaufmann, Rutkow, Spira, & Mojtabia, 2013) with some reports suggesting that police officers experience an average of three traumatic events for every 6 months of their police service (Patterson, 2001). Indeed, compared with members of the general population, police are at significantly greater risk of experiencing traumatic events such as violent confrontations, threats, attending violent deaths, reporting deaths to next of kin, handling dead bodies, making instantaneous life and death decisions, and dealing with abused children (Korre Korre, Farioli, Varvarigou, Sato & Kales,2014). In addition, police officers have the significant social responsibility

Police Psychology, Edited by Marques and Paulino. https://doi.org/10.1016/B978-0-12-816544-7.00006-1

of upholding the law and keeping the peace in a manner that is seen to be fair and reasonable (Violanti et al., 2017). Given the stressful nature of policing and heightened risk of experiencing trauma, it has often been suggested that police officers are at an increased risk of suicide, especially when compared with members of the general population (Violanti, 2007).

In order to test the police at high-risk hypothesis, there have been a number of epidemiological studies that have attempted to identify the rate of suicide among police officers compared with the general population. This research has been characterized by a wide variation in findings. Estimates of the rates of suicide within policing have varied, ranging from 5.8 suicides per 100,000 (Heiman, 1975) to over 200 per 100,000 (Nelson & Smith, 1970). Similarly, work comparing rates of police suicide to those of the general population have also yielded varying results. A number of early studies found that the rate of suicide among police officers was between 1.8 and three times greater than that of the general population (Guralnick, 1963; Mohandie & Hatcher, 1999; Slovenko, 1999). However, later research has found lower rates of suicide among police as compared with the general population (Marzuk, Nock, Leon, Portera, & Tardiff, 2002; Tiesman, Hendricks, Bell, & Amandus, 2010). For example, in a study of New York City police officers, the suicide rate for police was 14.9 per 100,000 as compared with a rate of 18.3 per 100,000 for the general population (Marzuk et al., 2002). It is not therefore clear whether police are at greater risk of suicide than the general population.

It is important to consider what may account for this variation in findings. Hem, Berg, and Ekeberg (2001) noted that this may be a product of a number of methodological limitations within the various studies. Some police suicide rates have been calculated from inadequate sample sizes, some studies estimating rates from sample sizes of 10 or fewer suicides. Calculated rates from small sample sizes are likely to be unreliable estimates since small sample sizes are subject to significant chance fluctuations. The aforementioned study estimating a police suicide rate of 200 per 100,000 (Nelson & Smith, 1970) is an example of such a study.

Another methodological limitation in the literature has been variation in the time periods considered. Some studies have explored data in a single calendar year, others over broader time periods such as a decade and in some cases many decades. Relatedly some studies have examined data drawn from the recent past while others have examined data going back to before the 1940s. Given changes in population demographics both within policing and the general population, studies examining old datasets are perhaps of historical interest and useful for examining broad trends but perhaps say little about contemporary policing or society.

Policing involves a wide range of different work. Some officers are regularly exposed to the sorts of trauma described above, while others are rarely exposed to such situations. The majority of studies of police suicide rates do not distinguish between roles and regard the police as a single homogenous group. If suicide risk in policing relates to the levels of exposure to trauma, failing to account for the heterogeneity of police samples in terms of risk of exposure to trauma may underlie the observed variation in suicide rates across studies.

Finally, a major difficulty in previous research has been a failure to utilize appropriate comparison groups. It is perhaps too simplistic to compare police with the general population given the heterogeneity of both groups. As mentioned, police vary in job roles; however, the general population is likely to be significantly more heterogenous. The general population is likely to contain both employed and unemployed individuals, police cohorts are by definition all in employment. The general population also consists of a much wider age range as compared with policing including older and retired individual. Police cohorts generally consist of individuals (around 80%) aged between 20 and 40 years. One particularly important way in which police differ from the general population is in what is known as the healthy worker effect (Demers, Heyer, & Rosenstock, 1992). This refers to the lower relative mortality that is observed in occupational cohorts because one generally has to be in good health in order to secure and maintain employment. Indeed, police officers are often selected using relatively strict criteria related to their physical and mental health. As such one might expect that, a priori, police officer cohorts should be healthier than the general population. The effect of all of this is that comparing police suicide rates to the general population may well be highly misleading (Violanti, Vena, Marshall, & Petralia, 1996).

Some researchers have argued that comparing police suicide rates to the general population is so misleading as to be rather meaningless. Instead they argue, better designed studies are needed that identify appropriate control groups. Such studies include controlling for age, gender, and occupational differences between policing and other cohorts (Aamodt & Stalnaker, 2001). Interestingly, in studies where adequate controls have been made for differences in the demographics between police and the general population observed suicide rates have been similar leading many to suggest that police are at no greater risk of suicide compared with the general population (Aamodt & Stalnaker, 2001).

Other research has compared suicide rates between police and those in occupational groups that have similar socioeconomic status, health benefits, entry requirements, and similar risk of exposure to trauma such as firefighters (Demers, Heyer, & Rosen- Stock, 1992; Roberts, 2018). These studies have shown that other occupations such as the military or firefighting have similar if not greater risks of suicide than police (Johnson et al., 2005).

A reasonable conclusion from the more empirically sound suicide rate research would seem to be therefore that police as a group are at no greater risk of suicide than the general population. However, this ignores the heterogeneity of police and police roles. Recent research has begun to explore differences in suicide rates among police cohorts based on demographic characteristics.

Demographics of police suicide
Gender

Policing is a male-dominated occupation with the ratio of men to women in most Western police agencies being around 4:1 (Brown, 2017). Without controlling for this ratio, most research on police suicide suggests a greater number of suicides are men and there has been an associated focus upon male suicide in much of the police suicide research (Violanti, Owens, McCanlies, Fekedulegn, & Andrews, 2018). However, where consideration has been made of the relative risk of suicide between men and women results have tended to suggest that women police officers are at greater risk (Roberts, 2018; Violanti, Mnatsakanova, & Andrew, 2013; Violanti, Robinson, & Shen, 2013). It has been suggested that this may be explained by a higher risk of depression—a known correlate of suicide—among women in general (Pratt & Brody, 2014) and women police officers in particular (Steyn, 2012; Violanti et al., 2008). This of course begs the question as to what may be contributing to elevated depression levels among women police officers. It has been argued that this might reflect the extent to which the particular needs of women officers are being met (or not) within policing. Some evidence has suggested that women police officers may be particularly sensitive to the social stressors of shift work, and social isolation as well as how their work interacts with childcare and other family obligations, while this does not appear to be the case for male officers (Dormann & Zapf, 2002). There is also evidence that the concerns of women police officers can be further compounded by working in a white male—dominated culture that stresses masculinity, ideals of strength and toughness, and devalues women (Brown, 2017; Faircloth & Clark, 2016). This creates negative consequences for women including exclusion and a lack of appropriate support (Faircloth & Clark, 2016). Interestingly a recent report on an Australian policing agency identified precisely such a context for women, and this was associated with poor mental and physical health outcomes including suicide (Victorian Human Rights Commission, 2016). We will return to the role of police culture in suicide later in this chapter.

Minority police officers

There have been few studies that have explored suicide among minorities within policing. Certainly, this ought to be of interest because, as the experience of women officers shows, being a minority may well confer additional and different risks to well-being that are not shared by the majority. Of course, minority status varies across different policing cohorts worldwide and on a rage of different criteria such as sexuality. In many Western jurisdictions such as the United States, United Kingdom, Germany, and Nordic countries, minority status refers to primarily to black and other ethnic minority groups (Burke & Mikkelsen, 2007), although LBGTIQ (Lesbian, Bisexual, Gay, Transgender, Intersex, and Queer) groups also form significant minorities in policing.

In the West, there has been some research looking at suicide rates among racial minority groups in policing. African American women in US police agencies have been found to have higher suicide rates than the general population (Violanti, 2010). Hispanic police officers also had a higher suicide rate than the male Hispanic population in the United States (Violanti, 2010). However, due to the relatively small numbers of minority officers in these studies, it is hard to make strong conclusions about the role of ethnicity and suicide in policing. There is a dearth of research exploring suicide among LBGTIQ police cohorts despite high rates of depression being found among police officers in these groups (Pratt & Brody, 2014). Certainly, more research is needed to explore the experience of minorities within policing and associations minority status may have with suicide.

Age and career stage

Limited research has explicitly examined the associations between age and career stage for police suicide. It appears that suicides cluster within the 40–44 years age groups with individuals having between 15 and 19 years' service (O'Hara, Violanti, Levenson, & Clark, 2013). This suggests that early-middle aged individuals in the middle of their career are at particular risk. These findings appear to be consistent with research showing greatest levels of job dissatisfaction among mid-career workers in a range of different industries (Schaible, 2018) and within policing in particular (Schaible, 2018). Although job dissatisfaction alone may not be sufficient to account for suicide, there may be characteristics of policing that make such dissatisfaction particularly acute and intolerable for officers. Certainly, the factors that might give rise to greater mid-career dissatisfaction are worthy of further study.

Epidemiological research: summary

Taking the results of the various epidemiological studies of police suicide together, how might it be summarized? First, the results of these studies over time have been inconsistent due to a number of methodological issues. Future research should take account of police demographics and variations in job roles and use adequate comparison groups.

When adequate comparison groups have been used the findings seem to show that police are at no greater risk of suicide than the general population. This finding is interesting and perhaps appears to fly in the face of the aforementioned healthy worker effect. The healthy worker effect is likely to be particularly strong within policing. Police agencies go to considerable lengths to identify individuals who are the most psychologically resilient, mentally well, and physically fit. Indeed, pre-existing positive health status appears to reduce the risk of experiencing psychological distress when faced with traumatic events, in addition, psychological distress is also reduced if one expects to experience traumatic events in one's work (not an unreasonable expectation for police officers; Kessler et al., 2005).

If police officers are, a priori, more able to deal with the effects of trauma, it might therefore be expected the suicide rate should be lower than that for the general population, at least to the extent that suicide among police is related to traumatic experiences. That it is not begs the question why not. A number of explanations can be offered. It could be that police may experience so much more trauma than the general population that eventually individual coping ability is overwhelmed and persistent experiences of trauma and stress lead to suicide. Certainly, there is some evidence that some police officers experience very high levels of trauma in their careers that eventually take their toll leading to various psychological problems including suicidal ideation and suicide attempts (Burke & Mikkelsen, 2007). Another, explanation might be that suicide is not just associated with traumatic experiences, but other factors may be involved that serve to increase suicide risk. Indeed, demographic research is perhaps supportive of this view to the extent that different genders, ethnicities, age groups, and career stages differ in risk of suicide. It is to a consideration of these factors that we now turn.

Factors associated with police suicide

Research on the factors associated with police officer suicide has taken two distinct paths. One path has been studies of completed suicides and factors that were associated with these. Another path has considered suicidal ideation (thoughts about suicide and making plans for suicide). The advantage of research on suicidal ideation is that individuals reporting this can give a richer description of the context and background to the thoughts than can be obtained when studying completed suicides. However, it is important to note that experiencing suicidal ideation does not guarantee that an individual will ever attempt suicide (CDC, 2013), care must therefore be used in interpreting these findings with reference to suicide. That said research on suicidal ideation and completed suicides in policing have produced rather similar findings. In the discussion below, we will draw on both bodies of literature. Factors related to the risk of police suicidal ideation and suicide can be grouped into work- and nonwork-related factors.

Work-related factors

These are factors associated with suicide and suicidal ideation that are associated with experiences at work. These include the management styles of police leaders, work patterns experienced by police officers including shift work- and other work-related structures, experience of operational stresses related to day-to-day police work such as traumatic experiences, and the culture of policing as it relates to police officer mental health.

Management styles

Police organizations are frequently hierarchical where authority is vested firmly in an individual's rank (Violanti, 2007). Rules, regulations, excessive formality, and routine procedures are a core of everyday activity. A significant body of research has identified the style of management experienced by police officers as being strongly related to their mental health status. Mental health problems are more likely where police officers regularly experience poor management practices such as unfair decision-making by managers, enactment of seemingly arbitrary rules, poor consultation with staff by managers, constantly shifting priorities, and administrative inefficiency. For example, Gershon, Barocas, Canton, Li, and Vlahov (2009) found that symptoms of clinical depression among officers were best predicted by poor management practices rather than experience of critical incidents. Amaranto, Steinberg, Castellano, and Mitchell (2003) also found that officers cited stressors such as low morale, lack of acknowledgment for achievements, and barriers to advancement and promotion as major sources of stress rather than experiences of violent or traumatic events.

Relatedly, much research has found that police organizations are unresponsive to the psychological needs of their staff, especially when staff are experiencing psychological difficulties (Violanti & Aron, 1994). Studies have found that it is how police managers respond to experiences of trauma rather than the trauma itself that predicts symptoms of mental health problems. For example, Carlier, Lamberts, and Gersons (1997) interviewed police officers who developed clinical depression, PTSD, and suicidal ideation as a result of a critical incident. They found that most officers did not attribute their symptoms to the incident per se, but to the complete absence of support from their police department. Carlier et al. (1997) concluded that manager's responses are critical, and where individuals are left to feel isolated, unsupported, and disempowered by a lack of response this increased the risk of trauma and suicidal ideation. Violanti et al. (2017) also found that lack of support from managers and poor administrative systems were associated with hopelessness in a cohort of police officers. Where individuals had symptoms of PTSD, these were exacerbated, and helplessness was significantly increased where individuals experienced limited support and even criticism from managers. It therefore seems that authoritarian, insensitive management practices where little support is offered to those experiencing distress compounds mental health problems can increase the risk of suicidal ideation and suicide among police officers.

Work patterns

Policing can involve working long and sometimes erratic hours, shift work, long periods of repetitive work, and carrying out roles for which an individual has no or minimal training (Violanti et al., 2008). All of these aspects of police work have been shown to lead to stress among police officers. Shift work in particular has been explored by a number of researchers, and findings indicate that it may lead to sleep deprivation and an increased risk of suicidal ideation (Violanti et al., 2008). To date, no studies have explored links between shift work, repetitive work, and conducting tasks for which one is inadequately trained and suicide; however, the broader associations between these factors, stress, and suicidal ideation means that research on this is needed.

Experiences of operational stressors

This refers to the stressors police officers experience as a result of day-to-day policing. As stated, police officers are at greater risk of experiencing traumatic events than most members of the general population. It is, however, noteworthy that a large amount of police work can be routine, repetitive, and without exposure to trauma. When traumatic events happen, for most police officers these are sudden breaks from everyday routine. Negotiating the transitions from routine to traumatic events is likely to substantially elevate stress levels, and some work suggests that those officers who must do so regularly are at elevated risk of long-term negative psychological and physiological consequences (Burke & Mikkelsen, 2007). Relatedly, exposure to critical events raises the risk of substance abuse, PTSD, aggressive behavior, and suicidal ideation (Violanti, Castellano, O'Rourke, & Paton, 2006).

Research has also demonstrated a link between symptoms of PTSD characterized by flashbacks, intrusive thoughts about an event, emotional numbing and increased anxiety, and suicidal ideation among police officers (Violanti, Castellano, O'rourke, & Paton, 2006). That said, although most police officers will experience a traumatic event during their career, by no means do all police officers show symptoms of PTSD. Estimates of PTSD in policing suggest between 7 and 19% of officers, show symptoms that satisfying the DSM IV (Diagnostic and Statistical Manual of Mental Disorders, version 4) criteria for PTSD (Violanti et al., 2006). Similarly, not all officers with PTSD experience suicidal ideation nor do all individuals with PTSD attempt suicide. It does seem that where individuals experience PTSD symptoms and use alcohol as a means of coping with symptoms, there is an increased risk of suicidal ideation. Individuals with PTSD symptoms were four times more likely to experience suicidal ideation where they used than others who did not use alcohol (Violanti, 2004).

The culture of policing

Police officers are trained to be strong and resilient and to run toward danger rather than avoid it. As such the job is replete with messages that have been described as toxic masculinity stressing strength and competence and avoiding showing signs of weakness (Faircloth & Clark, 2016). As a result, there is a culture within policing that implicitly and even explicitly discourages help seeking behavior and even making admissions of distress (Hackett & Violanti, 2003). There are several reasons why police officers avoid contacting mental health professionals. There is a mistrust of mental health professionals with many police officers questioning their competence to understand the specific pressures of law enforcement. In addition, trusting others is seen as a sign of weakness, where psychological symptoms are ignored as they damage self-perceptions of strength. Officers also fear losing their job, being overlooked for promotion or of being transferred out of operational roles. This environment is deeply problematic for officers with any form of psychological distress, and it is one that can serve to exacerbate symptoms (Waters & Ussery, 2007). This situation may be even worse for those who may be considered as "nontraditional" police officers. This includes members of minorities and women officers who, within a culture of toxic masculinity, are likely to be exposed to negative and derogatory comments and actions and are likely to be expected to fail due to their "difference" (Brown, 2017; Faircloth & Clark, 2016). For these individuals, any sign of weakness is likely to be severely damaging to them and reporting of distress is even less likely than for other officers (Faircloth & Clark, 2016). This may account for the higher risk of suicide among these groups.

Nonwork-related factor

This includes factors associated with suicide and suicidal ideation that result from experiences outside of police work. Included here are family stresses related to close familial relationships and alcohol use by police officers as a stress coping strategy.

Family problems

The interaction between police officers and their families can compound stressful effects of police work. It is not unusual for police officers to "take out" work stresses upon close relatives and partners. For example, Arias and Pape (2001) found relationship problems were common among police officers with 60% of partners in the sample reporting experiencing emotional and physical abuse. Similarly, Berg, Hem, Lau, Loeb, and Ekeberg (2003) noted that many police officers in their sample repressed their anger and frustration at work and redirected it toward family members. However, those officers who were involved in healthy relationships were resistant to workplace stressors and were unlikely to bring work problems home. This suggests that healthy relationships outside of the workplace can have an inculcating effect against workplace stresses. Berg et al. (2003) also found that suicidal ideation was most common among separated or divorced individuals who were experiencing a range of emotional problems associated with work such as anger, depression, and anxiety. Janik and Kravitz (1994) found police officers who had a history of suicide attempts were much more likely to have a history of marital discord than others. Thus it seems that where police officers are involved in poor personal relationships outside of the police, these can act as additional sources of stress to further compound work-related stress. Where they are involved in warm loving relationships these can have an inoculating effect against work stresses.

Alcohol use

Alcohol use has been part of policing culture for many years and is often regarded as a coping strategy (Lindsay & Shelley, 2009), although it does appear to be associated with an increased risk of suicide. For example, excessive consumption of alcohol has been associated with an increased risk of suicidal ideation among those who use alcohol to cope with symptoms of traumatic stress (Violanti, 2004). Cantor, Tyman, and Slater (1995) found that 50% of police officers in their sample who died by suicide were reported to have alcohol problems.

Reducing the risk of police suicide

Taking these strands of research together it seems that while police officers are more likely than the average person to be exposed to traumatic events, these events produce symptoms of traumatic stress in only a minority of officers. Police officer suicide is therefore not simply a product of traumatic stress experiences. Instead suicidal ideation is exacerbated, and suicide risk increased as a result of a complex interaction between an interrelated collection of personal vulnerabilities, work and family problems, and the culture of policing. Personal variables include individual vulnerabilities such as the presence of mental health problems such as anxiety, depression and traumatic stress, and/or abuse of alcohol as a coping mechanism. Job-related variables include occupational stressors such as authoritarian and unsympathetic management practices. Family problems include issues such as abusive personal relationships exacerbated by an individual's personal distress. Police culture includes a broad insensitivity to distress and reluctance among officers to seek help. How then can the risk of suicide among police be reduced, what preventative strategies might prove fruitful?

Given the multidimensional complexity of the factors associated with police suicide, any preventative interventions must of necessity be multidimensional in approach. Approaches that address just one or two factors are unlikely to succeed. Preventative efforts must also be aimed at both individual and organizational levels.

Given the significance of workplace culture, approaches that aim to reduce the stigma of mental health problems are likely to be useful in challenging negative attitudes toward mental health problems. Approaches that seek to normalize mental health problems as simply forms of illness that are experienced in some form by most people may prove useful to challenge stigma. Use of high-profile individuals from within and outside policing, who have experienced mental health problems can be a useful strategy, and this has been used by a number of police forces (and mental health charities) worldwide. Many police officers report that insensitivity to their experiences of trauma by managers and colleagues exacerbated their suffering. Again, this would appear to be a situation where education of managers is needed so that they understand the importance of offering support to colleagues and of taking traumatic experiences seriously.

Educating staff to recognize signs of distress and mental illness as well as effective coping strategies are likely to be valuable (Violanti, Owens, McCanlies, Fekedulegn, & Andrew, 2018). In addition to this, where officers may be distrustful of mental health practitioners, peer support programs may prove valuable (Davidson et al., 1999). This can be as simple as encouraging colleagues to check up on each other through to more formal strategies of mentorship. Beyond this, an openness from police organizations is needed that allows for regular interaction with mental health practitioners so that their approaches may be demystified, and officers become comfortable with them. Similarly, a willingness from police organizations to work with mental health charities, police unions and other external agencies would be helpful in removing stigma.

To the extent that poor management and leadership practices are considered to be stressful for police officers, suicide prevention might be enhanced by examining leadership and management practices and police culture. Within the occupational sciences, so-called organizationally just workplaces provide environments where workplace stress is reduced, cooperation is enhanced, and trust in managers is high (Colquitt et al., 2013; Roberts & Herrington, 2013). Such workplaces feature clearly articulated processes and procedures, that are fairly applied, rewards are fairly distributed, staff are given adequate information to make decisions, and staff are given a voice in interactions with superiors that is listened and responded to (Colquitt et al., 2013). Developing such management practices does fly in the face of the police culture that favors rank-based hierarchies and authority based upon rank, but given the trauma to officers, damage to morale and operational efficiency that suicides entail, it is perhaps worth a try.

Given that women officers appear to be at heightened risk of suicide there would seem to be a need to review how police culture is implicated in this and to challenge and change practices and procedures that are disadvantageous to women. It is certainly possible that women and other minorities are particularly reluctant to signal personal distress in this culture and so "suffer in silence" until it is too late. Existing suicide prevention approaches may not be relevant or sensitive to the needs of women and may require revision.

The association between intimate partner problems and suicide needs consideration by police agencies. Certainly, prevention approaches that are limited to the workplace may be too limited. If organizations are able to offer support and interventions that can help prevent or manage intimate partner problems, helping maintain strong relationships, this is known to mitigate against the worst excesses of police officer stress and may be valuable in preventing suicide. It may be that police officer training could include an element of training on how to develop and maintain healthy personal and intimate relationships, especially when faced with stressful events. Although not core police business, this could have significant effects downstream.

Alcohol has traditionally been used by police officers as a coping strategy. Again, there is a role for education of officers to allow them to understand how they are using alcohol and when that use is becoming dangerous. Certainly, using alcohol to disguise or hide symptoms of suffering is a danger sign and officers should be made aware of this.

Officers at midstages of their careers appear to be particularly at risk of suicide. This suggests a need for intervention strategies that are targeted at mid-career officers. In many jurisdictions, officers are given stress management training, but this may be a one-size-fits-all approach that is not targeted toward those who may be most vulnerable. There are likely to be particular issues that are relevant to mid-career officers, it is known that job dissatisfaction, burnout, and cynicism reach their highest levels at mid-career and identifying strategies to help officers to cope with these stresses would seems to be valuable. It may be that organizations need to examine their progression and career development programs and procedures and consider ways of enhancing the experience of those in mid-career who feel that their careers have stalled. Opportunities for secondment, developing new skills, and adult education programs may be helpful here.

In many jurisdictions, police officers have access to lethal means such as guns. An important aspect of suicide prevention may be to manage access to weapons, at least in the workplace. This has often been done by restricting access to weapons for those considered most at risk of suicide (Miller & Hemenway, 2008). While this approach has been used successfully in a number of instances (Daigle, 2005), in the case of police there are many potential challenges. Restricting firearm access at work may be possible but may be more challenging given the high levels of private gun ownership among police officers in some jurisdictions. This is where interaction with and education of other family members regarding an individual's vulnerability and the need to restrict their access to lethal suicidal means at home may therefore be a useful strategy. Means restriction strategies can be simple such as ensuring that unloaded firearms are locked in a secure cabinet and ammunition is kept separately. In this case, should an individual enter a suicidal crisis, if a loaded firearm is not immediately accessible this may allow an opportunity for intervention (Hawton, 2007). This is especially compelling given that often suicidal crises are very short lived, with around 48% of suicide attempt survivors reporting that their crisis lasted less than 10 minutes between deciding to attempt suicide and the actual attempt (Deisenhammer et al., 2009).

Finally, police organizations should invest in postvention strategies. These are strategies designed to help individuals and the organization to cope in the aftermath of a suicide. This is an important part of suicide prevention (Violanti et al., 2018) as following a suicide of a colleague, the entire agency is likely to be highly emotionally charged, with many traumatized by the events. Postvention includes debriefings, sharing of information by managers and mental health professionals, and publication of methods for preventing future suicides (Loo, 2001). All too frequently agencies are silent, seemingly determined to hide or forget about a suicide as it "reflects badly" upon them. Postvention is known to help colleagues, friends, and family deal with the aftermath of a suicide and allows organizations to begin to adjust to the loss and to grieve (Loo, 2001).

Conclusions

This chapter has considered much of what is known about police suicide and some of the methods that may be used to prevent suicide and manage their effects upon police officers and their organizations. It seems that police officers are at no greater risk of suicide than properly matched controls, although given the healthy worker effect relevant to police officers, police might be expected to have lower suicide rates than observed. It does not appear that police officer suicide is just related to their greater likelihood of experiencing traumatic events but is related to a complex interaction between a number of factors related to individual experiences of stress and trauma, police leadership and management strategies, the quality of social relationships among police officers and their intimates, police officer use of aberrant coping strategies, and police culture. Women, minorities, and mid-career officers appear most at risk.

There is, however, much research still to do. There is a need for better controlled studies into the epidemiology of police suicide. Explorations of the rates of suicide among minorities within policing and the impact of police culture upon such individuals are important and are lacking. More research is needed into the factors associated with police officer suicide such as the impact of shift work on suicide and why it is that mid-career individuals appear at heightened risk. The association between police culture and suicide needs more detailed exploration, particularly the processes through which the culture is maintained and serves to limit disclosure of distress, and studies are needed into effective approaches to undermining negative cultural messages about distress within policing. The high relative risk of suicide among police women is a significant concern, and research needs to explore this more fully and to design prevention strategies that are applicable to women officers. The design and proper evaluation of evidence-based suicide prevention strategies for policing in general is also important.

Police officer suicide is a highly traumatic and politically charged event. Organizations naturally struggle to deal with the aftermath and are often under pressure to "do something." This at times can lead to rapidly conceived, nonevidence-based interventions that can do little to prevent suicide. This is because, as illustrated here, the factors implicated in police suicide risk interact in complex ways. As such any interventions or prevention strategies needs to be broad-based and focus upon organizational, cultural, group, and individual factors rather than being attempts to respond to one or two factors perceived to be important. Only then will organizations have any chance of reducing the toll that police officer suicide exerts upon them and their officers.

References

Aamodt, M. G., & Stalnaker, N. A. (2001). Police officer suicide: Frequency and officer profiles. In D. C. Shehan, & J. I. Warren (Eds.), *Suicide and law enforcement* (pp. 383–398). Washington, D.C.: Federal Bureau of Investigation.

Amaranto, E., Steinberg, J., Castellano, C., & Mitchell, R. (2003). Police stress interventions. *Brief Treatment and Crisis Intervention, 3*(1), 47–53.

Arias, I., & Pape, K. T. (2001). Psychological abuse: Implications for adjustment and commitment to leave violent partners. In K. D. O'Leary, & R. D. Maiuro (Eds.), *Psychological abuse in violent domestic relations* (pp. 137–152). New York: Springer.

Berg, A. M., Hem, E., Lau, B., Loeb, M., & Ekeberg, J. (2003). Suicidal ideation and attempts in Norwegian police. *Suicide Life and Life Threatening Behavior, 33*(3), 302–312.

Brown, J. (2017). Discriminatory experiences of women police. A comparison of officers serving in England and Wales, Scotland, Northern Ireland and the Republic of Ireland. In women police. In M. Natarajan (Ed.), *Women police*. New York: Routledge.

Burke, R. J., & Mikkelsen, A. (2007). Suicidal ideation among police officers in Norway. *An International Journal of Police Strategies & Management, 30*, 228–236.

Cantor, C. H., Tyman, R., & Slater, P. J. (1995). A historical survey of police suicide in Queensland, Australia, 1843–1992. *Suicide and Life-Threatening Behavior, 25*(4), 499–507.

Carlier, I. V., Lamberts, R. D., & Gersons, B. P. (1997). Risk factors for posttraumatic stress symptomatology in police officers: A prospective analysis. *The Journal of Nervous and Mental Disease, 185*(8), 498–506.

Centers for Disease Control and Prevention (CDC). (2013). *Web-based injury statistics query and reporting system (WISQARS)* [Online]. National Center for Injury Prevention and Control. CDC (producer) http://www.cdc.gov/injury/wisqars/index.html.

Colquitt, J. A., Scott, B. A., Rodell, J. B., Long, D. M., Zapata, C. P., Conlon, D. E., et al. (2013). Justice at the millennium, a decade later: A meta-analytic test of social exchange and affect-based perspectives. *Journal of Applied Psychology, 98*(2), 199–236.

Coman, G., & Evans, B. (1991). Stressors facing Australian police in the 1990s. *Police Studies: International Review of Police Development, 14,* 153–165.

Daigle, M. S. (2005). Suicide prevention through means restriction: Assessing the risk of substitution: A critical review and synthesis. *Accident Analysis & Prevention, 37*(4), 625–632.

Davidson, L., Chinman, M., Kloos, B., Weingarten, R., Stayner, D., & Tebes, J. K. (1999). Peer support among individuals with severe mental illness: A review of the evidence. *Clinical Psychology: Science and Practice, 6*(2), 165–187.

Deisenhammer, E. A., Ing, C. M., Strauss, R., Kemmler, G., Hinterhuber, H., & Weiss, E. (2009). The duration of the suicidal process: How much time is left for intervention between consideration and accomplishment of a suicide attempt? *Journal of Clinical Psychiatry, 70*(1), 19–24.

Demers, P. A., Heyer, N. J., & Rosen- Stock, L. (1992). Mortality among firefighters from three northwestern United States cities. *British Journal of Industrial Medicine, 49,* 664–670.

Dormann, C., & Zapf, D. (2002). Social stressors at work, irritation, and depressive symptoms: Accounting for unmeasured third variables in a multi-wave study. *International Social Science Journal, 75*(1), 33–55.

Faircloth, P. K., & Clark, E. (2016). Gender role conflict and job satisfaction among police officers: Research and clinical implications for counselors and other mental health practitioners. *Alabama Counseling Association Journal, 30*(3), 4–21.

Gershon, R. R., Barocas, B., Canton, A. N., Li, X., & Vlahov, D. (2009). Mental, physical, and behavioral outcomes associated with perceived work stress in police officers. *Criminal Justice and Behaviour, 36*(3), 275–289.

Guralnik, L. (1963). *Mortality by occupation and cause of death among men 20 to 64 years of age. United States Vital Statistics Special Reports* (Vol. 53 (5)). Washington, DC: U.S. Public Health Service, National Vital Statistics Division.

Hackett, D. P., & Violanti, J. M. (Eds.). (2003). *Police suicide: Tactics for prevention.* New York: Charles C Thomas Publisher.

Hawton, K. (2007). Restricting access to methods of suicide: Rationale and evaluation of this approach to suicide prevention. *Crisis, 28*(S1), 4–9.

Hartley, T. A., Violanti, J. M., Sarkisian, K., Andrew, M. E., & Burchfiel, C. M. (2013). PTSD symptoms among police officers: associations with frequency, recency, and types of traumatic events. *International journal of emergency mental health, 15*(4), 241–253.

Heiman, M. F. (1975). The police suicide. *Journal of Police Science and Administration, 3,* 267–273.

Hem, E., Berg, A. M., & Ekeberg, Ø. (2001). Suicide in police — a critical review. *Suicide and Life Threatening Behaviour, 31*(2), 224–233.

Janik, J., & Kravitz, H. M. (1994). Linking work and domestic problems with police suicide. *Suicide and Life-Threatening Behavior, 24,* 267–274. https://doi.org/10.1111/j.1943-278X.1994.tb00751.x.

Johnson, S., Cooper, C., Cartwright, S., Donald, I., Taylor, P., & Millet, C. (2005). The experience of work-related stress across occupations. *Journal of Managerial Psychology, 20*(2), 178–187.

Kaufmann, C. N., Rutkow, L., Spira, A. P., & Mojtabai, R. (2013). Mental health of protective services workers: Results from the national epidemiologic survey on alcohol and related conditions. *Disaster Medicine and Public Health Preparedness, 7*(1), 36–45.

Kessler, R. C., Berglund, P., Delmer, O., Jin, R., Merikangas, K. R., & Walters, E. E. (2005). Lifetime prevalence and age of onset distributions of DSM-IV disorders in the National Comorbidity Survey Replication. *Achieves of General Psychiatry, 62*(6), 593–602.

Korre, M., Farioli, A., Varvarigou, V., Sato, S., & Kales, S. N. (2014). A survey of stress levels and time spent across law enforcement duties: Police chief and officer agreement. *Policing: Journal of Policy Practice, 8*(2), 109–122.

Lindsay, V., & Shelley, K. (2009). Social and stress-related influences of police officers' alcohol consumption. *Journal of Police and Criminal Psychology, 24*, 87–92.

Loo, R. (2001). A meta-analysis of police suicide rates: Findings and issues. *Suicide and Life-Threatening Behaviour, 33*(3), 313–325.

Marzuk, P. M., Nock, M. K., Leon, A. C., Portera, L., & Tardiff, K. (2002). Suicide among New York City police officers, 1977–1996. *American Journal of Psychiatry, 159*(12), 2069–2071.

Miller, M., & Hemenway, D. (2008). Guns and suicide in the United States. *New England Journal of Medicine, 359*(10), 989–991.

Mohandie, K., & Hatcher, C. (1999). Suicide and violence risk in law enforcement: Practical guidelines for risk assessment, prevention and intervention. *Behavioral Sciences & the Law, 17*(3), 357–376.

Nelson, P., & Smith, W. E. (1970). The law enforcement profession: An incident of high suicide. *Omega, 1*, 293–299.

O'Hara, A. F., Violanti, J. M., Levenson, R. L., Jr., & Clark, R. G. S. (2013). National police suicide estimates: Web surveillance study III. *International Journal of Emergency Mental Health, 15*(1), 31–38.

Patterson, G. T. (2001). The relationship between demographic variables and exposure to traumatic incidents among police officers. *The Australasian Journal of Disaster and Trauma Studies, 2*, 1–9.

Pratt, L., & Brody, D. (2014). *National center for health statistics: Depression in the US household population, 2009–2012. NCHS data brief # 172.* available at: www.cdc.gov/nchs/products/databriefs/db172.htm.

Roberts, K. A. (2018). Correlates of law enforcement suicide in the United States: A comparison with army and firefighter suicides using data from the national violent death reporting system. *Police Practice and Research*, 1–13.

Roberts, K., & Herrington, V. (2013). Organizational and procedural justice: A review of the literature and its implications for policing. *Journal of Policing, Intelligence and Counter Terrorism, 8*(2), 115–130.

Schaible, L. M. (2018). The impact of the police professional identity on burnout. *Policing: An International Journal of Police Strategies & Management, 41*(1), 129–143.

Sledjeski, E. M., Speisman, B., & Dierker, L. C. (2008). Does number of lifetime traumas explain the relationship between PTSD and chronic medical conditions? Answers from the national comorbidity survey-replication (NCS-R). *Journal of Behavioral Medicine, 31*(4), 341–349.

Slovenko, R. (1999). Police suicide. *Medicine & Law, 18*, 149–151.

Steyn, R. (2012). Gender differences in PTSD diagnostic criteria and suicidal ideation in a South African Police Sample. *Journal of Psychology in Africa, 22*(2), 235–238.

Tiesman, H. M., Hendricks, S. A., Bell, J. L., & Amandus, H. A. (2010). Eleven years of occupational mortality in law enforcement: The census of fatal occupational injuries, 1992–2002. *American Journal of Industrial Medicine, 53*(9), 940–949.

Victorian Human Rights Commission. (2016). Independent review into sex discrimination and sexual harassment, including predatory behaviour. In *Victoria police*. Melbourne: VHRC.

Violanti, J. M. (2004). Predictors of police suicide ideation. *Suicide and Life-Threatening Behavior, 34*(3), 277–283.

Violanti, J. M. (2007). *Police suicide: Epidemic in blue* (2nd ed.). Springfield, IL: Charles C. Thomas.

Violanti, J. M. (2010). Police suicide: A national comparison with fire-fighter and military personnel. *Policing: An International Journal of Police Strategies & Management, 33*(2), 270–286.

Violanti, J. M., & Aron, F. (1994). Ranking police stressors. *Psychological Reports, 75*(2), 824–826.

Violanti, J. M., Castellano, C., O'rourke, J., & Paton, D. (2006). Proximity to the 9/11 terrorist attack and suicide ideation in police officers. *Traumatology, 12*(3), 248–254.

Violanti, J. M., Charles, L. E., Hartley, T. A., Mnatsakanova, A., Andrew, M. E., Fekedulegn, D., et al. (2008). Shift-work and suicide ideation among police officers. *American Journal of Industrial Medicine, 51*(10), 758–768.

Violanti, J. M., Charles, L. E., McCanlies, E., Hartley, T. A., Baughman, P., Andrew, M. E., et al. (2017). Police stressors and health: A state-of-the-art review. *Policing: An International Journal of Police Strategies & Management, 40*(4), 642–656.

Violanti, J. M., Mnatsakanova, A., & Andrew, M. E. (2013). Suicidal ideation in police officers: Exploring an additional measure. *Suicidology Online, 4*(1), 33–41.

Violanti, J. M., Owens, S. L., McCanlies, E., Fekedulegn, D., & Andrew, M. E. (2018). Law enforcement suicide: A review. *Policing: An International Journal of Police Strategies & Management, 42*(2), 141–164.

Violanti, J. M., Robinson, C. F., & Shen, R. (2013). Law enforcement suicide: A national analysis. *International Journal of Emergency Mental Health, 15*(4), 289–297.

Violanti, J. M., Vena, J. E., Marshall, J. R., & Petralia, S. (1996). A comparative evaluation of police suicide rate validity. *Suicide and Life-Threatening Behavior, 26*, 79–85.

Waters, J. A., & Ussery, W. (2007). Police stress: History, contributing factors, symptoms, and interventions. *Policing: An International Journal of Police Strategies & Management, 30*(2), 169–188.

Psychology applied to policing issues

Psychological jurisprudence and the role of police psychology in community psychology

7

Bruce A. Arrigo and Brian G. Sellers

Introduction

Police psychology is an established field of behavioral science inquiry and clinical forensic practice (Bartol, 1996; Kitaeff, 2011; Mitchell & Dorian, 2016). Interestingly, the field's pivotal role in addressing the critical concerns of community psychology has yet to be probed or problematized. These are the concerns of resiliency, empowerment, and inclusion; civic justice and virtue; public and communal good; reflexivity and praxis (Fryer, Duckett, & Pratt, 2004; Kagan, Burton, Duckett, Lawthom, & Siddiquee, 2011; Prilleltensky & Nelson, 1997). This lack of erudition is surprising, especially since police-citizen encounters represent the intersection of these two divisions of psychology, and these divisions are ripe for much needed theoretical integration and conceptual model making.

In order to preliminarily further these important objectives, the ensuing chapter first reviews the scientific literature on police psychology, and it then examines where and how this literature has advanced or contributed to the imperatives of community psychology. For our purposes, these imperatives are targeted toward the human justice needs and the social welfare requisites of children and adolescents. Next, the chapter describes what psychological jurisprudence (PJ) is by way of its theoretical convictions and methodological commitments, and it explains what the solution-focused actions of PJ are by way of its prescriptions for policy and practice. This chapter concludes by proposing how the explanatory and predictive properties of PJ can bridge the divide between the science of police psychology and the praxis of community psychology. This is the investigative juncture where the mutual, relational, and communal dimensions of *police/suspect-citizen/suspect* interactions are the object of reconsideration and the subject of reconceptualization.

Policing youth: A police psychology review

At the outset, we note that the field of police psychology has thus far produced a limited body of scientific research addressing police-youth interactions. This

Police Psychology, Edited by Marques and Paulino. https://doi.org/10.1016/B978-0-12-816544-7.00007-3

conclusion obtains notwithstanding the fact that these relational encounters are frequent and inevitable. Law enforcement personnel are regularly involved in the everyday lives of children and teens through routine contact with them in their homes, on the streets, in shopping malls, at schools, and even through the monitoring of their activities on social media websites, like Facebook (McKitten & Thurau, 2017; Thurau, 2009). Moreover, aggressive policing strategies used in community interactions—especially including confrontations with youthful residents of low-income, minority neighborhoods—have sparked considerable concern from social and behavioral scientists (Brunson, 2007; Carr, Napolitano, & Keating, 2007; Gau & Brunson, 2010; McKitten & Thurau, 2017; Schuck, 2013). These concerns emphasize the negative influence that such corrosive exchanges engender between community members and police officers, cultivating a destructive and dangerous cycle of police-citizen relations (Brunson, 2007; Carr et al., 2007; Gau & Brunson, 2010; Schuck, 2013).

The above issues lead to important research questions. Perhaps chief among them is how the science of police psychology legitimately and meaningfully responds to the praxis imperatives of community psychology. The ensuing literature review summarily explores this prescient matter, focusing on police-youth interactions. Based on our assessment of the extant literature, police psychology research examining these encounters falls into five principal categories. These categories consist of the following domains of empirical inquiry and analysis: (1) the perceptual cues and interpersonal skills of police officers; (2) the attributions, prejudices, and stereotypes/typing by police officers; (3) the personality of law enforcement personnel; (4) policing, stress management, and exposure to aggression and violence; and (5) the psychology of recruiting, selecting, and training police officers.

The perceptual cues and interpersonal skills of police officers

Although police officers acknowledge that children and adolescents experience or are prone to some developmental anomalies that adversely affect them, officers still generally relate to youths in the same manner that they interact with adults, especially in interrogation contexts (Cleary, 2017; Cleary & Warner, 2016; McKitten & Thurau, 2017; Meyer & Reppucci, 2007; Thurau, 2009). To be clear, however, vulnerable adolescents are developmentally immature and cognitively impaired in numerous ways: (1) more susceptible to peer influence, (2) high reward sensitivity (preference for immediate rewards and gratification), (3) elevated levels of sensation-seeking, (4) lower impulse control or self-regulation, and (5) inhibited future orientation, making more likely immediate short-term thinking and reasoning rather than perceived long-term consequences for decision-making and action-taking (Cleary, 2017; McKitten & Thurau, 2017; Sellers & Arrigo, 2009). As such, youth are highly sensitive to police coercion, possess a diminished understanding of the interrogation process and its significances, are disposed to proffering false confessions, and fail to fully comprehend the police custody encounter (Cleary, 2017).[1] Moreover, when faced with stressful police-citizen interactions, officers can experience selective attention expressed through alterations in visual perception (e.g., tunnel vision) and auditory exclusion (e.g., inattentional deafness) (Kitaeff, 2011; Porter, Brinke, & Gustaw, 2010). These incidents can cause officers to narrowly focus on direct or indirect threat cues and respond with subconscious, intuitive ("gut instinct") choice and action, rather than conscious, rational decision-making that is reflective and logical (Kitaeff, 2011; Porter et al., 2010). Additionally, given such taxing conditions, officers are more prone to critical thinking errors (e.g., oversimplification of the situation, overgeneralization of stereotypes, unwarranted assumptions produced from emotion, and hasty conclusions based on insufficient evidence at hand). These errors can result in enhanced emotional reactions (Kitaeff, 2011; Thurau, 2009), and these reactions can lead to failed police-youth encounters, including questionable, and even deadly, use-of-force occurrences (Fine et al., 2003; Thurau, 2009).

The attributions, prejudices, and stereotypes/typing by police officers

Disproportionate minority contact is a well-documented problem that has been examined within the juvenile justice literature (e.g., McKitten & Thurau, 2017; Thurau, 2009). Consistent with this literature is the police psychology research on attribution, prejudice, and stereotyping. This research indicates that officers unconsciously assign (and perhaps consciously in cases of overt racism) higher levels of intentionality and dispositional character flaws to the actions of minority and impoverished youth than they do to Caucasian and affluent youth, whose equivalent behavior is often attributed to situational factors or overall immaturity (Graham & Lowery, 2004; McKitten & Thurau, 2017; Thurau, 2009). Moreover, police-youth interactions often occur under "legally and causally ambiguous circumstances" (Thurau, 2009, p. 34) where judgments are made hastily with limited information, rendering these judgments susceptible to unconscious stereotyping (Graham & Lowery, 2004). In addition to race, socioeconomic status is considered to be a powerful determinant of

---

[1] Thus, given the scientific evidence, it would be extremely appropriate for law enforcement officers to employ "developmentally appropriate, trauma-informed, and equitable standards" when engaged in police/youth interactions (McKitten & Thurau, 2017, p. 3). Regrettably, this is not the norm in the United States, and only California, Connecticut, New Jersey, Maryland, Virginia, and Florida provide officers with some form of guidance for policies regarding police-youth encounters.

disproportionate rates of indigent youth arrests (Garrett & Short, 1975; Thurau, 2009). Developing relationships with members of stereotyped youth groups is perhaps one of the best ways to challenge unconscious stereotyping, and its deployment is essential to effective community policing and community psychology fieldwork (McKitten & Thurau, 2017; Thurau, 2009).[2]

The personality of law enforcement personnel

The research on police psychology and personality shows that nearly all law enforcement agencies are subjected to rules, regulations, or accreditation standards requiring psychological evaluations of candidates (Bartol & Bartol, 2019). In fact, 38 states mandate psychological evaluations for officers, typically in the form of personality inventories (e.g., the MMPI-2, MMPI-2-RF, or IPI) especially during the preemployment screening process (Arrigo & Claussen, 2003) and in fitness-for-duty determinations (Bartol & Bartol, 2019). One debate within the police psychology literature is whether officer personality is predispositional, shaped by job experiences or a combination of both (e.g., Twersky-Glasner, 2005). Some research indicates that successful police officer applicants possess common personality traits, such as assertiveness (dominance), potential for social mobility (capacity for status), self-confidence (strong social presence), and a sense of self-worth (strong self-acceptance) (Arrigo & Claussen, 2003; Hogan & Kurtines, 1975; Mufson & Mufson, 1988; Twersky-Glasner, 2005). However, research also points out that officers may exhibit a sense of isolation/alienation, masculinity/machismo, authoritarian behavior, suspiciousness, and cynicism/pessimism as a product of worksite culture (Reiner, 2010; Skolnick, 2000). Indeed, officers may rarely feel integrated within the communities they patrol—regardless of their policing efforts—and may instead feel increased alienation and isolation, especially if the public's perception of them is negative (Ankony & Kelley, 1999; Twersky-Glaner, 2005). Perhaps more importantly, police psychology research has yet to acknowledge how the predominant traits associated with officer personality significantly differ from, and even conflict with, the coping behaviors associated with adolescents (Thurau, 2009). These coping behaviors include, among others, impulsivity, shortsightedness, sensation-seeking, egocentricity, fragile self-image, and hypermasculinity (McKitten & Thurau, 2017; Thurau, 2009).[3]

---

[2] Regrettably, however, current reliance on aggressive police tactics in impoverished communities of color continues to create and/or reinforce distrust of officers (e.g., Straub, 2008).

[3] For example, youth transitioning from childhood to adolescence often experience "dips" in personality maturity (Soto & Tackett, 2015, p. 360), whereby their levels of agreeableness, conscientiousness, and openness to experience decline during adolescence while neuroticism (i.e., anxiety) tends to rise, making them more likely to engage in social aggression (Thurau, 2009).

Policing, stress management, and exposure to aggression and violence

The police psychology research investigating stress management and exposure to aggression and violence indicates that expressions of disrespect, hostility, and provocation by youth toward police are a significant element of these interactions (McKitten & Thurau, 2017; Schuck, 2013; Thurau, 2009). For impoverished, urban youth, combativeness with the police is a prevalent feature of their daily activity (McKitten & Thurau, 2017; Thurau, 2009). In far too many instances, officers are perplexed by this hostility and become angry when juveniles characterize them as "bad guys" (Thurau, 2009, p. 37). Police do not necessarily understand that in order to survive their sense of powerlessness, many impoverished minority youth manifest hypermasculine behaviors and façades that enable them to cope with problems of self-image and feelings of despair (Thurau, 2009). Moreover, youths exhibit less cognitive control than their adult counterparts when presented with threatening conditions and negative emotional arousal (Cohen et al., 2016). Regrettably, without this knowledge of adolescent behavior, officers typically respond to displays of hostility and disrespect by choosing to arrest rather than utilize deescalation interventions (Gatti, Tremblay, & Vitaro, 2009). In fact, police are given few tools to employ beyond arrest in interactions with youth (McKitten & Thurau, 2017; Thurau, 2009). In response, some scholars have suggested that officers need to learn how to recognize the fragility of adolescent egos (including their sense of vulnerability) in order to decrease their need to express themselves through hypermasculine demonstrations of dominance and acts of violence (McKitten & Thurau, 2017; Spencer, Fegley, Harpalani, & Seaton, 2004; Thurau, 2009).[4]

The psychology of recruiting, selecting, and training police officers

Police psychology research on recruitment, selection, and training illustrates the fact that law enforcement officers are not given any specific or systemic direction on how to interact with youth, including how to interpret adolescent misbehavior and developmental immaturity (McKitten & Thurau, 2017; Thurau, 2009). Instead, police are taught to treat juveniles the same way they treat adults (Cleary, 2017; Thurau, 2009). Furthermore, although police are trained to be problem solvers, they often employ reactive approaches that are hasty and punitive when confronted with adolescent misconduct or defiance (Thurau, 2009). These questionable resolutions follow even though it is well recognized that children and teens lack the emotional

---

[4] Thus, the bravado of youth should be recognized as a "weapon of the weak" (Thurau, 2009, p. 37) used by kids to overcome feelings of shame in order to strengthen their weakened ego sourced in ontological inferiority (Scott, 1985; Spencer et al., 2004).

competence necessary to address complicated situations, and unsurprisingly, often respond inappropriately to this complexity (Cleary, 2017; Goldstein et al., 2015; Thurau, 2009). Police academies do not specifically address how to anticipate a youth's opposition and resistance to authority; consequently, officers are often ill-prepared for these interactions (McKitten & Thurau, 2017; Thurau, 2009). In addition, although mental illness is the number one youth disability, police personnel are not adequately trained to identify the psychological issues that vulnerable children and troubled teens experience (Kutcher & McDougall, 2009; McKitten & Thurau, 2017).[5]

The five principal categories of police psychology research addressing police-youth interactions are problematic on multiple relational fronts, especially when considering the human justice needs and social welfare requisites of children and teens. For many youth, particularly those of color living in urban areas, patrol officers symbolize the oppressive rules and structural obstacles these children and teens must overcome in order to survive in today's society (McKitten & Thurau, 2017; Schuck, 2013; Thurau, 2009). Not surprisingly, therefore, these youth tend to challenge authority figures they perceive to exacerbate their pervasive sense of helplessness expressed through repeated bouts of anger and hostility (Thurau, 2009). Indeed, recent approaches to policing youth, especially juveniles residing in impoverished African American and Latino communities, are distinguished by enhanced militarism coupled with excessive displays of force and coercion (Kappeler & Kraska, 2015; Kraska, 2007). These police tactics intend to solidify the power of the state while systematizing the prevailing relations of social, racial, and economic exchange (Adelman & Yalda, 2000; Thurau, 2009). In addition, some youth are inclined to perceive confrontations with the police as yet another proclamation of their powerlessness, resulting in exhibitions of pride when arrested in order to save face with peers and to avoid cohort rejection (Schuck, 2013; Thurau, 2009). Officers rarely perceive a youth's disrespectful behavior—which may be unrelated to the officer's own choices and actions—as an indication of the juvenile's need to reaffirm a sense of peer group belonging (Schuck, 2013; Thurau, 2009). Unfortunately, and in far too many instances, police officers depend on threat deescalation tactics to apprehend developmentally immature and cognitively impaired youth rather than utilizing

---

[5] These concerns have lead some investigators to propose that rather than adopting a reactive "command and control" response to youth misbehavior and crime, police need to learn about the potential of "connect and collaborate" approaches to community policing (McKitten & Thurau, 2017; Thurau, 2009, p. 40). The latter approach is more sensitive to adolescent development and psychology, which creates opportunity to reduce the trauma associated with arrest, while increasing the use of community-based alternatives that aim to develop networks of care and trust among law enforcement and the communities they protect and serve (McKitten & Thurau, 2017; Thurau, 2009). Therefore, the current script for law enforcement training needs to change into one that empowers the police with the practice techniques of better "reading" (i.e., faster and more accurately) juvenile situational encounters, mindful of adolescent developmental immaturity (McKitten & Thurau, 2017; Thurau, 2009, p. 42).

alternative problem-solving techniques and/or strategies (McKitten & Thurau, 2017; Thurau, 2009).

Community psychology is predicated on the notion that a person's optimal flourishing is best explained through an appreciation of the social contexts and human settings into which one is placed and out of which one creates shared meaning (Kagan et al., 2011; Orford, 2008). These are contexts and settings in which prospects for understanding, displays of healing, and opportunities for change require a commitment to *situated* manifestations of social justice (Fryer et al., 2004). These manifestations promote personal liberation and mutual well-being (Nelson & Prilleltensky, 2010). They depend on the presence of reflexivity and the work of praxis (Prilleltensky & Fox, 1997). Experiencing these critical possibilities begins with "an approach that tries to understand a [given] social reality through introduction of another, more penetrating frame of reference" (Kagan et al., 2011, p. 12). To date, the empirics of police psychology have overlooked or ignored these essential community psychology insights, rendering police-citizen interactions, especially encounters with youth, the subject of inadequate scientific knowledge production.

Psychological jurisprudence: on theory, method, and practice

PJ offers a radical framework (a critical frame of reference) for mutually, relationally, and communally experiencing social justice in various contexts or settings (Arrigo, 2013, 2015; Arrigo & Sellers, 2018). These contexts are situated in prisons between criminal offender and correctional therapist (Polizzi, Draper, & Andersen, 2014), in treatment facilities between recovering addict and substance abuse counselor (Pycroft, 2010), in state psychiatric hospitals between involuntarily hospitalized patient and mental health staff provider (Arrigo & Davidson, 2017), and even in the social relations or "lifelines" that maintain desistance communities (Weaver & McNeill, 2015, p. 95). These situated contexts hold the potential for generating dynamic and transformative (as opposed to devitalizing and finalizing) forms of human relatedness (Arrigo & Sellers, 2018). PJ's reformist framework includes a set of theoretical convictions (e.g., the society-of-captives thesis), methodological commitments (e.g., the jurisprudence of virtue), and policy prescriptions (e.g., the ethic of citizenship) (Arrigo, Bersot, & Sellers, 2011). In what follows, we briefly outline the core elements of this critical framework.

As theory, PJ both reevaluates and rediagnoses the status of "madness" in society. We all know its definition. Madness is doing the same thing over and over again and expecting a different result. But, what if the condition (i.e., madness) reappeared because of a steadfast and ubiquitous allegiance to a fixed and false belief (a delusion) that a different and better result had been undeniably achieved. In pertinent part, this is the belief that subscribing to a precrime society (McCulloch & Wilson, 2015; Zedner, 2007) will make justice an actuarial inevitability, and that this inevitability will guarantee both personal freedom and public safety (Ashworth & Zedner, 2015). In a precrime society, risk management is based on the predictive analytics and the surveillance technology of the digital sciences. In this informational reality, prevention and precaution are the decisional moorings of a secured (i.e., hyperreal) justice for one and all.[6]

However, according to PJ as theory, a destructive fear is nurtured by maintaining this delusion. This is the fear that socioculturally anchors Simon's (2009) governing-through-crime perspective. When digital forms of discipline and authority are omnipresent by way of justice system informational practices, then would-be offending and would-be offenders are unremittingly suspect. Problematically, this fear normalizes the "creeping criminalization of everyday life" (Presdee, 2001, p. 159) in ways that hold captive (especially ontologically and epistemologically) *the kept* and *their keepers* as well as *the watched and their watchers*. This is the captivity of all human subjectivity reasoned as the object of potential threat or hazard (Beck, 2009; O'Malley, 2010). This risk-averse mentality produces a society of captives that, in the extreme, morphs into the captivity of society (Arrigo & Milovanovic, 2009). Indeed, under conditions of *hypersecuritization*, freedom is an illusion and safety is undone. All that remains are "environments of enclosure" (Deleuze, 1992, p. 3), including cyber mechanisms of bio-digital control.[7]

As method, PJ seeks to clarify captivity's madness and to overcome the delusion that is its tangible support. To empirically realize these objectives, PJ rereads (deconstructs) the texts of hypersecuritization. These texts are case, statutory, and policy constructions of identity-making and rights-claiming, adjudicated as justice-rendering and its proper administration (Arrigo, 2015). However, once these texts are deconstructed by way of underlying judicial temperament, and still further, embedded jurisprudential ethic, "the laws of captivity" (Arrigo & Polizzi, 2018, p. 1) become increasingly evident. These laws specify what the normative expectations of human relatedness are, thereby defining the acceptable (conscionable) circumstances into and out of which the kept and their keepers, the watched and their watchers are to interact within situated contexts or settings. As we have demonstrated, however, the ethical underpinnings of these expectations and circumstances transform subjectivity into source and product of totalizing confinement (Arrigo

---

[6] This is not to dismiss the important socioeconomic effects of neoliberal theory in furthering a culture of madness (Simon, 2009; Sellers & Arrigo, 2018c). Instead, we draw attention to the informationalizing of risk.

[7] As we have argued elsewhere, "[u]nder these normalizing conditions, subjectivity (humanity) is reduced to the cyber-laws of passwords, and subjectivity (humanness) is repressed through the cyber-logics of profiles" (Sellers & Arrigo, 2018a, p. 136).

et al., 2011). This confinement imprisons epistemologically, and it incapacitates ontologically, reproducing for all of its participants a jurisprudence of docility.[8] Indeed, the excesses of this jurisprudence codify subjects into "docile bodies, bodies of abject utility [, rendering them] mere functionaries of the state" (Foucault, 1977, p. 210).

To stave off docility borne of hypersecuritization, PJ responds by relying on and cultivating a jurisprudence of virtue (Farrelly & Solum, 2008; Solum, 2003).[9] This jurisprudence, sourced in Aristotelian ethics (1976), reconceives the exegetical project of identity-making and rights-claiming. At issue are the ways in which the law can (and should) adjudicate disputes by promoting human flourishing and by building collective character (Arrigo, 2015). This emphasis on flourishing and character challenges established and taken-for-granted legal logics (e.g., reliance on interest-balancing rhetoric and duty-based rationales), maintaining that such moralism incompletely misses the opportunity to grow citizenship.[10] Recent applications of PJ's Aristotelian-sourced method of inquiry and analysis have reexamined sex offender laws (Bersot & Arrigo, 2015), state statutes affecting women's reproductive rights (Arrigo & Waldman, 2015), and zero tolerance public education policy (Sellers & Arrigo, 2018b).

---

[8] In their study investigating the social impact of surveillance in three UK schools, McCahill and Finn (2010) provide several examples of docility's reach. Describing the spatial (as opposed to temporal) strategies of social control at one site, they noted the following." [O]ne of the main functions of surveillance practices on th[e] site was to keep pupils in the school or in the classroom. This involved the 'manipulation of space' whereby all of the main entrances and exits were gated and locked and only teachers were allowed to move freely from one part of the school to another through the use of a 'fob key'. The school also had ID cards which had photographs of students on the front along with two small circles, a green circle which indicates that they have parental permission to leave the school premises at dinner time, and a red circle which means that they are not allowed to leave the site (Caretaker). The cards are then checked by one of the teachers (not the school security) who have been assigned to 'gate duty' over the dinner time period. These strategies were supported by the 'direct supervision' or 'focused attention' given to pupils by teachers patrolling the school with radios to keep them in the classroom/school" (p. 274).

[9] Virtue jurisprudence is a normative philosophy about the law, legal actors/actions, and legal rule-making (Arrigo, 2015). It is derived from aretaic concepts (Amaya & Hock Lai, 2013; Farrelly & Solum, 2008; Solum, 2003). Aretaic concepts are principled traits of human flourishing (e.g., living courageously, generously, benevolently, justly). When these noble traits are exercised habitually, they remind us of who we could be uniquely, collectively, and interdependently (Arrigo, 2013, 2015; Solum, 2003).

[10] Dependence on the logic of virtue changes the way in which legal texts (i.e., cases, statutes, and/or policies) are constructed and how legal judgments are reached. Consider the following observations: "[W]hen psychiatrically disordered convicts are placed in long-term disciplinary isolation, how and for whom does this practice exhibit courage, compassion, and generosity? When criminally adjudicated sex offenders are subsequently subjected to protracted civil commitment followed by multiple forms of communal inspection and monitoring, how and for whom is dignity affirmed, stigma averted, and healing advanced? When cognitively impaired juveniles are waived to the adult system, found competent to stand trial, and sentenced and punished accordingly, what version of nobility is celebrated and on whom is this goodness bestowed?" (Arrigo, 2013, p. 687).

As practice, PJ promotes an ethic of citizenship. This ethic redirects the law and its social control agents (e.g., police officers, mental health therapists, substance abuse counselors) to affirm the needs of individuals and to dignify the demands of society. This is citizenship that promotes healing, celebrates moral fiber, and seeks to generate dynamic and transformative manifestations of virtue for victims, offenders, and the communities to which all are bound (Arrigo et al., 2011; Farrelley & Solum, 2008). What this means, therefore, is that questions of generosity, benevolence, courage, compassion, and care, etc., would be central to how competing legal interests were weighed, how compelling legal duties were assigned, and how a situated justice was prescriptively achieved.

Still further, at the level of judicial (including US Supreme Court) decision-making, proponents of PJ and its ethic of citizenship have proposed that the courts incorporate the communal strategies of common sense justice, therapeutic jurisprudence, and restorative justice into their legal reasoning (Arrigo et al., 2011). These three strategies of "ethical activism" (Bersot & Arrigo, 2015, p. 41) are heavily steeped in the Aristotelian humanism of virtue jurisprudence. Common sense justice dignifies the subjective dimensions of the law and regards their significances as genuine expressions of the ordinary citizen's felt regard for what is just and fair. Therapeutic jurisprudence empowers courtroom actors to discern where and how the law might function as an agent of reform aimed at producing healing outcomes and prosocial change for all legal disputants. Restorative justice celebrates the role of mutual empathy, shared compassion, and even communal forgiveness in repairing the human injury that follows from criminal misconduct and the social harm that follows from transgressive acts. When these initiatives are dynamically rather than statically administered, they seek to engender within situated social contexts and human settings an appreciation for evolving habits of aretaic character (Arrigo, 2015).[11]

Psychological jurisprudence: bridging police psychology and community psychology

The police-youth encounter includes a number of situated contexts and human settings (e.g., at homes, in schools, on streets) in which mutual, relational, and communal manifestations of social justice can emerge. In what follows, we provisionally explain how the critical framework of PJ can enable the science of police

---

[11] Consequently, these three strategies intend to promote resolutions that repair citizenship by preventing norm violators from feeling "alienated, more damaged, disrespected, disempowered, less safe and less cooperative with society" (Braswell, Fuller, & Lozoff, 2001, p. 142). At the same time, these strategies hold the potential to advance for all participants the experience of personal growth, mutual understanding, human connectedness, a common sense of responsibility, and redemptive purpose (Arrigo et al., 2011). As proponents of virtue jurisprudence remind us, shared and ongoing experiences such as these hold the nearest promise of enhancing prospects for individual human flourishing and societal well-being (Amaya & Hock Lai, 2013; Farrelly & Solum, 2008).

psychology to better address the praxis imperatives of community psychology. Where useful and appropriate, we revisit the literature on police-youth interactions to further our explanation or describe illustrations of the same to contextualize our argument. Three questions warrant a preliminary response.

How can the theory of PJ inform the science of police psychology in ways that enable it to better address the praxis imperatives of community psychology?

Police encounters with children and adolescents are the source of considerable societal inquiry and concern. It is not simply the case that far too many citizens believe "anything can happen with police around" (Fine et al., 2003, p. 141) or that "police militarism" has become "normalized" (Kappeler & Kraska, 2015, p. 268). Instead, the issue is how both views—often fueled by media-hyped reporting that constructs reality sensationally—reflect and reinforce the mutual distrust that law officers and community members increasingly engender toward one another. In the instance of police-youth interactions, this distrust rises to the level of reciprocal suspicion in which the communication that ensues and the interventions that follow reduce the situated context or setting to a set of police/suspect-citizen/suspect exchanges of risk to be managed. In these exchanges, "criminalized scrutiny," "predatory surveillance," and a "siege" mentality permeate the interactional dynamics (Ruck, Harris, Fine, & Freudenberg, 2008, p. 15).

Consistent with the theory of PJ, we argue that these interactional dynamics are harm generating (devitalizing) and injury producing (finalizing). They (these dynamics) nurture the fixed false belief (the delusion) that hypersecuritization mediated by digital technology (e.g., body cameras worn by the police, tracking devices worn by juveniles, cell phones deployed for sousveillance purposes) can quiet any possible fight and can quell any potential fear that the watched and their watchers might otherwise experience (Sellers & Arrigo, 2018a). Presumably, the actuarial justice of precaution and prevention unrelentingly prevails (Ashworth & Zedner, 2015). What remain, however, are proliferating "environments of enclosure" (Deleuze, 1992, p. 3) in which a "profound mistrust of the state" is guaranteed, "with casualties including a diminished belief in democracy, cynical views about a 'broad-based' common good, and little memory of or imagination for a public sphere .... "(Ruck et al., 2008, pp. 15—16). As the theory of PJ reminds us, this is the precrime society dangerously at work. In this society, police-youth encounters reproduce a recurring madness. This is the madness of shared suspicion as source and product of hypersecuritization reified through its diffuse cyber mechanisms of bio-digital control. The science of police psychology would do well to consider how the forces of mutuality (i.e., police/suspect-citizen/suspect exchanges) are mediated virtually (rather than viscerally) on the streets, in homes, and/or at schools. Mutuality is a core component of community psychology's praxis imperatives.

How can the method of PJ inform the science of police psychology in ways that enable it to better address the praxis imperatives of community psychology?

The texts of hypersecuritization, diagnosed by way of the society-of-captives thesis, include the set of laws, statutes, and regulatory procedures that construct the identity and specify the rights of police officers and/or community members in situated contexts and human settings. Some of these texts include laws that interpret the constitutionality of stand your ground or stop and frisk statutes. Some of these regulatory procedures include use of force or critical incident debriefing protocols. As method, PJ questions what types of (judicial) temperament and what forms of (jurisprudential) ethic can be unearthed in these texts such that "the laws of captivity" reveal themselves (Arrigo & Polizzi, 2018, p. 1).[12]

Consistent with the deconstructive methodology of PJ, the question, then, is begged: What are the normative expectations of human relatedness that are lodged within the texts of police-youth encounters where matters of identity-making and rights-claiming are adjudicated by way of case law, statute enactment, or regulatory procedure? More specifically, do the relational dimensions of these laws (of captivity) principally advance a calculation of stakeholder interests and/or an assignment of stakeholder duties? And finally, to what extent, if at all, does virtue jurisprudence as a requisite for human flourishing and character building inform the identities that are adjudicated (for police officers, for youth citizens, for other community stakeholders) and the rights that are adjudicated (for police officers, for youth citizens, for other community stakeholders) by way of judicial decision, legislative outcome, and/or administrative protocol? An empirical (i.e., qualitative, textual, and interpretative) assessment of these discursive matters helps to disclose the relational parameters of how docility is bio-digitally codified as a cyber system of thought.[13] The science of police psychology would do well to consider how this docility sets limits to and imposes denials on other forms of relatedness within the manifold contexts and/or settings of police-youth encounters. Relationality is a core component of community psychology's praxis imperatives.

How can the practice strategies of PJ inform the science of police psychology in ways that enable it to better address the praxis imperatives of community psychology?

As a matter of overarching strategy or intervention, PJ employs an ethic of citizenship. This citizenship includes a set of practices (i.e., restorative justice, therapeutic jurisprudence, common sense justice) utilized for the purpose of redirecting legal actors and social control agents (e.g., patrol officers) to settle disputes and resolve conflicts by promoting human flourishing and by supporting character building. Policing youth at schools, in homes, or on the streets would therefore require the *recommunalization* of stakeholders through techniques of integrity-based

---

[12] In particular, this chapter draws preliminary attention to the policing of risk in the digital age (Ericson & Haggerty, 2008; O'Malley, 2010) where both law officer and youth citizen interrelate with preknowledge that they are both reduced to and repressed by the "mutual suspect" master status each bio-digitally assigns to the other.

[13] We suggest that body cameras worn by police officers reproduce nothing more than the "simulation of surveillance" (Bogard, 1996). We maintain that tracking devices worn by children and adolescents "carnivalize" hypersecuritization (Presdee, 2001). We argue that cell phones deployed for sousveillance purposes bio-digitize (i.e., depersonalize, devitalize), and therefore depoliticize (finalize), the embodiment or visceral-ness of injustice (e.g., Johnson, 2017).

ethical engagement. Among other things, this "virtue-centered" (Farrelly & Solum, 2008, p. 182) approach to police-youth interactions would work to achieve reconciliation by emphasizing the shared, collective, and interdependent values of living compassionately or caring altruistically or forgiving courageously.[14]

Thus, with respect to the science of police psychology, it is insufficient to use conscientiousness as a preemployment screening measure to predict which applicants would make successful cadets (Arrigo & Claussen, 2003). Moreover, it is inadequate to teach field officers "in ways that build trust within those communities least likely to willingly assist the police" (Lyons, 2002, p. 530). Instead, as a manifestation of habit-forming virtue and situated social justice, an ethic of citizenship reflexively and dynamically makes the activism of recommunalization central to transforming the police-youth encounters that ensue. Realizing this public good is a core component of community psychology's praxis imperatives.

Conclusions

This chapter critically examined how the theory, method, and practice strategies of PJ could enable the science of police psychology to better address the praxis directives of community psychology. For the purpose of our inquiry, these imperatives were targeted toward the human justice needs and the social welfare requisites of children and adolescents. Although clearly provisional, this chapter explored how the mutual, relational, and communal dimensions of PJ could bridge the divide between these two seemingly disparate and disconnected divisions of psychology. The challenge that awaits academic researchers and policy experts is to consider how the diagnostic framework of PJ is or could be relevant in the age of digital technology where both the watched and their watchers experience ubiquitous surveillance.[15] If

---

[14] Examples of such citizenship are discernible. Consider community-oriented policing initiatives, such as law enforcement—assisted diversion (LEAD). LEAD interventions compassionately divert drug offenders away from confinement and into community-based therapeutic and support services (i.e., adequate housing, healthcare, job training, counseling, medical treatment, and mental health support; Clifasefi, Lonczak, & Collins, 2017). Additionally, police use of restorative justice practices aim to repair community relationships harmed by law violations. In these instances, officers serve as mediators/facilitators whereby citizens (i.e., neighbors) become involved in the decision-making rather than the traditional criminal justice system making the decision for them. Such initiatives as these seek to strengthen capacity building that cultivates communal connectedness, victim restoration, responsiveness to citizen needs, and the empowerment of offenders with competency development and personal growth goals (Nicholl, 1999). This is police discretion infused with ethical activism.

[15] For example, this surveillance would produce (has produced?) mass "environments of enclosure" (Deleuze, 1992, p. 3) (e.g., at home or at work, in schools or in places of worship, on streets, and in parks), including proliferating cyber mechanisms of bio-digital control. What theory, method, and set of practices exist to explain, predict, and/or resolve the madness that follows from sustaining this hypersecuritization?

police/suspect-citizen/suspect dynamics are to be abated, this challenge warrants systematic and resolute attention.

References

Adelman, M., & Yalda, C. (2000). Seen but not heard: The legal lives of young people. *PoLAR: Political & Legal Anthropology Review, 23*(2), 37−58. https://doi.org/10.1525/pol.2000.23.2.37.

Amaya, A., & Hock Lai, H. (2013). In *Law, virtue, and justice*. UK: Hart Publishing.

Ankony, R. C., & Kelley, T. (1999). The impact of perceived alienation on police officers' sense of mastery and subsequent motivation for proactive enforcement. *Policing: An International Journal of Police Strategies & Management, 22*, 120−134. https://doi.org/10.1108/13639519910271193.

Arrigo, B. A. (2013). Managing risk and marginalizing identities: On the society-of-captives thesis and the harm of social dis-ease. *International Journal of Offender Therapy and Comparative Criminology, 57*(6), 672−693.

Arrigo, B. A. (2015). Responding to crime: Psychological jurisprudence, normative philosophy, and trans-desistance theory. *Criminal Justice and Behavior: International Journal, 42*(1), 7−18.

Arrigo, B. A., Bersot, H. Y., & Sellers, B. G. (2011). *The ethics of total confinement: A critique of madness, citizenship and social justice*. New York: Oxford.

Arrigo, B. A., & Claussen, N. (2003). Police corruption and psychological testing: A strategy for pre-employment screening. *International Journal of Offender Therapy and Comparative Criminology, 47*(3), 272−290.

Arrigo, B. A., & Davidson, L. (2017). Commentary on community mental health and the common good. *Behavioral Sciences & the Law, 35*(4), 364−371.

Arrigo, B. A., & Milovanovic, D. (2009). *Revolution in penology: Rethinking the society of captives*. Lanham, MD: Rowman & Littlefield.

Arrigo, B. A., & Polizzi, D. (2018). Introduction to the special issue: On the "laws of captivity." *New Criminal Law Review: An Interdisciplinary and International Journal, 21*(4).

Arrigo, B. A., & Sellers, B. G. (2018). Psychological jurisprudence and the relational problems of de-vitalization and finalization: Rethinking the society of captives thesis. In A. Mills, & K. Kendall (Eds.), *Mental health in prisons: Critical perspectives on treatment and confinement* (pp. 73−101). UK: Palgrave MacMillan.

Arrigo, B. A., & Waldman, J. L. (2015). Psychological jurisprudence and the power of law: A critique of North Carolina's woman's right to know act. *Duke Journal of Gender Law & Policy, 22*(1), 55−88.

Ashworth, A., & Zedner, L. (2015). *Preventive justice*. London, UK: Oxford University Press.

Bartol, C. (1996). Police psychology: Then, now and beyond. *Criminal Justice and Behavior, 23*(1), 70−89.

Bartol, C. R., & Bartol, A. M. (2019). Introduction to forensic psychology: Research and application (5th ed.). Thousand Oaks, CA: Sage.

Beck, U. (2009). *World at risk*. Cambridge, UK: Polity Press.

Bersot, H. Y., & Arrigo, B. A. (2015). Responding to sex offenders: Empirical findings, judicial decision-making, and virtue jurisprudence. *Criminal Justice and Behavior: International Journal, 42*(1), 32–44.

Bogard, W. (1996). *The simulation of surveillance: Hypercontrol in telemetric societies.* Cambridge: Cambridge University Press.

Braswell, M., Fuller, J., & Lozoff, B. (2001). *Corrections, peacemaking, and restorative justice: Transforming individuals and institutions.* Cincinnati, OH: Anderson Publishing Co.

Brunson, R. K. (2007). Police don't like black people: African-American young men's accumulated police experiences. *Criminology, 6,* 71–102.

Carr, P. J., Napolitano, L., & Keating, J. (2007). We never call the cops and here is why: A qualitative examination of legal cynicism in three Philadelphia neighborhoods. *Criminology, 45,* 445–480.

Cleary, H. M. D. (2017). Applying the lessons of developmental psychology to the study of juvenile interrogations: New directions for research, policy, and practice. *Psychology, Public Policy, and Law, 23*(1), 118–130.

Cleary, H. M. D., & Warner, T. C. (2016). Police training in interviewing and interrogation methods: A comparison of techniques used with adult and juvenile suspects. *Law and Human Behavior, 40*(3), 270–284. https://doi.org/10.1037/lhb0000175.

Clifasefi, S. L., Lonczak, H. S., & Collins, S. E. (2017). Seattle's law enforcement assisted diversion (LEAD) program: Within-subjects changes on housing, employment, and income/benefits outcomes and associations with recidivism. *Crime & Delinquency, 63*(4), 429–445. https://doi.org/10.1177/0011128716687550.

Cohen, A. O., Breiner, K., Steinberg, L., Bonnie, R. J., Scott, E. S., Taylor-Thompson, K. A., & Casey, B. J. (2016). When is an adolescent an adult? Assessing cognitive control in emotional and nonemotional contexts. *Psychological Science, 27,* 549–562. https://doi.org/10.1177/0956797615627625.

Deleuze, G. (1992). Postscript on the societies of control. *October, 59*(10), 3–7.

Ericson, R. V., & Haggerty, K. D. (2008). *Policing the risk society.* Oxford: Clarendon Studies in Criminology.

Farrelly, C., & Solum, L. (Eds.). (2008). *Virtue jurisprudence.* UK: Palgrave Macmillan.

Fine, M., Freudenberg, N., Payne, Y., Perkins, T., Smith, K., & Wanzer, K. (2003). "Anything can happen with police around": Urban youth evaluate strategies of surveillance in public places. *Journal of Social Issues, 59*(1), 141–158.

Foucault, M. (1977). *Discipline and punish: The birth of a prison.* New York: Pantheon.

Fryer, D., Duckett, P., & Pratt, R. (2004). Critical community psychology: What, why and how? *Clinical Psychology, 38,* 39–43.

Garrett, M., & Short, J. F. (1975). Social class and delinquency: Predictions of outcomes of police-juvenile encounters. *Social Problems, 22,* 367–383.

Gatti, U., Tremblay, R. E., & Vitaro, F. (2009). Iatrogenic effect of juvenile justice. *Journal of Child Psychology and Psychiatry, 50*(8), 991–998.

Gau, J. M., & Brunson, R. K. (2010). Procedural justice and order maintenance policing: A study of inner-city young men's perceptions of police legitimacy. *Justice Quarterly, 27,* 255–279.

Goldstein, N. E. S., Kelly, S. M., Peterson, L., Brogan, L., Zelle, H., & Romaine, C. R. (2015). Evaluation of Miranda waiver capacity. In K. Heilbrun, D. DeMatteo, & N. E. S. Goldstein (Eds.), *APA handbook of psychology and juvenile justice* (pp. 467–488). Washington, DC: American Psychological Association.

Graham, S., & Lowery, B. S. (2004). Priming unconscious racial stereotypes about adolescent offenders. *Law and Human Behavior, 28*, 483–494.

Hogan, R., & Kurtines, W. (1975). Personological correlates of police effectiveness. *Journal of Psychology, 91*, 289–295.

Johnson, R. (2017). *Embodied social justice*. New York: Routledge.

Kagan, C., Burton, M., Duckett, P., Lawthom, R., & Siddiquee, A. (2011). *Critical community psychology*. West Sussex, UK: Wiley-Blackwell.

Kappeler, V. E., & Kraska, P. B. (2015). Normalising police militarisation, living in denial. *Police and Society, 25*(3), 268–275. https://doi.org/10.1080/10439463.2013.864655.

Kitaeff, J. (Ed.). (2011). *Handbook of police psychology*. New York: Routledge.

Kraska, P. B. (2007). Militarization and policing—its relevance to 21st Century police. *Policing: Journal of Policy Practice, 1*(4), 501–513. https://doi.org/10.1093/police/pam065.

Kutcher, S., & McDougall, A. (2009). Problems with access to adolescent mental health care can lead to dealings with the criminal justice system. *Pediatric Child Health, 14*(1), 15–18.

Lyons, W. (2002). Partnerships, information, and public safety: Community policing in a time of terror. *Policing: An International Journal of Police Strategies & Management, 25*(3), 530–542.

McCahill, M., & Finn, R. (2010). The social impact of surveillance in three UK schools: 'angels', 'devils' and 'teen mums'. *Surveillance and Society, 7*(3/4), 273–289.

McCulloch, J., & Wilson, D. (2015). *Pre-crime: Pre-emption, precaution, and the future*. London: Routledge.

McKitten, R., & Thurau, L. (2017). *Where's the state? Creating and implementing state standards for law enforcement interactions with youth*. Cambridge, MA: Strategies for Youth. Retrieved from www.strategiesforyouth.org.

Meyer, J. R., & Reppucci, N. D. (2007). Police practices and perceptions regarding juvenile interrogation and interrogative suggestibility. *Behavioral Sciences & the Law, 25*, 757–780. https://doi.org/10.1002/bsl.774.

Mitchell, C. L., & Dorian, E. H. (Eds.). (2016). *Police psychology and its growing impact on modern law enforcement*. Hershey, PA: Information Science Reference.

Mufson, D. W., & Mufson, M. A. (1988). Predicting police officer performance using the Inwald personality inventory: An illustration from Appalachia. *Professional Psychology: Research and Practice, 29*(1), 59–62. https://doi.org/10.1037/0735-7028.29.1.59.

Nelson, G., & Prilleltensky, I. (Eds.). (2010). *Community psychology: In pursuit of liberation and well-being*. Basingstoke Hampshire, UK: Palgrave.

Nicholl, C. G. (1999). *Toolbox for implementing restorative justice and advancing community policing*. Washington, DC: U.S. Department of Justice, Office of Community Oriented Policing Services.

Orford, J. (2008). *Community psychology: Challenges, controversies, and emerging consensus*. Chichester, UK: Wiley-Blackwell.

O'Malley, P. (2010). *Crime and risk*. London, UK: SAGE.

Polizzi, D., Draper, M., & Andersen, M. (2014). Fabricated selves and the rehabilitative machine: Toward a phenomenology of the social construction of offender treatment. In B. A. Arrigo, & H. Y. Bersot (Eds.), *The Routledge handbook of international crime and justice studies* (pp. 231–255). UK: Taylor and Francis.

Porter, S., Brinke, L., & Gustaw, C. (2010). Dangerous decisions: The impact of first impressions of trustworthiness on the evaluation of legal evidence and defendant culpability. *Psychology, Crime and Law, 1*, 1–15. https://doi.org/10.1080/10683160902926141.

Presdee, M. (2001). *Cultural criminology and the carnival of crime*. London: Routledge.

Prilleltensky, I., & Nelson, G. (1997). Community psychology: Reclaiming social justice. In D. Fox, & I. Prilleltensky (Eds.), *Critical psychology: An introduction* (pp. 166–184). Thousand Oaks, CA: Sage.

Pycroft, A. (2010). *Understanding and working with substance misusers*. London, UK: SAGE.

Reiner, R. (2010). The politics *of* the police (4th ed.). Oxford, UK: Oxford University Press.

Ruck, M., Harris, A., Fine, M., & Freudenberg, N. (2008). Youth experiences of surveillance: Cross-national analysis. In M. Flynn, & D. Brotherton (Eds.), *Globalizing the streets: Cross-cultural perspectives on youth, social control, and empowerment* (pp. 15–30). New York: Columbia University Press.

Schuck, A. M. (2013). A life-course perspective on adolescents' attitudes to police: DARE, delinquency, and residential segregation. *Journal of Research in Crime and Delinquency, 50*(4), 579–607. https://doi.org/10.1177/0022427813481977.

Scott, J. C. (1985). *Weapons of the weak: Everyday forms of peasant resistance*. New Haven, CT: Yale University Press.

Sellers, B. G., & Arrigo, B. A. (2009). Adolescent transfer, developmental maturity, and adjudicative competence: An ethical and justice policy inquiry. *Journal of Criminal Law and Criminology, 99*(2), 435–488.

Sellers, B. G., & Arrigo, B. A. (2018a). Postmodern criminology and technocrime. In K. F. Steinmetz, & M. R. Nobles (Eds.), *Technocrime and criminological theory* (pp. 133–146). New York: Routledge.

Sellers, B. G., & Arrigo, B. A. (2018b). Virtue jurisprudence and the case of zero tolerance disciplining in U.S. public education policy: An ethical and humanistic critique of captivity's laws. *New Criminal Law Review: An Interdisciplinary and International Journal, 21*(4).

Sellers, B. G., & Arrigo, B. A. (2018c). Zero tolerance, social control, and marginalized youth in American schools: A critical reappraisal of neoliberalism's theoretical foundations and epistemological assumptions. *Contemporary Justice Review: Issues in Criminal, Social, and Restorative Justice, 21*(1), 60–79.

Simon, J. (2009). *Governing through crime: How the war on crime transformed American democracy and created a culture of fear*. New York: Oxford University Press.

Skolnick, J. (2000). Code blue. *The American Prospect, 11*(10), 1.

Solum, L. B. (2003). Virtue jurisprudence: A virtue-centered theory of judging. *Metaphilosophy, 34*, 178–213.

Soto, C. J., & Tackett, J. L. (2015). Personality traits in childhood and adolescence: Structure, development, and outcomes. *Current Directions in Psychological Science, 24*(5), 358–362. https://doi.org/10.1177/0963721415589345.

Spencer, M. B., Fegley, S., Harpalani, V., & Seaton, G. (2004). Understanding hypermasculinity in context: A theory-driven analysis of urban adolescent males' coping responses. *Research in Human Development, 1*(4), 229–257.

Straub, F. (2008). Policing cities: Reducing violence and building communities. *Police Chief, 75*(11). Retrieved from http://youthlinkusa.org/press/YOUTHLINK-press-11-2008-ThePoliceChiefMagazine.pdf.

Thurau, L. H. (2009). Rethinking how we police youth: Incorporating knowledge of adolescence into policing teens. *Children's Legal Rights Journal, 29*(3), 30–48.

Twersky-Glasner, A. (2005). Police personality: What is it and why are they like that? *Journal of Police and Criminal Psychology, 20*(1), 56–67.

Weaver, B., & McNeill, F. (2015). Lifelines: Desistance, social relations, and reciprocity. *Criminal Justice and Behavior, 42*(1), 95–107.

Zedner, L. (2007). Pre-crime and post-criminology. *Theoretical Criminology: An International Journal, 11*(2), 261–281.

The role of psychological science in public order policing

Neil Williams and Clifford Stott

Introduction

The seminal modern works on public order policing were arguably Peter (Tank) Waddington's *Strong Arm of the Law* (Waddington, 1991) and his subsequent work *Liberty and Order* (Waddington, 1994). The latter is first and foremost a rich and detailed first-hand account and analysis of an impressive and ground-breaking ethnography with the London Metropolitan Police Public Order Unit. It draws out the now familiar idea that the central motivation driving police decision-making in the public order context was a rather banal form of pragmatism revolving around the dynamics of what is referred to as *on the job* and *in the job* trouble. On the job trouble is conceptualized as the "public disorder" or confrontation that officers may have to routinely confront in the course of their duty, whereas in the job trouble described the potential political ramifications of disorder for commanders and the force as a whole. *Liberty and Order* sets out a whole series of case study examples to illustrate and substantiate this central thesis. There are too many to describe here but they are varied and compelling. Nonetheless, these examples point toward another important contribution that has been less well developed conceptually and evidentially. Specifically, this body of work points toward the centrality of police psychology in their actions toward crowds. For example, Waddington points out that police perceptions that disorder was "more or less uncontrollable" in turn "placed police commanders in a position of some helplessness and explains why they invested so much in trying to exert extensive control over the event" (Waddington, 1994, p. 160).

Classical perspectives and reactionary policing

The idea of the centrality of police psychology in public order policing was developed further by Stott and Reicher (1998a) who conducted a qualitative analysis of a series of interviews with 26 public order trained police officers from the UK. The study aimed to address three specific questions:

1. What were the general theories of crowd action articulated by police officers?
2. How do crowd contexts affect the practicalities of policing?

Police Psychology, Edited by Marques and Paulino. https://doi.org/10.1016/B978-0-12-816544-7.00008-5

3. How do these police theories and practicalities articulate with each other and affect the ways in which crowds are policed?

On the basis of their analysis, the authors identified three consistent themes evident in the way officers talk about crowds and their role in policing them. First, while officers described crowds' composition as generally heterogeneous, they consistently characterized this in terms of two social categories, an antisocial and violent minority which could exploit the potential mindlessness of the otherwise peaceful majority. It was evident that this psychological perspective mirrored dominant "classical" theories of the crowd. On the one hand, the minority group's behavior was described in terms of a convergence of those with preexisting motivations to create disruption and disorder (Allport, 1924). On the other, the majority were described as ordinary people who become pathological as a result of the anonymity assumed to be inherent from being within a crowd. Essentially, as a consequence of their anonymity and submergence within the crowd, the majority are open to the disease-like spread of pernicious ideas and behaviors through "contagion" (Le Bon, 1960; Zimbardo, 1969). As one police commander put it when describing his experience of policing a major riot in Central London:

> *The fever of the day, the throwing and everything else, they get locked together and think "oh we are part of this"'. Something disengages in their brain. I am not a medical man or an expert in crowd behaviour, but something goes, and they become part of the crowd.*

Stott & Reicher (1998a), p. 517.

Second, as a consequence of these assumed mechanisms, all crowds, despite their heterogeneity of composition, were described as potentially conflictual, and the crowd homogeneously dangerous. The final theme, and in line with Waddington's proposition, was the practicalities of policing that flowed from officers' psychological perspectives. To begin with, if crowds are potentially dangerous and volatile, then it was understood that strict control of them was necessary and if minor incidents of conflict developed it should be quelled via the rapid and relatively undifferentiated use of force. Moreover, if a crowd is homogeneously dangerous, then the decision to treat the crowd as a single entity is a logical one. Given this perspective, officers inevitably saw the cause of crowd conflict as a result of factors inherent to the crowd itself. In effect, there was no reason for them to reflexively consider the role that police tactics might play in the production and escalation of conflict.

Adding further quantitative evidence, Drury, Stott, and Farsides (2003) conducted a questionnaire survey of 80 public order trained police officers, also from the United Kingdom. As with the previous study, the data supported the idea that officers saw the composition of crowds as mixed but composed of a violent minority, and a mindless majority. While these data suggested that officers did not overtly endorse the view of the crowd as a homogeneous threat, it did confirm that they advocated the quick assertion of control against the crowd as a whole in order to prevent any potential conflict from escalating. Moreover, crowd policing methods were not considered to contribute to the escalation of conflict (Drury et al., 2003).

Given the two studies were conducted exclusively with British officers it is arguable that these forms of police psychology are only evident within a UK context. However, Prati and Pietrantoni (2009) translated the survey and distributed it to Italian police officers trained in policing public order. In addition to further validating and exploring the generalizability of the earlier studies, their survey data also allowed them to assess the effects of experience of crowd policing on officers' psychological perspectives on the crowd. The study supported the idea that police officers perceive crowds as populated by a dangerous minority capable of exploiting a relatively mindless majority. As such, these police officers saw a need to rely heavily on coercion in order to control the volatility of the crowd. Interestingly, Prati and Pietrantoni (2009) demonstrated that officers with more experience of policing crowds were also more likely to view the crowd from this "classical perspective" than their less experienced counterparts.

Arguably, this evidence within and across the police is evidence of what Prati and Pietrantoni (2009) referred to as a "commonsense" understanding. Yet, as such, it begs a commonsense question. As Milgram and Toch (1969) pointed out, if processes of anonymity lead to irrationality among crowd members and the uncritical spread of ideas and behaviors why do police officers not also become influenced by these same psychological processes? This important and far-reaching question itself reflects the broader limitations of these classical theoretical perspectives on the crowd and their lack of explanatory power. In other words, despite evidence that they are dominant in the psychological perspectives of police officers involved in policing crowds it has been increasingly recognized that such theories are themselves incapable of explaining the behavior of crowds (Reicher, 1982). Indeed, it must be recognized that these classical theories have been largely rejected by the academic community. They were developed at the end of the 19th century at a time when the emerging industrial capitalist social order was increasingly threatened by revolutions "from below," manifest most clearly in the form of the crowd. In this context the crowd became a salient social, political, and intellectual concern particularly to the elite middle classes keen to protect their newfound wealth and opportunity. As such, these classical theories were initially developed as a means through which a technology of social control could be developed and as such it is argued where they predominate they do so not because they explain but because they exculpate the authorities and legitimize coercive forms of social control (Barrows, 1981; Nye, 1975; Stott & Drury, 2017).

Perhaps more importantly, research also highlights that these forms of police psychology are problematic because they actually drive forms of police action that produce confrontation. For example, during a major demonstration in London against a new form of taxation, a peaceful demonstration developed into major rioting involving thousands of people in active confrontation against the police. Analysis of the dynamics through which that riot came about showed very powerfully that police intervention using relatively indiscriminate coercive force played a critical role. Moreover, research also highlighted that the decision to intervene in this way was partly a function of the police commander's interpretation of the situation in terms of classical theory. Witnessing minor incidents of confrontation, he had assumed that as a function of contagion processes this would spread to the crowd as a whole. As a consequence, he took a decision to intervene against the crowd, but in so doing inadvertently created forms of police action that shaped the very conflict they were seeking to avoid. In other words, police psychology acted as a form of self-fulfilling prophecy (Stott & Drury, 2000).

The social identity approach—a new way of understanding the crowd

In the late 20th century, a new way of understanding the psychology of crowds began to emerge. The Social Identity Model (SIM) of crowd behavior (Reicher, 1982, 1984, 1987) was developed to address the limitations of classical theory and build an explanation of the ideological form and normative limits of collective action during the 1980 St Paul's Riots in Bristol. The data collected by Reicher showed that there were clear patterns evident in the behavior of the rioters, and that far from being a mindless and random explosion, the rioters acted in a coordinated fashion, only attacking property which symbolized outside wealth and societal oppression, while the "police were the only [human] targets of collective attack" (Reicher, 1987, p. 192). Reicher concluded that these targets were seen by rioters as the physical embodiment of an ongoing unjust, oppressive, and racist social system (1984, 1987). The study was the first to identify how the actions of the crowd were based on a clearly defined, shared common social identity. Thus, Reicher (1996a) contended that:

> People do not lose their identity in the crowd but rather shift from acting in terms of personal identity to acting in terms of the relevant social identity. Correspondingly, people do not lose control over their behaviour in the crowd, but rather control shifts to those values and understandings by which this identity is defined. (p. 328)

Despite this important advance in theoretical understanding, the SIM was not able to explain changes in the normative behavior of the crowd, particularly the important transition from peaceful norms into a riot. As such, an analysis of a peaceful student protest which turned violent in London in 1990 (Reicher, 1996b) laid the foundation for the Elaborated Social Identity Model (ESIM) of crowd behavior. At an empirical level, the study highlighted how a peaceful demonstration against the abolition of student grants escalated into a major riot as a direct outcome of aggressive and indiscriminate police interventions against the crowd as a whole. At a theoretical level the study demonstrated the importance of intergroup interaction in reshaping the form and content of the social identity enabling collective action in the crowd. Moreover, the transition into collective conflict was not a result merely of mechanisms inherent in the crowd but resulted from the dynamics of the intergroup interactions over time. Moreover, by analyzing the conflict in its context, Reicher was able to demonstrate that police action and their psychological perspective, while intended to prevent violence, was actually implicated in its cause. Thus, in order to explain the developmental changes of crowd action it is important to recognize crowd events "are typically intergroup encounters and therefore the position of any one party must be understood in relation to the ongoing intergroup dynamic" (Drury & Reicher, 1999, p. 383).

The SIM is effectively an application and development of Self-categorization Theory (SCT) (Turner, Hogg, Oakes, Reicher, & Wetherell, 1987). SCT is a theory of the self and proposes that people have a variety of social identities that enable them to make sense of and orient meaningfully toward the group-level social context within which they may find themselves. For example, in societies organized and structured in terms of racial categories people often utilize those ethnic categories to define themselves and act toward others. Like SCT, the ESIM, and the SIM, view "social categories as context-dependent social judgements, based upon a social actor's background ideology and motivations, and ... are dynamic in both form and content" (Stott, Adang, Livingstone, & Schrieber, 2007, p. 76; see also, Reicher, 2001, pp. 182—208; Turner, Oakes, Haslam, & McGarty, 1994). Once salient in the self-system, SCT proposes that people conform to the defining dimensions of that social category and see others who do so as common in-group members. This social identity or self-categorization is actively constructed at the psychological level from background beliefs that flow into a set of comparative judgments within each specific social context. Given this intimate relationship between social identity and the social context, when that context changes, so too does the form (who is considered a common in-group member) and content (what is considered as normative for the in-group) of the social identity enabling collective action.

Accordingly, a specific self-categorization becomes salient in the self-system as a result of the *meta-contrast ratio* defined as:

> *The ratio of the average difference perceived between members of the category and the other stimuli (the mean inter-category difference) over the average difference perceived between members within the category (the mean intra-category difference) and provides a simple quantitative measure of the degree to which any subset of stimuli will tend to be cognised as a single unit, entity, or group (i.e., perceptually categorised).*

Turner et al. (1987), p. 47

In this way, the MCR explains how the social context plays a direct role not just in self-definition but also in social influence processes underpinning the emergent normative dimensions of collective action. Given this inter-relationship, as the social context changes (e.g., through police coercive intervention during a crowd event) then what it means to be a category member, the behaviors that are normative for that category and who is influential or prototypical also change. Put slightly differently, outgroups—such as the police—have the power to act *toward* a crowd in ways that impact directly upon the social identity dynamics driving collective action *in* that crowd. Thus, through its focus on the intergroup dynamics of crowd events ESIM adopts what can be referred to as a "process" model of identity; collective action in a crowd is not merely an outcome of cognitive processes but also "dependent upon the nature of power relations in the inter-group context" (Stott & Drury, 2000, p. 266; see also Reicher, 1987, 1996a; Reicher & Levine, 1994a, 1994b).

Thus, according to Stott, Drury, and Reicher (2011):

> *ESIM can be summarised as follows: people's sense of their social position (so-cial identity) changes to the extent that, in acting on their identity (participating in a crowd event), they are repositioned as a consequence of the understandings and reactions of an outgroup (treated as oppositional by the police). This reposi-tioning lead both to a new identity and new forms of inter and intragroup action (intergroup hostility, variations in 'prejudice' and conflict). (p. 297)*

Across a program of research surrounding a series of crowd events, involving England fans at the FIFA World Cup (Stott & Reicher, 1998a, 1998b), antipoll tax demonstrators (Drury & Reicher, 1999; Stott & Drury, 2000), and antiroad campaigns (Drury & Reicher, 2000), a similar pattern of intergroup interaction and psychological change was identified. The pattern can be summarized as follows:

1. At time 1 a physical crowd is constituted by smaller, relatively heterogeneous psychological groups united by an identity defined in terms of relatively peaceful objectives and norms.
2. The same crowd is perceived as a homogenous threat by the authorities (police) who have the power to act on the basis of this understanding leading them to exercise force in a relatively undifferentiated manner.
3. This action against the crowd by the authorities at time 1 is perceived as unwarranted and indiscriminate by sections of the crowd.
4. As a result of the shifting intergroup context (i.e., police action) the social identity enabling collective action in the crowd at time 2 also changes along two important dimensions.
5. Conflict toward the police comes to be seen as legitimate by crowd participants (e.g., a reassertion of rights) and those engaging in conflict against the outgroup are seen as common in-group members.
6. The boundaries of identity shift to be more inclusive and the psychological unity creates empowerment enabling crowd members to act against the police.

Taken together this research helps identify a series of issues that highlight the role of police psychology in the dynamics of crowds. On the one hand, police psychological perspectives are often informed by outdated classical theories of the crowd. This in turn feeds forms of police action which are essentially counterproductive and dangerous in that they appear to play an important role in the production of collective violence. Scientific research on crowd psychology has begun to show very powerfully how and why this is the case. Thus, we now move on to explore how the social identity-based research on crowds has begun to reshape police psychological perspective and behaviors toward crowds and the apparent benefits that accrue from this.

ESIM and football crowds: policing and self-regulation

A significant component of the early empirical and theoretical development of ESIM was made possible through a series of studies of what is often referred to as football *hooliganism*. Early academic theories of crowd violence at football suggested that collective conflict in this context was the result of the convergence of the "rough working class". Dunning, Murphy and Williams (1988) proposed that there were sections of society relatively untouched by "civilizing processes," through which, across the 20th century, the working classes had gradually adopted nonviolent middle-class norms and values (cf. Elias & Jephcott, 1978). They asserted that hooliganism was the result of young men from this rough working class converging onto the football terraces of their towns and cities to exercise a form of violent territorialism against similar groups from other towns and cities, visiting to support their teams. While Dunning and colleagues' (1988; cf. Dunning, 1994) work on football crowd conflict explains violent crowd behaviors in terms of class structure and socialization practices, this *hooligan* model essentially shares Allport's (1924) classical perspective that violence is a result of the convergence of those already predisposed toward violent confrontation (in this case through prior socialization processes).

From this viewpoint, the very presence of these fans poses a risk to the public order (Stott, West & Radburn, 2018). Accordingly, preventing football crowd disorder is a matter of identifying hooligans and stopping them from converging onto the football terraces. It is perhaps unsurprising then that the policing approach that predominates in football relies heavily upon the surveillance, categorization, and coercive control of so called *risk fans* (Hopkins, 2014; Hopkins & Hamilton-Smith, 2014, James & Pearson, 2015; Stott & Pearson, 2006, 2007, p. 218). However, the official UK and European police definition of a risk fan is somewhat problematic: a "person, known or not, who can be regarded as posing a possible risk to public order or antisocial behavior, whether planned or spontaneous, at or in connection with a football event" (Council of Europe, 2010, p. 21). It could be argued that far from providing a nuanced way of identifying fans that are inclined toward the production of disorder this definition is so broad it could be applied to anyone who goes to, or even watches, a football event. Moreover, it begs the question of what circumstances are likely to provoke or undermine any individual tendencies that may or may not be present.

Any understanding of collective conflict in terms of the hooligan crowd member's disposition also has several explanatory limitations. First, it cannot account for the specificities of a given incident: when it is likely to occur, if and how it spreads to involve others or the form it takes. Second, it is unable to explain the complete absence of violence when so called hooligans or risk fans are present or why it is that collective violence in the football context develops when those involved are not known to the police as hooligans or risk fans (Stott & Reicher, 1998b).

Stott and Reicher's (1998b) study of football crowd conflict on the island of Sardinia during the 1990 Italian World Cup Finals (Italia 90) demonstrated how ESIM could help advance theoretical understanding beyond the hooligan account. With English club sides still banned from European competition due to the Heysel stadium disaster,[1] the Italian authorities mobilized upwards of 7000 Italian police officers to keep the notorious English hooligans in check. While serious rioting did develop during England's residency on the island, Stott and Reicher argue that the dynamics and form of these riots could not be understood merely in terms of the pre-existing violent dispositions of English hooligans (c.f. Williams, Dunning, & Murphy, 1989). They assert that the rioting was better understood as the outcome of specific patterns of intergroup interactions between fans and police over time. England fans understanding themselves to be behaving legitimately—by gathering together, drinking, and celebrating their identity as supporters—were systematically confronted by other groups, locals, and police, in ways that the England fans understood as illegitimate and indiscriminate attacks on the category as a whole. Subsequently, as a direct result of these intergroup interactions, fans, who had initially eschewed violence, were drawn into conflict with the police (Stott & Reicher, 1998b).

It was also evident that prior to the tournament the police and significant components of the local population held and expressed the view that the majority of English fans traveling to the island were hooligans. As a result, large numbers of England fans experienced heavy handed and indiscriminate policing and hostility from locals over a period of days prior to England's second match of the tournament against Holland. This in turn created a social context in which England fans felt police actions were illegitimate and as a consequence that it would be legitimate to confront police given the opportunity. Just prior to this match, around 6000 England supporters began to march en masse toward the stadium. Fearing disorder, the Italian police attempted to block the route of the march using their batons to disperse the crowd. However, given England fans were gathered together and felt they had a legitimate right to march to the stadium peacefully, they felt empowered and that it was legitimate to confront the police, forcing them to retreat. In the context of this riot it was only police targets that were subjected to collective attack. Thus, the study suggested that collective conflict at football should not be viewed merely as a result of relatively fixed identities emerging from the macrosocial context (i.e., the rough working class). Rather those more powerful explanatory models of conflict require an analysis of the intergroup interactions between crowd participants and those who police them during the crowd events. Moreover, the study once again highlighted the importance of police psychology, by demonstrating that the police perspective of football crowds as inherently violent led them to police them as

---

[1] For more details, see https://www.britannica.com/place/Heysel-Stadium.

such, through which collective violence emerged as "a self-fulfilling prophecy"[2] (Stott & Reicher, 1998b, p. 374).

According to Stott, Hutchison, and Drury (2001), further evidence of the importance of these social psychological dynamics came when both England and Scotland qualified for the 1998 World Cup in France (France 98). The tournament provided a unique opportunity to extend the ESIM understanding of football crowd behavior by comparing the two supporter groups. While there are many differences in English and Scottish football culture, the domestic football leagues in both countries have problems of group conflict, yet the supporters of the Scottish national team no longer have the same reputation as those of the English team, despite sharing a very similar supporter demographic (Giulianotti, 1991; 1994).

England were drawn to play their opening match of France 98 against Tunisia in the southern city of Marseilles. As the tournament began, large numbers of England fans began to gather in the Old Port area of the city. During these early stages there appear to have been hostile interactions between some England fans and locals of North African descent, mostly likely racist provocations and insults from a relatively small contingent of England fans. However, as other England fans continued to arrive in significant numbers throughout the first few days into the Old Town, perhaps as a result of the earlier provocations, local youths began unprovoked attacks on England fans across the Old Port area. During these confrontations the police did little if anything to intervene or if they did, they launched attacks against England fans. In this context, England fans found themselves faced with a lack of protection from the police or as a target of what they experienced as unjustified police aggression. As a result collective violence began to emerge.

As was observed at Italia 90, the research highlighted a pattern in which the identity underpinning the emergence of collective violence was embedded in an intergroup context defined in terms of opposition to illegitimate outgroup actions. This context of "common fate" for England fans appears to have empowered those prepared to confront aggressive outgroups, and rendered them as prototypical, and hence influential, in-group members (Stott et al., 2001). Contrastingly, Scottish fans had been praised for their behavior at the UEFA European Football Championships in Sweden in 1992 (cf. Giulianotti, 1994) and were now famous for their creation of a boisterous but nonviolent "carnival" atmosphere surrounding football games (cf. Giulianotti, 1991). With their now positive reputation preceding them, police and locals were apparently much more welcoming. However, it was also evident that the heavy drinking and boisterous behavioral norms of the Scots were not dissimilar to the collective behavior among England fans. Yet while those behaviors were interpreted by police as hooliganism in the England context they were interpreted as benign in the other. The Scottish fans' experiences of being allowed to collectively express their identity without provoking a hostile response from

---

[2] Defined by the Cambridge Dictionary as "something that you cause to happen by saying and expecting that it will happen."

locals or police led to a perception of intergroup legitimacy which was paralleled by displays of a strong self-regulation culture. In effect, in this context of intergroup legitimacy the Scottish supporters started "self-policing." It was apparent that this form of norm enforcement was, at least in part, in order to maintain the positive reputation of their own group. Indeed, violence in this context was still seen as legitimate, but only toward those other Scottish supporters who had transgressed ingroup norms. As one Scottish supporter described concerning another who had acted violently toward a local:

> *The guy with the Tunisian top got the ball and … the Scottish guy stuck his fuckin' head on him ….Next thing there was about twenty, thirty guys with kilts on bootin' fuck out of the Scottish guy … nobody wanted to know him, just thought he was a complete wank. [Conversation Scotland supporter, 16 June 1998, Bordeaux].*
>
> **Stott et al. (2001), p. 372.**

However, it should be caveated that when Scotland fans did experience contexts of intergroup illegitimacy they too displayed evidence of similar shifts toward seeing conflict as both appropriate and normative for their category as a whole. The study therefore provided evidence as to how perceptions of outgroup legitimacy could make nonconflictual people within the crowd more influential in a potentially volatile situation, subsequently disempowering those who actively sought conflict, and vice versa in situations of perceived outgroup illegitimacy. Thus, it became evident that the ESIM could "account not only for the presence, but also the absence, of collective 'disorder'" (Stott et al., 2001, p. 359).

Euro 2000: High and low-profile policing

Having developed a theory and evidence-based approach to understanding collective violence in this context, the research work moved on to try to use this knowledge to inform and address police psychology and action. This "action research"—oriented approach was in part made possible by a structured observational analysis of crowd behavior conducted during the UEFA European Football Championships in Belgium and the Netherlands in 2000 (Euro, 2000), which offered an opportunity to compare the effect of contrasting policing styles upon supporters as they moved between cities (Adang & Cuvelier, 2001). The study identified two different styles of policing employed across the eight different host cities. According to the observational data collected, they suggested that a "friendly but firm" or *low-profile* policing approach was used in five cities, while a more *high-profile* style was recorded in the other three. The study defined the contrast between the two styles in terms of the relative distance from, visibility of riot uniforms to and levels of verbal contact with supporters. In high-profile cities police tended to maintain greater distance from the supporters, appear more often and in greater numbers in riot gear and demonstrated lower levels of friendly informal interactions with crowds, whereas in low-profile cities the patterns were reversed (Adang & Cuvelier, 2001).

Their quantitative structured observational data showed that for matches categorized by the authorities as *low risk*, high-profile cities tended to be characterized by three times as many visible police officers deployed onto the streets than in the low-profile cities (an average of 30 officers per 100 fans vs. 10 officers per 100 fans, respectively). In high-profile cities, riot police were also more visible (one out of five samples vs. one out of ten samples) as were police riot vehicles (62% vs. 42% of samples). For matches judged by the authorities to pose an increased risk, these ratios roughly trebled such that in high-profile cities the average number of officers increased to 90 per 100 fans present but only to 30 per 100 in the low-profile cities (Adang & Cuvelier, 2001, p. 62). Perhaps most interestingly, their study was also able to detect a clear relationship between the different styles of policing and the number of violent incidents; for fixtures categorized as high risk there was no detectable difference between observed levels of disorder and the police profile. In other words, in high-risk scenarios trebling the visible presence of police officers had no measurable impact upon the levels of disorder. However, the study also observed that the highest levels of disorder occurred surrounding fixtures classified as low risk by the authorities but where high-profile policing had been deployed. Thus, in low-risk scenarios, low-profile policing was not only associated with better outcomes, high-profile policing was either less effective or actually exacerbated problems.

These findings provide clear empirical support for the benefit of a low-profile policing approach. It is interesting to note that all of the low-profile cities were located in the Netherlands, whereas the high-profile cities were mostly in Belgium. When these two different policing styles are contrasted with the arrest figures for England fans during the tournament, there is also a radical difference: only 6 were arrested in the Netherlands compared with 965 in Belgium (Stott & Pearson, 2007, p. 146).

Further research suggested these stark differences were again linked to police psychological perspectives in that the Belgian police had expected England fans to be either potential hooligans or very likely to engage in disorder, thus they had policed them in a relatively uniform manner, treating all supporters as potentially dangerous and volatile and confronting fans for merely engaging in otherwise peaceful normative expressions of their football fan identity. Stott (2003) conducted a questionnaire survey of Belgian Gendarmerie officers that was used to explore their psychology toward England fans as a social category. With over 8000 officers deployed in Belgium alone, one of the primary influences on the social context into which England fans arrived was the Gendarmerie (Stott, 2003).

 The survey data suggested that the majority of the supporters attending the championships were not thought to pose any major level of threat to public order. Nonetheless, the survey identified that the fan groups of Turkey, Germany, and England were all perceived to pose significantly higher levels of threat than the fans of any other nations attending the tournament. Moreover, fixtures involving England were seen by the officers to pose the highest likelihood of disorder. The survey also suggested that these Gendarmerie expected that in the context of the tournament around two-thirds of England fans would ultimately become involved in violent disorder at some point and that roughly one in two of them were expected to be hooligans actively seeking to incite it. Perhaps it is unsurprising then that there was particularly clear consensus among these officers that there was going to be disorder surrounding the match between England and Germany when they played each other in the city of Charleroi.

When asked to describe England fans, the police consensus was that they were volatile, dangerous, and aggressive. Moreover, over one-third of England fans were expected to become violent when consuming alcohol, who, when gathering in large boisterous groups, were likely to pose a significantly higher threat to public order and be seen as significantly more intimidating to the general public than the supporters of other teams. Any boisterous activity involving England fans was seen as significant evidence of the presence of hooligans, more so than if those groups were say German or Romanian, for example. When asked about the cause of disorder with England supporters, provocation by German supporters and organized hooligan conspiracies were seen as relevant causal factors. However, the mere presence of English hooligans and heavy alcohol consumption were given the strongest mean likelihood ratings. There was also agreement that boisterous groups of England fans required strict forms of policing, with early forceful intervention essential.

The fact that the questionnaires were distributed after the events does limit the extent to which we can view officers' responses as a genuine representation of their previously held expectations. Some responses could have been influenced by events and may be more representative of postevent justifications or what Waddington calls *postriot ideology* (Waddington, 1991, p. 234; see also Stott, 2016b). But none the less this study does add further support for the idea that the police perception had implications because it led them to interpret otherwise peaceful supporters as potentially problematic and to police them accordingly.

Application Euro 2004—changing police psychology of the crowd

Reicher, Stott, Cronin, and Adang (2004) postulate that the success of the low-profile strategy was down to a number of factors that can be summarized as a set of principles, based on all the ESIM research discussed so far, Reicher et al. (2004) advocated a new approach to policing crowds which reconceptualized the approach as one of crowd management rather than crowd control. The new approach consisted of four conflict reducing principals:

- Education
  - Officers should learn about the social identities present within the crowd and be aware of their sensitivities and behavioral norms.
- Facilitation

> — The policing of crowds must be orientated toward facilitating the legitimate intentions of those present.
- Communication
  > — Officers must communicate with crowd participants throughout the event.
- Differentiation
  > — If police intervention does become necessary, then it must be correctly targeted at those causing trouble and not the whole crowd.

These principles raise important questions about how such theoretical strategic intentions can be tactically implemented by police practitioners. Hoggett and Stott (2012) argue that the most compelling example of their successful implementation can be found in the policing operation for fans attending the UEFA European Football Championships in Portugal in 2004 (Euro, 2004). Consistent with Adang and Stott (2004), the *Polícia de Segurança Pública* (PSP) decided to innovate and develop a low-profile policing model based on current scientific research and theory. Instead of policing in a manner influenced by the hooligan model that was characteristic of previous tournaments, the PSP embraced a theory-led approach in which a model of dynamic risk assessment was coupled with a graded tactical approach (Reicher et al., 2004, 2007; Stott & Pearson, 2007, p. 218; Stott, Adang, Livingstone, & Schreiber, 2007, 2008).

Along with a program of research led by the second author, ESIM was used to create a graded model of tactical intervention that focused initially on officers in normal uniform focused on facilitation and communication. This enabled police to establish and maintain a proportionate police presence that reflected the current behavior of the members of the crowd. It also allowed police to undertake ongoing dynamic risk assessments monitoring for and gathering information on the presence or absence of any threats to public order posed by individuals or small groups. Such tactics would allow for the early identification of emerging tensions, which, if necessary, could be dealt with by larger squads of police. This would increase the likelihood that if police use of force was necessary, it would be differentiated and proportionate while also fostering a sense of police legitimacy within the fan groups. Moreover, where such legitimacy was perceived it was predicted that fans would tend to enforce the maintenance of nonviolent norms (i.e., they would "self-police") (Stott & Pearson, 2007, p. 218).

In order to evaluate the success of this theory-led approach, both qualitative (Stott, Adang, Livingstone & Schrieber, 2007) and quantitative (Stott, Adang, Livingstone & Schrieber, 2008) data were gathered during the tournament. Using an ethnographic semistructured observational framework, Stott et al. (2007) constructed a consensual account of police deployment and the subsequent behavioral norms of England fans during match days in areas under the jurisdiction of the PSP. This was then contrasted to data collected in Albufeira, an area under the jurisdiction of the Portuguese Gendarmerie force, the *Guarda Nacional Republicana* (GNR) which had jurisdiction over Portugal's rural areas and smaller towns. In contrast to the PSP, the GNR approach relied on the use of high-profile police deployments similar to that seen in Belgium in Euro (2000). These observational accounts were then supplemented by phenomenological analysis of fan data collected from England supporters which was used to explore the evolving content of their social identity and its relationship to the surrounding social contexts.

Three key incidents were observed by the research team in areas under the jurisdiction of the PSP which highlighted the success of their approach in avoiding collective disorder. In all three incidents it was evident that some fans began to instigate conflict. However, rather than leading to more widespread disorder, these attempts were undermined; in the first two cases by England fans who effectively self-policed, and in the third by a proportionate and specifically targeted police intervention. The study highlights how the ESIM-informed tactics employed by the PSP helped them to avoid the undifferentiated use of force against large crowds, which earlier studies had pinpointed as being pivotal in initiating and escalating crowd conflict. Stott and colleagues argue that within those "cities a form of England fan identity was apparent that was defined in terms of 'non-violent' football fandom, similarity with fans of other nations and positive social relations with the police" (Stott et al., 2007, p. 91). They go on to suggest that it was this context of legitimate intergroup relations, created and facilitated by the low-profile approach that meant attempts by confrontational groups to influence the wider England fan base toward conflict failed. To put it simply, those fans attempting to create confrontation and violence were disempowered by a widespread perception of legitimate policing. Speaking to the success of the policing approach, in areas under the PSP's jurisdiction there were no major incidents of collective conflict. As one England fan described it:

> *All the fans were policed very well, it was obvious they had done their homework, were not out to cause rather to deter trouble, unlike certain other forces, Belgium and Slovakia, to name but two. They had learnt from the way that the Dutch [Police] worked so well in Euro (2000) and should be commended ... if only we could experience it wherever we went in Europe. (Post-tournament email survey, RH).*
>
> **Stott et al. (2007), p. 87**

Perhaps unsurprisingly, where collective conflict did emerge, it did so in areas controlled by the GNR. Despite not hosting an England match, two riots involving England fans occurred in the coastal resort of Albufeira, in the southern Algarve region of Portugal. The events were characterized by an escalation of conflict against the GNR, with initially peaceful fans being drawn into the concurrent escalation of relatively undifferentiated coercive police intervention. In contrast to the match cities, the shared social identity evident among England fans in Albufeira was defined in terms of the inappropriateness or illegitimacy of police action (Stott et al., 2007, p. 91).

In addition, Stott, Adang, Livingstone, and Schreiber (2008) conducted a quantitative analysis of policing at Euro 2004. Consistent with the approach used by Adang and Cuvelier (2001) at Euro 2000, a program of structured observations was undertaken in order to assess the overall pattern of policing and the effect on supporters across all of the tournament venues. This was supplemented by a survey-based study of England fans' perceptions of policing prior to and after the tournament. The study showed that across all observed fixtures around 56% of samples saw a visible police presence during crowd events. Of those samples there was an average of 5.5 officers per 100 fans. The pattern differed for matches considered normal risk as opposed to increased risk, with an average of 4.5 officers and 6.9 officers per 100 fans, respectively. In all the samples collected none observed police officers in full riot gear. This reflected the genuinely low visibility of riot police across the entire tournament. Most interestingly, across a total of 1896 observational samples taken (997 samples from seven normal risk matches and 899 samples from seven increased risk matches), only 0.4% samples record an incident of disorder, all of which were rated as small by the observers. This statistic is highly significant when compared with the 10% rate of disorder recorded in the 664 samples taken at Euro 2000. Stott et al. (2008) also demonstrate interesting psychological transformations among fans. In particular, when England fans traveled to the tournament they perceived a lack of similarity between fans and the police. However, after experiencing legitimate policing during of the tournament, when measured again these fans now saw themselves as very similar to police. In other words, the experience had transformed what had previously been a hostile and polarized relationship between fans and police into one where fans effectively identified with the police.

The challenge of change

The success of the Euro 2004 tournament in terms of the absence of collective disorder among fans is now widely acknowledged in policy circles throughout Europe (Stott & Pearson, 2007, p. 218). However, we use it here to explore Tank Waddington's earlier propositions regarding the importance of police psychology. Our research suggests police psychology of the crowd is often (mis)informed by classical theory, which as a result leads to fundamental misunderstanding, poor police decision-making, and action toward crowds that are counterproductive. Indeed, as we have asserted such perspectives are not just wrong, they are dangerous because they can act as a kind of self-fulfilling prophecy. We have gone on to reinforce these contentions about the centrality of police psychology by showing what can happen when you change it. Through an extended program of action-oriented research the psychological perspectives of the police were transformed by being informed about the importance of intergroup and social identity dynamics. With this perspective and knowledge in place the PSP in Portugal developed a highly sophisticated and successful policing approach, both at the strategic and tactical level. Our research at the tournament allowed us to understand that it was effective because it was capable of managing crowd dynamics in ways that avoided the mistakes of the past and enabled the tournament to pass off without any incidents of widespread rioting, except in those areas controlled by the GNR whose psychological perspectives and actions had not been informed by ESIM theory.

Evidence of this important relationship between police psychology and crowd dynamics is also evident in the policing of football fans in the United Kingdom. In 2002, Cardiff City Football Club (CCFC) had the highest number of arrests and football banning orders of any club in England and Wales (Stott, Hoggett & Pearson, 2012), and the longstanding reputation of their fans for collective violence meant they were seen as highly problematic for the authorities. Nonetheless, following two serious incidents of disorder with hundreds of CCFC fans, in May 2001 and January 2002 respectively, South Wales Police (SWP) came to understand that their then current model was according to a Chief Superintendent in the force "a real failure in policing" (Stott et al., 2012, p. 387). As a result, SWP decided to develop a multistakeholder initiative designed to try to address the underlying problems. Working with CCFC, the fans and the local authorities, a series of reforms were initiated. Shortly after these changes began to be implemented, Stott and colleagues (2012) began a longitudinal 3-year ethnographic study of the policing and collective action of CCFC fans between 2005 and 2008. Their analysis suggests that one of the most important changes was a move by the police away from a reliance on a deterrence model toward one which focused more on dialogue and facilitation. As one club official put it:

> *[Previously] There was no contact, no dialogue, there was nothing. Then they [the police] stopped that. They started talking to fans and … the [police] would interact with the fans, go to the fans meetings, the fans then thought "we know why they [the police] are here now they are not here to beat us up, there not here to bludgeon us, there here for a reason", and the fans reacted accordingly.*
>
> **Stott et al. (2012), p. 387.**

Thus, as we have seen elsewhere, changes in police understanding led to changes in police action over time. In this case, these reforms began to impact upon the intergroup context which led to increasing levels of shared perceived police legitimacy among fans. Stott et al. (2012) argue that this in turn appears to have fed into changes in the intragroup dynamics among a previously "radicalized" community of football fans, empowering a culture of self-regulation and disempowering so called hooligans. The dramatic changes in normative fan behavior, meant that within two seasons, major incidents of disorder had all but disappeared when Cardiff played at their home stadium which allowed the police to reduce the cost of policing games by approximately 50%. As one police commander put it:

> *This time four years ago, we'd have been policing this game with what, 6–8 PSUs[3] and here we are doing it with three tomorrow. It [the dialogue approach] is a win win, the club are saving money because they are not paying for the same number of officers at games and we're saving, with the overall wider community of South Wales also benefiting as there's less officers being subtracted from their*

---

[3] The number of officers in a PSU is 25.

communities to police the football. What I can't understand is why my colleagues
around the country are perhaps not taking the same view. SWP, C. Supt, 01
Stott et al. (2012), p. 388

As the statement above points out, despite a growing body of theory, research, and evidence, the UK police appear to have resisted attempts to update their own doctrines on public order policing. In other words, even in light of the knowledge made available to the police, practices simply remained the same. For example, in 2009 the national training for police public order commanders in the United Kingdom was using classical theory to (mis)inform trainees about the underlying dynamics of crowds. It was not until a member of the public was killed as a result of police use of force during the dispersal of a protest in Central London that year that this situation changed. Subsequently, a national inquiry into the policing of the G20 grew into a national review of public order policing (HMIC, 2009). Drawing upon the research discussed above, one of the core recommendations of that report was that classical theory should be rejected and ESIM theory should form the conceptual basis for public order policing in the UK. A second recommendation was that police should advance their capacity for communication and dialogue during crowd events. As a result, new units of officers called Police Liaison Teams (PLTs) were developed. These units were designed to promote dialogue with those in the crowd and rapidly began producing positive outcomes that have seen them spread across the UK in terms of the policing of protest. It has been argued that PLTs at protest events "allowed for an improved capacity for proactive public order management, encouraged 'self-regulation' in the crowd, and avoided the unnecessary police use of force at moments of tension" (Gorringe, Stott, & Rosie, 2012, p. 111).

However, once again, a conservatism toward reform in the police is evident. Hoggett and West (2018) note growing recognition that the way in which football in the UK is policed needs to change in line with those witnessed toward protests. However, despite the evidence of the success of PLTs in reducing intergroup tensions at protests (Gorringe et al., 2012) there is still a significant resistance to the adoption of PLTs within the policing of football in the UK (Hoggett & West, 2018; Stott, West & Radburn, 2018). During field work on the use of PLTs at football among the few forces willing to innovate in this direction, Stott, Havelund, and Williams (2018) noted that officers "openly expressed their view that PLT did not have a place in policing football" (p. 12). However, the irony of this should be emphasized. A lot of the ESIM research which has informed the creation of PLTs was conducted at football crowd events, so to question the appropriateness of their use in football seems illogical.

It is widely understood that most police practices are shaped by local customs, opinions, theories, and subjective impressions, and that on the whole the police have not shown an enthusiasm for evidence-based reform (cf. Sherman, 1998). Hoggett and Stott (2012) suggest that it is not the actual nature nor the availability of evidence that acts as a barrier to public order policing reform. Instead, it is the nature of the police organization itself combined with an often apparent inability of academia to find a successful way to work together with the police. Canter (2008) highlighted this issue with regards to police and academic cooperation, suggesting that both parties perceive themselves as the one-eyed king in the kingdom of the blind. But once again, perhaps there are lessons to be learned from work on crowds. In order to counter this problem, Hoggett and Stott (2012) suggest that "policing it-self needs to generate the capacity for knowledge development" (p. 180) by working with social scientists in a framework of knowledge coproduction whereby trust and communication are improved. This idea was reinforced by the work of Kalyal (2019) in Canada on resistance to evidence-based practice (EBP) in the Canadian police. After conducting an in-depth interview study with executive level police officers and members of police research organizations, Kalyal (2019) concluded by empha-sizing the importance of "maintaining effective communication within and outside the organisation … [in order to] reduce misconceptions that prevent EBP from tak-ing root in police organisations" (p. 12).

It is this partnership and knowledge coproduction approach that has underpinned the most recent studies of dialogue and facilitation-based policing approaches to do-mestic football in both the UK and Sweden. Specifically, a project called Enabling an Evidence-Based Approach to the Policing of Football (ENABLE) has been devel-oped that adopts a Participant Action Research approach that includes police officers as genuine stakeholders in the research teams. The several studies derived from ENABLE projects in Sweden (cf. Stott, Havelund, & Williams, 2018), the UK (cf. Stott, Pearson, & West, 2018), and Switzerland (cf. Brechbühl, 2018), have all added further evidence of the value of an ESIM-led "dialogue and facilitation" approach. However, these studies also highlight the issue of hostility that dialogue officers face from within their own organizations. The language used by these offi-cers' colleagues to describe them as the "hugging police" (Stott et al., 2016) or "pink and fluffy" (Stott, 2016a) is just one example that speaks to the nature of their rela-tionship with the police organization and its "canteen culture" (cf. Waddington, 1999), which resonates with the broader issues of the resistance to change in the po-lice service at large (College of Policing, 2015).

Hoggett and West (2018), when analyzing a trial deployment of PLTs at football by the West Midlands Police also draw attention to what Cronin and Reicher (2006, 2009) referred to as the *accountability dynamics* of policing public order. Cronin and Reicher (2006, 2009) had earlier highlighted the impact that these accountability dy-namics played within all levels of the police organization, especially in com-manders' decision-making processes during both tabletop public order practice exercises and actual operations. The commanders' ability to run public order oper-ations was constrained by the accountability demands of a broad range of audiences, both within (junior officers, senior officers, potential internal inquiries) and outside the police (e.g., local communities, local and national politicians, media) who often placed very different demands upon them (Cronin & Reicher, 2009, p. 239). In ef-fect, as the operations developed decision-making by commanders was driven as much by the consequences of their actions among their colleagues and political mas-ters as it was about actually preventing disorder.

Moreover, it was suggested that at different points in the police organizational hierarchy these accountability demands differed and this in itself created a certain amount of intragroup tension. For example, the senior officers appeared far more concerned with the accountability they held of external audiences, such as the public and the press than was the case for junior officers. Commanders even iterated the idea of *acceptable damage* in that junior officers had to sustain a level of injury necessary for outside audiences to see that police officers were reacting to crowd violence rather than provoking it. Whereas, for junior officers, there was no amount of acceptable damage and the idea that commanders were exposing them to it simply to protect their own position was intolerable. Cronin and Reicher's analysis showed that over the course of an operation, senior officers would prioritize the audiences that wield the most power over them and their organization at different times depending upon the contingency. Thus, we would argue that the resistance to change is perhaps because change often means going against the institutional orthodoxy and therefore exposing innovative commanders to risk.

Conclusions

In this chapter, we have set out to demonstrate that when it comes to crowds, police psychology matters. As we have sought to evidence throughout, when a classical psychological perspective underpins the policing or reactive control of crowds, then the violence which police fear and seek to prevent can ironically become a self-fulfilling prophecy. However, as we have shown with our earlier discussion, when the police inform their psychology and practice to proactively manage crowds from a social identity perspective this can help to undermine such conflictual dynamics. It is important to stress, however, that we are not seeking to position this approach as a *panacea*. What ESIM-based policing approaches can achieve is a reduction in the probability of disorder escalating, enabling the police to act quickly to problem solve and de-escalate conflictual situations before they can become widespread. This corresponds with the plethora of other potential benefits that can flow from this ESIM-led approach, such as reduced policing costs, the ability to use the officers not drafted into public order to help police their local communities, or the long-term increased perceptions of police legitimacy within the community.

When discussing the challenge of change we have then sought to highlight how there is some complexity to the relationship between police psychology and action in the context of crowds. When it comes to managing crowds, police psychology is important. However, we must also note that understanding the police psychological perspectives of the crowd is just part of the issue; we must recognize the need to understand the organizational and political factors that drive police action. Just as Waddington (1991, 1994) recognized, police accountability and organizational responsibility is very important in this context. If we want a genuine understanding of the complexity of public order policing, we have to accept that there is a program of work that is needed to expand Waddington's initial proposition.

The one thing that we can state with confidence is that, just as one cannot fully understand the dynamics of crowd action if one regards the crowd as a single homogenous category (Drury & Reicher, 1999, 2000; Reicher, 2001, pp. 182–208) so one cannot understand the dynamics of crowd policing if one treats the police as homogenous and ignores intra-group disputes. (Cronin & Reicher, 2009, p. 251)

So, to conclude, certainly police psychology matters. However, in the case of policing crowds, psychology is not all that matters. If we are to fully understand the relationship between police and the policing of crowds, we must be cognizant that there is a need for interdisciplinarity to understand how this psychology and behavior is shaped, enabled, and constrained by its social and political context.

References

Adang, O., & Cuvelier, C. (2001). *Policing Euro 2000: International police co-operation, information management and police deployment.* Tandem Felix.

Adang, O., & Stott, C. (2004). *Preparing for Euro 2004: Policing international football matches in Portugal* (Unpublished report for the Portuguese Public Security Police).

Allport, F. H. (1924). The group fallacy in relation to social science. *American Journal of Sociology, 29*(6), 688–706.

Barrows, S. (1981). *Visions of the crowd in late nineteenth century France.* London: Yale (Yale University Press).

Brechbühl, A. (2018). Spielbericht FC Zürich – FC Basel *vom 13.05.2018.* Universitat Bern (Unpublished Report for Research Unit Violence at Sport Events Switzerland).

Canter, D. (2008). In the kingdom of the blind. In D. Canter, & R. Žukauskiene (Eds.), *Psychology and law bridging the gap.* London: Ashgate Publishing.

College of Policing. (2015). *Leadership review: Interim report, March.*

Council of Europe. (2010). *Council resolution of 3rd June 2010 concerning an updated handbook with recommendations for international police cooperation and measures to prevent and control violence and disturbances in connection with football matches with an international dimension, in which at least one Member State is involved.* Official Journal of the European Union, 2010/C 165/01. Available from: http://eur-lex.europa.eu/legal-content/EN/TXT/?uri= CELEX%3A32010G0624(01).

Cronin, P., & Reicher, S. (2006). A study of the factors that influence how senior officers police crowd events: On SIDE outside the laboratory. *British Journal of Social Psychology, 45*(1), 175–196.

Cronin, P., & Reicher, S. (2009). Accountability processes and group dynamics: A SIDE perspective on the policing of an anti-capitalist riot. *European Journal of Social Psychology, 39*(2), 237–254.

Drury, J., & Reicher, S. (1999). The intergroup dynamics of collective empowerment: Substantiating the social identity model of crowd behavior. *Group Processes & Intergroup Relations, 2*(4), 381–402.

Drury, J., & Reicher, S. (2000). Collective action and psychological change: The emergence of new social identities. *British Journal of Social Psychology, 39*(4), 579–604.

Drury, J., Stott, C., & Farsides, T. (2003). The role of police perceptions and practices in the development of "public disorder" 1, 2. *Journal of Applied Social Psychology, 33*(7), 1480–1500.

Dunning, E. (1994). Sport in space and time:" civilizing processes", trajectories of state-formation and the development of modern sport. *International Review for the Sociology of Sport, 29*(4), 331–345.

Dunning, E., Murphy, P., & Williams, J. (1988). The roots of football hooliganism. *An historical and sociological study.*

Elias, N., & Jephcott, E. (1978). *The civilizing process* (Vol. 1). Oxford: Blackwell.

Giulianotti, R. (1991). Scotland's tartan army in Italy: The case for the carnivalesque. *The Sociological Review, 39*(3), 503–527.

Giulianotti, R. (1994). Scoring away from home: A statistical study of Scotland football fans at international matches in Romania and Sweden. *International Review for the Sociology of Sport, 29*(2), 171–199.

Gorringe, H., Stott, C., & Rosie, M. (2012). Dialogue police, decision making, and the management of public order during protest crowd events. *Journal of Investigative Psychology and Offender Profiling, 9*(2), 111–125.

Her Majesty's Chief Inspectorate of Constabulary (HMIC). (2009). *Adapting to protest: Nurturing the British model of policing.* London: Central Office for Information.

Hoggett, J., & Stott, C. (2012). Post G20: The challenge of change, implementing evidence-based public order policing. *Journal of Investigative Psychology and Offender Profiling, 9*(2), 174–183.

Hoggett, J., & West, O. (2018). Police liaison officers at football: Challenging orthodoxy through communication and engagement. *Policing: Journal of Policy Practice.*

Hopkins, M. (2014). Ten seasons of the football banning order: Police officer narratives on the operation of banning orders and the impact on the behaviour of 'risk supporters'. *Policing and Society, 24*(3), 285–301.

Hopkins, M., & Hamilton-Smith, N. (2014). Football banning orders: The highly effective cornerstone of a preventive strategy. In M. Hopkins, & J. Treadwell (Eds.), *Football hooliganism, fan behaviour and crime: Contemporary issues* (pp. 222–248). Basingstoke: Plagrave.

James, M., & Pearson, G. (2015). Public order and the rebalancing of football fans' rights: Legal problems with pre- emptive policing strategies and banning orders. *Public Law,* (3), 458–475.

Kalyal, H. (2019). 'One person's evidence is another person's nonsense': Why police organizations resist evidence-based practices. *Policing: Journal of Policy Practice.*

Le Bon, G. (1960). *The crowd: A study of the popular mind. 1895.* Reprint. New York: Viking.

Milgram, S., & Toch, H. (1969). Collective behavior: Crowds and social movements. In G. Lindzey, D. Gilbert, & S. T. Fiske (Eds.), *The handbook of social psychology* (Vol. 4, pp. 507–610). Reading, MA: Addison Wesley.

Nye, R. (1975). *The origins of crowd psychology.* Beverly Hills, CA: SAGE.

Prati, G., & Pietrantoni, L. (2009). Elaborating the police perspective: The role of perceptions and experience in the explanation of crowd conflict. *European Journal of Social Psychology, 39*(6), 991–1001.

Reicher, S. D. (1982). The determination of collective behaviour. *Social Identity and Intergroup Relations,* 41–83.

Reicher, S. D. (1984). The St Pauls riot: An explanation of the limits of crowd action in terms of a social identity model. *European Journal of Social Psychology, 14,* 1–21.

Reicher, S. D. (1987). Crowd behaviour as social action. In J. C. Turner (Ed.), *Rediscovering the social group: A self categorisation theory* (pp. 171−202). Oxford: Basil Blackwell.

Reicher, S. D. (1996a). Social identity and social change: Rethinking the contexts of social psychology. In P. W. Robinson (Ed.), *Social groups and identities: Developing the legacy of Henri Tajfel* (pp. 317−336). Oxford: Butterworth-Heinemann.

Reicher, S. D. (1996b). 'The Battle of Westminster': Developing the social identity model of crowd behaviour in order to explain the initiation and development of collective conflict. *European Journal of Social Psychology, 26*, 115−134.

Reicher, S. D. (2001). *Crowds and social movements. Blackwell handbook of social psychology.* Group processes.

Reicher, S., & Levine, M. (1994a). Deindividuation, power relations between groups and the expression of social identity: The effects of visibility to the out-group. *British Journal of Social Psychology, 33*(2), 145−163.

Reicher, S., & Levine, M. (1994b). On the consequences of deindividuation manipulations for the strategic communication of self: Identifiability and the presentation of social identity. *European Journal of Social Psychology, 24*(4), 511−524.

Reicher, S., Stott, C., Cronin, P., & Adang, O. (2004). An integrated approach to crowd psychology and public order policing. *Policing: An International Journal of Police Strategies & Management, 27*(4), 558−572.

Reicher, S., Stott, C., Drury, J., Adang, O., Cronin, P., & Livingstone, A. (2007). Knowledge-based public order policing: Principles and practice. *Policing: Journal of Policy Practice, 14*, 403−415.

Sherman, L. W. (1998). *Evidence-based policing.* Washington, DC: Police Foundation.

Stott, C. (2003). Police expectations and the control of English soccer fans at "Euro 2000". *Policing: An International Journal of Police Strategies & Management, 26*(4), 640−655.

Stott, C. (2016a). *Independent review of the policing of football in Staffordshire.* Staffordshire PCC Football Response. Retrieved from https://staffordshire-pcc.gov.uk/wp-content/uploads/2016/06/Staffordshire-OPCC-Football-Policing-Review-2016-ABF-1.pdf.

Stott, C. (2016b). Revisiting the classics: Policing coercion and liberty: A review of PAJ Waddington's liberty and order (1994) and policing citizens (1999). *Policing and Society, 26*(1), 114−119.

Stott, C., Adang, O., Livingstone, A., & Schreiber, M. (2007). Variability in the collective behaviour of England fans at Euro 2004: 'Hooliganism', public order policing and social change. *European Journal of Social Psychology, 37*(1), 75−100.

Stott, C., Adang, O., Livingstone, A., & Schreiber, M. (2008). Tackling football hooliganism: A quantitative study of public order, policing and crowd psychology. *Psychology, Public Policy, and Law, 14*(2), 115.

Stott, C., & Drury, J. (2000). Crowds, context and identity: Dynamic categorization processes in the 'poll tax riot'. *Human Relations, 53*(2), 247−273.

Stott, C., & Drury, J. (2017). Contemporary understanding of riots: Classical crowd psychology, ideology and the social identity approach. *Public Understanding of Science, 26*(1), 2−14.

Stott, C., Drury, J., & Reicher, S. (2011). From prejudice to collective action. In J. Dixon, & M. Levine (Eds.), *Beyond prejudice: Extending the social psychology of conflict, inequality and social change* (pp. 286−303).

Stott, C., Hoggett, J., & Pearson, G. (2012). 'Keeping the peace' social identity, procedural justice and the policing of football crowds. *British Journal of Criminology, 52*(2), 381−399.

Stott, C., Havelund, J., Lundberg, F., Khan, S., Joern, L., Hogget, J., et al. (2016). *Policing football in Sweden: Enabling an evidence based approach.* Retrieved from http://enable-research.org/wp-content/uploads/2016/08/Policing-Football-in-Sweden-2016.pdf.

Stott, C., Havelund, J., & Williams, N. (2018). Policing football crowds in Sweden. *Journal of Scandinavian Studies in Criminology and Crime Prevention,* 1–19.

Stott, C., Hutchison, P., & Drury, J. (2001). 'Hooligans' abroad? Inter-group dynamics, social identity and participation in collective 'disorder' at the 1998 World Cup finals. *British Journal of Social Psychology, 40*(3), 359–384.

Stott, C., & Pearson, G. (2006). Football banning orders, proportionality, and public order policing. *The Howard Journal of Criminal Justice, 45*(3), 241–254.

Stott, C., & Pearson, G. (2007). *Football 'hooliganism': Policing and the war on the 'English disease'.* London: Pennant Books.

Stott, C., Pearson, G., & West, O. (2018). Enabling an evidence based approach to policing football in the UK. *Policing: An International Journal of Police Strategies & Management.*

Stott, C., & Reicher, S. (1998a). Crowd action as intergroup process: Introducing the police perspective. *European Journal of Social Psychology, 28*(4), 509–529.

Stott, C., & Reicher, S. (1998b). How conflict escalates: The inter-group dynamics of collective football crowd violence. *Sociology, 32*(2), 353–377.

Stott, C., West, O., & Radburn, M. (2018). Policing football 'risk'? A participant action research case study of a liaison-based approach to 'public order'. *Policing and Society, 28*(1), 1–16.

Turner, J. C., Hogg, M. A., Oakes, P. J., Reicher, S. D., & Wetherell, M. S. (1987). *Rediscovering the social group: A self-categorization theory.* Basil Blackwell.

Turner, J. C., Oakes, P. J., Haslam, S. A., & McGarty, C. (1994). Self and collective: Cognition and social context. *Personality and Social Psychology Bulletin, 20*(5), 454–463.

Waddington, P. A. J. (1991). *The strong arm of the law: Armed and public order policing.* Oxford University Press.

Waddington, P. A. J. (1994). *Liberty and order: Policing public order in a capital city.* London: University College London Press.

Waddington, P. A. J. (1999). Police (canteen) sub-culture. An appreciation. *British Journal of Criminology, 39*(2), 287–309.

Williams, J., Dunning, E., & Murphy, P. (1989). *Hooligans abroad* (2nd ed.). London: Routledge.

Zimbardo, P. G. (1969). The human choice: Individuation, reason, and order versus deindividuation, impulse, and chaos. In *Nebraska symposium on motivation.* University of Nebraska Press.

Improving police procedures for dealing with mental illness

Ronald Roesch and Ilvy Goossens

Introduction

This chapter will focus on the ways police agencies have responded to calls that involve individuals with mental health issues. Interactions between police and individuals with mental illness have been increasing over the past few decades. A disproportionate number of these encounters results in arrest, and this has contributed to a substantial increase of jail inmates with mental health issues. The reasons for this will be highlighted as well as efforts to train police to deal more effectively with individuals whose mental health issues may be a central feature of the police/citizen interaction.

It is of historical relevance to note that mental hospitals in the United States and Canada were created in large part due to reformers like Dorothea Dix who were concerned with the jail incarceration of individuals with mental illness. Dix and other social reformers in the mid-1800s were successful in getting some 15 US states and some provinces in Canada to construct mental hospitals, thus creating an alternative to jail for individuals with mental health issues. Over time, however, this initially positive event resulted in large facilities that tended to create a class of chronic mental patients who were isolated from their communities for years, often decades. Beginning in the 1960s, the movement that came to be known as deinstitutionalization focused on getting patients out of the hospital and back to the community. In addition, changes in civil commitment laws made involuntary commitment more difficult (Appelbaum, 1994). The result of these two forces was that mental hospitals, which had become an option for police to bring a person with mental health issues, were no longer possible. While the goals of deinstitutionalization were admirable, the reality was that the community mental health resources were not prepared and insufficiently funded to provide services to those in need in their communities (Ogloff & Roesch, 1992; Roesch & Golding, 1985). The inadequacy of community mental health services has likely improved in the past few decades, but it is notable that the 2009 report of the American Psychiatric Association's Task Force on Outpatient Forensic Services concluded that "The evidence is clear: too many mentally ill individuals are incarcerated, post-release treatment is inadequate, as evidenced by lack of follow up and poor outcomes, and recidivism rates are too high. We can only conclude that at-risk patients are not being

Police Psychology, Edited by Marques and Paulino. https://doi.org/10.1016/B978-0-12-816544-7.00009-7

served adequately in existing outpatient treatment programs" (Hoge, Buchanan, Kovasznay, & Roskes, 2009, p. 10).

Ironically, we may now have come full circle. Mental hospitals did serve as an alternative to jail but when mental hospitals closed or their populations drastically reduced, individuals with mental health concerns in the community often end up in jails (Roesch, 1995; Steadman, Osher, Robbins, Case, & Samuels, 2009). This phenomenon has been referred to as the criminalization of the mentally ill (Abramson, 1972; Teplin, 1984), although as Peterson, Skeem, Kennealy, Bray, and Zvonkovic (2014) have pointed out, only a small percentage of the crimes committed by individuals with mental illness are directly motivated by symptoms of mental illness. Teplin was one of the first to examine the criminalization hypothesis. In her 1983 review of the literature, she found support for the thereto intuited hypothesis that individuals with mental health concerns are being processed through the criminal justice, rather than mental health systems. In a subsequent study of 1382 recorded police encounters, Teplin (1984) found that individuals with mental health problems were significantly more likely to be arrested than citizens without mental health problems for similar offenses. One limitation of this study is that characterization of individuals with mental health problems was based on officer's perceptions rather than a formal diagnosis.

Research since Teplin's seminal research has questioned the criminalization hypothesis. For example, Engel and Silver (2001) analyzed two large datasets that allowed for an examination of other factors that might mitigate the relationship between mental illness and police decisions about arrest. This includes factors such as whether individuals with mental health issues are more likely to engage in dangerous or violent behavior, especially when using alcohol or drugs. Engel and Silver argue that these factors increase the risk of arrest for all citizens, independent of the presence of mental disorder. They found that when controlling for a wide range of relevant factors (e.g., using force, male gender, under influence of alcohol/drugs), individuals with mental health issues were not more likely to be arrested.

While the distinction made by Engel and Silver (2001) is an important one to recognize in understanding arrest rates, it is clear that there has been an increase in the number of contacts between police and individuals with mental health issues. Reuland and Cheney (2005) noted that police in New York City respond to a call involving persons with mental illness every 6.5 minutes. Research generally indicates that police interventions with persons with mental illness represent a relatively small percentage of police contacts, but police officers spend a disproportionate amount of time dealing with these contacts (Reuland, Schwarzfeld, & Draper, 2009). Charette, Crocker, and Billette (2011) reported that these interventions comprised 3% of 8485 police interventions in Montreal during their 3-day study period, but these interventions consumed twice as much time for arrests and over three times more time if hospitalization was the disposition option. In a subsequent study published in 2014, these same authors analyzed over 6000 police interventions and found that although individuals with mental illness were less frequently involved in serious offenses, these interventions were more likely to lead to arrest, compared with encounters with individuals without mental illness. They also documented that interventions involving individuals with mental illness used 87% more resources than for those required for the comparison group.

While deinstitutionalization and inadequate community mental health options are factors accounting for increases in police involvement in mental health crises situations, other factors are also at play. It is likely that the move toward community policing as well as homelessness have contributed to a rise in contacts between police and citizens with mental health issues (Adelman, 2003; Perlin & Lynch, 2016). Police officers are often placed in the role of gatekeepers as they must make decisions about whether to arrest an individual or refer them to the mental health system (Lamb, Weinberger, & DeCuir, 2014). The increase in police encounters with individuals with mental illness that has taken place since deinstitutionalization has resulted in a corresponding increase in the number of jail inmates with mental health concerns. In a 2012 Canadian Community Health Survey, 34.4% of Canadian citizens with a mental or substance use disorder self-reported police contact (Boyce, Rotenberg, & Karam, 2015, pp. 1–25). The Treatment Advocacy Center estimates that Americans with severe mental illness are three times as likely to be in jail than in a hospital (Moran, 2010), and they are more likely to be rearrested (Eno Louden & Skeem, 2012). A similar situation exists in many other countries (Blaauw, Roesch, & Kerkhof, 2000; Corrado, Cohen, Hart, & Roesch, 2000), making mental health issues in prisons and jails a global health concern (Fazel & Danesh, 2002; Fazel & Seewald, 2012). In the North American context, an estimated 6%–14% of prisoners, far surpassing the community average, have a serious mental illness (i.e., major depression, bipolar disorder, schizophrenia, schizoaffective disorder, psychotic disorder) (Prins, 2011). While there is evidence of the iatrogenic effect of imprisonment itself (e.g., Fazel, Grann, Kling, & Hawton, 2011), many individuals enter correctional services with preexisting mental health concerns (e.g., Martin, Dorken, Wamboldt, & Wooten, 2012). This points to a systemic trend toward overincarceration of mental illness—for which police involvement is the first point of contact (Munetz & Griffin, 2006).

Although both police and the general public may have the view that there is a strong relationship between mental illness and violence (Watson, Corrigan, & Ottati, 2004), it is important to keep in mind that persons with mental illness are not typically violent or a threat to the community. Research shows that people with mental illness are somewhat more likely to be violent but the substantial majority are not violent (see Swanson, McGinty, Fazel, & Mays, 2015 for a review), although it should be noted that the co-occurrence of a substance abuse disorder or homelessness can increase the risk for violence (Elbogen & Johnson, 2009; Steadman et al., 1998). Individuals with mental health issues may be at a greater risk for being victims of violence. In one of the largest studies to date ($N = 4480$), Desmarais, Van Dorn et al., 2014 found that individuals with mental illness are more likely to be victims than perpetrators of violence. In their study, approximately one in four individuals with mental illness reporting committed violence—most of which was perpetrated in a residential treatment facility—and one in three individuals reported being victimized.

Public perceptions of the police

In a Canadian study, Desmarais, Livingston et al., 2014 focused on the perceptions of the police held by individuals with mental health issues. They conducted a survey of 244 participants who met the inclusion criteria of a current diagnosis of schizophrenia, schizoaffective disorder, delusional disorder, bipolar disorder, or other psychotic disorder, were aged 19–75 years, and spoke and understood English. They compared their responses with a national sample of Canadians' personal experiences of crime and perceptions of the criminal justice system. They matched the national survey participants to their sample by age, sex minority status, education, income, and geographic location. They found that their sample, compared with the national sample, had a significantly higher number of police contacts, were more likely to be perpetrators but also victims of crime, and gave police high ratings for promptly responding to calls but the lowest ratings for treating people fairly. Overall, the study found that ratings of confidence in the police and evaluations of their performance were lower among study participants compared with the sample drawn from the national survey. The authors concluded that the differences between the groups point to the need to improve the ways in which police interact with individuals with mental health issues. It is important to note that this study did not include jurisdictions in which Crisis Intervention Training (CIT), which will be discussed later in this chapter, has been implemented. Since one of the goals of CIT is to improve these interactions, it would be of interest to replicate this study in communities with and without officers trained in CIT.

The experience of citizens with mental illness of a prior police interaction, rather than mere contact, may affect behavior during subsequent interactions (for a review, see Desmarais, Livingston et al., 2014; Desmarais, Van Dorn et al., 2014). Regardless of outcome (e.g., arrest vs. warning), the appraisal of these interactions is shaped by the view of being treated justly and fairly; this is known as perceived *procedural justice* (Tyler & Fagan, 2008). Examining 139 people suffering from mental illness with lived experience with police, Watson and Angell (2013) found that greater perceived procedural justice led to decreased resistance and increased police cooperation. There have been only a few studies that have attempted to extrapolate factors negatively associated with perceived procedural justice (Livingston et al., 2014; Watson & Angell, 2013; Watson, Angell, Vidalon, & Davis, 2010), perceived coercion (e.g., threats, physical force), experiencing mental health crisis, apprehension/arrest, and negative pressure from officers seem to be more important than individual factors (e.g., sociodemographics, homelessness, substance use). While there is a trend in the literature to describe the overall positive experience of police interaction (e.g., Boyce et al., 2015; Livingston et al. 2014), it is worth noting that persons with mental illness tend to have a somewhat poorer *expectation* of police contact (e.g., Desmarais, Livingston et al., 2014; Desmarais, Van Dorn et al., 2014; Thompson & Kahn, 2016; Watson, Angell, Morabito, & Robinson, 2008). Highlighting, once again, the importance of police interaction, Watson et al. (2008) conclude that while persons with mental illness "feel vulnerable and fearful of police ... the way police treated them mattered" (p. 449).

Use of force

Most police-citizen interactions do not result in the use of force or in injuries to either police or members of the public. For example, Kerr, Morabito, and Watson (2010) conducted a study of police officer encounters with individuals with mental illness in four Chicago Police Department districts. They found that the number of injuries sustained by either police or citizens was quite small, with the majority of most injuries being mild and not requiring any medical care. However, while most situations are resolved uneventfully, people with mental illness do seem to be overrepresented in police fatalities and use-of-force incidents (Fuller, Lamb, Biasotti, & Snook, 2015; Morabito & Socia, 2015). An estimated one in four police fatalities in the United States involve a person with mental illness; making persons with mental illness 16 times more likely to be shot by police than others interaction with police (Fuller et al., 2015). Similarly, a large-scale Australian study of use-of-force incidents ($N = 4267$) in Victoria indicated that more than one in three people on whom the police used force suffered from a mental disorder (Kesic, Thomas, & Ogloff, 2013). Examining potential moderators of this risk, Morabito and Socia (2015) studied all "use-of-force" reports from Portland police (2008−11), 11.5% of which involved mentally ill suspects. Of these, 12% resulted in officer injury and 28% resulted in suspect injury, compared with 7% and 18% in encounters with nonmentally ill suspects. Study results indicated that substance use increased the likelihood of injury for suspects (up to 65% increase) and police officers (up to 13% increase), respectively (Morabito & Socia, 2015). Notably, use-of-force incidents with suspects with mental illness were more likely to involve resistance compared with suspects without mental illness (74% and 47%, respectively).

Some of these violent encounters may be due to intentional behavior by the individual with the goal of being killed by a police officer. This phenomenon is known as *suicide by cop* (Lord, 2004; McKenzie, 2006). Mohandie, Meloy, and Collins (2009) conducted a national US study of over 700 officer-involved shootings and found that more than one-third were the result of suicide by cop. These cases were likely to have a high incidence of weapon possession by the victim, with most of these involving a firearm. The authors also noted that about 20% simulated weapon possession in order to accomplish their suicidal intent. The CIT discussed elsewhere in this chapter is certainly helpful in providing police with skills to handle these situations without the use of lethal force. Another training option is providing police officers with simulated experiences in these situations. In Canada, for example, most police agencies train officers with use-of-force simulators, which use life-size screens to project different scenarios likely to be encountered by officers (Bennell, Jones, & Corey, 2007). This format can include scenarios involving individuals with mental health issues, including incidents involving attempts at suicide by cop. The training allows officers to respond to scenarios depicting various levels of threat in real time. Feedback on their performance is provided, with discussion of their decision-making and how they might have handled the situation differently.

Johnson (2011) examined whether police were more likely to use force in encounters with citizens with mental health issues, compared with citizens without any mental health issues. He found that police were more likely to use force with the former group, but also noted that this group was also more likely to act violently, resist the police, and possess a weapon. He added that after these behaviors were controlled for statistically, there were no differences for the use of force between the two groups.

Compton et al. (2014b) examined use of force by officers with and without CIT in a sample of encounters with individuals who may have had a serious mental illness, a substance abuse problem, or a developmental disability. A total of 180 officers approximately evenly split between those with and without training were involved in over 1000 encounters with individuals described as having behavioral disorders. Some degree of force was used in 97 of 406 encounters by trained officers, compared with 126 of 406 encounters by nontrained officers. The researchers found that although CIT training was not predictive of level of force, CIT-trained officers were more likely to report verbal engagement or negotiation as the highest level of force they used. They were also less likely to use arrest, particularly when physical force was used, as they were more often relied on referral or transport to mental health services as an alternative to arrest.

Police training
Memphis model

Although it is evident that the increased police contact with individuals with mental illness is a systemic issue, various police departments have taken it upon themselves to develop specific training and response models to better respond to mental health–related calls. The predominant model for training police to optimize interactions with individuals with mental illness is CIT. The first and best-researched program to develop this approach was in Memphis, Tennessee. The Crisis Intervention Team, often referred to as the Memphis Model, is regarded as the prototype for the several thousand communities that have since implemented it (Compton, Bahora, Watson, & Oliva, 2008), although there is considerable variability in how the program is structured and delivered in different communities (Cross et al., 2014). The Memphis program was developed in 1988 by Randolph Dupont, a psychiatrist at the University of Tennessee, and Major Sam Cochran of the Memphis Police Department, after a man with a history of mental health and substance abuse issues was fatally shot by Memphis police. The goal of CIT is to improve police response to citizens with mental health issues, to increase safety of both police officers and citizens, and to increase the use of community alternatives to arrest (Dupont & Cochran, 2000).

In the original program, police officers were provided with 40 h of classroom lectures as well as experiential de-escalation training in handling interactions with individuals dealing with mental health crises. Officers either volunteer or less frequently are assigned to receive this training. Once trained, shifts are scheduled so that at least one trained officer is available to respond to calls that may involve an individual with a mental health crisis. The goal of a CIT program is to have about 20%–25% of police officers completing the CIT training.

The curriculum includes lectures on such topics as clinical issues related to mental illnesses, medications and side effects, alcohol and drug assessment, co-occurring disorders, developmental disabilities, family/consumer perspective, suicide prevention, civil commitment, personality disorders, posttraumatic stress disorders (Dupont, Cochran, & Pillsbury, 2007). Scenario-based skill training is also included to gain skills in de-escalation. Police dispatchers are separately trained on how to receive and dispatch calls involving individuals with mental illness and crisis situations.

An essential component of the Memphis Model is the involvement of the community (Dupont et al., 2007). The Memphis program solicited participation from consumers/individuals with a mental illness, family members who had first-hand knowledge and experience in dealing with mental illness in their families, and groups such as the National Alliance on Mental Illness and the National Mental Health Association that advocate for issues regarding mental illness and aim to improve the quality of life of individuals impacted by mental illness. The program relies on the mental health community to provide training and ongoing support to police officers. These include psychologists, psychiatrists, physicians, social workers, counselors, pastoral counselors, alcohol/drug counselors, educators, trainers, and criminologists. Most of these professionals provide training voluntarily as a means of keeping down the costs of CIT training.

Another aspect of the CIT model is to designate an emergency mental health receiving facility, to provide an alternative to arrest (Dupont et al., 2007). The facility ensures a minimal turnaround for officers and needs to have access to a range of emergency mental health and general health options, including alcohol and drug emergency services.

In addition to the basic 40-hour training program, CIT also follows up with regular sessions to further enhance skills. This includes extended/advanced suicide CIT, advanced developmental disabilities, new developments in psychiatric medications, advanced verbal skill training (crisis hotline), and advanced scenario training (Dupont et al., 2007).

The Memphis Model recommends ongoing evaluation and research to measure the impact of CIT programs. One study examined differences between officers who volunteered for CIT training with those who were assigned (Compton, Bakeman, Broussard, D'Orio, & Watson, 2017). The authors noted that CIT officers in general were more likely to be female and had prior experience in the mental health field. The authors followed up with officers 2 years after their training and found that volunteer officers held significantly different opinions and attitudes about mental illness. Specifically, they showed greater self-efficacy, better de-escalation skills, and made better referral decisions. An interesting finding was that even when physical force was used, the volunteer officers were more likely to refer to community treatment programs and less likely to make an arrest. The authors concluded that law enforcement agencies should consider providing mental health response training to all officers but limit the CIT training to officers who volunteer for it.

Compton et al. (2014a) compared officers with and without CIT training on their knowledge and attitudes about serious mental illness, and how effective they felt about deescalating crisis situations and making referrals to mental health services. In a total sample of nearly 600 officers in six police departments in Georgia (the United States), they found that CIT-trained officers had better scores on measures of knowledge about mental illnesses and their treatments, felt higher levels of self-efficacy in interacting with individuals with psychosis or who might be suicidal, exhibited less stigma about mental illness, and scored higher on de-escalation skills and referral decision-making. Bonfine, Ritter, and Munetz (2014) were also interested in the impact that CIT had on officers' attitudes and their confidence in their ability to deal with situations involving a mental health crisis. The researchers conducted a survey of 57 officers who had completed CIT training in an Ohio community. They found that the officers viewed CIT positively, that it was perceived to have an impact on personal and community safety. They also reported feeling more confident in their abilities because the knowledge and skills taught in CIT made them better prepared to respond to mental health situations.

Although it is appealing to support CIT based on its rational and the promising studies cited in this chapter, Cross et al. (2014) note that overall little research has been conducted on the effectiveness of CIT in reducing injuries to officers or citizens or increasing the use of diversion from jail. They comment that some of the studies, including the ones reviewed in this chapter, are methodologically weak due to their small sample sizes and lack of comparison groups. However, they acknowledge that there is support that CIT improves officer knowledge about mental illness as well as their confidence in their abilities to interact with individuals in acute phases of mental illness. They propose a research agenda that would examine whether changes in knowledge and attitudes translates to changes in the way police interact with individuals with mental illness. We add to these limitations that there is likely considerable heterogeneity between various CIT programs; there is currently no literature base available evaluating the various components of CIT and how other programs deviate from the original Memphis Model. Variations in outcomes may thus be influenced by variations in the programming, or the application thereof. Taheri (2016) also noted the methodological limitation of the extant research, particularly in terms of the outcomes or impact of the training on outcomes. Taheri's (2016) meta-analysis of the extant CIT evaluations suggests that the training had no impact on use of arrest or on officer use-of-force, concluding that "the weight of the current research evidence shows neither significant benefits, nor harms, of the CIT model"

(p. 90). It seems that at this point, CIT is a program that has been implemented in many communities in the United States, but research is needed that will provide information on the extent to which CIT is meeting the goals of reducing arrests, use of force, and injury reduction.

While CIT training can be costly, there are indications that the benefits may offset the costs. For example, the cost benefits of CIT were the focus of a study by El-Mallakh, Kiran, and El-Mallakh (2014). They analyzed data from Louisville, Kentucky, 9 years after this city initiated CIT. They compared costs associated with officer training, increased emergency psychiatry visits, and hospital admissions with savings resulting from diverted hospitalizations and reduced arrests. Police had an average of 2400 CIT calls annually. They reported that the overall costs were $2,430,128, while the annual savings were $3,455,025, resulting in a total of $1,024,897 in annual cost savings. The bulk of the savings were due to reduced admissions to hospitals, psychiatric facilities, and jails.

While CIT can be an effective response to the escalation of police contacts with individuals with mental health issues, some see CIT as a first step in a systemic revision of the approach of police with individuals with mental illness. Many authors are calling for communities to go beyond simply providing CIT to police officers. Steadman and Morrissette (2016) comment that training alone will not lead to a more integrated approach that focuses on reducing trauma and unnecessary use of hospitals and jails. Rather, these authors call for behavioral health and law enforcement personnel to work together to develop a comprehensive crisis care continuum. They identify three needs they believe are necessary for a community crisis care continuum. They comment:

> For a truly appropriate response, a number of other elements beyond police training are needed: avoiding police involvement when it really is not needed, offering police community-based alternatives to jail when some type of transportation from the encounter is called for, and providing respite options for consumers and their families with differing lengths of time and varying intensities of services. (p. 3)

Watson, Compton, and Draine (2017) analyzed CIT programs in terms of whether they could be considered evidence-based practices, which are based on randomized, controlled trials and allow for systematic reviews/meta-analyses to evaluate effectiveness. Based on the research available at the time of their study, Watson et al. concluded that CIT can be considered an evidence-based practice in improving police officer knowledge and attitudes as well as well as better skills and decision-making in dealing with mental health crises that arise in police calls. However, the authors concluded that there was insufficient research to evaluate other outcomes, such as subject-level outcomes of reduced injuries, reduced criminal justice involvement, and improved mental health treatment linkage and engagement. Additionally, research has not addressed agency-level and community-level outcomes (e.g., community relations, cost, resource use, community confidence in police). Despite the limited availability of research on some outcomes, Watson and colleagues support the continued adoption of this model. They call for more research on the outcomes in which there is limited data. They also comment on the trend to train all officers on CIT. They note that this is not consistent with the Memphis Model, although there is no research to inform this issue. Another area in need of research is how the model can be implemented in rural communities.

Alternative models

While the Memphis Model is perhaps the most commonly used one in the United States, there are two other programs that have also been implemented. Steadman, Deane, Borum, and Morrissey (2000) compared the Memphis Model to the Birmingham (Alabama) and Knoxville (Tennessee) models of CIT. In the *Birmingham model*, civilian mental health professionals are recruited and employed by police departments. They are not police officers, do not wear uniforms, carry guns, or drive a marked police car. They are best considered civilian mental health teams who operate from the police department. Birmingham CIT units respond to mental health emergencies and provide crisis intervention services. The *Knoxville model* is a mental health—based unit specializing in evaluation of mental illness. The Knoxville team consists of a single evaluation unit ("reception center") with especially trained mental health professionals employed by the police. The Knoxville CIT team serves a five-county area in Tennessee and responds to calls for assistance and assessment in the field and jail; as jails did not have a mental health program integrated in their service. Steadman et al. (2000) compared the effectiveness of these three mental health policing response models and found that all three were effective in reducing the number of inappropriate arrests of those with mental health issues as well as facilitate collaboration between the mental health service providers and police. The researchers attributed the success of the programs to two factors. One was the availability of a mental health service that police could bring individuals in need of assistance, which reduces officer time to deal with mental health crisis situations. The other factor was that police embraced the notion that a mental health response should be a core component of the police role.

Vancouver-based *Car 87* is another specialized joint police-mental health program. The program, originated in 1978 in Vancouver (Canada), consists of a single specialized mobile unit where a police officer is partnered with a registered (psychiatric) nurse (Adelman, 2003). The team provides on-site assessment, intervention, and community linkage (e.g., mental health referral, emergency intervention) for calls involving a person with mental illness. To date, there have been no published studies evaluating the success of these teams. However, reports detail the uptake of similar models across Canada (e.g., Adelman, 2003), with the Royal Canadian Mounted Police, and the further development of similar models for youth; Yankee-10 and Yankee-20, pairing a police officer with a youth probation officer and an outreach worker with the BC Ministry of Children and Family Development, respectively.

A few notable drawbacks and differences of various training and response models have been highlighted in Adelman's 2003 report. Aside from a general lack of research into their effectiveness, there are a number of other factors police departments may want to consider when exploring implementation of one of these models. For example, the author notes that resources could be a considerable issue in models where a single team is responsible for an entire catchment area (Birmingham model, Car 87). Some models require an initial investment (e.g., Knoxville: all officers require basic training) for the model to be implemented as intended. Across models, a positive working relationship between police and mental health agencies seems beneficial. However, the Memphis Model and Car 87 seems to rely most heavily on formalized collaborations with mental health services. Depending on the structures in place, police departments may want to consider the coverage required (e.g., Memphis Model includes after-hours coverage), existing resources or the lack thereof (e.g., Knoxville model had to instate a reception center), and the most beneficial type of intervention required (e.g., Birmingham is focused on crisis resolution; Car 87 often results in hospitalization and triaging to longer-term community services).

Conclusions

It is now well-documented that interactions between police and citizens with mental health issues have increased over the past few decades. There are multiple reasons for this increase, including deinstitutionalization, homelessness, and insufficient community mental health and social services for persons with mental health and substance abuse issues. Historically, police and jail personnel had little training to prepare them to deal more effectively with this population. This has changed, with a number of programs to provide police with CIT and jails with the ability to identify and provide needed services to those with mental health and substance abuse issues.

While training police to more effectively deal with individuals with mental health concerns is important, it should be kept in mind that we will not likely have a significant impact on the increasing use of arrest of this population unless the broader systemic issues are also addressed. This includes mental health programs as well as programs addressing other issues that contribute to contacts with police in mentally ill populations. Homelessness, for example, is a major contributor to criminalization of mental illness—there is a high percentage of individuals without a permanent residence at the time of arrest (Roy, Crocker, Nicholls, Latimer, & Ayllon, 2014; Zapf, Roesch, & Hart, 1996). This is likely due to the high rate of mental health issues among homeless individuals and the fact that they are more likely to be on the streets and thus come into contact with police due to their living circumstances. Results from At Home/Chez Soi, a multisite Canadian social housing study focused on homeless mentally ill populations, indicated that in the 6 months prior to study inclusion, approximately half had at least one contact with the justice system (Roy et al., 2016). Of these, 27% had been arrested, 20% had been charged with a criminal offense, and 23% had been detained in a police cell for less than 24 hours (Roy et al., 2016). Nijdam-Jones, Nicholls, Crocker, Roy, and Somers (2017) noted that over 40% of homeless mentally ill individuals had contact with forensic psychiatric services. As Prins (2011) commented, providing housing could prevent many of the police encounters that often lead to arrest. A good example of the impact that providing a stable home would have is the Housing First program created in Vancouver, British Columbia. Research on this program found that providing housing for homeless adults with a mental disorder resulted in a significant reduction in emergency room visits and reoffense rates (Russolillo, Patterson, McCandless, Moniruzzaman, & Somers, 2014; Somers, Rezansoff, Moniruzzaman, Palepu, & Patterson, 2013).

In conclusion, police training programs have had moderate success but they are limited in that they do not address the underlying issues that have led to the increased level of police contact with individuals with mental health issues. In our view, more attention needs to be paid to providing community alternatives to arrest but also to programs that prevent police/citizens with mental health encounters. This would include increasing community mental health and social services resources so that appropriate treatment can be provided, providing more social housing to decrease homelessness, and creating opportunities for employment.

References

Abramson, M. F. (1972). The criminalization of mentally disordered behavior: Possible side-effect of a new mental health law. *Hospital and Community Psychiatry, 23,* 101−107.

Adelman, J. (2003). *Study in blue and grey: Police interventions with people with mental illness: A review of challenges and responses.* Vancouver, BC: Canadian Mental Health Association.

Appelbaum, P. S. (1994). *Almost a revolution: Mental health law and the limits of change.* New York: Oxford University Press.

Bennell, C., Jones, N. J., & Corey, S. (2007). Does use-of-force simulation training in Canadian police agencies incorporate principles of effective training? *Psychology, Public Policy, and Law, 13,* 35−58.

Blaauw, E., Roesch, R., & Kerkhof, A. (2000). Mental health in European prison systems: What arrangements have countries made to deal with mental disorders in jails and prisons? *International Journal of Law and Psychiatry, 23,* 649−663.

Bonfine, N., Ritter, C., & Munetz, M. R. (2014). Police officer perceptions of the impact of crisis intervention team (CIT) programs. *International Journal of Law and Psychiatry, 37,* 341−350.

Boyce, J., Rotenberg, C., & Karam, M. (2015). *Mental health and contact with police in Canada, 2012.* Juristat: Canadian Centre for Justice Statistics. Retrieved from http://proxy.lib.sfu.ca/login?url=https://search.proquest.com/docview/1696027336?accountid=13800.

Charette, Y., Crocker, A. G., & Billette, I. (2011). The judicious judicial dispositions juggle: Characteristics of police interventions involving people with a mental illness. *Canadian Journal of Psychiatry, 56,* 677−685.

Compton, M. T., Bahora, M., Watson, A. C., & Oliva, J. R. (2008). A comprehensive review of extant research on Crisis Intervention Team (CIT) programs. *Journal of the American Academy of Psychiatry and Law, 36,* 47−55.

Compton, M. T., Bakeman, R., Broussard, B., D'Orio, B., & Watson, A. C. (2017). Police officers' volunteering for (rather than being assigned to) Crisis Intervention Team (CIT) training: Evidence for a beneficial self-selection effect. *Behavioral Science and Law, 35,* 470–479.

Compton, M. T., Bakeman, R., Broussard, B., Hankerson-Dyson, D., Husbands, L., Krishan, S., et al. (2014a). The police-based crisis intervention team (CIT) model: I. Effects on officers' knowledge, attitudes, and skills. *Psychiatric Services, 65,* 517–522.

Compton, M. T., Bakeman, R., Broussard, B., Hankerson-Dyson, D., Husbands, L., Krishan, S., et al. (2014b). The police-based crisis intervention team (CIT) model: II. Effects on level of force and resolution, referral, and arrest. *Psychiatric Services, 65,* 523–529.

Corrado, R. R., Cohen, I. M., Hart, S. D., & Roesch, R. (2000). Comparative examination of the prevalence of mental disorders among jailed inmates in Canada and the United States. *International Journal of Law and Psychiatry, 23,* 633–647.

Cross, A. B., Mulvey, E. P., Schubert, C. A., Griffin, P. A., Filone, S., Winckworth-Prejsnar, K., et al. (2014). An agenda for advancing research on crisis intervention teams for mental health emergencies. *Psychiatric Services in Advance,* 1–7.

Desmarais, S. L., Livingston, J. D., Greaves, C. L., Johnson, K. L., Verdun-Jones, S., Parent, R., et al. (2014a). Police perceptions and contact among people with mental illnesses: Comparisons with a general population survey. *Psychology, Public Policy, and Law, 20,* 431–442.

Desmarais, S. L., Van Dorn, R. A., Johnson, K. L., Grimm, K. J., Douglas, K. S., & Swartz, M. S. (2014b). Community violence perpetration and victimization among adults with mental illnesses. *American Journal of Public Health, 104,* 2342–2349.

Dupont, R., & Cochran, S. (2000). Police response to mental health emergencies—barriers to change. *Journal of the American Academy of Psychiatry and the Law, 28,* 338–344.

Dupont, R., Cochran, S., & Pillsbury, S. (2007). *Crisis intervention team core elements.* Memphis, TN: University of Memphis School of Urban Affairs and Public Policy, Department of Criminology and Criminal Justice, CIT Center. Retrieved November 21, 2018 from http://cit.memphis.edu/pdf/CoreElements.pdf.

El-Mallakh, P. L., Kiran, K., & El-Mallakh, R. S. (2014). Costs and savings associated with implementation of a police crisis intervention team. *Southern Medical Journal, 107,* 391–395.

Elbogen, E. B., & Johnson, S. C. (2009). The intricate link between violence and mental disorder results from the National Epidemiologic Survey on Alcohol and Related Conditions. *Archives of General Psychiatry, 66,* 152–161.

Engel, R. S., & Silver, E. (2001). Policing mentally disordered suspects: A reexamination of the criminalization hypothesis. *Criminology, 39,* 225–252.

Eno Louden, J., & Skeem, J. (2012). How do probation officers assess and manage recidivism and violence risk for probationers with mental disorder? An experimental investigation. *Law and Human Behavior, 37,* 22–34.

Fazel, S., & Danesh, J. (2002). Serious mental disorder in 23 000 prisoners: A systematic review of 62 surveys. *The Lancet, 359,* 545–550.

Fazel, S., Grann, M., Kling, B., & Hawton, K. (2011). Prison suicide in 12 countries: An ecological study of 861 suicides during 2003–2007. *Social Psychiatry and Psychiatric Epidemiology, 46,* 191–195.

Fazel, S., & Seewald, K. (2012). Severe mental illness in 33 588 prisoners worldwide: Systematic review and meta-regression analysis. *The British Journal of Psychiatry, 200,* 364−373.

Fuller, D. A., Lamb, H. R., Biasotti, M., & Snook, J. (2015). *Overlooked in the undercounted: The role of mental illness in fatal law enforcement encounters.* Treatment Advocacy Center: Officer of Research & Public Affairs. Retrieved from https://www.researchgate.net/publication/291331905_Overlooked_in_the_Undercounted_The_Role_of_Mental_Illness_in_Fatal_Law_Enforcement_Encounters.

Hoge, S., Buchanan, A., Kovasznay, B., & Roskes, E. (2009). *Outpatient services for the mentally ill involved in the criminal justice system: A report of the Task force on outpatient forensic services.* Arlington, VA: American Psychiatric Association.

Johnson, R. R. (2011). Suspect mental disorder and police use of force. *Criminal Justice and Behavior, 38,* 127−145.

Kerr, A. N., Morabito, M., & Watson, A. C. (2010). Police encounters, mental illness, and injury: An exploratory investigation. *Journal of Police Crisis Negotiations, 10,* 116−132.

Kesic, D., Thomas, S. D., & Ogloff, J. R. (2013). Estimated rates of mental disorders in, and situational characteristics of, incidents of nonfatal use of force by police. *Social Psychiatry and Psychiatric Epidemiology, 48,* 225−232.

Lamb, H. R., Weinberger, L. E., & DeCuir, W. J., Jr. (2014). The police and mental health. *Psychiatry Online, 1−22.* Retrieved from https://ps-psychiatryonline-org.proxy.lib.sfu.ca/doi/10.1176/appi.ps.53.10.1266. on 11/27/18.

Livingston, J. D., Desmarais, S. L., Verdun-Jones, S., Parent, R., Michalak, E., & Brink, J. (2014). Perceptions and experiences of people with mental illness regarding their interactions with police. *International Journal of Law and Psychiatry, 37,* 334−340.

Lord, V. B. (2004). *Suicide by cop: Inducing officers to shoot.* Flushing, NY: Looseleaf Law.

Martin, M. S., Dorken, S. K., Wamboldt, A. D., & Wooten, S. E. (2012). Stopping the revolving door: A meta-analysis on the effectiveness of interventions for criminally involved individuals with major mental disorders. *Law and Human Behavior, 36,* 1−12.

McKenzie, I. K. (2006). Forcing the police to open fire: A cross-cultural/international examination of police-involved, victim-provoked shootings. *Journal of Police Crisis Negotiations, 6,* 5−25.

Mohandie, K., Meloy, J. R., & Collins, P. I. (2009). Suicide by cop among officer-involved shootings. *Journal of Forensic Science, 54,* 456−462.

Morabito, M. S., & Socia, K. M. (2015). Is dangerousness a myth? Injuries and police encounters with people with mental illnesses. *Criminology & Public Policy, 14,* 253−276.

Moran, M. (2010). Jail more likely than hospital for severely mentally ill. *Psychiatric News, 45,* 1−2.

Munetz, M. R., & Griffin, P. A. (2006). Use of the sequential intercept model as an approach to decriminalization of people with serious mental illness. *Psychiatric Services, 57,* 544−549.

Nijdam-Jones, A., Nicholls, T. L., Crocker, A. G., Roy, L., & Somers, J. M. (2017). History of forensic mental health service use among homeless adults with mental illness. *International Journal of Forensic Mental Health, 16,* 69−82.

Ogloff, J. R. P., & Roesch, R. (1992). Using community mental health centers to provide comprehensive mental health services to local jails. In J. R. P. Ogloff (Ed.), *Law and psychology: Broadening of the discipline* (pp. 241−260). Durham, NC: Carolina Academic Press.

Perlin, M. L., & Lynch, A. J. (2016). Had to be held down by big police": A therapeutic juris-prudence perspective on interactions between police and persons with mental disabilities. *Fordham Urban Law Journal, 43*, 685—710.

Peterson, J. K., Skeem, J., Kennealy, P., Bray, B., & Zvonkovic, A. (2014). How often and how consistently do symptoms directly precede criminal behavior among offenders with mental illness? *Law and Human Behavior, 38*, 439—449.

Prins, S. J. (2011). Does transinstitutionalization explain the overrepresentation of people with serious mental illnesses in the criminal justice system? *Community Mental Health Journal, 47*, 716—722.

Reuland, M., & Cheney, J. (2005). *Enhancing success of police-based diversion programs for people with mental illness*. Delmar, NY: GAINS Technical Assistance and Policy Analysis Center for Jail Diversion.

Reuland, M., Schwarzfeld, M., & Draper, L. (2009). *Law enforcement responses to people with mental illnesses: A guide to research-informed policy and practice*. New York: Council of State Governments Justice Center.

Roesch, R. (1995). Mental health interventions in pretrial jails. In G. M. Davies, S. Lloyd-Bostock, M. McMurran, & C. Wilson (Eds.), *Psychology, law and criminal justice: International developments in research and practice* (pp. 520—531). Berlin: De Greuter.

Roesch, R., & Golding, S. L. (1985). The impact of deinstitutionalization. In D. P. Farrington, & J. Gunn (Eds.), *Current research in forensic psychiatry and psychology: Aggression and dangerousness* (pp. 209—239). NY: Wiley.

Roy, L., Crocker, A. G., Nicholls, T. L., Latimer, E. A., & Ayllon, A. R. (2014). Criminal behavior and victimization among homeless individuals with severe mental illness: A systematic review. *Psychiatric Services, 65*, 739—750.

Roy, L., Crocker, A. G., Nicholls, T. L., Latimer, E., Gozdzik, A., O'Campo, P., et al. (2016). Profiles of criminal justice system involvement of mentally ill homeless adults. *International Journal of Law and Psychiatry, 45*, 75—88.

Russolillo, A., Patterson, M., McCandless, L., Moniruzzaman, A., & Somers, J. (2014). Emergency department utilisation among formerly homeless adults with mental disorders after one year of housing first interventions: A randomised controlled trial. *International Journal of Housing Policy, 14*, 79—97.

Somers, J. M., Rezansoff, S. N., Moniruzzaman, A., Palepu, A., & Patterson, M. (2013). Housing First reduces re-offending among formerly homeless adults with mental disorders: Results of a randomized controlled trial. *PLoS One, 8*. Retrieved from on 11/28/18. https://journals.plos.org/plosone/article/file?id=10.1371/journal.pone.0072946&type=printable

Steadman, H. J., Deane, M. W., Borum, R., & Morrissey, J. (2000). Comparing outcomes of major models of police responses to mental health emergencies. *Psychiatric Services, 51*, 645—649.

Steadman, H. J., & Morrissette, D. (2016). Police responses to persons with mental illness: Going beyond CIT training. *Psychiatric Services, 67*, 1054—1056.

Steadman, H. J., Mulvey, E. P., Monahan, J., Robbins, P. C., Appelbaum, P. S., Grisso, T., et al. (1998). Violence by people discharged from acute psychiatric inpatient facilities and by others in the same neighborhoods. *Archives of General Psychiatry, 55*, 393—401.

Steadman, H. J., Osher, F. C., Robbins, P. C., Case, B., & Samuels, S. (2009). Prevalence of serious mental illness among jail inmates. *Psychiatric Services, 60*, 761—765.

Swanson, J. W., McGinty, E. E., Fazel, S., & Mays, V. M. (2015). Mental illness and reduction of gun violence and suicide: Bringing epidemiologic research to policy. *Annals of Epidemiology, 25*, 366—376.

Taheri, S. A. (2016). Do crisis intervention teams reduce arrests and improve officer safety? A systematic review and meta-analysis. *Criminal Justice Policy Review, 27*, 76−96.

Teplin, L. (1984). Criminalizing mental disorder: The comparative arrest rate of the mentally ill. *American Psychologist, 39*, 794−803.

Thompson, M., & Kahn, K. B. (2016). Mental health, race, and police contact: Intersections of risk and trust in the police. *Policing: An International Journal of Police Strategies & Management, 39*, 807−819.

Tyler, T. R., & Fagan, J. (2008). Legitimacy and cooperation: Why do people help the police fight crime in their communities. *Ohio State Journal of Criminal Law, 6*, 231−275.

Watson, A. C., & Angell, B. (2013). The role of stigma and uncertainty in moderating the effect of procedural justice on cooperation and resistance in police encounters with persons with mental illnesses. *Psychology, Public Policy, and Law, 19*, 30−39.

Watson, A. C., Angell, B., Morabito, M. S., & Robinson, N. (2008). Defying negative expectations: Dimensions of fair and respectful treatment by police officers as perceived by people with mental illness. *Administration and Policy in Mental Health and Mental Health Services Research, 35*, 449−457.

Watson, A. C., Angell, B., Vidalon, T., & Davis, K. (2010). Measuring perceived procedural justice and coercion among persons with mental illness in police encounters: The Police Contact Experience Scale. *Journal of Community Psychology, 38*, 206−226.

Watson, A. C., Compton, M. T., & Draine, J. N. (2017). The crisis intervention team (CIT) model: An evidence-based policing practice? *Behavioral Science and Law, 35*, 431−441.

Watson, A. C., Corrigan, P. W., & Ottati, V. (2004). Police officers' attitudes toward and decisions about persons with mental illness. *Psychiatric Services, 55*, 49−53.

Zapf, P. A., Roesch, R., & Hart, S. D. (1996). An examination of the relationship of homelessness to mental disorder, criminal behavior, and health care in a pretrial jail population. *Canadian Journal of Psychiatry, 41*, 435−440.

Communication as a weapon for resolving hostage and barricaded situations

10

Michel St-Yves, Jeff Thompson and Lynne Bibeau

Introduction

In the past, police interventions during hostage-taking and barricade situations were often limited to a single warning — "immediately get out with your hands up, if you do not cooperate we will move in" — and the Special Weapons and Tactics (SWAT) would indeed proceed if the barricaded people did not comply. This tactical intervention (action-reaction type of decision) was ending crisis situations rather quickly but also resulted in wounded and/or deaths on both sides much too often (Schlossberg, 1979; St-Yves & Michaud, 2012). Today, the philosophy of intervention has changed and aims to use communication as a weapon to resolve these crisis situations. This approach is the most efficient, the cheapest, and the one that saves the most lives (Hare, 1997).

Communication is the method by which hostage takers and law enforcement negotiators engage in a transactional "dialogue" as each party seeks to define the interaction, exert control and influence over the other, manage the relational parameters of trust and power, present their desired image, and achieve their desired outcome. As such, crisis/hostage negotiation *is* a communicative event (Rogan, 2012).

This chapter describes how police crisis negotiators intervene when they find themselves confronted by high-risk situations, particularly those involving mentally disturbed individuals who are armed, barricaded, with or without hostages. Although the choice of response is closely tied to the immediacy of risk, the emphasis will be placed on the most efficient and usually least risky alternative: communication.

"Talk to Me": A new approach

Dr (and detective) Harvey Schlossberg and Captain Frank Bolz of the New York City Police Department (NYPD) are often cited as pioneers in the field of police crisis negotiation. They were the first to develop, in 1973, a crisis intervention team whose intervention was essentially based on communication and peaceful surrender. They

Police Psychology, Edited by Marques and Paulino. https://doi.org/10.1016/B978-0-12-816544-7.00010-3

suggested three guiding principles: (1) contain the incident (confine, control, and limit the besieged individual's movements); (2) understand the motivation and personality of the besieged individual; and (3) stall for time — to optimize negotiation and/or SWAT intervention. Today, this approach still constitutes the foundation of crisis negotiations (McMains & Mullins, 2015; Schlossberg, 1979). Communication and peaceful intervention are key goals, and the police response revolves around delaying tactical intervention, minimizing confrontation, engaging in dialogue, asking open-ended questions, and remaining nonjudgmental. This approach is the most effective and economical, and best protects life (Hare, 1997). Thus was born a new philosophy: "As long as no immediate threat to life exists, negotiations are acceptable" (McMains & Mullins, 2015, p. 9). Since then, this model of intervention — based essentially on the use of communication tools to peacefully resolve crises — has inspired all police forces around the world. The number of people injured or killed during these interventions has decreased drastically. The success of this approach is such that the number of people injured or killed during a negotiation is less than 1% (Thompson, 2014c). On the other hand, tactical interventions, including the use of chemical weapons, are responsible for relatively high rates of injuries and deaths (Greenstone & Leviton, 2002).

Today, most major city police departments have specialized crisis-response teams based on the principles established by Schlossberg and Bolz. Reputable Crisis Negotiation Teams (CNT) proudly display mottos such as "Listening is our weapon" (Research, Assistance, Intervention, Dissuasion [RAID] — National French Police), "Pax per conloquium" (resolution through dialogue — FBI) and "Talk to me" (for the NYPD). These mottos show the extent to which communication plays a major role in police intervention and gives meaning to their mission as peace officers (St-Yves & Michaud, 2012).

Crisis/hostage negotiation strategies

Most negotiation models have been developed to facilitate business negotiations. A business negotiation is a confrontation of divergent interests between an offer and a demand that each side attempts to make compatible, through a game of mutual concessions, until a satisfactory agreement is reached. Business negotiation models have proven their utility in all kinds of interventions with rational individuals who seek gains in contexts involving political or ransom demands, or in hostage-takings by criminals caught in the act of committing other crimes. The role of negotiators in such cases is to focus on the content of the demands, the "substance" of the problem (hostages, deadlines, conditions), and they draw heavily on business practices. These so-called traditional models are, however, of little use when it comes to dealing with mentally disturbed individuals. The vast majority of crisis interventions nevertheless involve such individuals (Thompson, 2014c) and the strategies for achieving a peaceful surrender in such cases are essentially based on crisis intervention. The focus then shifts to psychological aspects, and the intervention is based on listening, empathy, and communication, but once again using a significant number of the fundamental methods of any type of negotiation.

Defusing the crisis step by step

In crisis situations the person in distress usually moves through three classical stages: (1) the acute stage (generally emotional); (2) problem-solving (more rational and focused on solving the problem); and (3) acceptance or resignation (including the ability to accept and face consequences). Most crisis intervention models follow this pattern and have been developed in accordance with these natural — indeed universal — stages of human crises, which are often set off by deep psychological distress (for a review of the various models used in crisis/hostage negotiation see Grubb, 2010 and Johnson, Thompson, Hall, & Meyer, 2017). The most frequently encountered mental disorders in crisis situations are mood disorders, such as depression (three out of four people verbalize suicidal intentions), and paranoid schizophrenia (Soskis & Van Zandt, 1986; St-Yves & Collins, 2012).

The models of intervention are varied but all have in common the use of the basic elements, but essential, to communicate well (see St-Yves & Veyrat, 2012 for a review of some practical and effective models). The first common tool is always active listening. When negotiators effectively use active listening skills, it allows them to build rapport and demonstrates empathy with the subject, both which are critical to achieving the goal (voluntary compliance and a peaceful surrender).

Active listening

Law enforcement crisis hostage negotiation team (CHNT) members have to use a set of communicative skills strategically and genuinely in order to achieve their goal (Giebels & Taylor, 2010; Lanceley, 2004; McMains & Mullins, 2015; Noesner & Webster, 1997).

Importantly, the expert negotiator must also be able to adapt the use of these skills based on the context of that particular incident as well as the changing dynamics of the situation as it evolves (Dolnik, 2003; Donohue & Taylor, 2003; Giebels & Taylor, 2010; Thompson, 2014b).

In these crisis incidents, the negotiation team must have a goal and a plan to achieve it. This process is universal in law enforcement CHNT training across the world. The intention is to produce a behavioral change in the subject in order to reach to peaceful and voluntary compliance (St-Yves & Veyrat, 2012).

For a negotiator to be successful in achieving peaceful resolution he/she must use a specific set of microactive listening skills (Taylor & Donohue, 2006; Thompson, 2018b; Vecchi, Van Hasselt, & Romano, 2005). These skills involve avoidance of robotic manner or a style that is aloof or inauthentic. Instead, the negotiator must strive to create rapport with the subject by utilizing specific microactive listening skills. The negotiator has to know the specific microactive listening skills, use them together in clusters, be able to adapt their use based on the evolving context, and importantly use them genuinely.

Law enforcement crisis hostage negotiation is both an "art" and a "science" (St-Yves & Veyrat, 2012). It is not an ad hoc approach where one tries to figure out what to do as the negotiation proceeds. There is a science, backed by data, about which skills will work, why they work, and how. The art form is applying those skills to an individual's unique style that includes taking into account the context. Negotiators cannot afford to "wing it" — the work of crisis hostage negotiators is much too serious where life and death is often teetering on a delicate balance where the negotiator's actions can nudge it in either direction.

Active listening is one of the most important communication skill sets a negotiator must successfully employ when engaging the subject during a crisis incident (Johnson et al., 2017). Research has also consistently demonstrated active listening as being critical to successfully and peacefully resolve conflicts and disputes (Thompson, 2015). Active listening avoids rushing toward a conclusion. Instead, it demonstrates understanding and respect by building rapport and trust as well as possessing empathy (Thompson, Ebner, & Giddings, 2017; Vecchi et al., 2005).

Active listening explained

Active listening is effective and affective (Giebels & Taylor, 2010; Grubb, 2010; Thompson, 2014a & 2018b). It allows the negotiator to gain valuable information from the subject — such as the "why" behind their positions or their "wants." It develops rapport and demonstrates empathy (Thompson et al., 2017). Active listening is an approach that allows the negotiator to do the following with the subject: gain more information, improve understanding of their point of view, and work cooperatively with them. A negotiator who is actively listening looks and sounds interested, adapts the subject's point of view, and clarifies the subject's thoughts and feelings (Thompson et al., 2017).

Active listening entails listening more than talking. Some refer to this as the "80/20 Rule" (Hammer, 2007; Thompson, 2014b). It means, generally, a negotiator should listen 80% of the time while speaking only 20%. Although it is not a hard and fast rule, it serves as an important reminder that allowing the subject to speak (and letting them know they have been heard and understood) is critical to de-escalating their tense negative emotions. Further, when a negotiator is speaking less, he is able to evaluate his words and project with purpose and strategy. It is important to stress that although these skills are developed and adapted from therapeutic settings (Grubb, 2010; Hersen & Van Hasselt, 1998; St-Yves, Tanguay, & St-Pierre, 2001; Vecchi et al., 2005), these skills are used by negotiators in a specific manner where the negotiator does not lose focus of the goal (Giebels & Taylor, 2010).

Active listening encourages the subject to keep talking and indicates that the negotiator is following the conversation. It is not confrontational, and signals to the subject that the negotiator is attentive and interested in what the subject has to say (Greenstone, 1995). Each of these contributes to building trust with the person and developing rapport while also demonstrating empathy.

The impact of emotions

Crisis incidents are situations that are tense, and potentially volatile. The actions of the subject are often dictated by their overwhelming emotions creating a crisis for that person. A crisis is a "condition of instability or danger; a dramatic emotional upheaval in a person's life."[1] It is important to remember that a crisis is individually based. Many people experience similar situations yet only for some will it arise to a crisis. It can be due to a variety of reasons including having a mental illness (diagnosed or not), previous experiences, an inability to cope with stress, or a recent triggering event. Using active listening skills in these situations can move the subject from actions based on their negative, overwhelming emotions to one that is more rationally based (see Figure 10.1). This can then increase the negotiator's ability to influence a behavioral change in the subject to achieve the goal—again voluntary compliance (Giebels & Noelanders, 2004; Vecchi et al., 2005).

The actions of the negotiator, regardless of whether they are positive or negative, can affect the actions of the other person — this is called "emotional contagion" (Hatfield, Cacioppo, & Rapson, 1993). Each person involved in the crisis can produce emotional contagion. Therefore, the negotiator needs to be aware of this and their own emotions and of this possible effect. By remaining calm and using effective verbal and nonverbal communication (Thompson, 2015), the negotiator can impact the subject and reduce his negative emotions and tension (Bodie, Vickery, Cannava, & Jones, 2015; Johnson et al., 2017) while also returning a sense of self-control back to the subject (St-Yves & Veyrat, 2012).

Rapport and empathy

A negotiator is able to further stabilize the negative emotions of the subject by building rapport and demonstrating empathy. The use of active listening skills slows down the situation, establishes a connection with the subject, and creates a climate of caring and understanding, allowing the negotiator to influence the subject (Fuselier, 1981; St-Yves & Veyrat, 2012). Moving the latter toward more rational cognitions and positive behaviors is crucial.

Rapport is established between two people who are mutually attentive to each other, share positive feelings, and do not constantly interrupt each other or speak at

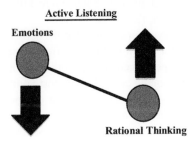

FIGURE 10.1

Impact of active listening on emotions and rational thinking

---

[1] Definition from Dictionary.com.

the same time (Tickle-Degnen & Rosenthal, 1990). This last aspect can be referred to as coordination (St-Yves, 2014). Positivity does not mean the negotiator is seeking to become friend with the subject but rather the negotiator's words and actions are spoken with respect and empathy. When a negotiator is giving the other person their attention, it demonstrates listening and understanding while it is also tactically safe.

Empathy is another important term to understand and for negotiators to use correctly (Misino & DeFelice, 2004). Empathy means understanding the perspective and emotions of another person. Importantly, empathy is not the same as sympathy (feeling sorry for someone). Empathy is important for negotiators to display as it helps him or her to "connect" with the people they are interacting with (Vecchi et al., 2005) while not becoming overwhelmed with the crisis the subject is experiencing (Ivey, Ivey, Zelaquett, & Quirk, 2012; Soskis & Van Zandt, 1986). Empathy is also strategic during crisis incidents; demonstrating empathy can help reduce negative emotions and contribute to gaining voluntary compliance. Empathy is displayed primarily through using active listening skills that involves both verbal and nonverbal cues (Thompson et al., 2017).

Aside from containing both verbal and nonverbal cues, active listening can be confusing as to what exactly it is and what it consists of. The following section removes this veil of ambiguity that can cloak active listening and details the individual "parts" that make up the "whole" of active listening.

Implementing active listening: the PRIME SOS+ acronym

The PRIME SOS+ acronym is a mnemonic device designed to assist the negotiator with recalling each of the microskills (Thompson, 2014a & 2018b). PRIME stands for the active listening: *Paraphrasing, Reflecting, "I" messages, Minimal encouragers, Emotional labeling.* SOS is for *Summarize, Open-ended questions, and Silences.* The "+" represents positive effect on the subject. These nine microskills are further explained below. They are adapted from a negotiation method created and taught by the Federal Bureau of Investigation (FBI) and elsewhere. The PRIME SOS+ builds on these versions as well as crisis counselors and crisis management professionals' perspectives and insight. Each microskill is explained below and adapted from Thompson's work (2014a & 2018b).

Paraphrasing: This involves repeating what the subject said in a much shorter format that is in the negotiator's own words. An effective paraphrase does not minimize what the subject has experienced. The negotiator should ensure to include the emotion the subject is experiencing as well: "You lost your job and it's really upsetting because you dedicated so many years to the company"; "You are annoyed because you feel like you didn't do anything wrong."

Reflecting/Mirroring: When the subject is finished speaking, reflecting and mirroring is much shorter than paraphrasing as it includes repeating the last few words the person said. If the person concluded by saying "… What they did is ridiculous and this really made me angry," the negotiator would say: "It really made you angry."

"I" messages: This is used to counteract statements made by the subject that are not conducive toward working collaboratively. This provides a "timeout" or reality check for the subject letting them know that the negotiator is trying to work together and they, from the negotiator's perspective, are not. It is important to be mindful when using this as to not do it in a way (be aware of voice tone) that is aggressive and creates an argument. For example, "I feel___ when you ___ because ___."

"I" messages can also be used to acknowledge positive actions and statements of the subject which then encourages more of it. The above example can be modified in the following way: "I appreciate that you let (a hostage) go, because you stayed true to your word and it shows me that you are genuinely wanting to end this peacefully."

Minimal encouragers: These are verbal statements such as "mmm," "okay," and "I see" and nonverbal gestures like head nodding (P.S. visual contact is rare in crisis/hostage negotiation). These encouragers demonstrate the negotiator is following what the subject is saying without interrupting him. It further establishes the building of rapport with the subject by subtly inviting the person to continue speaking: "mmm," "I see," "okay," "really," "yeah," "uh-huh."

Emotional labeling: It is important that the emotions of the subject be acknowledged. Think of emotional labeling as the opposite of saying "I understand." Instead, it is demonstrating the negotiator understands. Identifying the subject's emotions validates what they are feeling instead of minimizing it. By labeling and acknowledging their emotions, it helps reduce the subject's actions being grounded in their emotions to a more balanced and rationally thinking process. For example, "You sound frustrated," "It sounds like you're aggravated by this," "You feel disrespected."

When using emotional labeling, it is important to not ask the emotion ("are you mad by what happened?" or "did that frustrate you?"). This can make the negotiator come across as disconnected and not following along with the story. This can greatly hinder any development of rapport.

Summarize: Summarizing is an extended version of paraphrasing. It provides a review of what the subject said including the elements important to him or her as well as acknowledging their emotions. Summarizing validates for the subject that they have been heard and understood. This is critical to do as it can bring a sense of relief to the subject and reduce their actions being dictated by their emotions.

Summarizing is also a valuable tool for a negotiator to use when he or she is unsure what to do or say next. Summarizing what the person has said has multiple benefits in this situation. First, it buys time and, as already stated, slows the process down which is an important element in contributing to a peaceful resolution.

Next, summarizing can further contribute to the negotiator building rapport and developing trust. Rapport and trust then allow the negotiator to eventually move toward influencing the person to reappraise their situation and consider alternatives to a resolution and suggestions from the negotiator.

Open-ended questions: Asking open-ended questions solicits the subject to speak longer and thus it can help diffuse the tension as well as provide the negotiator with valuable information and insight into their perspective of the situation.

"What happened?"; "Then what happened?"; "Can you tell me more about …"

If the goal is to de-escalate the subject's tense negative emotions, using open-ended questions can assist the process by allowing him to take his time by telling his story.

Silence/Effective pauses: Part of listening includes utilizing silence and pausing before taking your turn to speak. Also described as part of dynamic inactivity,[2] silence allows the other subject to continue speaking while combining it with pausing prior to speaking helps calm a situation.

Keep in mind if the subject is acting out his emotions, he most likely will not be able to put his thoughts into words together as quickly as the negotiator (who is thinking more rationally). Providing the subject with time (silence) allows him to collect his thoughts.

Again, remember that calming the situation is critical as it helps move the person from acting out his emotions to a mindset that is more rationally based.

+ (Positive strength statements): Negotiators want to not only acknowledge the negative emotions the person in crisis is experiencing through emotional labeling, but they also need to eventually counter the subject's negative perspective of the situation that often can include feelings of being alone, hopelessness, and helplessness. Positive strength statements involve countering that perspective by helping to provide another positive viewpoint. Examples include "This is a lot for anyone to have to handle, it takes real courage to speak to me today."; "You are not alone, I'm here and I am here to help you. You do not have to take this all on by yourself."; "I'm impressed by your strength in having been through so much."; "People care about you."; "It's courageous for you to share that with me. I appreciate you trusting me."

It is important to note that employing positive strength statements is something new and emerging for law enforcement hostage negotiators to discern and utilize. Although it is something that has been long established in training for crisis counselors (Gregory, 2015; Kam, 2017; Thompson, 2014a & 2018b), it is a new skill that negotiators can employ as a tactic to assist with influencing the subject to see their situation from another perspective.

Each of the microactive listening skills detailed above often are enhanced when being used in clusters (Bodie et al., 2015). For example, an emotional label followed up by an open-ended question can demonstrate to the subject that the negotiator understands how they are feeling and they want to hear more. Although each microskill is important, some researchers have placed a greater importance on some above others, yet even among them the lists differ (Bodie et al. 2015; St-Yves & Veyrat, 2012; Vecchi et al., 2005).

Research on the use of active listening skills by negotiators produced a list of recommended behaviors, as well as behaviors negotiators should avoid (Johnson et al., 2017). Table 10.1 shows a sample of what the negotiators shared.

---

[2] Dynamic inactivity is a term originally used by NYPD HNT cofounder Dr Harvey Schlossberg. It refers to a negotiation tactic where it seems no overt activity is occurring but in reality there is planned and calculated subtle actions and words being used to reduce the need for physical force to be used.

Table 10.1 Behaviors to engage in and to avoid.

Behaviors to engage in:	Behaviors to avoid:
1. Use active listening skills 2. Appear calm 3. Remain emotionally stable 4. Be relaxed but firm 5. Control vocal tone and body language 6. Express empathy, show sincere concern for their well-being 7. Treat subject with respect 8. Recognize the subject's motives 9. Be nonjudgmental and honest without making assumptions 10. Use the subject's name	1. Being confrontational (arguing, yelling, and or interrupting) 2. Using certain words, generally, including police jargon and religion 3. Lying or making promises that cannot be kept 4. Saying "I understand" or "calm down" or "no" 5. Blaming, judging, or accusing 6. Expressing disinterest or rushing the process 7. Being demanding or minimizing other's concerns

From "talk to me" to "text me"

As a negotiating instrument, speech has an important role and it is not just about words and their meanings. The inflection of the voice, the tone, the rhythm also play an important role in the communication (Divasto, 1996; Wargo, 1990). After all our emphasis on the verbal communication and active listening skills for negotiators, today we are "obliged" to look at a particular way of communicating: texting! Internet and cellular data have greatly influenced how the younger people are "connecting" with each other, anytime, anywhere, and this is also generalizing to older generations. Today, almost all people born after 1980 have never used a rotary telephone. Those who are used to landline phones may still feel a little lost in this age of cyberspace and modern communication technologies. This illustrates just how the development of communications has transformed our lives and the world we live in. Thus, it is also influencing some negotiation strategies (Christol, 2009).

Today, many people are using text messages and social media to communicate, especially among adolescents and young adults (Ebner, 2017). In a study of teenagers reaching out via text messaging to Tel-Jeunes, a crisis support organization, the findings revealed that it not only meets their needs while in crisis but it also showed that the texted based option is essential in providing them support (Thoër et al., 2017). This does not preclude the continuation of the intervention by telephone later. In the United States, crisis counselors with Crisis Text Line (a crisis counseling service that is text-based) have exchanged more than 75 million messages with people in crisis (Thompson, 2018a). The work of these crisis counselors has many similarities to that of law enforcement negotiators.

In certain crisis situations, texting may be the only way to initiate a contact. Some individuals may be more comfortable texting to establish the first contact with the police negotiator. To begin with, this may feel less engaging or simply reflecting that some people are so used to texting as opposed to talking on their cell phone. Perhaps it is like a comfortable "distance" or a just the right "interpersonal connection" for an increasing number of people?

You may have observed that the popular attitude about "picking up the phone" or "taking text messages" appears to be different. In the Canadian/American culture, people seem at ease not answering the phone and also hanging up when contradicted. To the contrary, people seem to not resist looking at a text message as it enters on their cell phone and they may very well write back a few words or send an emoticon spontaneously or shortly after receiving the message. Currently, there are no scientific studies on law enforcement negotiators negotiating with subjects via text messages yet with the data available in similar settings (via Crisis Text Line), it is an area that is worth exploring. Some negotiation teams have experienced engaging subjects through text messaging and do not report major disadvantages.

Perhaps texting requires a little more concentration and may in fact be useful to slow down the subject emotional reaction. Texting back a response may also be slightly delayed on both parts which is not a problem. It even allows time to weigh one's words. Empathy remains in the repertoire of interventions, but it will translate into the choice of words and emoticons. Habitual text users — the new generations — have some abbreviations and expressions perhaps not known by the negotiator. This is overcome by simply asking to clarify if need be or searching the Internet as replies are not expected to be instantaneous.

One of the concerns using text messages is often the nonexclusive communication with the negotiator. Indeed, other people can also text or communicate via social media with the subject. As long as the negotiation team gets to monitor (Christol, 2009) the impact of these others on the subject, this can be dealt with.

Negotiation teams ought to be knowledgeable of contemporary social and technological advances, be creative and use the new technologies. Texting may replace some of the "older" negotiation apparatus, and this may facilitate the important "connection" between a negotiator and a subject. Nevertheless, verbal negotiation is still the method of choice. Although some suggest the negotiator should try convincing the subject to eventually switch from texting to talking (Shonk, 2018), it must also be a method that negotiators are comfortable with when communicating with subjects because if texting is the method the subject is most comfortable with, the negotiator must be equally comfortable.

Risk assessment in crisis/hostage negotiation

Be it a 50 minutes long or a 30 hours long operation, the negotiator will have given back some hope to the subject and the opportunity to peacefully and with dignity solve the acutely stressful and at-risk situation that the subject has created for himself. A barricaded distressed or mentally ill individual armed with a sharp object or a firearm, emotionally reactive, often under the influence of alcohol or drugs is far from what clinicians manage in their offices. This is what negotiators do manage. As they talk with subjects and work toward achieving the objective, they also remain aware of the fluctuating risk for auto-destructive and/or heteroaggressive subject's behaviors within this high-risk situation. The context presented here is the most common encountered. The threat that a subject may represent is assessed based on the context, the individual characteristics, his speech and behaviors. It borrows indicators from the field of general threat assessment and management literature where academics and practitioners join their expertise (Meloy & Hoffmann, 2014).

The negotiation team must obtain as much information as possible regarding "who" the individual is (Michaud, St-Yves, & Guay, 2008; Miller, 2005; Walker, Kennedy, Vassilev, & Rogers, 2018): Does he have any violent or criminal history? Any medical/psychiatric history? Any suicidal history? Information about his occupational history is important (e.g., recently unemployed, military background,...). What triggered this crisis? What were the subject's first actions reported in the present situation (e.g., Did he hurt someone? Any gunshots?). How confrontational is the subject with the police? Are there any persons significant to him—any social support? According to Juliano and Yunes (2014), this is usually an important protective factor. Does he keep using substances as the negotiation is in process? Information may come directly and quickly from a subject who is willing to talk, as it may come via social media, from relatives, friends, etc. Having this type of information will help the negotiator establish a good rapport with the subject. Knowing the "who" is mainly knowing the static risk factors (unchangeable characteristics) but also some dynamic risk factors (elements on which the negotiator may have an impact) (Meloy, 2000). Everything the negotiator says is in fact a way to manage the "threat" and to de-escalate the crisis. This is the most effective and safest way to end such crisis.

The whole crisis negotiation process — PRIME SOS+ helps get the subject out of the spinning negative and self-centered painful thinking. As the crisis state is being defused, the individual regains the capacity to think of meaningful people and/or aspects of his life worth recomposing himself.

The negotiator is one member — a very important one — of a team assessing the threatening situation. The commander is of course in charge of the whole operation. The team's structure can include a forensic psychologist in assisting with providing suggestions and with making the threat assessment. The beginning and the end of the intervention are the most at-risk moments of the incident. At the start, the individual is likely emotionally unstable while trust is not yet established between him and the negotiator. At the time of surrender even a collaborative subject may behave in a surprising manner by not respecting instructions already discussed in details, be it intentionally provoking a suicide by cop, or somehow causing disorganization by a sudden burst of stress or fear, thus putting himself and the SWAT officers at risk. Frequently when the subject is behaving and thinking more rational, is well informed and reassured, the result will be him surrendering peacefully.

A hostage situation represents a higher level of preoccupation. The more affective proximity or intimacy between the subject and the person(s) taken hostage, the more likely the threat can be acted upon. This is the "intimacy factor" (Calhoun & Weston, 2003; 2016) that should be considered here as in any threat analysis.

Therefore, domestic contexts are more at risk. In such unstable and emotionally charged situations, hostages' reactions may also increase the risk of violence. Other hostage events may be circumstantial and/or "instrumental" often with unrealistic demands as in an active shooting like in the Orlando Pulse Bar in the United States (Patrick, 2016) and the Lindt Café in Sydney, Australia (New South Wales Department of Justice, 2017). Those become special topics to address and are not the scope of the present chapter (Chedid, 2014; Lowther, 2015).

Some authors have identified alarm indicators of a negotiation not progressing and/or increasingly at risk for a suicide, a suicide by cop, or violence toward hostages and law enforcement (Dolan & Fuselier, 1989; Noesner & Dolan, 1992; Strentz, 1995). These are: the subject shows a continuous defiance and provocation of the negotiator, maintains his unrealistic demands or keeps threatening, communicates only in a superficial or instrumental way, shortens the interaction with the negotiator, rejects all insinuations to a solution or to a future, keeps blaming others including law enforcement for his situation, becomes more detached, suddenly puts pressure to see the negotiator or fixes a time for his surrender without an agreement to the safety measures. If there are hostages, the way the subject is treating them may indicate an improving or deteriorating situation. All of these indicators taken at the reverse would suggest stability or progression toward a peaceful surrender. Therefore, the negotiation team and the tactical intervention must adjust their plan accordingly as the incident progresses.

A negotiation is a "live" threat assessment. Although no specific tools yet exist, scientific threat assessment studies for risk factors and protective factors, and several actuarial and structured professional judgment tools (Skeem & Monahan, 2011) can provide transferable knowledge to the context of crisis/hostage negotiation.

Conclusions

The majority of crisis situations involve people in distress, often depressive, who threaten to die by suicide. Active listening is a collection of skills that negotiators must command an expertise in utilizing with a discernible ability to adapt when necessary based on the context and changing dynamics of the evolving incident.

A negotiator uses these skills strategically (Grubb, 2010). When most untrained in this art and science think the negotiator should work toward compliance as expeditiously as possible, the negotiator instead uses active listening to slow down the situation, to de-escalate the tense and negative emotions the subject is experiencing, to build rapport and demonstrate empathy, all for the purpose of influencing a behavioral change in the subject to achieve the goal: gaining voluntary compliance. In this final stage, the negotiator will do everything to allow this person to preserve or restore his dignity — it is sometimes in the subject's eyes all that remains to him.

References

Bodie, G. D., Vickery, A. J., Cannava, K., & Jones, S. M. (2015). The role of "active listening" in informal helping conversations: Impact on perceptions of listener helpfulness, sensitivity, and supportiveness and discloser emotional improvement. *Western Journal of Communication, 79,* 1—23.

Calhoun, F. S., & Weston, S. W. (2003). *Contemporary threat management: A practical guide for identifying, assessing, and managing individuals of violent intent.* San Diego, CA: Specialized Training Services.

Calhoun, F. S., & Weston, S. W. (2016). *Threat assessment and managing strategies, identifying the howlers and hunters.* Boca Raton, FL: CRC Press.

Chedid, C. (2014). *Barricade hostage case studies.* Retrieved from https://www.researchgate.net/publication/318969835.

Christol, T. (2009). Negotiating through text messaging. *Law & Order, 57*(6), 80—85.

Divasto, P. V. (1996). Negotiating with foreign language-speaking subjects. *FBI Law Enforcement Bulletin, 65,* 11—15.

Dolan, J. T., & Fuselier, G. D. (1989). A guide for first responder to hostage situations. *FBI Law Enforcement Bulletin, 58,* 9—13.

Dolnik, A. (2003). Contrasting dynamics of crisis negotiations: Barricade versus kidnapping incidents. *International Negotiation, 8,* 495—526.

Donohue, W. A., & Taylor, P. J. (2003). Testing the role effect in terrorist negotiations. *International Negotiation, 8,* 527—547.

Ebner, N. (2017). Negotiating via text messaging. In C. Honeyman, & A. K. Schneider (Eds.), *The negotiator's desk reference.* St Paul, MN: DRI Press.

Fuselier, G. W. (1981). A practical overview of hostage negotiations (Part I). *FBI Law Enforcement Bulletin, 50,* 2—6.

Giebels, E., & Noelanders, S. (2004). *Crisis negotiations: A multiparty perspective.* Veendendaal, Netherlands: Universal Press.

Giebels, E., & Taylor, P. J. (2010). Communication predictors and social influence in crisis negotiations. In R. G. Rogan, & F. J. Lanceley (Eds.), *Contemporary theory, research and practice of crisis and hostage negotiation* (pp. 59—77). United Kingdom: Hampton Press.

Greenstone, J. L. (1995). Crisis intervention skills: Training for police negotiators. *Police Chief, 62*(8), 30—34.

Greenstone, J. L., & Leviton, S. C. (2002). *The elements of crisis intervention: Crises and how to respond to them* (2nd ed.). Pacific Grove, CA: Brooks Cole.

Gregory, A. (2015). *R u there? A new counseling service harnesses the power of the text message.* The New Yorker. Retrieved from: https://www.newyorker.com/magazine/2015/02/09/r-u.

Grubb, A. (2010). Modern day hostage (crisis) negotiation: The evolution of an art form within the policing arena. *Aggression and Violent Behavior, 15,* 341—348.

Hammer, M. (2007). *Saving lives: The SAFE model for resolving hostage and crisis incidents.* Westport, CT: Praeger Security International.

Hare, A. (1997). Training crisis negotiators: Updating negotiation techniques and training. In R. G. Rogan, M. R. Hammer, & C. R. Van Zandt (Eds.), *Dynamic processes of crisis negotiation: Theory, research and practice* (pp. 151—160). Westport, CT: Praeger Security International.

Hatfield, E., Cacioppo, J. T., & Rapson, R. L. (1993). Emotional contagion. *Directions in Psychological Science, 2*, 96–100.

Hersen, M., & Van Hasselt, V. B. (1998). *Basic interviewing: A practical guide for counselors and clinicians*. Mahwah, NJ: Erlbaum.

Ivey, A. E., Ivey, M. B., Zalaquett, C. P., & Quirk, K. (2012). *Essentials of intentional interviewing: Counseling in a multicultural world*. Belmont, CA: Brooks/Cole Cengage Learning.

Johnson, K. E., Thompson, J., Hall, J. A., & Meyer, C. (2017). Crisis (hostage) negotiators weigh in: The skills, behaviors, and qualities that characterize an expert crisis negotiator. *Police Practice and Research, 19*(5), 472–489.

Juliano, & Yunes. (2014). Reflections on the social support network as a mechanism for protection and promotion of resilience. *Ambiente & Sociedade, 17*(3). Retrieved from http://www.scielo.br/scielo.php?pid=S1414753X2014000300009&script=sci_arttext&tlng=en.

Kam, H. (2017). *Automation in training? Elementary!*. Retrieved from https://www.crisistextline.org/blog/sherlock.

Lanceley, F. J. (2004). *Negotiation lessons learned by an FBI hostage negotiator*. Negotiator Magazine. Retrieved from http://www.negotiatormagazine.com/article235_1.html.

Lowther, M. (2015). *Negotiating with islamic extremists*. Retrieved from http://www.patc.com/weeklyarticles/print/2015_Negotiating1_Lowther.pdf.

McMains, M. J., & Mullins, W. C. (2015). *Crisis negotiations: Managing critical incidents and hostage situations in law enforcement and corrections*. New York: Routledge.

Meloy, R. (2000). *Violence risk & threat assessment : A practical guide for mental health & criminal justice professionals*. San Diego, CA: Specialized Training Services.

Meloy, R., & Hoffmann, J. (2014). *International handbook of threat assessment* (Oxford).

Michaud, P., St-Yves, M., & Guay, J. P. (2008). Predictive modeling in hostage and barricade incidents. *Criminal Justice and Behavior, 35*(9), 1136–1155.

Miller, L. (2005). Hostage negotiation, psychological principals and practices. *International Journal of Emergency Mental Health, 7*(4), 277–298.

Misino, D., & DeFelice, J. (2004). *Negotiate and win: Proven strategies from the NYPD's top hostage negotiator*. New York: McGraw-Hill.

New South Wales Department of Justice. (2017). *Inquest into the deaths arising from the Lindt Café siege. Findings and recommendations*. Retrieved from http://www.lindtinquest.justice.nsw.gov.au/Documents/findings-and-recommendations.pdf.

Noesner, G. W., & Dolan, J. T. (1992). First responder negotiator training. *FBI Law Enforcement Bulletin, 61*(8), 1–4.

Noesner, G. W., & Webster, M. (1997). Crisis intervention: Using active listening skills in negotiations. *FBI Law Enforcement Bulletin, 66*, 13–17.

Patrick, W. L. (June 15, 2016). *Orlando Shooter's homophobia, ideology or identity?*. Retrieved from https://www.psychologytoday.com/us/blog/why-bad-looks-good/201606/orlando-shooter-s-homophobia-ideology-or-identity.

Rogan, R. G. (2012). The communicative dynamics of crisis negotiation: Research, theory and application. In M. S. Yves, & P. Collins (Eds.), *The psychology of crisis intervention for law enforcement officers* (pp. 51–81). Montreal, Canada: Carswell.

Schlossberg, H. (1979). Police response to hostage situations. In J. T. O'Brien, & M. Marcus (Eds.), *Crime and Justice in America* (pp. 87–102). New York: Pergamon Press.

Shonk, K. (2018, November 20). *Negotiation examples: How crisis negotiators use text messaging*. Retrieved from https://www.pon.harvard.edu/daily/batna/with-no-good-batna-police-negotiators-accept-texts/.

Skeem, J., & Monahan, J. (2011). Current direction in violent risk assessment. *Current Directions in Psychological Sciences, 20*(1), 38–42.

Soskis, D. A., & Van Zandt, C. R. (1986). Hostage negotiation: Law enforcement's most effective nonlethal weapon. *Behavioral Sciences & the Law, 4*, 423–435.

St-Yves, M. (2014). Rapport in investigative interviews: Five fundamental rules to achieve it. In M. St-Yves (Ed.), Investigative interviewing: The essentials *(1-27)*. Toronto, Canada: Carswell.

St-Yves, M., & Collins, P. (2012). *The psychology of crisis intervention for law enforcement officers*. Toronto, Canada: Carswell.

St-Yves, M., & Michaud, P. (2012). From Munich to Columbine: A portrait of contemporary police responses to crisis situations. In M. St-Yves, & P. Collins (Eds.), *The psychology of crisis intervention for law enforcement officers* (pp. 3–22). Toronto, Canada: Carswell.

St-Yves, M., Tanguay, M., & St-Pierre, J. (2001). Le rythme de la crise/Following the rhythm of a crisis. *Revue Internationale de Police Criminelle/International/Criminal Police Review, 491*, 4–9.

St-Yves, M., & Veyrat, J. P. (2012). Negotiation models for crisis situations. In M. St-Yves, & P. Collins (Eds.), *The psychology of crisis intervention for law enforcement officers* (pp. 23–51). Toronto, Canada: Carswell.

Strentz, T. (1995). *The cyclic crisis negotiation time line*. Law and Order. March.

Taylor, P. J., & Donohue, W. A. (2006). Hostage negotiation opens up. In A. Schneider, & C. Honeymoon (Eds.), *The negotiator's fieldbook* (pp. 667–674). New York: American Bar Association Press.

Thoër, C., Noiseux, K., Siche, F., Palardy, C., Vanier, & Vrgnaud, C. (2017). Online text-based psychological intervention for youth in Quebec. *Sante Ment Que, 42*(1), 337–354.

Thompson, J. (2014a). Active Listening: Using "PRIME SOS" to recall the critical skills of crisis & hostage negotiators. In *Paper distributed during law enforcement hostage negotiation trainings*.

Thompson, J. (2014b). Applying hostage and crisis negotiation intervention strategies in commercial dispute resolution. *Alternatives to the High Cost of Litigation, 4*(32), 63–65, 52.

Thompson, J. (2014c). "Crisis" or "hostage" negotiation? The distinction between two important terms. *FBI Law Enforcement Bulletin, 3*(83). https://leb.fbi.gov/articles/featured-articles/crisis-or-hostage-negotiation-the-distinction-between-two-important-terms.

Thompson, J. (2015). *Nonverbal communication and the skills of effective mediators: Developing rapport, building trust, and displaying professionalism*. Thesis (PhD Doctorate). Brisbane, Australia: Griffith University. Retrieved from https://www120.secure.griffith.edu.au/rch/items/364d6bce-686c-4ad5-8968-64a732300f96/1/.

Thompson, J. (2018a). *Crisis counselor skills: Helping people in crisis in 160 characters or less*. Retrieved from https://www.mediate.com/articles/thompson-crisis-counselor.cfm.

Thompson, J. (2018b). Active Listening: Using "PRIME SOS+" to recall the critical skills of crisis & hostage negotiators. In *Paper distributed during law enforcement hostage negotiation trainings*.

Thompson, J., Ebner, N., & Giddings, J. (2017). Nonverbal communication in negotiation. In C. Honeyman, & A. K. Schneider (Eds.), *The negotiator's desk references*. St Paul, MN: DRI Press.

Tickle-Degnen, L., & Rosenthal, R. (1990). The nature of rapport and its nonverbal correlates. *Psychological Inquiry, 1*, 285–293.

Vecchi, G. M., Van Hasselt, V. B., & Romano, S. J. (2005). Crisis (hostage) negotiation: Current strategies and issues in theory and practice. *Aggression and Violent Behavior: A Review Journal, 10*(5), 533–551.

Walker, S., Kennedy, A., Vassilev, I., & Rogers, A. (2018). How do people with long-term mental health problems negotiate relationship with network members at times of crisis? *Health Expectations, 1*(21), 336–346.

Wargo, M. G. (1990). Communication skills for hostage negotiators. *Police Marksman, 52*(2).

Contributions of psychological science to enhancing law enforcement agencies' response to intimate partner violence

11

Mauro Paulino, Paulo Barbosa Marques, Miguel Oliveira Rodrigues and Stephen J. Morewitz

Introduction

Intimate partner violence (IPV) takes on a worldwide scope and is undoubtedly one of the most shocking crimes with complex implications for victims, the community, the health system, and social and judicial services (Ali & Naylor, 2013; Chan & Cho, 2010; Dillon, Hussain, Loxton, & Rahman, 2013; Eckhardt et al., 2013; Tjaden & Thoennes, 2000). Every 9 seconds, somewhere in the United States, a woman is assaulted by her intimate partner or ex-partner. More than 8.7 million women are assaulted every year (Paulino, 2016; Roberts, 1998; Yeager, Robets, & Roberts, 2015).

According to European statistics, one in four women is a victim of IPV, and investigations conducted by the World Health Organization estimate that throughout their life history, women experience various types of abuse, for which the prevalence is around 15%–71% (Garcia-Moreno, Jansen, Ellsberg, Heise, & Watts, 2005).

Echoing similar results from other countries (e.g., Catalano, 2012; Hulme, Morgan, & Boxall, 2019; Sinha, 2013), in the Portuguese context, women appear to be the main victims (80%) and men the main aggressors (85%). An average of 28,000 cases were reported to the Portuguese police, making domestic violence the second most prevalent crime against persons in Portugal (Gabinete do Secretário-Geral do Sistema de Segurança Interna, 2010, 2011, 2012, 2013, 2014, 2015, 2016, 2017, 2018, and 2019; Gomes & Duarte, 2018). According to a report published by the Observatório de Mulheres Assassinadas—União de Mulheres Alternativa e Resposta, the Portuguese observatory on femicide, from Jan. 2004 to Dec. 2018, a total of 503 women were victims of femicide (UMAR, 2019). Thus, IPV can be seen as the crime that most victimizes and kills women in the Portuguese context.

Police Psychology, Edited by Marques and Paulino. https://doi.org/10.1016/B978-0-12-816544-7.00011-5

The consequences of IPV can cross generations, because witnessing or being exposed to interparental violence, in general, has been associated with emotional, behavior, and learning problems in children (Carlson, Voith, Brown, & Holmes, 2019; Carpenter & Stacks, 2009; Margolin, 2005; Margolin & Gordis, 2000; McTavish, MacGregor, Wathen, & MacMillan, 2016; Paulino, 2016; Sani, 2018). Between Jan. 2010 and Dec. 2018, Portuguese law enforcement agencies (LEAs) responded to as many as 84.767 domestic violence incidents in which children were present (Castanho, 2019). This exposure to IPV leaves the children at risk for significant harm and may lead to child protection procedures. In 2019, 22,14% of the incidents reported to Portuguese child welfare and protection institutions, the Comissões de Protecção de Crianças e Jovens, were related to IPV, constituting the second leading cause of referral to the child protection system that year and the top cause for the past 5 years (Comissão Nacional de Promoção dos Direitos e Proteção das Crianças e Jovens, 2020).

Considering these facts, there is a need to adopt a more comprehensive and specialized approach to the prevention, investigation, prosecution, and follow-up of this emerging crime in the main LEAs by creating specialized services and units. In Portugal, the two police organizations that respond to cases of IPV are the Republican National Guard (GNR) and the Public Security Police (PSP). The GNR largely polices nonurban areas and has created special programs aimed at implementing proximity policing strategies and promoting a feeling of safety within the community. Moreover, this gendarmerie force developed special investigation teams (Investigation and Support to Vulnerable Victims Teams) at the district and local levels to respond to reports of violence against women. Some 443 officers were engaged in these teams during the most recent evaluation by the Group of Experts on Action against Violence against Women and Domestic Violence (GREVIO) (GREVIO, 2019). The PSP is city-based and pursues an intervention model linking crime prevention and proximity policing. The model special focuses on protecting vulnerable groups and victims of IPV through the work of Proximity and Victim Support Teams. In addition, both the GNR and the PSP incorporate Safe School Program Teams. The missions of these teams are to strengthen bonds between LEAs and citizens and prevent situations that may result in criminal offences, notably by raising awareness of issues related to gender equality and violence against women. The total number of professionals of the PSP with specific responsibilities related to domestic violence cases was 562 at the time of GREVIO's evaluation (GREVIO, 2019).

The complex nature of IPV warrants the attention of police organizations worldwide. An accurate understanding of this crime and an appreciation of the harm it causes to victims and their children is essential if officers are to be effective in carrying out their core policing activities of keeping victims safe and bringing offenders to justice (Her Majesty's Inspectorate of Constabulary, 2014). LEAs need to have the proper tools, resources, training, and partnerships in place to be successful in the prevention, response, investigation, and prosecution of IPV. Creating, implementing, and developing training on an IPV department policy ensures that an agency is prepared to respond successfully and effectively to preparing these complex cases and reinforces the safety of the community it serves (Artinopoulou, Koufouli, & Michael, 2018; Westera & Powell, 2017). According to the International Association of Chiefs of Police (IACP, 2018):

> *Training is necessary for all personnel, sworn and non-sworn, who have contact with intimate partner violence victims, including dispatch and communications, initial responder, and supervisors as well as those who investigate these crimes. All officers should receive ongoing training that specifically addresses the realities, dynamics, and investigations of these crimes, resources available to victims, common suspect behavior, and legal developments pertaining to intimate partner violence. Responders at every level need to recognize that they are accountable to the victim. (p. 7)*

With this perspective in mind, the police response to IPV cases should be as competent as possible and benefit from the contributions of psychological science.

Particularities of police intervention in the context of intimate partner violence

Research indicates that from 15% to more than 50% of all police calls result from situations of IPV, constituting the single largest category of calls received by police (Klein, 2009). Because this form of violence occurs mainly in the private space of the home, and considering the vulnerability of the victim, this problem requires police authorities to take particular care with regard to their immediate protection and security, their rights, and the guarantee of the correct collection of evidence (Rodrigues & Paulino, 2018).

The complexity and demand of the activity require the police to arrive at the scene, discriminate between conflicting stories, examine the psychological state of the victim, assess the potential dangerousness of the alleged perpetrator, and provide necessary support and guidance to the victim (Arrigo & Shipley, 2005). In addition, most victims of IPV are assaulted over time, posing challenges to the investigation of victims' ability to recall specific events. Interviewing victims of repeated violence requires specific and scientifically supported techniques and strategies, an example of which is cognitive interviewing (Hartwig, Dawson, Wrede, & Ask, 2011; Marques, 2018; Milne, Griffiths, Clarke, & Dando, 2019).

In Portugal, we observed a small number of studies, analyses, and assessments of different organizations engaged in policing and criminal justice, namely LEAs. There are a few exceptions to the scarcity of research conducted in the Portuguese context; this chapter will focus further attention on the unique contribution of these initiatives. Later in this chapter, we will briefly describe and explain one study in which the competencies of police officers responding to IPV have been investigated. First, we will summarize conclusions to be drawn from official reports that evaluate the intervention of various Portuguese public services, including of LEAs, which have acted in homicide cases within the context of IPV. These reports are the result of work carried out by a team created by the Government of Portugal known as the Equipa de Análise Retrospetiva de Homicídio em Violência Doméstica (EARHVD), which conducts domestic violence homicide reviews in a way similar to that in other jurisdictions (e.g., Australian Human Rights Commission, 2016; Home Office, 2016). The measures and/or recommendations resulting from the team analysis are systematized according to different areas: health, internal administration, justice, social security, and gender equality. The respective reports are sent to members of the government responsible for these areas and are publicly available. Some failures in the procedures of police work have been reported and resulted in recommendations to LEAs.

As part of its first report, the EARHVD states that the IPV risk assessment should be carried out by specialized professionals with experience in the topic' this indicates that in cases in which this does not prove viable, it must be supervised by a professional with proper expertise and experience within a period not exceeding 48 hours. Measures for implementing the protection and safety plan designed for the victim, as well as any incidents related to their adoption, must be registered in a document to be attached to the criminal file, so that it is possible to know and control its effective execution. Another aspect covered by this report was the important recommendation for police officers to avoid conducting interviews with victims and offenders on the same day. To protect the victim better, this procedure should be carried out on different days (EARHVD, 2017).

According to the fourth report of the same team, it is recommended that LEAs seriously consider adequate training in the fields of IPV, violence against women, and domestic violence, to improve frontline police officers' knowledge about the characteristics and dynamics of this form of violence. Moreover, proper training will increase the quality of their performance in the reception and care of the victim, collection of evidence, risk assessment, and design and implementation of the safety plan. EARHVD further advises LEAs to report any incident or intervention related to the possible existence of violence in interpersonal relationships, even if it does not lead to the start of a legal procedure (EARHVD, 2018a).

With regard to its fifth report, EARHVD (2018b) recommends that in cases of violence against women and domestic violence, direct or indirect involvement or affected children should be investigated. Furthermore, the violence risk assessment and the adoption of appropriate security measures that consider the specific needs of children should be accomplished by LEAs, as well as the report of incidents to the Portuguese child protection system and/or the competent judicial authority, to protect and promote their rights.

In an analysis of the international context, we find important manuals developed by the United Nations (United Nations Office on Drugs and Crime, 2010a, 2010b) that introduce a training model and specific guidelines for police officers to respond effectively and appropriately to IPV. The contribution of these manuals leads to potential far-reaching improvements in the way LEAs prevent and prosecute domestic violence by including measures to prevent violence against women, forms of response, research, and resources to meet the needs of victims during and after an incident. Some of the programmatic content indicates the clear need for police officers to know how to define contexts, know the statistics and various forms of violence against women, understand the vulnerabilities of these victims, recognize the wide variety of factors that contribute to this violence, and broadly describe the legislation and responses of judicial authorities to violence against women and international conventions on violence against women. They also alert the police to identify possible gaps in local and national legislation, recognize the impact of these faults, and seek to promote the necessary improvements.

Historically, many police organizations have lacked the training opportunities, resources, and support needed to address IPV effectively. In addition, some less obvious forms of abuse (e.g., verbal and emotional abuse, coercive control, financial abuse) receive less attention than others owing to erroneous beliefs and misunderstandings about this crime and the realities of its victims and perpetrators. An exploratory study on the attitudes and perceptions of police officers about the occurrences of IPV mainly in urban areas of the western zone of the United States obtained troubling results. Some of the findings showed a high level of frustration over the time that calls for IPV and associated bureaucracy occupy in the general context of incidents in which the police is involved. Officers seem confused about the complexities of IPV, and a significant number of respondents (93%) support the idea that too many IPV cases consist of verbal family arguments that require no police intervention. Another area of concern emerges from the results showing that most police officers in the sample expressed doubts that specialized training would help them respond more competently to cases of IPV (Gover, Paul, & Dodge, 2011).

McPhedran, Gover, and Mazerolle (2017) conducted a cross-national examination of American and Australian police officers' attitudes toward IPV. Bivariate analyses were conducted to determine whether attitudes varied by the country and gender of the responding officers. The results indicated that the gender of the respondents does not lead to significant differences in their attitudes about IPV. The findings of Gover and colleagues (2011) also lend support to earlier suggestions that (a) the amount of time and resources consumed by IPV incidents may represent a significant concern for police; (b) the ability to use discretion to decide the most appropriate course of action when responding to IPV remains an area of concern for law enforcement officers; and (c) most officers surveyed in both police departments believe that too many IPV calls relate to verbal arguments (McPhedran et al., 2017). A common view among male officers in Australia is that IPV should be handled as a private matter. Jennett (2012) offers a potential explanation for this misconception, stating that officers themselves are drawn from the general community and some continue to hold attitudes about IPV that indicate an unwillingness to interfere in the "private" domain of intimate relationships. Goodman-Delahunty and Crehan (2016) examined Australian client advocates and legal practitioners' experiences with the New South Wales Police Force complaint system and came to the key conclusion regarding these discretionary decisions when responding to IPV. The authors stated in their conclusions that many police officers seem to believe that their responsibilities when responding to this crime are matters of discretion rather obligation. However, failure to investigate or inadequate investigation was the second most common form of misconduct identified in an audit of the LEA's handling of domestic and family violence complaints.

Therefore, enhancing knowledge regarding attitudes of police officers toward IPV is recommended to implement improvements in training programs and better responses to this serious and pervasive crime (McPhedran et al., 2017).

IPV is underreported to LEAs (Tjaden & Thoennes, 2000). The way police responds to this crime is decisive in whether and how the victims seek help and determine their future intention to involve the police. Prior studies highlighted several factors affecting IPV victims' decisions and barriers to police reporting, such as situational and personal factors, including the type of abuse (e.g., physical or psychological abuse), fear of escalation and further violence from the offender, economic dependence on the abuser, and fear that involving police may disrupt the family or result in the removal of their children (Wolf, Ly, Hobart, & Kernic, 2003). Therefore, understanding the perspective of those exposed to IPV is critical to developing practice standards as well as informing law enforcement officers. Saxton, Olszowy, MacGregor, MacQuarrie, and Wathen (2018) used a subset of data from the first pan-Canadian survey on IPV to examine (a) rates of reporting to the police; (b) experiences with, and perceived helpfulness of, police; (c) rates of involvement with the criminal and family law systems, including protection orders; and (d) experiences with, and perceived helpfulness of, the justice system. The authors concluded that despite overall satisfaction, many victims are often unhappy with some aspect of the police intervention. Despite low reporting rates, victims of IPV who come into contact with the police are often in need of immediate protection, which further stresses the vital role LEAs have in this type of crime, by stopping the violence and empowering victims to make decisions that will increase their safety and help them end the cycle of abuse. The importance of police response to IPV is reflected by the extensive body of empirical evidence on risk assessment and management by police (Belfrage et al., 2012; Kebbell, 2019; Storey, Kropp, Hart, Belfrage, & Strand, 2014).

In Canada, Ballucci, Gill, and Campbell (2017) analyzed the support and resistance of police officers to risk assessment tools in IPV cases, because the success of such strategies depends on their attitudes, knowledge, and perceptions regarding risk tools and IPV. The results showed some negative perceptions and attitudes toward the risk assessment instruments and toward the perception of the crime itself.

In the United Kingdom, since 2013, Her Majesty's Inspectorate of Constabulary (HMIC) conducts an inspection on the police response to situations of IPV. In this inspection, HMIC collected data and reviewed files from 43 LEAs in England and Wales; interviewed 70 victims of this crime, who participated in focus groups; and surveyed more than 500 victims online, as well as around 200 professionals working with victims of IPV. In this analysis of LEAs, in addition to the interviews, focus groups were held with frontline personnel and included unannounced visits to police stations to test the implemented approaches. In short, the findings indicated that the LEAs' general response to victims of IPV was not effective enough, pointing to unacceptable failures in essential policing activities, crime investigation, and crime prevention, including errors that could lead perpetrators to escape the law, as well as weaknesses in maintaining victims' safety (Her Majesty's Inspectorate of Constabulary, 2014). In 2017, the third report in a series of thematic reports that examined the police response to UK domestic violence victims, Her Majesty's Inspectorate of Constabulary and Fire and Rescue Services (HMICFRS, 2017) inspection, concluded that seven of the 43 LEAs still had a "cause of concern" (i.e., a serious or critical shortcoming in the LEA practice, policy, or performance) regarding response to this crime. Moreover, HMICFRS' inspection identified a total of 33 of 43 forces that had aspects that fell short of the expected standard (i.e., areas for improvement). Some of the most troubling findings related to downgrading the severity of calls and conducting the violence risk assessment inappropriately (e.g., HMICFRS raised concerns about the practice of conducting the initial risk assessment over the telephone), a practice that may be putting already vulnerable victims at an even greater risk. Cases were also detected in which police officers did not detain suspects in situations in which this would be appropriate, thus not bringing them to justice. It is crucial that police officers fully appraise the wider situation and understand that sometimes victims might not want the intimate partner to be arrested because of the *coercive control* exerted by him. The HMICFRS (2017) inspection states that potentially intolerable consequences for victims of IPV can result from the failure of police officers to exercise their power of arrest.

Past research showed that police officers were less inclined to arrest in domestic than nondomestic assaults. According to Eigenberg, Scarborough, and Kappeler (1996), victims of IPV apparently had to work harder to provide evidence of victimization before perpetrators were arrested. To eliminate police inaction in cases of IPV, several jurisdictions implemented mandatory arrest policies for law enforcement responses toward this crime. Current research on the topic indicates that domestic violence arrest rates have risen as a direct result of the implementation of mandatory arrest laws. However, research also suggests that these laws may have counterproductive effects on the response to IPV. It seems that such domestic violence laws influence a broader range of cases than intended and resulted in higher dual arrest rates, a situation in which both parties to an incident are arrested (Hirschel, Buzawa, Pattavina, & Faggiani, 2008). Recent reforms, such as primary aggressor laws mandating that officers determine who the primary aggressor is in the incident, have reduced the prevalence of unjust victim arrest. Nevertheless, evidence also suggests that when law enforcement officers are instructed to arrest the primary aggressor, they are often reluctant to make any arrest (Hirschel, McCormack, & Buzawa, 2017).

Dolon, Hendricks, and Meagher (1986) surveyed 125 police officers and found that a variety of factors directly influenced officers' arrest decisions. In order of importance, they are: (1) use of violence against the police; (2) commission of a felony; (3) use of a weapon; (4) serious injury to the victim; (5) likelihood of future violence; (6) frequent calls for police assistance from the household; (7) offender intoxicated with alcohol or drugs; (8) disrespect toward police officers; (9) previous injury to victim or damage to property; (10) previous legal action (restraining order);

and (11) victim insisting on arrest. In another study, Feder (1997) surveyed 297 South Florida police officers and found that the most significant factors contributing to their decision to arrest were belief in the utility of police involvement, knowledge of the department's arrest policy, and attitudes toward women. This suggests that police officers decisions are influenced by gender schemas, stereotypes, and norms. Research on violence in general demonstrates that social norms reflect paternalistic and protective attitudes toward women, by showing that people evaluated violence from a man to a woman more negatively than violence from a woman to a man (e.g., Felson & Feld, 2009). Russell (2018) asked 273 police officers from 27 states in the United States to complete an online research study and examined how disputants' gender and sexual orientation influence respondents' perceptions of IPV. Results showed that police perceptions of potential danger, likelihood of past or future harm to the intimate partner, and victim credibility are influenced by disputant gender and sexual orientation. In another contribution to the study of arrest practices, Tatum and Pence (2015) examined 3200 IPV calls and concluded that severity of crime, presence of children, presence of an injunction, and victim injury increased the likelihood of an arrest. Research on police officers' attitudes toward IPV brings another variable into the equation. It is apparent that the risk for injury represents a significant police concern when responding to IPV; around 76% of American officers and 79% of Australian officers agreed that they were more likely to be injured at an IPV call than any other call (McPhedran et al., 2017). It is reasonable to suggest that the fear of injury may have an impact on police officers' response to IPV incidents.

It is clear that police officers need to reflect critically on a multiplicity of factors when responding to an IPV incident. It might be helpful to assess the potential risk for violence in the decision to arrest, because it helps an officer to understand better the risk posed and the dynamics of violence in a given case (Gill, Campbell, & Balluci, 2019).

Prediction and management of risk for intimate partner violence

The first and most important goal of police intervention in IPV is to ensure the safety and protection not only of the victim(s) but also of all actors, including the police themselves. A thoroughly collection of all information available about the IPV incident or complaint allows conducting, as comprehensively as possible, an effective risk assessment. The protection and safety of the victim are a priority and the reason why LEAs must be able to conduct an adequate assessment of the likelihood of IPV perpetration, repeated victimization, and escalation of frequency or severity of abuse, including the risk for intimate partner homicide.

Risk assessment in IPV is thus composed of a process of collecting and analyzing information about the people involved, with the initiative to make decisions according to the risk for recurrence of violence (Kropp, 2008; Kropp, Hart, Webster, & Eaves, 1995). In this sense, risk assessment in IPV involves five basic principles (Whittemore & Kropp, 2002): (1) it should use multiple sources of information; (2) it should consider risk factors supported in the literature; (3) it should be victim informed; (4) it can be improved by using decision-support tools or guidelines; and (5) it should lead to risk management.

The first principle of risk assessment requires the evaluator, technician, professional, using several methods, to obtain multiple sources of information. In an ideal concept, the risk assessment of IPV should be based on interviews with the abuser and victim, the criminal record consultation, the psychological assessment, and other sources of information considered relevant by the evaluator.

A second principle is based on the fact that the evaluator must consider only evidence-based risk factors (Kropp, 2008), according to theoretical and empirical support where he can assimilate and identify multiple information (e.g., history of violent behavior against family members; history of physical, sexual, or emotional violence against intimate partners; use or access to weapons; antisocial attitudes and behaviors; unstable relationships, including a history of separation or divorce; stressful life events, including financial problems, unemployment, or recent loss; victim or witness of IPV in childhood; evidence of mental health problems or personality disorders; resistance to change and motivation for treatment; attitude supporting violence against women; stalking behaviors).

The third principle points to the relevance of risk assessment procedures' attempt to interview the victim or obtain the victims' version of the facts from alternative sources. A risk assessment based solely on information provided by the perpetrator of IPV should be made with extreme caution, because this may minimize or even deny their responsibility and thus lead to an underestimate of risk to the victim. A comprehensive and fair attempt to assess the risk of violence reasonably should allow comparison between the victim's and accused's version of events.

The fourth principle is related to the recommendation to use structured risk assessment instruments, because in this appraisal of risk, the evaluator should be able to communicate his conclusions about the level of risk. The use of evidence-based risk assessment tools avoids potential pitfalls of the procedure by imposing the necessary structure without eliminating some discretion when conducting the task.

The fifth principle has to do with the idea that effective management of the risk posed by the perpetrator and victim safety must not end with a risk assessment. In fact, reporting offenders' risk without the proposal of tangible measures to manage that risk is insufficient. At this stage, the decision-making process can be reviewed and explained, and risk assessment will guide this process. This should be documented in detail and within the reach of the various professionals involved. Here, the evaluators should appropriately select the risk management strategies, with the implementation of four main activities (Kropp, 2008): (1) monitoring and surveillance; (2) evaluation and treatment; (3) control and supervision; and (4) victim safety plans.

In a contribution to the field, the European Institute for Gender Equality (EIGE, 2019) prepared a guide providing LEAs with practical guidelines and recommendations regarding how to develop and implement risk assessment and risk management approaches. Within this framework, the European Institute for Gender Equality included core principles to be considered followed by recommendations to the police on improving risk management, considering the gendered dynamics of IPV and adopting a victim-centered approach. Table 11.1 presents the main principles to be considered by LEAs in their risk assessment and risk management strategies.

Risk factors for severe intimate partner violence

The growing development of risk assessment instruments is based on the premise that certain individual and environmental characteristics or circumstances can be used to predict the risk for future offending behaviors, with particular importance in police activity (Campbell, Gill, & Ballucci, 2018; Hilton, Pham, Jung, Nunes, & Ennis, 2020; Kebbell, 2019; Kropp, 2008; Perez Trujillo & Ross, 2008).

Several scientific contributions help to clarify risk factors related to the occurrence of serious violence or homicide, which must be mastered by police officers when dealing with IPV. It is essential to assess factors carefully, such as an increase in the frequency and intensity of aggressions, extreme minimization or denial of spousal assault history, the need for mental health monitoring and intervention, drug and alcohol abuse, death threats, coercive control, stalking, imposition of continued deprivation of liberty, torture, use of dangerous instruments or weapons, prior record of violence, past violation of conditional release or community supervision, psychopathy, chaotic family environment, and abuse in the family of origin, among others (Belfrage & Rying, 2004; Belfrage & Strand, 2008; Campbell et al., 2003; Capaldi, Knoble, Shortt, & Kim, 2012; Dutton & Hart, 1992; Grann & Wedin, 2002; Morewitz, 2004, 2008; Paulino, 2016, 2017; Saunders, 1995).

There are studies indicating that when lethal outcomes occur for victims, violence has increased in frequency or severity in the month preceding the homicide. This is why it is necessary to discriminate whether episodes of violence have occurred more frequently or severely over time, especially in the past month (Paulino, 2016).

Based on the main risk factors identified in the literature, Saavedra and Fonseca (2013) point out that within the Portuguese context, the use of weapons and death threats is associated with episodes of severe and repeated violence: men who make credible death threats have a greater risk for the recurrence of violence. Moreover, aggressors who have used or threatened to use weapons have a greater risk for recurrence of violence and an increased risk for intimate partner homicide. These assumptions corroborate the conclusions of Campbell et al. (2003) showing that threatening the victim with a weapon and previous threats to kill the victim are factors that more closely predict intimate partner femicide.

In a study of 19 cases of intimate partner homicides, as part of the validation process of the Portuguese domestic violence risk assessment form, Ficha de Avaliação

Table 11.1 Core principles for police risk assessment and risk management of intimate partner violence.

Guidelines on risk assessment	**Principle 1** Prioritizing victim safety	Recognize and effectively assess the risk of repeat victimization, intimidation and retaliation in the context of intimate partner violence and ensure that victims receive the most effective support possible to reduce that risk. In this way, risk assessment is not an end in itself but an entry point for female victims to the victim support system, regardless of risk level.
	Principle 2 Adopting a victim-centered approach	Ensure that risk assessment leads to the identification of a victim's specific needs. In turn, this informs appropriate risk management strategies by the police that are tailored to the needs and situation of the victim and the perpetrator.
	Principle 3 Carrying out gender-competent risk assessment	Risk assessment practices must reflect an understanding of how gender relations and women's inequality shape women's and children's experiences of intimate partner violence. Gender-competent police officers understand the gender dynamics of violence against women and are capable of predicting lethality.
	Principle 4 Adopting an intersectional approach	Risk assessment should include consideration of the circumstances and life experiences of each individual. The personal characteristics of a victim are crucial in identifying victims' individual safety needs and possible barriers to accessing support and protection.
	Principle 5 Considering children's experiences	Risk assessment should be child competent in that it routinely and robustly takes into account the impact of abuse on children and informs risk management strategies that address their individual safety needs.
Recommendations on risk management	**Principle 1** Gender-specific approach to risk management	Police officers are capable of understanding the gender dynamics of intimate partner violence and can develop, with the contribution of victims and the collaboration of other relevant agencies, strategies that ensure victims' safety from physical and psychological violence.
	Principle 2 Individualized approach	Police officers take into consideration individual characteristics such as race, disability, age, religion, immigration status, ethnicity and sexual orientation, and implement interventions aimed at preventing victims' secondary victimization.
	Principle 3 evidence-based approach	Delivering victim safety and reduced reoffending requires an evidence-based approach to policing intimate partner violence. Such an approach requires good data and proportionate monitoring and evaluating risk management strategies and interventions, to better prevent repeat victimization.
	Principle 4 Outcome-focused approach	The processes of risk management must be underpinned by a consistent focus on the main purposes of risk management: Victim safety and reduced reoffending.
	Principle 5 Coordinated multi-agency response	Multi-agency mechanisms are a prominent strategy for effectively responding to intimate partner violence. These mechanisms may take the form of informal multiagency cooperation on a case-by-case basis between, for example, police and a local victim services organization or of formal referral processes for victims that are underpinned by negotiated working protocols across multiple stakeholders.

Adapted from European Institute for Gender Equality, EIGE. (2019). A guide to risk assessment and risk management of intimate partner violence against women for police. Luxembourg: Publications Office of the European Union.

de Risco em Situações de Violência (RVD), it was observed that in 73.7% of cases there were previous episodes of violence and coercive control, and extreme jealousy and stalking behaviors; in 47.4% of cases, the first episode of violence occurred 1 year before the homicide; in 63.2% of cases, there was an increase in the frequency or severity of the violence in the month before the homicide; in 57.9% of cases, the perpetrator had a firearm or easy access to one; and perpetrators had previously threatened the victim with a weapon in 52.6% of cases (DGAI, 2013).

In addition, previous attempts to asphyxiate the victim (or other family members) also presents a high risk for lethality, because research has shown that strangulation is a key method to establish coercive control, and it is often a precursor to femicide (Campbell et al, 2003; Campbell, Glass, Sharps, Laughon, & Bloom, 2007; Dobash, Dobash, & Cavanagh, 2009; Glass et al., 2008; Klein, 2009; Messing, Patch, Wilson, Kelen, & Campbell, 2018; Thomas, Joshi, & Sorenson, 2014).

Another important factor concerns the existence of previous acts of sexual violence by the aggressor. Some studies indicate that victims of IPV who have experienced sexual violence are more likely to experience more severe or even lethal episodes of physical violence (Campbell et al., 2007; Spencer & Stith, 2020).

An equally risk-enhancing factor is present in cases in which the perpetrator is very controlling, reveals obsessive jealousy, and displays persistent pursuit or stalking behaviors (e.g., Monckton Smith, 2020; Monckton-Smith, Szymanska, & Haile, 2017). The context in which several intimate partner homicides occur is one of male coercive control, which is often triggered by loss of control owing to impending separation or real or imagined infidelity (Johnson, Eriksson, Mazerolle, & Wortley, 2019; Sheehan, Murphy, Moynihan, Dudley-Fennessey, & Stapleton, 2015). According to Campbell et al. (2003), "When the worst incident of abuse was triggered by the victim's having left the abuser for another partner or by the abuser's jealousy, there was a nearly 5-fold increase in femicide risk" (p. 1091). Studies conducted in several countries indicate that one-third to one-half of all women killed by partners had separated or were planning to separate at the time of the murder (Campbell et al., 2003; Dobash et al., 2009; Johnson & Hotton, 2003; Wilson & Daly, 1993).

In these cases, the perpetrator cannot accept the actual or suspected termination of an intimate relationship, nor is he able to cope with rejection by his female partner. Often, he commits suicide after killing what he perceives to be his "extended self" (Palermo, 1994).

In an analysis of 22 articles between 2012 and 2018 on homicide-suicide in the context of IPV, Zeppegno et al. (2019) identified that occurrences were committed predominantly by men, usually married, cohabiting, or recently separated from the partner, with a medium to low-paying job. The victim is usually the current or former partner. In fact, the killing of women by men who then take their own lives (femicide-suicide) is the most common form of homicide-suicide (Bossarte, Simon, & Barker, 2006; Violence Policy Center, 2012). Building on this idea, another risk factor should be mentioned: prior perpetrator suicide threats (Koziol-McLain et al., 2006). Research conducted within the Portuguese context analyzing 19 intimate partner homicides indicated the presence of suicide-homicide threats by the perpetrator in 52.6% of cases (DGAI, 2013).

Another important risk factor may arise from the victim's pregnancy. IPV during pregnancy appears to be a risk factor for severe IPV, including attempted or completed femicide (Martin, Macy, Sullivan, & Magee, 2007).

Campbell et al. (2003) examined all consecutive femicide police or medical examiner records from 1994 through 2000 in 11 US cities and concluded that pregnancy significantly increased women's risk for becoming a victim of intimate partner homicide. Evidence from this 11-city study also showed that male perpetrators who abuse their pregnant intimate partners seem to be particularly dangerous and more likely to commit homicide.

According to the research, women abused during pregnancy are four times more likely to experience severe violence, including beatings, suffocation, armed attacks, and sexual violence (Barnish, 2004). Perpetrators may also engage in "reproductive coercion" behaviors and force or manipulate the intimate partner into becoming pregnant (i.e., pregnancy coercion); prevent the intimate partner from using contraception or tampering with contraceptives (i.e., birth control sabotage); or force the victim into an unwanted pregnancy or to abort against her will (i.e., control of pregnancy outcomes) (Miller & Silverman, 2010; Paulino, 2016).

Another important risk factor is related to the variability of social, cultural, and religious norms, values, or beliefs, in which tolerance or censorship of violence may differ according to the social, cultural, or racial/ethnic minority group or professed religion to which the victim belongs (Do, Weiss, & Pollack, 2013; Ellison, Trinitapoli, Anderson, & Johnson, 2007; Vandello & Cohen, 2003). Prior research suggested that in cultures of honor, IPV is more tolerated (Dietrich & Schuett, 2013; Vandello & Cohen, 2003). Honor ideology is also associated with an increased likelihood of men actually engaging in violent and sexually coercive behaviors toward women (Brown, Baughman, & Carvallo, 2018). Regarding religious variations, evidence shows that men who hold much more conservative theological views than their partners are especially likely to perpetrate IPV (Ellison, Bartkowski, & Anderson, 1999).

Risk assessment tools for intimate partner violence

With the premise of prevention, it becomes important to determine what steps should be taken to minimize risks. The use of risk assessment instruments by police officers has the potential to make an enormous difference regarding how IPV is policed (Kebbell, 2019). Risk assessment tools allow LEAs to allocate their often limited resources based on the estimated level or extent of harm to victims. Moreover, because it is an evidence-based procedure, it grants a framework of reasonableness and objectivity to the decisions of less experienced frontline police officers, providing a certain structure to their intervention in IPV occurrences (Kebbell, 2019).

Several risk assessment instruments for IPV have been developed and validated in a variety of settings. For the purpose of this chapter, we will mention tools that tend to produce the most reliable risk estimates for predicting future IPV. In particular, there is sufficient evidence supporting the use of these instruments (Graham, Sahay, Rizo, Messing, & Macy, 2021; Hanson, Helmus, & Bourgon, 2007; Hilton et al., 2020; Messing & Thaller, 2013; Nicholls, Pritchard, Reeves, & Hilterman, 2013):

- Brief Spousal Assault Form for the Evaluation of Risk (B-SAFER) (Kropp, Hart, & Belfrage, 2005)
- Danger Assessment (DA) (Campbell, Webster, & Glass, 2009)
- Domestic Violence Risk Appraisal Guide (DVRAG) (Hilton, Harris, Rice, Houghton, & Eke, 2008)
- Domestic Violence Screening Instrument (DVSI/DVSI-R) (Williams & Houghton, 2004; Williams & Grant, 2006)
- Ontario Domestic Assault Risk Assessment (ODARA) (Hilton et al., 2004)
- Spousal Assault Risk Assessment (SARA) (Kropp et al., 1995)

Most of these risk measures are not appropriate for use by LEA because they were designed for clinical purposes (e.g., SARA) or are too lengthy for use by frontline police officers (e.g., DA, DVRAG). Among commonly available tools, only ODARA and B-SAFER were developed especially for use by law enforcement officials to assess risk for IPV (Kebbell, 2019; Nicholls et al., 2013; Storey et al., 2014).

Messing and Thaller (2013) examined the average predictive validity weighted by sample size of five IPV risk assessment tools and concluded that ODARA is the most predictive instrument, followed by SARA and DA. However, B-SAFER was not included in this research.

The predictive validity of B-SAFER was examined in a study focused on a Swedish police setting and showed area under the curve values of around 0.70 and significant associations between B-SAFER total scores and subsequent psychological and physical violence (Storey et al., 2014). According to Kebbell (2019), ODARA and B-SAFER are comparable in predictive validity.

We now present a brief overview of these two tools and introduce the instrument used within the Portuguese context.

Ontario Domestic Assault Risk Assessment

ODARA is a 13-item actuarial tool developed in collaboration with the Ontario Provincial Police. This instrument was designed to predict general IPV and is intended for use by police officers when responding to an IPV occurrence. The items require assessors to collect and review information such as criminal records, history of IPV incidents, and general antisocial behavior of the offender. The 13 ODARA items are scored as 1 or 0 according to the presence or absence, respectively, of risk factors: confinement of the victim during index assault; existence of threat to harm or kill anyone at the index assault; victim concern about future offences; victim and/or offender have more than one child together; victim has a biological child with someone other than the offender; offender has committed assault on the victim while she was pregnant; offender has more than one indicator of a substance abuse problem; victim faces at least one barrier to support; offender has a prior violent incident against a nondomestic victim (offender is violent outside the home); offender has a prior domestic assault in a police report or criminal record (against current or former partner or partner's child); offender has a prior nondomestic incident of assault in a police record or criminal record (against any person other than a partner or a partner's child); offender has a prior custodial sentence of 30 days or more; and evidence of failure on current or prior conditional release (including bail, parole, probation, or pretrial release order) or conditions of a restraining order. If the final score is 7 or above, the person is in the highest risk category.

Brief Spousal Assault Form for the Evaluation of Risk

B-SAFER, also known in some European countries as the Police Version of SARA, is a structured professional judgment instrument developed to assess and manage IPV risk in criminal justice settings. This tool was developed in 2005 to assist police in undertaking risk management decisions, because the authors considered that SARA might not be the most advantageous tool for use by LEA, because it is relatively long and entails specific judgments about psychopathology (Kropp et al., 2005). Thus, on the basis that the instrument was time-consuming and requires clinical skills to complete it proficiently, a number of modifications were made to the SARA to make it more appropriate for police settings.

The B-SAFER is composed of 10 items divided in two sections: perpetrator risk factors (items 1−5) and psychosocial adjustment (items 6−10). Risk factors are described as being present (coded as 2), partly present (coded as 1), or absent (coded as 0) in the current (i.e., within the past 4 weeks) and past situation (i.e., more than 4 weeks ago). The latest version of the B-SAFER (version 2) includes a third section containing five victim vulnerability factors (e.g., unsafe living situation and inadequate access to resources) in an attempt to accommodate police officers' feedback condemning the absence of such factors in the former version (Kropp, Hart, & Belfrage, 2010; Storey & Strand, 2012). The aim of assessing victim vulnerability is to protect victims from repeat violence (Storey & Strand, 2017).

To determine the nature or degree of risk, police officers must collect information available by consulting the offender and victim involved in the IPV episode, or through other sources of information available (e.g., witnesses, police reports). Once all information is systematized and risk factors are assessed, a global risk assessment is conducted. Although total scores can be derived from summing scores; the instrument does not apply cutoff scores to determine the nature of the risk posed by the perpetrator. The main focus is on preventing IPV, and it requires police officers to determine appropriate risk management strategies based on the identified risk factors (Kropp et al., 2005).

Portuguese domestic violence risk assessment form

In Portugal, as of Nov. 1, 2014, a domestic violence risk assessment tool was implemented and replaced the form created in 2006, which was not of mandatory completion. The current instrument, which is mandatory in all cases of IPV, is the RVD. It has two versions, one that is used in a first complaint (RVD-1L) and another for revaluation (RVD-2L) (Rodrigues & Paulino, 2018). In addition to RVD, there are three relevant support manuals not only in the context of this instrument, but also in the broader framework of a model of policing that involves this crime: the RVD—Manual de Aplicação da Ficha de Avaliação de Risco (available and directed to support and/or guide police officers in the correct application of the instrument), the Manual de Policiamento da Violência Doméstica, and the Manual de Apoio para o Plano de Segurança para Vítimas de Violência Doméstica" (Procuradoria-Geral Distrital de Lisboa, 2015).

In addition to risk factors, this instrument has a list of safety-promoting measures intended to contribute to risk management. As mentioned, when a complaint of domestic violence is made, the police officer must fill out all 20 items in the RVD. After they are duly filled, this risk assessment tool may indicate three distinct levels of risk: low, medium, or high. According to these categories, the risk is revaluated within a maximum of 60 days for low-risk situations, within a period not exceeding 30 days for medium-risk cases, and 72 hours for high risk for harm (Rodrigues & Paulino, 2018).

Inattention to investment in a framework for risk assessment and risk management of IPV can lead to neglect of protection policies, unawareness and lack of technical skills for professionals carrying out duties in the area of IPV, lack of knowledge of specificities of assessment and intervention with certain groups of victims, particularly vulnerable ones and, for obvious reasons, serious cases of victimization and lethality (Saavedra & Fonseca, 2013). In a risk scenario such as IPV, police must take appropriate protective measures providing self-protection that are part of an important and necessary *safety plan*, an instrument that must be victim-informed, as we discuss further in the next section.

Safety planning with intimate partner violence victims

Safety planning is a major outcome of the IPV risk assessment, and LEAs have a role in helping to develop and support safety plans as part of risk management procedures (EIGE, 2019).

A safety plan is an instrument based on the definition and provision of guidelines for self-protection and prevention of risk and danger to a specific victim, considering a characterization of the current situation reported, as well as relevant information collected from other sources, defining strategies for security assessed by the victim as possible to be executed, within various contexts in which victimization may occur, without increasing the possible risk for violence. A safety plan alone does not guarantee the physical and mental integrity of an IPV victim, but when properly developed and personalized, it can make the difference in the possible avoidance of serious injuries or even the difference between life and death.

In consonance with the Portuguese law, LEAs must be aware of all safety plans applied in the respective areas of intervention, as well as of any changes that may be introduced in them.

According to Davies (2017), these plans frequently rely on physical separation and a victim abandoning a relationship to increase safety. The author states that this almost exclusive focus on physical violence may result in limited safety or even increase the vulnerability of some victims (e.g., a plan might reduce the risk for violence but leave a victim homeless and with no source of income to survive if other measures are not considered).

We highlight the importance of this safety plan being worked out in negotiation with victims and according to their circumstances, because each case is unique. The victim should be informed about safety measures and instructions in a format that the professional understands as more accessible to the victim's specific idiosyncrasies and needs and the particularities of each case. Each victim's perspective and priorities for safety involve her risk analysis, life circumstances, and plans. These are unique to each victim. Understanding that context for each victim is important to decide what strategies will be relevant (Davies, 2017; EIGE, 2019).

In this sense, police officers must work with victims on a range of safety scenarios (Paulino & Rodrigues, 2016):

- *Safety during the episode of violence* (e.g., screaming for help, asking people to call the police; protecting the most vulnerable parts of the body; establishing the safest route out of the home and practice escaping that way);
- *Safety after the aggression* (e.g., moving to the hospital to document injuries; reporting the crime; seeking the support of a professional or institution specialized in victim support);
- *Daily safety when you continue to live with the abuser* (e.g., register or memorize useful phone numbers; program your phone with speed dial numbers to request help more quickly; share the situation with neighbors, requesting that they contact the police when they realize or listen to suspicious noises; create a code combined with the children, neighbors, friends, or family to call the police; select less risky places, avoiding the kitchen, garage, or other places with knives or other objects that can serve as a weapon);
- *Safety when the victim prepares to leave home* (e.g., choose the most appropriate day to leave, considering the routines of the aggressor; have documents and important items prepared in a safe place, including documentation of past police reports; guaranteeing a safe place, and if there are children, talk to them about leaving, so that they feel less anxious);
- *Safety after leaving the abuser* (e.g., hide the contacts or address from the aggressor; install an alarm; ask the police and the court so that the new address does not appear in the documents to which the attacker has access; inform relatives and neighbors that he or she no longer lives with the aggressor, so that if the abuser is seen in the immediate vicinity of the victim's home, they should contact the police; change routines and routes; contact the children's teachers and inform them of the situation, anticipate escape plans if the aggressor appears in the workplace or elsewhere);

- *Safe house or shelter safety* (e.g., not disclosing the shelter's address or location; not receiving visits in the shelter or in the surrounding area, because there is a risk that the offender follows the person trusted by the victim; not using the ATM, credit cards, or bank accounts common in the safe house area; avoid places normally used by the aggressor or people known to the aggressor; prefer walking on more busy streets);
- *Safety for the victim returning to the area of origin* (e.g., avoid place normally used by the aggressor; in case of being chased by the abuser, move to the nearest public square or police station and call the police; having the number of the nearest police station in hand; frequently changing schedules and routes to work and schools).
- *Safety on social media* (e.g., avoid sharing posts or pictures that might show where victim is staying or living; use social network tools to block the abuser; turn off social networks' geolocation features).

In practice, risk identification and safety planning are not distinct and separate processes; they are generally undertaken in a fluid and integrated manner. The questions you ask a victim and the actions you take toward safety planning help them to be aware of the risk they face and increase their safety, as well as that of their children. As we will discuss in the next section, intervention that directly targets children exposed to IPV may be warranted.

Children of intimate partner violence: victims that cannot be forgotten

Exposure to interparental violence is recognized by scientific research to be a factor of family stress with negative implications in the global adjustment of children and adolescents (Artz et al., 2014; Holt, Buckley, & Whelan, 2008; McCormick, Cohen, & Ashton, 2018; Moylan et al., 2010). We expect that police forces have a sustained sense of that impact and perceive children to be equally the victims of a crime.

It is urgent to deconstruct an adult-centered view of IPV, because the number of children and adolescents exposed to the phenomenon referred to competent child protection authorities is increasingly becoming evident (Chanmugam, 2016; Comissão Nacional de Promoção dos Direitos e Proteção das Crianças e Jovens, 2020).

Research has shown that childhood exposure to IPV is associated with short- and long-term health consequences, including an impact on cognitive, behavioral and emotional systems, leading to a range of internalizing and externalizing behavior problems (Fong, Hawes, & Allen, 2019; Holt et al., 2008; Herrenkohl, Sousa, Tajima, Herrenkohl, & Moylan, 2008; Ruiz & Pereda, 2021), contributing to the concept of the *silent* or *invisible* victim (Groves, Zuckerman, Marans, & Cohen, 1993; Osofsky, 1995).

McCormick et al. (2018) provide strategies for police to minimize negative effects on children when arresting an offender parent owing to IPV. The authors recommend transitioning toward more specialized units that empower concerted responses between police officers and child experts, to reduce the harm of exposure to these particular adverse childhood experiences (ACEs). For example, knowing that exposure to a parent's arrest forms key ACEs, frontline police officers should provide specialized support (e.g., the presence of a psychologist) or plan the intervention so that the act of detention is done in a discreet manner and, if possible, the child is not present.

It is important be aware of the specific impact on a child being exposed to interparental violence, because there is a wide range of invisible situations to which the child might be subjected, such as staying in a corner listening, being in their room trying to sleep and listening to the sound of the conflict, seeing the marks of violence the next day, and experiencing a strange or negative dynamic in the parents' relationship. Exposure to interparental violence thus constitutes a form of psychological and emotional abuse, because it terrifies the child. By creating an atmosphere of oppression and fear, it forces the child to live in a hostile and dangerous environment in which seeing or hearing violent interpersonal events constitutes a negative model that validates and encourages violent behavior.

Moreover, exposure to interparental violence should be strongly considered in delicate procedures such as divorce proceedings and *regulating parental responsibilities*, because sometimes the phenomenon may elucidate the reason for a negative attitude or even a refusal to live with or visit one of the parents. To understand the child's refusal to visit and to grant his or her safety and psychological balance and well-being, it would be desirable for police officers to be better prepared and trained to deal with calls for noncompliance with the parental responsibility agreement. This means that it is vital to have the child as the core of the entire process.

Experience has clearly shown that violence continues after separation or divorce, and those children are directly victimized when they seek to protect their mother or indirectly witness violence. In a legislative framework that favors the joint exercise of parental responsibilities, IPV victims are forced to contact the aggressor, make joint decisions regarding their children, and comply with coercive visits, even in the face of the child's refusal, under penalty of being prosecuted for the crime of subtraction of minors.

It is also important to include children in the risk assessment and risk management procedures, because it has proved to be fundamental in preventing multiple forms of violence against children, and thus is a determining factor in their future. The appraisal practice should be evidence-based, cautious of all historical and dynamic risks, and reasoned with a view to avoiding inappropriate interventions (Chan, 2012; Norris, Griffith, & Norris, 2017). The use of specific tools for this purpose contributes positively to the predictive assessment, particularly when different methods of assessment are combined (D'Andrade, Austin, & Benton, 2008; Vial, Assink, Stams, & van der Put, 2019).

Certain factors (e.g., separation or divorce) related to high-risk or even lethal situations are mentioned in various studies of homicides in the context of IPV (Campbell et al., 2003; Christianson, Azad, Leander, & Selenius, 2013). The risk of lethality for children has deserved concern in several studies. In a report from

Women's Aid, 29 children from 13 families were reported to have been killed in England and Wales between 1994 and 2004 as a result of contact or residence arrangements (Saunders, 2004). Women's Aid (2016) reviewed serious case reviews for England and Wales, published between Jan. 2005 and Aug. 2015, and found that 19 children in 12 families were killed by IPV abusers (all perpetrators were fathers) after informal or supervised contact arrangements.

The decision to kill a child (i.e., filicide) occurs frequently as a form of revenge in the context of separation and in a history of IPV (Dawson, 2015).

Adhia, Austin, Fitzmaurice, and Hemenway (2019) analyzed the homicide of children aged 2–14 years in 16 states from the United States during 2005–14, resulting in a total of 1386 victims, 280 of which were associated with narratives of violence between intimate partners. Of the 280 victims, 54.3% were child homicides related to IPV, in which the perpetrator also killed or attempted to kill the partner. These aggressors were more likely to use firearms and commit suicide. The authors state that the US National Violent Death Reporting System underestimates cases of child homicide in the context of IPV, when in fact many cases suggest the need for services to intervene before violence results in fatal incidents.

Jaffe, Campbell, Olszowy, Hazel, and Hamilton (2014) concluded that adult homicides and child homicides in the context of IPV have similar warning signs, and it is essential to understand these signs and guide risk assessment equally for children. The same authors argue that all stakeholders must cooperate and adopt a coordinated action to ensure that safety and prevention plans at different levels include children. In fact, proper safety planning for children is another important aspect to be considered by police authorities involved in assisting victims of IPV. Considering the negative effects of IPV exposure on children, if police officers aim to consider children's emotional needs in safety planning, they must master important communication skills. These are covered in the next section.

Communication with victims of intimate partner violence

It is estimated that 85% of police time is used in some form of communication; yet, the time devoted to this competence in police training is around 2% (Rand Corporation, 1975). Westera, Kebbell, Milne, and Green (2014) point out that by far, the most important factor for being an effective police officer is related to communication skills, particularly how to communicate effectively with a variety of people (e.g., victims, suspects, colleagues, experts).

Accordingly, considering that IPV victims often seek the police in an evident phase of crisis, it is imperative that their attendance, practical assistance and information, support by police specialized teams, and referral to special support services be as competent as possible, because the manner in which police carry out this task will certainly affect recovery from this crisis (APAV, 2010; Gover et al., 2011; Paulino & Rodrigues, 2016; Yeager et al., 2015). In addition, as a person in need of help, the victim has assumptions about the nature of police intervention and expects recognition about his or her precarious situation, understanding, and encouragement. If police officers fail to establish rapport or engage in an empathetic relationship and active listening about the victims' narrative, interaction with the LEA might be seen as negative or result in so-called *secondary victimization*. In such a scenario, the victim will probably consider that he or she has not been treated appropriately, according to the situation and needs, precisely by those who should provide professional care. This experience may culminate in aggravation of psychological damage resulting from the initial victimization.

The reactions of humans to traumatic events are not uniform, but a number of indicators help the professional to perceive the degree of vulnerability of a certain person. These indicators have a cumulative effect in the sense that the greater their presence, the greater the probability of the traumatic event having increased severity. Some of these indicators are often present in the aftermath of an IPV incident, making it a traumatic or distressing event (e.g., lack of social or family support; vulnerabilities related with idiosyncratic psychological features; personal circumstances such as economic dependency from the intimate partner).

In a crisis situation, police officers can be trained and therefore more aware of a set of communication skills and techniques that may be particularly useful in reducing the emotional activation of victims, as well as in establishing adequate rapport. For example, an approach such as Psychological First Aid might be a supportive and practical response to a victim of IPV, stabilizing emotions to collect evidence that may be needed (e.g., testimonial evidence).

Before any intervention, police personnel should start the conversation gently by revealing the officer's name, and then ask and use the name of the victim. In this first contact, the officer must demonstrate a compassionate and empathetic attitude, transmitting to the victim a genuine interest in the victim's concerns and showing willingness to promote the necessary actions to address the victim's needs, problems, and expectations. When questioning, it is important to use open questions so that the victim can openly develop his or her narrative. To help the victim's reasoning, use strategies such as paraphrasing, small encouragements, naming, and validating what the victim is feeling. After a period of listening to the victim's narrative of events, it may be useful to summarize and prove the full comprehension of the account. Additional questions may arise based on the information police personnel gathers; the use of focused, direct, or closed questions may help in elucidating aspects enunciated vaguely, generically, or confusingly. On the other hand, it is important for the police to adopt a serene stance, in the sense that the officer must be able to understand that sometimes a silence in the discourse can be organizing, and once respected, it can result in an account that addresses aspects not mentioned earlier. When confronted with the victim's dismay, it may be necessary to motivate and positively influence change, promoting a sense of self-efficacy and self-control in managing the situation. Likewise, this sense of self-control is recovered if police personnel are able to reduce uncertainty, through the important task of providing all necessary information and referring the victim to the people or entities most able to provide the necessary support.

Despite the challenges inherent in the specialization of police functions, it is possible to identify several advantages associated with such differentiation in the reception and support services or units, such as increasing accountability, competence, and effectiveness, which are particularly beneficial to victims, but also improve the cohesion and morale of specialized units. Because many police departments have identified that a significant part of calls for service include IPV incidents, specialized units constitute a prudent organizational strategy to deal effectively with this crime, which involves protection and support to the victim and also the investigation and prosecution of perpetrators.

Communication by technological means also have an important role in building awareness of the phenomenon through the use of the Internet and social networking as tools to communicate with the community about IPV. By using their websites, LEAs can disseminate useful information about IPV (e.g., IPV dynamics, what to do, safety plans, myths and facts about IPV, helpful contacts).

Comparing intimate partner violence perceptions: experts, victims, and police officers

In pursuit of the definition of a profile of police competencies to provide effective support to victims of IPV, in 2012, a group of participants with different roles in this phenomenon were interviewed: experts in the field of IPV, with the necessary skills; women victims of IPV to describe the missing skills; and police officers to present their perceptions about the presence or absence of key competencies. In a second phase of the research, in 2018, the police officers were interviewed again.

The study was conducted using a qualitative–quantitative paradigm and the Delphi method. In the first phase of the research, the sample was composed of three distinct groups: the group of experts in the field of IPV ($n = 14$), women victims of IPV ($n = 100$), and police officers ($n = 100$).

With regard to experts, we used the focus group methodology (Kreuger & Casey, 2009) to collect qualitative information about experts' perceptions of competencies needed by police when working in the field of IPV.

With regard to the victims, the research included women who had reported the crime to the PSP during the first half of 2012, in which the incident had resulted in police intervention at the home of the various participants: victim, perpetrator, and child(ren), if they existed.

We nonrandomly selected a sample of frontline police officers who were more likely to deal with IPV situations in their daily duties, patrol police officers who normally responded to IPV calls. The police officers sample participated in both phases of the study (i.e., in 2012 and 2018). In terms of sample characterization, most participants were male ($n = 98$), from low-rank categories (e.g., constable; $n = 52$), with 11–15 years of service ($n = 51$), with 51 or more interventions in cases of IPV ($n = 80$), and with academic qualifications at the level of secondary education ($n = 93$).

Expert perceptions

The experts included in the research identified a set of 44 "exactly necessary" competencies (Table 11.2) to be observed to provide an efficient response to IPV: 17 competencies of the knowledge list, 16 of the skills list, and 11 of the attitudes list.

Victims and police officers perceptions: convergences and divergences

Questionnaires administered to the victims of IPV were based on these competencies, as defined by the experts. These questionnaires asked participants about the degree of satisfaction regarding assistance provided by the police when the police responded to their situation. The instrument consisted of a Likert scale scored from 1 to 5 (*very unsatisfied, unsatisfied, moderately satisfied, very satisfied,* and *extremely satisfied*). Criteria used to determine the presence or absence of a given competence were defined according to the following model: values lower than moderately satisfied established the lack or absence of the competence, and values equal to or greater than moderately satisfied determined the existence of the competence in the police response.

In the questionnaire administered to law enforcement officers, which was also based on competencies defined by the experts, the police officers were asked about the degree of knowledge they believed they possessed regarding the competencies presented. This was also measured using a Likert scale rated from 1 to 5 (*none, below average, medium, good,* and *excellent*). Thus, in a format that we can define as self-assessment, the criteria and indicators used to determine the presence or absence of a given competence were defined according to the following model: values lower than medium established the lack or absence of the competence, and values equal to or greater than this central criterion determined the existence or verification of the competence.

From the perspective of the victim, and based on the 44 competencies defined by the experts, 30 competencies were perceived to be lacking and only 14 competencies were accomplished. The victims pointed out the absence of 12 competencies on knowledge, 11 on skills and seven on attitudes.

With regard to the LEAs, 25 competencies come with positive evaluations and the remaining 19 refer to negative evaluations. These police officers perceived that they accomplished eight competencies of knowledge, seven of skills and 10 of attitudes.

To achieve a better understanding about differences in the perceptions of the presence or absence of certain competencies in police response, and based on the previous table defined by experts, we compared the self-assessment made by police officers and the victims' perceptions.

Both groups (i.e., police officers and victims) consider that competencies C1, C2 and C16 (knowledge competencies) to be present. On the other hand, both groups agree that C4, C5, C7, C8, C9, C11, C12, and C13 are lacking. Regarding skills competencies, both groups agree on the presence of H1, H2, H15, and H16 and consider

Table 11.2 Profile of final competencies identified by experts.

Knowledge competencies

C1 - knowing the concept and notions of intimate partner violence (IPV) and how to identify its forms, types, and dynamics

C2 - knowing about IPV legislation and how to act in the presence of this crime

C3 - knowing the concept of the *victim's statute*

C4 - knowing the concept of crisis intervention in IPV incidents

C5 - knowing about the psychological aspects and mechanisms (e.g., resilience, beliefs) of the victims

C6 - knowing the concept of privacy regarding approaching and safeguarding the victim

C7 - knowing about aggressor's strategies

C8 - knowing about communication and specific types of language used in the field of IPV

C9 - knowing the concept of *secondary victimization*

C10 - knowing the concept of *risk assessment*

C11 - knowing the concept of *safety plan*

C12 - knowing the concept of working in network and partnership

C13 - knowing about institutions that support the victims of IPV, and their functions and actions

C14 - knowing the concept of professional ethics

C15 - knowing about teamwork

C16 - knowing about your own frames of reference (e.g., stereotypes, prejudices, value judgments, experiences, perceptions about IPV)

C17 - knowing about producing a police report in the specific case of IPV

Skill competencies

H1 - identifying the crime of domestic violence and its dynamics

H2 - acting on the crime of domestic violence based on current legislation, and applying all mechanisms provided by the law (e.g., in detention situations, being able to formulate an opinion on the need to apply protective measures)

H3 - informing the victim about legal proceedings

H4 - analyzing the victim's statute and informing about it

H5 - performing crisis intervention in IPV situations (and all immediately inherent intervention procedures)

H6 - interpreting psychological aspects (e.g., resilience, beliefs) of victims

H7- providing privacy and safety in victim support (e.g., knowing that you have to separate the victim from the abuser, talking to each other at different times and locations)

H8 - identifying aggressor's strategies and acting appropriately

H9 - using the correct communication method in an occurrence of IPV (applying communication techniques depending on the victim; making her feel as if she were unique and not just another victim)

H10 - acting to avoid secondary victimization

H11 - undertaking risk assessments

H12 - executing the safety plan

H13 - acting in a way to work in network and partnership

Table 11.2 Profile of final competencies identified by experts.—*cont'd*

H14 - contacting and knowing how to contact institutions that provide assistance and support to victims of IPV

H15 - acting correctly facing knowledge of their own frames of reference (e.g., stereotypes, prejudices, value judgments, experiences, perceptions regarding IPV)

H16 - interpreting information collected or observed in an IPV incident

Attitude competencies

A1 - commitment: being predisposed to accomplish their duties and ensure all necessary efforts for the victim and with the victim

A2 - ethics: have a predisposition to act socially and professionally in a correct and loyal way

A3 - kindness: being predisposed to treat the victim in a respectful, sincere, and dignified manner

A4 - professional empathy: being predisposed to put yourself in the victim's shoes in a professional way, understanding his or her problems and aspirations

A5 - dynamism: being willing to what is necessary to overcome obstacles and achieve goals

A6 - team spirit: being willing to share information and responsibility for results, promoting solid and positive relationships, and seeking cooperation (only with the team or entities with direct intervention in the situation, to guarantee confidentiality and discretion)

A7 - communicability: being willing to listen carefully and convey ideas with clarity, objectivity, and security (specific communication techniques)

A8 - continuing education: having a predisposition to keep up to date through formal education (technical courses in the field of IPV)

A9 - honesty: being predisposed to explain to the victim how police and judicial intervention in IPV really takes place

A10 - courage: being willing to defend truth and justice for the victim

A11 - emotional intelligence: being predisposed to use emotions to work in their favor, using them to guide behavior and reasoning to improve the desired outcomes

H5, H6, H8, H9, H11, H12, H13, and H14 to be absent. More interesting are the disparate results showing that police officers assume H3, H4, and H7 to be present, whereas the victims consider them to lack these skills. Concerning attitudes, the results illustrate an agreement between groups in the presence of competencies A2, A6, A9, and A10, and equal agreement regarding the absence of A8. In addition, although police officers perceive A1, A3, A4, A5, A7, and A11 competencies as being present, victims' perceptions point in a different direction and consider that these attitudes to be missing in the police response.

Police officers perceptions: comparison 2012—18

Comparing the results from 2012 with 2018, regarding participants in the police officers' sample ($n = 100$), in terms of the presence or absence of the 44 competencies, research results showed that 27 competencies are perceived to be present and the other 17 are assumed to be lacking. This means that after 6 years of professional experience, police officers were perceived to have acquired only two more competencies in their repertoire: *knowing the concept of risk assessment* (C10) and one of the skill competencies: undertake risk assessments (H11).

An analysis of the data provides results that are worrying, because they suggest that frontline police officers perceive that 39% of competencies that experts establish as being essential and desirable in police response to IPV are lacking. By way of illustration, we mention the absence of competencies related to crisis intervention, psychological aspects and mechanisms of victims, notions of communication and specific types of language used in the field of IPV, the concept of secondary victimization, elaboration of a safety plan, networking and partnership, knowledge about institutions to support victims IPV, the lack of predisposition to keep up to date through specific training in the area of IPV. In fact, this competence in the field of attitudes (i.e., A8) is likely to be of the most concern. Even though the results show gaps, especially in the domain of knowledge and skills, which could be filled with proper training; if police officers' don't show a predisposition for continuous learning and training, then the solution to the problem proves to be more difficult.

Within the Portuguese context, disinvestment in training in several areas of policing is well-known. For example, Marques and Milne (2019) conducted a study with police officers from different LEAs, in which they also collected the opinions of prosecutors and judges, and reached a conclusion regarding the existence of a significant gap in training in investigative interviewing. However, in their research, a significant percentage of police officers expressed a desire to obtain training in this specific area. Although there are areas of policing that may prove to be more attractive to police personnel, the use of contemporary pedagogic methods and a competency-based education framework can promote greater motivation for attendance to continuous training. In the particular case of IPV, a field that is constantly benefiting from the contributions of scientific evidence, keeping up-to-date is critical to responsibilities in ever-evolving modern policing.

Conclusions

Over the past few decades, the negative impact of IPV on societies has been overwhelming. As we have tried to show, the tentacles of this reality extend to the victim of violence and also often reach the most vulnerable, as happens in the case of children exposed to interparental violence, who are condemned to significant consequences that may endure over the life span.

For its part, society and its various agents were not inert by just contemplating the phenomenon: political decision-makers sought to develop legislative measures that were more capable of providing greater protection to victims. Multiple persons and associations (e.g., nongovernmental organizations) have emerged to provide assistance and comfort to victims. The scientific community has sought to deepen knowledge about IPV in its multiple facets, and provide evidence-based tools that proved to be central to the activity of the various stakeholders. Moreover, LEAs and their professionals took a quantum leap forward in the way they respond to this crime. If we perform the exercise of comparing the way in which contemporary police view a phenomenon that not many decades ago remained closed and silenced by four walls, we may easily conclude that the evolution was enormous. Today, we have trained police officers better, become better equipped with communication skills, trained to use evidence-based tools such as risk assessment instruments, and, above all, become more aware that they must discard stereotypes and preconceived ideas about IPV that may greatly affect the justice of their interventions.

Risk assessment and management are not free from ethical challenges, limits, and dilemmas. They are procedures that involve collecting information about the people involved and the subsequent decision-making process according to the identified risk. The use of risk assessment tools by LEAs can make a significant difference in preventing severe physical and/or psychological injuries. Psychological science has contributed several risk assessment approaches and tools, risk management interventions, and various strategies to protect the victims of IPV. Police personnel should benefit from robust training at this level, as well as regular initiatives in the updating and discussion of cases. It is essential to master risk factors associated with this type of violence, particularly those that provide an increased likelihood of high risk, to avoid serious or lethal outcomes.

Recognition of the competence that LEAs and their specialized units have acquired in the field of IPV has been deserving of recognition and has resulted in an expansion of powers: the ability to adopt urgent measures to ensure the safety of the victim. Implementation of the RVD instrument in the Portuguese context is a good example of how the practice informed science to produce science-informed practice. Through the study of risk factors present in real cases of homicide in IPV contexts, psychological research efforts contributed to developing an evidence-based risk assessment instrument (i.e., the RVD), which includes in its form practical measures such as proposing to the public prosecutor to promote a more severe coercive measure against the perpetrator, proposing that searches and seizures be carried out, and referring the victim to teleassistance protection services. The training methodology used in learning the RVD framework was equally innovative, based on a logic of *train the trainers* in RVD, which later disseminated knowledge in different jurisdictions. It was the first time that the Ministry of Internal Affairs standardized a police procedure for the two main security forces (i.e., PSP and GNR).

However, despite all of the credit due to these important initiatives, we cannot be eternally satisfied with their success and fail to continue to avoid further IPV incidents, which are countless and many times lethal. Several years have passed since the adoption of the RVD framework, and as mentioned earlier, it is essential to promote a culture of continuous training for police officers: first, because the competencies in question are perishable, and second, because research has shown new risk factors and realities that deserve increased attention (e.g., studies on stalking; coercive control).

The research on police competencies presented here is elucidative in demonstrating that police officers perceive that they have acquired only two new competencies in the field of IPV in several years of service. These are associated with the practice of risk assessment and are easily explained by training in RVD that occurred in 2014, when the study occurred.

The specialized literature on competencies states that an organizational culture should define the core competencies of the organization itself and communicate them to its personnel, who must commit to acquiring them. Perhaps for this reason, organizations and their leaders should seek to develop capable people. Human capital is the most important valuable asset of police organizations, and the education of police personnel is an investment that makes LEAs more accountable to the communities they serve, and thus more responsive to their needs, in turn increasing public confidence.

Psychological science, as this chapter illustrates, has closely followed this maturing process in the response to IPV, contributing with theory and tools that are the result of years of research on the subject. However, although policing is a human interaction-driven activity, psychology continues to occupy a residual space in the training curricula of LEAs. If police organizations intend to become more effective in the response to IPV incidents over the next decades, we must incorporate more psychological concepts into the initial and continuing training schemes.

References

Adhia, A., Austin, S. B., Fitzmaurice, G. M., & Hemenway, D. (2019). The role of intimate partner violence in homicides of children aged 2−14 years. *American Journal of Preventive Medicine, 56*(1), 38−46.

Ali, P., & Naylor, P. (2013). Intimate partner violence: A narrative review of the biological and psychological explanations for its causation. *Aggression and Violent Behavior, 18,* 373−382.

Arrigo, B., & Shipley, S. (2005). *Introduction to forensic psychology: Issues and controversies in crime and justice* (2nd ed.). San Diego: Elsevier Academic Press.

Artinopoulou, V., Koufouli, A., & Michael, I. (2018). *Towards a victim-centered police response - training manual.* Greece: European Public Law Organization.

Artz, S., Jackson, M., Rossiter, K., Nijdam-Jones, A., Géczy, I., & Porteous, S. (2014). A comprehensive review of the literature on the impact of exposure to intimate partner violence for children and youth. *International Journal of Child, Youth and Family Studies, 5*(4), 493−587.

Associação Portuguesa de Apoio à Vítima [APAV]. (2010). *Manual Alcipe - Para o atendimento de mulheres vítimas de violência.* Lisboa: APAV.

Australian Human Rights Commission. (2016). *A national system for domestic and family violence death review.* Retrieved from: https://www.humanrights.gov.au/our-work/sex-discrimination/publications/national-system-domestic-and-family-violence-death-review.

Ballucci, D., Gill, C., & Campbell, M. (2017). The power of attitude: The role of police culture and receptivity of risk assessment tools in IPV calls. *Policing: A Journal of Policy and Practice, 11*(3), 242–257.

Barnish, M. (2004). *Domestic violence: A literature review.* London: HM Inspectorate Probation.

Belfrage, H., & Rying, M. (2004). Characteristics of spousal homicide perpetrators: A study of all cases of spousal homicide in Sweden 1990-1999. *Criminal Behaviour and Mental Health, 14,* 121–133.

Belfrage, H., & Strand, S. (2008). Structured spousal violence risk assessment: Combining risk factors and victim vulnerability factors. *International Journal of Forensic Mental Health, 7*(1), 39–46. https://doi.org/10.1080/14999013.2008.9914402

Belfrage, H., Strand, S., Storey, J. E., Gibas, A. L., Kropp, P. R., & Hart, S. D. (2012). Assessment and management of risk for intimate partner violence by police officers using the Spousal Assault Risk Assessment Guide. *Law and Human Behavior, 36*(1), 60–67. https://doi.org/10.1037/h0093948

Bossarte, R. M., Simon, T. R., & Barker, L. (2006). Characteristics of homicide followed by suicide incidents in multiple states, 2003-04. *Injury Prevention, 2,* 33–38. https://doi.org/10.1136/ip.2006.012807

Brown, R. P., Baughman, K., & Carvallo, M. (2018). Culture, masculine honor, and violence toward women. *Personality and Social Psychology Bulletin, 44*(4), 538–549. https://doi.org/10.1177/0146167217744195

Campbell, M. A., Gill, C., & Ballucci, D. (2018). Informing police response to intimate partner violence: Predictors of perceived usefulness of risk assessment screening. *Journal of Police and Criminal Psychology, 33*(2), 175–187.

Campbell, J., Glass, N., Sharps, P., Laughon, K., & Bloom, T. (2007). Intimate partner homicide: Review and implications of research and policy. *Trauma, Violence & Abuse, 8*(3), 246–269.

Campbell, J., Webster, D., & Glass, N. (2009). The danger assessment: Validation of a lethality risk assessment instrument for intimate partner femicide. *Journal of Interpersonal Violence, 24,* 653–674.

Campbell, J., Webster, D., Koziol-McLain, J., Block, C., Campbell, D., Curry, M., et al. (2003). Risk factors for femicide in abusive relationship: Results from a multisite case control study. *American Journal of Public Health, 93,* 1089–1097.

Capaldi, D. M., Knoble, N. B., Shortt, J. W., & Kim, H. K. (2012). A systematic review of risk factors for intimate partner violence. *Partner Abuse, 3*(2), 231–280. https://doi.org/10.1891/1946-6560.3.2.231

Carlson, J., Voith, L., Brown, J. C., & Holmes, M. (2019). Viewing children's exposure to intimate partner violence through a developmental, social-ecological, and survivor lens: The current state of the field, challenges, and future directions. *Violence Against Women, 25*(1), 6–28. https://doi.org/10.1177/1077801218816187

Carpenter, G. L., & Stacks, A. M. (2009). Developmental effects of exposure to intimate partner violence in early childhood: A review of the literature. *Children and Youth Services Review, 31*(8), 831–839. https://doi.org/10.1016/j.childyouth.2009.03.005

Castanho, A. (April 1, 2019). Exposição à violência doméstica e a transmissão intergeracional do trauma. In *Encontro de Abertura do Mês da Prevenção dos Maus Tratos na Infância. Communication conducted at the meeting of Comissão Nacional de Promoção dos Direitos e Proteção das Crianças e Jovens (CNPDPCJ), Lisboa, Portugal.*

Catalano, S. (2012). *Intimate partner violence, 1993-2010*. Bureau of Justice Statistics. Retrieved from: http://www.ncdsv.org/images/BJS_IPV1993-2010_11-2012.pdf.

Chan, K. (2012). Evaluating the risk of child abuse: The child abuse risk assessment scale (CARAS). *Journal of Interpersonal Violence, 27*(5), 951−973.

Chan, K., & Cho, E. (2010). A review of cost measures for the economic impact of domestic violence. *Trauma, Violence & Abuse, 11*(3), 129−143.

Chanmugam, A. (2016). Children and young people in domestic violence shelters. *Geographies of Children and Young People, 12*, 19−43.

Christianson, S., Azad, A., Leander, L., & Selenius, H. (2013). Children as witnesses to homicidal violence: What they remember and report. *Psychiatry, Psychology and Law, 20*(3), 366−383.

Comissão Nacional de Promoção dos Direitos e Proteção das Crianças e Jovens. (2020). *Relatório Anual de Avaliação da Atividade das Comissões de Proteção de Crianças e Jovens (CPCJ) no ano de 2019*. Lisboa: CNPDPCJ.

D'Andrade, A., Austin, M., & Benton, A. (2008). Risk and safety assessment in child welfare. *Journal of Evidence-Based Social Work, 5*(1−2), 31−56.

Davies, J. (2017). *Victim-defined safety planning: A summary*. Hartford, CT: Greater Hartford Legal Aid.

Dawson, M. (2015). Canadian trends in filicide by gender of the accused, 1961-2011. *Child Abuse & Neglect, 47*, 162−174.

DGAI. (2013). *Análise Retrospetiva de Homicídios ocorridos em Relações de Intimidade*. Lisboa: Direção Geral de Administração Interna.

Dietrich, D. M., & Schuett, J. M. (2013). *Culture of honor and attitudes toward intimate partner violence in Latinos*. SAGE Open. https://doi.org/10.1177/2158244013489685

Dillon, G., Hussain, R., Loxton, D., & Rahman, S. (2013). Mental and physical health and intimate partner violence against women: A review of the literature. *International Journal of Family Medicine, 2013*, 313909. https://doi.org/10.1155/2013/313909

Dobash, E., Dobash, R., & Cavanagh, K. (2009). Out of the blue: Men who murder an intimate partner. *Feminist Criminology, 4*(3), 194−225.

Dolon, R., Hendricks, J., & Meagher, M. S. (1986). Police practices and attitudes toward domestic violence. *Journal of Police Science and Administration, 14*(3), 187−192.

Do, K. N., Weiss, B., & Pollack, A. (2013). Cultural beliefs, intimate partner violence and mental health functioning among Vietnamese women. *International Perspectives in Psychology: Research, Practice, Consultation, 2*(3). https://doi.org/10.1037/ipp0000004

Dutton, D., & Hart, S. (1992). Risk markers for family violence in a federally incarcerated population. *International Journal of Law and Psychiatry, 15*, 101−112.

Eckhardt, C., Murphy, C., Whitaker, D., Sprunger, J., Dykstra, R., & Woodard, K. (2013). The effectiveness of intervention programs for perpetrators and victims of intimate partner violence. *Partner Abuse, 4*(2), 196−231.

Eigenberg, H. M., Scarborough, K. E., & Kappeler, V. E. (1996). Contributory factors affecting arrest in domestic and non-domestic assaults. *American Journal of Police, XV*(4), 27−54.

Ellison, C. G., Bartkowski, J. P., & Anderson, K. L. (1999). Are there religious variations in domestic violence? *Journal of Family Issues, 20*(1), 87−113. https://doi.org/10.1177/019251399020001005

Ellison, C. G., Trinitapoli, J. A., Anderson, K. L., & Johnson, B. R. (2007). Race/ethnicity, religious involvement, and domestic violence. *Violence Against Women, 13*(11), 1094−1112. https://doi.org/10.1177/1077801207308259

Equipa de Análise Retrospetiva de Homicídio em Violência Doméstica [EARHVD]. (2017). *Relatório final: Dossiê n.o 1/2017-AC*. Lisboa: EARHVD.

Equipa de Análise Retrospetiva de Homicídio em Violência Doméstica [EARHVD]. (2018a). *Relatório final: Dossiê n.o 4/2017-VP*. Lisboa: EARHVD.

Equipa de Análise Retrospetiva de Homicídio em Violência Doméstica [EARHVD]. (2018b). *Relatório final: Dossiê n.o 1/2018-AC*. Lisboa: EARHVD.

European Institute for Gender Equality, EIGE. (2019). *A guide to risk assessment and risk management of intimate partner violence against women for police*. Luxembourg: Publications Office of the European Union.

Feder, L. (1997). Domestic violence and police response in a pro-arrest jurisdiction. *Women & Criminal Justice, 8*(4), 79–98. https://doi.org/10.1300/J012v08n04_04

Felson, R., & Feld, S. (2009). When a man hits a woman: Moral evaluations and reporting violence to the police. *Aggressive Behavior, 35*, 477–488.

Fong, V. C., Hawes, D., & Allen, J. L. (2019). A systematic review of risk and protective factors for externalizing problems in children exposed to intimate partner violence. *Trauma Violence & Abuse, 20*(2), 149–167. https://doi.org/10.1177/1524838017692383

Gabinete do Secretário-Geral do Sistema de Segurança Interna. (2010). *Relatório Anual de Segurança Interna (RASI) - 2009*. Lisboa: SGMAI.

Gabinete do Secretário-Geral do Sistema de Segurança Interna. (2011). *Relatório Anual de Segurança Interna (RASI) - 2010*. Lisboa: SGMAI.

Gabinete do Secretário-Geral do Sistema de Segurança Interna. (2012). *Relatório Anual de Segurança Interna (RASI) - 2011*. Lisboa: SGMAI.

Gabinete do Secretário-Geral do Sistema de Segurança Interna. (2013). *Relatório Anual de Segurança Interna (RASI) - 2012*. Lisboa: SGMAI.

Gabinete do Secretário-Geral do Sistema de Segurança Interna. (2014). *Relatório Anual de Segurança Interna (RASI) - 2013*. Lisboa: SGMAI.

Gabinete do Secretário-Geral do Sistema de Segurança Interna. (2015). *Relatório Anual de Segurança Interna (RASI) - 2014*. Lisboa: SGMAI.

Gabinete do Secretário-Geral do Sistema de Segurança Interna. (2016). *Relatório Anual de Segurança Interna (RASI) - 2015*. Lisboa: SGMAI.

Gabinete do Secretário-Geral do Sistema de Segurança Interna. (2017). *Relatório Anual de Segurança Interna (RASI) - 2016*. Lisboa: SGMAI.

Gabinete do Secretário-Geral do Sistema de Segurança Interna. (2018). *Relatório Anual de Segurança Interna (RASI) - 2017*. Lisboa: SGMAI.

Gabinete do Secretário-Geral do Sistema de Segurança Interna. (2019). *Relatório Anual de Segurança Interna (RASI) - 2018*. Lisboa: SGMAI.

Garcia-Moreno, C., Jansen, H., Ellsberg, M., Heise, L., & Watts, C. H. (2005). *WHO multi-country study on women's health and domestic violence against women*. Geneva: World Health Organization.

Gill, C., Campbell, M. A., & Ballucci, D. (2019). Police officers' definitions and understandings of intimate partner violence in New Brunswick, Canada. *The Police Journal: Theory, Practice and Principles*. https://doi.org/10.1177/0032258X19876974

Glass, N., Laughon, K., Campbell, J., Block, C. R., Hanson, G., Sharps, P. W., et al. (2008). Non-fatal strangulation is an important risk factor for homicide of women. *Journal of Emergency Medicine, 35*(3), 329–335. https://doi.org/10.1016/j.jemermed.2007.02.065

Gomes, S., & Duarte, V. (2018). *Female crime and delinquency in Portugal: In and out of the criminal justice system*. Gewerbestrasse, Switzerland: Palgrave Macmillan.

Goodman-Delahunty, J., & Crehan, A. C. (2016). Enhancing police responses to domestic violence incidents: Reports from client advocates in New South Wales. *Violence Against Women, 22*(8), 1007–1026. https://doi.org/10.1177/1077801215613854

Gover, A., Paul, D., & Dodge, M. (2011). Law Enforcement Officers' attitudes about domestic violence. *Violence Against Women, 17*(5), 619–636.

Graham, L. M., Sahay, K. M., Rizo, C. F., Messing, J. T., & Macy, R. J. (2021). The validity and reliability of available intimate partner homicide and reassault risk assessment tools: A systematic review. *Trauma, Violence, & Abuse, 22*(1), 18–40. https://doi.org/10.1177/1524838018821952

Grann, M., & Wedin, I. (2002). Risk factors for recidivism among spousal assault and spousal homicide offenders. *Psychology, Crime & Law, 8*(1), 5–23. https://doi.org/10.1080/10683160208401806

GREVIO. (2019). *GREVIO's (baseline) evaluation report on legislative and other measures giving effect to the provisions of the Council of Europe Convention on Preventing and Combating Violence against Women and domestic violence(Istanbul convention) – Portugal*. Strasbourg: Secretariat of the monitoring mechanism of the Council of Europe Convention on Preventing and Combating Violence against Women and Domestic Violence.

Groves, B. M., Zuckerman, B., Marans, S., & Cohen, D. J. (1993). Silent victims children who witness violence. *Journal of the American Medical Association, 269*(2), 262–264. https://doi.org/10.1001/jama.1993.03500020096039

Hanson, R. K., Helmus, L.,., & Bourgon, G. (2007). *The validity of risk assessments for intimate partner violence: A meta-analysis*. Retrieved from the Public Safety Canada Website: http://www.publicsafety.gc.ca/res/cor/rep/vra_ipv_200707-eng.aspx.

Hartwig, M., Dawson, E., Wrede, O., & Ask, K. (2011). Interviewing victims of repeated domestic violence: Investigators' beliefs and strategies. *Psychiatry, Psychology and Law, 19*, 672–681.

Her Majesty's Inspectorate of Constabulary [HMIC]. (2014). *Everyone's business: Improving the police response to domestic abuse*. United Kingdom: HMIC.

Her Majesty's Inspectorate of Constabulary and Fire & Rescue Services [HMICFRS]. (2017). *A progress report on the police response to domestic abuse*. London: HMICFRS.

Herrenkohl, T. I., Sousa, C., Tajima, E. A., Herrenkohl, R. C., & Moylan, C. A. (2008). Intersection of child abuse and children's exposure to domestic violence. *Trauma, Violence & Abuse, 9*(2), 84–99. https://doi.org/10.1177/1524838008314797.

Hilton, N. Z., Harris, G. T., Rice, M. E., Houghton, R. E., & Eke, A. W. (2008). An in depth actuarial assessment for wife assault recidivism: The Domestic Violence Risk Appraisal Guide. *Law and Human Behavior, 32*, 150–163.

Hilton, N. Z., Harris, G. T., Rice, M. E., Lang, C., Cormier, C. A., & Lines, K. J. (2004). A brief actuarial assessment for the prediction of wife assault recidivism: The Ontario Domestic Assault Risk Assessment. *Psychological Assessment, 16*, 267–275.

Hilton, N. Z., Pham, A., Jung, S., Nunes, K., & Ennis, L. (2020). Risk scores and reliability of the SARA, SARA-V3, B-SAFER, and ODARA among Intimate Partner Violence (IPV) cases referred for threat assessment. *Police Practice and Research*. https://doi.org/10.1080/15614263.2020.1798235

Hirschel, D., Buzawa, E., Pattavina, A., & Faggiani, D. (2008). Domestic violence and mandatory arrest laws: To what extend do they influence police arrest decisions? *Journal of Criminal Law and Criminology, 98*(1), 255–298.

Hirschel, D., McCormack, P. D., & Buzawa, E. (2017). A 10-year study of the impact of intimate partner violence primary aggressor laws on single and dual arrest. *Journal of Interpersonal Violence.* https://doi.org/10.1177/0886260517739290

Holt, S., Buckley, H., & Whelan, S. (2008). The impact of exposure to domestic violence on children and young people: A review of the literature. *Child Abuse & Neglect, 32*(8), 797−810. https://doi.org/10.1016/j.chiabu.2008.02.004

Home Office. (2016). *Multi-agency statutory guidance for the conduct of domestic homicide reviews.* Retrieved from: https://www.gov.uk/government/publications/revised-statutory-guidance-for-the-conduct-of-domestic-homicide-reviews.

Hulme, S., Morgan, A., & Boxall, H. (2019). Domestic violence offenders, prior offending and reoffending in Australia. In *Trends & issues in crime and criminal justice no. 580.* Canberra: Australian Institute of Criminology. https://aic.gov.au/publications/tandi/tandi580.

IACP. (2018). *Intimate partner violence response policy and training guidelines.* https://www.theiacp.org/resources/document/intimate-partner-violence-response-policy-and-training-content-guidelines.

Jaffe, P., Campbell, M., Olszowy, L., Hazel, L., & Hamilton, A. (2014). Paternal filicide in the context of domestic violence: Challenges in risk assessment and risk management for community and justice professionals. *Child Abuse Review, 23,* 142−153.

Jennett, C. (2012). From a man's castle to a woman's refuge: Changing police attitudes to domestic violence. *Independent Scholars Association of Australia (ISAA) Review, 11*(2), 29−44.

Johnson, H., Eriksson, L., Mazerolle, P., & Wortley, R. (2019). Intimate femicide: The role of coercive control. *Feminist Criminology, 14*(1), 3−23. https://doi.org/10.1177/1557085117701574

Johnson, H., & Hotton, T. (2003). Losing control: Homicide risk in estranged and intact intimate relationships. *Homicide Studies, 7,* 58−84.

Kebbell, M. (2019). Risk assessment for intimate partner violence: How can the police assess risk? *Psychology, Crime and Law, 25*(8), 829−846. https://doi.org/10.1080/1068316X.2019.1597087

Klein, A. (2009). *Special report: Practical implications of current domestic violence research.* Washington, DC: U.S. Department of Justice, National Institute of Justice.

Koziol-McLain, J., Webster, D., McFarlane, J., Block, C. R., Ulrich, Y., Glass, N., et al. (2006). Risk factors for femicide-suicide in abusive relationships: Results from a multisite case control study. *Violence & Victims, 21*(1), 3−21.

Kreuger, R., & Casey, M. (2009). *Focus groups: A practical guide for applied research.* London: Sage Publications.

Kropp, P. R. (2008). Intimate partner violence risk assessment and management. *Violence & Victims, 23,* 202−220.

Kropp, P. R., Hart, S. D., & Belfrage, H. (2005). *Brief spousal assault form for the evaluation of risk (B-SAFER): User manual.* Vancouver, Canada: Proactive Resolutions Inc.

Kropp, P. R., Hart, S. D., & Belfrage, H. (2010). *Brief spousal assault form for the evaluation of risk (B-SAFER), version 2: User manual.* Vancouver, Canada: Proactive Resolutions Inc.

Kropp, P. R., Hart, S. D., Webster, C. D., & Eaves, D. (1995). *Manual for the spousal assault risk assessment guide* (2nd ed.). Vancouver, BC: British Columbia Institute on Family Violence.

Margolin, G. (2005). Children's exposure to violence: Exploring developmental pathways to diverse outcomes. *Journal of Interpersonal Violence, 20*(1), 72–81. https://doi.org/10.1177/0886260504268371

Margolin, G., & Gordis, E. B. (2000). The effects of family and community violence on children. *Annual Review of Psychology, 51*(1), 445–479.

Marques, P. B. (2018). A Entrevista Cognitiva: Um método de recolha de testemunhos mais completos e fidedignos. In M. Paulino, & L. Alho (Eds.), *Comportamento Criminal e Avaliação Forense* (pp. 1–19). Lisboa: Pactor.

Marques, P. B., & Milne, R. (2019). The investigative interview's contribution to law enforcement. *European Law Enforcement Research Bulletin, 18*, 91–106.

Martin, S. L., Macy, R. J., Sullivan, K., & Magee, M. L. (2007). Pregnancy-associated violent deaths: The role of intimate partner violence. *Trauma, Violence, & Abuse, 8*(2), 135–148. https://doi.org/10.1177/1524838007301223

McCormick, A., Cohen, I., & Ashton, S. (2018). Modifying the 'how' of an arrest: Reducing the interacting effects of childhood exposure to intimate partner violence and parental arrest. *Police Practice and Research*. https://doi.org/10.1080/15614263.2018.1555479

McPhedran, S., Gover, A. R., & Mazerolle, P. (2017). A cross-national comparison of police attitudes about domestic violence: A focus on gender. *Policing: An International Journal, 40*(2), 214–227. https://doi.org/10.1108/PIJPSM-06-2016-0083

McTavish, J. R., MacGregor, J. C. D., Wathen, C. N., & MacMillan, H. L. (2016). Children's exposure to intimate partner violence: An overview. *International Review of Psychiatry, 28*(5), 504–518. https://doi.org/10.1080/09540261.2016.1205001

Messing, J. T., Patch, M., Wilson, J. S., Kelen, G., & Campbell, J. (2018). Differentiating among attempted, completed, and multiple nonfatal strangulation in women experiencing intimate partner violence. *Women's Health Issues, 28*(1), 104–111. https://doi.org/10.1016/j.whi.2017.10.002

Messing, J. T., & Thaller, J. (2013). The average predictive validity of intimate partner violence risk assessment instruments. *Journal of Interpersonal Violence, 28*(7), 1537–1558. https://doi.org/10.1177/0886260512468250

Miller, E., & Silverman, J. G. (2010). Reproductive coercion and partner violence: Implications for clinical assessment of unintended pregnancy. *Expert Review of Obstetrics & Gynecology, 5*(5), 511–515. https://doi.org/10.1586/eog.10.44

Milne, B., Griffiths, A., Clarke, C., & Dando, C. J. (2019). The cognitive interview: A tiered approach in the real world. In J. J. Dickinson, N. S. Compo, R. N. Carol, B. L. Schwartz, & M. R. McCauley (Eds.), *Evidence based investigative interviewing* (pp. 56–73). New York: Routledge.

Monckton Smith, J. (2020). Intimate partner femicide: Using foucauldian analysis to track an eight stage progression to homicide. *Violence Against Women, 26*(11), 1267–1285. https://doi.org/10.1177/1077801219863876

Monckton-Smith, J., Szymanska, K., & Haile, S. (2017). *Exploring the relationship between stalking and homicide*. Project Report. Cheltenham: University of Gloucestershire in association with Suzy Lamplugh Trust.

Morewitz, S. J. (2004). *Domestic violence and maternal and child health: New patterns of trauma, treatment, and criminal justice responses*. New York: Springer US.

Morewitz, S. J. (2008). *Death threats and violence: New research and clinical perspectives*. New York: Springer US.

Moylan, C. A., Herrenkohl, T. I., Sousa, C., Tajima, E. A., Herrenkohl, R. C., & Russo, M. J. (2010). The effects of child abuse and exposure to domestic violence on adolescent internalizing and externalizing behavior problems. *Journal of Family Violence, 25*(1), 53—63. https://doi.org/10.1007/s10896-009-9269-9

Nicholls, T. L., Pritchard, M. M., Reeves, K. A., & Hilterman, E. (2013). Risk assessment in intimate partner violence: A systematic review of contemporary approaches. *Partner Abuse, 4,* 76—168.

Norris, G., Griffith, G., & Norris, H. (2017). Risk assessment in youth justice: A child-centered approach to managing interventions. In W. Petherick, & G. Sinnamon (Eds.), *The psychology of criminal and antisocial behavior* (pp. 211—231). San Diego: Elsevier Academic Press.

Osofsky, J. D. (1995). Children who witness domestic violence: The invisible victims. *Social Policy Report, 9,* 1—20. https://doi.org/10.1002/j.2379-3988.1995.tb00035.x

Palermo, G. B. (1994). Murder-suicide—an extended suicide. *International Journal of Offender Therapy and Comparative Criminology, 38*(3), 205—216. https://doi.org/ 10.1177/0306624X9403800303

Paulino, M. (2016). *Forensic psychology of spousal violence.* San Diego: Elsevier Academic Press.

Paulino, M. (2017). Domestic violence: Psychological issues related to the victim and offender. In W. Petherick, & G. Sinnamon (Eds.), *The psychology of criminal and antisocial behavior* (pp. 343—359). San Diego: Elsevier Academic Press.

Paulino, M., & Rodrigues, M. (2016). *Violência Doméstica: Identificar, Avaliar e Intervir.* São Pedro do Estoril: PrimeBooks.

Perez Trujillo, M., & Ross, S. (2008). Police response to domestic violence: Making decisions about risk and risk management. *Journal of Interpersonal Violence, 23*(4), 454—473. https://doi.org/10.1177/0886260507312943

Procuradoria-Geral Distrital de Lisboa. (2015). *Relatório violência Doméstica, julho 2015.* Lisboa: Procuradoria-Geral Distrital de Lisboa.

Rand Corporation. (1975). *The criminal process* (Vols. 1—3) (Santa Monica: California).

Roberts, A. R. (1998). *Battered women and their families: Intervention strategies and treatment programs* (2nd ed.). New York: Springer.

Rodrigues, M., & Paulino, M. (2018). Evolução das Polícias Portuguesas na Avaliação de Risco nas relações de violência doméstica: Da Teoria à Praxis. In M. Paulino, & L. Alho (Eds.), *Comportamento Criminal e Avaliação Forense* (pp. 205—238). Lisboa: Pactor.

Ruiz, R. A., & Pereda, N. (2021). Exposure to family violence and risk factors for recidivism in juvenile offenders. *Victims and Offenders.* https://doi.org/10.1080/15564886.2021. 1888168

Russell, B. (2018). Police perceptions in intimate partner violence cases: The influence of gender and sexual orientation. *Journal of Crime and Justice, 41*(2), 193—205. https:// doi.org/10.1080/0735648X.2017.1282378

Saavedra, R., & Fonseca, M. (2013). Avaliação do risco e gestão da segurança nos serviços de apoio à vítima: Mulheres vítimas de violência nos relacionamentos íntimos. In A. Sani, & S. Caridade (Eds.), *Violência, Agressão e Vitimação: Práticas para a Intervenção* (pp. 273—295). Coimbra: Almedina.

Sani, A. (2018). Exposição da criança à violência doméstica: (Re)conhecimento e (re)ação atuais. In I. Dias (Ed.), *Violência doméstica e de género: Uma abordagem multidisciplinar* (pp. 81—96). Lisboa: Pactor.

Saunders, D. (1995). Prediction of wife assault. In J. Campbell (Ed.), *Assessing dangerousness: Violence by sexual offenders, batterers and child abusers* (pp. 68—95). Thousand Oaks, CA: Sage.

Saunders, H. (2004). *Twenty-nine child homicides: Lessons still to be learnt on domestic violence and child protection*. Bristol: Women's Aid.

Saxton, M. D., Olszowy, L., MacGregor, J. C. D., MacQuarrie, B. J., & Wathen, C. N. (2018). Experiences of intimate partner violence victims with police and the justice system in Canada. *Journal of Interpersonal Violence*. https://doi.org/10.1177/0886260518758330

Sheehan, B. E., Murphy, S. B., Moynihan, M. M., Dudley-Fennessey, E., & Stapleton, J. G. (2015). Intimate partner homicide: New insights for understanding lethality and risks. *Violence Against Women, 21*(2), 269–288. https://doi.org/10.1177/1077801214564687.

Sinha, M. (2013). *Family violence in Canada: A statistical profile, 2011. Section 3: Intimate partner violence* (Catalogue no. 85-002-X). Retrieved from Statistics Canada website: http://www.statcan.gc.ca/pub/85-002-x/2013001/article/11805-eng.pdf.

Spencer, C. M., & Stith, S. M. (2020). Risk factors for male perpetration and female victimization of intimate partner homicide: A meta-analysis. *Trauma, Violence, & Abuse, 21*(3), 527–540. https://doi.org/10.1177/1524838018781101

Storey, J. E., Kropp, P. R., Hart, S. D., Belfrage, H., & Strand, S. (2014). Assessment and management of risk for intimate partner violence by police officers using the brief spousal assault form for the evaluation of risk (B-SAFER). *Criminal Justice and Behavior, 41*, 256–271. https://doi.org/10.1177/0093854813503960

Storey, J. E., & Strand, S. (2012). The characteristics and violence risk management of women arrested by the police for intimate partner violence. *European Journal of Criminology, 9*(6), 636–651. https://doi.org/10.1177/1477370812453403

Storey, J. E., & Strand, S. (2017). The influence of victim vulnerability and gender on police officers' assessment of intimate partner violence risk. *Journal of Family Violence, 32*(1), 125–134.

Tatum, K., & Pence, R. (2015). Factors that affect the arrest decision in domestic violence cases. *Policing: An International Journal, 38*(1), 56–70. https://doi.org/10.1108/PIJPSM-07-2014-0075

Thomas, K. A., Joshi, M., & Sorenson, S. B. (2014). "Do you know what it feels like to drown?": Strangulation as coercive control in intimate relationships. *Psychology of Women Quarterly, 38*(1), 124–137. https://doi.org/10.1177/0361684313488354

Tjaden, P., & Thoennes, N. (2000). Prevalence and consequences of male-to-female and female-to-male intimate partner violence as measured by the national violence against women survey. *Violence Against Women, 6*(2), 142–161. https://doi.org/10.1177/10778010022181769

União de Mulheres Alternativa e Resposta [UMAR]. (2019). *Observatório de mulheres assassinadas (OMA): Dados 2018*. Lisboa: UMAR.

United Nations Office on Drugs and Crime. (2010a). *Training curriculum on effective police responses to violence against women (Criminal Justice Handbook Series)*. New York: UNODC.

United Nations Office on Drugs and Crime. (2010b). *Handbook on effective police responses to violence against women (Criminal Justice Handbook Series)*. New York: UNODC.

Vandello, J. A., & Cohen, D. (2003). Male honor and female fidelity: Implicit cultural scripts that perpetuate domestic violence. *Journal of Personality and Social Psychology, 84*(5), 997–1010. https://doi.org/10.1037/0022-3514.84.5.997

Vial, A., Assink, M., Stams, G. J. J. M., & van der Put, C. (2019). Safety and risk assessment in child welfare: A reliability study using multiple measures. *Journal of Child and Family Studies, 28*, 3533–3544. https://doi.org/10.1007/s10826-019-01536-z

Violence Policy Center. (2012). *American roulette: Homicide-suicide in the United States*. Washington, DC: Author.

Westera, N., Kebbell, M., Milne, B., & Green, T. (2014). Towards a more effective detective. *Policing and Society, 26*(1), 1—17.

Westera, N., & Powell, M. B. (2017). Prosecutors' perceptions of how to improve the quality of evidence in domestic violence cases. *Policing and Society, 27*(2), 157—172. https://doi.org/10.1080/10439463.2015.1039002

Whittemore, K. E., & Kropp, P. R. (2002). Spousal assault risk assessment: A guide for clinicians. *Journal of Forensic Psychology Practice, 2*(2), 53—64. https://doi.org/10.1300/J158v02n02_03

Williams, K. R., & Grant, S. R. (2006). Empirically examining the risk of intimate part-ner violence: The revised domestic violence screening instrument (DVSI-R). *Public Health Reports, 121*, 400—408.

Williams, K. R., & Houghton, A. B. (2004). Assessing the risk of domestic violence reoffend-ing: A validation study. *Law and Human Behavior, 28*, 437—455.

Wilson, M., & Daly, M. (1993). Spousal homicide risk and estrangement. *Violence & Victims, 8*(1), 3—16.

Wolf, M. E., Ly, U., Hobart, M. A., & Kernic, M. A. (2003). Barriers to seeking police help for intimate partner violence. *Journal of Family Violence, 18*(2), 121—129. https://doi.org/10.1023/A:1022893231951

Women's Aid. (2016). *Nineteen child homicides: What must change so children are put first in child contact arrangements and the family courts*. Bristol: Women's Aid.

Yeager, K., Robets, A., & Roberts, B. (2015). A comprehensive model for crisis intervention with battered women and their children. In K. Yeager, & A. Roberts (Eds.), *Crisis intervention handbook: Assessment, treatment and research* (4th ed., pp. 459—501). New York: Oxford University Press.

Zeppegno, P., Gramaglia, C., di Marco, S., Guerriero, C., Consol, C., Loreti, L., et al. (2019). Intimate partner homicide suicide: A mini-review of the literature (2012—2018). *Current Psychiatry Reports, 21*(3), 1—13.

The contribution of psychological science in police responses of sexual assaults

12

Julien Chopin and Eric Beauregard

Introduction

Sexual offending represents one of the most difficult crimes to investigate by the police due in part to the various complexities involved. For instance, contrary to most forms of crime, the sole presence of forensic evidence (e.g., DNA) is often not enough to charge and convict a suspect. In many cases, the notion of consent needs to be debated, which more often than not, comes down to the word of the victim against the offender. Therefore, it becomes of the utmost importance to develop various techniques that can be used by the police in their effort to find the truth and charge the right suspect.

Research on sexual violence has traditionally focused its efforts on improving our understanding of the various risk factors related to this form of offending as well as how to best treat and manage these offenders. However, some researchers have conducted innovative research applied specifically to the investigation of sexual crimes. In this chapter, we discuss several elements surrounding the investigation of sexual crimes. First, the chapter starts by reviewing some of the misconceptions about "sex offenders" that may mislead an investigation. Then, we discuss the various studies on suspect prioritization, while also reviewing some of the studies on geographic profiling and crime linkage analysis. This chapter also covers investigative interviewing specific to sexual crimes, focusing on the witnesses, the victims, and the suspects. Moreover, the chapter includes a section on some of the indicators of false rape allegations as well as false confessions. Finally, this chapter discusses the investigation of online sexual crimes.

Misconceptions about sex offenders

Sexual crimes are often considered by law enforcement as special due to the perception that sex offenders are different compared with the general population of criminals (Harris & Grace, 1999). This notion of the sex offender as "special"

Police Psychology, Edited by Marques and Paulino. https://doi.org/10.1016/B978-0-12-816544-7.00012-7

or "unique" has led to several misconceptions about these offenders that may erroneously influence the criminal investigation process of sexual crimes.

One of the most popular misconceptions about sex offenders concerns their level of recidivism. They are often considered some of the most dangerous criminals because their level of recidivism is thought to be higher. In the last few decades, there have been many studies that have measured and discussed the level of recidivism of sex offenders. In one of the first reviews of the literature, Furby, Weinrott, and Blackshaw (1989) found recidivism levels varied considerably — between 4% and 56%— depending on the methodology and the definition of recidivism used. However, in a seminal meta-analysis using a sample size of 23,393 individuals, Hanson and Bussiere (1998) found an average recidivism rate of 13.4% for sexual offenders who committed a new sexual crime using a follow-up period of 5 years after their first offense. Even for adolescent sex offenders, Sipe, Jensen, and Everett (1998) found that only about 10% committed a new sex offense in adulthood. Similar findings were replicated in several longitudinal studies on adolescent sex offenders, which demonstrated that the continuation of sex offending into adulthood was rare, ranging from zero to 12% (Lussier & Blokland, 2014; Lussier, van den Berg, Bijleveld, & Hendriks, 2012; Piquero, Farrington, Jennings, & Diamond, 2012; Zimring, Jennings, Piquero, & Hays, 2009; Zimring, Piquero, & Jennings, 2007). Several studies have also compared sex offenders' level of recidivism with other types of offenders. Langan and Levin (2002) found that the level of recidivism for sex offenders is among the lowest compared with burglars, robbers, and thieves. In the study by Sample and Bray (2003), levels of recidivism for sex offenders were compared to a series of other types of offenders (i.e., homicide, robbery, nonsexual assault, kidnap, stalking, burglary, larceny, property damage, public order). Their findings on the percentages for rearrest for any other offense within 1, 3, and 5 years showed that sex offenders were not the most prolific recidivists compared with other types of offenders, but rather, were comparable to the lower recidivism rates of stalkers and kidnappers. In summary, many studies show that despite common beliefs, sex offenders' recidivism rates are not higher than other types of offenders—quite the opposite. This level of recidivism is largely influenced by the operational definition chosen, the follow-up period, the type of data used (e.g., official vs. self-report), as well as the specific subgroup of sex offenders examined (e.g., sadistic rapists, child molesters, homosexual pedophiles). This is important for the criminal investigation as it suggests that sex offenders are not all "serial" offenders and that the strategy to look for known sex offenders when a sexual crime has been committed may only prove useful in a minority of cases (see Beauregard & Martineau, 2013).

Another persistent misconception about sex offenders is to consider all of them as "specialist," neglecting the versatility of their criminal career (see Lussier, 2005). For instance, Beauregard, DeLisi, and Hewitt (2017) analyzed the criminal career of nonviolent sexual offenders and violent sexual offenders. Their results showed that although nonviolent sex offenders were mainly involved in other sexual assaults, they were also found to engage in fraud, assault, break and enter, and theft. On the other hand, violent sexual offenders were mainly involved in assault, break and enter, theft, and fraud and engaged less frequently in sexual crimes. Furthermore, the nonviolent sex offenders were involved in approximately 15 crimes and had 4.30 convictions on average, whereas violent sex offenders were involved in 17.31 crimes and had 5.13 convictions, on average (Beauregard et al., 2017). They also found that nonviolent sexual offenders were more often specialists (63.3%), whereas violent sexual offenders were more often versatile offenders (63.9%), similar to sexual murderers (68.2%) (Beauregard et al., 2017). This versatility is particularly important for the criminal investigation. Sex offenders not only commit other crimes than sexual crimes, but they may also switch the type of victim they target (Beauregard, Leclerc, and Lussier, 2012). The fact that some sex offenders are "crossovers" when selecting victims suggests a certain heterogeneity among them (see e.g., Chopin & Beauregard, 2018; 2019a, 2019b). For example, some offenders might choose to target both child and adult victims based on the criminal opportunity (Stephens, Reale, Goodwill, & Beauregard, 2017). This becomes especially important for police to consider, as a known sex offender who has previously only targeted adult victims may still be at risk of offending against a child. Thus, prioritizing suspects should not be made based on assumptions that sex offenders will only target specific victims (e.g., stranger/acquaintance, male/female, or adult/child).

Accordingly, another misconception of sex offenders is that they constitute a homogeneous group. The classical representation of sex offenders is that of a criminal, specialized in sex offenses, committing his crimes against stranger victims (Craun & Theriot, 2009). Despite the fact that many people think that sexual crimes are committed by stranger offenders, many studies have shown the opposite. The objective risk to be sexually assaulted by an acquaintance is far greater than to be sexually assaulted by a stranger, especially in cases involving children (Craun & Theriot, 2009). Sexually assaulting a child that is a complete stranger to the offender is usually more difficult as the offender needs access to the child who is often supervised by adults. Thus, it becomes easier for offenders to attack children that are known or for which the offender is familiar with the family, as trust will be easier to gain in these situations. The heterogeneity of sex offenders has been observed in research on their modus operandi (e.g., Beauregard, Proulx, Rossmo, Leclerc, & Allaire, 2007) as well as their motivation, varying depending on whether the victim was a child, an adult, or an elderly person (Chopin & Beauregard, 2018, 2019a; Reid, Beauregard, Fedina, & Frith, 2014). The research on the pathways to sexual aggression (see Proulx, Beauregard, Lussier, and Leclerc, 2014) has shown that sex offenders present various pathways to commit their crimes and that these pathways are not only influenced by the type of victims targeted but also the lifestyle of the offenders. This is something that could prove important in the criminal investigation and eventually in the prioritization of suspects.

Suspect prioritization

When a sexual crime is committed and reported to the police, a judicial procedure is opened, and a criminal investigation will follow. One of the major tasks of investigators is to identify the suspect so that charges may be laid to eventually convict the offender. When the suspect is unknown, it is possible that the investigation will produce a high number of suspects. In such cases, it becomes important to use techniques that will facilitate the prioritization of suspects. Among these techniques, criminal profiling and crime linkage analysis are probably the most prevalent. Criminal profiling is defined as an investigative tool used by the police to identify characteristics (e.g., behavioral, demographic, psychological) of an unknown offender based on various types of data (Bartol & Bartol, 2013). These different types of data generally include crime scene information, police databases, geospatial data, and interviews. Profiling can be divided into five areas: crime scene profiling, psychological profiling, suspect-based profiling, equivocal death analysis, and geographic profiling.

Criminal profiling is a technique used to identify offenders' characteristics (i.e., behavioral, psychological, and demographic) on the basis of evidence found during the crime commission process. As with psychological profiling, it is a tool used to determine the dangerousness of individuals. This type of tool is used on known individuals and is mainly based on threat assessment (i.e., credibility and seriousness of a threat) and risk assessment (i.e., evaluation of individuals with deviant behaviors presenting risks for society) (Bartol & Bartol, 2013). On the other hand, suspect-based profiling is a technique used to establish links between the type of criminal activities and some suspect characteristics (Harcourt, 2003). Whereas, equivocal death analysis is a postmortem psychological analysis (Bartol & Bartol, 2013) and is used in cases of suspect suicide where the goal is to analyze if it is a true suicide or if foul play is involved (i.e., analysis of the reasons/motivations of why the suspect did it) or a homicide (e.g., staging) (Bartol & Bartol, 2013). Finally, geographic profiling corresponds to the process used to link spatial data with an offender's information. It uses the crime scene locations associated with the crime in order to predict the general area where the offender lives. In terms of research, this type of profiling is probably the one that has been the most tested and empirically validated, and it is a tool that presents strong theoretical foundations (see Rossmo, 2000).

Geographic analyses and sexual crimes

Several scholars have investigated the distance between the offender's living place and the crime scene (for a complete review, see Beauregard, Proulx, & Rossmo, 2005). Generally, findings indicate that sexual offenders do not travel far to assault their victims. This phenomenon is known as the distance decay pattern and has been observed in several studies (Alston, 1994; Andresen, Frank, & Felson, 2014; Block, Galary, & Brice, 2007; Chopin & Caneppele, 2018, 2019; Chopin, Caneppele, & Beauregard, 2020; Davies & Dale, 1995; LeBeau, 1987a, 1987b, 1987c, 1992). One exception to this distance pattern was firstly observed by Turner (1969) and described as the "buffer zone." The buffer zone can be described as the area around the offender's residence where committing a crime is perceived to be too risky due to the possibility of being recognized.

Findings of studies examining the relationships between individual and crime characteristics and the spatial behaviors of offenders have found that younger offenders travel less than older ones (Andresen et al., 2014; Davies & Dale, 1995; Gabor & Gottheil, 1984; Rossmo, Davies, & Patrick, 2004; Warren et al., 1998). As to sexual crimes specifically, studies have shown that marital status appears to provide strong explanatory power for the distance traveled by sex offenders (Ciavaldini, 1999; Gravier, Mezzo, Abbiati, Spagnoli, & Waeny, 2010; Chapko, Somse, Kimball, & Massanga, 1999; Newton Taylor, DeWit, & Gliksman, 1998). For instance, Gabor and Gottheil (1984) found that married offenders traveled farther than others. In addition, studies have shown that in cases where victims were sexually assaulted in their residences, the offenders tended to live close by (e.g., Chopin & Caneppele, 2018, 2019; Chopin, Beauregard, Bitzer, and Reale, 2019; LeBeau, 1987a). When offenders are strangers to victims, they tend to travel farther to commit the crime than when they are acquaintances (Duwe, Donnay, & Tewksbury, 2008). Generally, sexual crimes occur in places where offenders could be alone with their victims and that offer an easy escape plan (Ceccato, 2014).

A few studies (Amir, 1971; Andresen, Felson, & Frank, 2012; Chopin & Caneppele, 2018, 2019; Chopin et al., 2019) have applied sexual crimes to the crime mobility triangle methodology (i.e., linking offenders', victims' and crime locations addresses), first proposed by Burgess (1925). In their study, Chopin and Caneppele (2018) have found that for sexual assault against adult victims, crime characteristics are more strongly associated with spatial behavior than for victims or offenders characteristics. However, the findings were quite different for sexual crimes against children where spatial patterns of offenders were strongly associated with victims' lifestyle (Chopin & Caneppele, 2019). Moreover, by analyzing the individual characteristics, modus operandi processes, and the spatial behaviors involved in sexual homicides, Chopin et al. (2019) identified a four-category typology that could prove useful in the investigation of these crimes (i.e., farming, hunting, trapping, and picking). When connecting various elements of the crime, the offender, and his spatial behaviors, this can be useful for the criminal investigation, more specifically when trying to link crimes to the same offender.

Crime linkage analysis: the ViCLAS example

Crime linkage analysis is another method for police to identify suspects. This tool is mainly used for crimes of a serial nature, such as extrafamilial sexual crimes. Crime linkage analysis is a process to identify crimes sharing similarities to determine if they could have been committed by the same offender. Links between cases are established on the basis of different factors such as the crime scene description, the modus operandi, and the forensic evidence. Over the past two decades, police databases have been created to facilitate crime linkage analysis. The two most commonly used crime linkage systems are the Canadian Violent Crime Linkage Analysis System (ViCLAS) and the American Violent Crime Apprehension Program (ViCAP) (Collins, Johnson, Choy, Davidson, & MacKay, 1998). The ViCLAS system has been adopted by several police forces across the world like Australia, Austria, Belgium, Canada, the UK, France, Germany, the Netherlands, Switzerland (partially), and the United States (in two states) (Bartlett & Mears, 2011; Bennell & Woodhams, 2015; Snook, Luther, House, Bennell, & Taylor, 2012; Woodhams & Bennell, 2015). This system is based on a theoretical process of operational intelligence described by Ribaux (2014) where data are collected, integrated in the intelligence system, and where analysts can proceed to a series of analyses to detect cases that are connected to the same individual. The results are then transmitted to investigators who make decisions during their investigation. Victims', offenders', and crime characteristics are collected in order to compare the entirety of the case and identify similarities that could offer links between several cases and thus, identify a serial offender.

Research evaluating such systems has identified some weaknesses and methodological issues. For instance, the amount of information used for linkage analysis may cause a phenomenon called linkage blindness—defined as the inability of police forces to link cases where all the information is available (Egger, 1984). Snook, Cullen, Bennell, Taylor, and Gendreau (2008) discussed the $N = 1$ phenomenon, where data collection is too specific, making each case unique and impossible to link with others. Also, by analyzing the construct validity of the system, Chopin and Aebi (2017) found that the system is not totally efficient at identifying series of sexual crimes and therefore still needs improvement. Furthermore, Chopin (2017) showed that it is possible to drastically reduce the amount of data used in the ViCLAS tool without any efficiency losses. Ultimately, research surrounding the reliability of the data introduced in the Canadian ViCLAS system has shown that it is quite variable (Martineau & Corey, 2008; Snook et al., 2012).

Lastly, in their study, Chopin and Aebi (2017) found that the type of data (i.e., sociodemographic, physical, situational behavioral) lead to differences in the ease of collection. More specifically, objective data like sociodemographic and situational information were easier to collect and analyze by police forces compared with psychological and behavioral information. As suggested by Deslauriers-Varin, Bennell, and Bergeron (2018), crime linkage tools are interesting in an investigative perspective but must be improved to increase their capacity to help investigators to identify and prioritize suspects of sexual crimes.

Investigative interview

In sexual crimes like rapes, the testimonies of witnesses and victims are crucial in order to identify the offender and solve the crime. The information that can be provided by the victims and witnesses during the criminal investigation are important in two ways. First, when the offender is a stranger— the combination of forensic evidence and the testimonies increases the probability of identifying and arresting the suspect. Second, when the offender and the victim are acquainted, the most difficult task is not to identify the suspect but to prove the absence of consent from the victim

(Hazelwood & Burgess, 2016; Westera & Kebbell, 2014). Therefore, the interviewing of victims and witnesses becomes of the utmost importance for the criminal investigation of sexual crimes.

In a study comparing 3243 solved rapes to 1111 unsolved rapes, Chopin, Beauregard, Bitzer, and Reale (2019) found that cases where victims spent more time with the offenders were more likely to be solved. They also found that cases where victims had verbal interactions and visual contact with the offenders were more likely to be solved. This confirmed the fact that when victims more precisely describe their offenders, the better the chances of solving the crime. In that perspective, victim interviews are crucial to collect useful information and to solve crimes. Similarly, findings observed in a study by Sommers and Baskin (2011) on the influence of forensic evidence on the processing of rape incidents demonstrate the importance of victim testimony in case outcomes. More specifically, the authors found that a victims' willingness to testify and the level of victim injury were better indicators of case outcomes than whether there was available forensic evidence. Although victim testimony can be one of the best tools for investigators to help identify the perpetrator, cases of mistaken identification—wherein the victim identifies the wrong person—is the leading cause of wrongful convictions, potentially accounting for 70% of the overturned convictions documented to date. Therefore, the role of the investigator in verifying victim information is also paramount to avoid misidentification. This, among other reasons, is why techniques used to interview victims are very important to collect accurate and key information about the crime. It has been suggested that the less efficient victims' interviews were characterized by domination from the interviewer. In particular, interview where investigators asked close-ended questions to victims were shown to be inefficient (Wright & Alison, 2004). As a consequence, this type of questioning leads the investigator to only explore his hypothesis without considering other important elements that could be known by the victim or the witnesses. To avoid this type of situation, specific techniques to interview victims have been elaborated. Among these techniques, one is particularly useful in cases of sexual crimes: the cognitive interview (Fisher, Geiselman, Raymond, & Jurkevich, 1987). Fisher and Geiselman (1992) based their technique on a four-step methodology. The first step consists of the victim remembering the context of the assault by rethinking in detail about the crime process using mental reconstruction. The goal here is to provide as much information as possible on the physical and personal context of the crime. In the second step, the victim is encouraged to provide detail, even partial, to complete the information collected during the first step. The third step consists of describing the crime process under various perspectives (i.e., their own perspective and the perspective of other potential witnesses). Finally, the last step consists of providing details about the crime process under various temporal perspectives. During the interview, it is recommended for interviewers not to interrupt the victims and/or the witnesses in order to collect as much information and detail as possible that could lead to solving the crime. The cognitive interview has been tested with different types of population (i.e., children, adults, elderly people) and has shown that it was effective to obtain more information from victims and witnesses without jeopardizing its quality (Akehurst, Milne, & Kohnken, 2003; Fisher, Geiselman, & Amador, 1989; Robinson & McGuire, 2006).

Interviewing suspects

In sexual crimes, the interview of suspects is especially important as it can lead to a conviction even in the absence of physical evidence. Research has shown that in approximately one-third of sexual assault cases, the guilt of the suspect was established from the offender's confession (Cassell, 1996; Leo, 1995). To obtain a confession from the suspect, it is necessary to possess good training as well as a great understanding of the facts associated with the case as suspects charged with sexual crimes are less likely to confess their crimes compared with other types of crime (Deslauriers-Varin, Beauregard, & Wong, 2011; Moston, Stephenson, & Williamson, 1992; Sigurdsson & Gudjonsson, 1994). In addition, research has shown that the attitude of police investigators during interviews can impact the outcome of the case. On the one hand, findings indicated that situations where investigators have a good and positive approach with the suspects—which includes respect and lack of judgment—are more likely to result in a confession. On the other hand, situations where interrogators have violent, negative, and disrespectful interview strategies are less likely to result in a confession (Holmberg & Christianson, 2002; Kebbell, Alison, & Hurren, 2008; Oxburgh & Ost, 2011; Westera & Kebbell, 2014). However, it is important to keep in mind that the outcome of the interrogation does not only depend on the interrogator's behavior. Research (Holmberg & Christianson, 2002; Moston et al., 1992; Phillips, Brown, James, & Goodrich, 1998) found that several other characteristics may influence the outcome. For example, situations where the suspect decides to talk spontaneously without the presence of a lawyer is more likely to result in a confession. Similarly, cases where objective evidence is recovered are more likely to result in a confession. Situations where interrogators are using strategies involving moral justification, psychological excuses, identification of contradictory information combined with empathic and respectful behavior are also more likely to lead to a confession. Research on confession has also identified some suspect characteristics associated with a greater likelihood of confession. On the one hand, individuals who are white, young, with no criminal history, presenting personality disorders (e.g., schizoid personality, introverted personality), having consumed psychoactive substances prior to the crime, and have targeted victims that are male or victims not from a criminogenic environment (e.g., prostitution, drug abuse) are more likely to confess their crimes (Beauregard, Deslauriers-Varin, & St-Yves, 2010; Holmberg & Christianson, 2002; Pearse, Gudjonsson, Clare, & Rutter, 1998; Phillips et al., 1998; St-Yves, 2002). On the other hand, Beauregard et al. (2010) found that suspects with versatile criminal history were less likely to confess their crimes.

Although the confession of the suspect in sexual crime is of the utmost importance in order to charge and convict the offender, it is important to understand the potential dangers associated with some interrogation strategies (e.g., Reid technique). If the goal of the interrogation is to obtain a confession, it is important to be able to recognize when the interrogator is at risk of extracting a false confession.

False confessions

The false confession can be defined as a situation where an innocent person confessed to a crime that he did not commit. Although this situation may appear as completely irrational, research has shown that in one quarter of exonerated cases, people have made a false confession (Kassin, 2008). There are four possibilities to objectively identify a false confession. The first is when it has been objectively established that the crime did not occur. The second is when the alleged offender did not have the capacity (spatiotemporal) to be present at the crime scene at the moment of the offense. The third possibility is when another individual has been found guilty by objective evidence. Finally, another possibility is when objective evidence (e.g., DNA evidence) exonerates the alleged offenders. The literature presents several types of false confession and risk factors associated with them.

The *voluntary false confessions* describe situations where innocent people confess using false criminal facts without external pressure. These false confessions can occur in two types of situations. First, intentional false confessions can be related to the suspect's mental disorder (e.g., psychosis), the search for recognition, or a feeling of guilt due to previous criminal acts (Kassin & Gudjonsson, 2004). Second, intentional false confessions may be explained by the need to protect somebody (e.g., family members) from a difficult situation (Kassin & Gudjonsson, 2004). In the *compliant false confession,* the false confession is the outcome of the police interview. In this situation, the suspect confesses false crimes to escape uncomfortable situations, or to obtain a reward promised by the police (Kassin & Gudjonsson, 2004). Such rewards may take different forms, like eating, making a phone call, or simply leaving the interview room. Kassin and Gudjonsson (2004) suggested that young, desperate, socially dependent or phobic individuals are more at risk to falsely confess in this context. The *internalized false confession* corresponds to a situation where an innocent and highly suggestible individual is convinced during a police interview that he has committed a crime. This type of false confession occurs in cases where the suspect experience a distrust of his memory called "memory distrust syndrome" as explained by Gudjonsson and MacKeith (1982). Thus, the police investigator claims to detain very precise information on the suspect's past and convinces him to accept a wrong reality (Ost, Costall, & Bull, 2001).

Although these four types of false confession are not widespread, it is important to understand there are some risk factors which have been associated with the likelihood of falsely confessing to a crime. In terms of personality, two factors are mainly associated with the false confession: submission and suggestibility (Leo, 2009). Some people have the propensity to be influenced into submission in a stressful situation. In the case of a police interview, submissive behaviors can result in situations where people will lie and falsely confess to crimes to avoid confrontation with authority figures. People who are highly suggestible present a weaker memory than others and tend to be more anxious. They confess false facts because they are influenced by the suggestions of the investigators during the interview and they end up accepting that it is the truth. These personality traits are especially influenced by the withdrawal of psychoactive substances (alcohol/drugs) and the lack of sleep (Kassin & Gudjonsson, 2004). Two scales have been created to identify these people: The Gudjonsson Compliance Scale and the Gudjonsson Suggestibility Scale (Gudjonsson, 1984, 1989).

In their study, Drizin and Leo (2004) showed that young people are more at risk to falsely confess with more than half of false confessions made by people under 25 years. Young people are more sensitive to coercive interviews and are subject to be more compliant with a figure of authority. Research has also shown that adolescents and young adults are more sensitive to suggestibility and have a greater propensity to merge truth and fictional facts that could be suggested by an authority figure like police investigators.

In the review published by Kassin and Gudjonsson (2004), mental disorders and mental retardation have been linked to false confessions. Drizin and Leo (2004) found that approximately 22% of false confessions were made by people with mental retardation. Kassin and Gudjonsson (2004) suggested that people with mental retardation have a weaker memory and attention span leading to false confessions. These people seem more sensitive to the suggestions made by authority figures. Finlay and Lyons (2002) explained in their study that people with mental retardation have difficulties evaluating the consequences of their false declarations. These people also have problems understanding the role of the police investigators during interviews and generally consider them as allies. Thus, they are more likely to confess false facts in order to please police investigators. Kassin and Gudjonsson (2004) also explained that some people with psychiatric disorders are at risk to falsely confess. Their perception of reality may be impaired, impacting the capacity for them to determine reality and fiction.

A false confession can have disastrous consequences for the case under investigation. Therefore, it becomes important to be able to recognize signs associated with these false confessions. Particularly with sexual crimes, investigators are often confronted with a "he said, she said" situation, where physical evidence has little to no impact on the case. This is especially evident in cases where the victim and perpetrator are known to one another. Although the investigator should try to get a confession—a genuine one—out of the suspect, in some situations, he will also have to assess the veracity of the victim's statement. Despite not being frequent, some alleged victims will make a false rape allegation. Similar to cases of false confessions, investigators need to be equipped to recognize some of the red flags associated with such false allegations.

False rape allegations

One of the most challenging and controversial issues related to sexual crime investigations is the identification of false rape allegations. A false allegation can be defined as "the description of an event that the complainant knows never actually occurred" (Rumney, 2006, p. 130). This definition suggests the conscious or malicious motive of the individual making the false claim.

The prevalence of false allegations in cases of sexual assault is not easy to establish. Several studies have tried to measure this phenomenon but the discrepancies between the results are especially important to consider. For instance, Rumney (2006) identified a set of 20 studies that measured the prevalence of false allegations in rape cases in the UK and Scotland. Among this corpus of research, the lower rate of false allegations was 1.5% (Theilade & Thomsen, 1986), whereas the higher rate was 90% (Stewart, 1981). Two studies in the United States estimated the rate of false rape allegations to be between 8% and 20% (Greenfield, 1997; Russell & Bolen, 2000). A study in Denmark showed that the percentage of false allegations of rape was between 1.5% and 10% (Theilade & Thomsen, 1986), whereas in a New Zealand study, Jordan (2004) found that 38% of rape and sexual assault cases were deemed by the police as possibly true or false, 33% were deemed as false, and in 8% the complainants confirmed the false allegation.

Studies have identified various motivations behind false rape allegations: revenge, the need of attention, providing an alibi, money, alcohol and drugs abuse, psychological troubles, and false memories (Aitken, Burgess, & Hazelwood, 1999; Bronson, 1918; Kanin, 1994; Loftus, 2003; Loftus & Ketcham, 1991, 1994; St-Yves, 2007). The identification of false rape allegations is generally based on simple indicators used by the police, and many of these could be considered as subjective and stereotypical (St-Yves, 2007). The first of them is the confession (Raphael, 2008). It is the simplest situation that occurs when the false victim confesses to having lied and makes a false declaration. The second indicator is the existence of scientific evidence proving that the statement was false. Finally, the last indicator is the victim's credibility. Some victim's characteristics may raise doubt to the victim's allegation (e.g., psychological disorders).

Several researchers have tried to identify factors associated with false rape allegations to help police investigations. Generally, scholars have identified three categories that could permit the identification of false allegations: the victimology, the offender's description, and the modus operandi characteristics.

The characteristics that distinguish true rape victims from false complainants are mainly based on the lifestyle and psychological aspects. Generally, false complainants are more likely to present various problems in their personal and social life. A number of false complainants have social difficulties (e.g., few friends and social resources), marital problems (e.g., unstable relationship), psychological troubles and/or professional complications (e.g., pathological liar, personality disorders) (Jordan, 2004; Ledray, 1994; McDowell & Hibler, 1987). Hunt and Bull (2012) have shown that true rape victims are more often intoxicated with alcohol and drugs compared with false complainants. On the opposite, a study by St-Yves and Beauregard (2015) identified that the alcohol consumption of victims is a good predictor of false allegations of rape. This difference could be due to the type of data used in each study. The delay between the crime commission and the complaint by the victims is also a good predictor, wherein the longer the delay, the greater the risk of a false allegation (Hunt & Bull, 2012; Jordan, 2004; McDowell & Hibler, 1987). In their study, Hunt and Bull (2012) showed that when complaints are filed in the 24 hours following the aggression, it is five times more likely to be genuine than to be false. On the opposite, St-Yves and Beauregard (2015) did not find evidence that complaint delays predicted false allegations. They justified this result by the nature of data, including stranger and acquaintance victims (St-Yves & Beauregard, 2015).

Several studies (Ledray, 1994; McDowell & Hibler, 1987; St-Yves & Beauregard, 2015) have found that offenders' descriptions in cases of false rape allegations are especially unclear. In their study, McDowell and Hibler (1987) found that false complainants gave a stereotypical description of the offenders and often described them as strangers. However, Kanin (1994) found that when the motivation is based on revenge, the fallacious offender is described as an acquittance. St-Yves and Beauregard (2015) found on the contrary that true victims are more able to describe specific aspects of offenders (e.g., smell of alcohol).

Some interesting differences were also observed in the modus operandi description of false rape allegations. False victims are generally more likely to describe a surprise approach as the strategy used by the offender, whereas true victims more often report a con approach (Hunt & Bull, 2012; St-Yves & Beauregard, 2015). False victims will more often report resistance on their behalf and excessive verbal and physical violence used by offenders, whereas genuine victims generally choose to cooperate because they are afraid and they want to save their life (Alison & Marshall, 2006; Kocsis, Cooksey, & Irwin, 2002; McDowell & Hibler, 1987; Prentky & Knight, 1991). Despite the supposed use of verbal and physical violence by offenders, fallacious victims report less serious injuries (superficial in most cases) that are generally self-inflicted (Ledray, 1994). Fallacious victims experience more difficulties describing the sexual acts performed during the aggression and frequently will simply mention the occurrence of vaginal penetration (De Zutter, Horselenberg, & Van Koppen, 2014). In their study, St-Yves and Beauregard (2015) showed that allegations where the victim reported that the offender used strategies to avoid police detection were generally genuine allegations.

Strategies used in sexually related online crimes

With the relatively recent development of technology, a new type of sexual crime has been identified: online sexual crimes. As a result, the identification of online sexual offenders has drastically increased in the last two decades. Although more research has been conducted lately on this form of sexual violence, these crimes represent a new challenge for law enforcement. Some of the tools that have been already discussed do not readily apply for these investigations. Thus, it becomes important to develop specific strategies to investigate these crimes.

First, it is important to define what child pornography is. Krone (2004, p. 2) defines child pornography as the "material that describes or depicts a person under 16 years of age, who appears to be less than 16, in a manner that would offend a reasonable adult." In Canada, child pornography is defined as "A photographic, film, video or other visual representation, whether or not it as made by electronic or mechanical means, (i) that shows a person who is or is depicted as being under the age of 18 and is engaged in or is depicted as engaged in explicit sexual activity, or (ii) the dominant characteristics of which is the depiction, for a sexual purpose, of a sexual organ or the anal region of a person under the age of 18" (Criminal Code, 1985, s. 163 (1) (a)). In his report, Lanning (2010) suggested that children are exploited online in three different ways: (1) dissemination of online pornography, (2) offenders engaged in inappropriate communication with children, such as attempting to engage in real-word meetings (i.e., luring), and (3) establishment and/or development of networks sharing pedo-pornographic contents.

A five-level scale, the COPINE typology, has been developed to detail the various types of child pornography content based on the level of severity (Sentencing Advisory Panel, 2002). The first step concerns images of nudity or of erotic posing without sexual activity. The second step includes content of sexual activity between children or solo masturbation by a child. The third step includes content with nonpenetration sexual acts between children and adults. The fourth step describes content with acts of sexual penetration between adults and children. Finally, the last category includes acts of bestiality and/or sadism on child victims (Sentencing Advisory Panel, 2002).

In addition to the identification of the type of material that can be found online, it is important to be able to identify the offenders behind this content. Despite the fact that we do not have a plethora of knowledge on specific offenders' characteristics, these offenders have been classified according to some typologies.

Wolak, Mitchell, and Finkelhor (2003) showed that the typical profile of arrested offenders is a white male who is less than 25 years old that acts alone. However, Krone (2004) described different types of online sexual offenders. The *browser* comes across child pornography unintentionally and decides to keep it. This category looks like the normal situational offenders described by Lanning (2010). The second category described by Krone (2004) is the *private fantasy*. This category includes people with sexual fantasies involving children but no offenses are committed. These offenders possess sexual content involving children but generally they do not share it. The third category is the *trawler*. With these offenders, there is no specific security measure put in place and they typically use a restricted network. Among these offenders there are the *sexually omnivorous*, the *sexually curious*, and the *libertarian*. The fourth category described by Krone (2004) is the nonsecure collector. These people access pedo-pornographic content and share it from open sources. On the opposite, the *secure collector* uses security measures to collect illegal content. The next category is labeled the *online groomer*. These offenders initiate online contact with a child to have a virtual and/or physical sexual relationship. The *physical abuser* category includes people that sexually abuse children and record it for personal use (not to share). The *producer* category includes people that also physically abuse children and share images to other users of pedo-pornography.

The last category of this typology is the *distributor*. These people do not necessarily have an interest in child pornography but are interested in profiting from these offenses.

Cooper, Putnam, Planchon, and Boies (1999) suggested a three-level psychological typology of child pornography users. The first level concerns *recreational users* for which access to child pornography content does not persistent over time. The second, labeled *at-risk users*, includes vulnerable people developing an interest in child pornography but not on the Internet. The last group, the *sexual compulsives*, have a specific interest in children as sexual object and are active consumers of online child pornography.

These typologies help to recognize that online sexual violence is not a homogeneous phenomenon. The distinction between various types may become helpful for the investigation of these crimes. For instance, the investigation of online pedo-pornography contents is mainly based on various digital sources of evidence. The most popular source of digital evidence is the offender's computer. Investigators and technicians inspect hard drives to find evidence of pedo-pornography use and possession. Handheld devices represent another type of digital evidence. These devices (e.g., mobile phone, digital cameras) can store pornographic data involving children or have filmed scenes of sex between adults and children. Investigators may also analyze servers to find evidence. For instance, the analysis of a suspect's server may allow investigators to access the users IP addresses, or recorded pornographic content. The last type of digital evidence that can be investigated is the online activity. Investigators use digger engine software to monitor online activities involving sexual abuse of children. This monitoring allows to identify only sex offenders with their IP addresses and enables investigators to collect evidence of online criminal activities.

In the study by Krone (2005), four types of police operations have been detailed according to the type of offenders targeted by law enforcement. The first one targets individuals possessing digital content related to child pornography. These investigations are the most traditional and investigators generally use the offender's computers to find evidence. Wortley and Smallbone (2012) mentioned that this type of investigation is initiated by complaints from the public, computer repairers, victims, or hackers having access to the offenders' computers. The second type of investigation targets covert groups of offenders (Krone, 2005) and are conducted in a similar way. Once one member of a criminal group is identified, he can lead police investigators to other group members through the forensic evidence collected. Krone (2005) mentioned that covert groups have different levels of security to avoid police detection. These operations are initiated when nonmembers discover a group and report it to the police or when police investigators work on individual cases. The third type of investigation targets the website subscribers in order to have a list of websites involving pedo-pornography. The goal here is to obtain individual information on users of these websites. Lanning (2010) suggested that people using these websites are the least experienced offenders because they do not take any precautions to save their personal information. The fourth type of operation is police stings.

The goal of these operations is to actively solicit online offenders—not only by identifying them—but also to generate a feeling of insecurity when they consult these types of sites. It reminds them that there is not true anonymity on the Internet, and they can be easily identified and denounced to their local police (Krone, 2005).

There have also been a number of vigilante efforts by media or private organizations that attempt to help detect online sexual crimes. For example, in Quebec, a series of articles describing undercover operations sponsored by the media were publicized in an effort to catch online predators (Fortin & Lanthier, 2013). Also, in 2013, an international organization "Terre des Hommes" used a computer-generated 10-year-old girl named "Sweetie" to identify over 1000 adults across 71 countries who attempted to solicit her for sexual purposes. These efforts can help police catch potential suspects; however, they can also lead to unintended consequences such as misidentification, collateral victimization (e.g., attacks on family members of friends of the publicly ousted suspects), and violence.

Conclusions

Despite the various challenges associated with the investigation of sexual crimes, several psychology-based tools have been developed over the years in order to help investigators in their quest to solve these crimes. Importantly, research on sex offenders has helped to dispel some of the misconceptions or the "myths" that have influenced the investigation of sexual crimes in the past. Guided by strong empirical findings, the police can now rely on evidence-based techniques that can help them solve sexual crimes—from the identification of the offender, to his interrogation, and ultimately, his confession. Moreover, the research has provided tools for when investigators are dealing with deceit. More specifically, how should they recognize that a suspect is falsely confessing to a crime he has not committed? In an even more sensitive situation, what are some indicators that the alleged victim is actually lying? The research on these two aspects of witness and perpetrator interviewing are particularly important in the investigation of sexual crimes, as being accused of a sexual crime may have long-term and permanent consequences for the individual who is being accused. Finally, it was also important to develop strategies to investigate these crimes where very often, the offender does not necessarily meet in person the victim but commit his crimes on the Internet. As knowledge on these offenders is relatively scarce, it is crucial to tailor some of the investigative strategies to their unique modus operandi.

Future studies need to continue to focus on offenders who commit sexual crimes and develop tools that may help the investigation of these crimes. This is why the collaboration between the police and academics becomes so important, with one benefiting the other. In the future, it will be important to look at some of the limitations associated with the tools described in this chapter, propose ways to resolve them, and hopefully, improve the investigation of sexual crimes.

References

Aitken, M. M., Burgess, A. W., & Hazelwood, R. R. (1999). False rape allegations. In R. R. Hazelwood, & A. W. Burgess (Eds.), *Practical aspects of rape investigation: A multidisciplinary approach* (2 ed.). CRC Press.

Akehurst, L., Milne, R., & Kohnken, G. (2003). The effects of children's age and delay on recall in a cognitive or structured interview. *Psychology, Criminal and Law, 9*(1), 97–107.

Alison, L. J., & Marshall, B. C. (2006). Structural behavioural analysis as a basis for discriminating between genuine and simulated rape allegations. *Journal of Investigative Psychology and Offender Profiling, 3*(1), 21–34.

Alston, J. D. (1994). *The serial rapist's spatial pattern of target selection* (PhD). Burnaby: Simon Fraser University.

Amir, A. (1971). *Patterns in forcible rape.* Chicago: University of Chicago Press.

Andresen, M. A., Felson, M., & Frank, R. (2012). The geometry of offending and victimization. *Canadian Journal of Criminology and Criminal Justice, 54*(4), 495–510. https://doi.org/10.3138/cjccj.2011.E36.

Andresen, M. A., Frank, R., & Felson, M. (2014). Age and the distance to crime. *Criminology and Criminal Justice, 14*(3), 314–333. https://doi.org/10.1177/1748895813494870.

Bartlett, H., & Mears, E. (2011). *Sexual violence against people with disabilities: Data collection and barriers to disclosure.* Dublin: Rape Crisis Network Island.

Bartol, C. R., & Bartol, A. B. (2013). *Criminal & behavioral profiling.* Thousand Oaks: CA: Sage.

Beauregard, E., & Martineau, M. (2013). A descriptive study of sexual homicide in Canada: Implications for police investigation. *International Journal of Offender Therapy and Comparative Criminology, 57*(12), 1454–1476.

Beauregard, E., DeLisi, M., & Hewitt, A. N. (2017). Sexual murderers: Sex offender, murderer, or both? *Sexual Abuse,* 1079063217711446.

Beauregard, E., Deslauriers-Varin, N., & St-Yves, M. (2010). Interactions between factors related to the decision of sex offenders to confess during police interrogation: A classification-tree approach. *Sexual Abuse, 22*(3), 343–367.

Beauregard, E., Proulx, J., & Rossmo, K. (2005). Spatial patterns of sex offenders: Theoretical, empirical, and practical issues. *Aggression and Violent Behavior, 10*(5), 579–603. https://doi.org/10.1016/j.avb.2004.12.003.

Beauregard, E., Proulx, J., Rossmo, K., Leclerc, B., & Allaire, J. F. (2007). Script analysis of the hunting process of serial sex offenders. *Criminal Justice and Behavior, 34*(8), 1069–1084. https://doi.org/10.1177/0093854807300851.

Bennell, C., & Woodhams, J. (2015). Crime linkage research: Where to from here? In J. Woodhams, & C. Bennell (Eds.), *Crime linkage: Theory, research, and practice.* Boca Raton: CRC Press.

Block, R., Galary, A., & Brice, D. (2007). The journey to crime: Victims and offenders converge in violent index offences in Chicago. *Security Journal, 20*(2), 123. https://doi.org/10.1057/palgrave.sj.8350030.

Bronson, F. R. (1918). False accusation of rape. *American Journal of Urology and Sexology, 14,* 509–510.

Burgess, E. W. (1925). Can neighborhood work have a scientific basis. In R. E. Park, E. W. Burgess, & R. D. McKenzie (Eds.), *The city: Suggestions for investigation of human behavior in the urban environment* (p. 148). Chicago, IL: University of Chicago Press.

Cassell, P. G. (1996). *Miranda's social costs: An empirical reassessment* (Vol. 90, pp. 387—499). Northwestern University Law Review.

Ceccato, V. (2014). The nature of rape places. *Journal of Environmental Psychology, 40*, 97—107. https://doi.org/10.1016/j.jenvp.2014.05.006.

Chapko, M. K., Somse, P., Kimball, A. M., & Massanga, M. (1999). Predictors of rape in Central African Republic. *Health Care for Women International, 20*, 71—79. https://doi.org/10.1080/073993399245971.

Chopin, J. (2017). *La gestion des liens entre les crimes sexuels de prédations: Repenser ViCLAS sous la perspective du paradigme situationnel [Identifying links among predatory sexual crimes: Rethinking ViCLAS under the situational paradigm perspective].* Lausanne: Université de Lausanne (Doctoral thesis).

Chopin, J., & Aebi, M. F. (2017). The tree that hides the forest? Testing the construct validity of ViCLAS through an empirical study of missing data. *Policing: Journal of Policy Practice, 13*(1), 55—65. https://doi.org/10.1093/police/pax062.

Chopin, J., & Beauregard, E. (2018). Sexual abuse of elderly victims investigated by the police: From motives to crime characteristics. *Journal of Interpersonal Violence.* https://doi.org/10.1177/0886260518821456.

Chopin, J., & Beauregard, E. (2019a). Sexual homicide of children: A new classification. *International Journal of Offender Therapy and Comparative Criminology.* https://doi.org/10.1177/0306624X19834419.

Chopin, J., Beauregard, E., Bitzer, S., & Reale, K. (2019). Rapists' behaviors to avoid police detection. *Journal of Criminal Justice, 61*, 81—89. https://doi.org/10.1016/j.jcrimjus.2019.04.001.

Chopin, J., & Beauregard, E. (2019b). Elderly sexual abuse: An examination of the criminal event. *Sexual Abuse: A Journal of Research and Treatment.* https://doi.org/10.1177/1079063219843899. Advance online publication.

Chopin, J., & Caneppele, S. (2018). The mobility crime triangle for sexual offenders and the role of individual and environmental factors. *Sexual Abuse: A Journal of Research and Treatment.* https://doi.org/10.1177/1079063218784558.

Chopin, J., & Caneppele, S. (2019). Geocoding child sexual abuse: An explorative analysis on journey to crime and to victimization from French police data. *Child Abuse & Neglect, 91*, 116—130. https://doi.org/10.1016/j.chiabu.2019.03.001.

Chopin, J., Caneppele, S., & Beauregard, E. (2020). *An Analysis of Mobility Patterns in Sexual Homicide.* Homicide Studies, *24*(2), 178—202. https://doi.org/10.1177/1088767919884601.

Ciavaldini, A. (1999). *Psychopathologie des agresseurs sexuels.* Paris: Masson.

Collins, P. I., Johnson, G. F., Choy, A., Davidson, K. T., & MacKay, R. E. (1998). Advances in violent crime analysis and law enforcement: The Canadian violent crime linkage analysis system. *Journal of Government Information, 25*(3), 277—284. https://doi.org/10.1016/S1352-0237(98)00008-2.

Cooper, A., Putnam, D. E., Planchon, L. A., & Boies, S. C. (1999). Online sexual compulsivity: Getting tangled in the net. *Sexual Addiction & Compulsivity: The Journal of Treatment and Prevention, 6*(2), 79—104.

Craun, S. W., & Theriot, M. T. (2009). Misperceptions of sex offender perpetration: Considering the impact of sex offender registration. *Journal of Interpersonal Violence, 24*(12), 2057—2072.

Davies, A., & Dale, A. (1995). *Locating the stranger rapist.* London: Home Office Police Department.

De Zutter, A., Horselenberg, R., & Van Koppen, P. J. (2014). Filing false vice reports: Distinguishing true from false allegations of rape. *The European Journal of Psychology Applied to Legal Context, 9*(1), 1−14.

Deslauriers-Varin, N., Beauregard, E., & Wong, J. (2011). Changing their mind about confessing to police: The role of contextual factors in crime confession. *Police Quarterly, 14*(1), 5−24.

Deslauriers-Varin, N., Bennell, C., & Bergeron, A. (2018). Crime linkage et profilage criminel [Crime linkage and criminal profiling]. *Les Cahiers de la Sécurité et de la Justice, 43,* 81−90.

Drizin, S. A., & Leo, R. A. (2004). The problem of false confession in the post-DNA world. *North Carolina Law Review, 82,* 891−1007.

Duwe, G., Donnay, W., & Tewksbury, R. (2008). Does residential proximity matter? A geographic analysis of sex offense recidivism. *Criminal Justice and Behavior, 35*(4), 484−504. https://doi.org/10.1177/0093854807313690.

Egger, S. A. (1984). A working definition of serial murder and the reduction of linkage blindness. *Journal of Police Science and Administration, 12*(2), 348−355.

Finlay, W. M., & Lyons, E. (2002). Acquiescence in interviews with people who have mental retardation. *Mental Retardation, 40*(1), 14−29.

Fisher, R. P., & Geiselman, R. E. (1992). *Memory enhancing techniques for investigative interviewing: The cognitive interview.* Charles C Thomas Publisher.

Fisher, R. P., Geiselman, R. E., & Amador, M. (1989). Field test of the cognitive interview: Enhancing the recollection of actual victims and witnesses of crime. *Journal of Applied Psychology, 74*(5), 722.

Fisher, R. P., Geiselman, R. E., Raymond, D. S., & Jurkevich, L. M. (1987). Enhancing enhanced eyewitness memory: Refining the cognitive interview. *Journal of Police Science and Administration, 15*(4), 291−297.

Fortin, F., & Lanthier, V. (2013). Leurre informatique : Auteurs, victimes et environnement technologique. In F. Fortin (Ed.), *Cybercriminalité : Entre inconduite et crime organise* (pp. 135−156). Montréal: Presses Internationales Polytechnique.

Furby, L., Weinrott, M. R., & Blackshaw, L. (1989). Sexual offender recidivism: A review. *Psychological Bulletin, 105,* 3−30.

Gabor, T., & Gottheil, E. (1984). Offender characteristics and spatial mobility: An empirical study and some policy implications. *Canadian Journal of Criminology, 2,* 267−281.

Gravier, B., Mezzo, B., Abbiati, M., Spagnoli, J., & Waeny, J. (2010). *Prise en charge thérapeutique des délinquants sexuels dans le système pénal vaudois: Etude critique* (Retrieved from Lausanne).

Greenfield, L. A. (1997). *Sex offenses and offenders: An analysis of data on rape and sexual assault: Sex offenses and offenders.* Washington, DC: US Department of Justice. Groth, AN (1979). Men who rape: The psychology of the offender.

Gudjonsson, G. H. (1984). A new scale of interrogative suggestibility. *Personality and Individual Differences, 5*(3), 303−314.

Gudjonsson, G. H. (1989). Compliance in an interrogative situation: A new scale. *Personality and Individual Differences, 10*(5), 535−540.

Gudjonsson, G. H., & MacKeith, J. A. (1982). False confessions: Psychological effects of interrogation. *Reconstructing the Past: The Role of Psychologists in Criminal Trials,* 253−269.

Hanson, R. K., & Bussiere, M. T. (1998). Predicting relapse: A meta-analysis of sexual offender recidivism studies. *Journal of Consulting and Clinical Psychology, 66*(2), 348–362.

Harcourt, B. E. (2003). *The shapping of chance: Actuarial models in criminal profiling at the turn of the twenty-first century* (Vol. 70, pp. 105–128). University of Chicago Law Review.

Harris, J., & Grace, S. (1999). *A question of evidence?: Investigating and prosecuting rape in the 1990s.* London: Home Office.

Hazelwood, R. R., & Burgess, A. W. (2016). *Practical aspects of rape investigation: A multi-disciplinary approach.* CRC Press.

Holmberg, U., & Christianson, S. (2002). Murderers' and sexual offenders' experiences of police interviews and their inclination to admit or deny crimes. *Behavioral Sciences & the Law, 20*(1-2), 31–45.

Hunt, L., & Bull, R. (2012). Differentiating genuine and false rape allegations: A model to aid rape investigations. *Psychiatry, Psychology and Law, 19*(5), 682–691.

Jordan, J. (2004). Beyond belief? Police, rape and women's credibility. *Criminal Justice, 4*(1), 29–59.

Kanin, E. J. (1994). False rape allegations. *Archives of Sexual Behavior, 23*(1), 81–92.

Kassin, S. M. (2008). False confessions: Causes, consequences, and implications for reform. *Current Directions in Psychological Science, 17*(4), 249–253.

Kassin, S. M., & Gudjonsson, G. H. (2004). The psychology of confessions: A review of the literature and issues. *Psychological Science in the Public Interest, 5*(2), 33–67.

Kebbell, M., Alison, L., & Hurren, E. (2008). Sex offenders' perceptions of the effectiveness and fairness of humanity, dominance, and displaying an understanding of cognitive distortions in police interviews: A vignette study. *Psychology, Crime and Law, 14*(5), 435–449.

Kocsis, R. N., Cooksey, R. W., & Irwin, H. J. (2002). Psychological profiling of offender characteristics from crime behaviors in serial rape offences. *International Journal of Offender Therapy and Comparative Criminology, 46*(2), 144–169.

Krone, T. (2004). *A typology of online child pornography offending.* Canberra: Australian Institute of Criminology.

Krone, T. (2005). *International police operations against online child pornography.* Canberra: Australian Institute of Criminology.

Langan, P., & Levin, D. (2002). *Recidivism of prisoners released in 1994.* Washington, DC: US Department of Justice, Bureau of Justice Statistics. NCJ.

Lanning, K. V. (2010). *Child molesters: A behavioral analysis.* Retrieved from: http://www.missingkids.com/content/dam/pdfs/publications/nc70.pdf.

LeBeau, J. L. (1987a). The journey to rape: Geographic distance and the rapist's method of approaching the victim. *Journal of Police Science and Administration, 15,* 129–136.

LeBeau, J. L. (1987b). The methods and measures of centrography and the spatial dynamics of rape. *Journal of Quantitative Criminology, 3*(2), 125–141, 0784-4518/87/0600~0125505.o.

LeBeau, J. L. (1987c). Patterns of stranger and serial rape offending: Factors distinguishing apprehended and at large offenders. *Journal of Criminal Law and Criminology, 78,* 309, 0091-4169/87/7802-309.

LeBeau, J. L. (1992). Four case studies illustrating the spatial-temporal analysis of serial rapists. *Police Studies, 15,* 124.

Ledray, L. E. (1994). Rape or self-injury? *Journal of Emergency Nurcing, 20*(2), 88–90.

Leo, R. A. (1995). Inside the interrogation room. *Journal of Criminal Law and Criminology, 86,* 266.

Leo, R. A. (2009). False confessions: Causes, consequences and implications. *Journal of the American Academy of Psychiatry and the Law, 37*(3), 332–343.

Loftus, E. (2003). Our changeable memories: Legal and practical implications. *Nature Reviews Neuroscience, 4*(3), 231.

Loftus, E., & Ketcham, K. (1991). *Witness for the defense.* New York: St. Martin's Press.

Loftus, E., & Ketcham, K. (1994). *The myth of repressed memory: False memories and allegations of abuse.* New York: St. Martin's.

Lussier, P. (2005). The criminal activity of sexual offenders in adulthood: Revisiting the specialization debate. *Sexual abuse. A Journal of Research and Treatment, 17*(3), 269–292.

Lussier, P., & Blokland, A. (2014). The adolescence-adulthood transition and Robins's continuity paradox: Criminal career patterns of juvenile and adult sex offenders in a prospective longitudinal birth cohort study. *Journal of Criminal Justice, 42,* 153–163.

Lussier, P., van den Berg, C., Bijleveld, C., & Hendriks, J. (2012). A developmental taxonomy of juvenile sex offenders for theory, research, and prevention: The adolescent-limited and the high-rate slow desister. *Criminal Justice and Behavior, 39,* 1559–1581.

Martineau, M. M., & Corey, S. (2008). Investigating the reliability of the violent crime linkage analysis system (VICLAS) crime report. *Journal of Police and Criminal Psychology, 60,* 51–60.

McDowell, C. P., & Hibler, N. S. (1987). False allegations. In R. R. Hazelwood, & A. W. Burgess (Eds.), *Practical aspects of rape investigation: A multidisciplinary approach.* New York: Elsevier.

Moston, S., Stephenson, G. M., & Williamson, T. M. (1992). The effects of case characteristics on suspect behaviour during police questioning. *British Journal of Criminology, 32*(1), 23–40.

Newton Taylor, B., DeWit, D., & Gliksman, L. (1998). Prevalence and factors associated with physical and sexual assault of female university student in Ontario. *Health Care for Women International, 19*(2), 155–164. https://doi.org/10.1080/073993398246485.

Ost, J., Costall, A., & Bull, R. (2001). False confessions and false memories: A model for understanding retractors' experiences. *Journal of Forensic Psychiatry, 12*(3), 549–579.

Oxburgh, G., & Ost, J. (2011). The use and efficacy of empathy in police interviews with suspects of sexual offences. *Journal of Investigative Psychology and Offender Profiling, 8*(2), 178–188.

Pearse, J., Gudjonsson, G. H., Clare, I., & Rutter, S. (1998). Police interviewing and psychological vulnerabilities: Predicting the likelihood of a confession. *Journal of Community & Applied Social Psychology, 8*(1), 1–21.

Phillips, C., Brown, D., James, Z., & Goodrich, P. (1998). *Entry into the criminal justice system: A survey of police arrests and their outcomes.* London: Home Office, Research and Statistics Directorate.

Piquero, A. R., Farrington, D. P., Jennings, W. G., Diamond, B., & Craig, J. (2012). Sex offenders and sex offending in the Cambridge study in delinquent development: Prevalence, frequency, specialization, recidivism, and (dis)continuity over the life-course. *Journal of Crime and Justice, 35,* 412–426.

Prentky, R. A., & Knight, R. A. (1991). Identifying critical dimensions for discriminating among rapists. *Journal of Consulting and Clinical Psychology, 59*(5), 643.

Raphael, J. (2008). Book review: Taylor Jr., S., & Johnson, KC (2007). Until proven innocent: Political correctness and the shameful injustices of the duke lacrosse rape case. New York: St. Martin's. *Violence Against Women, 14*(3), 370–375.

Reid, J. A., Beauregard, E., Fedina, K. M., & Frith, E. N. (2014). Employing mixed methods to explore motivational patterns of repeat sex offenders. *Journal of Criminal Justice, 42*(2), 203–212.

Ribaux, O. (2014). *Police scientifique: Le renseignement par la Trace [forensic science: Intelligence through the forensic evidence]*. Lausanne: Presses polytechniques et universitaires romandes.

Robinson, J., & McGuire, J. (2006). Suggestibility and children with mild learning disabilities: The use of the cognitive interview. *Psychology, Crime and Law, 12*(5), 537–556.

Rossmo, K. (2000). *Geographic profiling*. New York: CRC Press.

Rossmo, K., Davies, A., & Patrick, M. (2004). *Exploring the geo-demographic relationship between stranger rapists and their offences (Special Interest Series)*. London: Policing and Reducing Crime Unit, Home Office.

Rumney, P. N. S. (2006). False allegations of rape. *The Cambridge Law Journal, 65*(1), 128–158.

Russell, D. E. H., & Bolen, R. M. (2000). *The epidemic of rape and child sexual abuse in the United States*. Sage.

Sample, L. L., & Bray, T. M. (2003). Are sex offenders dangerous? *Criminology & Public Policy, 3*(1), 59–82.

Sentencing Advisory Panel. (2002). *The panel's advice to the court of appeal on offences involving child pornography*. London: Sentencing Advisory Panel.

Sigurdsson, J. F., & Gudjonsson, G. H. (1994). Alcohol and drug intoxication during police interrogation and the reasons why suspects confess to the police. *Addiction, 89*(8), 985–997.

Sipe, R., Jensen, E. L., & Everett, R. S. (1998). Adolescent sexual offenders grown up: Recidivism in young adulthood. *Criminal Justice and Behavior, 25*(1), 109–124.

Snook, B., Cullen, R. M., Bennell, C., Taylor, P. J., & Gendreau, P. (2008). The criminal profiling illusion — what's behind the smoke and mirrors? *Criminal Justice and Behavior, 35*(10), 1257–1276. https://doi.org/10.1177/0093854808321528.

Snook, B., Luther, K., House, J. C., Bennell, C., & Taylor, P. J. (2012). The violent crime linkage analysis system a test of interrater reliability. *Criminal Justice and Behavior, 39*(5), 607–619. https://doi.org/10.1177/0093854811435208.

St-Yves, M. (2002). Interrogatoire de police et crime sexuel: Profil du suspect collaborateur [police interrogation and sexual crimes: The profile of the collaborative suspect]. *Revue Internationale de Criminologie et de Police Technique et Scientifique, 1*, 81–96.

St-Yves, M. (2007). Les fausses allégations de viol: Quand la victime devient l'auteur du crime. In M. St-Yves, & M. Tanguay (Eds.), Psychologie de l'enquête criminelle: La recherche de la vérité. *Cowansville: Les Éditions Yvon Blais*.

St-Yves, M., & Beauregard, E. (2015). Les fausses allégations d'aggression sexuelle: Vers un modèle statistique de prédiction. *Revue Internationale de Criminologie et de Police Technique, 68*, 23–40.

Stephens, S., Reale, K., Goodwill, A. M., & Beauregard, E. (2017). Examining the role of opportunity in victim cross-over sex offenders. *Journal of Criminal Justice, 52*, 41–48. https://doi.org/10.1016/j.jcrimjus.2017.07.010.

Stewart, C. H. (1981). A retrospective survey of alleged sexual assault cases. *Police Surgeon, 28*, 32–35.

Theilade, P., & Thomsen, J. L. (1986). False allegations of rape. *Police Surgeon, 30*, 17–22.

Turner, S. (1969). Delinquency and distance. In T. Sellin, & M. Wolfgang (Eds.), *Delinquency: Selected studies* (pp. 11–27). New York: Wiley.

Warren, J., Reboussin, R., Hazelwood, R. R., Cummings, A., Gibbs, N., & Trumbetta, S. (1998). Crime scene and distance correlates of serial rape. *Journal of Quantitative Criminology, 14*(1), 35–59. https://doi.org/10.1023/A:1023044408529.

Westera, N. J., & Kebbell, M. (2014). Investigative interviewing in suspected sex offences. In *Investigative interviewing* (pp. 1–18). Springer.

Wolak, J., Mitchell, K., & Finkelhor, D. (2003). *Internet sex crimes against minors: The reponse of law enforcement*. New Hampshire: National Center for Missing and Exploited Children.

Woodhams, J., & Bennell, C. (2015). Time to consolidate and reflect. In J. Woodhams, & C. Bennell (Eds.), *Crime linkage: Theory, research, and practice*. Boca Raton: CRC Press.

Wortley, R., & Smallbone, S. (2012). *Child pornography on the internet* (Retrieved from Washington, DC: US).

Wright, A. M., & Alison, L. (2004). Questioning sequences in Canadian police interviews: Constructing and confirming the course of events? *Psychology, Crime and Law, 10*(2), 137–154.

Zimring, F. E., Jennings, W. G., Piquero, A. R., & Hays, S. (2009). Investigating the continuity of sex offending: Evidence from the second Philadelphia birth cohort. *Justice Quarterly, 26*, 58–76.

Zimring, F. E., Piquero, A. R., & Jennings, W. G. (2007). Sexual delinquency in Racine: Does early sex offending predict later sex offending in youth and young adulthood? *Criminology & Public Policy, 6*, 507–534.

Psychology in criminal investigation

Beyond reasonable doubt: how to think like an expert detective

13

Ivar Fahsing

Introduction

Most of the available research on criminal investigation work has been conducted from a criminological perspective. Probably, impelled by a general concern over the effectiveness of the law enforcement system, this line of research has been mainly descriptive, aiming to capture the overt nature of policing and unveil actual police practices, for instance, comparisons between clear-up rates for different types of crime drawn from national databases (Burrows, Tarling, Mackie, Lewis, & Taylor, 2000; Greenwood, Chaiken, & Petersilia, 1977). Although informative as to the official outcome, this view takes little account of the methods used by an investigator, nor does it take account of the complexity of the case or indeed its seriousness. In national databases, a theft of a bottle of soda counts as one detection as does murder, yet the pressure, competence, process, and resources required to investigate each crime are completely different (O'Neill, 2011).

In order to gain a better understanding of the criminal investigation process, and prevent serious malpractice from reoccurring, it is important to study the psychological underpinnings of investigators' judgments and decision-making. Moreover, it is necessary to identify the underlying sources and cognitive mechanisms through which prejudices and biases operate. Next, what cultural safeguards and methodological countermeasures may help detectives operate safer but still effectively during criminal investigations? Finally, how can these be implemented in a rugged decision-landscape? This chapter will not answer all these questions, but at least identify some of the fundamental challenges and touch upon some promising developments and, finally, address some knowledge-based advice for a safer practice.

Lessons from a craft tradition

In order to understand why there is so little research on how detectives actually do their job, we have to dive back to the murky alleys where the profession first began. Although, modern criminal investigation is a highly regulated activity defined by law in its commencement, undertakings, and purpose; a number of sociological

Police Psychology, Edited by Marques and Paulino. https://doi.org/10.1016/B978-0-12-816544-7.00013-9

and criminological studies indicate that traditional detective work did not always thrive in "the light of day" (Leo, 2008; Maguire, 1994; Reiner, 1997). The central characteristic of the job is essentially the same today as it has always been, namely to constantly deliver when the crowds want someone to blame. As pointed out by Maguire (1994): "Despite the changes in recent years, the CID[1] clearly remains highly results-oriented: what matters, above all else, the very *rasion d'être* of the detective branch, is to arrest criminals" (p. 44). Moreover, becoming a detective was in itself a promotion that kept you away from the uniform and the streets -but only if you blended in and performed (Rachlin, 1996). As stated by one of Maguire's (1994) detective interviewees: "A sus[pect] a day keeps the helmet away" (p. 44).

The environment in which detectives operate involves daily exposure to grave violence, appalling abuse, and hard-nosed suspects, all of which may encourage rapid goal-directed thinking (Ask, Granhag, & Rebelius, 2011) and deep emotional involvement (Ask & Granhag, 2007a; Hobbs, 1988). In addition, major crime inquiries are burdened with a high workload, constant time pressure, and almost absurd media attention (Innes, 2003). Hence, the detective branch created work cultures with a premium placed on quick, stereotyped, and resource-saving solutions (Barrett & Hamilton-Giachritsis, 2013; Mortimer, 1993; Mortimer & Shepherd, 1999). A recent study in Norway by Knutsson (2013) shows that expediency measures such as clearance days and conviction rates are still dominating the official publications reflective of quality in criminal investigations. Similar measures prevail also in England and Wales (Carson, 2007; O'Neill, 2018; Tong, 2009) and in the US (Epstein, 2017; Simon, 2012).

In line with this tradition of oversuspiciousness and expediency, the traditional detective practice picked up a tendency toward guilt assumption in combination with confirmatory investigation strategies (Brookman & Innes, 2013; Griffiths & Rachlew, 2018; Kassin, Goldstein, & Savitsky, 2003; Leo, 2008; Oxburgh, Fahsing, Haworth, & Blair, 2016). Accordingly, traditional detective cultures ran an investigation as a constantly on-going "information game" against the suspect, the defense, and the courts (Hobbs, 1988; Kleinig, 2001). It somehow became a privilege for the police to leave out the information that did not fit with their main theory (Kassin et al., 2010). Leo (2008) describes how American detectives seem to view an interrogation as a game where the final goal was achieved with little or no objective collection of information. The ultimate goal is to make the suspect accept and adhere to the theory of guilt—to make him confess. This outsmarting game was "structured to promote incrimination, if necessary, over truth-finding" (Leo, 2008, p. 23). Accordingly, detectives developed a culture of not publicly revealing their actual motivation, strategies, or tactics (Alison, Kebbell, & Leung, 2008; Rachlew, 2003; Soufan, 2011). The notion of never disclosing more than absolutely necessary is still an important cultural artifact of the profession. Personal commitment to winning "the game" is also regarded as vital; the more severe the crime, the higher the

---

[1] Criminal Investigation Department.

cultural status of "winning" the case and the personal responsibility for "restoring justice" (Corsianos, 2001, 2003; Rachlin, 1996). This might sound like outright police corruption, but the constant battle between crime control and due process runs much deeper than that (Brodeur, 2010; Packer, 1968). The adversary system used in common law countries and beyond has from its early commencement been criticized for the risk of turning the pursuit of justice into an unfair game where the end goal of victory compromises the quality of justice (Langbein, 2003; Pound, 1909). As stated by van Koppen (1995): "Basically, this is a process in which the evidence is used to verify the indictment; not one which is the innocence of the defendant is falsified" (p. 588).

A related issue is what Klockars (1980) defined as "The Dirty Harry Problem." This kind of practice may take many forms, but it ultimately means that detectives might drift into professional cultures where the perceived good end of solving brutal crimes permits ethically, politically, or legally dubious means for its achievement. These darker sides of detective work are portrayed in BBC's TV series *Life on Mars* with the sometimes frighteningly passionate Detective Chief Inspector Gene Hunt as "Dirty Harry" (BBC, 2008). Although this production is fictional, the same culture and similar methods are represented in numerous official documents (e.g., Chatterton, 2008; Royal Commission on Criminal Justice, 1993; Royal Commission on Criminal Procedure, 1981), books (e.g., Leo, 2008; Rachlin, 1996; Tong, Bryant, & Horvath, 2009; van Koppen, 2008), and journal articles and book chapters (e.g., Baldwin, 1993; Oxburgh et al., 2016; Rachlew, 2003; Stelfox & Pease, 2005). As stated by Her Majesty's Inspector of Constabulary: "An emphasis on sanction detection levels has undoubtedly to a degree produced the unintended effect of officers spending time investigating crimes with a view to obtaining a detection, even when that is clearly not in the public interest" (Flanagan, 2008, p. 10).

Bittner (1970) described police work as a "tainted occupation" with an inherent drive toward a practice of discretion, building on prejudice rather than the strict rules of law. At the same time, the massive US Rand Criminal Investigation Studies in the 1960s and 1970s concluded that detective work did not have any practical impact even on clearance rates as 97% of the solved cases were solved by patrol officers, the public, or clerks (Greenwood et al., 1977; Isaacs, 1967). These findings were supported by UK research (Bottomley & Coleman, 1981; Burrows & Tarling, 1987). Morris (2007) noted that: "Investigation … remains an artisan craft devoid of any higher intellectual content" (p. 24).

It should, therefore, come as no surprise that both prosecutors and police officers dismissed research as being hostile, biased and wasted (Bradley & Nixon, 2009). Consequently, police cultures bear a rather restrained relationship to research in general, and to the social sciences in particular (Canter & Zukauskiene, 2007; Stelfox, 2007). Higher education was seen as "upper-class". It was also considered unproductive and outright dangerous as it typically made you more rigid, less practical, less street-smart, and less productive (Hobbs, 1988). In line with this, the detective job was modeled upon and practiced as a hardcore craftsmanship. The internal notion of "the good detective" was simply that some officers had a "nose" for the job, while others simply did not (O'Neill, 2018; Tong & Bowling, 2006). Thus, managers were constantly on the outlook to identify newcomers " with the right combination of persistence, intuition and practical experience should be able to quickly interpret the information at hand in almost any case and solve it using "expedient case construction"—most often synonymous with getting a confession (Mortimer & Shepherd, 1999; Sear & Williamson, 1999). This somewhat gloomy backdrop might help explain why there is so little research on the inner cores of detective work and why the drive from within the organizations has not been bigger. Hence, despite much of the groundbreaking research of investigative interviewing and the rather warm receivement of these principles in parts of the police, it would be a grave overstatement to claim that investigative work, in general, is evidence led.

In any investigation, complex or straightforward, detective work involves solving three interrelated problems: (1) what happened, (2) who did it, and (3) can it be proven beyond reasonable doubt? As mentioned above, in some cases strongly incriminating evidence is already available from the outset of an investigation. These cases are what Innes (2003) termed "self-solvers." In such circumstances, there are typically witnesses to the crime, who can identify a suspect in combination with the presence of substantial, and incriminating physical evidence. Self-solving investigations tend to be structured around three main stages of investigative activity: initial response directed toward establishing whether a crime has actually taken place; gathering evidence in the form of interviews and inquiries; and finally, case construction which involves establishing an account of what has occurred to be presented in court.

In contrast, "whodunit" investigations are cases where no obvious suspect or "self-solving" set of cues is present at the outset of the investigation. Instead, investigators must rely on secondary sources of information, typically in the form of vague witness statements and ambiguous physical evidence (Roach, 2014). The quality of this initial information might "make or break" the investigation (Wells & Lindsay, 1980; Wells, Lindsay, & Ferguson, 1979). Accordingly, a great deal of the forensic psychological research has addressed different methods for enhancing the accuracy and detail of witness accounts (e.g., Kassin, Tubb, Hosch, & Memon, 2001; Loftus & Palmer, 1974; Penrod, Loftus, & Winkler, 1982; Turtle, Read, Lindsay, & Brimacombe, 2008), and how to assess the reliability of such information (e.g., Christianson, 1992; Gabbert, Hope, & Fisher, 2009; Steblay, 1992; Wells, 1978). Consequently, the shortcomings of criminal investigation have often been attributed to unreliable witness statements, coercive interrogations of suspects, and poor interviewing skills (e.g., Fahsing & Rachlew, 2009; Griffiths & Rachlew, 2018, pp. 154−178; Gudjonsson, 1994; Kassin et al., 2010; Milne & Bull, 1999; Oxburgh et al., 2016; Sear & Williamson, 1999). When investigations go wrong, however, it is an even more fundamental feature that also seems to fail, namely the detectives' judgments, decision-making, and overall supervision of the case. In research for the British Royal Commission on Criminal Justice (RCCJ), Maguire and Norris (1992) identified decision-making as one of the most common reasons for miscarriages of justice. They suggested that detective training should address this issue in a more fundamental way. Later, a number of subsequent studies from different traditions have identified decision-making abilities as the core in the making of an effective detective (Ask, 2006; Canter & Alison, 1999; Dean, 2000; Innes, 2003; Irvine & Dunningham, 1993; O'Neill, 2011; Rossmo, 2009; Smith & Flanagan, 2000; Westera, Kebbell, Milne, & Green, 2016). This shift was termed *Investigative Psychology* (Canter, 1994) and introduced new ways of how psychology could contribute to the investigation, prosecution, and reduction of crime. Parts of this new approach were specifically directed toward detectives' cognitive tasks such as investigative decision-making and offender profiling (Canter, 2000; Canter & Alison, 1999). Hence, a more inward focus directed toward the thinking styles of the detectives was emerging.

In a seminal study of the personal qualities required to succeed as a Senior Investigating Officer (SIO)[2], Smith and Flanagan (2000) identified 22 core skills. They clustered these skills into three groups: (1) *investigative ability*, seen as reacting to incoming information to devise and prioritize inquiries; (2) *knowledge levels*, which relate to what the SIO must know (e.g., the crime type or legal points that must be proved); and (3) *management skills*, which include competencies with human and other resources. Unfortunately, these important findings were never subjected to any further methodological conceptualization based on experimental "what-works" research.

As mentioned above, the detectives' decision environment is often far from ideal. Crego and Alison (2004) describe officers' frustration with "having to continuously fight for staff or run an enquiry on a shoestring" (p. 219) not to mention the "complexity involved in handling the intrusiveness of the media" (p. 217). Innes (2003) illustrates how murder squad officers experience pressure from a number of sources:

> There is always a considerable time pressure involved, therefore police officers strive to identify suspects quickly and to identify and protect all potential crime scenes and evidence from being destroyed or decaying in quality. There is always financial pressure to "get a result" as quickly as possible. (p. 658)

Innes (2003) also refers to the pressures that come from having to handle huge amounts of incoming information at the beginning of an investigation, with most of this information probably proving to be irrelevant to the critical aspects of the inquiry.

In such a challenging decision environment, it is a paradox that most detectives have to rely on their own intuition, mere persistence, and culturally shared rules of thumb (Tong & Bowling, 2006). We have learned a great deal about how investigations typically fail and the challenges that investigators face in the complex reality of policing. There are countless studies telling detectives what not to do, but very little

---

[2] SIO—Senior Investigating Officer is the primary operational decision maker in large-scale investigations in England and Wales.

positive guidance is provided. It should therefore come as no surprise that some cases go terribly wrong.

Detectives are simply human

A common denominator can be noted between different accounts of criminal investigative failures; investigators strive to confirm their initial hypothesis, while seemingly ignoring or downplaying conflicting information. Research on human judgment and decision-making teaches us that most people, much of the time, act in ways that systematically depart from strict logic and rationality. To cope with uncertainty, people tend to rely on a limited number of heuristics and principles that reduce complexity thereby generating simpler judgment and decision strategies. In everyday life, heuristics are quite helpful as they generally make our decisions more effective by guiding us in the right direction more often than not (Gigerenzer & Todd, 1999; Simon, 1977). However, in high-stake situations, where information is limited, the same heuristics, due to a number of known biases, may be just as fatal as they are helpful.

The term *confirmation bias* was introduced in 1960 by Peter Wason, who after a series of experiments on hypothesis testing concluded that participants showed a preference for confirmation over falsification (Wason, 1960, 1968). Subsequent research has consistently shown a strong preference for positive testing strategies (Nickerson, 1998). A number of studies show a robust inclination toward a belief consistent interpretation of available information (Klayman & Ha, 1987) and the search for new information (Klayman, 1995; Nisbett & Ross, 1980; Wason & Johnson-Laird, 1972). In many situations, the confirmation bias might feel useful as it reflects adaptive behavior and reduces the cognitive load required to evaluate and execute complex decisions. Just like the rest of the "fast and frugal" psychological heuristics and mechanisms, it filters and integrates new information to form a coherent system of values, beliefs, and actions. The confirmation bias is sometimes so strong that beliefs persist even after the information that formed the beliefs has been firmly discredited or completely withdrawn (Nickerson, 1998). The psychological and social investments in establishing and maintaining beliefs is too high to abandon them just because the underlying information is later proven to be false or irrelevant (Jonas, Schulz-Hardt, Frey, & Thelen, 2001; Lord, Ross, & Lepper, 1979; Wason & Johnson-Laird, 1972). In a series of experiments, Smedslund (1963), Jenkins and Sainsbury (1969), and Sainsbury (1971) showed that the *presence* of instances has more influence on our judgments than their *absence*—like in the popular saying: "out of sight—out of mind." They named this the *feature-positive effect*. In forensic settings, this disregard of the diagnostic value of negative information was first demonstrated by Wells and Lindsay (1980) in an archival study of lineups. They found that positive lineup identifications of suspects were considered far more informative than non-identifications. This fundamental tendency toward positive testing strategies can lead to an *illusion of correlation* even for totally unrelated details, items, or events.

Even when there is no prior personal or situational relevant reason to confirm a hypothesis, people seem to favor confirmation as the default testing strategy. This is brilliantly illustrated by Wason's card selection experiments, where the participants were asked to determine whether or not four cards complied with a rule. For example, participants were instructed that four cards had a number on one side, and a letter on the other. The pertinent rule was that if there was a vowel on one side, then there must be an even number on the other. The following cards were subsequently presented: A, K, 4, and 7. The participant was instructed to turn over as few cards as possible in order to test whether or not the rule applied to the set of cards. Strikingly, a vast majority of participants chose a double confirmation strategy and turned the cards A and 4. The correct and most effective solution to this problem was to turn the A and the 7. Turning A provides the only necessary opportunity to confirm the hypotheses and turning the 7 offers the only direct opportunity to falsify the rule by finding a vowel on the backside (Wason, 1968). The phenomenon has proven strikingly robust across diverse domains of human thinking, including logical problem-solving (Hastie & Dawes, 2010; Hoffer, 1951; Lord et al., 1979; Wason, 1968), social interaction (Darley & Gross, 1983; Snyder & Swann, 1978), medical reasoning (Dawes, 1996), military intelligence (Cook & Smallman, 2008) and in courts and police investigations (Ask & Granhag, 2005; Nickerson, 1998; Rassin, Eerland, & Kuijpers, 2010). Kassin et al. (2003) describe how US detectives rapidly form impressions of guilt, and then they do everything they can to find evidence to support their prevailing theory. Likewise, in a study of more than a 1000 suspect interviews in the Metropolitan Police, Stephenson and Moston (1993) found that in 70% of the cases the detectives were convinced of guilt prior to the interview. At an early stage, they become convinced of a suspect's guilt, and with that mind-set seek evidence which might confirm it. McConville, Sanders, and Leng (1991) also describe how British detectives act as *agents of crime* more than strict upholders of the law. The evidence is not simply discovered—but rather *selected* and *produced*. Similarly, Brodeur (2010) notes that Canadian detectives routinely were willing to neglect rules in order to ensure a conviction if they considered the suspect to be guilty. Similar practices have seemingly prevailed in the rest of the criminal justice system too, in order to ensure that "justice is done" and the "right" suspect is convicted—even if the means to secure convictions were dubious (Chatterton, 2008; van Koppen, 1995).

A typical example of such endemic tunnel vision occurred in a high-profile criminal investigation in Beatrixpark in Schiedam, the Netherlands (van Koppen, 2008). In June 2000, a 10-year-old girl and her friend, an 11-year-old boy, were abducted and sexually assaulted. The girl was tragically killed, but the boy managed to escape after having played dead. The surviving boy ran from the scene of the crime following the attack and waved down a passing cyclist. The cyclist immediately notified the authorities and the police began an investigation. At first, the surviving boy was accused of lying about the offense and subjected to confession-oriented interrogations. However, when the detectives uncovered that the cyclist previously had been warned in the park for approaching young children in suspicious circumstances, their focus rapidly moved to him. Police investigators were now convinced that the suspect was the perpetrator, despite the surviving child providing a description unlike him and not identifying him as the perpetrator. In addition, the DNA found on the crime scene did not match the man on the bike. Nevertheless, the police were so convinced of the man's guilt that they actively disregarded all the evidence that could have proven his innocence. Him reporting the crime was seen as a failed and cunning delusion strategy, the child's no matching description and lack of identification was explained away as possible signs of trauma, and the DNA evidence was seen as suggestive of an accomplice. Neither the prosecution nor the police mentioned this evidence in court, and they also failed to inform the defense about it. Hence, the cyclist was convicted. Years later, DNA was matched to a known criminal who was arrested for two violent rapes in a neighboring town. He confessed spontaneously to the murder and sexual assaults, and the confession was later backed up by convincing evidence. He was later convicted. The poor man on the bike, who initially had reported the crime, was indeed innocent.

From the above, we can learn that flaws in detectives' decision-making are not necessarily mainly due to bad will or corrupted cultures. The search or interpretation of evidence in ways that are partial to existing beliefs or the hypothesis at hand is a looming risk to any human investigator—no matter the context or stakes involved. This fundamental tendency is, however, quite strongly regulated by a number of internal and external factors. Let us see how this is reflected in psychological research on detectives and decision-making.

Research on detectives' decision-making

As mentioned above, detectives operate in a rather harsh environment and few other professional groups must routinely handle as many competing tasks, cope with as strong external pressures or risk as severe future consequences (Alison & Crego, 2008). An account of detectives' decision-making must, therefore, recognize the potential influence that comes from a number of situational factors.

Most criminal investigations are carried out under some form of time pressure stemming from various sources such as handling a number of cases simultaneously, the natural temporal decay in information quality, clearance pressures, and more explicit and formal ones, such as adhering to court rulings limiting days suspects may stay in custody. Detectives must therefore constantly negotiate the need for thoroughness, against the requirement to maintain an acceptable production of cases.

Psychological research has consistently found that time pressure affects the quality of decision-making (Svenson & Maule, 1993). A number of studies in psychology show that time pressure reduces the decision maker's flexibility (Bruner, Goodnow, & Austin, 1956; Kaplan, Wanshula, & Zanna, 1993). Specifically, the ability to generate and test alternative hypotheses is likely to be hampered under time pressure (Dougherty & Hunter, 2003; Thomas, Dougherty, Sprenger, & Harbison, 2008). Hence, time pressure complicates the challenge to keep an open mind and avoid premature conclusions. In a series of seminal experimental studies using crime vignettes, Ask and Granhag (2005); Ask and Granhag (2007b); Ask, Granhag, et al. (2011) have found that time pressure makes detectives more selective toward hypothesis-consistent information, less able to generate alternative explanations of criminal evidence, and more persistent in their initial belief regarding guilt and less adaptive toward new and relevant information. Whereas colleagues working without time pressure adjusted their position accordingly. Subsequent research has shown that merely a perceived social expectation to work quickly, rather than actual time pressure, might produce similar effects. Professional investigators who were exposed to social norms promoting efficiency (vs. thoroughness) were less systematic in their processing of case-relevant information and less aware of this influence. Thus, it appears that the *need for speed* inherent in the investigative environment has some obvious detrimental effects and other more subtle influences on detectives' evidence evaluation and decision-making.

According to Klein and Hoffmann (1993), experienced decision makers can perform at high levels despite time pressure. Alison, Doran, Long, Power, and Humphrey (2013) tested this notion in a study of English detectives. They found that time pressure reduced hypothesis generation in a computer-based rape investigative scenario and level of professional experience did *not* moderate the effects. An explanation for this discrepancy in findings might be differences in task composition among the two studies in combination with the notion that in some tasks it is probably acceptable not to explicitly consider all alternatives and simply choose the one the expert recognizes as right (Chi, Feltovich, & Glaser, 1981). Moreover, being an expert does not necessarily mean that one's decisions are always correct (Lipshitz, Klein, Orasanu, & Salas, 2001).

Another central aspect of human cognition is the extent to which a phenomenon is driven by "hot" motivational forces as opposed to "cold" cognitive mechanisms (Kunda, 1990). Detectives and prosecutors claim some kind of legally defined *objectivity*. This is probably fine as long as it comes to upholding a legally defined impartiality, but seems quite naive if it is understood as an ability to judge without biases or influence. It has long been recognized that human behavior is largely motivated by goals, and those goals can have a strong influence on cognitive processes (Kruglanski, 1996; Kunda, 1990). The social environment we operate in is an important source of goal activation (Klein & Kunda, 1993). The mere observation of another individual's behavior might automatically trigger an inference of which goal the individual is pursuing (Moskowitz & Grant, 2009), which in turn makes observers more likely to strive toward the same goal (Aarts, Gollwitzer, & Hassin, 2004). It also looks as people generally have little conscious insight into the cognitive processes that regulate goal activation. Besides, nonconscious goal activation has been found to predict both memory performance (Dijksterhuis, Aarts, Bargh, & Van Knippenberg, 2000) and creativity (Förster, Friedman, Butterbach, & Sassenberg, 2005; Hassin, Aarts, & Ferguson, 2005/3). As mentioned above, criminal investigations are goal-directed, although one may debate how to best define its ultimate goal (e.g., successful prosecution, solving the crime, punishing the offender, helping victims, etc.). In a series of experiments, Ask and colleagues have demonstrated how different forms of motivation like *emotions* (Ask & Granhag, 2007a; Ask & Pina, 2011), *efficiency norms* (Ask, Granhag, et al., 2011), and *prior suspicion* (Ask, Rebelius, & Granhag, 2008; Ask, Reinhard, Marksteiner, & Granhag, 2011; Marksteiner, Ask, Reinhard, & Granhag, 2011) significantly hampered participants' ability to generate alternative explanations of criminal evidence in a murder case scenario. Similarly, Dror, Peron, Hind, and Charlton (2005) found that their participants tended to detect matches more readily from otherwise vague and ambiguous fingerprints if the crime of which the suspect was accused was more severe. Hence, knowledge of crime severity may lead to an increased risk of tunnel vision or correlation by illusion. As another example, Meissner and Kassin (2002) found that police officers, who are convinced that a suspect is lying, cannot easily be brought to change their mind.

Similarly, Ask et al. (2008) found that their participants had more faith in DNA, video, and identification evidence if it produced incriminating information, compared with when the outcome of the same procedure was exonerating or inconclusive. As pointed out by Ask, Granhag, et al. (2011) and Ask, Reinhard, et al. (2011): "this strong normative emphasis on efficiency is likely to turn the social work environment into a chronic source of activation of efficiency goals, at the expense of more time-consuming accuracy goals" (p. 548). Findley and Scott (2006) argue that the dynamics, roles, and expectations inherent in the criminal procedure in itself promote tunnel vision against the suspect. These claims and findings are hardly surprising, but rather patterns deeply rooted in the principles of human memory and cognition. As stated by Simon (1947): "Rationality requires a choice among all possible alternative behaviors. In actual behavior, only a very few of all these possible alternatives come to mind" (p. 79).

Fig. 13.1 illustrates how judgments and conclusions in investigative settings may interfere with different internal and external factors. Naturally, the taxonomy has the anatomy of the human brain and cognitive structure as its base layer. As we move upwards, we go from general to more specific challenges. The influencing factors are increasingly dependent on the individuals and organizations involved (such as their motivation, training, tools, systems, organizational culture, etc.) and the information available and how it is processed by the detective(s). All these interact with factors such as the nature of the case (e.g., what happened, who's involved, community impact), the mental pressures created from inside the organization and from the outside. Finally, the case will depend on how the management style operates the available resources, knowledge, and experience. The illustration is far from complete, but it meant to illustrate how the evidence production in a specific case arises as an interaction between a number of internal and external factors.

In a study by Fahsing and Ask (2013), 35 highly experienced homicide detectives were asked to detail what they felt were the most important factors (tipping points) that *prematurely* might shift an investigation from a suspect identification stage to a

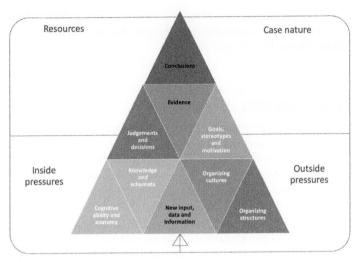

FIGURE 13.1

An illustration of how different factors may interact and influence the production of evidence during the investigation of a criminal case.

suspect verification stage. In effect, the verification stage assumes that the investigation has the right suspect and the material is then marshaled toward a court outcome. Two types of decisions were identified as typical and potentially *critical tipping points*: (1) decisions to point out, arrest, or charge a suspect and (2) decisions concerning main strategies and lines of inquiry in the case. Moreover, 10 individual factors (e.g., background, motivation, training, experience) and 14 situational factors (e.g., nature of the crime, the evidence present, who is involved) were reported as related to the likelihood of mind-set shifts, most of which correspond well with previous decision-making research. These critical and vulnerable stages of the investigative process are arguably also the most underresearched (Brodeur, 2010; O'Neill, 2018). In O'Neill's study of volume crime investigators (2011), investigators asked to rate 30 suggested skills, abilities, and characteristics required to be a successful investigator rated decision-making, motivation,[3] and communication as very important. All of these facets were ranked quite important or very important by at least 90% of respondents. Interestingly, very few studies or participants from detective environments actually point out the apparent lack of basic methods and guiding principles in their own practice. In science, method is always the starting point to evaluate the meaning or credibility of findings. Scientific method can be defined[4] in the following way: "a [...] investigation in which a problem is first identified and observations, experiments, or other relevant data are [...] used to construct or test

---

[3] There were several forms of motivation (e.g., commitment, persistence, etc.).

[4] Dictionary.com.

hypotheses that purport to solve it." Most police officers and detectives have no clue what method they use and which inherent strengths and weaknesses it might entail. They are simply trying to solve the case.

How should good detectives think?

As illustrated above, detectives operate in a very challenging and complex decision environment. It is a worrying paradox then that it exist very little methodological awareness or positive guidance of how to improve investigative judgements and decision-making. At present, there are virtually no available evidence-based methods and operational procedures.

This raises the fundamental question of how should good detectives think and decide? Interestingly, Sir Arthur Conan Doyle described the essence of such a method 150 years ago—the abductive logic applied by Sherlock Holmes: "How often have I said to you that when you have eliminated the impossible, whatever remains, however improbable, must be the truth?" Doyle (1890), p. 111.

It has been argued that this applied form of abductive logic or perhaps rather—*finding the inference to the best explanation*-should be the employed in any investigation (Canter & Alison, 1999; Carson, 2009; Fraser-Mackenzie, Bucht, & Dror, 2013; Snyder & Swann, 1978; Keppens & Schafer, 2004). The term *abduction* was coined by Charles Sanders Peirce in his lifelong work on the logic of science. Peirce described abduction as the first stage of any inquiry in which we try to generate theories which may then later be assessed. He said: "abduction is the process of forming explanatory hypotheses" (Peirce, 1965, p. 172). Although there is no reference in Peirce's writings on abduction to the notion of what constitutes the best explanation (Campos, 2009), it is clear that he thought of explanations as competing and more or less satisfactory-there might even be a best one. This is crucial in much modern work on abduction which encompasses a stage concerned with the assessment of tentative theories (Lipton, 2007). Abductive logic is widely recognized as a powerful mechanism for hypothetical reasoning in the absence of complete knowledge, and it is generally understood as reasoning from effects to causes. It also captures important issues such as reasoning with defaults and beliefs (Ciampolini & Torroni, 2004; Josephson & Josephson, 1994). Abduction has been described as "the logic of what might be" and unlike deduction, but similar to induction, the conclusions from an abductive argument might turn out to be false, even if the premises are true. Unlike induction, abductive logic allows for qualified and pragmatic guessing. In deductive reasoning, *the conclusion is a direct result of the facts presented.* Example: Tim cannot see (fact). The condition when you cannot see is known as blindness (fact). Hence, Tim is blind (deduction). In inductive reasoning, *the conclusion is derived from a fact, but an inference is added.* Example: Tim cannot see (fact). All people who cannot see have probably bumped into many objects compared with people who can see (inference). Tim will have more accidents than people who can see (induction). In abductive reasoning, *we try to presume potential facts by using supporting facts.* Example: Some people cannot see (fact). Tim continued walking into objects (supporting fact). Tim might possibly be blind (abduction). This explorative function and the absence of conclusive information make abductive inferences non-monotonic[5] and serving as argument to the best explanation (Eco, 1986; Harman, 1965; Kolko, 2011). Abduction, therefore, involves the creative process of inferring the most probable hypotheses that might explain or discover some (possibly new) phenomenon or observation. A medical diagnosis is a typical application of abductive reasoning: given a set of symptoms, what is the diagnosis that would best explain most of them? Sometimes the symptoms are so ambiguous or hard to test that there cannot be placed a clear diagnosis. Then the abductive process will have to (1) generate the best guesses based on what they know and (2) evaluate the competing hypotheses to find the best diagnosis. Typically, the inferences go beyond the information incorporated in the premises. Therefore, abduction entails both a logical and analytic dimension closely intertwined with more creative design and synthetic dimensions (Kolko, 2011; Patokorpi, 2006).

All we can expect of our "selective" abduction is that it tends to produce hypotheses for further examination that have some chance of turning out to be the best explanation (Rønn, 2013). Selective abduction will always produce hypotheses that give at least a partial explanation and therefore have at least some amount of initial plausibility. Hence, if there are reasonable grounds to suspect that someone is guilty of a crime, an investigation in form of an abductive process should commence and (1) identify what hypotheses are best supported by the available evidence and (2) identify, secure, and document information from sources of information with potential to falsify the hypotheses. The notion of considering the opposite (of guilt) also lies behind the presumption of innocence, a fundamental principle of fair trial (Stumer, 2010) and the burden of proof in criminal cases (Diesen, 2000; Kolflaath, 2015). Notably, all reasonable conflicting theories should be ruled out before a guilty verdict can be passed in a criminal court. As stated by Zuckerman & Roberts (2010), "the fact-finder has to follow a mental procedure of progressive elimination of explanations consistent with innocence" (p. 134). As an example, section 23(1) of the British Criminal Procedure and Investigations Act (1996) code of practice states: "where a criminal investigation is conducted, the investigator must take all reasonable steps for the purposes of the investigation and pursue all reasonable lines of enquiry, whether these point toward or away from the suspect." In fact, this fundamental legal obligation to actively "consider the opposite" of guilt is a norm for the evaluation of evidence in most modern democracies (Klamberg, 2015; Langbein, 2003). This normative quality dimension, embedded in principles from early Roman Law (Stumer, 2010), can only be understood as a warning against biased or premature decisions in criminal cases. As noted by Packer (1968), "The

---

[5] Nonmonotonic inferences are defeasible; in contrast to deductive inferences, the conclusions drawn may be withdrawn in the light of further information, even though all original premises are retained.

presumption of innocence is a direction to officials of how they are to proceed, not a prediction of the outcome" (p. 161).

The information gathered in criminal investigations is often both ambiguous and fragile (Dror & Cole, 2010; Innes, 2003). Therefore, the burden of proof cannot be understood as truly *deductive* elimination of all possible alternatives to guilt (Jackson, 1988). The available data will simply not always allow for this (Innes, 2003); hence, criminal investigation should be understood as a pragmatic and abductive process aiming to identify the most reasonable explanation for the available information. As proposed by a number of studies on detective work (Carson, 2007; Fahsing, 2016; Hald & Rønn, 2013; Innes, 2003; Jones, Grieve, & Milne, 2008), abductive logic serves well as a model in depicting the criminal investigation as a highly fragile, creative, and synthetic process. Like other abductive problems, criminal investigations are often complicated by a large number of potential explanations for an observation, the constant influx of new information, and the many possible ways to combine, test, and develop competing hypotheses about the most likely explanation. According to this view, all tentative hypotheses should be formed on the basis of initially available information and the detectives' available schemata of potential crimes and their noncriminal alternatives. Ideally, such hypotheses should subsequently include assumptions about all likely situations, potential perpetrators, modes of conduct, and motives behind an offense. The aim is to keep track of alternative explanations of the evidence and to remind the detective of all the different avenues of enquiry which should be exhausted.

In the next stage, the detective decides which inquiries to be carried out to best discriminate between the different explanations. In subsequent stages, all the competing hypotheses should be tested with investigative actions and refined through attempts of both verification and falsification. Accordingly, Shaklee and Fischhoff (1982) suggested that one of the most effective strategies for reducing judgmental biases is to make individuals systematically consider alternatives—a debiasing strategy recommended already by the 17th-century philosopher Francis Bacon (Lord, Lepper, & Preston, 1984). This so-called "Baconian approach to probability" argues that regardless of how many favorable results exist for a hypothesis, it only takes one unfavorable result to disprove it. Hence, reliable evidential tests should be designed to eliminate any hypothesis that is under consideration. The hypothesis that best resists the most concerted efforts to eliminate it is the one which we should hold with most confidence. Such a procedure encourages the decision maker to generate evidence that supports alternative outcomes, resulting in a more balanced and objective evaluation of the relevant evidence at the time of judgment.

The importance of such a legally defined obligation to promote accuracy goals in the criminal justice process is supported by numerous studies demonstrating that persons asked to test a single hypothesis select different information than subjects asked to test the same hypothesis against specific alternatives (Bassok & Trope, 1984; Kruglanski & Mayseless, 1988). Hence, the search for diagnostic information is context-dependent. Thus, a systematic consideration of all the competing options should lead people to use a more thorough and qualitatively better judgmental process (Hirt & Markman, 1995).

A number of subsequent studies have proven this strategy effective for reducing the negative effects of several known cognitive sources of error, such as, for example, confirmation bias (Lord et al., 1984), hindsight bias (Sanna & Schwarz, 2003), and overconfidence (Koriat, Lichtenstein, & Fischhoff, 1980). The "consider the alternatives strategy" goes beyond the task at a hand (Hirt, Kardes, & Markman, 2004; Keeney & Raiffa, 1993) and can stimulate creative thinking and analytical problem-solving by invoking changes in mind-sets (Markman, Lindberg, Kray, & Galinsky, 2007; Markman, McMullen, & Elizaga, 2008).

The required *burden of proof* is met if the investigation can rule out all reasonable alternatives to guilt beyond reasonable doubt (Diesen, 2000; Klamberg, 2011; Roberts & Zuckerman, 2010). The phrase *beyond* (reasonable doubt) indicates that the hypothesis of guilt must be proven to go longer (i.e., be stronger and explain more) than all other competing hypotheses put forward in the case. Therefore a suggested core methodology for both criminal investigation, prosecution, and trial:

a) establish the suspicion based on law and available evidence,
b) think abductively, always consider innocence and identify all competing explanations which might fit the evidence,
c) identify, gather, and cross-check all new information to show how the evidence supports or weakens the competing hypotheses.

As stated by Jones et al. (2008), "investigations should document all relevant hypotheses identified in the case … and the inquiry should seek to disprove each one: the remaining one is probably the strongest theory" (p. 20).

Generic models and supporting tools for investigative judgments and decision-making

At a global level, detective work would benefit from the development of a shared conceptual model of investigative decision-making. After all, the fundamental crime hypotheses to prove or disprove are the same no matter where or when you operate as a detective. For example, to prove murder beyond reasonable doubt in a missing person investigation you will have to disprove illness, accident, suicide, or that the person is still alive.

Some initial attempts have been made to capture the essential elements of how to think and decide in criminal investigations. These range from prescriptive and general guidelines to more detailed and descriptive models. An example of the former is Canter and Alison's (1999) advice that "good thinking is represented by a thorough search for alternatives without favouring what one already has in mind" (p. 30). An example of the latter is Innes' (2003) description of major crime inquiries as a five-stage sequence: (1) the collection of available evidence from the crime scene and witnesses (*initial response*); (2) the rapid acquisition of potentially relevant information (*information burst*); (3) the identification of potential prime suspects (*suspect development*); (4) the evaluation of evidence necessary to charge one of the suspects (*suspect targeting*); and (5) the construction of a full narrative account of the crime for use in court (*case construction*).

In an attempt to combine both prescriptive and descriptive elements, Dean (2000) formulated a five-stage process model in his studies of experienced Australian detectives. He called the stages "the 5 C's": (1) *collecting* data; (2) *checking* the data for relevance, accuracy, and reliability; (3) *connecting* data from different sources; (4) *constructing* all relevant competing explanations/hypotheses; and (5) *considering* all explanations, gauging them against available data and identifying information gaps. Dean, Fahsing, and Gottschalk (2006) subsequently validated the model insofar as detectives from Norway and Singapore acknowledged the model as a good illustration of their daily work. Fahsing (2016) subsequently modified Dean's process into a cyclic process description for investigative tasks. The Investigative Cycle (see Fig. 13.2) is described as an iterative problem-solving process that may help detectives focus on the diagnostic process and strive for accuracy. Fahsing also added a sixth C to the model—*consult*—to highlight the necessity of consulting others for a critical view on one's own judgments. This "devil's advocate" approach, whereby others' dissenting opinions are actively sought, has proven to be an

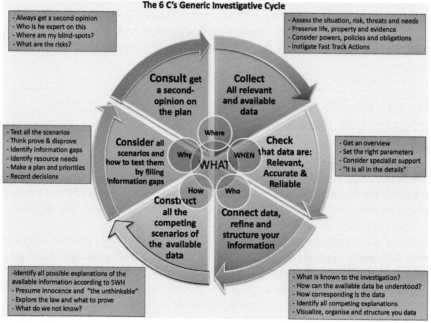

FIGURE 13.2

The Investigative Cycle as proposed by Fahsing (2016).

effective debiasing strategy in complex decision-making (Bollen, 2010; Herbert & Estes, 1977; Schwenk, 1990). As can be seen in Fig. 13.2, the Investigative Cycle aims to remind the detective to answer the six key investigative questions—the "6 W's": Who did What to whom? Why, hoW, Where, and When did it happen? In order to keep the number of competing hypotheses as low as possible, it is wise always to start your search for alternatives with considering "what might have happened" and then follow on with the rest of the refining questions. To handle the "what" question is of course also a fundamental legal requirement for establishing legal grounds for suspicion and even commencing an investigation since this renders which paragraph of the law you suspect might be broken.

Now, your questions can be further explored in a systematic investigation process involving six interlinked steps. The iterative process of hypotheses refinement, information gathering and retesting should ideally run as long as there is legally obtainable information available and a need to strengthen the case construction (Diesen, 2000; Klamberg, 2011; Roberts & Zuckerman, 2010).

The Investigative Cycle is now part of all investigative education programs at the Norwegian Police University College (Bjerknes & Fahsing, 2017). Moreover, following the enquiry into the wrongful convictions of alleged serial murder Sture Bergwall in Sweden and Norway, the Director of Public Prosecutions in Norway strongly recommended an implementation of the Investigative Cycle in combination with documented hypothesis-driven investigation plans (Riksadvokaten, 2017).

Another proposed tool that may facilitate a systematic approach to hypothesis testing is the Analysis of Competing Hypotheses (ACH) method. Originally designed primarily for use by practitioners within the intelligence field (Heuer, 2014), ACH uses a matrix to display the weighting of alternative explanations and conclusions for a given problem (see Fig. 13.3). Drawing on the fundamental investigative principle of cross-checking information from different sources (Dean, 2005; Gordon & Hayward, 1968), ACH makes explicit what evidence is used, how evidence is considered, and how it relates to all the competing hypotheses in the case. In a first step, all possible alternative hypotheses are generated. To uphold the legally required presumption of innocence, a null hypothesis (H0) assuming that the suspect has not committed the crime must be among the hypotheses considered. Second, the items of evidence with the greatest probative value with regard to a given hypothesis are identified. Third, particular focus is placed on identifying evidence that may disprove or weaken a given hypothesis. The latter step aligns the ACH method with the scientific ideal of "falsification" (Townsley, Mann, & Garrett, 2011) and aids investigators in addressing the standard burden of proof in criminal cases. Because the considered hypotheses are mutually competitive, the weakening of one hypothesis necessarily entails the strengthening of others. Hence, the progressive elimination of explanations consistent with innocence helps rule out any reasonable doubt that may prevent the conviction of a guilty perpetrator.

None of the models above have been experimentally tested in randomized controlled trials. It should, therefore, be a prioritized goal for future research to test the effect of such prescriptive and descriptive models and tools.

Information gap	Action	Priority	H1 (Murder)	H (Kidnap)	H3 (Accident)	H4 (Illness)	H5 (Suicide
Did anyone have a motive?	Interviews of family and friends	High	Consistent	Consistent	Inconsistent	Inconsistent	Inconsistent
Any signs of illness or decease?	Interviews of family and friends	High	Consistent	Consistent	Inconsistent	Inconsistent	Inconsistent
Any travel planning activities?	Check accounts and records	High	Consistent	Consistent	Inconsistent	Inconsistent	Inconsistent
Any signs of fight or violence?	Crime scene analysis	High	Consistent	Consistent	Consistent	Consistent	Neutral
Does she have friends abroad?	Interviews of family and friends	High	Consistent	Consistent	Inconsistent	Inconsistent	Neutral
Does she have a passport?	Check accounts and records	High	Consistent	Consistent	Inconsistent	Inconsistent	Neutral

FIGURE 13.3

An example ACH matrix which uses a coloring scheme for evidence evaluation to facilitate interpretation.

A related question is how to transfer this knowledge and theories into the daily practice of detectives and prosecutors. First of all, the urgent need for change and development has to be acknowledged and addressed by politicians and the top level management. Next, we have to define more explicitly what actually characterize a high-quality investigation and a good detective. Finally, we need systems, technology, and methods to implement, uphold, review, and further develop knowledge-based practice.

There is little research on early predictors of what makes a good detective and few formal systems in place to translate knowledge into sound investigative practice and acknowledge detective expertise (De Poot & van Koppen, 2002; Fahsing & Rachlew, 2009; O'Neill & Milne, 2014; Tong, 2009). Due to the lack of formal systems for recruitment, reviews, and authorization, the level of performance and expertise is often seen as synonymous with years of professional experience (Fahsing & Ask, 2016; Stelfox, 2007).

England and Wales, however, have turned their experiences from justice failures into reforms with programs specifically directed toward standardization of core investigative methods, procedures, and accreditation of police investigators (ACPO, 2000; ACPO, 2002; ACPO, 2005; ACPO, 2007; ACPO, 2010; ACPO, 2012). An initiative under the British Police Reform Act 2002 was the Professionalising Investigation Programme (PIP), which was formally launched by the Association of Chief Police Officers and the National Centre for Policing Excellence in 2005. The proclaimed aim of PIP was "to enhance the crime investigation skills and ability of police officers and staff involved in the investigative process and to drive through new standards of investigation at all levels" (NCPE, 2005, p. 1). This was to be achieved by providing training in and assessment of professional investigative procedures designed to assist investigators in making accountable decisions and minimizing the risk of errors.

Although very little of the content was so-called evidence-based, the documentation and national standardization of all working procedures in criminal investigations is probably the one of the most important steps ever done to improve investigative practice anywhere. Documented operational procedures and accreditation of competence levels are perhaps the most fundamental moves from a craftsmanship tradition toward a more full-blooded profession.

The implementation of the PIP program was reviewed by Flanagan (2008) who concluded that it had established a body of knowledge for investigative practice and delivered a recognizable framework to professionalize the investigative process which had been previously absent. According to Flanagan (2008), PIP provided the opportunity to "deliver the right people, with the right skills in the right place at the right time" (p. 6). What this means in practice is not clear and there is very little evidence available to further support the claim or the true effect of the new framework. Despite the apparent lack of scientific evidence for the advice given in previous reforms in England and Wales, no other government or police service in the world has so openly stated a need for a change in policy when it comes to investigative decision-making.

Fahsing and Ask (2016) wanted to explore and test the difference in decision-making competence between England and Norway—where no similar reforms had taken place. On the other hand, the basic police training in Norway is a 3-year bachelor while in England it is typically a 25-week training course with subsequent mentoring. The first study compared senior detectives' insight and awareness of the fragility of the decision-making process in major crime investigations. The results showed quite a high level of practical awareness which on many areas connected well to the available psychological literature. The consensus between the two detective cohorts was generally found to be surprisingly high (see Fahsing & Ask, 2013). Using a quasi-experimental design with two real life—inspired crime scenarios, Fahsing and Ask also compared the operational quality of investigative decisions made by experienced homicide detectives and novice police officers in England and Norway. In England, the PIP-accredited homicide detectives vastly outperformed novice police officers in the number of adequate investigative hypotheses and actions reported. In Norway, however, bachelor-educated police novices did marginally better than highly experienced (but non-accredited) homicide detectives. Fahsing and Ask (2016) suggested that the most obvious difference between the experienced detectives from each country was the process of development of detective expertise and standardized investigative practice. SIOs in the UK (since 2005) were the product of the PIP development process, whereas Norwegian detectives had no similar national standards or developmental program. The authors proposed that the investigative practice in Norway, and probably also in most other countries, could be strongly enhanced by implementing a reform and development process similar to the PIP.

Conclusions

In this chapter, I have described how investigative decision-making can be understood and improved through better application of the knowledge we possess both from research and from the field. The available research has identified several elements of investigators' work environment that aggravate the risk of confirmation bias. These kinds of challenges and processes will always be associated with uncertainty, subjective influences, and systematic biases. A few attempts have been made to study countermeasures of bias and tools to aid detectives' reasoning processes, but most suggested measures and tools remain largely untested. This chapter has focused mostly on how we more safely can move the conclusion of any investigation beyond reasonable doubt by a more transparent, systematic and conscious information processing, use of abductive logic and documented evidence production through active use of hypothesis testing. The tested empirical effect of these potential safeguards in applied settings remains to be seen, but used in combination they might increase the quality of the case, strengthen the principles of fair trial, and reduce the risk of errors. If the need for a new paradigm is ignored, the potentially harmful consequences are considerable. First, shallow processing of evidence—an inevitable consequence of information overload—may increase the risk of stereotyping in criminal investigations. The efficiency-promoting goals that characterize the police culture may make detectives favor hypotheses and information supporting guilt. Exonerating evidence or information supporting a noncriminal explanation may be ignored or go undetected. Innocent citizens, unfortunate enough to become the subject of such an investigation, may be seriously disadvantaged and wrongfully convicted. Second, the competing investigative hypotheses and actions that do not receive sufficient attention during an investigation may dramatically weaken the prosecution's case and open up unnecessary and potentially exonerating speculations in court. Only the guilty suspect will benefit from this.

References

Aarts, H., Gollwitzer, P. M., & Hassin, R. R. (2004). Goal contagion: Perceiving is for pursuing. *Journal of Personality and Social Psychology, 87*(1), 23–37.

ACPO. (2000). *Murder investigation manual.* Wyboston, UK: Association of Chief Police Officers.

ACPO. (2002). *Investigation of volume crime manual.* Wyboston, UK: Association of Chief Police Officers.

ACPO. (2005). *Major incident room standardised administrative procedures manual.* Wyboston, UK: Association of Chief Police Officers.

ACPO. (2007). *Practice advice on critical incident management.* Wyboston, UK: Association of Chief Police Officers.

ACPO. (2010). Skills for justice: Policing professional framework: *Senior investigation officer.*

ACPO. (2012). *Practice advice on core investigative doctrine* (2. *edition*). Wyboston, UK: Association of Chief Police Officers and National Policing Improvement Agency.

Alison, L., & Crego, J. (2008). *Policing Critical Incidents. Leadership and critical incident management*. Cullompton, Devon: Willan Publishing.

Alison, L., Doran, B., Long, M. L., Power, N., & Humphrey, A. (2013). The effects of subjective time pressure and individual differences on hypotheses generation and action prioritization in police investigations. *Journal of Experimental Psychology: Applied, 19*(1), 83.

Alison, L., Kebbell, M., & Leung, J. (2008). A facet analysis of police officers' self-reported use of suspect-interviewing strategies and their discomfort with ambiguity. *Applied Cognitive Psychology, 22*(8), 1072−1087.

Ask, K. (2006). *Criminal investigation: Motivation, emotion and cognition in the processing of evidence*. Sweden: Department of Psychology, Göteborg University.

Ask, K., & Granhag, P. A. (2005). Motivational sources of confirmation bias in criminal investigations: The need for cognitive closure. *Journal of Investigative Psychology and Offender Profiling, 2*(1), 43−63.

Ask, K., & Granhag, P. A. (2007a). Hot cognition in investigative judgments: The differential influence of anger and sadness. *Law and Human Behavior, 31*, 537−551.

Ask, K., & Granhag, P. A. (2007b). Motivational bias in criminal investigators' judgments of witness reliability. *Journal of Applied Social Psychology, 37*(3), 561−591.

Ask, K., Granhag, P. A., & Rebelius, A. (2011). Investigators under influence: How social norms activate goal-directed processing of criminal evidence. *Applied Cognitive Psychology, 25*, 548−553.

Ask, K., & Pina, A. (2011). On being angry and punitive: How anger alters perception of criminal intent. *Social Psychological and Personality Science, 2*(5), 494−499.

Ask, K., Rebelius, A., & Granhag, P. A. (2008). The "elasticity" of criminal evidence: A moderator of investigator bias. *Applied Cognitive Psychology, 22*(9), 1245−1259.

Ask, K., Reinhard, M.-A., Marksteiner, T., & Granhag, P. A. (2011). Elasticity in evaluations of criminal evidence: Exploring the role of cognitive dissonance. *Legal and Criminological Psychology, 16*(2), 289−306.

Baldwin, J. (1993). Police interview techniques − establishing truth or proof? *British Journal of Criminology, 33*, 325−351.

Barrett, E. C., & Hamilton-Giachritsis, C. (2013). The victim as a means to an end: Detective decision making in a simulated investigation of attempted rape. *Journal of Investigative Psychology and Offender Profiling, 10*(2), 200−218.

Bassok, M., & Trope, Y. (1984). People's strategies for testing hypotheses about another's personality: Confirmatory or diagnostic? *Social Cognition, 2*, 199−213.

BBC. (2008). *Life on Mars*. Retrieved from: http://www.bbc.co.uk/programmes/b006t85s.

Bittner, E. (1970). *The functions of police in modern society*. Chevy Chase, MD: National Institute of Mental Health.

Bjerknes, O. T., & Fahsing, I. (2017). *Etterforskning. Prinsipper, metoder og praksis* (Vol. 1). Bergen: Fagbokforlaget.

Bollen, M. (2010). *Tunnelvisie als bedrijfsrisico*. Deventer: Kluwer.

Bottomley, A. K., & Coleman, C. (1981). Understanding crime rates. *Farnborough: Gower, 208*, 70−96.

Bradley, D., & Nixon, C. (2009). Ending the "dialogue of the deaf": Evidence and policing policies and practices. An Australian case study. *Police Practice and Research: International Journal, 10*(5−6), 423−435.

Brodeur, J.-P. (2010). *The policing web*. New York: Oxford University Press.

Brookman, F., & Innes, M. (2013). The problem of success: What is a "good" homicide investigation? *Policing and Society, 23*(3), 292–310.

Bruner, J. S., Goodnow, J. J., & Austin, G. A. (1956). *A study of thinking.* New York, NY: John Wiley & Sons.

Burrows, J., & Tarling, R. (1987). The investigation of crime in England and Wales. *British Journal of Criminology, 27*(3), 229–251.

Burrows, J., Tarling, R., Mackie, A., Lewis, R., & Taylor, G. (2000). *Review of police forces' crime recording practices.* Home Office Research Study.

Campos, D. G. (2009). On the distinction between Peirce's abduction and Lipton's Inference to the best explanation. *Synthese, 180*(3), 419–442.

Canter, D. (1994). *Criminal shadows: Inside the mind of the serial killer.* HarperCollins.

Canter, D. (2000). Investigative psychology. In J. A. Siegel, P. J. Saukko, & G. C. Knupfer (Eds.), *Encyclopedia of forensic sciences* (Vol. 3, pp. 1091–1097). New York: Academic Press.

Canter, D., & Alison, L. (1999). *Profiling in policy and practice.* Aldershot: Ashgate.

Canter, D., & Zukauskiene, R. (2007). *Psychology and law; bridging the gap.* Hampshire, UK: Ashgate Publishing Ltd.

Carson, D. (2007). Models of investigations. In T. Newburn, T. Williamson, & A. Wright (Eds.), *Handbook of criminal investigation* (pp. 407–425). Devon: Willan.

Carson, D. (2009). Detecting, developing and disseminating detectives' "creative" skills. *Policing and Society, 19*(3), 216–225.

Chatterton, M. (2008). *Loosing the detectives: Views from the frontline.* Surbiton, UK: Police Federation.

Chi, M. T. H., Feltovich, P. J., & Glaser, R. (1981). Categorization and representation of physics problems by experts and novices. *Cognitive Science, 5*, 121–152.

Christianson, S.-Å. (1992). Emotional stress and eyewitness memory: A critical review. *Psychological Bulletin, 112*(2), 284–309.

Ciampolini, A., & Torroni, P. (2004). Using abductive logic agents for modeling the judicial evaluation of criminal evidence. *Applied Artificial Intelligence: AAI, 18*(3–4), 251–275.

Cook, M. B., & Smallman, H. S. (2008). Human factors of the confirmation bias in intelligence analysis: Decision support from graphical evidence landscapes. *Human Factors: The Journal of the Human Factors and Ergonomics Society, 50*(5), 745–754.

Corsianos, M. (2001). Conceptualizing "justice" in detectives' decision making. *International Journal of the Sociology of Law, 29*(2), 113–125.

Corsianos, M. (2003). Discretion in detectives' decision making and "high profile" cases. *Police Practice and Research: International Journal, 4*(3), 301–314.

Crego, J., & Alison, L. (2004). Control and legacy as functions of perceived criticality in major incidents. *Journal of Investigative Psychology and Offender Profiling, 1*, 207–225.

Darley, J. M., & Gross, P. H. (1983). A hypothesis-confirming bias in labeling effects. *Journal of Personality and Social Psychology, 44*(1), 20–33.

Dawes, R. M. (1996). *House of cards. Psychology and psychotheraby bulit on myth.* New York: Free Press.

De Poot, C., & van Koppen, P. J. (2002). *The criminal investigation process.* Presented at the 12th European conference on psychology and law, (Leuven, Belgium).

Dean, G. (2000). *The experience of investigation for detectives (PhD).* Brisbane, Australia: Queensland University of Technology.

Dean, G. (2005). The "Cross+check" system: Integrating profiling approaches for police and security investigations. *Journal of Police and Criminal Psychology, 20*(2), 20–43.

Dean, G., Fahsing, I., & Gottschalk, P. (2006). Profiling police investigative thinking: A study of police officers in Norway. *International Journal of the Sociology of Law, 34*(4), 221–228.

Diesen, C. (2000). Beyond reasonable doubt: Standard of proof and evaluation of evidence in criminal cases. *Scandinavian Studies in Law*, (40), 169–180.

Dijksterhuis, A., Aarts, H., Bargh, J. A., & Van Knippenberg, A. (2000). On the relation between associative strength and automatic behavior. *Journal of Experimental Social Psychology, 36*(5), 531–544.

Dougherty, M. R. P., & Hunter, J. (2003). Probability judgment and subadditivity: The role of working memory capacity and constraining retrieval. *Memory & Cognition, 31*(6), 968–982.

Doyle, A. C. (1890). *The sign of the four*. London, UK: The Strand Magazine.

Dror, I. E., & Cole, S. A. (2010). The vision in "blind" justice: Expert perception, judgment and visual cognition in forensic pattern recognition. *Psychonomic Bulletin & Review, 17*(2), 161–167.

Dror, I. E., Péron, A. E., Hind, S.-L., & Charlton, D. (2005). When emotions get the better of us: The effect of contextual top-down processing on matching fingerprints. *Applied Cognitive Psychology, 19*(6), 799–809.

Eco, U. (1986). *Semiotics and the philosophy of language*. Indiana University Press.

Epstein, J. (2017). The national commission on forensic science: Impactful or ineffectual. *Seton Hall Law Review, 48*, 743.

Fahsing, I. (2016). The Making of an expert detective. Thinking and deciding in criminal investigations (PhD). University of Gothenburg. Retrieved from https://gupea.ub.gu.se/handle/2077/47515.

Fahsing, I., & Ask, K. (2013). Decision making and decisional tipping points in homicide investigations: An interview study of British and Norwegian detectives. *Journal of Investigative Psychology and Offender Profiling, 10*(2), 155–165.

Fahsing, I., & Ask, K. (2016). The making of an expert detective: The role of experience in English and Norwegian police officers' investigative decision-making. *Psychology, Crime and Law, 22*(3), 203–223.

Fahsing, I., & Rachlew, A. A. (2009). Investigative interviewing in the Nordic region. In B. Milne, & S. Savage (Eds.), *International developments in investigative interviewing*. Devon, UK: Willan Publishing.

Findley, K. A., & Scott, M. S. (2006). The multiple dimensions of tunnel vision in criminal cases. *Wisconsin Law Review, 291*, 291–397.

Flanagan, R. (2008). *The review of policing: Interim report*. London, UK: Her Majesty's Inspector of Constabulary.

Förster, J., Friedman, R. S., Butterbach, E. B., & Sassenberg, K. (2005). Automatic effects of deviancy cues on creative cognition. *European Journal of Social Psychology, 35*(3), 345–359.

Fraser-Mackenzie, P. A. F., Bucht, R., & Dror, I. E. (2013). Forensic judgement and decison-making. In T. R. Zentall, & P. H. Crowley (Eds.), *Comparative decison making*. Oxford: Oxford Scholarship Online.

Gabbert, F., Hope, L., & Fisher, R. P. (2009). Protecting eyewitness evidence: Examining the efficacy of a self-administered interview tool. *Law and Human Behavior, 33*(4), 298–307.

Gigerenzer, G., & Todd, P. M. (1999). *Simple heuristics that make us smart*. New York: Oxford University Press.

Gordon, T. J., & Hayward, H. (1968). Initial experiments with the cross-impact matrix method of forecasting. *Futures, 1*(2), 100–116.

Greenwood, P., Chaiken, J., & Petersilia, J. (1977). *The criminal investigation process.* Lexington, Mass: D.C. Heart.

Griffiths, A., & Rachlew, A. (2018). From interrogation to investigative interviewing: The application of psychology. In *The psychology of criminal investigation.* Routledge.

Gudjonsson, G. H. (1994). The effects of interrogative pressure on strategic coping. *Psychology, Crime and Law, 1*(4), 309–318.

Hald, C., & Rønn, K. V. (2013). *Om at opdage — metodiske refleksjoner over politiets undersøkelsespraksis.* Copenhagen: Samfundslitteratur.

Harman, G. H. (1965). The inference to the best explanation. *Philosophical Review,* 88–95.

Hassin, R. R., Aarts, H., & Ferguson, M. J. (2005/3). Automatic goal inferences. *Journal of Experimental Social Psychology, 41*(2), 129–140.

Hastie, R., & Dawes, R. M. (2010). *Rational choice in an uncertain world: The psychology of judgment and decision making.* Thousand Oaks, CA: SAGE.

Herbert, T. T., & Estes, R. W. (1977). Improving executive decisions by formalizing dissent: The corporate devil's advocate. *Academy of Management Review, 2*(4), 662–667.

Heuer, R. J., Jr. (2014). *Structured analytic techniques for intelligence analysis.* CQ Press.

Hirt, E. R., Kardes, F. R., & Markman, K. D. (2004/5). Activating a mental simulation mindset through generation of alternatives: Implications for debiasing in related and unrelated domains. *Journal of Experimental Social Psychology, 40*(3), 374–383.

Hirt, E. R., & Markman, K. D. (1995). Multiple explanation: A consider-an-alternative strategy for debiasing judgments. *Journal of Personality and Social Psychology, 69*(6), 1069.

Hobbs, D. (1988). *Doing the business: Entrepreneurship, detectives and the working class in the East end of London.* Oxford: Oxford University Press.

Hoffer, E. (1951). *The true believer.* New York: Harper and Row.

Innes, M. (2003). *Investigating murder: Detective work and the police response to criminal homicide.* Oxford, UK: Oxford University Press.

Irvine, B., & Dunningham, C. (1993). Human factors in the quality control of CID investigations. In *Royal commission on criminal justice research study* (Vol. 21). London: HMSO.

Isaacs, H. (1967). A study of communications, crimes, and arrests in a metropolitan police department. *Task Force Report: Science and Technology,* 88–106.

Jackson, J. D. (1988). Two methods of proof in criminal procedure. *The Modern Law Review, 51*(5), 549–568.

Jenkins, H. M., & Sainsbury, R. S. (1969). The development of stimulus control through differential reinforcement. In J. N. Mackintosh, & W. K. Honig (Eds.), *Fundamental issues in associative learning* (pp. 123–167). Halifax: Dalhousie University Press.

Jonas, E., Schulz-Hardt, S., Frey, D., & Thelen, N. (2001). Confirmation bias in sequential information search after preliminary decisions: An expansion of dissonance theoretical research on selective exposure to information. *Journal of Personality and Social Psychology, 80*(4), 557–571.

Jones, D., Grieve, J., & Milne, B. (2008). The case to review murder investigations. *Policing, 2*(4), 470–480.

Josephson, R.,J., & Josephson, G.,S. (1994). *Abductive inference: Computation, philosophy, technology.* New York: Cambridge University Press.

Kaplan, M. F., Wanshula, L. T., & Zanna, M. P. (1993). Time pressure and information integration in social judgment: The effect of need for structure. In O. Svenson, & A. J. Maule

(Eds.), *Time pressure and stress in human judgment and decision making* (pp. 255—267). New York: Plenum Press.

Kassin, S. M., Drizin, S. A., Grisso, T., Gudjonsson, G. H., Leo, R. A., & Redlich, A. D. (2010). Police-induced confessions: Risk factors and recommendations. *Law and Human Behavior, 34*(1), 3—38.

Kassin, S. M., Goldstein, C. C., & Savitsky, K. (2003). Behavioral confirmation in the inter-rogation room: On the dangers of presuming guilt. *Law and Human Behavior, 27*(2), 187—203.

Kassin, S. M., Tubb, V. A., Hosch, H. M., & Memon, A. (2001). On the "general acceptance" of eyewitness testimony research. *American Psychologist, 56*(5), 405—416.

Keeney, R. L., & Raiffa, H. (1993). *Decisions with multiple objectives: Preferences and value trade-offs.* Cambridge University Press.

Keppens, J., & Schafer, B. (2004). Murdered by persons unknown — speculative reasoning in law and logic. In T. Gordon (Ed.), *Legal knowledge and information systems. Jurix 2004: The seventeenth annual conference* (pp. 109—118). Amsterdam: IOS Press.

Klamberg, M. (2011). *Fact-finding in international criminal procedure — how collection of evidence may contribute to testing of alternative hypotheses.* https://doi.org/10.2139/ssrn.1847710.

Klamberg, M. (2015). The alternative hypothesis approach, robustness and international crim-inal justice — a plea for a "combined approach" to evaluation of evidence. *Journal of International Criminal Justice, 13*(3), 535—553.

Klayman, J. (1995). Varieties of confirmation bias. In R. H. A. D. L. M. Jerome Busemeyer (Ed.), *Psychology of learning and motivation* (Vol. 32, pp. 385—418). Academic Press.

Klayman, J., & Ha, Y.-W. (1987). Confirmation, disconfirmation, and information in hypoth-esis testing. *Psychological Review, 94*(2), 211—228.

Klein, G. A., & Hoffmann, R. (1993). Seeing the invisible: Perseptual/cognitive aspects of expertise. In M. Rabinowitz (Ed.), *Cognitive sience foundations of instruction* (pp. 203—226). Mahwah, NJ: Lawrence Erlbaum Associates.

Kleinig, J. (2001). The blue wall of silence: An ethical analysis. *International Journal of Applied Philosophy, 15*(1), 1—23.

Klein, W. M., & Kunda, Z. (1993). Maintaining self-serving social comparisons: Biased reconstruction of one's past behaviors. *Personality and Social Psychology Bulletin, 19*(6), 732—739.

Klockars, C. B. (1980). The dirty Harry problem. *The Annals of the American Academy of Political and Social Science, 452*(1), 33—47.

Knutsson, J. (2013). Måling av effektivitet i etterforskning: Delrapport i «Etterforskningsprosjektet» *(PHS Forskning 2013 No. 8278081042)* (Vol. 3). Oslo: Politihøgskolen.

Kolflaath. (2015). En metode for bevisbdømmelsen i straffesaker. In R. Aarli, M.-A. Hedlund, & S. E. Jebens (Eds.), *Bevis i straffesaker. Utvalgte emner* (pp. 507—534). Oslo: Gyldendal Akademisk.

Kolko, J. (2011). *Exposing the magic of design: A practitioner's guide to the methods and theory of synthesis.* Oxford University Press.

van Koppen, P. (1995). Judges' decision-making. In R. Bull, & D. Carson (Eds.), *Handbook of psychology in legal contexts* (pp. 581—607). Chichester, UK: Wiley.

van Koppen, P. J. (2008). Blundering justice. In R. N. Kocsis (Ed.), *Serial murder and the psy-chology of violent crimes* (pp. 207—228). New Jersey: Humana Press.

Koriat, A., Lichtenstein, S., & Fischhoff, B. (1980). Reasons for confidence. *Journal of Experimental Psychology: Human Learning & Memory, 6*(2), 107−118.

Kruglanski, A. W. (1996). Goals as knowledge structures. In P. M. Gollwitzer, & J. A. Bargh (Eds.), *The psychology of action: Linking cognition and motivation to behavior* (pp. 599−618). New York: Guilford Press.

Kruglanski, A. W., & Mayseless, O. (1988). Contextual effects in hypothesis testing: The role of competing alternatives and epistemic motivations. *Social Cognition, 6*(1), 1−20.

Kunda, Z. (1990). The case for motivated reasoning. *Psychological Bulletin, 108*(3), 480−498.

Langbein, J. H. (2003). *The origins of adversary criminal trial.* Oxford, UK: Oxford University Press.

Leo, R. A. (2008). *Police interrogation and American justice.* Cambridge (US): Harvard University Press.

Lipshitz, R., Klein, G., Orasanu, J., & Salas, E. (2001). Taking stock of naturalistic decision making. *Journal of Behavioral Decision Making, 14*(5), 331−352.

Lipton, P. (2007). Alien abduction: Inference to the best explanation and the management of testimony. *Episteme; Rivista Critica Di Storia Delle Scienze Mediche E Biologiche, 4*(3), 238−251.

Loftus, E. F., & Palmer, J. C. (1974). Reconstruction of automobile destruction: An example of the interaction between language and memory. *Journal of Verbal Learning and Verbal Behavior, 13*(5), 585−589.

Lord, C. G., Lepper, M. R., & Preston, E. (1984). Considering the opposite: A corrective strategy for social judgment. *Journal of Personality and Social Psychology, 47*(6), 1231−1243.

Lord, C. G., Ross, L., & Lepper, M. R. (1979). Biased assimilation and attitude polarization: The effects of prior theories on subsequently considered evidence. *Journal of Personality and Social Psychology, 37*(11), 2098.

Maguire, M. (1994). The wrong message at the wrong time? The present state of investigative practice. In D. Morgan, & G. M. Stephenson (Eds.), *Suspicion and silence: The right to silence in criminal investigations.* London, UK: Blackstone Press Limited.

Maguire, M., & Norris, C. (1992). *The conduct and supervision of criminal investigations. Royal commission on criminal justice research study number 5.* London, UK: HMSO.

Markman, K. D., Lindberg, M. J., Kray, L. J., & Galinsky, A. D. (2007). Implications of counterfactual structure for creative generation and analytical problem solving. *Personality and Social Psychology Bulletin, 33*(3), 312−324.

Markman, K. D., McMullen, M. N., & Elizaga, R. A. (2008/3). Counterfactual thinking, persistence, and performance: A test of the reflection and evaluation model. *Journal of Experimental Social Psychology, 44*(2), 421−428.

Marksteiner, T., Ask, K., Reinhard, M.-A., & Granhag, P. A. (2011). Asymmetrical scepticism toward criminal evidence: The role of goal- and belief-consistency. *Applied Cognitive Psychology, 25,* 541−547.

McConville, M., Sanders, A., & Leng, R. (1991). *Case for the prosecution (1991): Police suspects and the construction of criminality.* London: Routledge.

Meissner, C. A., & Kassin, S. M. (2002). "He's guilty!": Investigator bias in judgments of truth and deception. *Law and Human Behavior, 26*(5), 469−480.

Milne, R., & Bull, R. (1999). *Investigative interviewing: Psychology and practice.* Chichester, UK: Wiley.

Morris, B. (2007). History of criminal investigation. In T. Newburn, T. Williamson, & A. Wright (Eds.), *Handbook of criminal investigation* (pp. 15–40). Devon: Willan Publishing.

Mortimer, A. (1993). "A case of . . .": Patterns in police officers' perceptions of offences. *Issues in Criminological and Legal Psychology, 18*, 13–29.

Mortimer, A., & Shepherd, E. (1999). Frames of mind: Schemata guiding cognition and conduct in the interviewing of suspected offenders. In A. Memon, & R. Bull (Eds.), *Handbook of the psychology of interviewing* (pp. 293–315). Chichester, UK: Wiley.

Moskowitz, G. B., & Grant, H. (2009). *The psychology of goals.* New York: Guilford Press.

NCPE. (2005). *Professionalising investigation programme information pack.* Wyboston, UK: National Centre for Policing Excellence.

Nickerson, R. S. (1998). Confirmation bias: A ubiquitous phenomenon in many guises. *Review of General Psychology: Journal of Division 1, of the American Psychological Association, 2*(2), 175–220.

Nisbett, R., & Ross, L. (1980). *Human inference: Strategies and shortcomings of social judgment.* Englewood Cliffs, NJ: Prentice-Hall.

Oxburgh, G. E., Fahsing, I., Haworth, K., & Blair, J. P. (2016). Interviewing suspected offenders. In G. E. Oxburgh, T. Myklebust, T. Grant, & R. Milne (Eds.), *Communication in investigative and legal contexts: Integrated approaches from forensic psychology, linguistics and law enforcement* (pp. 135–158). Chichester, UK: Wiley-Blackwell.

O'Neill, M. (2011). *What makes a successful volume crime investigator?* (Unpublished PhD Thesis).

O'Neill, M. (2018). *Key challenges in criminal investigation.* Policy Press.

O'Neill, M., & Milne, B. (2014). Success within criminal investigations: Is communication still a key component?. In *Investigative interviewing* (pp. 123–146). Springer.

Packer, H. L. (1968). *The limits of the criminal sanction.* Stanford, CA: Stanford University Press.

Peirce, C. S. (1965). *Pragmatism and pragmaticism* (Vol. 5). Belknap Press of Harvard University Press.

Penrod, S. D., Loftus, E. F., & Winkler, J. (1982). The reliability of eyewitness testimony. In N. L. Kerr, & R. M. Bray (Eds.), *The psychology of the courtroom* (pp. 119–168). New York: Academic Press.

Pound, R. (1909). Some principles of procedural reform. *Ill. LR, 4*, 388.

Rachlew, A. (2003). *Norske politiavhør i et internasjonalt perspektiv. 4.* Tidsskrift for Strafferett.

Rachlin, H. (1996). *The making of a detective.* New York, NY: Random House Publishing Group.

Rassin, E., Eerland, A., & Kuijpers, I. (2010). Let's find the evidence: An analogue study of confirmation bias in criminal investigations. *Journal of Investigative Psychology and Offender Profiling, 7*(3), 231–246.

Reiner, R. (1997). Media made criminality. In M. Maguire, R. Morgan, & R. Reiner (Eds.), *The oxford handbook of criminology* (2nd ed.). Oxford, UK: Oxford University Press.

Riksadvokaten. (2017, July 6). *Rapport om norsk politi og påtalemyndighets behandling av straffesakene mot Sture Bergwall – Riksadvokatens vurderinger, videre oppfølging og pålegg.* Retrieved from: https://www.riksadvokaten.no/wp-content/uploads/2017/10/Bergwall-rapporten-oppfølging.pdf.

Roach, J. (2014). The devil and the detail. Local analysis of homicide for investigators and policy makers. *Journal of Homicide and Major Incident Investigation, 9*(1), 86–102.

Roberts, P., & Zuckerman, A. (2010). *Criminal evidence*. Oxford: OUP.

Rønn, K. V. (2013). Mistanke Hypoteser og forklaringer i opdagelsesarbeidet. In C. Hald, & K. V. Rønn (Eds.), *Om at opdage — metodiske refleksioner over politiets undersøgelsespraksis* (pp. 255–300). Copenhagen: Samfundslitteratur.

Rossmo, D. K. (2009). *Criminal investigative failures*. Boca Raton, FL: CRC Press.

Royal Commission on Criminal Justice. (1993). *Report CM 2263*. London, UK: HMSO.

Royal Commission on Criminal Procedure. (1981). *Report CMND 8092*. London, UK: HMSO.

Sainsbury, R. (1971). The "feature positive effect" and simultaneous discrimination learning. *Journal of Experimental Child Psychology, 11*(3), 347–356.

Sanna, L. J., & Schwarz, N. (2003). Debiasing the hindsight bias: The role of accessibility experiences and (mis)attributions. *Journal of Experimental Social Psychology, 39*(3), 287–295.

Schwenk, C. R. (1990). *Effects of devil's advocacy and dialectical inquiry on decision making: A meta-analysis — ScienceDirect*. https://doi.org/10.1016/0749-5978(90)90051-A.

Sear, L., & Williamson, T. (1999). British and American interrogation strategies. *Interviewing and Deception, 67*–81.

Shaklee, H., & Fischhoff, B. (1982). Strategies of information search in causal analysis. *Memory & Cognition, 10*(6), 520–530.

Simon, H. A. (1947). *Administrative behavior: A study of decision-making processes in administrative organisation* (Vol. 1). New York: The Free Press.

Simon, H. A. (1977). The logic of heuristic decision making. In *Models of discovery* (pp. 154–175). Dordrecht: Springer Netherlands.

Simon, D. (2012). *In Doubt: The psychology of the criminal justice process*. Cambridge, MA: Harvard University Press.

Smedslund, J. (1963). The concept of correlation in adults. *Scandinavian Journal of Psychology, 4*(1), 165–173.

Smith, N., & Flanagan, C. (2000). The effective detective: Identifying the skills of an effective SIO *(police research series Paper 122.)*. London, UK: Policing and Reducing Crime Unit.

Snyder, M., & Swann, W. B. (1978). Hypothesis-testing processes in social interaction. *Journal of Personality and Social Psychology, 36*(11), 1202–1212.

Soufan, A. (2011). *The black banners: The inside story of 9/11 and the war against al-Qaeda*. New York, NY: W. W. Norton & Company.

Steblay, N. M. (1992). A meta-analytic review of the weapon focus effect. *Law and Human Behavior, 16*(4), 413–424.

Stelfox, P. (2007). Professionalizing criminal investigation. In T. Newburn, T. Williamson, & A. Wright (Eds.), *Handbook of criminal investigation* (pp. 628–650). Devon: Willan Publishing.

Stelfox, P., & Pease, K. (2005). Cognition and detection: Reluctant bedfellows? In M. J. Smith, & N. Tilley (Eds.), *Crime science: New approaches to preventing and detecting crime*. Cullompton, UK: Willan.

Stephenson, G. M., & Moston, S. J. (1993). Attitudes and assumptions of police officers when questioning criminal suspects. *Issues in Criminological and Legal Psychology, 18*, 30–36.

Stumer, A. (2010). *The presumption of innocence: Evidential and human rights perspectives*. Bloomsbury Publishing.

Svenson, O., & Maule, A. J. (1993). *Time pressure and stress in human judgment and decision making*. New York: Plenum Press.

Thomas, R. P., Dougherty, M. R., Sprenger, A. M., & Harbison, J. I. (2008). Diagnostic hypothesis generation and human judgment. *Psychological Review, 115*(1), 155—185.

Tong, S. (2009). Assessing performance: Quantity or quality? In S. Tong, R. P. Bryant, & M. Horvarth (Eds.), *Understanding criminal investigation*. Chichester, UK: John Wiley Sons Ldt.

Tong, S., & Bowling, B. (2006). Art, craft and sience of detective work. *Police Journal, 79*, 323—329.

Tong, S., Bryant, R. P., & Horvath, M. A. H. (2009). *Understanding criminal investigation*. Chichester, UK: John Wiley & Sons.

Townsley, M., Mann, M., & Garrett, K. (2011). The missing link of crime analysis: A systematic approach to testing competing hypotheses. *Policing, 5*(2), 158—171.

Turtle, J., Read, J. D., Lindsay, D. S., & Brimacombe, C. A. E. (2008). Toward a more informative psychological science of eyewitness evidence. *Applied Cognitive Psychology, 22*(6), 769—778.

Wason, P. C. (1960). On the failure to eliminate hypotheses in a conceptual task. *The Quarterly Journal of Experimental Psychology, 12*(3), 129—140.

Wason, P. C. (1968). Reasoning about a rule. *The Quarterly Journal of Experimental Psychology, 20*(3), 273—281.

Wason, P. C., & Johnson-Laird, P. N. (1972). *The psychology of reasoning: Structure and content*. Cambridge, MA: Harvard University Press.

Wells, G. L. (1978). Applied eyewitness-testimony research: System variables and estimator variables. *Journal of Personality and Social Psychology, 36*(12), 1546—1557.

Wells, G. L., & Lindsay, R. C. (1980). On estimating the diagnosticity of eyewitness nonidentifications. *Psychological Bulletin, 88*(3), 776—784.

Wells, G. L., Lindsay, R. C., & Ferguson, T. J. (1979). Accuracy, confidence, and juror perceptions in eyewitness identification. *Journal of Applied Psychology, 64*(4), 440—448.

Westera, N. J., Kebbell, M. R., Milne, B., & Green, T. (2016). The prospective detective: Developing the effective detective of the future. *Policing and Society, 26*(2), 197—209.

Developing a psychological research base for criminal investigations: academics and practitioners working together

Nathan Ryan and Mark Kebbell

Introduction

With the rate of technological advancement, the readily available access to information and the ever-changing nature of crime, there is a need for police to achieve and maintain the most current evidence-based strategies. The complex nature of this environment and the task that is required of police investigators means that the need to collaborate with academics to develop empirically sound research that can inform practice and have real-world applications is extremely valuable. A failure to keep up with the changing environment would mean that criminals would gain an advantage over authorities and increase their chances of avoiding capture. Further, ineffective practices may lead to wrongful convictions (Gross, Jacoby, Matheson, Montgomery, & Patil, 2005) and in turn a reduction in the public's confidence in the police reducing their legitimacy as law enforcers (Innes, 2010; Jang, Joo, & Zhao, 2010). This is particularly relevant in the case of violent crimes such as homicide which the reduction of and ability to solve these cases can be seen as directly affecting the public's perception of the effectiveness of police and in turn the public's perception of legitimacy (Dawson, 2018; Jang et al., 2010).

There have been many areas of policing where academics and practitioners have come together to advance knowledge and improve outcomes. One example is research conducted by Westera, Kebbell, Milne, and Green (2014a) into the various roles of detectives. In this study, the researchers interviewed detectives to identify the various traits and skills that combine to make an effective detective. Ultimately, there are benefits for both researcher and practitioner in this style of research. Academics gain valuable insight into a previously unseen aspect of policing and can progress research into other areas or use this information to guide future research that can have a more applied focus. For the police there is the benefit of gaining

Police Psychology, Edited by Marques and Paulino. https://doi.org/10.1016/B978-0-12-816544-7.00014-0

an evidence base to assist with recruiting suitable individuals for the role and identifying areas that detectives need to develop to optimize their performance (Westera, Kebbell, Milne, & Green, 2014b). Further, the implementation of new technology by police can open new streams of data for academics and also provide research opportunities.

The implementation of visual recording equipment by police departments has allowed detailed analysis of areas such as the application of the investigative interviewing process, the quality of information generated by witnesses and suspects, and how this impacts perceptions of evidence (Westera, Kebbell, & Milne, 2011), and in the case of body-worn cameras, interactions with the public and the decision-making of police in the field (Richards, Roberts, Britton, & Roberts, 2017). Essentially the introduction of the video recorded interview has allowed researchers to assess and improve the practice and policy of police to improve outcomes by viewing these recorded interviews and developing a model to address any shortcomings (Baldwin, 1992; Clarke & Milne, 2001). Further, the recorded interview has been shown to provide more complete and reliable accounts from witnesses (Westera, Kebbell, & Milne, 2013) and, in the case of rape victims, removed the stress of having to provide testimony in court (Kebbell, O'Kelly, & Gilchrist, 2007). This research demonstrates the benefits that academics and practitioners can achieve when working together to improve outcomes. In this chapter, we discuss the process of conducting practical, police research using a real example of an investigative interviewing research project. In this example, a problem was brought to our attention by an experienced, senior police investigator. The problem was how best to conduct suspect interviews in missing body homicide cases. The issue raised was one of a lack of evidence to inform practice in these cases. This example of research demonstrates how a practitioner-inspired problem can be investigated by bringing together the theoretical knowledge of researchers with the practical experience of police to develop a research project that is useful and can be applied.

A model for "real-world" enquiry

The examples provided in the previous section demonstrate some of the benefits for collaborations between academics and practitioners. "Real-world research" differs to the traditional model of scientific enquiry which is theory driven and is conducted in controlled environments. The scope for real-world research is much broader and is based in applied fields such as criminology and psychology (Robson & McCartan, 2016). This style of research is more likely to use problems inductively through the experience of practitioners. Fig. 14.1 displays a model of a "real-world" enquiry process that starts with the identification of an area of enquiry and integrates the experience of practitioners at various stages (Robson, 1995).

The first step is to identify a "problem of concern." This line of enquiry could come from anywhere but is generally started from an issue identified in the real world, rather than a gap in the academic literature. This may seem an obvious

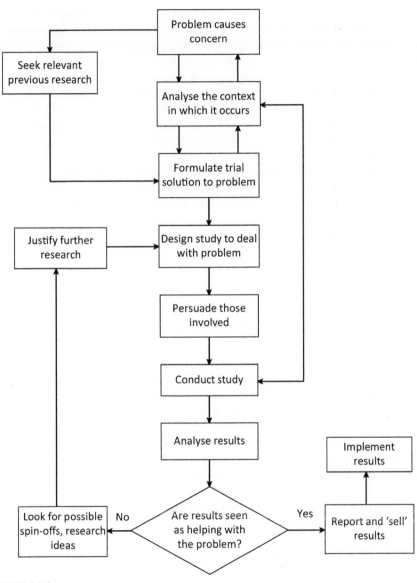

FIGURE 14.1

Real-world enquiry model.

starting point. However, there are examples where there has been little collaboration between police and academics. For instance, very little empirical work has been done with detectives concerning how they solve crime (there are some notable exceptions, see Chapter 13 and Fahsing & Ask, 2013). This is not because academics are not interested in detectives, as there is an extensive literature on the fictional detective Sherlock Holmes. Indeed, this academic literature on Sherlock Holmes is much more extensive than on real detectives. The gap seems to be because of a failure of researchers and police to develop research projects together.

The involvement of police at the outset is essential as police have a unique understanding of the issues they face. Police get to see parts of the community that academics do not, namely, crime tends to be hidden from view. For example, domestic violence and sexual violence occur behind closed doors and are not apparent to the public and academics. Similarly, offending patterns are dynamic and can change rapidly. An example of this is thefts of cars. As cars have become harder to steal because of immobilizers, criminals have taken to breaking into houses to steal the keys to vehicles. Police were aware of this change more quickly than academics.

There have certainly been some successes. Shortly, we will outline an example of a positive research program concerning investigations in missing body homicide cases from conception of the problem to solutions. Of course, this is not the only example. For instance, Fox and Farrington (2015) report a study where they worked with police to develop offender profiles that were used to improve detection rates for burglary. In this study, they collaborated with police to identify statistical patterns in offending behaviors. An example of this was offenders they labeled as "Opportunistic." These offenders could be identified at burglaries because they made their way into a property because it had been left open, stole low value items, and showed no preparation or use of tools. Offenders in this category tended to be young, male, with prior theft and shoplifting offenses, and without a car. In contrast, an "Organized" group of offenders were identified. These could be identified at the scene because they left a clean, but forced entry, had brought tools to the scene, did not leave evidence behind, and took high value items that would often need a "fence" to dispose of. These offenders tended to be older, specialize in burglary, cohabit or have a partner, and have a car. Using the typology, police crime analysts were able to draw up lists of potential suspects. This strategy increased the arrest rate to three times that of a control site, a substantial improvement in this difficult-to-solve crime. This example illustrates how researchers and police can work together to solve problems causing concern (see Chapter 18).

Formulation
Identifying a problem

The research in the case example presented in this chapter was identified as being in need of research by an experienced investigative interviewer who was also an interview advisor. Over the course of his career, the interviewer had worked on cases where a perpetrator had admitted, or had been found guilty of, a murder and had hidden the victim's remains. However, while the murderer was willing to disclose the location of these remains, investigators had been unsuccessful in gaining the information required to identify where the body could be found. From these experiences, the practitioner identified a need to develop an evidence-based interview protocol that was specific to these circumstances. The experience of the practitioner was that once a perpetrator admitted to the murder and that they knew where the victim's remains could be found, investigators did not know how to proceed other than getting the perpetrator to direct them to the scene or use various untested methods of gaining information about the location of the deposition site. Not having an evidence-based guideline for an investigative interview created a whole host of issues, such as the contamination of memory potentially, exposure to possibly previously unknown information that could be used to deceive the investigators, and lacking a systematic approach that could facilitate accurate recall. Nevertheless, the original problem was not sufficiently clear to conduct a program of research. The next step in the process, therefore, was to define the problem.

The practitioner was an active participant throughout the research process including the design phase. This maintained a practical perspective and prevented drift into the purely theoretical (even though it could be argued that if a theory is true it should be able to be applied in practical situations). For this phase, the research team discussed what was practical, what can be achieved within certain timeframes and budgets. Initially, the desire was to investigate the entire interview process in missing body homicide cases; however, that was too broad in terms of resources and time. For instance, deception, is a field of research where there are already existing evidence-based procedures (Vrij & Fisher, 2016) that could be overlaid in a missing body homicide case. Therefore, the decision was made to include only cases that involved "willing" interviewees. Once deception was no longer on the research agenda, this narrowed the objective down to memory retrieval techniques. The question became, how do we improve the memory retrieval of perpetrators in these cases? Related to this question was how these cases differ from other types of cases such as robbery or rape?

Perhaps the most important questions were, however, "Is this research important enough to warrant further enquiry?" and, "Does something already exist that fulfill the needs of these cases?" The process of answering the previous questions is one of research, both in academic journals, the "gray" literature (e.g., police documents and government reports) and publicly available information such as the media.

Researching the background

A first question is whether the problem warrants further enquiry? The parameters around determining this lie in the prevalence of these cases, the amount of public interest in these cases, and the impact on victim's families and the broader community. Generally, these cases are rare. Although there are no definitive statistics on how many intentional homicide cases involve a missing body and a willing perpetrator, it is well known that homicide is a comparatively rare crime compared with other types of crime such as assault. The rate of homicide in Australia (the country the research was conducted in) is around 1 in 100,000. This is low compared with the global rate of 6 in 100,00 (UNODC, 2013). Of these homicides, most cases in Western countries are referred to as "self-solvers," that being there is a clear suspect, a clear motive, and evidence to solve the crime. It could be assumed that cases where the body of the victim is missing would not fall into this category of homicide, while a body is not necessary for a conviction, finding the body would make it easier to convict. Therefore, missing body homicide cases fall into a rarer subset of an already relatively rare crime. The assumed prevalence rates alone might indicate that the research may have minimal value.

Indeed, the decision of what is of importance to research has become a research topic itself. Research by Lawrence Sherman and his colleagues at the University of Cambridge has sought to identify what are the most consequential crimes in terms of the harm they cause and the most important offenders to target (Sherman, 2007). Sherman's work provides an important framework to guide police and academic research because it provides a way of measuring the consequences of different crimes and different criminals. Of course, not all research needs to be focused on the most harmful crimes and criminals, we need to understand less serious crimes too. However, it would be concerning if most research is focused on the least serious crimes and criminals.

With regard to missing body homicide cases, it became clear that there is great public concern in these cases and there is a great impact on victims' families and the community. In the words of Sherman (2007), these offenses caused a great deal of "harm." One example of a missing body homicide case where the perpetrator was willing to disclose the location of the victim's remains was the murder of Matthew Leveson. Matthew Leveson died and had his remains disposed of by Michael Atkins in Sydney in 2007 (State Coroner's Court of New South Wales, 2017). After an investigation, Atkins, the suspected perpetrator, was charged with Leveson's murder but was acquitted due to a lack of evidence. Subsequently, a Coroner's inquest into the investigation was started in 2008 but was suspended and resumed in 2015. It was during this inquest that Atkins was compelled to give evidence about the death of Leveson. Atkins perjured himself but was granted immunity from further prosecution for the perjury or for the murder, if he disclosed the whereabouts of Leveson's remains (State Coroner's Court of New South Wales, 2017). This removed any motivation for Atkins to lie about the whereabouts of Leveson's remains and provided an incentive to do so. Atkins ultimately disclosed the location of the body deposition site, claiming that Leveson overdosed on drugs and Atkins panicked and hid the body (State Coroner's Court of New South Wales, 2017).

At this point, a period of 10 years had passed between the death of Leveson and the attempt to locate his remains, therefore, the location of the deposition site was not easily found. During Atkin's first visit, he identified three possible deposition sites (State Coroner's Court of New South Wales, 2017). Search teams were deployed but were unsuccessful at locating the remains. A second attempt was made with investigators employing relaxation techniques with Atkins in a bid to improve his recollection of the location. This eliminated one possible location. A new search effort was launched, but again was unsuccessful. A third site visit was conducted. With the advice of a forensic psychologist, the investigators chose to conduct a reenactment of the events, using the car used by Atkins to dispose of Leveson's remains and drive to the scene with a weighted dummy. Atkins was then required to drag the dummy into the bushland and place it at the deposition site. A third search attempt was launched. In the last hour of the last day of this final search, the remains of Leveson were found. In total the search effort lasted 6 months, and 7,500 m^2 of soil was searched, excavated, and sieved (State Coroner's Court of New South Wales, 2017). The Leveson case held nationwide interest, and the suffering of the Leveson family was apparent.

Current interview techniques

A literature review of the investigative interviewing literature showed that there are many interview models in use by practitioners. This literature review relied on access to journal articles. Sadly, many academic journals are kept behind paywalls, meaning that access to these articles is very expensive for police. This gives another incentive for police to work with academics who typically have access via their University. The review showed several commonly used interview models in the academic literature: Conversation management (CM), the Cognitive Interview (CI)/ Enhanced Cognitive Interview (ECI), and the PEACE model (Fisher & Geisleman, 1992; Shephard & Griffiths, 2013). Essentially, each of these models overlap in their use of the mnemonics developed by Fisher and Geisleman (1992) with the development of the CI/ECI. The issue found with the research around these interviewing models is that, with the exception of one research study, no research has looked at the retrieval of memory for location. This may not seem like an important distinction to the practitioner, but in the field of cognitive psychology this distinction is important and will be addressed later. The common research paradigm used to study the CI is to play participants a visual recording of a mock crime event, then allocate them to one of several interview conditions and measure the information generated by correct information, incorrect information, confabulations, and omissions (Ginet & Verkampt, 2007; Köhnken, Milne, Memon, & Bull, 1999; Memon, Meissner, & Fraser, 2010; Odinot, Memon, La Rooy, & Millen, 2013).

Spatial versus episodic memory

Simply put, episodic memory is the memory of events and spatial memory is the memory for relationships between objects in space (Thorndyke, 1981; Thorndyke & Hayes-Roth, 1982; Tversky, 2003). To someone who is not familiar with this distinction this might seem not an important distinction. After all, the memory of an event may also contain aspects of spatial memory such as in the case of a bank robbery, where the perpetrator is standing, how far the witness is from the bank teller, etc. However, while this is overlaid with the memory of the event, the way that the spatial memory is encoded differs from that of an episodic memory (Jones & Martin, 2009; Kelly, Avraamides, & Loomis, 2007; Robin et al., 2015; Ruddle, Volkova, Mohler, & Bülthoff, 2011; Tversky, 2003). As a person moves through an environment, they are judging distances and angles and encoding them. This can happen in several ways and will change as a person becomes familiar with an environment (Meilinger, Frankenstein, Wantanabe, Bülthoff, & Hölscher, 2015; Mou & McNamara, 2002). When a person moves through an unfamiliar environment, they tend to judge distances, angles, and relationships between objects by the positioning of their physical selves, i.e., the distance from themselves to a street corner, known as an egocentric perspective. As a person becomes familiar with the environment, they may start to encode the memory in the form of relationships between objects external to themselves, i.e., the distance between a street corner and a house, known as an allocentric perspective (Mou & McNamara, 2002). All of this is done in a specific frame of reference. This refers to the division in the way a spatial memory has been encoded based on either an eye-level view or a topographical view. If a memory has been encoded at the eye level, it is best retrieved at this same level (Meilinger et al., 2015; Thorndyke & Hayes-Roth, 1982). The same is true of a topographical encoding of the memory. If a spatial memory has been encoded via the use of a map, it is best retrieved using a topographical method, a map (Thorndyke & Hayes-Roth, 1982).

The link between physically interaction with an environment and the retrieval of spatial memory was evidenced in a study conducted by Kelly et al. (2007). In this study, they explored a phenomenon known as the "sensorimotor alignment effect." Kelly and colleagues found that participants were much better at remembering the location of the objects if they remained at the orientation in which they were encoded (Kelly et al., 2007). It must be noted that this is only one example of the role sensorimotor systems play in the encoding and retrieval of spatial memory (Burgess, 2006; Ruddle et al., 2011). However, this has important implications for the field of investigative interviewing in missing body homicide cases as the orientation of an interviewee may play a role in the ability to retrieve spatial information and this may affect the outcomes of locating a victim's remains. These were some of the theoretical perspectives we brought to the design stage.

Design

While there is a wealth of research in the investigative interviewing and memory fields, it is clear that there was no synthesis of the two and that this was an issue that is salient for investigators in missing body homicide cases. Therefore, the need to conduct research on an effective way to interview in these cases was needed. If there is no research to demonstrate the best way to interview people in this context, what were practitioners doing? And, what are the issues that practitioners deem important in these cases? These questions are important to place parameters around any experimental designs that might test interviewing techniques. Previous research has shown that interviewees and legal professionals are reluctant to accept some interviewing techniques as they feel that they are misunderstood in a courtroom (Kebbell, Milne, & Wagstaff, 1999). Therefore, it is important to test methods that will be used, essentially a synthesis between the theoretical literature and the applied.

Analyze the context

The first step in analyzing the context was to consult with practitioners and ask them about how they interview and what issues they face in these cases. This was the focus of the first study. Eleven homicide detectives were interviewed with direct experience in missing body homicide cases or prominent homicide cases where a key object in the investigation was missing (weapon) and needed to be located (Ryan, Westera, Kebbell, Milne, & Harrison, 2016). Again, as we mentioned in the beginning of this chapter, involving police at the outset was critical to ensuring the research would provide findings that were useful to police. The importance of talking to police about what is important is not confined to the current program of research. Another example, of using interviews to find out what matters, is illustrated by Hunter, May, and Hough (2019). Hunter and colleagues interviewed police officers about using evidence-based practice. The interviews revealed practical challenges, such as putting those educated in evidence-based research back in frontline roles that may not have occurred to the researchers otherwise. The point of this being that the interviews were useful in helping to identify what was important. In our research, the investigators were asked to give detail about a specific case they were involved in, how they interviewed the suspect, what they thought went well, what they thought went wrong, what they could improve on next time, and what advice they would give to someone about to conduct an interview in these circumstances.

The results showed that practitioners were divided about whether to take the suspect on-site (taking them into the field) or interview them off-site (in an interview room). This is an important distinction as the previously mentioned research into spatial memory suggested that the sensorimotor nature of encoding will have an effect of the retrieval of the interviewee (Jones & Martin, 2009; Kelly et al., 2007; Ruddle et al., 2011; Tversky, 2003). Therefore, from a theoretical perspective, the choice to take a suspect to the site is clear, they must be taken to the site to help facilitate memory retrieval. However, there was also a list of practical concerns identified that make this a much more complex issue. Problems with the security of the suspect, staff, and public were all worthy of consideration (Ryan et al., 2016). Often these cases cause outrage in the public and have intense coverage in the media. Due to this, the suspect may be well known and may draw negative attention to themselves from interested parties that cause danger to all involved. Further, the community impact on returning a suspect to the site in an emotionally charged situation may damage relationships between the police and the public or cause general stress to members of the community. Often there are memorials constructed and vigils held at locations important to the investigation and the probability of encountering the public would be high (Ryan et al., 2016). There were also issues with the ECI/CI and their acceptability as evidence.

Consistent with previous research, the practitioners found that certain aspects of the ECI/CI were not useful to them because the interviewees found them difficult or were confused by their purpose (Kebbell et al., 1999; Ryan et al., 2016). The reverse order and change perspectives mnemonics were rarely if ever used by practitioners. Several cited instances where interviewees became confused and the instructions needed to be restated or the process abandoned altogether (Ryan et al., 2016). Further, it was a commonly held belief that the presentation of the evidence in court when using the full CI would be confusing to jurors and may jeopardize the chances of a successful conviction. It was found that practitioners chose what mnemonics to apply based on the circumstances they are presented. While most were consistent with their use of interview strategy in an off-site setting, including the use of maps and sketch plans to get spatial information, when taking the suspect to the site, there were no consistent strategies and the use of the ECI/CI mnemonics were largely unused.

From this study, there were many avenues of research that could have been pursued. Ultimately the choice of which area to pursue came back to one of need. Which area is most in need of research? The off-site interviews were being conducted in a systematic, evidence-based way (albeit lacking adequate spatial research), whereas the on-site interview seemed to have little to no consistency and no research to support the retrieval of spatial memory. From this point, it was determined to investigate an on-site interviewing strategy. Spending time interviewing police about a problem helps to develop a useful program of research. Perhaps as importantly, the interviews are means for the police and the researchers to get to know one another, establish rapport and trust. The importance of an honest relationship cannot be underestimated.

Formulate a trial solution to the problem and design the study

The ECI/CI has been proven to be an effective interview technique in many settings for willing interviewees (or willing suspects; one of the parameters of our research). Therefore, the first step in exploring this issue was to test the ECI in a situation that simulates a missing body homicide scenario. When considering the previous research, it was clear that the practitioners are reluctant to use the reverse order and change perspective mnemonics, so these were not included in the study. Further, the previous research had participants engage in an episodic memory task (watching a video of a crime event) where our research required something mainly focused on spatial memory retrieval. Again, the desire was to create something that could be applied by practitioners and previous spatial memory research had been conducted largely in a VR environment. It was decided that using a real-world setting would provide the study with a more ecologically valid result. Therefore, a natural bush-land setting was used.

To replicate a missing body homicide is impossible. We cannot ask participants to commit a murder and hide a body, therefore, the goal was to induce the mind-set of someone in that situation. A mock scenario was used to engage the participant in the thought process involved in hiding an object from someone who was searching for it. A timeframe of 1 hour to choose a location and hide the object was introduced to put some pressure around the task and the size of the object to be hidden, a white sack filled with empty drink bottles was chosen to replicate the size of a human torso or small child. No weight was added to the bag. This decision was made due to the difference in motivation between a participant in an experiment and someone who has committed a homicide. It is believed that a participant would not have the same level of motivation and therefore would not drag a weighted sack as far as a person in an actual homicide.

The example we have chosen for this chapter concerns an interview with some-one who is cooperating with police. This is easy to get participants to simulate because experimental participants are already cooperative. However, more chal-lenging aspects of interviewing can also be tested. For instance, Vrij and colleagues have conducted studies looking at detection of deception using students that are motivated to lie by being asked to steal money and then to deny doing so (Vrij et al., 2008). Some researchers have gone further and used real, high-stake lies (e.g., Wright Whelan, Wagstaff, & Wheatcroft, 2014). Wright Whelan et al. (2014) looked at public appeals for help with missing or murdered relatives. They found that some behaviors discriminated between honest and deceptive appeals. Deceptive appeals contained more equivocal language, gaze aversion, head shaking and speech errors, and expressions of hope of finding the missing relative alive. From an evidence base of these studies like these, Vrij and Fisher (2016) were able to identify lie detection techniques that have potential for use. The potential for experimentally studying ways of improving policing is limitless, and the growth of the "evidence-based policing" movement is giving new examples every day (Sherman, 2015).

Conduct the study

The study required participants to enter a large section of natural bushland and hide the sack under the premise that they had committed a murder and were disposing of incriminating evidence. They were told that after an hour had elapsed another partic-ipant was to enter the bushland and attempt to locate their object. Participants were then required to return to the bushland 30 days later and locate their object after be-ing randomly allocated to either an ECI or free recall condition. The distance be-tween where they had initially hidden the sack in the first phase and where they had indicated they had hidden the sack in the second phase was measured. Further the quantity and quality of the information generated from these interviews were also coded an analyzed. The results showed that participants were no more accurate in locating their object in the ECI condition than the free recall condition. However, the amount of information generated, and the level of detail provided through the ECI, was significantly higher than the free recall condition.

Analyze the results

At this stage of the research process the question is "are the results helping?" Although the ECI did not improve the participants' accuracy in locating the object, it did increase the amount of information and detail generated. In some cases, particularly in the fine-grain detail of landmarks on the journey to the deposition site, the level of information generated in the ECI condition was three times that of the free recall condition. This is a great increase in the amount of information generated. Information is the lifeblood of any criminal investigation and increasing the amount of information generated by a perpetrator in this situation may have great benefits for investigators. Therefore, the answer to this question is "yes." Although there was no direct improvement in the likelihood of locating the victim's remains (the participants finding the exact location), an increased level of information and detail will add to the pool of evidence at the investigators' disposal. Therefore, the preferred interview technique in this scenario is the abbreviated version of the ECI. However, more research needs to be conducted as the current technique needs to be refined to improve the ultimate outcome for investigators—finding the body.

Reporting, selling, and implementing the results

As identified in the first study, there is a need to develop an interviewing protocol for missing body homicide cases. The two studies reported here are now being used to inform the development of a missing body homicide manual for practitioners. This research is in its infancy, and any manual created will need to be amended as the research is refined. As, such the research has been implemented through the production of this manual, with a possibility of investigating its effectiveness in the future by consulting practitioners who have used the protocol. This is essentially a never-ending cycle. After, the protocol as new research comes to light, seek feedback on the amendments, and conduct more research to seek improvements.

The question of whether the research is helping with the problem should not be a yes or no response: it is rarely a clear answer. As demonstrated in this research, the main goal of increasing accuracy was not achieved. However, the results arguably help with the problem. The use of the ECI will increase the amount of coarse and fine-grain details regarding key information that can assist in locating a victim's remains. In this way, the response to this stage of the model should be open. Although, in its current form, this could be immediately used to assist investigators in generating more information within the investigative interview, there should be a refinement of the process through the feedback from reporting, selling, and implementing the results. There should also be a search for other research questions that can assist with the problem. In this example, patterns in the hiding behaviors of the participants were noticed. This opened another line of enquiry, another search of the literature and another research project. This is to investigate if the behavior of the participants contains patterns that may also assist investigators. Similar, to those of the opportunistic/organized classifications mentioned above, patterns of hiding behaviors may also yield valuable information to narrow search areas and increase the probability of locating a victim's remains. This involved the comparison on experimental data and secondary data collected by investigators. Again, the process of linking researcher with practitioners to achieve a practical outcome that benefits both research and practice.

Research is of no consequence unless the findings make some difference. Even negative findings can be helpful if it discourages others from wasting time on something that will not be useful. Nevertheless, for research to make a difference the findings must be communicated. Academics can be useful here for three reasons. First, they have the luxury of the time to write articles. For many police officers, their case load is too high for them to devote time to recording what they have done and what was the influence. Second, academics offer a stability of focus. Academics tend to specialize and maintain an interest in a subject over a long time, whereas police officers are often transferred or promoted to different roles. This means that the police officers' interests, enthusiasm, and experience are lost while academics are able to see a project through, and record the results, so they are available for people in the future. Third, the rigor of academic research and reporting can give a credibility to ideas that might otherwise be lacking—especially in a hierarchical organization such as the police where lower ranked officers may be overlooked. The implementation process is critical to the research having been worthwhile, and this stage must not be neglected (Powell, Davies, & Nutley, 2016).

Conclusions

We will end with a quote from Sherman and Murray (2015). They point out, "It is a hallmark of a science-based profession that its members conduct and publish research" (p. 7). It is not a coincidence that Sherman is an academic and Murray is a police officer. In this chapter, we have outlined how academics and police can work together to do just that—with regard to practical, important problems. This was achieved through the model for real-world enquiry (Fig. 14.1) that uses relationships with practitioners to identify a problem, analyze the context, formulate a potential solution-based existing evidence, develop a way of testing this "solution" and refining it based on the results of research and practitioner feedback (Robson, 1995). This is important for police who then have access to the research literature, academic knowledge and rigor, and findings that are published and consolidated. This is also important for academics who gain access to what is happening in their community and what are the most important challenges with regard to crime (Kebbell & Westera, 2017). Most importantly, academics and police working together can be beneficial for the public by creating a knowledge base that can be used to investigate crime more effectively to ensure those who have committed serious offenses are held to account.

References

Baldwin, J. (1992). *Video taping interviews with suspects: A national evaluation*. London: Home Office.

Burgess, N. (2006). Spatial memory: How egocentric and allocentric combine. *Trends in Cognitive Sciences, 10*(12), 551–557. https://doi.org/10.1016/j.tics.2006.10.005.

Clarke, C., & Milne, R. (2001). *A national evaluation of the PEACE investigative interviewing course*. London: Home Office.

Dawson, A. (2018). Police legitimacy and homicide: A macro-comparative analysis. *Social Forces, 97*(2), 841–866.

Fahsing, I., & Ask, K. (2013). Decision making and decisional tipping points in homicide investigations: An interview study of British and Norwegian detectives. *Journal of Investigative Psychology and Offender Profiling, 10*, 155–165.

Fisher, R. P., & Geisleman, R. E. (1992). *Memory-enhancing techniques for investigative interviewing*. Springfield: Charles C Thomas.

Fox, B. H., & Farrington, D. P. (2015). An experimental evaluation on the utility of burglary profiles applied in active police investigations. *Criminal Justice and Behavior, 42*, 156–175.

Ginet, M., & Verkampt, F. (2007). The cognitive interview: Is its benefit affected by the level of witness emotion? *Memory, 15*(4), 450–464. https://doi.org/10.1080/09658210601092670.

Gross, S. R., Jacoby, K., Matheson, D. J., Montgomery, N., & Patil, S. (2005). Exonerations in the United States 1989 through 2003. *Journal of Criminal Law and Criminology, 95*(2), 523–560.

Hunter, G., May, T., & Hough, M. (2019). Are the police embracing evidence-informed practice? A view from England and Wales. *Policing and Society, 29*, 251–265.

Innes, M. (2010). A 'mirror' and a 'motor': Researching and reforming policing in an age of austerity, policing. *Journal of Policy Practice, 4*(2), 127–134.

Jang, H., Joo, H.-J., & Zhao, J. (2010). Determinants of public confidence in police: An international perspective. *Journal of Criminal Justice, 38*, 57–68.

Jones, G. V., & Martin, M. (2009). Spatial recall improved by retrieval enactment. *Psychometric Bulletin & Review, 16*(3), 524–528. https://doi.org/10.3758/PBR.16.3.524.

Kebbell, M. R., Milne, R., & Wagstaff, G.,F. (1999). The cognitive interview: A survey of its forensic effectiveness. *Psychology, Crime and Law, 5*(1–2), 101–115. https://doi.org/10.1080/10683169908414996.

Kebbell, M., O'Kelly, C., & Gilchrist, E. (2007). Rape victims' experiences of giving evidence in English courts: A survey. *Psychiatry, Psychology and Law, 14*(1), 111–119. https://doi.org/10.1375/pplt.14.1.111.

Kebbell, M. R., & Westera, N. (2017). The 'worst of the worst': Detectives' beliefs about dangerous violent offenders and how to deal with them. *Psychiatry, Psychology and Law, 24*, 843–852.

Kelly, J. W., Avraamides, M. N., & Loomis, J. M. (2007). Sensorimotor alignment effects in the learning environment and in novel environments. *Journal of Experimental Psychology: Learning, Memory, and Cognition, 33*(6), 1092–1107. https://doi.org/10.1037/0278-7393.33.6.1092.

Köhnken, G., Milne, R., Memon, A., & Bull, R. (1999). The cognitive interview: A meta-analysis. *Psychology, Crime and Law, 5*, 3–27. https://doi.org/10.1080/10683169908414991.

Meilinger, T., Frankenstein, J., Wantanabe, K., Bülthoff, H. H., & Hölscher, C. (2015). Reference frames in learning from maps and navigation. *Psychological Research, 79*, 1000–1008. https://doi.org/10.1007/s00426-014-0629-6.

Memon, A., Meissner, C. A., & Fraser, J. (2010). The cognitive interview: A meta-analytic review and study space analysis of the past 25 years. *Psychology, Public Policy, and Law, 16*(4), 340–372. https://doi.org/10.1037/a0020518.

Mou, W., & McNamara, T. P. (2002). Intrinsic frames of reference in spatial memory. *Journal of Experimental Psychology: Learning, Memory, and Cognition, 28*(1), 162–170. https://doi.org/10.1037//0278-7393.28.1.162.

Odinot, G., Memon, A., La Rooy, D., & Millen, A. (2013). Are two interviews better than one? Eyewitness memory across repeated cognitive interviews. *PLoS One, 8*(10). https://doi.org/10.1371/journal.pone.0076305.

Powell, A., Davies, H., & Nutley, S. (2016). Missing in action? The role of the knowledge mobilisation literature in developing knowledge mobilisation practices. *Evidence and Policy, 13*, 201–223. https://doi.org/10.1332/174426416X14534671325644.

Richards, P., Roberts, D., Britton, M., & Roberts, N. (2017). The exploration of body-worn video to accelerate the decision-making skills of police officers within an experimental learning environment. *Policing, 12*(1), 43–49.

Robin, J., Hirshhorn, M., Rosenbaum, R. S., Winocur, G., Mosovitch, M., & Grady, C. L. (2015). Functional connectivity of hippocampal and prefrontal networks during episodic and spatial memory based real-world environment. *Hippocampus, 25*, 81–93. https://doi.org/10.1002/hipo.22352.

Robson, C. (1995). *Real world research: A resource for social scientists and practitioner-researchers*. Oxford: Blackwell Publishers Ltd.

Robson, C., & McCartan, K. (2016). *Real world research*. In (Fourth ed). GB: Wiley Etextbooks.

Ruddle, R. A., Volkova, E., Mohler, B., & Bülthoff, H. H. (2011). The effect of landmark and body-based sensory information on route knowledge. *Memory & Cognition, 39*, 686–699. https://doi.org/10.3758/s13421-010-0054-z.

Ryan, N. C., Westera, N. J., Kebbell, M., Milne, R., & Harrison, M. (2016). Where is the body? Investigative interviewing strategies in missing body homicide cases. In *International investigative interviewing research group (iIIRG), London, 22–24 June, presented 24 June 2016*.

Shephard, E., & Griffiths, A. (2013). *Investigative interviewing: The conversation management approach*. New York: Oxford University Press.

Sherman, L. W. (2007). The power few: Experimental criminology and the reduction of harm. *Journal of Experimental Criminology, 3*, 299–321.

Sherman, L. W. (2015). A tipping point for "totally evidenced policing" ten ideas for building an evidence-based police agency. *International Criminal Justice Review, 25*, 11–29.

Sherman, L. W., & Murray, A. (2015). Evidence-based policing: From academics to professionals. *International Criminal Justice Review, 25*(1), 7–10.

Thorndyke, P. W. (1981). Distance estimations from cognitive maps. *Cognitive Psychology, 13*, 526–550.

Thorndyke, P. W., & Hayes-Roth, B. (1982). Differences in spatial knowledge acquired from maps and navigation. *Cognitive Psychology, 14*, 560–589.

Tversky, B. (2003). Body and mind. In C. Freska, W. Brauer, C. Habel, & K. F. Wender (Eds.), *Spatial cognition III* (pp. 1–10). Berlin: Springer Berlin Heidelberg.

UNODC (United Nations Office on Drugs and Crime). (2013). *Global study on homicide*. Retrieved from: www.unodc.org/documents/gsh/pdfs/2014_GLOBAL _HOMICIDE_ BOOK_web.pdf.

Vrij, A., & Fisher, R. P. (2016). Which lie detection tools are ready for use in the criminal justice system? *Journal of Applied Research in Memory and Cognition, 5*, 302–307.

Vrij, A., Mann, S. A., Fisher, R. P., Leal, S., Milne, R., & Bull, R. (2008). Increasing cognitive load to facilitate lie detection: The benefit of recalling an event in reverse order. *Law and Human Behavior, 32*, 253–265.

Westera, N. J., Kebbell, M. R., & Milne, R. (2011). Interviewing rape complainants: Police officers' perceptions of interview format and quality of evidence. *Applied Cognitive Psychology, 25*(6), 917–926.

Westera, N., Kebbell, M., & Milne, B. (2013). Losing two thirds of the story: A comparison of the video recorded police interview and live evidence of rape complainants. *Criminal Law Review, 4*, 290–308.

Westera, N. J., Kebbell, M. R., Milne, R., & Green, T. (2014a). Towards a more effective detective. *Policing and Society: An International Journal of Research and Policy, 26*(1), 197–207.

Westera, N. J., Kebbell, M. R., Milne, R., & Green, T. (2014b). The prospective detective: Developing the effective detective of the future. *Policing and Society: An International Journal of Research and Policy, 26*(2), 197–209.

Wright Whelan, C., Wagstaff, G. F., & Wheatcroft, J. M. (2014). High-stakes lies: Verbal and nonverbal cues to deception in public appeals for help with missing or murdered relatives. *Psychiatry, Psychology and Law, 21*, 523–537.

Threat assessment in law enforcement: advances in the appraisal and management of violence risk by police

15

Caroline Logan

Introduction

The process of threat assessment and management is the application of a set of investigative and operational techniques by practitioners—such as law enforcement professionals—to identify, evaluate, and mitigate the potential for targeted violence (e.g., Fein & Vossekuil, 1998; Meloy & Hoffmann, 2014). The objective of the undertaking is to ensure the safety of a known or identifiable target (or targets) from one or more individuals—from private persons to organized groups—who have presaged in some way their intention to cause harm to that target by some means and at some time (e.g., Cornell & Datta, 2017). Threat assessment scenarios may include, for example, the safety of an individual from the specific threat of another (e.g., a person who has previously been the victim of intimate partner violence, or of long-term stalking and harassment), or the well-being of a celebrated figure at a public event with limited participant screening (e.g., a politician at a rally, a monarch on a public walkabout, a famous singer on an open stage). However, the range of scenarios to which threat assessment and management processes can be applied is necessarily broad. Additional scenarios may include the security of members of the general public and the integrity of landmark buildings and infrastructure during mass gatherings or demonstrations in the context of civil unrest or disharmony (e.g., in relation to a large sporting event, or national celebration, or political demonstration), or during times of high congestion (e.g., over- and underground trains and stations, airports and on aeroplanes, roads, bridges, and tunnels), or in locations or at times of significance (e.g., in schools, workplaces, and social gatherings such as nightclubs, during rush hour, public holidays, religious festivals and locations, or in relation to a contentious political issue or in times of civil unrest and disharmony). And attack may be threatened in the form of physical or psychological harm, material or reputational damage or destruction, or harm by way of denial of service (e.g., electronic or cyberattack). Each of these situations and more are ones that require

Police Psychology, Edited by Marques and Paulino. https://doi.org/10.1016/B978-0-12-816544-7.00015-2

comprehensive and accountable threat assessments and the preparation of robust, proportionate and effective management plans (Meloy & Hoffmann, 2014).

However, threat assessment and management is a challenging process in the law enforcement arena. Protecting specific individuals, the general public, and key locations and services in their communities from harm comes at a cost—for example, to liberty, freedom of movement, and to the capacity to engage with the people, places, or the services they seek to access (van der Meer & Deikhuis, 2014). Therefore, these costs have to be justified and proportionate to the threat posed. Also, if threats are enacted despite management plans being in place, processes from beginning to end will be subject to scrutiny, sometimes at the highest level. Thus, threat assessment and management practice must be transparent, accountable, and defensible, and underpinned by the best and most up-to-date evidence relating to what is relevant to the nature and mitigation of the threat posed. Comprehensive information-gathering protocols, clear guidance on individual practice, and a context of continuous research and evaluation are essential to provide reassurance about the quality, legality, and validity of professional practice. So, how should threat assessment and management be undertaken in order to provide such reassurances to those who are the major stakeholders in the process? What works in threat assessment and management? And how might the field of threat assessment and management usefully develop in the coming years?

This chapter begins by describing and differentiating threat assessment and management from the closely related task of *risk* assessment and management. Both tasks share a fundamental drive to prevent bad things from happening, but they differ in terms of their focus, how the process is carried out, who has primacy over the undertaking, and the range of outcomes expected. Therefore, the purpose of both kinds of assessment and management activity is delineated, their intended outcomes specified, and the guiding principles they share and that are specific to threat assessment are examined. The chapter then explores methods—tradecraft—in threat assessment and management in law enforcement and offers suggestions for some ways in which the field can learn from that which focuses more on risk, in particular, in respect of the application of the structured professional judgment approach. This chapter concludes with a discussion of the challenges faced by law enforcement professionals attempting to implement threat assessment and management practices in services that are subject to higher levels of scrutiny and public accountability than ever before.

Preventing harm: the convergence of risk and threat assessment and management in modern law enforcement

In general, the term threat assessment and management refers to understanding and acting in response to a credible threat of deliberate harmful action by one or more people against a specific victim or target, who may be one person (e.g., a named politician) or a group representative of the target (e.g., any politician or person on their staff) or a similarly representative building (e.g., the Palace of Westminster), location (e.g., the area around Parliament Square in Central London), or event (e.g., the State Opening of Parliament) (Meloy, Hart, & Hoffmann, 2014). The focus of threat assessment and management is understanding the relationship between the potential perpetrator(s) and the target (or victim) and the context in which this relationship exists; the objective of the task is the prevention of harm or damage through the preemptive manipulation of physical, procedural, and relational variables. Threat assessment and management activity takes place in a broad operational context—it is the daily activity of law enforcement professionals, among others, both in the public and in the private sectors. However, it is also the work of those with responsibility for buildings and infrastructure, energy and communications, the built and natural environments, and the climate. This chapter will focus on threat assessment and management in the law enforcement context and in relation to people as targets, although the principles discussed herein will have relevance to its practice across all areas.

The specific focus of threat assessment and management activity is the interplay among the victim or target, their relationship with the perpetrator(s), and on the nature, meaning, and purpose of the threat posed in the context in which it occurs (Cornell & Datta, 2017; Meloy et al., 2014). Therefore, the focus of activity is on a premeditated or targeted threat—the harm intended is planned by the perpetrator and is deliberately directed at that subject. The threat is usually appraised using live observations of the behavior of involved parties, and also the context of their interactions. That is, threat assessment and management is frequently a real-time undertaking, a dynamic interaction of information and understanding, action, feedback, further action, and round and around until the situation is regarded as managed (van der Meer & Deikhuis, 2014). However, the information derived from evaluative inquiries is likely to be incomplete and possibly conflicting, and it may not involve direct contact with the perpetrator if and until the identity of that person is known and they consent to some form of questioning. Further, threat mitigation activity is frequently actioned under pressure of time—it is reactive because the threat may be imminent or likely to materialize (if it does) in the short (minutes, hours) to medium term (days, weeks), rather than in the longer term (months to years). Victim safety plans are a critical part of threat management planning. And given the nature of the threats posed and against the targets identified, the impact of not preventing the harmful outcome from occurring may be profound (e.g., loss of life, loss of service, violent disorder, loss of morale or hope, reputational damage, or destruction). The requirement in threat assessment and management, therefore, is for approaches that offer guidance to law enforcement professionals on threat detection, the key variables relevant to threat mobilization, and clear and transparent decision-making processes around threat mitigation and management. Such guidance offers professionals the opportunity to exercise their discretion about understanding and moderating the dynamic threat posed while ensuring that the decisions made and the action taken are accountable, defensible, and as free from biased thinking as possible (Meloy et al., 2014).

Risk assessment and management shares many of the same principles and theoretical evidence base as its threat-focused counterpart (Meloy et al., 2014); indeed, they could be considered comparable or overlapping activities and the terms may be used interchangeably although it would, in many instances, not be entirely correct to do so. So, what distinguishes risk assessment and management from threat assessment and management? The focus of the former activity is far more on the perpetrator than on the victim and the situations in which the targeted threat may materialize. And while threat assessment and management are prepared for and actioned in real-time, risk assessment is generally more reflective, using the individual's past behavior to inform one's considered understanding about their possible future behavior and its mitigation against known or unknown victims. Therefore, the focus of a risk assessment is on a person's potential to act harmfully against others, either in a premeditated way or in a way that may be more impulsive and unplanned. Consequently, the product of a risk assessment is generally for the use of judicial decision-making bodies such as multidisciplinary teams, mental health tribunals, Parole Board hearings, multiagency public protection teams (such as sexual offender management units or probation teams), and the Courts, in order to plan the risk management of that individual. While the professional undertaking a threat assessment and actioning in real-time the management requirements indicated is generally a person with responsibility for implementing the law (e.g., a law enforcement or security officer), the professional undertaking a risk assessment is generally a mental health or corrections practitioner such as a psychologist, a psychiatrist, a social worker or probation officer, or a psychiatric nurse. As such, they are often able to access the individual directly and over a prolonged period, as well as extensive historical records about their life and activities to date, and they are likely to have the time to review such material ahead of a deadline (e.g., a formal review or court hearing). A number of important sets of guidance have been prepared for the use of risk assessment practitioners—such as the HCR-20^{V3} (Douglas, Hart, Webster, & Belfrage, 2013; see below)—who assist in highlighting variables or risk factors that should be taken into account in order to understand past behavior and to comment usefully on one's inductions about his or her future potential and its management, while avoiding excessively biased decision-making (Douglas et al., 2014). And practitioners offering such comments are held to account on the basis of the evidence base for the specific method they have used as well as their application of that method to the individual case.

Thus, the risk assessment and management of a perpetrator of intimate partner violence for the purposes of legal proceedings in relation to that person may have much in common with the threat assessment and management activity in relation to the safety of that person's rehomed partner and children. In this scenario, information about the perpetrator and victims will inform the action taken to keep both adults and their children safe. However, threat assessment and management activity in relation to the safety of members of the British royal family and senior political figures at the annual Remembrance Day service in Whitehall in London may bear little resemblance to the risk assessment eventually carried out on the individual arrested for declaring online their plan to kill the Prime Minister when he or she seeks discharge from their *Mental Health Act* section under whose conditions they were subsequently detained.

The similarities and differences between threat and risk assessment and management in practice are captured in a number of important resources (e.g., Cornell & Datta, 2017; Meloy et al., 2014; Mitchell & Palk, 2016; Reddy et al., 2001) and summarized in Table 15.1.

Principles of threat assessment and management

The objectives of threat—and indeed, risk—assessment and management are to protect victims from harm, to ensure the safety of those undertaking to enforce the law, and to safeguard individuals from engaging in harmful acts that are as much against their own interests as anyone else's (Hart & Logan, 2011). Such preventative activity is underpinned by a number of common principles (Logan, 2021). First, the sole purpose of threat assessment is to guide management, and the purpose of threat management is harm limitation or (ideally) harm prevention. Assessing threat in relation to a victim or target without any intention of managing the concerns raised is both reckless and unethical; assessment must be for the purpose of driving action. *Therefore, it is insufficient to compile or check lists of threat (or risk) factors in the absence of attention to how evidence of their presence will be turned into a harm preventative plan.*

Second, the assessment and management of threat should be a dynamic and real-time undertaking—it should mirror as closely as possible the live or dynamic nature of the situation under scrutiny (van der Meer & Deikhuis, 2014). Initial efforts to mitigate threat will inform the understanding evaluators have of its occurrence, which will in turn inform the development and redevelopment of bespoke management plans. *Therefore, threat assessment and management should be a continuous or live process rather than one that is static or snapshot.*

Third, the information collected about the threat to be prevented should extend over the range of characteristics that the empirical and practice literatures tell us are important to the victim(s), the perpetrator(s), and the situations under consideration. Further, individual variables or factors do not operate in isolation from one another, or in isolation from protective factors. *Therefore, the potential for any harmful event to occur is about the real-time interplay of context and individuals, and of threat enhancing and reducing factors, and we should use research and good practice to inform threat assessment and management guidance for current and future professionals.*

Fourth, the threat of violence may be assessed at different points in the evolution of that potential—before the specific threat is detected, on its detection or discovery, on its initial investigation, at the point at which a plan of action is prepared and implemented to mitigate the specific threat, and at regular and periodic points thereafter. Further, different agencies (e.g., police, mental health services, security

Table 15.1 Similarities and differences between threat and risk assessment and management.

	Threat assessment and management	Risk assessment and management
Objective	Identifying, understanding, and managing the vulnerabilities of a victim (or victims) to targeted or predatory violence by a known or unknown perpetrator and in the context—including the nature of the association or relationship between victim and perpetrator—and the physical setting in which violence may occur	Understanding and managing the risks posed by a known individual who has a history of harmful behavior (impulsive or predatory), against a future victim whose identity may or may not already be known, in order to prevent that harm potential being realized
Evaluator	Mainly law enforcement and security professionals	Mainly practitioners in (forensic) mental health, corrections, and social services
Assessment evidence	Derived from a range of sources, and may not include any direct contact with the perpetrator(s); the evidence used generally emphasizes dynamic physical, procedural, social, and relational information, collated around a developing time line—starting with the identification or detection of the threat	Also derived from a range of sources, but often including an interview with the potential (sole) perpetrator; evidence will include a detailed study of the past behavior and motives of that person, as well as relevant health and mental health, relationship, and educational and employment data, in order to inform an understanding of future harm potential and when and why it might be realized—the risk is being assessed because the person's past behavior creates realistic concerns about their potential for violence again in the future, such as when they leave prison or secure mental healthcare
Assessment context	Operational, in order to guide frontline action; information about the nature of the threat directly informs decision-making about threat management, which is likely to be directly acted upon	Consultative, in order to assist legal decision-making, often over lengthy time frames
Process	Often rapid and real-time, a continual process of intelligence-gathering, evaluation, initial action, and reevaluation, in order to guide threat management in an evolving situation	More slow or nonurgent, for a specific purpose or date (e.g., a forthcoming annual review, a court hearing weeks or months hence); a review of relevant information, an interview with the client and other relevant parties, the preparation of a report, its examination in legal or similar proceedings, in order to inform decision-making about the conditions to be imposed on the liberty of its subject

Table 15.1 Similarities and differences between threat and risk assessment and management.—*cont'd*

	Threat assessment and management	Risk assessment and management
Assessment structure	Flexible, discretionary, focused on the relationship between the victim(s) and perpetrator(s); idiographic or case-driven (inductive)	Assessment options range from fixed, nondiscretionary, nomothetic, group-focused, and deductive through to discretionary, idiographic, individual-focused, and inductive
Flaws	The threat assessment and management process applies some structure to some assessments, depending on the nature of the threat and the time frame for its management; the exercise of discretion without structuring professional judgment raises the risk of a number of sources of bias (including availability, confirmatory, and predictable world biases) in decision-making	The risk assessment and management process attempts to manage the risk of bias by the application of guidance to the selection, appraisal, combination, and use of relevant information to inform risk management; the application of such guidance is usually mandatory in the health and corrections settings in which their users work
Timescale	Evaluations are based on narrow time frames (often the present and immediate future), updated regularly or continuously on the basis of new information about relevant physical, procedural, social, and relational factors in relation to the victim, as well as motivational and other dynamic variables about the perpetrator(s), when identified	Evaluations focus on long time periods—past and future—with a focus on individual, dispositional, and historic factors relevant to the specific harmful behavior to be prevented (e.g., nonsexual violence, sexual violence, suicide) in the person with a history of violence
Outcomes	• A plan of action toward threat mitigation based on an understanding of the threat posed to the victim(s) or target by the perpetrator(s), if known • Consensus about case prioritization in the short term (minutes to hours) in order to determine the urgency and extent or level of concern and response	• An informed opinion, with evidence, usually in the form of a written report and oral testimony, which is used to inform action over a period of time—from days to months, possibly years—outcomes from which will be used to refine the original opinion and risk mitigation strategies

agencies) may have access to quite different kinds of information (e.g., intelligence data, behavioral observations, informant information, the self-report of the potential perpetrator) and management options (e.g., the creation of a physical barrier between the target and a potential perpetrator, the psychiatric treatment of the perpetrator). Each evaluation is a complex undertaking, requiring the balancing of multiple forms of evidence and contingencies. Guidance, sensitive to the requirements of each stage and evidence type, is a protection against the failure to take important elements of the process into consideration (Gawande, 2011). *Therefore, different sets of guidance, focusing on different kinds of threats as well as outcomes and priorities, are required at different stages in the task of understanding and managing threat; no single set of guidance can achieve all the requirements of the harm prevention process in one agency or jurisdiction.*

Fifth, threat (and risk) assessment and management requires an understanding of the outcome to be prevented (e.g., an act of intimate partner violence or stalking, a mass casualty attack in a school or workplace, an act of politically or ideologically motivated violence), the practice of threat (or risk) assessment and management, and the interests and requirements of essential partners in the harm prevention process (van der Meer & Deikhuis, 2014). Such practice also requires outcomes to be specified at an organizational level. *Therefore, expertise in one area (e.g., stalking) is not a guarantee of good practice in the other (e.g., multiagency cooperation in the management of stalking risk), and competent threat and risk managers have to be proficient in multiple areas.*

Sixth, threat assessment and management in relation to potentially spectacular outcomes (e.g., risk to life at a public event) is an activity likely to be subject to the highest level of scrutiny by multiple agencies with competing agendas (e.g., police ombudsmen, security services, politicians, the courts, the media). *Therefore, the task of assessing and managing threat should be transparent and accountable in order to facilitate reasonable scrutiny and defendable practice, and to nurture continued support from these essential stakeholders.*

Finally, evaluation is critical to demonstrating good practice and evidencing it to those stakeholders—from the public who fund their protection through taxation through to politicians who legislate for their safety and security. *Therefore, no process for understanding threat with a view to its mitigating should be implemented without regard for how improved practice may be measured and demonstrated.* Making time for evaluation, however, and respecting the scientific process can be a challenge in a fast-paced harm prevention setting.

Methods of threat assessment and management: tradecraft for law enforcement professionals

There are varying forms of guidance available to assist the law enforcement professional trying to understand and manage the threats to which they are alerted. All the guidance currently available imposes a degree of structure on the information-gathering and evaluation process in order to ensure transparency and heighten accountability—and to guarantee that empirical evidence and best practice principles are applied in each case and in a consistent way. The structure applied to the threat assessment and management process may be modest, as when the threat is in the early stages of investigation and its nature is not yet clear or the threat is of a form that is infrequently occurring and on which there has been little previous research or even experience. In such a scenario, the threat may be explored through a case consultation with knowledgeable and experienced peers: *here is my case, let us discuss what we understand about it, and explore together what we can do to manage the threat.* However, less formal consultation processes may be at risk of biased decision-making; for example, because the range of information available to discuss is incomplete, or some pieces of information have more saliency than others in the minds of some of the reviewers, or because reviewers highlight only the information that confirms to their view of the problem, or because of the inclination to perceive order or rules where they have not been proven to exist (Meloy et al., 2014). Where the situation is critical—that is, there is a need for prompt action—or the potential outcomes are severe, a more formal examination provides the opportunity for clearer and verifiable decision-making and therefore, some important safeguards against such risks.

The formality of a threat assessment and management process comes from the application of guidance prepared and agreed in advance to support decision-making in just the kinds of situation characterized by the threat at hand. As suggested above and in Gawande (2011), the application of such guidance offers a degree of protection against failure; that is, it prompts the exploration of all topics and actions deemed necessary in a case like this, thus providing a safeguard against missing something obvious or important that would be unlikely to be overlooked in a less heated or demanding moment. The formality of the process is further certified by it being underpinned as far as possible by evidence—of what is relevant to the nature of the threat posed in the setting in which it is to be assessed and managed, derived from a combination of empirical research and best practice case work. In these two ways, formal threat assessment and management procedures structure the way that professionals identify, collect, weigh, and combine the most potentially relevant information about the threat in order that their evaluations reflect the most up-to-date practice and legal requirements.

In the practice of risk assessment and management, two kinds of formal evaluation are available—*nondiscretionary* and *discretionary* (Hart & Logan, 2011). These approaches to evaluation reflect the guidance given on weighing and combining information in order to reach a judgment that will inform risk management regardless of what information is considered and its sources (Meehl, 1954/1996). In the nondiscretionary approach—also known as the actuarial, mechanical or automated, or algorithmic approach (Grove & Meehl, 1996)—decision-making about risk is accomplished according to the application of fixed and explicit rules determined in advance and based entirely on empirical research on the nature of the risk to be prevented (Meehl, 1954/1996). This approach has very little to offer the threat assessment and management field because it relies on the existence of a substantial empirical evidence base, which is not present, and because it offers very little guidance to planning or decision-making in relation to threat management.

In the discretionary approach, decision-making about risk reflects the professional judgment of the practitioner structured by guidance derived from both the empirical *and* the practice literatures. The practitioner is therefore supported to make decisions about risk that are informed by guidance developed by their learned peers and by the requirements of the specific situation in which risk is being assessed and is to be managed. The most respected manifestation of the discretionary approach to risk assessment and management is the structured professional judgment approach (Hart, Douglas, & Guy, 2016). Essentially, this approach provides guidelines (rather than fixed rules) for evaluators to follow in their negotiation of the case in hand. There are many sets of structured professional guidelines available to practitioners to apply in the risk assessment and management field. One of the best known and most widely used is the *Historical, Clinical, Risk Management-20 Violence Risk Assessment Guide* (HCR-20^{V3}) (Douglas et al., 2013; Douglas et al., 2014). The HCR-20^{V3} guides practitioners to identify and understand the relevance of key historical factors about the individual at risk of violence toward others (such as their history of violence, their mental health problems, and their response to interventions in the past), also clinical variables (such as their insight and their stability—or instability), and the variety of risk management parameters (such as their access to and attitudes toward professional support). However, while the HCR-20^{V3} is invaluable to practitioners working in forensic mental health and correctional settings, it is not suitable for use by law enforcement professionals. This is because of the advanced clinical skills required to understand the relevance of some of the risk factors to threatening behavior (e.g., mental health problems, personality difficulties) and because its application has been optimized to risk assessment and management in mental health and criminal justice settings. As a template for the structured professional judgment approach to the prevention of violence, it is nonetheless an excellent example.

What formal methods are available for use in a threat assessment context that exemplifies the structured professional judgment approach? There are several available. For example, the potential for workplace violence may be explored and the product of those explorations used to underpin threat management using the *Workplace Assessment of Violence Risk* (White, 2014; White & Meloy, 2010)—referred to as the WAVR-21 because it has 21 items. The WAVR-21 consists of a range of factors that are thought to enhance (risk factors) and counteract (protective factors) the threat of workplace violence. Assessors are guided in their understanding of factors such as motives for violence (item 1), homicidal ideas, violent fantasies or preoccupation (item 2), violent intentions and expressed threats (item 3), weapons skill and access (item 4), and preattack planning and preparation (item 5). Following a review of all 21 items and a determination of their presence in the individual case, assessors proceed to an evaluation of the nature of the threat posed, its severity, frequency or duration, imminence, as well as likelihood. Given the form of several of the items—entitlement and other negative traits (item 10), depression and suicidality (item 13), paranoia and other psychotic symptoms (item 14)—responsibility for an evaluation based on the application of the WAVR-21 must be held by a clinician, such as a suitably trained, experienced, and supervised psychologist or psychiatrist. However, law enforcement professionals have a significant role to play in gathering relevant information for the use of the clinician and in flagging the need for such an evaluation in the first place.

An alternative set of structured professional guidance that is suitable for direct use by experienced and knowledgeable law enforcement professionals is the *Brief Spousal Assault Form for the Evaluation of Risk* (B-SAFER) (Kropp & Cook, 2014; Kropp, Hart, & Belfrage, 2005; Thijssen & De Ruiter, 2011). The B-SAFER is a set of guidance for the assessment and management of the risk of spousal assault. Assessors are supported in their examination of 10 factors organized into two clusters—intimate partner violence (items 1–5) and psychosocial adjustment (items 6–10)—relevant to spousal assault. Items include a history of violent acts (item 1), a history of violent threats of thoughts (item 2), and escalation (item 3), and a history of general criminality (item 6), intimate relationship problems (item 7), and employment problems (item 8). Assessors are then guided through their consideration of a range of risk management strategies, including monitoring and surveillance options, control and supervision strategies, assessment and treatment, and victim safety plans. The evaluation concludes with a determination of the level of case prioritization (that is, a statement about the level of concern in this case if no intervention is taken), the level of concern about life-threatening violence as an outcome, the prospect of imminent violence, and the identity of the perpetrator's most likely victims.

A similar set of guidance from the same expert scholar-practitioner stable, and also suitable for use by law enforcement professionals, is the *Assessment of Risk for Honour Based Violence*, also known as the PATRIARCH (Belfrage & Ekman, 2013; Belfrage, Strand, Ekman, & Hasselborg, 2012; Kropp, Belfrage, & Hart, 2013). Structured and operationalized in the same way as the B-SAFER, the PATRIARCH directs the attention of assessors toward factors more relevant to honor-based violence than spousal assault. Consisting of 15 items across three clusters—focusing on the nature of honor-based violence (items N1 to N5), perpetrator risk factors (items P1 to P5), and victim vulnerability factors (items V1 to V5)—it covers areas such as violent attitudes or thoughts, presently or in the past (item N1), problems with cultural integration (item P1), and inconsistent attitudes and behavior in the victim (item V1).

Further examples of the application of structured professional judgment approaches to understanding threat or risk relate to stalking and harassment. They are the *Stalking Risk Profile* (SRP) (James, Farnham, & Wilson, 2014; MacKenzie et al., 2009; McEwan et al., 2018) and the *Guidelines for Stalking Assessment and Management* (SAM) (Foellmi, Rosenfeld, & Galietta, 2016; Kropp & Cook, 2014; Kropp, Hart, & Lyon, 2008; Kropp, Hart, Lyon, & Storey, 2011). However, while the SAM may be used by law enforcement professionals, like the WAVR-21, the SRP is solely for use by clinicians; this is due to of the specialized nature of some of the areas in which evaluation is required. Therefore, the authors of the SRP have helpfully produced the *Screening Assessment for Stalking and Harassment* (SASH) (Hehemann, van Nobelen, Brandt, & McEwan, 2017; McEwan, Strand, MacKenzie, & James, 2017), which may be used by law enforcement and security professionals as well as mental health practitioners. All three guides draw the attention of assessors to factors relating to the nature of the stalking activity (e.g., communications, approaches, contact), perpetrator characteristics (e.g., anger, obsessed, relationship problems), and victim vulnerability factors (e.g., inconsistent behavior toward the perpetrator, the safety of living conditions, distress). And all three guides—the SAM, the SRP, and the SASH—walk the assessor through into risk management, thus ensuring that assessment informs the action taken to mitigate threat and that the whole process is transparent and evidence-based.

Two additional areas that are significantly in development and are of particular interest and relevance to law enforcement professionals internationally are threat assessment and management in relation to violent extremism and in relation to human trafficking and illegal migration. With respect to violent extremism, there are clear applications of the structured professional judgment approach to understanding and managing risk and threat (Hart, Cook, Pressman, Strang, & Lim, 2017; Logan & Lloyd, 2019). Indeed, given the range of activities potentially relevant to violent extremism—from attack planning and implementation, as a lone actor or as part of a coordinated group or movement, through to the logistical or financial facilitation of the attack plans of others and the radicalization of vulnerable individuals to encourage their support, tolerance, and perhaps their eventual use of targeted and ideologically motivated violence—it is arguable that the flexibility and discretion offered by such an approach makes it the only one suitable for this arena. However, given that law enforcement professionals engaged in understanding and managing the threat of violent extremism are invariably working in partnership with other intelligence-gathering agencies and that, for reasons of national security, their joint endeavors cannot be openly discussed, researched, or published—or only to a limited extent—there are significant challenges in the development and publication of relevant guidance. There is guidance available—for example, the *Violent Extremism Risk Assessment-Second Edition Revised* (VERA-2R) (Pressman, Duits, Rinne, & Flockton, 2016), the *Extremism Risk Guidance-22+* (ERG-22+) (Lloyd & Dean, 2015), also the *Multi-Level Guidelines* (MLG) (Cook, Hart, & Kropp, 2013), and the *Terrorist Radicalization Assessment Protocol-18* (TRAP-18) (Meloy & Gill, 2016; Meloy, Roshdi, Glaz-Ocik, & Hoffmann, 2015). But it is not applicable in all jurisdictions, or to more than a narrow range of the threats presented for management to law enforcement professionals. In addition, much of this guidance is unsuitable for use with the limited range of information that law enforcement professionals usually have available to them. Notably, testing the quality of the guidance as applied in different jurisdictions and scenarios without the assistance of the wider community of academic and practitioner peers, which has significantly informed the development of guidance such as the HCR-20^{V3}, makes demonstrating the veracity of new processes a challenge. Therefore, some creativity is required in identifying the most suitable guidance and incorporating it into practice—in addition to a sound theoretical and evidential basis for the development of new and bespoke guidance in this area (Logan & Lloyd, 2019).

With regard to human trafficking and illegal migration, law enforcement professionals are faced with a further set of challenges in their efforts to detect and track criminality, often involving multiple agencies operating across state or international borders and cultures, involving victims who can be as motivated to remain undiscovered as its perpetrators, although for very different reasons, and all severely testing prosecutorial processes. This field of threat assessment and management incorporates such scenarios as the deception, abduction, and trafficking of vulnerable adults, mainly women, and children for the purpose of commercial slavery including sexual slavery and enforced prostitution, extending to survival-sex/rape, for the financial benefit of others, through to the payment by victims of war, social upheaval, environmental crisis, disaster, or change, or economic disadvantage of corrupt individuals or organized crime groups to facilitate illegal and often highly dangerous cross-border travel in search of safety or opportunity. Negative attitudes toward if not the criminalization of victims (as willing commercial sex workers or an illegal immigrants) and the lack of any or appropriate facilities for those rescued or arrested in the course of crime detection and pursuit, have the potential to discourage good practice in the assessment and management of the threat of trafficking and illegal migration (e.g., Countryman-Roswurm & Bolin, 2014).

Current guidance on the assessment and management of threat in relation to human trafficking and illegal migration is superficial and generally narrow in range, focusing more on detection than on understanding and management (e.g., United Nations Office on Drugs and Crime, 2009). However, more advanced systems are in development taking better account of modern-day trafficking and illegal migration scenarios. For example, Ibanez and Suthers (2014, pp. 1556–1565) discuss a procedure for the detection of indicators of domestic human trafficking, focusing on online communication data and the reliance by organized crime groups on technology to facilitate their activities. And McKenzie (2019) discusses at length the financial indicators of human trafficking and the use of advanced data analytics toward detection and curtailment, including prosecution. However, the unification of threat assessment and management in this area awaits more detailed consideration and evaluation.

Unfortunately, despite their availability, it is not always possible to implement formal assessments such as the WAVR-21, the B-SAFER, the PATRIARCH, the SAM or the SRP, the VERA-2R, or the TRAP-18—as when the situation requires urgent management because the threat is imminent or when formal assessments are either inadequate for the purpose or nonexistent. What basic guidance can law enforcement professionals follow in order to structure their judgment in respect of the threat detected such that it is as informed and defensible as possible across a variety of threat scenarios?

As proposed above, threat assessment is the set of investigative and operational techniques used by practitioners such as law enforcement professionals to identify, evaluate, and mitigate the potential for targeted violence (e.g., Fein & Vossekuil, 1998; Meloy & Hoffmann, 2014). What are the investigative and operational techniques to which this definition refers? And how can we ensure that the essence of the structured professional judgment approach guides this less formal evaluation process?

First, on the detection or discovery of a threat, law enforcement professionals can apply a comprehensive information-gathering framework to what is known and unknown, emerging, and required to be known about the situation at hand. Such a knowledge base provides a platform for subsequent and informed decision-making. The information-gathering framework should include at least the following prompts, to be adapted depending on the nature of the specific threat posed and the time available.

i. Nature: What is the nature of the threat or threats to be prevented (or minimized)? Is the victim (or victims) identifiable? Is the perpetrator (or perpetrators) identifiable? What is known about where the threat will be actioned, and when?

ii. Severity: How severe might be the outcomes were this threat to be realized?

iii. Time, imminence: How long has this threat been in development or present? How soon might this threat be realized? (A time line will be helpful to visualize the development of events and situations over time, to flag missing information and sources, and to assist in understanding how antecedents give rise to consequences, and with what knock-on effects) (see Hart, Gresswell, & Braham, 2011).

iv. Information: What do we know now? What information do I have and can I access, from whom and over what time frame, given our understanding of the threat posed? What are the key information sources—and of these, which are critical in this case? What are the most pressing information gaps? What circumstances appear to be enhancing the threat? What circumstances appear to be mitigating the threat now? (That is, why has the threatened action not yet been carried out?) (Subject matter experts, either in law enforcement or in allied professions such as mental health, are valuable sources of guidance on the specific kinds of information that may be relevant to the threats posed in the individual case—for example, in a stalking case, a subject matter expert may be able to offer valuable advice on understanding the role of mental health problems in the threat posed and in its management).

v. Intent: If the identity of the perpetrator (perpetrators) is known, what would appear to be his or her intention in targeting this victim (victims)? What does it appear that the perpetrator(s) hopes to achieve?

vi. Capability: How realistic is this threat—can it be actioned by those posing the threat, do they have the capability to do so?

vii. Planning and preparation: What would appear to be the practical arrangements made to date to carry out the threat made?

viii. Outcomes: What are the necessary and desirable outcomes of this situation? What evidence would indicate that these outcomes had been achieved?

Second, on the basis of what is emerging about the threat posed to the target or targets identified, law enforcement professionals should prepare hypotheses—ideally, more than one—that may account for the reason why this threat is being posed to this target now. That is, what range of motives may account for the threat as it is currently understood? Common aspirations among those who use violence or the threat of violence include the satisfaction of revenge or retribution, status, a sense of justice, excitement, status, self-esteem, and so on (e.g., Logan, 2020). It is important that what is prepared at this stage are hypotheses—*possible* explanations—rather than definitive statements. Therefore, hypotheses would be presented in circumspect language (e.g., "Given what we know now, it appears that this public figure's stalker is angry with her because she is denying that they have ever had a relationship, which he believes—erroneously—that they have had, and therefore his motive in threatening her is to make her agree with him and to stop hurting him with her denials" *or* "Given what we know now, it may also be the case that this public figure's stalker is enjoying the fear he believes his behavior is causing in her—recent changes she has made in her daily routine may be taken as evidence that he is powerful and in control and this makes him feel good"). This stage of the threat assessment process is an opportunity to connect the pieces of information together and over time to gain an impression of the evolution of the threat and the potential next steps in its progression. An examination of possible motives in this way can enhance appreciation of the nature of the threat posed and the circumstances in which that threat may play out.

Third, as proposed above, the reason for assessing and understanding the nature of the threat posed is in order to do something about it; that is, threat management is the *raison d'être* of threat assessment. What are the component parts of a threat management plan that will ensure its comprehensive application toward prevented harm? Consistent with the structured professional judgment approach used in risk management in clinical and correctional settings (e.g., Douglas et al., 2013), threat management should consist of a range of options including but not limited to (1) direct interventions with the victim(s) and/or perpetrator(s), (2) situation management, (3) observations or surveillance, and (4) victim safety plans. Direct interventions are specific actions that are intended to alter one or more of the variables that are enhancing the potential for the threat to be realized or to increase the potency of variables that have an inhibiting influence. Further, direct interventions may be focused on the victim or victims, or they could be directed at the perpetrator(s)—or both. For example, in the case of a stalker, direct interventions may include compulsory mental health interventions for that person to address anger or mood issues or substance misuse problems, which appear to fuel that person's grievance against their victim.

Situational management strategies involve restrictions on the individual's ability to operationalize the threats they have made. For example, the stalker may be served with a legal requirement to keep a certain distance from his or her victim, or alternatively, may be denied access to the Internet or detained in custody in order to restrict their opportunity to threaten that person. But situational management can also include enhancements to the individual's circumstances to make actioning their threats less attractive or desirable. For example, the stalker may be supported into employment or rehoused in order to provide him or her with more positive outlets for their interests and energy if boredom or resentment due to their material circumstances were a factor in their focus on that victim.

Threat management using monitoring, observation, or surveillance strategies involves determining what will be taken as evidence of a change—escalation—in the threat level and implementing early warning systems in order to detect those changes when they occur. When tripped, such notifications should trigger a reappraisal of the threat. For example, the stalking victim might be told to monitor their email communications and telephone calls from unknown sources and to flag suspicious messages to the police for further investigation. Alternatively, the stalker may be required to attend meetings or therapy sessions or his or her local police station on a regular basis, and any breaches or evidence or noncompliance will be taken as an indication of a change—potential elevation—in the threat posed to the victim.

Finally, victim safety planning is key to threat management; that is, what can the intended target of the detected threat do to harden themselves to the potential for harm? Victim safety plans may involve a wide range of interventions from improvements to physical security around the target, enhancements to procedures for sounding the alarm about elevated risk, and managing the relationship (such as via communications) between the perpetrator and the victim. For example, the victim of the stalker may be coached on his or her communications with this individual and on the consistency of what they say and do, the security of key premises and modes of transport improved, and domestic and personal alarm systems introduced and regularly tested.

Fourth, in the context of services trying to manage multiple threats at any one time, which is commonly the case with law enforcement services who are required to prioritize threats for assessment and management on a weekly if not daily even hourly basis, there is a requirement for an agreed system of case prioritization. The structured professional judgment approach to risk assessment and management advocates case prioritization rather than the allocation of a risk level—low, moderate or medium, high—because the latter assumes a static level of risk and may confound severity of outcome with imminence of risk. Case prioritization implies a more dynamic system whereby cases may move up or down the priority list dependent, not on a judgment of overall level of risk, but need for effort or action to prevent threatened harm. Therefore, a high-priority case would indicate that urgent action is required. This would be in contrast to a low-priority case, which implies instead that threat is in the course of being managed and that no additional action is required right now. A low-priority case is not the same as a low-risk case, where the latter implies more that risk is negligible or inconsequential, which could be very misleading.

Therefore, formal threat assessment and management requires a degree of structure in order to ensure that the process is as considered, evidence-based, and reliable as possible and yet also flexible and adaptable to the circumstances of the situations to which it is applied. As discussed above, a number of formal threat assessment and management processes that may be applied to the work of law enforcement professionals have been prepared and are published and researched and, as such, offer a degree of reassurance that evidence-based practice is being implemented in the cases in which they are used. Transparency, accountability, and defensible practice are encouraged by their application. However, not all situations lend themselves to such time-consuming and information- and resource-hungry evaluations. Therefore, as suggested here, broader guidance is required—and this may be derived from the structured professional judgment approach that appears to be effective and helpful in other and related arenas. But is it always possible to exercise best practice in threat assessment and management in law enforcement settings? And if not, can the barriers to doing so be identified and their influence minimized? It is to such challenges that we will now turn.

The challenges of threat assessment and management in a law enforcement setting

Law enforcement is one of the most noble, exciting, and diverse areas of occupational activity. However, it is also a complex environment with high-stakes outcomes. Further, the work of law enforcement professionals is rarely a matter of them working directly and alone with those who threaten the safety and security of their victims. Invariably, and necessarily, other organizations and parties—stakeholders—have a say in how threats are detected, assessed, understood, and managed. Therefore, the first and arguably the most challenging test of threat assessment and management is its operation across agencies, that is, working in partnership toward threat management. For example, in the case of a stalker, there may be a requirement for law enforcement agencies to work with the Courts (e.g., to agree to a legal order to restrict contact between stalker and the victim) and mental health services (e.g., to facilitate the stalker's access to treatment that he has been denied because of his behavior or refusal in the past). Challenges here come in the form of, for instance, information access and exchange across agencies (see James et al., 2014 for an example of how information can be shared and used across agencies). However, in the case of an act of terrorist violence, multiagency involvement extends to include security services and other governmental oversight agencies, in addition to political and public interests. Partnership working is complex in the best of circumstances, not least because each agency has a different set of working practices, legal and ethical requirements, information sharing protocols, and expectations about role, influence, and outcome. It is not possible to minimize that complexity by any meaningful degree; it will always exist. However, it is helpful to acknowledge the presence of this challenge in order to monitor its influence on proceedings on a day-to-day basis and, in so doing, to reduce its impact.

Second, the nature of the threats managed by law enforcement professionals is diverse—from the threat of violence in the workplace and in educational establishments to all kinds of relational violence, to threats of harm against public figures, threats to specific and nonspecific targets, the threat of terrorism and mass or forced migration, threats to infrastructure and operation, threats in the short, medium, and long term, and so on. The diversity of the threats to be identified, assessed, understood, and managed means that it is a challenge to determine working practices that will apply in most situations in a way that supports evidence-based practice. That said, the risk assessment and management field can offer some pointers, and this chapter has endeavored to delineate what those pointers are. Thus, threat assessment and management in law enforcement can stand on the shoulders of the giants in other fields where harm prevention is the objective. The application of guidance based on the structured professional judgment approach is an example of how good practice in a strongly related area can be extended to the threat assessment and management field with good effect. However, some acknowledgment is necessary of the challenges of doing so and the adjustments required—such as investment in the training and supervision required of law enforcement professionals, and in the funding of subject matter expertise and training to support best practice in law enforcement teams.

Third, as proposed above, it is essential to evaluate threat assessment and management activity in law enforcement—because such an investment in time and resources can only be justified if it provides demonstrable benefits. Too often, novel threat assessment and management processes can be implemented at speed and altered in haste in response to the demands of a changing social or political climate, making it a challenge to maintain practices long enough to evaluate their impact and allow evidence rather than expediency to adjust what is done. Too often, it can feel as if the plane is flying while it is still being built. But what can be the most central challenge to quality work in threat assessment and management is agreeing with stakeholders what the outcomes of the activity are and how those outcomes will be measured and evidenced. Evidence of the effectiveness of threat assessment and management work is that a bad outcome did not occur—such an outcome was presaged but diverted at an early stage such that the full nature of the threat was not realized, the catastrophe averted. However, its nonoccurrence may be such as to make it unclear what contribution threat assessment and management activity made— and therefore, whether the effort and expense of the activity was justified in this and similar cases. It is too easy with effective service delivery of this kind for those more removed from the process to become complacent and to come to the view that the expense of such an endeavor is unjustified.

Therefore finally, and probably, the greatest challenge faced by law enforcement professionals trying to exercise the best possible practice in threat assessment and management is dealing with the expectations of those more distant from the daily activity of the task. This is especially the case when those individuals have influence over operational policies and procedures in the practice of teams, and in their funding. Such remote stakeholders are at risk of believing that the threat assessment and management task is simpler to understand and implement than it really is. Therefore, there is a very real possibility that good and thorough practice is curbed in the name of cost savings, a failure to grasp the reality of the task and its complexity, or impatience with its considerate and disciplined delivery. In this respect, the words of Nate Silver have never been more relevant:

> *The most calamitous failures of prediction usually have a lot in common. We focus on those signals that tell a story about the world as we would like it to be, not how it really is. We ignore the risks that are hardest to measure, even when they pose the greatest threats to our wellbeing. We make approximations and assumptions about the world that are much cruder than we realise. We abhor uncertainty, even when it is an irreducible part of the problem we are trying to solve.*
>
> **Silver (2012), pp. 19—20.**

Conclusions

This chapter has examined threat assessment and management in law enforcement. It has defined the process and attempted to differentiate it in general terms from the related task of risk assessment and management. The key principles of the task, such as the necessity of linking threat assessment to its management and the requirement for structure and guidance in what is a sophisticated and high-stakes activity have been described in some detail and emphasized. This chapter has concluded with a review of some of the challenges faced in implementing best practice in threat assessment and management in law enforcement settings, not least the effort of demonstrating that bad things did not happen as a direct result of the good work undertaken to make this the case.

But where to from here? This chapter concludes with two related recommendations for law enforcement professionals engaged in threat assessment and management activity. First, threat assessment and management is a task best undertaken by professionals of different kinds working together to create the most comprehensive understanding of the individual at risk. Multidisciplinary teamwork in this arena is strongly advised (James et al., 2014)—and should be funded accordingly. Multiple disciplines improve the opportunity for a more comprehensive understanding of the nature of the threat and its motivational drivers, and therefore the prospect of a more effective and proportionate threat management plan. Also, the involvement of multiple disciplines guards against unitary and potentially biased thinking. However, with the involvement of multiple disciplines comes the prospect of organizational partnerships and the need for clear service level agreements, spelling out areas of responsibility and accountability, and information sharing protocols, especially across different classification levels—and the prospect of interagency disputes if these are not established and agreed in advance. Partnerships too must be invested in, monitored, and nurtured.

Second and finally, we cannot arrest our way out of all the scenarios posed by those who choose to threaten violence as a way of expressing their feelings or controlling others. While the law is our most important guide and ally, arresting people and denying them their liberty can also make them more angry and grievance-fueled, thus potentially compounding their original motivation to threaten harm. And there are significant costs associated with legal action in this form. Often, arrest and incarceration are the only options that can safeguard the well-being of the victim or victims, making it the right option. But threat management is and should be more creative that simply locking down the person who threatens. Multidisciplinary teamwork creates the opportunity for more imaginative plans to divert the individual from a pathway toward violence and at an earlier stage, and to address some of the underlying causes of their desire to threaten and do harm, resulting in more enduring and comprehensive safety plans. In this way, there is a valuable and necessary convergence of threat and risk assessment in the service of prevented harm.

References

Belfrage, H., & Ekman, L. (2013). Threat assessment of targeted honour-based violence. In J. R. Meloy, & J. Hoffmann (Eds.), *International handbook of threat assessment* (pp. 260–271). New York: Oxford University Press.

Belfrage, H., Strand, S., Ekman, L., & Hasselborg, A. K. (2012). The PATRIARCH: Six-years experiences from the use of a checklist for the assessment of risk for patriarchal violence with honor as motive. *International Journal of Police Science and Management, 14*, 20–29. https://doi.org/10.1350/ijps.2012.14.1.250.

Cook, A. N., Hart, S. D., & Kropp, P. R. (2013). *Multi-Level Guidelines (MLG) for the assessment and management of group-based violence. User Manual.* Burnaby, BC: Mental Health, Law, and Policy Institute.

Cornell, D., & Datta, P. (2017). Threat assessment and violence prevention. In L. C. Wilson (Ed.), *The Wiley handbook of the psychology of mass shootings* (pp. 353–371). Chichester: John Wiley & Sons Ltd. https://doi.org/10.1002/9781119048015.ch19.

Countryman-Roswurm, K., & Bolin, B. L. (2014). Domestic minor sex trafficking: Assessing and reducing risk. *Child and Adolescent Social Work Journal, 31*, 521–538. https://doi.org/10.1007/s10560-014-0336-6.

Douglas, K. S., Hart, S. D., Webster, C. D., & Belfrage, H. (2013). *HCR-20: Assessing risk for violence* (3rd ed.). Vancouver: Mental Health, Law and Policy Institute, Simon Fraser University.

Douglas, K. S., Hart, S. D., Webster, C. D., Belfrage, H., Guy, L. S., & Wilson, C. W. (2014). *Historical-clinical-risk management-20*, version 3 (HCR-20V3): Development and overview. *International Journal of Forensic Mental Health, 13*, 93–108. https://doi.org/10.1080/14999013.2014.906519.

Fein, R. A., & Vossekuil, B. (1998). *Protective intelligence and threat assessment investigations: A guide for state and local law enforcement officials.* Washington DC: US Department of Justice.

Foellmi, M. C., Rosenfeld, B., & Galietta, M. (2016). Assessing risk for recidivism in individuals convicted of stalking offenses: Predictive validity of the guidelines for stalking assessment and management. *Criminal Justice and Behavior, 43*, 600–616. https://doi.org/10.1177/0093854815610612.

Gawande, A. (2011). *The checklist manifesto.* London: Profile Books Ltd.

Grove, W. M., & Meehl, P. E. (1996). Comparative efficiency of informal (subjective, impressionistic) and formal (mechanical, algorithmic) prediction procedures: The clinical-statistical controversy. *Psychology, Public Policy, and Law, 2*, 293–323. https://doi.org/10.1037/1076-8971.2.2.293.

Hart, S. D., Cook, A. N., Pressman, D. E., Strang, S., & Lim, Y. L. (2017). *A concurrent evaluation of threat assessment tools for the individual assessment of terrorism.* Canadian Network for Research on Terrorism, Security, and Society.

Hart, S. D., Douglas, K. S., & Guy, L. S. (2016). The structured professional judgement approach to violence risk assessment: Origins, nature, and advances. In A. R. Beech, & T. Ward (Eds.), *The Wiley handbook on the theories, assessment and treatment of sexual offending* (pp. 643–666). Chichester: Wiley-Blackwell. https://doi.org/10.1002/9781118574003.wattso030.

Hart, A. J., Gresswell, D. M., & Braham, L. G. (2011). Formulation of serious violent offending using multiple sequential functional analysis. In P. Sturmey, & M. McMurran (Eds.), *Forensic case formulation* (pp. 129–152). Chichester: Wiley-Blackwell. https://doi.org/10.1002/9781119977018.ch6.

Hart, S. D., & Logan, C. (2011). Formulation of violence risk using evidence-based assessments: The structured professional judgment approach. In P. Sturmey, & M. McMurran (Eds.), *Forensic case formulation* (pp. 83–106). Chichester: Wiley-Blackwell. https://doi.org/10.1002/9781119977018.ch4.

Hehemann, K., van Nobelen, D., Brandt, C., & McEwan, T. (2017). The reliability and predictive validity of the screening assessment for stalking and harassment (SASH). *Journal of Threat Assessment and Management, 4*, 164–177. https://doi.org/10.1037/tam0000085.

Ibanez, M., & Suthers, D. D. (2014). *Detection of domestic human trafficking indicators and movement trends using content available on open internet sources. 2014 47th Hawaii International Conference on System Sciences.* https://doi.org/10.1109/HICSS.2014.200. https://ieeexplore.ieee.org/abstract/document/6758797.

James, D. V., Farnham, F. R., & Wilson, S. P. (2014). The fixated threat assessment centre: Implementing a joint policing and psychiatric approach to risk assessment and management in public figure threat cases. In J. R. Meloy, & J. Hoffmann (Eds.), *International handbook of threat assessment* (pp. 299–320). New York: Oxford University Press.

Kropp, P. R., Belfrage, H., & Hart, S. D. (2013). *Assessment of risk for honour based violence (PATRIARCH): User manual.* Vancouver: ProActive Resolutions Inc.

Kropp, P. R., & Cook, A. N. (2014). Intimate partner violence, stalking, and femicide. In J. R. Meloy, & J. Hoffmann (Eds.), *International handbook of threat assessment* (pp. 178–194). New York: Oxford University Press.

Kropp, P. R., Hart, S. D., & Belfrage, H. (2005). *Brief spousal Assault form for the evaluation of risk (B-SAFER). User manual.* Vancouver: ProActive Resolutions Inc.

Kropp, P. R., Hart, S. D., & Lyon, D. R. (2008). *Guidelines for stalking assessment and management (SAM): User manual.* Vancouver: ProActive Resolutions Inc.

Kropp, P. R., Hart, S. D., Lyon, D. R., & Storey, J. E. (2011). The development and validation of the guidelines for stalking assessment and management. *Behavioral Sciences & the Law, 29*, 302–316. https://doi.org/10.1002/bsl.978.

Lloyd, M., & Dean, C. (2015). The development of structured guidelines for assessing risk in extremist offenders. *Journal of Threat Assessment and Management, 2*, 40–52. https://doi.org/10.1037/tam0000035.

Logan, C., (2020). Violence risk management and personality disorder. In J.S. Wormith, L.A. Craig and T. Hogue (eds.), What works in violence risk management: Theory, research and practice. Chichester: Wiley-Blackwell.

Logan, C., (2021). The assessment and management of risk of violent extremism. CREST Security Review, *11*, Summer 2021. https://www.crestresearch.ac.uk/magazine/risk/.

Logan, C., & Lloyd, M. (2019). Violent extremism: A comparison of approaches to assessing and managing risk. *Legal and Criminological Psychology, 24*, 141–161. https://doi.org/10.1111/lcrp.12140.

MacKenzie, R., McEwan, T. E., Pathe, M., James, D. V., Ogloff, J. R., & Mullen, P. E. (2009). *Stalking risk profile: Guidelines for the assessment and management of stalkers.* Melbourne, Australia: Monash University.

McEwan, T. E., Shea, D. E., Daffern, M., MacKenzie, R. D., Ogloff, J. R., & Mullen, P. E. (2018). The reliability and predictive validity of the *Stalking Risk Profile. Assessment, 25*, 259–276. https://doi.org/10.1177/1073191116653470.

McEwan, T. E., Strand, S., MacKenzie, R. D., & James, D. V. (2017). *Screening assessment for stalking and harassment (SASH): Guidelines for application and interpretation.* https://www.stalkingriskprofile.com/stalking-risk-profile/sash.

McKenzie, J. (2019). *Identifying and mitigating human trafficking risk through the use of financial institutions.* Utica College. Doctoral dissertation. https://search.proquest.com/openview/26645672dfcab5f88a8913f1d6291da3/1?pq-origsite=gscholar&cbl=18750&diss=y

Meehl, P. E. (1996). *Clinical versus statistical prediction: A theoretical analysis and a review of the literature.* Northvale, NJ: Jason Aronson. https://doi.org/10.1037/11281-000.

Meloy, J. R., & Gill, P. (2016). The lone-actor terrorist and the TRAP-18. *Journal of Threat Assessment and Management, 3*, 37–52. https://doi.org/10.1037/tam0000061.

Meloy, J. R., Hart, S. D., & Hoffmann, J. (2014). Threat assessment and threat management. In J. R. Meloy, & J. Hoffmann (Eds.), *International handbook of threat assessment* (pp. 3–17). New York: Oxford University Press.

Meloy, J. R., & Hoffmann, J. (2014). In *International handbook of threat assessment.* New York: Oxford University Press.

Meloy, J. R., Roshdi, K., Glaz-Ocik, J., & Hoffmann, J. (2015). Investigating the individual terrorist in Europe. *Journal of Threat Assessment and Management, 2*, 140–152. https://doi.org/10.1037/tam0000036.

Mitchell, M., & Palk, G. (2016). Traversing the space between threats and violence: A review of threat assessment guidelines. *Psychiatry, Psychology and Law, 23*, 863–871. https://doi.org/10.1080/13218719.2016.1164638.

Pressman, E., Duits, N., Rinne, T., & Flockton, J. (2016). *VERA-2R violent extremism risk assessment version 2 revised: A structured professional judgement approach.* Utrecht, The Netherlands: NIFP/DJI.

Reddy, M., Borum, R., Berglund, J., Vossekuil, B., Fein, R. A., & Modzeleski, W. (2001). Evaluating risk for targeted violence in schools: Comparing risk assessment, threat assessment, and other approaches. *Psychology in the Schools, 38,* 157–172. https://doi.org/10.1002/pits.1007.

Silver, N. (2012). *The signal and the noise: Why so many predictions fail-but some don't.* New York: Penguin.

Thijssen, J., & De Ruiter, C. (2011). Identifying subtypes of spousal assaulters using the B-SAFER. *Journal of Interpersonal Violence, 26,* 1307–1321. https://doi.org/10.1177/0886260510369129.

United Nations Office on Drugs and Crime. (2009). *Anti-human trafficking manual for criminal justice practitioners: Module 5 — risk assessment in trafficking in persons investigations.* https://www.unodc.org/documents/human-trafficking/TIP_module5_Ebook.pdf.

Van der Meer, B. B., & Diekhuis, M. L. (2014). Collecting and assessing information for threat assessment. In J. R. Meloy, & J. Hoffmann (Eds.), *International handbook of threat assessment* (pp. 54–66). New York: Oxford University Press.

White, S. G. (2014). Workplace targeted violence: Threat assessment incorporating a structured professional judgment guide. In J. R. Meloy, & J. Hoffmann (Eds.), *International handbook of threat assessment* (pp. 83–106). New York: Oxford University Press.

White, S. G., & Meloy, J. R. (2010). *Workplace assessment of violence risk-21 (WAVR-21): A structured professional guide for the workplace assessment of violence risk.* San Diego: Specialized Training Services.

Investigative interviewing: exploring the contamination timeline of witness memory

16

Gary Dalton and Rebecca Milne

Introduction

Criminal investigations involve collecting sufficient reliable evidence to find out what happened (if anything did happen) and who was involved (Kebbell & Milne, 1998; Milne & Bull, 2016). Crucial to any criminal investigation is the information provided by witnesses and victims normally gathered through interviewing techniques conducted by police personnel (Milne & Bull, 2016). Thus, it is important to conduct quality witness interviews to obtain high-quality witness evidence. For the remainder of this chapter, the term witness will be used to describe not only those who observe the crime but also those who fall victim to the crime. From the outset a witness's account can direct the investigation, inform decisions, and impact the latter stages of the investigation including outcomes reached in the court room (Shepherd & Griffiths, 2013). Thus, for the investigation to be successful, there is a need to gain accurate and detailed information from witnesses. This chapter will outline how memory can be contaminated during the interview process, but will also discuss the implications of research and how it can inform practice for the gathering of information throughout the investigative process (i.e., from the initial emergency call, to frontline communication, to the formal interview).

Witness memory involves personally experienced events which fall within the domain of episodic memory (Wheeler & Gabbert, 2017). Memory for experienced events is fallible and hence can be inaccurate and incomplete (Frenda, Nichols, & Loftus, 2011). Due to memory being constructive, recollections for events are easily contaminated or distorted by information encountered after the event took place. In addition, memory is not like a video recorder and so witnesses naturally forget details with their memory of the event changing over time (Loftus, 1979). Certain information will be forgotten, and this forgetting can occur quite quickly, meaning that even after a short delay, a witness might only remember the general gist of an event. A witness may also have memory gaps or omissions for information they did not attend to in the first place. As a

Police Psychology, Edited by Marques and Paulino. https://doi.org/10.1016/B978-0-12-816544-7.00016-4

result of these natural memory processes, police personnel face a difficult task in obtaining accounts from individuals, especially when they have witnessed complex events under challenging encoding conditions (Kontogianni, Hope, Taylor, Vrij, & Gabbert, 2018) or when there is a delay in gathering information from the witness (Wixted & Ebbesen, 1997).

Despite memory being reconstructive in nature, memory often forms the centerpiece of the criminal investigation (Howe, Knott, & Conway, 2018). For example, a witness will describe and later identify a perpetrator from memory, but will also report, during a police interview, what they remember about the event in question (e.g., a weapon being present, the location of the incident, and the number of people present). However, a criminal investigation will rarely involve the single interview of a witness by an investigator (Leeney & Mueller-Johnson, 2012). Instead, the investigation will consist of multiple interviews, which typically start with the original emergency call from the witness to the police. In this first interview the caller will be interviewed by the call handler to find out what happened. The call handler will then mobilize available units, and a frontline police officer will attend the scene and carry out a second interview to obtain more information. These details tend to be recorded in the officer's notebook, and nowadays it is likely that the interaction will also be recorded using body worn video (BWV) (Dalton & Ang, 2014). A statement will then be taken from the witness (either straight away or at a later date) and forms the third interview. Thus, police personnel must have good communication skills (e.g., avoiding leading questions) and attention to detail to reduce the likelihood of a witness's memory being contaminated across the investigation (O'Neill & Milne, 2014).

Contaminated witness memory can have serious consequences for an investigation and has been shown to contribute to a number of miscarriages of justice (Poyser, Nurse, & Milne, 2018; Savage & Milne, 2007). Thus, the current chapter will now explore each stage of the investigation process and see where memory contamination can occur and how easily those conducting interviews can influence the information and accuracy of this information reported by witnesses.

On the phone: the call handler interview

After a criminal event has taken place, a witness will typically report it via a phone call to the police emergency number (Ambler & Milne, 2006; Pescod, Wilcock, & Milne, 2013). The witness will have a brief interview with a call handler about the incident (Leeney & Mueller-Johnson, 2012), and the call handler will then determine the nature of the call and decide on the best course of action. The role of the call handler is to ensure public safety, mobilize the correct resources, and establish the location of the reported incident. This initial phone call is likely to be the first opportunity in which the witness can recall the event (Pescod et al., 2013). This initial stage of the investigation is therefore of critical importance because not only is it the stage when the witness's memory is most likely to be detailed and accurate and least likely to have been contaminated (Wixted & Ebbesen, 1997), but it is also the stage in which the criminal investigation commences (Wilcock, Bull, & Milne, 2008). However, it should be noted that information taken at this stage is often collected quickly and in circumstances where the witness might be highly traumatized. Such circumstances are not conducive to memory retrieval (Milne & Bull, 2016). In fact, call handling may be at greater risk of contamination than face-to-face interviewing because as demonstrated by Campos and Alonso-Quecuty (2006), memory retrieval on the telephone is more error prone than face-to-face communication.

Given the importance of this initial stage of the investigation, it is perhaps surprising that nearly all published research on witness interviewing has focused on the latter stages of the investigation (e.g., the formal police interview), with few studies examining communication by call handlers (Leeney & Mueller-Johnson, 2012). Research suggests that memory contamination can occur at the initial stage due to call handlers condensing, distorting, and sometimes elaborating reports of incidents (Ekblom & Heal, 1982). In a more recent study, the call logs written by the call handlers revealed that 21.6% of information mentioned by the caller about the perpetrator was missing, 5% of details had been changed, and 3% had actually been mistakenly added (Leeney & Mueller-Johnson, 2012). Call logs are important as officers will often use these rather than listening to the actual call to make investigative decisions (Ambler & Milne, 2006). Call handlers may also hold biases and therefore on some occasions may view the callers accounts as mistaken, deliberately untrue (e.g., hoax calls), or exaggerated (Waddington, 1993). Call handlers tend to prefer the use of closed questions when gathering information (Ambler & Milne, 2006; Johnson & Garner, 2003). Leeney and Mueller-Johnson (2012) focused on 40 phone calls (interviews) from an English police call center and found that call handlers used unproductive questioning techniques in 11.5% of the questions, including leading, suggestive, and forced choice question types. While closed questions can be helpful in minimizing information deemed irrelevant, they do run the risk of missing relevant unsolicited information (Fisher & Schreiber, 2007). On a more positive note, Leeney and Mueller-Johnson's (2012) sample were found to use scripts 42.5% of the time. When call handlers used these scripts, they asked fewer questions to elicit the same amount of information (i.e., they asked more open questions to elicit information and used fewer suggestive and leading questions). Thus, using evidence-based call scripts can provide structure to the call handler and promote good interview practice (Gabbert, Hope, Carter, Boon, & Fisher, 2016).

The need to improve the call handling interview is perhaps obvious. We know that the information retrieved by a witness in an initial retrieval attempt can affect information elicited during subsequent retrievals. Marsh, Tversky, and Hutson (2005) found that an inaccurate initial recall reduced the accuracy of a subsequent recall. Moreover, when there was an incomplete initial recall it sometimes resulted in an incomplete subsequent recall (Shaw, Bjork, & Handal, 1995). This has important implications for call handlers: if memory elicited during the call is incomplete or contains inaccuracies, then this can lead to difficulties during subsequent recall within more formal investigative interviews (Pescod et al., 2013).

Poor interviewing techniques, such as the use of leading questions by call handlers can also have a significant detrimental effect on witness memory (e.g., misinformation effect; Lindsay, 1990; Loftus & Palmer, 1974). Studies demonstrate that such questions have the potential to mislead police investigations (Frenda et al., 2011) and can lead to witness evidence being inadmissible in court (Gabbert et al., 2016). Hence, the use of poor interviewing techniques by call handlers can contaminate the memory of the witness. This will have a significant impact on the decision-making processes of the call handler leading to serious consequences for the future investigation (Milne & Bull, 2016). Additionally, if misinformation occurs prior to a detailed statement being taken, then this can increase the chance of the misinformation being recalled in subsequent retrieval attempts (Lane, Mather, Villa, & Morita, 2001). These (false) memories can be held with as much confidence as real memories even in the face of contradictory information (Schooler, 1994). Thus, if this initial albeit brief interview by the call handler is not conducted correctly, it can have a detrimental effect on a witness's ability to recall information at a later date. Consequently, this could have an impact on the direction and outcome of the investigation as well as the decisions made in the court room. To ensure an effective recall the call handler must protect against exposure to postevent misinformation (Gabbert, Hope, & Fisher, 2009).

In order to reduce the risk of memory contamination, psychologists have developed call handling interview protocols that aim to gather information quickly and without negatively affecting memory. Research has shown that recall elicited using open-ended questions is more likely to be accurate than recall elicited using specific questions (Lipton, 1977). Pescod et al. (2013) tested a new call handling protocol which contained the "report everything" component of the cognitive interview (CI) (see Section 16.4 for a full discussion of this technique). The "report everything" instruction has been found to encourage interviewees to report everything they can remember, including partially remembered details or details the witness deems trivial (Milne & Bull, 2002). Pescod et al. (2013) found that this new interview protocol increased the overall number of correct items recalled by witnesses when reporting the incident to police call handlers. Importantly, there was no increase in the number of confabulated items recalled. In addition, 80% of participants in the "report everything" condition recalled more correct information compared with those in the current call handling procedure condition. However, it is important to note that the "report everything" interviews did lead to a small but significant increase in incorrect information. Nevertheless, the accuracy rates remained high (i.e., 89%).

To summarize, call handling has received little attention in the research world, with many seeing it as purely a facilitator for an immediate police response. However, it is clear that call handling plays a vital role in the investigation (Leeney & Mueller-Johnson, 2012). When call handlers interview appropriately, they set the precedent for a good investigation, but when carried out poorly, they can hamper the investigation by contaminating memory and eliciting incorrect details. Thus, to move forward there is a need to develop evidence-based interview guidance for police call handlers. Work is currently being undertaken to develop bespoke evidence-based control room protocols for the Fire and Rescue Service (Shawyer et al., 2018) and should be an area considered within other emergency services, especially the police.

At the scene: the frontline interview

Following an emergency call, police officers are dispatched to the scene of an incident in order to obtain information on what occurred and who was involved. While these frontline officers will be responsible for the early investigative work (e.g., gathering information/evidence), it should be noted that they also have to, first and most importantly, try and resolve the incident itself (i.e., breaking up disturbances, ensuring the safety of individuals). During this initial interviewing phase, it is important that frontline police officers obtain the maximum quantity and quality of information from witnesses. However, this is by no means an easy task (Milne & Bull, 2006). These difficulties are exacerbated because as already noted, memory is fragile, and can be altered, changed, and manipulated. Hence, it is imperative for frontline police officers to recognize how easily they can contaminate memory and alter the reporting of information provided by witnesses.

Unfortunately, frontline police officers typically have the least amount of interview training and experience, but are responsible for conducting the greatest volume of interviews (Dando, Wilcock, & Milne, 2008). There is limited field research looking at police interviewing at the scene of the investigation. Thus, little is known about the interactions occurring between frontline officers and witnesses. The few field studies that have been conducted have found shortcomings in the way in which police officers interview witnesses, including the over reliance on asking closed questions (Myklebust & Alison, 2000) and using leading questions (Wright & Alison, 2004). Police officers themselves have reported feeling inadequately trained, ill-equipped, and under pressure when conducting witness interviews (Dando et al. 2008). It is only recently through the introduction of BWV that we can evaluate the types of questions being asked by frontline police officers during the gathering of information. This was not previously possible, as police officers typically only record, through a written statement, the responses provided by witnesses and do not record the specific questions used to elicit such information.

As a result of the advances in technology, it could be argued that BWV has transformed modern policing (Jennings, Fridell, & Lynch, 2014). BWV is currently being utilized worldwide in countries such as Australia, Singapore, the UK, and the United States. In the UK, budget constraints and recent government policies have accelerated this transformation and have resulted in BWV being adopted by numerous police forces. Cameras mounted on police uniforms (i.e., BWV) have been credited with creating greater transparency, efficiency, and effectiveness of police conduct (Drover & Ariel, 2015). Early studies in the United States focused on BWV reducing the number of complaints against the police (Katz et al., 2014) and reducing the use of force by police officers during interactions with members of the public (Ariel,

Farrar, & Sutherland, 2014). Recently, research has started to use BWV as a tool to examine the communication skills of frontline police officers and how information is elicited from witnesses. To date, research suggests that frontline officers often fail to deploy strategies to build rapid rapport with witnesses and tend to use inappropriate questions (e.g., closed, leading) to gather information (Dalton, Milne, Hope, Vernham & Nunan, 2021; Gabbert, Hope, LaRooy et al., 2016).

Dalton et al. (2021) examined the elicitation of person descriptions from witnesses being interviewed by frontline officers. This study obtained invaluable access to real-life BWV footage from officers operating within the UK police force. The footage available for analysis spanned a 20-month period and included over 2000 recordings. Crimes included assaults, domestic offences, sexual offences, and theft. Dalton et al. (2021) found that a witness's memory was being contaminated by frontline police officers as a result of witnesses being interviewed collectively, witnesses being interrupted during recall, and police officers providing feedback to witnesses about the event. Additionally, they found that approximately 50% of the questions asked by frontline police officers to elicit person description information were inappropriate (e.g., 23% were leading questions and 8% were forced choice questions). Fisher (1995) argues that interruptions discourage witnesses from providing extensive, detailed responses. If witnesses are constantly interrupted, then the witness may interpret this as indication that they only have a limited time to respond to the police officer, so may start to shorten their responses accordingly. Additionally, police officers should be warned against providing witnesses with feedback during the interview as it can inflate their confidence (Semmler, Brewer, & Wells, 2004). For example, when a witness is given explicit feedback, or even subtle cues, regarding their account, they are likely to adjust their confidence to reflect their belief that they were accurate (confirming feedback) or inaccurate (disconfirming feedback). Witness confidence can impact upon how the witness is perceived by the police and in court with higher confidence being associated with honesty (Wells, Lindsay, & Ferguson, 1979; Whitley & Greenberg, 1986). Frontline officers therefore need to be sensitive about providing feedback as memory can easily be distorted by postevent information (Frenda et al., 2011), which can later determine the outcomes of the case.

In dynamic incidents where there are multiple witnesses and importantly multiple police officers, it is paramount that witnesses are separated to avoid contamination of memory (Gabbert, Memon, & Wright, 2006; Loftus, 2003). Cowitnesses can affect how one witness remembers the event, and this can lead to memory conformity (Gabbert & Hope, 2013). Memory conformity refers to information about the incident that is acquired by a witness following the event (e.g., during discussions with other people) (Gabbert, Memon, & Allan, 2003). In some circumstances, one witness may report details learned from another in order to avoid the perceived social costs of disagreeing (Cialdini & Goldstein, 2004) or because they believe the new information is accurate (Deutsch & Gerard, 1955). The problem here is that witnesses may go on to report details that were learned through discussion with a cowitness because they have forgotten the source of the information (Zaragoza & Lane, 1994).

Even when there are not multiple police officers in attendance and hence only one police officer available to interview multiple witnesses, there are interview tools available to support the retrieval of information (e.g., the Self-Administered Interview (SAI)) (Gabbert et al., 2009). The SAI can be given out at the scene of the incident and is a protocol of instruction and questions drawing on the CI technique (e.g., report everything and context reinstatement) (see Section 16.4 for a full description) and designed to elicit a written free-recall statement. The SAI is particularly useful when there are multiple witnesses at the scene and when there is a lack of resources in terms of time, expertise, and personnel to conduct the interviews (Gabbert et al., 2016). Studies using the SAI have reported a significant increase in the completeness and accuracy of information (Gabbert et al., 2009; Krix et al., 2016). Moreover, the SAI protects the memory from potentially distorting postevent information (Gabbert et al., 2009, 2012; Hope, Gabbert, Fisher, & Jamieson, 2014).

To reduce the potential for memory contamination, frontline police officers should be asking appropriate questions (e.g., open and specific closed). This is because research has shown that the use of open questions allows for unlimited free recall responses from witnesses and produces information of higher accuracy than closed questions (Fisher, Falkner, Trevisan, & McCauley, 2000). As the memory for the incident is recent and less likely to have been contaminated (presuming the call handler has asked appropriate nonleading questions), a good quality interview at this stage is important because the completeness and accuracy of witness evidence decreases as the delay between witnessing an incident and recalling the incident increases (Wixted & Ebbesen, 1997). While there have been advances in effective interview practices, these have not always translated into improving frontline communication. Working with practitioners, Gabbert, Hope, LaRooy et al. (2016) developed an evidence-based Structured Interview Protocol (SIP) and related training, for use by frontline police officers. The SIP package promotes high-quality interview performance, reduces memory contamination, and has led to increased use of rapid rapport techniques, enhanced "engage and explain" skills, and an increase in appropriate question types, used in a structured manner.

A final evidence-based technique to enhance memory retrieval during frontline communication is a sketch plan. Sketch plans have been shown to be useful in helping witnesses to explain what they experienced, the location of people and objects (Dando et al., 2009). Sketch plans can also be used as an aid to mentally reinstate the context, as it encourages witnesses to generate their own retrieval cues while minimizing the cues elicited by the interviewer (e.g., during leading questions). Moreover, sketches have been found to be less demanding and less time consuming for interviewers than the full mental reinstatement of context (Dando et al., 2009; see Section 16.4 for a full discussion of this technique). This is particularly important when there are limited resources available or during complex crimes (e.g., when there is a need to interview multiple witnesses). Research has also shown that sketches can be used with a variety of witnesses, including those who are deemed vulnerable (Mattison, Dando, & Ormerod, 2018).

Regardless of the interview techniques utilized by frontline police officers, there are many uncontrollable witness factors that can affect how information is encoded at the scene of the incident, and thus these factors can later affect subsequent recall (see Gabbert et al., 2016 for a full discussion of witness factors). One such factor is the blood alcohol level of the witness, as intoxication can impair memory performance. Evans, Schrieber-Compo and Russano (2009) surveyed police officers and found 53% of respondents routinely dealt with intoxicated witnesses (on average four per week). In addition, Palmer, Flowe, Takarangi, and Humphries (2013) found that 33% of testimonies heard in court were made by witnesses who were intoxicated. Until recently, this has been an area largely ignored within the witness literature (Malpass et al., 2008). Research has shown that alcohol reduces the ability to encode episodic memories (Yuille & Tollestrup, 1990) and reduces our ability to form new long-term memories (White, 2003). Moreover, Clifasefi, Takarang, and Bergman (2006) found that intoxicated participants showed greater levels of attentional blindness than nonintoxicated participants. This is similar to research examining the presence of a weapon and the impact it has on encoding (e.g., witnesses are unable to recall details about the scene including details regarding the perpetrator because their attention is diverted to the weapon) (for a review on weapon focus, see Loftus, 1979 and Steblay, 1992).

One explanation for why alcohol can affect a witness's memory is Alcohol Myopia Theory (Steele & Josephs, 1990). The main assumptions of this theory are that alcohol depresses the central nervous system, and this inhibits brain activity. The neurons become less responsive to stimulation, and this reduces cognitive capacity. Thus, when witnesses are intoxicated they encode fewer details due to attention narrowing to "central" or "salient" stimuli (Harvey, 2016; Harvey, Kneller, & Campbell, 2013). Schreiber-Compo et al. (2011) examined the type of information affected by intoxication. Participants interacted with a bartender and were then immediately asked to complete a written free recall. In comparison with participants who were not given alcohol, participants who had been given alcohol were just as accurate for central details (e.g., descriptions of the bartender) but provided significantly less accurate peripheral details (e.g., information about the bar). However, it should be noted that the precise nature of the impairment caused by intoxication is not well understood and results are mixed (Hope & Sauer, 2014). For example, it is not clear whether alcohol consumption reduces the overall capacity of one's attention or whether it just hampers our ability to allocate attention.

A witness's level of stress at the scene of the incident may also affect witness memory. When frontline officers attend a scene the witness may still be experiencing physiological arousal. Research examining memory performance and stress has produced mixed results (see Deffenbacher, Bornstein, Penrd, & McGorty, 2004 for a review), but the overall consensus is that the effect of memory performance reflects an inverted U-shaped curve, with memory for events best when stress levels are moderate (Morley & Farr, 2012). That being said, high levels of stress have typically been shown to impair memory (Hope et al., 2016; Hope, Lewinski, Dixon, Blocksidge, & Gabbert, 2012). Stress has also been shown to increase levels of suggestibility. Morgan, Southwick, Steffian, Hazlett, and Loftus (2013) conducted a study involving 800 soldiers who were taking part in survival training. Soldiers who were exposed to misinformation were vulnerable to suggestion. For example, 27% of soldiers mistakenly reported that they were threatened with a weapon by their interrogator. Thus, witnesses exposed to high levels of stress will typically report significantly fewer details and exhibit increased memory errors in comparison with witnesses exposed to lower levels of stress. Nevertheless, research examining real-life witnesses has shown that stress does not always impair memory. Peace and Porter (2004) found that witnesses were able to remember details about an event as long as their memories were elicited using appropriate interviewing procedures (e.g., open-ended questions). Indeed, research examining the best ways to communicate with those who have witnessed a critical incident (e.g., a terror attack) found that transferring control of the interview to the witness was crucial to ensuring a therapeutic jurisprudence ethos of the interview process (Risan, Binder, & Milne, 2016; Smith & Milne, 2018).

In summary, the aim of gathering the initial account is to gather as much information as possible in order to help steer the rest of the investigation. However, it is important that frontline officers realize the importance of gathering accurate information and thus, employ techniques that facilitate rather than hinder memory. Frontline police officers need to be aware of the issues surrounding memory and need to refrain from using quick-fire questioning that contains leading questions. They also need to split witnesses up at the scene (utilizing techniques such as the SAI), avoid providing feedback, and need to take into account the circumstances surrounding the event (e.g., witness intoxication and stress).

At the police station: the formal interview

As discussed earlier in the chapter, witnesses can be interviewed multiple times across an investigation, from the call handler to the frontline officer. When questioned about how many times witnesses are interviewed, 82% of police officers responded with between two and six times (Brown, Lloyd-Jones, & Robinson, 2008). The next stage of the investigation, after the frontline interview, is typically the investigative (formal) interview. This formal interview differs from the call handler and frontline interviews in that it moves forward to not only uncovering what happened and who was responsible, but also to understanding why it happened. The why is particularly important because it helps legal decision makers to assess the grounds of liability (Gabbert et al., 2016). This formal interview like those before it can again lead to the contamination of witness memory. While in an ideal world a witness is interviewed in a neutral environment that is free from distractions, by a police officer that is well trained in interviewing, and who has unlimited time, this is not always possible (Milne & Bull, 2016). Thus, the best memory techniques are not always utilized and memory contamination can occur. Furthermore, research has repeatedly shown that police interviewers make errors that can limit the quantity and accuracy of the information obtained from witnesses (MacDonald, Snook, & Milne, 2017).

One reason memory contamination can be exacerbated during the formal interview is as a result of the length of delay between the encoding of the event and the retrieval of the event. Research has shown that as the period between encoding and retrieval increases, the amount and accuracy of information recalled significantly decreases (Tuckey & Brewer, 2003). A second reason for memory contamination is that the formal interview takes place following the event and so the risk of the witnesses receiving postevent information (e.g., from social media or other witnesses) also increases. One area of particular concern is the use of social media, with witnesses potentially looking up information online that could be incorrect and detrimental to the investigation. Thus, witnesses can mistakenly report information that they have not in reality experienced (both correct and incorrect information). A third reason for memory contamination during the formal interview is as a result of the questions being asked by police officers. As with frontline communication, research has shown that police officers tend to dominate the talk time, ask predominantly closed questions, and thus control the interaction (e.g., MacDonald et al., 2017), even after lengthy training (Griffiths, Milne, & Cherryman, 2011).

To reduce memory contamination, there are a number of evidence-based interview techniques available to the police (e.g., the CI; Geiselman et al., 1984). The CI is a well-established protocol for interviewing witnesses and comprises a series of memory retrieval and communication techniques that are designed to increase the amount of information gathered from a witness (Memon, Meissner, & Fraser, 2010). The original CI consisted of a set of four instructions that were given to the witness by the interviewer. It is based on established psychology principles of remembering and retrieval of information from memory. The CI approach addresses three primary psychological processes that underline interviews with cooperative interviewees: (1) the social dynamics between the witness and interviewer (e.g., rapport building), (2) the witness' and interviewers' cognitive processes (e.g., through use of sketches), and (3) facilitating communication between the witness and the interviewer (e.g., transferring control of information flow). Before outlining the instructions, it is important to note that, when using the CI in the field, it does not have to be applied to all witnesses in the same manner. This is because cognitive and social demands vary across situations and interviewees. For the CI to be effective, it needs to be implemented as a tool box of skills that are used strategically, including only those elements that are appropriate for the specific interview scenario. In addition, these elements can be modified or adapted based on the demands of the incident or witness (Fisher, Milne, & Bull, 2011).

One of the instructions of the CI is "the report everything instruction," which, as mentioned earlier in the chapter, encourages witnesses to report everything they remember, including details they feel irrelevant/trivial (Fisher & Geiselman, 1992; Milne, 2004). The rules of social communication and daily life conversations lead witnesses to think they should not dominate a conversation (Grice, 1975), and so they do not spontaneously report everything they can actually remember (Vrij,

Hope, & Fisher, 2014). Consequently, this instruction helps to promote a detailed response with good quality information as the interviewee realizes that in the formal interview a different set of communication rules apply, some of which are completely opposite to the usual ways of communicating. Another instruction is "the mental reinstatement of context" which asks witnesses to reconstruct in their minds the context, both physical (environmental) and personal (e.g., how they felt at the time) features of the event. Context can have a powerful effect on memory (e.g., in crime reconstructions), but to avoid memory contamination, questions and statements must not be leading or suggestive. Mental reinstatement has been shown to improve recall (Godden & Baddeley, 1975), with additional research showing an increase in the information recalled when witnesses close their eyes (Perfect et al., 2008; Vredeveldt et al., 2015). During the "report everything instruction," the use of sketch plans can be useful, especially if time is of the essence (Dando et al., 2008).

A further instruction is "the recalling of events in a variety of different orders." Once a witness has reported the event, they can be encouraged to report what happened in a variety of sequences (e.g., in reverse order recall from the end to the beginning of the event). This technique aims to counter the reconstructive nature of memory. When witnesses are asked to remember an event, their recall is influenced by prior knowledge, expectations, and the employment of scripts (e.g., what typically happens in certain situations). When an event is freely recalled, most people report the event in real time (i.e., in forward order). When recalling in this way, witnesses may use their script knowledge to help them recall the incident, which results in the recall of information (which maybe correct or incorrect) but in line with the script. Hence, the occurrence of script inconsistent information may not be recalled. The change order instruction invites the witness to examine the actual memory record, which in turn can result in the reporting of additional information which is incidental to the script (Fisher & Geiselman, 1992; Milne, 2016). A final instruction involves witnesses being given "the change perspective technique." People have a tendency to report events from their own psychological perspective, and therefore this technique requires the witness to recall the event from another perspective (e.g., the perpetrator). The change perspective technique has been shown to promote extensive retrieval (Anderson & Pichert, 1978).

In 1992, Fisher and Geiselman published an enhanced version of the CI (ECI) that included a framework for building rapport and communicating effectively with the witness (see Fisher & Geiselman, 1992; Milne & Bull, 1999 for a detailed description). Throughout the interview process, the interviewer is discouraged from interrupting the witness and is instructed to allow the witness to control the flow of information and to listen actively to what the witness has to say. This witness-centered interview approach is a major characteristic of the ECI.

There has been a wealth of laboratory research to document the CI's and ECI's ability to significantly improve the number of correct details recalled, while only slightly increasing the number of incorrect details (Kohnken, Milne, Memon, & Bull, 1999; Memon et al., 2010). In addition, the CI has been incorporated into numerous law enforcement agencies training for police officers worldwide (e.g., Australia, Ireland, Norway, New Zealand) (see Fisher et al., 2011). Research in the field has revealed that police officers trained in the CI gain more detailed information from witnesses (Fisher, Geiselman, & Amador, 1989). However, the CI is rarely implemented in its entirety and thus poor interviewing can still occur. This is due in part to a lack of witness interview training worldwide. For example, research has demonstrated that untrained interviewers, or trained interviewers who do not receive supervision or feedback about their interview techniques, tend to dominate the interview process and ask leading questions (Griffiths et al., 2011). Clifford and George (1996) analyzed real-world witness interviews and found that not one interview had applied all four CI memory enhancement techniques, after receiving a 4-day training session. Memon, Holley, Milne, Kohnken, and Bull (1994) also found that posttraining performance was inadequate, with police officers again not using all the CI techniques. The CI has, however, helped improve the ethos of best practice guidance in terms of questioning with police officers understanding the need to use open-ended questions and to avoid leading questions in their approach to gathering information from witnesses (MacDonald et al., 2016; Milne, Griffiths, Clarke, & Dando, 2019).

Another area that deserves more research attention is the method of recording the witness-police officer interaction. In most countries around the world, a police officer handwrites the witness' account while questioning the witness. The resultant product is a handwritten (or typed) police statement. However, the question that arises is whether or not this handwritten statement provides a true and accurate representation of memory. Research has shown that interviewing and more specifically writing a statement is cognitively demanding for the interviewer, which can result in information being omitted (Gregory, Compo, Vertefeuille, & Zambruski, 2011; Kohnken, Thurer, & Zoberbier, 1994). Moreover, McLean (1992) examined police statements and found that not one contained all the relevant information reported. Even with child witnesses, 25% of the forensically relevant information was missing (Lamb, Orbach, Sternberg, Hershkowitz, & Horowitz, 2000). In a more recent study, Milne, Nunan, Hope, Hodgkins, and Clarke (2017) examined 18 real criminal cases, including the recording and statements that were generated by the police officers. They found an overall accuracy rate of 73.2%. The inaccurate information included 14.5% omission errors, 7.2% new information, 4.8% distortions, and 0.3% contradictions. This is concerning as witnesses do not always detect the changes in information (Milne & Shaw, 1999; Wolchover & Heaton-Armstrong, 1997), which could later be confusing for the witness if they are presented with their statement in court and do not believe it to be a true representation of their original memory. As technology has now advanced somewhat, it is recommended that police officers should record (e.g., through the use of BWV) the statement for transparency and to avoid memory contamination (Westera, Kebbell, & Milne, 2011).

To summarize, the formal interview provides further issues associated with memory contamination. Human memory processes are fragile, and when the time between encoding and retrieval increases the risk of memory error also increases.

Postevent information, such as social media, are providing new challenges for the investigative process and ensuring the information is admissible in court. As with the call handler and frontline communication, appropriate questioning and enhanced interview techniques are essential to maximize the quantity and quality of information reported and recorded. The CI is one enhanced interview technique that is known to be effective, but practitioners need to see this as a flexible tool that can be adapted for use depending on the situation and interviewee. Research looking at the handwritten statement raises the point that all interviews should be recorded.

Conclusions

This chapter has discussed three key interviewing stages of an investigation (i.e., call handling, frontline communication, the formal interview) and the importance of applying cognitive and social psychology principles to this investigative process. Memory is fragile and subject to distortions from a variety of sources. Therefore, practitioners need to be made aware of the limitations of memory and the need to utilize investigative tools that are evidence-based, conducive to memory, and aid in the retrieval of both accurate and comprehensive information. To maximize impact and promote knowledge transfer activities, researchers and practitioners need to come together to disseminate findings, highlight current issues, and develop investigative techniques that are appropriately evaluated and relevant to those working in the field.

References

Ambler, C., & Milne, R. (2006). Call handling centres: An evidential opportunity or threat?. In *Paper presented at the second international investigative interviewing conference, Portsmouth (July, 2006).*

Anderson, R. C., & Pichert, J. W. (1978). Recall of previously unrecallable information following a shift perspective. *Journal of Verbal Learning and Verbal Behavior, 17*(1), 1–12. https://doi.org/10.1016/S0022-5371(78)90485-1.

Ariel, B., Farrar, W. A., & Sutherland, A. (2014). The effect of police body-worn cameras on use of force and citizens' complaints against the police: A randomised controlled trial. *Journal of Quantitative Criminology, 31*(3), 509–535. https://doi.org/10.1007/s10940-014-9236-3.

Brown, C., Lloyd-Jones, T. J., & Robinson, M. (2008). Eliciting person descriptions from eyewitnesses: A survey of police perceptions of eyewitness performance and reported use of interview techniques. *European Journal of Cognitive Psychology, 20*(3), 529–560. https://doi.org/10.1080/90541440701728474.

Campos, L., & Alonso-Quecuty, M. (2006). Remembering a criminal conversation: Beyond eyewitness testimony. *Memory, 14*, 27–36. https://doi.org/10.1080/09658210444000476.

Cialdini, R. B., & Goldstein, N. J. (2004). Social influence: Compliance and conformity. *Annual Review of Psychology, 55*(1), 591–621. https://doi.org/10.1146/annurev.psych.55.090902.142015.

Clifford, B. R., & George, R. (1996). A field evaluation of training in three methods of witness/victim investigative interviewing. *Psychology, Crime and Law, 2*(3), 231–248. https://doi.org/10.1080/10683169608409780.

Clifasefi, S. L., Takarangi, M. K. T., & Bergman, J. S. (2006). Blind drunk: The effects of alcohol on inattentional blindness. *Applied Cognitive Psychology, 20*(5), 697–704. https://doi.org/10.1002/acp.1222.

Dalton, G., & Ang, J. (2014). *An evaluation of how police forces utilise body worn video cameras.* Singapore: Home Team Behavioural Sciences Centre, Research Report: Singapore Police.

Dalton, G., Milne, R., Hope, L., Vernham, Z., & Nunan, J. (2021). 'He was just your typical average guy' Examining how person descriptions are elicited by frontline police officers. *Applied Cognitive Psychology, 35*(2), 517–525. https://doi.org/10.1002/acp.3778.

Dando, C., Wilcock, R., & Milne, R. (2008). The cognitive interview: Inexperienced police officers' perceptions of their witness/victim interviewing practices. *Legal and Criminological Psychology, 13*(1), 59–70. https://doi.org/10.1348/135532506X162498.

Dando, C., Wilcock, R., & Milne, R. (2009). The cognitive interview: Novice police officers' witness/victim interviewing practices. *Psychology, Crime and Law, 15*(8), 679–696. https://doi.org/10.1080/10683160802203963.

Deffenbacher, K. A., Bornstein, B. H., Penrod, S. D., & McGorty, E. K. (2004). A meta-analytic review of the effects of high stress on eyewitness memory. *Law and Human Behavior, 28*(6), 687–706. https://doi.org/10.1007/s10979-004-0565-x.

Deutsch, M., & Gerard, H. B. (1955). A study of normative and informational social influences upon individual judgement. *Journal of Abnormal and Social Psychology, 51*(3), 629–636. https://doi.org/10.1037/h0046408.

Drover, P., & Ariel, B. (2015). Leading an experiment in police body-worn video cameras. *International Criminal Justice Review, 25*(1), 80–97. https://doi.org/10.1177/1057567715574373.

Ekblom, P., & Heal, K. (1982). The police response to calls from the public *(Home Office research and Planning Unit Paper 9).* London: Home Office.

Evans, J. R., Schreiber-Compo, N., & Russano, M. B. (2009). Intoxicated witnesses and suspects: Procedures and prevalence according to law enforcement. *Psychology, Public Policy, and Law, 15*(3), 194–221. https://doi.org/10.1037/a0016837.

Fisher, R. P. (1995). Interviewing victims and witnesses of crime. *Psychology, Public Policy, and Law, 1*(4), 732–764. https://doi.org/10.1037/1076-8971.1.4.732.

Fisher, R. P., Falkner, K. L., Trevisan, M., & McCauley, M. R. (2000). Adapting the cognitive interview to enhance long-term (35 years) recall of physical activities. *Journal of Applied Psychology, 85*(2), 180–189. https://doi.org/10.1037/0021-9010.85.2.180.

Fisher, R. P., & Geiselman, R. E. (1992). *Memory-enhancing techniques for investigative interviewing: The cognitive interview.* Springfield, IL: Charles C. Thomas Books.

Fisher, R. P., Geiselman, R. E., & Amador, M. (1989). Field test of the cognitive interview: Enhancing the recollection of actual victims and witnesses of crime. *Journal of Applied Psychology, 74*(5), 722–727. https://doi.org/10.1037/0021-9010.74.5.722.

Fisher, R. P., Milne, R., & Bull, R. (2011). Interviewing cooperative witnesses. *Current Directions in Psychological Science, 20*(1), 16−19. https://doi.org/10.1177/0963721410396826.

Fisher, R. P., & Schreiber, N. (2007). Interview protocols to improve eyewitness memory. In M. P. Toglia, J. D. Read, D. F. Ross, & R. C. Lindsay (Eds.), *The handbook of eyewitness psychology: Volume 1 Memory for events* (pp. 53−80). Mahwah, NJ: Lawrence Erlbaum Associates.

Frenda, S. J., Nichols, R. M., & Loftus, E. F. (2011). Current issues and advances in misinformation research. *Current Directions in Psychological Science, 20*(1), 20−23. https://doi.org/10.1177/0963721410396620.

Gabbert, F., & Hope, L. (2013). Suggestibility and memory conformity. In A. M. Ridley, F. Gabbert, & D. J. La Rooy (Eds.), *Suggestibility in legal contexts: Psychological research and forensics implications* (pp. 63−83). Chichester: Wiley-Blackwell.

Gabbert, F., Hope, L., Carter, E., Boon, R., & Fisher, R. (2016). The role of initial witness accounts within the investigative process. In G. Ocburgh, T. Myklebust, T. Grant, & R. Milne (Eds.), *Communication in investigative and legal contexts: Integrated approaches from forensic psychology, linguistics and law enforcement* (pp. 107−131). Chichester, UK: Wiley-Blackwell.

Gabbert, F., Hope, L., & Fisher, R. P. (2009). Protecting eyewitness evidence: Examining the efficacy of a self-administered interview tool. *Law and Human Behavior, 33*, 298−307. https://doi.org/10.1007/s10979-008-9146-8.

Gabbert, F., Hope, L., Fisher, R. P., & Jamieson, K. (2012). Protecting against misleading post-event information with a self-administered interview. *Applied Cognitive Psychology, 26*(4), 568−575. https://doi.org/10.1002/acp.2828.

Gabbert, F., Hope, L., La Rooy, D., McGregor, A., Milne, R., & Ellis, T. (2016). Introducing a PEACE-complaint 'structured interview protocol' to enhance the quality of investigative interviews. In *Paper presented at the Ninth international investigative interviewing conference London (June, 2016)*.

Gabbert, F., Memon, A., & Allan, K. (2003). Memory conformity: Can eyewitnesses influence each other's memories for an event? *Applied Cognitive Psychology, 17*, 533−543. https://doi.org/10.1002/acp.885.

Gabbert, F., Memon, A., & Wright, D. B. (2006). Memory conformity: Disentangling the steps toward influence during a discussion. *Psychonomic Bulletin & Review, 13*, 480−485. https://doi.org/10.3758/BF03193873.

Geiselman, R. E., Fisher, R. P., Firstenberg, I., Hutton, L. A., Sullivan, S. J., Avetissian, I. V., et al. (1984). Enhancement of eyewitness memory: An empirical evaluation of the cognitive interview. *Journal of Police Science and Administration, 12*, 74−80.

Godden, D. R., & Baddeley, A. D. (1975). Context-dependent memory in two natural environments: On land and underwater. *British Journal of Psychology, 66*(3), 325−331. https://doi.org/10.1111/j.2044-8295.1975.tb01468.x.

Gregory, A. H., Compo, N. S., Vertefeuille, L., & Zambruski, G. (2011). A Comparison of US police interviewers' notes with their subsequent reports. *Journal of Investigative Psychology and Offender Profiling, 8*(2), 203−215. https://doi.org/10.1002/jip.139.

Grice, H. P. (1975). Logic and conversation. In P. Cole, & J. J. Morgan (Eds.), *Syntax and semantics* (Vol. 3). New York: Academic Press.

Griffiths, A., Milne, R., & Cherryman, J. (2011). A question of control? The formulation of suspect and witness interview strategies by advanced interviewers. *International Journal* of *Police Science and Management, 13*(3), 255–267. https://doi.org/10.1350/ijps.2011.13.3.219.

Harvey, A. J. (2016). When alcohol narrows the field of focal attention. *The Quarterly Journal of Experimental Psychology Section A, 69*(4), 669–677. https://doi.org/10.1080/17470218.2015.1040803.

Harvey, A. J., Kneller, W., & Campbell, A. C. (2013). The effects of alcohol intoxication on attention and memory for visual scenes. *Memory, 21*(8), 969–980. https://doi.org/10.1080/09658211.2013.770033.

Hope, l., Blocksidge, D., Gabbert, F., Sauer, J. D., Lewinski, W., Mirashi, A., et al. (2016). Memory and the operational witness: Police officer recall of firearms encounters as a function of active response role. *Law and Human Behavior, 40*(1), 23–35. https://doi.org/10.1037/lhb0000159.

Hope, L., Gabbert, F., Fisher, R. L., & Jamieson, K. (2014). Protecting and enhancing eyewitness memory: The impact of an initial recall attempt on performance in an investigative interview. *Applied Cognitive Psychology, 28*(3), 304–313. https://doi.org/10.1002/acp.2984.

Hope, L., Lewinski, W., Dixon, J., Blocksidge, D., & Gabbert, F. (2012). Witnesses in action: The effect of physical exertion on recall and recognition. *Psychological Science, 23*(4), 386–390. https://doi.org/10.1177/0956797611431463.

Hope, L., & Sauer, J. D. (2014). Eyewitness memory and mistaken identifications. In M. S. Yves (Ed.), *Investigative interviewing: Handbook of best practices* (pp. 97–124). Toronto: Carswell.

Howe, M. L., Knott, L. M., & Conway, M. A. (2018). *Memory and miscarriages of justice*. New York: Routledge.

Jennings, W. G., Fridell, L. A., & Lynch, M. D. (2014). Cops and cameras: Officer perceptions of the use of body-worn cameras in law enforcement. *Journal of Criminal Justice, 42*, 549–556. https://doi.org/10.1016/j.jcrimjus.2014.09.008.

Johnson, E., & Garner, M. (2003). *Review of FCC call handling procedures for CC21 project* (Unpublished report presented to Kent County Constabulary).

Katz, C. M., Choate, D. E., Ready, J. R., Nuño, L., Kurtenbach, C. M., & Kevin, S. (2014). *Evaluating the impact of officer worn body cameras in the Phoenix police department, final report*. Phoenix, AZ: Arizona State University.

Kebbell, M. R., & Milne, R. (1998). Police officers' perceptions of eyewitness performance in forensic investigations. *The Journal of Social Psychology, 138*(3), 323–330. https://doi.org/10.1080/00224549809600384.

Kohnken, G., Milne, R., Memon, A., & Bull, R. (1999). A meta-analysis on the effects of the cognitive interview. *Psychology, Crime and Law, 5*, 3–27.

Kohnken, G., Thurer, C., & Zoberbier, D. (1994). The cognitive interview: Are the interviewers' memories enhanced too? *Applied Cognitive Psychology, 8*(1), 13–24. https://doi.org/10.1002/acp.2350080103.

Kontogianni, F., Hope, L., Taylor, P. J., Vrij, A., & Gabbert, F. (2018). The benefits of a self-generated cue mnemonic for timeline interviewing. *Journal of Applied Research in Memory and Cognition, 7*, 454–461. https://doi.org/10.1016/j.jarmac.2018.03.006.

Krix, A. C., Sauerland, M., Raymaekers, L. H. C., Memon, A., Quaedflieg, C. W. E. M., & Smeets, T. (2016). Eyewitness evidence obtained with the self-administered interview is unaffected by stress. *Applied Cognitive Psychology, 30*, 103–112. https://doi.org/10.1002/acp.3173.

Lamb, M. E., Orbach, Y., Sternberg, K. J., Hershkowitz, I., & Horowitz, D. (2000). Accuracy of investigators' verbatim notes of their forensic interviews with alleged child abuse victims. *Law and Human Behavior, 24*(6), 699−708. https://doi.org/10.1023/A:1005556404636.

Lane, S. M., Mather, M., Villa, D., & Morita, S. K. (2001). How events are reviewed matters: Effects of varied focus on eyewitness suggestibility. *Memory & Cognition, 29,* 940−947. https://doi.org/10.3758/BF03195756.

Leeney, D. G., & Mueller-Johnson, K. (2012). Examining the forensic quality of police call-centre interviews. *Psychology, Crime and Law, 18*(7), 669−688. https://doi.org/10.1080/1068316X.2010.534478.

Lindsay, D. S. (1990). Misleading suggestions can impair eyewitness ability to remember event details. *Journal of Experimental Psychology: Learning, Memory, and Cognition, 16,* 1077−1083. https://doi.org/10.1037/0278-7393.16.6.1077.

Lipton, J. P. (1977). On the psychology of eyewitness testimony. *Journal of Applied Psychology, 62,* 90−95. https://doi.org/10.1037/0021-9010.62.1.90.

Loftus, E. F. (1979). The malleability of human memory: Information introduced after we view an incident can transform memory. *American Scientist, 67*(3), 312−320.

Loftus, E. F. (2003). Our changeable memories: Legal and practical implications. *Nature Reviews Neuroscience, 4,* 231−234. https://doi.org/10.1038/nrn1054.

Loftus, E. F., & Palmer, J. C. (1974). Reconstruction of automobile destruction − example of interaction between language and memory. *Journal of Verbal Learning and Verbal Behavior, 13,* 585−589. https://doi.org/10.1016/S0022-5371(74)80011-3.

MacDonald, S., Snook, B., & Milne, R. (2017). Witness interview training: A field evaluation. *Journal of Police and Criminal Psychology, 32*(1), 77−84. https://doi.org/10.1007/s11896-016-9197-6.

Malpass, R. S., Tredoux, C. G., Compo, N. S., McQuiston-Surrett, D., Maclin, O. H., Zimmerman, L. A., et al. (2008). Study space analysis for policy development. *Applied Cognitive Psychology, 22*(6), 789−801. https://doi.org/10.1002/acp.1483.

Marsh, E. J., Tversky, B., & Hutson, M. (2005). How eyewitness talk about events: Implications for memory. *Applied Cognitive Psychology, 19,* 531−544. https://doi.org/10.1002/acp.1095.

Mattison, M., Dando, C. J., & Ormerod, T. C. (2018). Drawing the answers: Sketching to support free recall by child witnesses and victims with autism spectrum disorder. *Autism, 22*(2), 181−194. https://doi.org/10.1177/1362361316669088.

McLean, M. (1992). *Identifying Patterns in witness interviews. Unpublished BA (Hons) dissertation, University of Hull.*

Memon, A., Holley, A., Milne, R., Kohnken, G., & Bull, R. (1994). Towards understanding the effects of interviewer training in the evaluating the cognitive interview. *Applied Cognitive Psychology, 8*(7), 641−659. https://doi.org/10.1002/acp.2350080704.

Memon, A., Meissner, C. A., & Fraser, J. (2010). The cognitive interview: A meta-analytic review and study space analysis of the past 25 years. *Psychology, Public Policy, and Law, 16*(4), 340−372. https://doi.org/10.1037/10020518.

Milne, R. (2004). *The enhanced cognitive interview: A step-by-step guide.* Portsmouth: University of Portsmouth.

Milne, R. (2016). *At a glance: The cognitive interview. Centre for research and evidence on security threats guide.* Retrieved from: http://www.crestresearch.ac.uk.

Milne, R., & Bull, R. (1999). *Investigative interviewing: Psychology and practice.* Chichester: Wiley.

Milne, R., & Bull, R. (2002). Back to basics: A componential analysis of the original cognitive interview mnemonics with three age groups. *Applied Cognitive Psychology, 16*, 743−753. https://doi.org/10.1002/acp.825.

Milne, R., & Bull, R. (2006). Interviewing victims of crime, including children and people with intellectual difficulties. In M. R. Kebbell, & G. M. Davies (Eds.), *Practical psychology for forensic investigations*. Chichester: Wiley.

Milne, R., & Bull, R. (2016). Witness interviews and crime investigation. In D. Groome, & M. W. Eysenck (Eds.), *An introduction to applied cognitive psychology*. London: Routledge.

Milne, R., Griffiths, A., Clarke, C., & Dando, C. (2019). The cognitive interview − a tiered approach in the real world. In B. Schwartz, J. Dickenson, N. Schreiber Compo, & M. McCauley (Eds.), Evidence-based investigative interviewing: *Routledge*. in press.

Milne, R., Nunan, J., Hope, L., Hodgkins, J., & Clarke, C. (2017). The whole truth and nothing but the truth: Transforming verbal interviews into written statements. In *Paper presented at the Annual conference of the European association of psychology and law, Mechelen (May, 2017)*.

Milne, R., & Shaw, G. (1999). Obtaining witness statements: The psychology, best practice and proposals for innovation. *Medicine, Science & the Law, 39*(2), 127−138.

Morgan, C. A., Southwick, S., Steffian, G., Hazlett, G. A., & Loftus, E. F. (2013). Misinformation can influence memory for recently experienced, highly stressful events. *International Journal of Law and Psychiatry, 36*(1), 11−17. https://doi.org/10.1016/j.ijlp.2012.11.002.

Morley, J. E., & Farr, S. A. (2012). Hormesis and amyloid-beta protein: Physiology or pathology? *Journal of Alzheimer's Disease, 29*(3), 487−492. https://doi.org/10.3233/JAD-2011-111928.

Myklebust, T., & Alison, L. (2000). The current state of police interviews with children in Norway: How discrepant are they from models based on current issues in memory and communication? *Psychology, Crime and Law, 6*, 331−351. https://doi.org/10.1080/10683160008409810.

O'Neill, M., & Milne, R. (2014). Success within criminal investigations: Is communication a key component? In R. Bull (Ed.), *Investigative interviewing* (pp. 123−146). New York: Springer.

Palmer, F. T., Flowe, H. D., Takarangi, M. T., & Humphries, J. E. (2013). Intoxicated witnesses and suspects: An archival analysis of their involvement in criminal case processing. *Law and Human Behavior, 37*(1), 54−59. https://doi.org/10.1037/lhb0000010.

Peace, K., & Porter, S. (2004). A longitudinal investigation of the reliability of memories for trauma and other emotional experiences. *Applied Cognitive Psychology, 18*(9), 1143−1159. https://doi.org/10.1002/acp.1046.

Perfect, T. J., Wagstaff, G. F., Moore, D., Andrews, B., Cleveland, V., Newcombe, S., et al. (2008). How can we help witnesses to remember more? It's an (eyes) open and shut case. *Law and Human Behavior, 32*(4), 314−324. https://doi.org/10.1007/s10979-007-9109-5.

Pescod, L., Wilcock, R., & Milne, R. (2013). Improving eyewitness memory in police call centre interviews. *Policing: Journal of Policy Practice, 7*, 299−306. https://doi.org/10.1093/police/pat013.

Poyser, S., Nurse, A., & Milne, R. (2018). *Miscarriages of justice: Causes, consequences and remedies*. Bristol: Policy Press.

Risan, P., Binder, P. E., & Milne, R. (2016). Regulating and coping with distress during police interviews of traumatized victims. *Psychological Trauma: Theory, Research, Practice, and Policy, 8*(6), 736–744. https://doi.org/10.1037/tra0000119.

Savage, S., & Milne, R. (2007). Miscarriages of justice – the role of the investigative process. In T. Newburn, T. Williamson, & A. Wright (Eds.), *Handbook of criminal investigation* (pp. 610–627). Cullompton: Willan.

Schooler, J. W. (1994). Seeking the core – the issues and evidence surrounding recovered accounts of sexual trauma. *Consciousness and Cognition, 3*, 452–469. https://doi.org/10.1006/ccog.1994.1026.

Schreiber-Compo, N., Evans, J. R., Carol, R. N., Kemp, D., Ham, L. S., & Rose, S. (2011). Alcohol intoxication and memory for events: A snapshot of alcohol myopia in real-world drinking scenario. *Memory, 19*(2), 202–210. https://doi.org/10.1080/09658211.2010.546802.

Semmler, C., Brewer, N., & Wells, G. L. (2004). Effects of postidentification feedback on eyewitness identification and nonidentification confidence. *Journal of Applied Psychology, 89*(2), 334–346. https://doi.org/10.1037/0021-9010.89.2.334.

Shaw, J. S., Bjork, R. A., & Handal, A. (1995). Retrieval induced forgetting in an eyewitness-memory paradigm. *Psychonomic Bulletin & Review, 2*, 249–253. https://doi.org/10.3758/BF03210965.

Shawyer, A., Milne, R., Dalton, G., May, B., Hope, L., & Gabbert, F. (2018). "My house is on fire" an examination of frontline communication in fire and Rescue control rooms. In *Paper presented at the Eleventh international investigative interviewing conference Porto (July, 2018)*.

Shepherd, E., & Griffiths, A. (2013). *Investigative interviewing: The conversation management approach*. Oxford: Oxford University Press.

Smith, K. M., & Milne, R. (2018). Witness interview strategy for critical incidents (WISCI). *Journal of Forensic Practice*. https://doi.org/10.1108/JFP-03-2018-0007.

Steblay, N. M. (1992). A meta-analytic review of the weapon focus effect. *Law and Human Behavior, 16*(4), 413–424. https://doi.org/10.1007/BF02352267.

Steele, C. M., & Josephs, R. A. (1990). Alcohol myopia: Its prized and dangerous effects. *American Psychologist, 45*(8), 921–933. https://doi.org/10.1037/0003- 066X.45.8.921.

Tuckey, M. R., & Brewer, N. (2003). The influence of schemas, stimulus ambiguity, and interview schedule on eyewitness memory over time. *Journal of Experimental Psychology: Applied, 9*(2), 101–118. https://doi.org/10.1037/1076-898X.9.2.101.

Vredeveldt, A., Tredoux, C. G., Nortje, A., Kempen, K., Puljevic, C., & Labuschagne, G. N. (2015). A field evaluation of the eye-closure interview with witnesses of serious crime. *Law and Human Behavior, 39*(2), 189–197. https://doi.org/10.1037/lhb0000113.

Vrij, A., Hope, L., & Fisher, R. P. (2014). Eliciting reliable information in investigative interviews. *Policy Insights from the Behavioral and Brain Sciences, 1*(1), 129–136. https://doi.org/10.1177/2372732214548592.

Waddington, P. (1993). *Calling the police: The interpretation of, and response to, calls for assistance from the public*. Aldershot, UK: Avebury.

Wells, G. L., Lindsay, R. C. L., & Ferguson, T. J. (1979). Accuracy, confidence and juror perceptions in eyewitness testimony. *Journal of Applied Psychology, 64*(4), 440–448. https://doi.org/10.1037/0021-9010.64.4.440.

Westera, N., Milne, R., & Kebbell, M. (2011). Interviewing witnesses will investigative and evidential requirements ever concord? *The British Journal of Forensic Practice, 13*(2), 103–113. https://doi.org/10.1108/14636641111134341.

Wheeler, R. L., & Gabbert, F. (2017). Using self-generated cues to facilitate recall: A narrative review. *Frontiers in Psychology, 8*, 1830. https://doi.org/10.3389/fpsyg.2017.01830.

White, A. M. (2003). What happened? Alcohol, memory blackouts, and the brain. *Alcohol Research & Health, 27*(2), 186–196.

Whitley, B. E., & Greenberg, M. S. (1986). The role of eyewitness confidence in juror perceptions of credibility. *Journal of Applied Social Psychology, 16*, 387–409. https://doi.org/10.1111/j.1559-1816.1986.tb01148.x.

Wilcock, R., Bull, R., & Milne, R. (2008). *Criminal identification by witnesses: Psychology and practice.* Oxford University Press.

Wixted, J. T., & Ebbesen, E. B. (1997). Genuine power curves in forgetting: A quantitative analysis of individual subject forgetting functions. *Memory & Cognition, 25*, 731–739. https://doi.org/10.3758/BF03211316.

Wolchover, D., & Heaton-Armstrong, A. (1997). Tape-recording witness statements. *New Law Journal, 6*, 855–857.

Wright, A. M., & Alison, L. (2004). Questioning sequences in Canadian police interviews: Constructing and confirming the course of events. *Psychology, Crime and Law, 10*(2), 137–154. https://doi.org/10.1080/1068316031000099120.

Yuille, J. C., & Tollestrup, P. A. (1990). Some effects of alcohol on eyewitness memory. *Journal of Applied Psychology, 75*(3), 268–273. https://doi.org/10.1037/0021-9010.75.3.268.

Zaragoza, M. S., & Lane, S. M. (1994). Source misattributions and suggestibility of eyewitness memory. *Journal of Experimental Psychology: Learning, Memory, and Cognition, 20*(4), 934–945. https://doi.org/10.1037/0278-7393.20.4.934.

Is confession really necessary? The use of effective interviewing techniques to maximize disclosure from suspects

17

Dave Walsh and Paulo Barbosa Marques

A system of criminal law enforcement which comes to depend on the "confession" will, in the long run, be less reliable and more subject to abuses than a system which depends on extrinsic evidence independently secured through skillful investigation.

United States Supreme Court in Escobedo v. Illinois (1964).

Introduction

More than half a century has passed since the abovementioned United States Supreme Court decision recognizing the value of a "skillful investigation," and yet, despite the existence of important safeguards in the contemporary criminal justice systems around the world, innocent suspects often succumb to accusatorial and deceptive interrogation methods (Smalarz, Scherr, & Kassin, 2016).

Psychological theory and research show that adopting an accusatorial interrogation approach is not only ineffective as a strategy for eliciting accurate and complete information but also when combined with confirmation bias, absence of supervision, and poor valuation of the evidence, may well result in false confessions (Gudjonsson, 2021; Vrij et al., 2017).

In the "white paper" on police interrogations and false confessions, Kassin et al. (2010) state the following:

Wrongful convictions based on false confessions raise serious questions concerning a chain of events by which innocent citizens are judged deceptive in interviews and misidentified for interrogation; waive their rights to silence and to counsel; and are induced into making false narrative confessions that form a sufficient basis for subsequent conviction.

Police Psychology, Edited by Marques and Paulino. https://doi.org/10.1016/B978-0-12-816544-7.00017-6

According to Leo (2008), false confessions start with the police. Once a confession is obtained during the interrogation process, criminal investigators tend to close their investigation, deem the case solved, and become extremely reluctant to expend further investigative efforts to strengthen the evidence in the case or to pursue any exculpatory evidence or other possible leads—even if the confession is internally inconsistent, is contradicted by external evidence, or is the result of coercive interrogation.

These biased police practices violate universal principles of criminal justice such as *in dubio pro reo*, which requires that defendants are *presumed* to be *innocent*, until proved to be otherwise guilty by the prosecution. This rule, stating that in doubt you must decide in favor of the defendant, means that *presumption of innocence* must be defeated by proof of guilt *beyond a reasonable doubt* before guilt can be regarded as established and a conviction can take place.

If we want to ensure that criminal investigations are not based upon preconceived beliefs or conclusions as to guilt or innocence but are guided by the facts, it is vital to establish the purposes of a criminal investigation.

According to Milne and Bull (2006), the key aim of an investigation is to establish the answer to two primary questions: (i) "What happened?" (if anything did happen) and (ii) "Who did it?"

Investigators need to perform a vast array of methodological and systematic procedures when undertaking criminal investigations. Inherent in such tasks are a keen attention to detail, good communication skills, and the ability to gather accurate and fulsome information from a number of sources (Innes, 2003; O'Neill & Milne, 2014). Therefore, if the investigators intend to gain relevant information from a suspect, they need to be able to interview appropriately.

The questioning of criminal suspects is a specialist task that can be very demanding. In many countries around the world, before the interview starts, every suspect must be informed of their right to silence and to seek legal advice. Under these circumstances, it requires great skill, and sometimes creativity, to obtain information relevant to criminal investigations without infringing on suspects' rights. The absence of training and expertise in investigative interviewing in several jurisdictions hinders the acquisition of advanced interview skills, resulting in the use of improper interviewing techniques often learned on the job (Marques & Milne, 2019). Moreover, many law enforcement agencies around the world have long advocated a "confession culture," characterized by the use of accusatorial and often "persuasive" interrogation techniques in the quest of a confession (Kassin et al., 2007; Leo, 2008; Meissner et al., 2014). Such techniques may violate suspects' rights and are more likely to elicit false confessions (Garrett, 2010; Gudjonsson, 2018; Kassin et al., 2010; Kassin & Gudjonsson, 2004).

Although it may be difficult to estimate the precise incidence rate of false confessions, there exist a disturbing number of documented cases in which defendants were convicted at trial in cases that contained evidence of confessions later proved to be false (Drizin & Leo, 2004; Garrett, 2010; Leo, 2008; Leo & Ofshe, 1998).

In the last decades, the scientific community has been working on this matter, and studies have accumulated that demonstrate the effectiveness of information-gathering approaches as an effective alternative to accusatorial interrogations. Research has demonstrated that such an information-gathering approach to suspect interviewing can significantly reduce the likelihood of false confessions (Meissner et al., 2014).

This accumulated knowledge has promoted the implementation of important reforms in police practices with regard to interviewing suspects. One good example of these developments is the creation of the PEACE model of investigative interviewing in England and Wales, a framework that we will further discuss in this chapter.

From obtaining a confession to establishing truth

Interviews with suspects of crime are an important element of police investigations. As advised earlier, they can be crucial in helping establish whether or not a ciminal act has occurred and may well provide evidence that enables the resolution of the criminal investigation. If the police gain admissions from suspects of wrongdoing, this might, on the face of it, reinforce the belief that they were right to suspect them. However, a reliance on confessions as the single or major influence in determining guilt has been found to be misplaced. Several countries (e.g., Norway, the United States of America, and the United Kingdom) report cases where confessions have been made to the police, and people have been convicted of crimes, only to find later that those convictions have to be overturned in light of new evidence (including that which led to the conviction of the actual perpetrator). Such events have led us to rightly question the purpose of police interrogations with suspects. They have also prompted inquiry as to whether the pursuit of confessions in such interviews is appropriate and whether the police's role is to search for the truth, including that where the outcome of the investigation may well suggest that a person is innocent. In this chapter, we examine one such country (England and Wales), where *interrogations* with suspects were once viewed primarily as opportunities to gain confessions from suspects. We detail an approach—*investigative interviewing*—that has led to such confessions being considered as less important to the resolution of criminal investigations, and where miscarriages of justice caused by unethical and coercive interviewing techniques (known to elicit false confessions) to be almost consigned to history (Poyser, Nurse, & Milne, 2018).

The emergence of investigative interviewing in England and Wales

Prior to the 1990s, the training of police officers concerning as to how to undertake interviews with victims, witnesses, or suspects in England and Wales broadly amounted to them learning from their more experienced colleagues (typically by watching these senior colleagues conduct such interviews). This had been the situation for many generations of police officers in this country. To the extent that police officers learned the established way of interviewing people, such an approach to training was fulfilled. Whether this approach was successful in prompting good interview techniques is, of course, quite another matter. Regardless, the effects of an introduction in that country of legislation that governed the rights of people detained by the police for questioning as criminal suspects (namely, the Police and Criminal Evidence Act 1984; henceforth, PACE) meant that such cascading from the experienced to the novice was no longer feasible. That is, PACE outlawed practices by the police that were found to be commonplace before its introduction (see, for example, Irving, 1980). These practices were also the ones that may well trigger either false confessions or accounts from interviewees (particularly from vulnerable ones). The techniques that were found to be of concern included the police advising suspects that they possessed evidence that in fact was not to hand (or overstating the strength of that evidence), being aggressive and accusatory, and undermining the suspect's self-esteem. In short, the aim of interviews with suspects was to gain confirmation of the police's belief in their guilt (Irving, 1980; Softley, Brown, Forde, Mair, & Moxon, 1980).

As a consequence of the implementation of PACE, police officers in England and Wales could no longer undertake such practices (and soon after the introduction of PACE, interviews with suspects were audio recorded, providing an evidential record of what the police did do in interviews with suspects). Importantly, senior officers could no longer pass these problematic techniques on to their junior counterparts. Police officers, irrespective of their experience, were then being told what they could no longer do (though not necessarily, why), and moreover, they were not advised as to what they could (or should) do. They deserved better. Studies carried out on police interviews with suspects in England and Wales, conducted at the turn of the 1990s, found those practices that were often demonstrated before the introduction of PACE had largely disappeared (Baldwin, 1993; Moston, Stephenson, & Williamson, 1992). However, these studies also found that police officers still continued to seek confessions as the main aim of these interviews, with little time spent on gathering an account from suspects. These interviewers were also generally assessed as being ineffective (Baldwin, 1993; Moston et al., 1992). An explanation for this malaise is argued to be that while those unethical practices found to be used by interviewers before the introduction of PACE were now outlawed, the motivation behind their usage (i.e., to gain confessions from suspects "known to the police as being guilty") had not. This attitude drove both interviewing and investigative practices. In Moston et al. (1992) study, the police were found to spend little time in gaining the suspects' side of the story. Instead, they were accusatory from the outset of the interview, very often revealing all the information/evidence in the early stages of the interview expecting or hoping that the suspect would just acknowledge their "guilt" and confess. Invariably, in this large-scale study that involved examination of over 1000 tape-recorded interviews (undertaken in the period 1989–90), suspects did not confess (probably because they saw the totality of the evidence and concluded it was weak). Baldwin (1993) also found a tendency for interviewers to employ confession-oriented strategies (again largely unsuccessfully employed) among the 600 tape-recorded interviews undertaken in the same time period as that of Moston and colleagues study. Only rarely in these studies was it found that suspects changed their position from that of initially denying allegations to that of admitting their involvement (and even more rare was such a shift in position due to police officers' interviewing skills).

Matters began to change in the early 1990s with the onset of a new training course rolled out across England and Wales. This 5-day course gave officers the basics of levels of awareness (and limited amount of opportunity to trial it under simulated conditions) of a framework called the PEACE model. This term was an acronym for the five phases of the framework. That is, **p**reparation and **p**lanning before the interview, **e**ngaging with the interviewee and **e**xplaining what the respective roles were to be expected of all those present during the interview, before gathering an **a**ccount (and if needed, clarifying and challenging that account), and then finally **c**losing the interview. Thereafter, an **e**valuation would be expected to take place both of the case and of the officer's own interview performance. Such training was the first time that officers in England and Wales had received formal coaching as to how undertake interviews.

The PEACE framework has been adopted in similar forms in other countries (such as Australia and New Zealand, Norway, the Republic of Ireland, and Canada, see Walsh, Oxburgh, Redlich, & Myklebust, 2016b). What is common about all these models is that they are underpinned by an aim of gaining, not confessions, but a detailed and reliable account from interviewees. As such, the framework would underpin interviews, whether with victims, witnesses, or suspects. In England and Wales, various studies have examined use of the framework in actual interviews conducted by police officers or other criminal investigators (see Clarke & Milne, 2001; Griffiths & Milne, 2006; Griffiths, Milne, & Cherryman, 2011; Leahy-Harland & Bull, 2017; Oxburgh, Williamson, & Ost, 2006; Soukara, Bull, Vrij, Turner, & Cherryman, 2009; Walsh & Bull, 2010, 2012a, 2012b, 2015; Walsh & Milne, 2008). Consistent across these studies was the findings that the malpractices that were often seen before the introduction of PACE (that were noted earlier) were rarely in occurrence after the introduction of the PEACE model. As such, the ethos of PEACE as an interview technique that respects interviewees is nonoppressive, is not confession oriented, and (thus) noncoercive and seems to have become an essential part of the investigative interviewing paradigm.

Developing an evidence base for the PEACE framework

While the PEACE model has come to be viewed as a framework possessing those above principles, concerns emerged that it was less clear as a procedural tool (particularly when it was first introduced). For example, guidance as to how to develop good questioning strategies was not obvious. That is to say that even though the PEACE model recommended open questioning types (and the avoidance of leading questions), it remained open to conjecture what (i) open questions were (see Oxburgh, Myklebust, & Grant, 2010); (ii) what other good question types were (and what were not); and (iii) (more importantly) what strategies were effective when using the array of question types (Griffiths & Milne, 2006). Nor was it clear how all the recommended techniques of the PEACE framework worked together (Kelly, Redlich, Miller, & Kleinman, 2013). Indeed, many studies (e.g., Clarke & Milne, 2001; Walsh & Bull, 2010) commonly found problems in its use in practice, such as those relating to investigators (i) providing intermittent and final summaries; (ii) developing a logical structure to the interview; and (iii) closing the interview effectively. Furthermore, rapport building was something that was often found in those studies of interviewer practice to be demonstrated ineffectively. Further, the matter that various definitions have been given in the literature as to what rapport building actually is, there was little guidance as to what interviewers should do to both build and maintain rapport.

Aside from such issues pertaining to how to deliver good interview techniques, it has also been found in practice that there are concerns relating two of the framework's five fundamental components (i.e., Planning and Preparation and Evaluation). Firstly, planning and preparation has been often found to be misunderstood and underutilized (see Clarke & Milne, 2001; Walsh & Milne, 2007). Yet, there has been an association found between its undertaking and the interview aim of gaining comprehensive information/evidence (Walsh & Bull, 2010). Walsh and Milne (2007) and Walsh and Bull (2011) both found that such inattention to this groundwork task was explained by interviewers as their having insufficient time to undertake the task (though they recognized and accepted that planning and preparation was an important task to fulfill). However, Kim, Walsh, Bull, and Bergstrom (2018) found in their study of South Korean investigators that investigators' propensity to plan was less associated with perceived time pressures, but more so with (i) organizational cultures (e.g., overt or more subtle messages that signal to interviewers that interview planning is not always necessary); (ii) officers' beliefs in their own ability to interview effectively without planning; and (iii) officers suggesting that they often conduct interviews having already made enough investigative enquiries and evidence gathering to know what had happened (without entertaining other possibilities or testing their hypothesis robustly).

Taken together, these factors of organizational culture, self-estimation of skills, and an apparent early need for cognitive closure (Kim, Alison, & Christiansen, 2020; Kruglanski & Fishman, 2009) were found in the Kim et al. (2018) study to be associated with encouraging negligence to the task of planning interviews. Furthermore, prior studies (Walsh & Bull, 2011; Walsh & Milne 2007) had found that investigators believe that most of the time they know that the suspect was guilty before they entered the interview room, contrary to the one of the main principles of the PEACE framework of retaining an open mind. Such presumptions of guilt are also thought to lead to insufficient preparation (and most probably these presumptions also lead their making insufficient investigative enquiries and failing to gather enough information/evidence because too often investigators likely had exercised during investigation this early need for cognitive closure). Nevertheless, how investigators make decisions during investigations, including how they assess incoming information and evidence and judge what further enquiries to make, remains a vastly underresearched area of study. One exception is that of Fahsing and Ask (2013), who found that open-mindedness that was initially exhibited by investigators when conducting homicide investigations tended to fade as prime suspects became identified. The consequence of the development by investigators of generating a single hypothesis (or one too that is prematurely generated), as to what happened to whom and by whom, and its impact on subsequent investigative interviews with suspects thus become obvious. That is, they are often the cause of investigative failure (see Rossmo, 2009).

Moreover (with regard to the second neglected area of research of the PEACE model that concerns the task of evaluation), both Walsh, King, and Griffiths (2017) and Griffiths and Walsh (2018) found self-assessments by investigators of their own skill levels to be consistently exaggerated when compared to independent assessments. In brief, investigators are not always good evaluators of their own interview performance (the second aforementioned concern with the basic steps of the PEACE framework). Indeed, as has been noted in Walsh et al. (2017), officers received little or no training in the evaluation task (as it related to the assessment of performance), and thus unsurprisingly admitted to undertaking evaluation only rarely, if at all (Walsh & Bull, 2010; Walsh & Milne, 2007). It can also be reasonably assumed that such little attention to the task of evaluation in training would mean interviewers placing insufficient emphasis on its undertaking. Those studies also found that investigators rarely received received much feedback on their performance from, say, their supervisors (see also Clarke & Milne, 2001).

Feedback on performance has been found in training and educational domains as an important feature of sustaining performance and skill learned in the training room. Equally, the tendency to be a reflective practitioner is a vital element not only of professionalism but also in longer term skills maintenance too. The point being that such neglect of attention to the evaluation element of the PEACE model may be connected to the continuing mediocrity of investigative interviewing, often found in field studies (see Walsh & Bull, 2010). Finally, it was more often than not those investigators, assessed independently as performing least skillfully in the study conducted by Walsh et al. (2017), that were found least likely both to be reflective of their own performance and also to offer action plans for self-improvement (Griffiths & Walsh, 2018). In that later study, there was a tendency found for these least skillful investigators to merely describe their performance (frequently inaccurately), attributing blame for any shortfalls (where they did acknowledge them) on matters they perceived as being outside of their control.

Notwithstanding these issues, the PEACE framework was largely embraced by investigative practitioners as it provided (for the first time) a structure for their undertaking of interviews. It also began to provide direction as to how to undertake interviews that promoted an ethical approach (while avoiding unethical interviewer behaviors). The framework also importantly promoted the idea that interviews with suspects were not confession oriented, but paid emphasis to an approach where the goals were those of obtaining detailed and reliable information from all interviewees. Hand in glove with these emerging developments was the usage of the term investigative interviewing, associated with information gathering approaches to questioning interviewees (such as PEACE), in contrast to the confrontational and accusatorial ones of interrogation. Nevertheless, the PEACE framework was absent of an evidence base as a forensic interview model upon its initial introduction, though many of the techniques were culled from social and cognitive psychology that had been previously utilized in other domains (such as counseling).

Reviews of the PEACE framework being conducted by investigators in the field have been undertaken (see Clarke & Milne, 2001; Griffiths & Milne, 2006; Soukara, Bull, Vrij, Turner, & Cherryman, 2009; Walsh & Bull, 2010, 2012a, 2012b, 2015; Walsh & Milne, 2007). Each of these studies has found that investigators no longer use those unethical tactics, found so present in interviews with suspects before the 1990s (that have often been reported as being associated with prompting false confessions). In short, they found information gathering by interviewers to be the foremost approach. At the same time, common concerns with interview skills were revealed in the separate studies that have already been noted in this chapter (such as rapport building, developing logical interview structures, and questioning strategies). Griffiths (2008), in his PhD thesis, also noted that these particular techniques (regularly noted as problematic for investigators to deploy skillfully in practice) were those he defined as higher order ones (because of their complexity). These particular techniques have also been noted as ones that investigators are least likely to mention when reflecting on their performance (Griffiths & Walsh, 2018). Since the task of reflection (as part of evaluating one' own performance) is known to be a key component in addressing areas for improvement of professional practice, their absence when undertaking such considerations might indicate investigator avoidance (or even nonrealization of the importance) of these more demanding aspects of interviewing.

Challenges to interviewers when conducting investigative interviews: rapport building

There have been, around the world, proliferation studies over the last 20 years or so that have been conducted that concern police interviews (both in vivo and in vitro). This part of this chapter will now cover some of these more recent studies that have examined (what has been argued to be) these more challenging interview tasks, starting with rapport building.

Definitions in the literature of rapport have not always been uniform. However, they have been found to cluster around that of a "working alliance" (Vanderhallen, Vervaeke, & Holmberg, 2011) that involves mutuality both of trust and respect between interview protagonists (Russano, Narchet, Kleinman, & Meissner, 2014). A further definition of rapport that has been regularly employed when examining investigative interviews is that of Tickle-Degnen and Rosenthal (1990), based on a theoretical model of rapport used in the therapeutic literature that encompasses aspects of positivity, mutual attentiveness (i.e., mutual interest in each other's goals and needs), and coordination. While nuanced differences in rapport definitions persist, there is a general agreement, which has been forged through the literature, as to the benefits of both building and maintaining rapport in interviews. Such benefits have been those pertaining to the gathering of more complete (and more reliable) information (Redlich, Kelly, & Miller, 2014; Walsh & Bull, 2012a). Further, using measures drawn from Miller and Rollnick's (2002) *motivational interviewing* paradigm, rapport in interviews with actual terrorist suspects has been found to overcome initial resistance (Alison, Alison, Noone, Entlib, & Christiansen, 2013). Additionally, rapport that has developed between interviewers and suspects has been found believed to help facilitate a pathway to suspects of serious crimes providing reliable confessions of their wrongdoing (Holmberg & Christianson, 2002; Kebbell, Alison, Hurren, & Mazerolle, 2010; Leahy-Harland & Bull, 2017). Furthermore, both interviewers and their interviewees consider rapport to be a fundamental requirement of interviews in assisting their working relationships (Goodman-Delahunty, Martschuk, & Dhami, 2014). In Alison et al. (2013) study, it was found that highly skilled interpersonal techniques significantly built rapport, whereas aggressive approaches (which the authors coined as "tough tactics") failed to do so, with those latter interview types often failing to achieve much either by way of cooperation or information.

Despite such consistency in the research as to the value of the inclusion of rapport in investigative interviews as an aid to create the climate where more information is provided by suspects, it has not always been found to be present when they are conducted. For example, in one study that examined the benefits of developing rapport, Walsh and Bull (2012a) examined 142 interviews conducted in the field. They found that interviews often overlooked opportunities to build rapport in the opening stages of an interview. Furthermore, interviewers made little effort to sufficiently ensure suspects understood their rights in the interview. The researchers found that this not only was a missed opportunity for rapport development but also reflected little regard toward suspects as to whether it mattered to interviewers that suspects understood their rights. That is, Walsh and Bull found that the officers advising suspects of their rights of interviewees were often spoken in a very scripted and mechanical fashion (probably to avoid interviewers getting the words or their meaning wrong). Once these rights had been given, interviewees were then invited by their interviewers to confirm their understanding, which they almost always provided in the affirmative (being the expected answer given by suspects believed to appear socially acquiescent and to avoid being viewed as either uncooperative or even stupid). In their study, Walsh and Bull noted that more skilled approaches tended to occur when interviewers meticulously went through the explanation of the rights incrementally to suspects, and in harmony with them, explaining (and duly empathizing with) the difficulties when suspects encountered the complexities involved in their understanding of their rights. When returning to definitions of rapport, it was such mutuality of cooperation between interviewers and interviewees in their striving for common goals (of ensuring suspects demonstrated understanding of their rights) that was often the platform for the establishment of subsequent rapport.

However, even when in these early stages of the interview rapport had been built, Walsh and Bull (2012a) found that it was not always the case that it was maintained. Tasks that were seen in some interviews as a continuance of the working alliance as the interview progressed were often undertaken in an unskillful manner. Indeed, their study found that 40% of those interviews where rapport had been rated as at least satisfactory in the opening stages (that is, the Engage and Explain phase of the PEACE model), were found to deteriorate, when the level of rapport skills was assessed in the subsequent Account phase. Interestingly, this study also found that interviews which did not commence with particularly good levels of rapport (caused, say, by either the nervousness or anxiety either of the interviewer or the interviewee, or both) could in time develop rapport with one another, as these anxieties eased. Indeed, interviews (where rapport in the Account phase was rated as being either good or excellent in that study, regardless of its earlier quality) were associated with significantly greater levels of information yield from interviewees, when compared to those interviews, where rapport was rated as unsatisfactory or poor in that Account phase. Further, in those interviews where rapport was rated either good or excellent in both Engage and Explain phases and the Account phase were over five times more likely to achieve the recommended goals of investigative interviewing (that is, the obtaining of comprehensive information) than those interviews where rapport was consistently unacceptable throughout its duration. Among the tasks in the Account phase, which Walsh and Bull found in their study to be often less skillfully undertaken by interviewers (which resulted in the undermining of rapport), were those concerned with the revealing of evidence or information held, confronting suspects with apparent inconsistencies (either with the evidence held or with what the suspects had already said), and also how interviewers dealt with resistance. We will return to these matters later in this chapter.

It is important to note here that not all suspects were found uncooperative and indeed, on a wider perspective, not all resistance should be viewed as signs of suspects concealing their guilt. In regard to the latter, Kebbell, Hurren, and Mazerolle (2006) conducted a small scale study in Australia with convicted sex offenders and found that only 20% of these offenders said that they entered interviews with a firm denial strategy, while half of their sample said they were undecided at that initial stage (with the remaining 30% advising that they had decided that they would admit their guilt). The authors found such decisions among the "undecided" half rested on the manner as to how they were treated in the interview. Those offenders, who said they felt that their interviewers were nonjudgmental and respectful, advised that they acknowledged their wrongdoing in the interviews. This finding is consistent with the study conducted in Sweden by Holmberg and Christianson (2002) also involving convicted offenders. In that study, an association was found between interviewing styles and the propensity to acknowledge guilt in the interview. That is, those, who said that their interviewers adopted an approach characterized by a humanitarian style, were more likely to be found as those who confessed when being questioned, whereas those interviewers (described by offenders as being either dominant or aggressive) were found significantly less associated with interviews that resulted in confessions.

Challenges to interviewers when conducting investigative interviews: disclosing evidence

The attitudes of interviewers are unlikely to be by themselves the sole pivot on which suspects confess. What tactics interviewers actually undertake in interviews with suspects is also reckoned important. In the United States of America, Leo (1996) had found that certain tactics used extensively in around two thirds of those 182 interviews examined in his study had led to suspects to providing information that incriminated them in criminal activity (and also promoted either partial or full confessions). One of these tactics, found in over 90% of the interviews, was the police *emphasizing contradictions*, either between the various statements the suspects provided or with the evidence they had in their possession. Other tactics, found equally as prominent in Leo's study, was *offering the suspect a moral justification or psychological excuse* and also *praise or flattery* and *appealing to the suspect's conscience*. In another study, Walsh and Bull (2012b) also analyzed how interviewers attempted to overcome suspects' denials as to suspected wrongdoing. They found that suspects who began interviews with denials and then partially or fully changed their perspectives toward confession did so when interviewers used a range of tactics that were consistent with those prescribed by the PEACE model (particularly when they used them skillfully). Those techniques not favored with the PEACE framework (because of their oppressive nature that could prompt false confessions, such as *maximization, minimization, intimidation, or scenario suggesting*) were very rarely found in Walsh and Bull's (2012b) study. Indeed, when, in those rare circumstances, they were found to be present, they were not found associated with any confession shifts. Indeed, these tactics were found to increase suspects' resistance. Moreover, of those techniques that were found in their study to have a positive relationship with movements toward confessions, it was the *"disclosure of evidence"* that was found most associated with acknowledgments by suspects of their wrongdoing.

The matter of disclosing evidence and its relationships with confessions in interviews has also featured in other studies. For example, Bull and Soukara (2010) examined the techniques undertaken by interviewers during each 5-minute segment throughout 40 interviews. Their sample was particularly selected since it was known that the suspect in those interviews had first denied any wrongdoing (only to admit to the same later in the interview). Bull and Soukara noted in these particular time segments that, either at the point of confession or in the 10 minutes prior to confessions, certain interviewer techniques were always evident in those interviews. While, as in Leo's (1996) study, *emphasizing contradictions* was often found utilized as a tactic by interviewers in these important time segments, the use of *open questions* and the undertaking of *evidence disclosure* (again) were also found to be always present. Associations between disclosing strong evidence and confessions from suspects have been found in several studies (Cassell & Hayman, 1996; Gudjonsson & Petursson, 1991; Kebbell et al., 2006; Moston et al., 1992; Sellers & Kebbell, 2009; Soukara et al., 2009; Walsh & Bull, 2012b).

Further, other studies analyzing various methods of evidence disclosure in interviews with suspects have been undertaken. These studies have found associations with increased information yielded from suspects (Bull & Leahy-Harland, 2012; Nystedt, Nielsen, & Kleffner, 2011; van der Sleen, 2009). Yet other studies have found that certain evidence disclosure strategies appear to optimize (more than other strategies) how credible are the accounts given by suspects (Dando, Bull, Ormerod, & Sandham, 2013; Granhag, Strömwall, Willén, & Hartwig, 2012; Hartwig, Granhag, Strömwall, & Kronkvist, 2006; Hartwig, Granhag, Strömwall, & Vrij, 2005; Sorochinski et al., 2014). However, while these range of studies all reflect the importance of evidence disclosure, it is less understood as to what particular methods of evidence disclosure are more effective than others.

In brief, the literature indicates there are essentially three methods of disclosure of evidence, being "early," "late," or "gradual." A more detailed explanation of these three different strategies has been provided by Bull (2014). In brief, "early" disclosure, as it might be imagined, refers to that evidence being wholly revealed shortly after the interview has commenced (Moston et al., 1992; Sellers & Kebbell, 2009; Leo, 1996). Sellers and Kebbell (2009) found that confessions by suspects were likely to occur in interviews where evidence was introduced at the interview's commencement, especially in those instances when suspects (in their laboratory-based study) viewed the evidence as persuasively powerful. This finding was in concert with that of an earlier study that was conducted by the police in England and Wales prior to the police being trained in the PEACE model (i.e., Moston et al., 1992) who also found suspects being advised at the outset of the interview of the evidence against them and then being asked for them to admit their guilt. Only when the evidence was viewed as strong were such admissions forthcoming. In almost all other interviews in Moston et al. (1992) study, suspects maintained a denial strategy in the face of repeated accusations by their interviewers. Often, in the face of these repeated denials from suspects, the interviewers gave up such lines of questioning and closed the interview.

Walsh and Bull (2015) found that interviews, where the evidence was introduced early, lasted significantly shorter than those where evidence was introduced either later in the interview or gradually. This may well be indicative that once the evidence had been fully disclosed early that there was little room for interviewers to add more (when that evidence was met with denials). On the one hand (having seen the evidence), the suspect denied any offending or in sight of the evidence could adjust their story to fit the disclosed evidence. Regardless, the interviewer had very few strategies remaining as to how to deal with such denials, while (on the other hand) if there was a confession, then the interview would come quickly thereafter to a close (since the interviewer's goal had apparently been obtained). Walsh, Milne, and Bull (2016a) found that investigators, expressing preference to disclose evidence early, said their choice was predicated on a confession strategy. More dangerously, early disclosure of evidence might prompt highly vulnerable suspects to change their stories and make false confession to fit with that evidence disclosed, no matter how inaccurate or incomplete that evidence was in revealing the full story (see Gudjonsson, 2003, for a full account of both "memory distrust syndrome" and "coerced-internalized" confessions). As if to emphasize the limited efficacy of early disclosure strategies, Walsh and Bull (2015) found that these early evidence disclosure interviews were conducted less skillfully and obtained less information than those interviews where the evidence was revealed either "later" or "gradually." Further, it was found that, despite that officers having stated that their apparent aim of providing such early evidence revelations is to gain quick admissions of guilt (see Walsh, Milne, & Bull, 2016a), these interviews were largely unsuccessful in actually prompting confessions from suspects.

The development of the SUE approach and the concerns with later evidence disclosure

Turning to "late" disclosure of evidence in interviews, this approach involves revealing the evidence, but only after a comprehensive account has been first sought from suspects (who are unaware of what, if any, evidence is possessed by the investigators that shows their possible involvement in the crime). Interviewers undertake a strategy that is said to ensure exhaustive coverage of all possible alibis and excuses before disclosing what evidence they held (Hartwig et al., 2005, 2006; Sorochinski et al., 2014). Defined as the Strategic Use of Evidence approach (or SUE), Hartwig et al. (2006) found that such "late" disclosure of evidence enabled investigators to be more accurate in detecting whether suspects were either lying or telling the truth (than was the case in their study where interviewers revealed evidence "early"). Indeed, while the scenario in their experiment was relatively simple, detection rates of lying were found at unprecedented rates of 85%, when compared to the literature (where rates are often found to hover around levels of chance). In explaining such findings, it is thought that interviewers (by not revealing what they knew) allowed suspects to make statements, which were either consistent or in contradiction with the as yet undisclosed evidence to hand. As such, suspects would have little room to satisfactorily explain any contradictions between what they have said and what then they came to learn that the interviewer actually knows, once the evidence held was revealed. Whether in real-life interviews suspects are regularly ignorant of the evidence what they know or believe that the police may hold is highly speculative. It is suspected as more the case that suspects may well provide information in interviews that accommodate such knowledge or suspicions. More research needs to be conducted that accommodates such likely realities. Furthermore, not all lies uncovered by interviewers in real-life cases reflect the guilt of suspects. Some suspects lie not to cover their own guilt, but to protect others (and indeed themselves) from repercussions should the truth emerge.

Nevertheless, there remains much in the SUE approach that is appealing. However, such potential in its undertaking in practice might be compromised somewhat by the increasing incidence of legal representation in interviews. Lessons from England and Wales may thus be salutary. Here, lawyers have had the right to be present in all interviews with suspects for well over 30 years. A picture has emerged that withholding evidence until later in interviews leads invariably to legal advice being given to suspects by their lawyers to make no comment in the face of police questioning. In response, investigators in this country have developed strategies to attempt to avoid suspects' silence in interviews (though there has been little research examining whether these attempts are successful). Regardless, officers tend to provide, before the interview commences, at least some details of the evidence held against them to their lawyers (and presumably, then relayed to suspects) ahead of the forthcoming interviews. Of course, lawyers may still advise suspects to make no replies when police officers ask questions, even in these circumstances where some evidence has been revealed by investigators to lawyers before the interview begins. Irrespective as to whether suspects choose to give answers to questions asked of them by the police, the matter remains that suspects may well have details of at least some of the evidence held against them. In that context, the SUE approach may become less effective, relying as it does on suspects' uttered contradictions and consistencies with the evidence that investigators have in their possession (of which suspects are thought to be unaware). That said, when suspects are highly cooperative, though deceitful, in interviews, the SUE approach holds much potential in identifying statement credibility. Withheld evidence, on the other hand, that is subsequently revealed only later to suspects when being interviewed may disrupt either rapport or cooperation (Goodman-Delahunty et al., 2014).

Legal representation of suspects in interviews and evidence disclosure

Sukumar, Wade, and Hodgson (2016) point out that this matter of disclosure to lawyers is not just an issue discrete to England and Wales. That is, suspects across all member states of the European Union have a fundamental legal right to know what information/evidence is held as a basis of their being detained (Council Directive 2012/13/EU on the access to information in criminal proceedings [2012] OJ L142/1) (Sukumar, Wade, & Hodgson, 2016). Wider still is the European Court of Human Rights (whose jurisdiction covers all 47 countries in the European Economic Area) where failure to advise the suspect of the possessed evidence has been argued to be a violation of their human rights under its Article 6; the right to a fair trial (and that includes those pretrial dimensions of police interviews). However, what is less prescriptive (and more the basis of argument between psychological and legal researchers, see Sukumar, Wade, & Hodgson, 2016) in these contexts is the specific amount of detailed information that suspects are entitled to receive before they are interviewed, whether they have their lawyer in attendance or they have elected not to be legally represented (reckoned to be around a half of those detained for questioning in England and Wales). Irrespective of one's standpoint in this matter, it remains that an increasing number of countries are incorporating into procedures this legal right of preinterview disclosure of held evidence. Sukumar, Wade, and Hodgson (2016) enquire whether there is scope within legal frameworks for certain disclosure to take place that might provide sufficient to enable suspects (and where applicable, their lawyers) to understand why they are suspected of involvement in a crime, but for certain key details to be held back by the police for them to be positioned to test the truthfulness of suspects during interviews.

What is revealed by investigators (and whether certain strategies are undertaken) prior to interviews with suspects has been scarcely the subject of research. One exception is the study of Sukumar, Hodgson, and Wade (2016) who were able to observe a small number of cases (N = 16) that included all interactions between lawyers and their clients, police, and lawyers, as well as the interviews between the police and suspects (where the lawyer remained present) involving three police forces in England and Wales. They found that the dialogue between the police and the lawyer was often punctuated with attempts by lawyers to gain more information from the police than they had initially provided. Some of these attempts were successful by more information being given. Alternatively, when lawyers learned from the police that requests for evidence were not able to be met, this provided information that such information/evidence was not in the possession of the police. In this event, lawyers could assess more accurately what evidence was held (including its totality). They were found to be able to advise their client on their own strategy in the police interview, including (where the evidence was viewed as weak) that of suspects remaining silent when questioned by the police. In the context of the SUE approach, the benefits of 'late evidence disclosure' may become less pronounced where suspects increasingly have lawyers accompanying them in interviews conducted by the police across the world. It, therefore, is of no surprise to see those SUE researchers now beginning to examine "drip feed" strategies of evidence disclosure in their research directions.

Recent studies, which have incorporated the origins of the SUE approach, have also examined further dimensions of that strategy (such as the manner of confrontation, whether confrontational or conversational in tone, as well as timing of evidence disclosure in interviews alongside increasingly sophisticated crime scenarios in attempt to narrow the gap between experimental and applied settings). These studies (e.g., May, Granhag, & Tekin, 2017; Tekin et al., 2015; Tekin, Granhag, Strömwall, & Vrij, 2016) have found a conversational tone (that keeps the suspects involved and responsive to the interviewer's questions) to be more effective than the confrontational approach at uncovering attempts by suspects at lying, as well as suspects supplying more information. These findings yet further emphasize the importance of avoiding accusatorial techniques in interviews. It has been also found that gradual evidence disclosure is at least as effective as the strategy of the initial SUE research findings that considered just deferred evidence presentation.

Gradual evidence disclosure

This mode of "gradual" evidence disclosure involves an incremental approach of "drip-feeding" evidence throughout the interview (Granhag et al., 2012). Walsh, Milne, and Bull (2016a) asked 224 British investigators which of "early" "late," and "gradual" evidence disclosure approaches they preferred, finding that the vast majority opted for a gradual approach. This may not be so surprising given that this cohort had received training in the PEACE model, which advocates such a phased method of evidence disclosure (but only after gaining a first account from suspects). What is of interest here is that prior their being PEACE trained, studies found that interviewers in England and Wales tended to introduce evidence by way of the "early" method (Baldwin, 1993; Moston et al., 1992). As we have already noted, these studies also found that when evidence was perceived as weak by them (in its totality) suspects very rarely admitted any guilt, nor did they often change their story from denials to admission. Attempts to gain from suspects their side of the story were also found rare in incidence. In contrast to these interviews conducted before the introduction of the PEACE framework, more recent studies of interviews conducted by PEACE trained investigators (e.g., Bull & Soukara, 2010; Walsh & Bull, 2012b) found shifts from denial to confession occurring later in the interview, presumably as suspects (having had the opportunity to provide an initial account) came to realize that continuing to deny was increasingly futile as evidence gradually emerged of their wrongdoing. Walsh and Bull (2015) found this was particularly the case when officers also undertook a "skillful" questioning strategy when revealing evidence that involved. These findings may well lead to the conclusion that the tactics recommended in the PEACE framework is more successful in moving resistant suspects to confess to crimes (without the use of unethical tactics), by first giving suspects opportunity to provide their versions of stories before gradually disclosing evidence and emphasizing the inconsistencies between that evidence and their given accounts.

Prior studies examining questioning strategies have tended to be confined to counting the number of various question types that have been observed in an interview (Clarke & Milne, 2001; Walsh & Milne, 2008). In contrast, Griffiths and Milne (2006) examined such matters by studying the arrangement of interviewer questions as they occurred in each interview. These authors, firstly, classified question types either as productive or nonproductive (in terms of likely information yield from interviewees), based upon the literature concerning question types (although Oxburgh et al., 2010 note the ambiguity of some definitions). Productive ones were defined by Griffiths and Milne as those such as open or probing, while nonproductive ones were those such as closed or leading questions. Griffiths and Milne advocated an approach where questioning (on each topic in the interview) would start with an open enquiry, followed by probing questions designed to seek out the required microdetail (while avoiding use of the nonproductive questions). Walsh and Bull (2015) found this approach to be strongly associated with interviews that were more successful in gathering comprehensive information, as well as (as was noted above) overcoming denials. However, what remains underresearched is how interviewee responses to various question types affect subsequent interviewer tactics and questioning. Indeed, while research has increased into practices, it remains the case that research has tended to focus upon selected activities (such evidence disclosure, questioning strategies, or rapport) and insufficiently upon the interactions of interviewer attitudes and the array of tactics that occur in interviews.

Development of a taxonomy of interview domains

In contrast, Kelly, Miller, Redlich, and Kleinman (2013) undertook endeavors to develop greater understanding of the whole interview process and structure to a model of investigative interviewing (by developing a taxonomy). Around 70 specific interrogation techniques were identified in their research, which they subsequently undertook to have these coded into six conceptual meso-level domains of *rapport and relationship building*, *context manipulation*, *emotion provocation*, *confrontation/competition*, *collaboration*, and *presentation of evidence*. Kelly et al. have argued that identification of these domains would be helpful to the gaining of better insight when studying interview practices. Redlich et al. (2014) undertook to survey investigators in the United States of America. They found that most participants recommended rapport and relationship building as tactics to be employed when interviewing suspects. Much less preferred as tactics were those domains often found in the literature to prompt confessions. These were *confrontation/competition* (i.e., being accusatorial) and *emotion provocation* (i.e., techniques involving the manipulation of suspects, such as maximization, minimization, and offering rationalizations).

In their later study of 29 interviews conducted by the police in the United States of America, Kelly, Miller, and Redlich (2016) coded tactics over each of 5-minute segments, not dissimilar to the methodology that had been used by Bull and Soukara (2010) that was reported earlier. Kelly et al. found (in line with their earlier self-report study) that the domain of *rapport and relationship building* was that most featured in the opening stages of interviews and was found to be positively associated with the level of cooperation from suspects. However, this particular domain was found to tail off in its usage as the interview progressed, with the emergence of other domains (i.e., *presentation of evidence* and *emotion provocation*). This finding was in line with those of Walsh and Bull (2012a) who (as has been noted) found that rapport was not always maintained. Indeed, Walsh and Bull (2012b) found that in the face of those interviews (where suspects did not shift at all toward confessions) that investigators undertook an increased usage of leading questions in their attempts to overcome resistance and prompt confessions (although in all interviews in their study these were largely unsuccessful ones). These attempts were identified as ones that saw a tactic of *information giving* undertaken by interviewers (i.e., their stating what they thought had actually happened), rather than *information gathering* (being the aims of the PEACE model).

In Kelly et al. (2016), they also found (in those interviews where confessions did occur) that there was a return to the usage of the domain of *rapport and relationship building* as the interview began drawing to a close. However, where the usage of the two domains in that central interview phase (i.e., *presentation of evidence* and *emotion provocation*) did not overcome suspects' denials, it was found that interviewers began to more often use the domain of *confrontation/competition* domain. Moreover, during (and for up to 15 minutes following) such domain presence levels of cooperation from suspects were found to decline. In line with findings of Walsh and Bull (2012b), that interviewing skill is an important variable (and not just its presence), Kelly et al. found that while evidence disclosure was used more often as a tactic in those interviews in their sample where denials occurred, it was found that when evidence was used more "thoughtfully" (and subtly) that confessions occurred, rather than when disclosed more as an immediate reaction to interviewer perceived inconsistencies. Indeed, Walsh and Bull (2015) had also found these same two types of gradual evidence disclosure in their study, which revealed that evidence coined as "gradual deferred" (where evidence was released in much more considered and highly strategic manner) was significantly more successful in gaining comprehensive accounts from suspects than the interviewer gradual "reactive" approach (or for that matter "late" or "early" evidence disclosures). The gradual "reactive" method tended to be characterized by "kneejerk" responses made by interviewers. That is, police officers confronted suspects with inconsistencies as soon as the suspects were viewed as providing them (i.e., those inconsistencies between either what they had said earlier in response to questions asked by the police or the evidence held).

Such findings as those revealed in the studies of Walsh and Bull (2015) and Kelly et al. (2016) again underline the importance of skilled evidence disclosure and also the benefits of rapport while addressing the problems of an accusatorial approach. Their findings further appear to justify the usage of the PEACE framework as the basis for an information gathering approach when interviewing suspects. Advocating information gathering techniques over accusatorial ones has been the conclusion of reviews of the literature in being more effective in gaining suspects' cooperation, gathering reliable and comprehensive information, and avoiding those tactics that have been found to risk false confessions (see Meissner, Kelly, & Woestehoff, 2015; Meissner, Redlich, Bhatt, & Brandon, 2012).

In Walsh and Bull's study (2010), these authors found that interviewers utilizing tactics prescribed in the PEACE framework in a skillful way were strongly associated to the obtaining of increased information. On the other hand, those less skillful interviewers very often failed to achieve these outcomes. While clearly more research is needed, initial efforts by researchers have commonly found endorsement of the PEACE information gathering approach and significantly less support for interrogational and accusatory approach. It is also to be noted that one of the driving forces behind the change to this interviewing model in England and Wales (that is, avoiding miscarriages of justice, prompted at least in part by false confessions) has been found to decrease dramatically since the introduction of the PEACE model in that country. Various field studies conducted there rightly may have found that interviewing standards are not uniformly more skilled. However, these studies have also found that the unethical approaches so prevalent (and reported as so likely to prompt false confessions and false convictions) before their introduction of the PEACE model are now a rare phenomenon. That alone represents some progress, but more is needed to understand why lessons learned in training by interviewers are not always sustained over time in the field. Research has largely been silent here.

Conclusions

Research concerning the PEACE framework as the fulcrum of the investigative interviewing method has found it to have been effective in steering interviews with suspects away from coercive approaches that saw police interrogations as merely confession centered to those where information gathering is the focus of police interviews with suspects. It is with some confidence that investigative interviewing can be said to have reduced the chance of miscarriages of justice occurring through false confessions. An investigative interviewing paradigm has also stressed the importance to investigators of conducting better investigations, rather than having an overreliance on suspects' confessions as the key to resolving crimes. That said, as has been reported here, why investigative interviewing practice remains of an uneven standard requires much further research. Some early thoughts have been offered. Nevertheless, moving away from an emphasis on confessions is seen as progressive. Such transformation in England and Wales has been largely underpinned by three factors. Firstly, the introduction of legislation (i.e., PACE) which safeguards the rights of suspects when being questioned, including that of the right to legal representation. Secondly, the mandatory recording of such interviews to act as a faithful evidential record of police encounters with suspects, that in England and Wales has served to protect all protagonists against accusations of malpractice. Thirdly, the demonstrated commitment of most senior police officers to reinforce an operational culture which values and promotes ethical practices and does not tolerate any malpractice as a justifiable means of resolving crimes. All three factors were integral to the change in England and Wales. None of them independently enabled the improvements.

Some suggestions for future research directions

Research concerning investigative interviews has tended to focus on certain techniques (such as evidence disclosure, rapport, or questioning strategies), examining them either in unison or individually. Further, research has tended to examine the "central activity" of account gathering, neglecting to examine other interview phases too, such as the opening rapport building stage. These emphases have led to a lacuna. Investigative interviews are a product of the dynamic interactions of attitudes, tactics, and strategies that are present throughout their duration. Kelly's work with his associates over the last few years does accommodate these very matters when measuring the ongoing nature of interviews through the lens of those key domains. More work is clearly needed, but a recent study suggests that such an approach can effectively examine investigative interviews conducted by PEACE-trained interviewers (Izotovas, Kelly, & Walsh, in press).

Further, it seems reasonable to assume that the legacy of the decision-making by investigators that occurs during investigations (and the investigative mindset that guides such decision-making) may affect preparations ahead of carrying out investigative interviews. These issues may well also affect the willingness of interviewers to reflect candidly on their own performance once interviews have been conducted. Research has regrettably neglected these two areas. In sum, skilled investigative interviewing requires skilled investigations as a prerequisite. Investigative professionalism is hall-marked by a willingness to learn and continuously improve from experiences.

Investigative interviewing research is still in its infancy in other areas (such as when dealing with those suspects viewed as vulnerable either through mental health or learning difficulties, in addition to the growing number of interviews conducted in the presence of an interpreter). Furthermore, the effects of the experience of suspects' incarceration, regardless of its length, on subsequent interviews are argued to require substantive awareness. We know that lengthy periods of isolation (e.g., in Japan, where suspects can be held for 23 days without charge) can increase suspects' vulnerability and susceptibility to their making false confessions. However, we remain unaware of either the beneficial or adverse effects of the varying incarceration experiences of suspects upon their subsequent investigative interviews, even when relatively short periods of time are involved (e.g., such as the case in England and Wales, where suspects can in only exceptional circumstances be detained for more than 24 hours). It, therefore, behooves the research community to continue endeavors that seek to establish more knowledge in order to enable practitioners to undertake more effective interviews in this array of demanding contexts. Furthermore, policy makers around the world need to heed the lessons of those countries who have so far embraced investigative interviewing. There, evidence exists that suggests strongly that false confessions may well have become increasingly rare. While our understanding is far from complete, what we know thus far concerning investigative interviewing suggests most persuasively that an approach that has at its core a respect for human rights, is ethical, is open minded, and searches for truth (rather than confessions) provides optimism for better justice outcomes. It is an approach that does not rely on confessions resulting from either coercion exercised by investigators on vulnerable or naïve suspects. It requires investigators to be skilled ones.

References

Alison, L., Alison, E., Noone, G., Entlib, S., & Christiansen, P. (2013). Why tough tactics fail and rapport gets results: Observing rapport-based interpersonal techniques (ORBIT) to generate useful information from terrorists. *Psychology, Public Policy, and Law, 19*, 411–431. https://doi.org/10.1037/a0034564

Baldwin, J. (1993). Police interview techniques: Establishing truth or proof? *British Journal of Criminology, 33*, 325–351.

Bull, R. (Ed.). (2014). *Investigative interviewing*. New York: Springer.

Bull, R., & Leahy-Harland, S. (2012). Analyses of real-life police interviews with suspects: Strategies used and suspect responses. In *Paper presented at the 5th international investigative interviewing research group conference, Toronto, 26-28th May, 2012.*

Bull, R., & Soukara, S. (2010). A set of studies of what really happens in police interviews with suspects. In G. D. Lassiter, & C. Meissner (Eds.), *Interrogations and confessions* (pp. 81–96). Washington, DC: American Psychological Association.

Cassell, P., & Hayman, B. (1996). Police interrogation in the 1990s: An empirical study of the effects of Miranda. *UCLA Law Review, 43*, 839–932.

Clarke, C., & Milne, R. (2001). National evaluation of the PEACE investigative interviewing course. In *Police research award scheme report no. PRAS/149*. London: Home Office.

Dando, C., Bull, R., Ormerod, T., & Sandham, A. (2013). Helping to sort the liars from the truth- tellers: The gradual revelation of information during investigative interviews. *Legal and Criminological Psychology*. https://doi.org/10.1111/lcrp.12016

Drizin, S. A., & Leo, R. A. (2004). The problem of false confessions in the post-DNA world. *North Carolina Law Review, 82*, 891−1007.

Fahsing, I., & Ask, K. (2013). Decision making and decisional tipping points in homicide investigations: An interview study of British and Norwegian detectives. *Journal of Investigative Psychology and Offender Profiling, 10*, 155−165.

Garrett, B. L. (2010). The substance of false confessions. *Stanford Law Review, 62*, 1051−1118.

Goodman-Delahunty, J., Martschuk, N., & Dhami, M. K. (2014). Interviewing high value detainees: Securing cooperation and disclosures. *Applied Cognitive Psychology, 28*, 883−897. https://doi.org/10.1002/acp.3087

Granhag, P.-A., Strömwall, L., Willén, R., & Hartwig, M. (2012). Eliciting cues to deception by tactical disclosure of evidence: The first test of the Evidence Framing Matrix. *Legal and Criminological Psychology, 18*, 341−355. https://doi.org/10.1111/j.2044-8333.2012.02047.x

Griffiths, A. (2008). *An examination into the efficacy of police advanced investigative interview training?*. Unpublished PhD thesis. University of Portsmouth.

Griffiths, A., & Milne, R. (2006). Will it all end in tiers? Police interviews with suspects in Britain. In T. Williamson (Ed.), *Investigative interviewing: Rights, research and regulation* (pp. 167−189). Cullompton: Willan.

Griffiths, A., Milne, B., & Cherryman, J. (2011). A question of control? The formulation of suspect and witness interview question strategies by advanced interviewers. *International Journal of Police Science and Management, 13*(3), 255−267. https://doi.org/10.1350/ijps.2011.13.3.219

Griffiths, A., & Walsh, D. (2018). Investigators' reflective portfolios: A reflection of their actual investigation skills? *Psychology, Crime and Law, 24*, 433−450.

Gudjonsson, G. H. (2003). *The psychology of interrogation and confessions: A handbook*. Chichester: Wiley.

Gudjonsson, G. H. (2018). *The psychology of false confessions: Forty years of science and practice*. John Wiley & Sons Ltd. https://doi.org/10.1002/9781119315636

Gudjonsson, G. H. (2021). The science-based pathways to understanding false confessions and wrongful convictions. *Frontiers in Psychology, 12*, 633936. https://doi.org/10.3389/fpsyg.2021.633936

Gudjonsson, G. H., & Petursson, H. (1991). Custodial interrogation: Why do suspects confess and how does it relate to their crime, attitude and personality? *Personality and Individual Differences, 12*, 295−306.

Hartwig, M., Granhag, P. A., Strömwall, L. A., & Kronkvist, O. (2006). Strategic use of evidence during police interviews: When training to detect deception works. *Law and Human Behavior, 30*, 603−619.

Hartwig, M., Granhag, P. A., Strömwall, L. A., & Vrij, A. (2005). Detecting deception via strategic disclosure of evidence. *Law and Human Behavior, 29*, 469−484. https://doi.org/10.1007/s10979-005-5521-x

Holmberg, U., & Christianson, S. (2002). Murderers' and sexual offenders' experiences of police interviews and their inclination to admit or deny crimes. *Behavioral Sciences & the Law, 20*, 31−45. https://doi.org/10.1080/1068316X.2017.1390115

Innes, M. (2003). *Investigating murder: Detective work and the police response to criminal homicide*. Oxford, UK: Oxford University Press.

Irving, B. (1980). Police interrogation. In *A case study of current practice, research study no. 2*. London: HMSO.

Izotovas, A., Kelly, C. E., & Walsh, D., The Domains of PEACE: Examining interviews with suspected sex offenders. *Journal of Police and Criminal Psycholog* (in press), https://doi.org/10.1007/s11896-021-09465-8.

Kassin, S. M., Drizin, S. A., Grisso, T., Gudjonsson, G. H., Leo, R. A., & Redlich, A. D. (2010). Police induced confessions: Risk factors and recommendations. *Law and Human Behavior, 34*, 3–38.

Kassin, S. M., & Gudjonsson, G. H. (2004). The psychology of confessions: A review of the literature and issues. *Psychological Science in the Public Interest, 5*, 33–67.

Kassin, S. M., Leo, R. A., Meissner, C. A., Richman, K. D., Colwell, L. H., Leach, A.-M., et al. (2007). Police interviewing and interrogation: A self-report survey of police practices and beliefs. *Law and Human Behavior, 31*, 381–400.

Kebbell, M., Alison, L., Hurren, E., & Mazerolle, P. (2010). How do sex offenders think the police should interview to elicit confessions from sex offenders? *Psychology, Crime and Law, 16*, 567–584. https://doi.org/10.1080/106831609029710554

Kebbell, M. R., Hurren, E. J., & Mazerolle, P. (2006). Sex offenders' perceptions of how they were interviewed. *Canadian Journal of Police and Security Services, 4*, 67–75.

Kelly, C., Miller, J., & Redlich, A. (2016). The Dynamic nature of interrogation. *Law and Human Behavior, 40*, 295–309. https://doi.org/10.1037/lhb0000172

Kelly, C. E., Miller, J. C., Redlich, A. D., & Kleinman, S. M. (2013). A taxonomy of interrogation methods. *Psychology, Public Policy, and Law, 19*(2), 165–178. https://doi.org/10.1037/a0030310

Kim, S., Alison, L., & Christiansen, P. (2020). The impact of individual differences on investigative hypothesis generation under time pressure. *International Journal of Police Science and Management, 22*(2), 171–182.

Kim, J., Walsh, D., Bull, R., & Bergstrom, H. (2018). Planning ahead? Factors influencing investigators' attitudes towards planning for interviews with suspects. *Journal of Police and Criminal Psychology, 33*, 158–174. https://doi.org/10.1007/s11896-017-9243-z.104

Kruglanski, A. W., & Fishman, S. (2009). The need for cognitive closure. In M. R. Leary, & R. H. Hoyle (Eds.), *Handbook of individual differences in social behavior* (pp. 343–353). The Guilford Press.

Leahy-Harland, S., & Bull, R. (2017). Police strategies and suspect responses in real-life serious crime interviews. *Journal of Police and Criminal Psychology, 32*(2), 138–151.

Leo, R. A. (1996). Inside the interrogation room. *Journal of Criminal Law and Criminology, 86*, 266–303.

Leo, R. A. (2008). *Police interrogation and American justice*. Cambridge: Harvard University Press.

Leo, R. A., & Ofshe, R. (1998). The consequences of false confessions: Deprivations of liberty and miscarriages of justice in the age of psychological interrogation. *Journal of Criminal Law and Criminology, 88*, 429–496.

Marques, P., & Milne, R. (2019). The investigative interview's contribution to law enforcement. *European Law Enforcement Research Bulletin, 18*, 91–106.

May, L., Granhag, P.-A., & Tekin, S. (2017). Interviewing suspects in denial: On how different evidence disclosure modes affect the elicitation of new critical information. *Frontiers in Psychology, 8*, 1154–1165.

Meissner, C. A., Kelly, C. E., & Woestehoff, S. A. (2015). Improving the effectiveness of suspect interrogations. *Annual Review of Law and Social Science, 11*, 211–233.

Meissner, C. A., Redlich, A. D., Bhatt, S., & Brandon, S. (2012). Interview and interrogation methods and their effects on true and false confessions. *Campbell Systematic Reviews*, 1–53. https://doi.org/10.4073/csr.2012.13

Meissner, C. A., Redlich, A. D., Michael, S. W., Evans, J. R., Camilletti, C. R., Bhatt, S., et al. (2014). Accusatorial and information-gathering interrogation methods and their effects on true and false confessions: A meta-analytic review. *Journal of Experimental Criminology, 10*(4), 459–486.

Miller, W., & Rollnick, S. (2002). *Motivational interviewing* (2nd ed.). New York: Guilford Press.

Milne, R., & Bull, R. (2006). Interviewing victims of crime, including children and people with intellectual difficulties. In M. R. Kebbell, & G. M. Davies (Eds.), *Practical psychology for forensic investigations*. Chichester: Wiley.

Moston, S., Stephenson, G. M., & Williamson, T. (1992). The effects of case characteristics on suspect behaviour during police questioning. *British Journal of Criminology, 32*, 23–40.

Nystedt, M., Nielsen, C. A., & Kleffner, J. K. (Eds.). (2011). *A handbook on assisting international criminal investigations*. Stockholm: Bernadotte Academy.

O'Neil, M., & Milne, R. (2014). Success within criminal investigations: Is communication still a key component? In R. Bull (Ed.), *Investigative interviewing* (pp. 123–146). New York: Springer.

Oxburgh, G. E., Myklebust, T., & Grant, T. (2010). The question of question of question types in police interviews: A review of the literature from a psychological and linguistic perspective. *International Journal of Speech Language and the Law, 17*, 45–66.

Oxburgh, G. E., Williamson, T., & Ost, J. (2006). Police officers' use of emotional language during child sexual abuse investigations. *Journal of Investigative Psychology and Offender Profiling, 3*, 35–45.

Poyser, S., Nurse, A., & Milne, R. (2018). *Miscarriages of justice: Causes, consequences and remedies*. Policy Press.

Redlich, A. D., Kelly, C. E., & Miller, J. C. (2014). The who, what, and why of human intelligence gathering: Self-reported measures of interrogation methods. *Applied Cognitive Psychology, 28*(6), 817–828. https://doi.org/10.1002/acp.3040

Rossmo, D. K. (2009). *Criminal investigative failures*. New York: CRC Press.

Russano, M., Narchet, F., Kleinman, S., & Meissner, C. (2014). Structured interviews of experienced HUMINT interrogators. *Applied Cognitive Psychology, 28*, 847–859. https://doi.org/10.1002/acp.3069

Sellers, S., & Kebbell, M. R. (2009). When should evidence be disclosed in an interview with a suspect? An experiment with mock-suspects. *Journal of Investigative Psychology and Offender Profiling, 6*, 151–160. https://doi.org/10.1002/jip.95

van der Sleen, J. (2009). A structured model of investigative interviewing of suspects. In R. Bull, T. Valentine, & T. Williamson (Eds.), *Handbook of psychology of investigative interviewing* (pp. 35–52). Chichester: Wiley.

Smalarz, L., Scherr, K. C., & Kassin, S. M. (2016). Miranda at 50: A psychological analysis. *Current Directions in Psychological Science, 25*, 455–460. https://doi.org/10.1177/0963721416665097

Softley, P., Brown, D., Forde, B., Mair, G., & Moxon, D. (1980). *Police interrogation: An observational study in four police stations*. London: HMSO.

Sorochinski, M., Hartwig, M., Osborne, J., Wilkins, E., Marsh, J., Kazakov, D., et al. (2014). Interviewing to detect deception: When to disclose the evidence? *Journal of Police and Criminal Psychology, 29*, 87–94. https://doi.org/10.1007/s11896-013-9121-2

Soukara, S., Bull, R., Vrij, A., Turner, M., & Cherryman, J. (2009). What really happens in police interviews with suspects? Tactics and confessions. *Psychology, Crime and Law, 15*, 493–506.

Sukumar, D., Hodgson, J., & Wade, K. A. (2016b). Behind closed doors: Live observations of current police station disclosure practices and lawyer-client consultations. *Criminal Law Review, 12*, 900–914.

Sukumar, D., Wade, K. A., & Hodgson, J. S. (2016a). Strategic disclosure of evidence: Perspectives from psychology and law. *Psychology, Public Policy, and Law, 22*(3), 306–313. https://doi.org/10.1037/law0000092

Tekin, S., Granhag, P. A., Strömwall, L. A., Mac Giolla, E., Vrij, A., & Hartwig, M. (2015). Interviewing strategically to elicit admissions from guilty suspects. *Law and Human Behavior, 39*, 244–252. https://doi.org/10.1037/lhb0000131

Tekin, S., Granhag, P. A., Strömwall, L. A., & Vrij, A. (2016). How to make perpetrators in denial disclose more information about their crimes. *Psychology, Crime and Law, 22*, 561–580. https://doi.org/10.1080/1068316X.2016.1168425

Tickle-Degnen, L., & Rosenthal, R. (1990). The nature of rapport and its nonverbal correlates. *Psychological Inquiry, 4*, 285–293.

Vanderhallen, M., Vervaeke, G., & Holmberg, U. (2011). Witness and suspect perceptions of working alliance and interviewing style. *Journal of Investigative Psychology and Offender Profiling, 8*(2), 110–130. https://doi.org/10.1002/jip.138

Vrij, A., Meissner, C. A., Fisher, R. P., Kassin, S. M., Morgan, C. A., & Kleinman, S. M. (2017). Psychological perspectives on interrogation. *Perspectives on Psychological Science, 12*(6), 927–955. https://doi.org/10.1177/1745691617706515

Walsh, D., & Bull, R. (2010). The interviewing of suspects by non-police agencies: What's effective? What is effective! *Legal and Criminological Psychology, 15*, 305–321.

Walsh, D., & Bull, R. (2011). Benefit fraud investigative interviewing: A self-report study of investigation professionals' beliefs concerning practice. *Journal of Investigative Psychology and Offender Profiling, 8*, 131–148.

Walsh, D., & Bull, R. (2012a). How do interviewers attempt to overcome suspects' denials? *Psychiatry, Psychology and Law, 19*, 151–168.

Walsh, D., & Bull, R. (2012b). Examining rapport in investigative interviews with suspects: Does its building and maintenance work? *Journal of Police and Criminal Psychology, 27*, 73–84. https://doi.org/10.1007/s11896-011-9087-x

Walsh, D., & Bull, R. (2015). The association between evidence disclosure, questioning strategies, interview skills, and interview outcomes. *Psychology, Crime and Law, 21*, 661–680. https://doi.org/10.1080/1068316X.2015.1028544

Walsh, D., King, M., & Griffiths, A. (2017). Evaluating interviews which search for the truth with suspects: but are investigators' self-assessments of their own skills truthful ones? *Psychology, Crime and Law, 23*, 647–665. https://doi.org/10.1080/1068316X.2017.1296149

Walsh, D., & Milne, R. (2007). Giving PEACE a chance. *Public Administration, 85*(2), 525–540.

Walsh, D., & Milne, R. (2008). Keeping the PEACE? A study of investigative interviewing practices in the public sector. *Legal and Criminological Psychology, 13*, 39–57.

Walsh, D., Milne, R., & Bull, R. (2016a). One way or another? Investigators' beliefs concerning evidence disclosure in interviews with suspects in England and Wales. *Journal of Police and Criminal Psychology, 31*, 127–140. https://doi.org/10.1007/s11896-015-9174-5

Walsh, D., Oxburgh, G., Redlich, A., & Myklebust, T. (2016b). *International developments and practices in investigative interviewing and interrogation*. London: Routledge.

Offender profiling: a review of the research and state of the field

18

Bryanna Fox

Introduction

Offender profiling (OP) is an investigative tool used by law enforcement, consultants, and academics to help identify the major personality, behavioral, and demographic characteristics of an offender based upon an analysis of the crime scene behaviors (Douglas & Burgess, 1986; Fox & Farrington, 2016, 2018; Ormerod, 1996). While OP has become a household name throughout much of the world, as it has been portrayed in several popular films (e.g., *The Silence of the Lambs*, *Along Came a Spider*), television shows (e.g., *Criminal Minds*, *Cracker*, *Mindhunter*), and books (e.g., the sprawling true crime genre), there is considerable controversy and debate surrounding the practice.

For instance, despite the attention and perceived credibility of OP, there are many misperceptions and myths regarding the practice. In the fictionalized accounts on TV, in books, and on the silver screen, OP is typically portrayed as a psychiclike talent possessed by just a lucky few investigators, informed by instinct, and used to accurately predict the features of an unknown suspect based upon the behaviors witnessed at the crime scene alone (Douglas & Burgess, 1986; Fox & Farrington, 2016; Ormerod, 1996).

While the overall purpose of OP portrayed in these accounts is mostly accurate, many other aspects of these portrayals are not. For example, many people believe OP is highly accurate, even though very little is actually known regarding the accuracy and utility of OP, and few rigorous evaluations of the practice have ever been conducted (Dowden, Bennell, & Bloomfield, 2007; Fox & Farrington, 2016, 2018). Furthermore, while OP may be used to prioritize and focus law enforcement's investigation of offenders, a profile is not considered a legal form of evidence to justify the arrest or prosecution of an offender in the United States; probable cause based upon other evidence is still needed to arrest a suspect (State v. Stevens, 2001, p. 817). Finally, while scholars and practitioners in the field of OP have generally agreed upon the purpose of the practice, determining the requisite background/training, methodology used to develop profiles, terminology used within profiles, and standardized profiles for various types of crimes have been challenging, to say the least.

Police Psychology, Edited by Marques and Paulino. https://doi.org/10.1016/B978-0-12-816544-7.00018-8

The goal of this chapter is to introduce readers to the practice of OP and overview prior evaluations which shed light on the accuracy and effectiveness of the practice. To begin, this chapter reviews the origin of the field of OP and various approaches to the practice (as well as their strengths and weaknesses), and finally, summarizes scientific evaluations of the accuracy and usefulness of OP when applied in the field.

Origins of offender profiling
Early days—the case of Jack the Ripper

The origins of OP can be traced back to the infamous "Jack the Ripper" murders, which took place in London, England, in 1888. In less than 4 months, five brutal slayings of women, all known to be prostitutes, took place within London's Whitechapel neighborhood. Given the similarity in the way the victims were killed (they were "ripped" open with a knife), the close proximity of the murders, and the short timeframe when they occurred, Dr. Thomas Bond, a physician who reviewed the crime scene photos and autopsy results, believed that these murders were all committed by the same offender. In fact, Bond coined a new term, "signature," to describe the crime scene behavior common across offenses, but not required to commit the crime and not present in most other offenses. In the case of Jack's murders, Bond suggested that the extensive mutilation, and in some cases, removal of internal organs, was his signature.

In addition to establishing one of the first methods to measurably link crimes to a single offender, Bond also used the signature to infer information about the personality, background, and demographics of the responsible offender. For instance, Bond believe that Jack was "a man of solitary habits, subject to periodic attacks of homicidal and erotic mania, and the character of the mutilations possibly indicating 'satyriasis' or uncontrollable sexual desire" (Bonn, 2017). He also believed that despite the extensive knife wounds, the killer had no formal medical training or knowledge of anatomy, given the lack of precision in the cuts. While the case of Jack the Ripper was not solved at the time, the behavioral analysis approach newly developed by Dr. Bond changed law enforcement investigations forever.

Clinical offender profiling—the FBI's Behavioral Science Unit

While the use of behavioral analysis by law enforcement and military intelligence increased since the Jack the Ripper case, the practice of OP was not officially established until 1976 by members of the Federal Bureau of Investigation's (FBI) Behavioral Science Unit (BSU). Back then, the BSU was responsible for training law enforcement executives at the FBI National Academy, conducting research on crimes and investigative techniques, and consulting on cases for local agencies across the country. It is out of this mission that the field of OP was born.

While consulting for police departments in the 1970s, BSU agents John Douglas and Robert Ressler decided to conduct "off the books field trips" to meet some of the worst offenders in the nation. For instance, while in California, Douglas and Ressler stopped by the local prison to speak to Ed Kemper, a serial killer who murdered college women and often severed off their heads. Rather than discussing evidence in the case or attempting to close additional unsolved crimes, the BSU agents asked Kemper about his childhood, background, and motivation for committing the crime. None of the new information was evidentiary; these interviews were only meant to provide context and identify patterns across the offenders' behaviors, backgrounds, personalities, and motivations.

After conducting interviews with 36 of the most infamous murderers, serial killers, assassins, and attempted killers, to include Charlie Manson, John Wayne Gacy, Sirhan Sirhan, and others, Douglas and Ressler began to identify patterns in the way certain crimes were committed, and the traits, backgrounds, and motivations of the offenders who commit them (see Hazelwood & Burgess, 1987; Ressler, Burgess, & Douglas, 1988). These individual factors include information about the offender's personality, age, race, gender, religion, marital status, and other social and behavioral factors, and are often developed through a deductive process where crime scenes are studied in extreme detail to develop highly specific and customized profiles applicable only to that case and offender (Holmes & Holmes, 1996). This led the BSU agents to propose that offenders who commit a specific crime style (e.g., organized or disorganized) are likely to possess certain background traits and behaviors, and established the field of OP.

Although no single definition of OP exists across in the field, most definitions agree that the goal is to establish links between types of crimes committed and the characteristics of offenders who commit those types of crimes. Hazelwood and Douglas (1980) defined the FBI's approach to profiling as an "educated attempt to provide investigative agencies with specific information as to the type of individual who committed a certain crime … A profile is based on the characteristic patterns or factors of uniqueness that distinguish certain individuals from the general population" (p. 22). The BSU suggested that this new investigative tool could be used by police to generate or narrow down the range of possible suspects by predicting a combination of characteristics that an offender is likely to possess based on elements of a crime scene alone.

As a result, the BSU proposed the first "offender profiles," suggesting that all murders, rapes, and arsons, and the offenders who commit them, can be categorized into the "organized" or "disorganized" profiles (Hazelwood & Douglas, 1980). Organized crimes are carefully planned, well prepared for (e.g., weapons or tools are brought along), deliberately executed (e.g., potential victims are assessed), and conducted in a methodical manner with any known evidence of the offense destroyed or concealed to prevent detection (Kocsis, Irwin, & Hayes, 1998). In many cases, the FBI profilers noted that organized offenses consist of three crime scenes: where the killer approached the victim, where the victim was killed, and where the victim's body was disposed of, further indicating the level of effort and premeditation put into these offenses. Organized crimes are committed by equally organized and meticulous offenders, who, according to the FBI profilers, are intelligent, charming, socially adept, and competent (Hazelwood & Douglas, 1980). These offenders are typically not known to police and go to inordinate lengths to cover their tracks and avoid apprehension (Bonn, 2018). Conversely, disorganized offenses are poorly planned or even impetuous, and the victims tend to be chosen at random. These offenses are often committed by inexperienced and reckless offenders near their homes, with little effort made to conceal the crime, often leaving a frenzied and chaotic crime scene typically with evidence left behind (Kocsis et al., 1998).

Applying the organized/disorganized profiles to real-world cases, consider the murders committed by Theodore Robert Bundy in the 1970s across the United States. Many young females were lured to the charming and attractive Ted Bundy, who was a law student and outwardly friendly. To prey on his victims, he would often ask a young woman for help, then hit her on the head and/or strangle her to death. Some victims he decapitated, and in some cases Bundy had sexual intercourse with his victims' dead bodies. Still, Bundy was cunning enough to avoid suspicion by traveling hundreds of miles to new locations to commit his murders. This is one reason why many victims have been attributed to Bundy, but he was never charged or convicted of their murders. Even after being arrested for homicide in Colorado in 1977, Bundy was able to escape by jumping out of the second story window of the Pitkin County Courthouse law library, which he was authorized to use to assist in his own legal defense. Bundy was later captured and moved to the Garfield County Jail in Colorado, where he again managed to escape by crawling through the ceiling ducts after losing considerable weight in order to make himself fit. In short, Bundy was a cunning, methodical, and premeditated killer whose charm and sophistication allowed him the ability to access victims and get away with his crimes.

In contrast, Richard Ramirez (also known as the Night Stalker) is more exemplar of a disorganized serial killer, as his murders were brutal, chaotic, and committed against victims who were selected at random. Specifically, Ramirez's first murder, committed in 1984 in San Francisco, was against a 9-year-old child who he raped, beat, stabbed to death, and then hung the body from a nearby pipe (Van Derbeken, 2009). He then went on to viciously murder 13 women (and witnesses) by stabbing, shooting, beating, strangling, and in many cases, raping the victims, often as they slept, who ranged in age from 16 to 83. In several cases, the victims were able to fight Ramirez and occasionally survive, and report the crimes to police. He also engaged in highly erratic behavior during his crimes, and made little effort to conceal his crime or responsibility for it. For instance, while raping an 81-year-old woman, Ramirez used her lipstick to draw the pentagram, a symbol of witchcraft, on her thigh and later on the walls. He also made a woman "swear on Satan" that she would not scream while he raped and sodomized her in front of her 3-year-old son, who Ramirez tied up in the room to watch (Carlo, 1996). Afterward he let the woman and her son go free.

Forensic evidence was frequently left at Ramirez's horrific crime scenes, to include blood, fingerprints, shoeprints (once on a victim's face), semen, guns, knives, and the victims' bodies. Ramirez was an equally unstable and chaotic figure, as he was believed to show an interest in "Satanism," dropped out of school in the ninth grade, and was fired from his job at a Holiday Inn after a hotel guest returned to his room to find Ramirez attempting to rape his wife (Carlo, 1996). While the hotel patron beat Ramirez senselessly, he and his wife did not return to California for the trial and all charges were dropped. Ramirez was later identified, and ultimately convicted, for his serial killings in part due to his rotten teeth. Ramirez's desistance from all personal hygiene around the age of 18, as well as his drug addictions, ultimately led to his mouth full of decaying and missing teeth, which was fright-inducing, but highly identifiable by his future victims and witnesses. Ramirez was found guilty for his killings and died of natural causes while on death row.

Evaluations of clinical profiles

The FBI's organized/disorganized profiles have come under scrutiny in recent years, as they were created using "experience, intuition, and educated guesswork" (Geberth, 1990, p. 492; Pinizzotto, 1984), not quantitative data and statistical methods (Fox & Farrington, 2016; Kocsis & Cooksey, 2002). Many experts in psychology, criminology, and law enforcement have therefore raised concerns about clinical profiling approaches, particularly as research suggests these profiles are about as accurate as a coin toss. For instance, in one of the best-known accuracy assessments of clinical offender profiles, Pinizzotto (1984) asked police to evaluate the 192 FBI profiles they used on their unsolved cases between 1971 and 1981. Results indicated that less than half of the cases were ever solved, and just 17% of the police felt the profiles directly aided in the identification of a suspect. Most notably, 17% of the profile recipients felt that the profiles "were not useful at all" (Pinizzotto, 1984).

Clinical profiles developed by non-FBI profilers appear to fare similarly in terms of accuracy and effectiveness in unsolved cases. For instance, Copson (1995) found that just 14% of the clinically developed profiles used by police in the United Kingdom helped solve the case. In Canada, 14% of the 29 surveyed officers reported that a profile helped focus the investigation, and 3% said the profiles provided accurate predictions about the responsible offender (Snook, Taylor, & Bennell, 2007). Trager and Brewster (2001) found that among the 48 American police officers they surveyed, 38% felt the clinical profiles that they used directly assisted in the identification of a suspect, though 25% said the profiles had actually hindered their investigation in some way.

A major limitation of this evaluation strategy is that police responding to these studies may be impacted by their perceptions of the accuracy of profiling and their impression of the profiler. For instance, the more an officer believes that profiling works or is impressed by the credentials of a profiler, the more correct and useful the profiles may appear to be (Kocsis & Middledorp, 2004). This concern was voiced by Campbell (1976), who stated that police may be more seduced by the credentials of the profiler than the profiles themselves (Petherick, 2006).

As a result, a second type of OP evaluation was developed to overcome the concern about biased perceptions impacting surveys conducted with profiler users. These studies compare the accuracy of profilers to individuals with relevant backgrounds and training such as psychologists, psychics, police officers, and college students to see who is most accurate when predicting traits of an offender based upon crime scene information. Pinizzotto and Finkel (1990) compared FBI profilers to detectives, and found that when it came to selecting offenders from a lineup based upon the description of the crime, the FBI profilers were most accurate. However, detectives were most accurate in predicting traits of offenders and had the most correct responses overall (Pinizzotto & Finkel, 1990). Studies by Kocsis and colleagues expanded upon this research and found that clinical-style profilers averaged a 46% total accuracy rate in terms of predicting traits of an offender based upon crime scene information, which is higher than the 40% average accuracy rate for college students and a 38% accuracy rate for psychics in the sample (Kocsis, 2006; Kocsis, Irwin, Hayes, & Nunn, 2000). However, these results also suggest that clinical profilers were wrong in their predictions more than 50% of the time.

In the first study to measure the true accuracy of profiles applied in police investigations by comparing specific predictions made in the profile to the characteristics of the arrested suspects, and identifying how many cases the profiles solved, Gudjonsson and Copson (1997) examined 184 profiled cases in the United Kingdom. The results showed that predictions made by clinical profilers were accurate approximately 66% of the time; however, the profiles led to an arrest in just 5 of the 184 cases. In other words, despite the relatively high accuracy rate in terms of correctly predicting the traits of offenders, there was only a 2.7% success rate when the profiles were actually applied in the field (Gudjonsson & Copson, 1997).

Statistical offender profiling

Due to the limitations and concerns over accuracy rates for clinically developed profiles, a more statistical approach to OP has recently been adopted by the field (see, e.g., Canter, 1995; Farrington & Lambert, 2000; Fox & Farrington, 2012). Statistical OP is based upon statistical regularities found between the way certain offenses are committed and the features of responsible offenders, based upon objective analysis of large datasets of crimes (Fox & Farrington, 2018). This inductive approach to profiling is based on the premise that statistical regularities among certain co-occurring features of crimes and offenders can be generalized to other unknown perpetrators of similar crime styles to aid in their identification (Holmes & Holmes, 1996). Furthermore, as this approach is based on statistical regularities between specific features of offenders and the types of crimes they commit from large datasets on prior crimes and offenders, it is not subjective or based upon a specific profiler's opinions and experiences to develop the resultant profiles (Holmes & Holmes, 1996). This scientific approach has been growing in popularity in the OP field (see, e.g., Bennell & Canter, 2002; Canter, 1995; Farrington & Lambert, 2000; Fox & Farrington, 2012) and has many advantages in terms of replicability, data-driven findings, and increased accuracy and utility when applied in the field.

Investigative psychology

Canter (1995) was the first to propose a more statistical approach to OP, when he proposed the "A to C equation", where A represents the actions related to a crime known to the police (e.g., crime location, method of entry, state of scene) and C refers to the characteristics of the responsible offender (e.g., criminal history, identifying traits). Canter (1995) believed that profiles of offenders can be developed and statistically linked to crime scene actions using a database of known offenses and offenders. When features of crimes committed by different individuals are similar, he felt that the offenders who commit those crimes must also share some common underlying traits, which can also be generalized to other unknown perpetrators of similar crime styles to aid in their identification (Canter, 1995; Holmes & Holmes, 1996). Through the use of statistical analysis of crime and offender data, unique subtypes of offenses and offenders can be developed and statistically linked together to develop scientifically informed offender profiles that can be more effective when used by police.

For instance, Canter and Kirby (1995) found unique statistical relationship exists between certain offenders' characteristics, such as previous convictions for indecent exposure or assault, and characteristics of rape offences (e.g., whether the offender bound up the victim). Canter went on to apply this statistical approach to identify unique subtypes of arsonists (Canter & Fritzon, 1998), property offenders (Canter & Alison, 2000), armed robbers (Alison, Rockett, Deprez,& Watts, 2000), and the relationship between murder crime scenes and the characteristics of responsible offenders (Salfati & Canter, 1999).

However, there have also been criticisms of investigative psychology, as two leading researchers in the field stated that there has not been an independently conducted, empirically robust, and scientifically peer-reviewed study that demonstrates that a sample of suitably qualified experts in investigative psychology can construct an accurate criminal profile of the characteristics of an unknown offender any better than individuals employing some other rivalling method of profiling (Kocsis & Palermo, 2016). In other words, investigative psychology has not been subjected to the same level of evaluation as other approaches to OP, and therefore it is unclear how much more accurate and effective the profiles truly are.

Geographic profiling

Geographic profiling uses statistical algorithms and mathematical formulas to predict the most likely home/operating base of an offender, or area the offender will strike in the future, based upon the locations of a prior series of crimes (Rossmo, 2000). In other words, geographic profilers aim to provide reliable information to police on probability estimates of where a suspect's residence might be or where he/she may offend next. To do this, geographic profilers rely on a variety of computer programs which use advanced statistics and data to produce "crime maps." One of these programs, *Criminal Geographic Targeting*, developed by Rossmo (1995), analyzes offenders' crime locations to produce a topographic map, assigning probabilities to different locations where the suspect may be residing or have his base for offending. *Geographical profiling* is spatial movement analysis of a single serial offender, while *geographical mapping* is spatial patterns analysis pertaining to a number of offenders over a period of time. Furthermore, it is possible to use a geographic profile in combination with a statistically generated offender profiler in order to provide more clarity to police on the features and location of the most likely offender (Rossmo, 2000). Using this information, police can customize their investigative strategies to be more effective and efficient. However, it should be noted that like investigative psychology, independent evaluation of the accuracy of geographic profiling has yet to take place.

Case linkage analysis

Another example of a statistically based approach to OP is crime linkage analysis (CLA). CLA, first developed by Bennell and Canter (2002), uses statistical analysis to link crimes to a single offender on the basis of commonalities seen in various crime scene behaviors. CLA typically uses receiver operating characteristic (ROC) analysis to evaluate behavioral similarity across offenses and determines the likelihood of case linkage (Bennell, Mugford, Ellingwood, & Woodhams, 2014). Next, an area under the ROC curve (AUC) analysis is used to determine the accuracy of the decision to link crimes to a serial offender (Bennell et al., 2014; Steadman et al., 2000). Given the statistical sophistication of CLA, this approach has been a rapidly growing area in the OP field.

A recent meta-analysis of the accuracy of CLA was conducted by Fox and Farrington (2018). Based upon 34 effect sizes derived from 18 studies identified using a thorough search of electronic databases and references for published literature on CLA from 2002 through 2016, the results of the meta-analysis indicated that CLA has been performed on five crime types (homicide, sex offenses, burglary, robbery, and car theft), using data from six different countries (the United Kingdom, Canada, the United States, Finland, South Africa, and Japan), and samples ranging in size from 49 to 720 offenses (Fox & Farrington, 2018). Most importantly, this meta-analysis indicated that the weighted mean effect size for all CLA studies was $AUC = 0.83$, suggesting that overall, CLA models are highly accurate (e.g., correctly link crimes to the same offender 83% of the time). Furthermore, 18% of the CLA studies indicated near perfect accuracy when linking crimes ($AUC = 0.90$ to 1.00) and 62% were highly accurate ($AUC = 0.70$ to 0.89) (Swets, 1988). This finding is very positive for the accuracy of CLA and suggests it is a validated statistical OP strategy that can reliably be utilized in law enforcement investigations.

Evidence-based offender profiling

Due to the objectivity and replicability associated with statistical profiling, but the lack of empirical evaluation of most statistically-derived profiles, Fox and Farrington (2012, 2016) established the evidence-based offender profiling (EBOP) approach. EBOP draws upon objective statistical classification techniques, such as Latent Class Analysis (LCA), to develop subtypes of offenses and offenders, and then evaluate the statistical relationships between these subtypes using statistical and experimental evaluations (Fox & Farrington, 2012, 2016).

In the first study to develop EBOP profiles, Fox and Farrington (2012) used LCA to identify subtypes in offender traits and crime scene behaviors among 405 burglaries in Florida. Results indicated that there were four burglary profiles, labeled: (1) organized, (2) disorganized, (3) opportunistic, and (4) interpersonal style offenses. Like the FBI's clinical profile for organized homicides, the organized style burglaries are premeditated and professional offenses where foresight and care were taken to reduce risks and increase gains (Fox & Farrington, 2012). Organized burglars typically bring tools to the crime scene (indicating the premeditation and preparation), use forced entry to enter a target, leave little or no evidence left behind, and steal high-value items that often require fencing/stolen goods network. These burglaries are often committed by older offenders with a long criminal history for theft and burglary, who tend to use manipulation and schemes to gain access to a property prior to the burglary (e.g., posing as salesmen or a utility worker to see inside and "case" a residence) or have a job that they would use to facilitate burglary (e.g., tree trimming, construction, plumbing, electrician, etc.). In many cases, the victim met the offender, though may not know him/her very well. There would often be two or more organized burglars committing the crime, in order to increase the amount of "loot" able to be stolen. For the same reason, organized burglars often had a car, which also allowed a quick getaway to a location further away from the victimized target (Fox & Farrington, 2012).

In contrast, disorganized style burglaries were highly spontaneous and haphazard, with little concern or effort taken to avoid apprehension or prevent evidence from being left behind. If a tool was needed, these burglars typically found something (e.g., a large rock, brick, etc.) or used their body (arms, hands, feet) to force entry. Once inside, the target was usually ransacked, leaving the scene in disarray and sending a clear indication that a burglary took place. Evidence was commonly left behind, and low-value items were often stolen. Disorganized burglars tend to be young with early onset of criminal behavior. They do not know the victim and select targets at random. Disorganized burglars are less likely to have cars, be employed, or have stability in their lives. The disorganized burglaries were also similar to the FBI's profile for disorganized homicides (Fox & Farrington, 2012).

Two additional profiles for burglary were identified using the EBOP method. Opportunistic burglaries demonstrated a lack of premeditation, as most of these burglars entered a dwelling when a door, window, or garage was left open, did not bring tools to the crime, often occurred at unoccupied residential dwellings, and low-value items were stolen. They are crimes of opportunity. Opportunistic burglars are young but have not committed many offenses in the past. They likely do not know the victim, did not premeditate their crime, tend not to have a car, and may commit these burglaries while skipping school or while bored over the summer months.

Finally, interpersonal style burglaries are highly unique in that the target of the crime was the victim, not his/her objects. Unlike other burglaries, interpersonal offenses typically occur at occupied residential dwellings at night and were motivated by anger or a dispute. These were highly confrontational, which is unusual for a property crime such as burglary. In many ways, the interpersonal burglar appears to be testing the waters for a more serious offense such as sexual battery, domestic violence, or homicide; many rapists and serial killers have burglary in their background (Schlesinger & Revitch, 1999). Interpersonal burglars tend to be adult aged and almost always know the victim (often females) and usually offend alone. Unlike other burglars, this group enjoys the thrill of being in an occupied dwelling with the victim, and may "case" the location to ensure the victim is inside. Interpersonal burglars are at highest risk for escalating to more severe crimes in the future.

After developing a statistical profile, the critical next step in the EBOP model is to replicate profiles developed for various crimes using new samples, and to test the effectiveness of the profiles in active police investigations using experimental evaluations (Fox & Farrington, 2016). Replication of the statistical profiles will help increase the reliability and confidence in the profiles, if consistency across samples and locations can be established, or will provide insight on the similarity and differences in behavior exhibited by offenders for otherwise dissimilar crimes. Applying and evaluating the impact of statistical profiles used in field investigations will shed light on the true impact of the profiles in the field when measured using a high-quality experimental evaluation.

While randomized controlled trials (RCTs) are the gold standard in experimental research and the preferred method when evaluating effects, as randomization allows true causality (i.e., knowing the treatment caused the change in outcome) to be established, RCTs are typically very difficult (or impossible) to conduct in criminal justice settings due to the time, resources, and cooperation needed to implement the design (Farrington & Welsh, 2006). Therefore, nonrandomized experiments are commonly used in social science research. This design involves collection of pre- and posttest measures for an outcome (e.g., crime arrest rates) for both the treatment (e.g., using the statistical profiles) and control (e.g., not using the statistical profiles) groups. This design should also include (1) additional covariates to improve matching between the conditions, (2) multiple pre- and posttreatment measures to get a more accurate effect size measure, and (3) multiple treatment or control groups for better comparisons. While the lack of randomization prevents causality from being definitively established, these elements address many of the major threats to internal validity. Therefore, conducting an experimental evaluation of the EBOP statistical profiles impact on arrest rates should be conducted using an RCT or nonequivalent group experimental design.

For instance, in the first and only scientific field experiment on the effectiveness of offender profiles applied in active police investigations to date, Fox and Farrington (2016) implemented the Fox and Farrington (2012) evidence-based burglary profiles were implemented in one police department in Florida while three others continued their standard policing techniques. After a 1-year follow-up, results of the experiment showed that the police department using the burglary profiles solved more than 260% more burglaries compared with the departments which did not use the profiles, despite all conditions having nearly identical arrest rates at the start of the experiment. Furthermore, the burglary arrest rate for the department using the profiles increased from 10% to over 30% in the posttest period, even after statistically controlling for prior arrest rates and burglary incidence rates. This experiment provides the best empirical evidence of the real-world utility of OP, although the results were based upon statistically generated EBOP burglary profiles, and results may differ for profiles developed using less sound statistical methods.

State of the field of offender profiling

A systematic review and meta-analysis of all 426 OP publications from 1976 through 2016 by Fox and Farrington (2018) aimed to evaluate the state of the field of OP and identify recurring profiles and effectiveness associated with profiles developed using varied approaches. This novel analysis revealed several important findings. First, the plurality of OP publications (46%) were published between 2006 and 2016, and not a single article in the past decade was authored by a member of the famed FBI Behavioral Science Unit (BSU). In fact, less than 5% of all OP publications were produced between 1976 and 1985, which was the "height" of OP conducted by FBI profilers in the BSU. With respect to the training of those publishing on OP, results indicate that most authors are psychologists (43%), followed by criminologists (17%), and those in other fields (12%). FBI special agents authored just 7% of all publications on OP.

The accuracy of the profiles can differ greatly depending upon the type of methods, data quality, and analytical technique that was utilized. Results of Fox and Farrington's (2018) analysis found that over half of all OP publications used no statistics of any kind, while 22% used basic descriptive statistics, and just over a quarter used advanced inferential statistics to develop profiles. Similarly, half of the 426 studies did not use any crime/offender sample, 43% drew upon a sample less than 400, and 7% used a sample of offenders that was 400 or greater. Nearly two-thirds (63%) of the publications were published in peer-reviewed journals, and the remaining 37% were not.

To identify recurring profiles with the body of literature on OP, an analysis of the 62 publications proposing new offender profiles was conducted (Fox & Farrington, 2018). Homicide, the crime most commonly profiled in OP publications (26%), most often yielded four total profiles, with recurring themes of *expressive, instrumental, visionary, hedonistic, power/control, traveling,* and *local* offenders. It should be noted that the organized/disorganized profiles, popularized by Douglas and Ressler of the FBI's BSU, were not found to be recurring profiles in the literature to date. Sexual homicide, a subtype in which victims are sexually assaulted (often in sadistic ways), three distinct profiles were commonly identified, with recurring profiles of *sadistic, sexual, anger/fury, power/control, organized,* and *disorganized* offender types. In this case, the organized/disorganized profiles were repeatedly found throughout multiple OP publications. Sexual assaults were the second most common crime to be profiled (13%), and four profiles were most often identified in the OP literature. The recurring profiles for sexual assault were *hostility, involvement, opportunistic, disorganized/chaotic, ritual,* and *power/control* types. About 5% of all OP publications profiled burglary, and four profiles were commonly identified, but only two recurring profiles were found across the literature: *opportunistic* and *disorganized/pilferer* type burglars. Finally, arson profiles comprised 3% of all OP publications, and again four profiles were most common in the literature. The recurring themes were *expressive, instrumental, crime concealment,* and *revenge* arson profiles.

In summary, results of the Fox and Farrington (2018) meta-analysis indicate that the field of OP appears to be on a much more scientific and statistically based path than it was four decades ago, when not a single publication used any type of advanced statistical analysis or evaluation technique.

Conclusions

While there is still much more to be done to understand the impact of offender profiling on unsolved cases and how police can leverage offender profiles to achieve the best results in their unique and specific cases, it would appear that statistically-generated behavioral profiles are more likely to lead to positive results than profiles created using subjective clinical methodologies alone. Consequently, the continuation of the current trajectory will help transform the field of OP from what some have referred to as a "pseudoscience" into an evidence-based discipline that produces results used to help police, understand criminal behavior, and make the world a safer place for all.

References

Alison, L., Rockett, W., Deprez, S., & Watts, S. (2000). Bandits, cowboys and Robin's men: The facets of armed robbery. In D. V. Canter, & L. J. Alison (Eds.), *Profiling property crimes* (pp. 75−106). Dartmouth: Ashgate.

Bennell, C., & Canter, D. V. (2002). Linking commercial burglaries by modus operandi: Tests using regression and ROC analysis. *Science and Justice, 42*(3), 153−164.

Bennell, C., Mugford, R., Ellingwood, H., & Woodhams, J. (2014). Linking crimes using behavioural clues: Current levels of linking accuracy and strategies for moving forward. *Journal of Investigative Psychology and Offender Profiling, 11,* 29−56.

Bonn, S. (December 4, 2017). Criminal profiling: The original Mind Hunters profiling killers dates back to Jack the Ripper. *Psychology Today*. Retrieved from https://www.psychologytoday.com/us/blog/wicked-deeds/201712/criminal-profiling-the-original-mind-hunters?amp.

Bonn, S. (June 17, 2018). Organized versus disorganized serial predators: The basis of FBI criminal profiling. *Psychology Today*. Retrieved from https://www.psychologytoday.com/us/blog/wicked-deeds/201806/organized-versus-disorganized-serial-predators.

Campbell, C. (1976). Portrait of a mass killer. *Psychology Today, 9*, 110–119.

Canter, D. V. (1995). *Criminal shadows: Inside the mind of the serial killer*. London, UK: HarperCollins.

Canter, D. V., & Alison, L. J. (2000). *Profiling property crimes* (Vol. 4). Aldershot, England: Ashgate Publishing.

Canter, D. V., & Fritzon, K. (1998). Differentiating arsonists: A model of firesetting actions and characteristics. *Journal of Criminal and Legal Psychology, 3*, 73–96.

Canter, D. V., & Kirby, S. (1995). Prior convictions of child molesters. *Science and Justice, 35*, 73–78.

Carlo, P. (1996). *The night stalker: The life and crimes of Richard Ramirez*. New York: Kensington Publishing Corp.

Copson, G. (1995). *Coals to newcastle? Part 1: A study of offender profiling*. London, England: Home Office, Police Research Group.

Douglas, J. E., & Burgess, A. E. (1986). Criminal profiling: A viable investigative tool against violent crime. *FBI Law Enforcement Bulletin, 55*, 9–13.

Dowden, C., Bennell, C., & Bloomfield, S. (2007). Advances in offender profiling: A systematic review of the profiling literature published over the past three decades. *Journal of Police and Criminal Psychology, 22*, 44–56.

Farrington, D. P., & Lambert, S. (2000). Statistical approaches to offender profiling. In D. V. Canter, & L. J. Alison (Eds.), *Profiling property crimes* (pp. 233–274). Aldershot, England: Ashgate Publishing.

Farrington, D. P., & Welsh, B. C. (2006). A half century of randomized experiments on crime and justice. *Crime and Justice, 34*(1), 55–132.

Fox, B., & Farrington, D. P. (2012). Creating burglary profiles using latent class analysis: A new approach to offender profiling. *Criminal Justice and Behavior, 39*, 1582–1611.

Fox, B., & Farrington, D. P. (2016). An experimental evaluation of the utility of burglary profiles applied in active police investigations. *Criminal Justice and Behavior, 42*, 156–175.

Fox, B., & Farrington, D. P. (2018). What have we learned from offender profiling? A systematic review and meta-analysis of 40 years of research. *Psychological Bulletin, 144*, 1247–1274.

Geberth, V. J. (1990). Serial killer and the revelation of ted Bundy. *Law and Order, 38*, 72–77.

Gudjonsson, G. H., & Copson, G. (1997). The role of the expert in criminal investigations. In J. L. Jackson, & D. A. Bekerian (Eds.), *Offender profiling: Theory, research and practice* (pp. 1–7). New York, NY: John Wiley.

Hazelwood, R. R., & Burgess, A. W. (Eds.). (1987). *Practical aspects of rape investigation: A multidisciplinary approach*. Boca Raton, FL: CRC Press.

Hazelwood, R. R., & Douglas, J. E. (1980). The lust murderer. *FBI Law Enforcement Bulletin, 49*, 18–22.

Holmes, R. M., & Holmes, S. T. (1996). *Profiling violent crimes: An investigative tool*. Thousand Oaks, CA: SAGE.

Kocsis, R. N. (2006). Validities and abilities in criminal profiling: The dilemma for David Canter's investigative psychology. *International Journal of Offender Therapy and Comparative Criminology, 50*, 458–477.

Kocsis, R. N., & Cooksey, R. W. (2002). Criminal psychological profiling of serial arson crimes. *International Journal of Offender Therapy and Comparative Criminology, 46*, 631–656.

Kocsis, R. N., Irwin, H. J., & Hayes, A. F. (1998). Organised and disorganised criminal behaviour syndromes in arsonists: A validation study of a psychological profiling concept. *Psychiatry, Psychology and Law, 5*, 117–131.

Kocsis, R. N., Irwin, H. J., Hayes, A. F., & Nunn, R. (2000). Expertise in psychological profiling: A comparative assessment. *Journal of Interpersonal Violence, 15*, 311–331.

Kocsis, R. N., & Middledorp, J. T. (2004). Believing is seeing III: Perceptions of content in criminal psychological profiles. *International Journal of Offender Therapy and Comparative Criminology, 48*, 477–494.

Kocsis, R. N., & Palermo, G. B. (2016). Criminal profiling as expert witness evidence: The implications of the profiler validity research. *International Journal of Law and Psychiatry, 49*, 55–65.

Ormerod, D. C. (1996). Psychological profiling. *The Journal of Forensic Psychiatry, 7*, 341–352.

Petherick, W. (2006). The fallacy of accuracy in criminal profiling. In W. Petherick (Ed.), *Serial crime: Theoretical and practical issues in behavioral profiling* (pp. 53–65). London, England: Elsevier Academic Press.

Pinizzotto, A. J. (1984). Forensic psychology: Criminal personality profiling. *Journal of Police Science and Administration, 12*, 32–40.

Pinizzotto, A. J., & Finkel, N. J. (1990). Criminal personality profiling: An outcome and process study. *Law and Human Behavior, 14*, 215–233.

Ressler, R. K., Burgess, A. W., & Douglas, J. E. (1988). *Sexual homicide: Patterns and motives.* Lexington, MA: Lexington Books.

Rossmo, D. K. (1995). *Geographic profiling: Target patterns of serial murderers.* Doctoral dissertation thesis. Canada: School of Criminology, Simon Fraser University.

Rossmo, D. K. (2000). *Geographic profiling.* Boca Raton, FL: CRC Press.

Salfati, C. G., & Canter, D. V. (1999). Differentiating stranger murders: Profiling offender characteristics from behavioral styles. *Behavioral Sciences and the Law, 17*, 391–406.

Schlesinger, L. B., & Revitch, E. (1999). Sexual burglaries and sexual homicides: Clinical, forensic, and investigative considerations. *Journal of the American Academy of Psychiatry and Law, 27*, 227–238.

Snook, B., Taylor, P. J., & Bennell, C. (2007). Criminal profiling belief and use: A study of Canadian police officer opinion. *Canadian Journal of Police and Security Services, 5*, 1–11.

Steadman, H. J., Silver, E., Monahan, J., Appelbaum, P. S., Robbins, P. C., Mulvey, E. P., & et al. (2000). A classification tree approach to the development of actuarial violence risk assessment tools. *Law and Human Behavior, 24*, 83–100.

Stevens, S.v. (2001). *Tennessee 78 S.W.*

Swets, J. A. (1988). Measuring the accuracy of diagnostic systems. *Science, 240*, 1285–1293.

Trager, J., & Brewster, J. (2001). The effectiveness of psychological profiles. *Journal of Police and Criminal Psychology, 16*, 20–28.

Van Derbeken, J. (October 23, 2009). Night stalker tied to slaying of S.F. Girl. *San Francisco Chronicle.* Retrieved from http://m.sfgate.com/news/article/Night-Stalker-tied-to-slaying-of-S-F-girl-3213197.php.

Conclusion
Police psychology and contemporary challenges in an uncertain world

Paulo Barbosa Marques and Mauro Paulino

In concluding this book, we do not seek to examine the themes covered thoroughly in each individual chapter of the book, but instead we concentrate on several contemporary issues that will demand further advice and support from police psychologists, if these psychologists are to play an active role in the increasingly diverse and complex environment that they serve.

The world is facing multiple challenges and many of the global threats are induced by people and involve a high degree of uncertainty. Since we are attempting to understand human behavior and how it affects most of the contemporary and emerging challenges facing law enforcement, police psychology should be expanded and further resourced.

We are living in an era of unparalleled resources and technological advancement. In recent years, significant global health gains have been achieved: life expectancy has increased in many parts of the world, 6 million fewer children under age 5 died in 2016 than in 1990, polio is on the verge of being eradicated, and 21 million people who are living with HIV are now receiving treatment. Economic and social development has enabled millions of people to escape extreme poverty and enabled many more countries to contribute to the global agenda (World Health Organization, 2019a). However, for too many people, this is also an era of insecurity. The world faces threats from high-impact health emergencies (e.g., epidemics, pandemics, conflicts, natural and technological disasters) and the emergence of antimicrobial resistance. More than 244 million people (more than 3% of the world's population) have migrated from their country of origin, and 65 million of these were forcibly displaced. Current data from the International Organization for Migration (IOM, 2017) indicates that in 2016 there were 40.3 million internally displaced people worldwide; 22.5 million are refugees and 2.8 million are seeking international protection and awaiting determination of their refugee status, referred to as asylum seekers.

The World Health Organization (2019b) and the World Economic Forum (2019) both listed *fragile and vulnerable settings* and *large-scale involuntary migration*, respectively, and its effects as one of their top risks for 2019. The potential risk of migration at such a massive scale is rooted in social, political, economic, and gender inequalities and other determinants.

In precarious socioeconomic conditions or situations involving persecution, people escaping conflict can be more easily deceived. Armed conflicts tend to have a negative impact on the livelihood of people living in the surrounding areas, even when they are not directly involved in the violence. Transnational organized crime groups know this and may target communities that are particularly vulnerable because of forced displacement, taking advantage of people's desperation (UNODC, 2018a). The costs of smuggling and the urgency of their migration may leave them vulnerable to abuse and, in the most severe cases, to trafficking situations (UNODC, 2018b).

Moreover, human trafficking has also played an increasing role in the operations of terrorist organizations, and their direct or indirect involvement with organized crime syndicates is used as part of the strategic objectives and ideology of terrorist groups and as a way to raise funds to support their activities (CTED, 2019). The European Union Serious and Organised Crime Threat Assessment (SOCTA) 2017 identifies migrant smuggling and trafficking in human beings as *specific priority crime threats*, which require the greatest concerted action to ensure the most effective impact (Europol, 2017).

The General Assembly of the United Nations noting existing, growing, or potential links between transnational organized crime and terrorism in some cases, has adopted the 2000 United Nations Convention against Transnational Organized Crime and its supplementary Protocols (Protocol to Prevent, Suppress and Punish Trafficking in Persons, Especially Women and Children, Protocol against the Smuggling of Migrants by Land, Air and Sea, and Protocol against the Illicit Manufacturing and Trafficking in Firearms, Their Parts and Components and Ammunition) with a view to promoting international cooperation in addressing those links.

The pursuit of criminal activities in support of terrorist activities is not a new phenomenon. However, the involvement of suspects with extensive criminal backgrounds and access to the resources and tools of organized crime networks in terrorism are particularly threatening in light of the fast pace of radicalization and the willingness to very quickly engage in terrorist attacks following the beginning of the radicalization process (Europol, 2017).

The mutations of contemporary societies could contribute to the materialization of the phenomenon of radicalization. The grounds of these changes are multiple and complex, with a combination of geopolitical, religious and societal factors, bringing along insecurity and precariousness.

Ultimately, the nexus between irregular and forced migration, transnational organized crime networks, which seize the opportunity to make large profits from trafficking in human beings and the smuggling of migrants, and terrorist organizations' efforts to radicalize, recruit and mobilize new members, introduces complexities and uncertainties that need to be taken into account. The complex and dynamic nature of these emergent hazards requires new techniques and a multistakeholder approach that is able to equip law enforcement agencies and their employees with the knowledge and skills they need to prevent and combat the international, multifaceted, unpredictable, highly developed, ambitious, and profitable cross-border crime.

So how does psychological science, and its practitioners, handle these challenges and balance the uncertainties in order to assist police organizations in carrying out their missions and making informed decisions about the risks they manage and where they focus their resources and energy? How can psychology inform policing and border management policies, procedures, and practices in an era of uncertainty?

First, psychologists must seek to understand and define the risks and minimize the consequences of such a volatile environment by providing police officers with the skills and tools necessary to improve judgment and decision-making and apt to protect themselves not just physically but also psychologically.

Almost three decades ago, Blau (1988) stressed that appropriate psychological training assists police agencies not only in the delivery of services and the advancement of the profession, but also in the prevention of damages to the public and the attenuation of civil liability. Aware of the need to incorporate psychological science contributions in the training of law enforcement personnel, agencies with important responsibilities in the field of law enforcement include the application of psychological research and principles in training activities aiming to promote practical experience of applying best practice techniques and proper professional behavior (see CEPOL, 2018; Frontex, 2019).

According to Tyler, Goff, and MacCoun (2015), the development of police research provides an example of how initially academic psychological theories and experimental laboratory-based research conducted by social psychologists can provide a powerful alternative to some of the traditional models that have dominated law enforcement agencies.

If police psychologists aspire to support the policing community in achieving a high degree of certainty in their decisions, the psychological models must speak to issues that are important to the actors in law enforcement agencies. In order to deal with the uncertainty of the contemporary landscape, frontline police officers must have superior multicultural and interpersonal skills capable of providing comfort with cultural diversity. Like many other professions, police work contains a mixture of legitimate and illegitimate claims that require differentiation (Lilienfeld & Landfield, 2008). Law enforcement organizations must avoid being seduced by pseudoscientific practices and increase the delivery of credible and scientifically verified practices.

For example, the sudden and unexpected increase in migratory pressure prompted psychologists and other social scientists to look at the migration, asylum, and border issues in an attempt to make border management more predictable and accountable (e.g., Jupe, Leal, Vrij, & Nahari, 2017; van Veldhuizen, Horselenberg, Landström, Granhag, & van Koppen, 2017), and to raise awareness and improve the lives of individuals and communities that have been affected by the ongoing crisis (e.g., American Psychological Association, 2014; British Psychological Society, 2018; Dando, Walsh, & Brierley, 2016). However, under the argument of continuous traffic growth, combined with the increased threat of illegal immigration and the impact that slow border crossings have on travelers' satisfaction, business, and trade, countries are turning to ever more ultramodern, but also controversial technologies (e.g., promises of automated deception detection), in order to protect their borders (e.g., the multimillion EU-funded project *iBorderCtrl*).

Despite the extent of scientific research on nonverbal communication, security and justice professionals in some jurisdictions have turned to programs, methods, and approaches that fail to reflect the state of the science. The consequences of the misuse of nonverbal communication are important enough to question the responsibility of organizations in the fields of security and justice that rely on the observation of behavioral indicators (or combinations of some of them) in face-to-face interactions to detect threats (Denault et al., 2019).

Following the September 11, 2001, attacks, the Transportation Security Administration (TSA) of the US Department of Homeland Security implemented, in numerous US airports, the Screening of Passengers by Observation Techniques (SPOT), a program aimed at identifying aviation security threats through monitoring the nonverbal behaviors and appearance of passengers. After the assessment of the scientific basis of SPOT by independent experts, in 2013 the US Government Accountability Office recommended that the US Congress consider the absence of scientific evidence on the effectiveness of identifying aviation security threats through the nonverbal behaviors of passengers in its SPOT funding decisions (US Government Accountability Office, 2013).

We can find some similarities between SPOT and the Automated Deception Detection system (ADDS) which is powered by a conversational agent avatar. ADDS is part of the iBorderCtrl (Intelligent Portable Control System) and in its proponents' words is "capable of quantifying the degree of deception on the part of the interviewee" (O'Shea et al., 2018). The main difference is that the behavior detection officers deployed in US airports are now replaced by a lie-detecting avatar.

We follow the conclusions of Denault et al. (2019) in questioning the investment in a program with no scientific evidence to substantiate its reliability, validity, and utility. The financial resources allocated to these programs could be invested in the development of new programs based on knowledge published in peer-reviewed scientific journals, as well as in programs with established effectiveness. For example, rather than being invested in "advanced border control agent avatars" of unknown effectiveness, these resources could be invested in the recruitment and training of border guards.

The Portuguese context provides another perspective. Although being at the forefront of smart border control technology (e.g., the Portuguese Vision-Box automated border control e-gates deployed at the airports on a global scale), the Immigration and Borders Service (SEF) has been facing an increasing number of passengers at Portuguese airports (and also the unprecedented arrival of irregular migrants, asylum seekers, and potential victims of trafficking in human beings and their offenders using air migration routes to the European Union) through the investment in human resources.

Organized crime groups regularly use air connections between African countries and EU Member States to facilitate underage trafficking in human being victims. As an example, several underage Angolan potential victims of trafficking were identified while trying to enter the EU via Lisbon and Porto international airports, unaccompanied or escorted by other Angolan citizens who, claiming to be their direct relatives, were using forged or look-alike Angolan documents — passports, ID cards, birth certificates, and travel documents.

The number of minors detected at Portuguese airports has been steadily increasing since 2014, with more than 20 entries per year following the same scheme. For Angolan victims, Portugal is used as a point of entry to the EU while the end destination of the minors is in other EU Member States, especially Belgium, France, Germany. Associates of the human trafficking network maintain a logistical base in the country to facilitate the initial stages of the exploitation process: housing the victims and organizing their further movements (Europol, 2018).

According to the US Department of State (2019), traffickers also exploit children from Eastern Europe, including those of Roma descent, for forced begging and forced criminal activity in Portugal. Authorities report that traffickers bring women and children, many from West Africa, to Portugal to claim asylum and obtain false documents before bringing them to other European countries for sex trafficking. Sub-Saharan trafficking networks increasingly use Portugal as a route into the Schengen area to exploit children for both sex trafficking and forced labor.

As mentioned previously, to address this and other unforeseeable events and factors that can have a profound and unpredictable impact on the situation at the border, SEF initiated the necessary recruitment and training measures to ensure that the required manpower is available and trained in accordance with the Common Core Curriculum for Border Guard Basic Training (Frontex, 2019). The Common Core Curriculum Basic is the first common curriculum including common skills and competencies for the basic training of law enforcement officers in the EU. It encompasses many topics from psychological sciences (e.g., applied psychology; guiding persons with nervous, aggressive, or deceptive behavior and psychologically unstable persons; influence of alcohol or drugs on behavior; stress management and critical incident response; crowd psychology; investigative interview). This set of abilities and aptitudes derived from psychology will also be of utmost importance in the many Frontex deployments in migration hotspots where Portuguese border guards participate.

A strong and proactive training environment, combined with the establishment of specialized teams (e.g., SEF's Anti-Trafficking in Human Beings Unit) may be a winning formula to help law enforcement agencies accomplish their missions. Recent police operations attest the added value of such an approach (e.g., Eurojust, 2019; Reuters, 2019; SEF, 2019a; SEF, 2019b).

Another example that agencies are increasingly recognizing the importance of psychology in effective integrated border management services is the IOM-funded project "Development of Integrated Psychological Services of the Border Police in the Republic of Moldova (SPINS)." IOM supported the General Inspectorates of Border Police (GIBP) of the Moldovan Ministry of Internal Affairs in restructuring and enhancing of its operational capacities for proper handling of its competences, especially in facilitating the regular movement of people through the Moldovan border while counteracting irregular migration. This support is an important prerequisite for combating transnational crime such as human smuggling and trafficking; terrorist threats; and the identification and interception of foreign fighters. It supports Moldova's overall capacity to ensure regular movement of Moldovans and foreigners through Moldovan borders and territory and ensure full observation of migrants' human rights, including their psychological well-being. This includes support for capacity building and creation of a self-sustainable system for development of the GIBP operational capacity, while also enhancing the agency's capacity and abilities for psychological support to its staff, as well as for the people crossing the border, in line with the best international and European standards and practices (IOM SEECA, 2018).

One important feature of the abovementioned project is the specific reference to the identification and interception of "foreign terrorist fighters" (FTFs). Moreover, a recent study highlighted how violent extremist networks exploit structural factors within the process of migration to radicalize migrants (Elshimi, Pantucci, Lain, & Salman, 2018). As stressed by the Parliamentary Assembly of the Council of Europe in its Resolution 2221 (2018), the absence of comprehensive migration policies significantly increases the likelihood of the spreading of violent extremism and radicalization of migrants. Factors like (1) bureaucratic administrative and legal procedures contributing to a precarious status as migrants become "illegal" and thus exposed to human rights abuses and other vulnerabilities or (2) the discrimination and stigmatization of labor migrants combined with economic exploitation and poverty can lead to feelings of marginalization, exclusion, and alienation. These and other factors can foster grievances that can be exploited by violent extremist entities. However, it is important to remember that migrants should not be perceived as an increasing terrorism risk, as has been asserted by media and politicians in many countries. Such a position only leads to increased stigmatization of an entire community or exposure to different forms of discrimination and violence on arrival and it will ultimately exacerbate the problem of radicalization. The return of FTFs and their families and the radicalization into violent extremism are two trends that law enforcement agencies around the world must be aware of.

The phenomenon of FTFs has expanded worldwide, with an estimated 40,000 individuals from more than 110 countries having traveled to Syria and Iraq, where they became affiliated with terrorist groups. The perceived imminent threat posed by the FTFs returning home or relocating to safe havens or other troubled parts of the world represents a major challenge to international peace and security.

In the words of Ganor (2004), terrorism is a form of psychological warfare. Terrorists try to harness uncertainty to advance their goals, by sowing the seeds of fear of random, highly unpredictable, and horrific future terrorist acts. If terrorism has a psychological dimension, police psychologists are at the forefront of efforts to assist law enforcement agencies in the prevention of radicalization and violent extremism. Ultimately, the fight against terrorism can only be won if we prevent young people from joining such organizations and if we manage to induce members of terrorist groups to leave their organizations (Schmid, 2005).

Multidimensional deradicalization initiatives may be an efficient approach with vulnerable young individuals or returning FTFs who have been exposed to all aspects of violent extremism and who may have experienced loss, be traumatized, and require psychological care. The psychological trauma caused by an event that acutely affects a person can trigger and increase dramatically the psychological susceptibility to violence and radical ideas.

It is important to take into account the psychological factors to explain mobilization. Such factors can help explain why one particular individual might become radicalized, while another from an analogous situation and background does not. Psychological and cognitive factors, such as one's self-image, a sense of identity and belonging, expectations, beliefs, and attitudes, are dynamic and shape how a person experiences and reacts to his or her environment and events. These factors can have an impact on the development of negative feelings of displacement, of "being odd," for instance, feelings of exclusion, rejection, relative deprivation, humiliation, victimization, injustice, frustration, revolt, or superiority. This can push someone to be more susceptible to the appeal of terrorism (OSCE, 2014).

Beyond the evolving repressive and security efforts, educational accompaniment and systematic psychological intervention could increase the likelihood of the individual disengaging from violent extremism and re-entering society without presenting a potentially enduring significant threat. Police psychologists should encourage policies which highlight the benefits of diversity and develop positive self-perceptions of individual identity free of any inferiority complexes among young people, in order to prevent alienation, a lack of a sense of belonging, marginalization and community isolationism from prevailing, and providing a fertile breeding ground for radicalization.

The focus on the underlying psychological mechanisms and dynamics of the radicalization process is critical. But if police psychologists want to help law enforcement agencies to execute policies that protect and empower our communities, they need to encourage initiatives designed to enhance *psychological resilience* and implement large-scale *community engagement* strategies.

The concept of resilience is worth mentioning in the prevention discourse and is key, as it provides a perspective on prevention that acknowledges the potential and agency of individuals and communities. However, according to Stephens, Sieckelinck, and Boutellier (2019), a clear framework for resilience in relation to violent extremism is missing. A social-ecological perspective on resilience represents a promising foundation that must be built upon if such a framework is to emerge. Doosje et al. (2016) outlined how factors at the micro (i.e., individual), meso (i.e., group), and macro (i.e., society) levels can play a role in a process of radicalization and deradicalization. The authors argue that it is crucial to take into account group membership and the intergroup context that forms the basis of radicalization. Moreover, particular awareness must be directed toward ensuring that attention is given not only to possibilities for change at the individual and community level but more particularly to what is required at an institutional and social level (Stephens et al., 2019).

Preventing and combating radicalization requires strong and strategic alliances and partnerships between all pertinent stakeholders at all levels of governance (local, regional, and national), including in civil society. At the core of the community, an engagement perspective is the strengthening of relationships between citizens and the institutions of the state. Consequently, much attention is given to the quality of the relationships between a community and the police. This encompasses recommendations such as that law enforcement officers should be capable of spending additional time within a community, acquiring a deep cultural understanding of the community they are serving. This extends in some cases to the recommendation that police officers should engage in partnership with those who may be embracing radical and extremist views and ideologies (Cherney, 2018).

The nature of globalization continues to evolve and present new challenges. These complex societal transformations may result in the decline of psychological well-being and augmented stress levels as a consequence of lack of control in the face of insecurity. Mental health problems can create a sense of danger and uncertainty and heighten social conflicts with family, peers, and neighbors which have the potential to negatively impact social cohesion.

These issues deserve more attention and imply a rise in the complexity of law enforcement duties and responsibilities. Police organizations would benefit from a comprehensive strategy that builds on the many contributions that psychologists in general, and police psychologists in particular, may undertake to meet the challenges we face now and in the future. Whether it is the migration crisis, or threats from serious and organized crimes like smuggling and trafficking in human beings, or terrorism and radicalization, if we are to meet our communities' needs, police psychologists must continue to adapt to the modern policing environment.

The psychologists collaborating with police organizations must adopt a consistent and professional attitude at all times in adhering to ethical and evidence-based practices. More importantly, they must contribute to and promote the improvement of police-community relations and public confidence in policing.

By mitigating uncertainty and helping to maintain a sense of control in a fast-changing world, police psychologists can make the difference in achieving a more fair and peaceful society and reinforcing the need for law enforcement agencies to rely on psychological science across their multiple domains of intervention, as discussed in this book.

References

American Psychological Association. (2014). *Report of the task force on trafficking of women and girls*. Washington, DC: American Psychological Association. Retrieved from http://www.apa.org/pi/women/programs/trafficking/report.asp.

Blau, G. L. (1988). Psychology in police training. *Journal of Police and Criminal Psychology, 4*(2), 21–24. https://doi.org/10.1007/BF02806552.

British Psychological Society. (2018). *Guidelines for psychologists working with refugees and asylum seekers in the UK: Extended version.* Retrieved from http://www.infocoponline.es/pdf/GuideRefugees.pdf.

CEPOL. (2018). *European union strategic training needs assessment 2019–2021.* Budapest: CEPOL European Union Agency for Law Enforcement Training. Retrieved from https://www.cepol.europa.eu/sites/default/files/EU-STNA%20Report.pdf.

Cherney, A. (2018). Police community engagement and outreach in a counterterrorism context. *Journal of Policing, Intelligence and Counter Terrorism, 13*(1), 60–79. https://doi.org/10.1080/18335330.2018.1432880.

CTED. (2019). *Identifying and exploring the nexus between human trafficking, terrorism, and terrorism financing.* Counter-Terrorism Committee Executive Directorate. Retrieved from https://www.un.org/sc/ctc/wp-content/uploads/2019/02/HT-terrorism-nexus-CTED-report.pdf.

Dando, C. J., Walsh, D., & Brierley, R. (2016). Perceptions of psychological coercion and human trafficking in the West Midlands of England: Beginning to know the unknown. *PLoS One, 11*(5), e0153263. https://doi.org/10.1371/journal.pone.0153263.

Denault, V., Plusquellec, P., Jupe, L. M., St-Yves, M., Dunbar, N. E., Hartwig, M., et al. (2019). The analysis of nonverbal communication: The dangers of pseudoscience in security and justice contexts. *Anuario de Psicología Jurídica.* https://doi.org/10.5093/apj2019a9. Ahead of print.

Doosje, B., Moghaddam, F. M., Kruglanski, A. W., Wolf, A., Mann, L., & Feddes, A. R. (2016). Terrorism, radicalization and de-radicalization. *Current Opinion in Psychology, 11*, 79–84. https://doi.org/10.1016/j.copsyc.2016.06.008.

Elshimi, M. S., Pantucci, R., Lain, S., & Salman, N. L. (2018). *Understanding the factors contributing to radicalisation among Central Asian labour migrants in Russia.* London: Royal United Services Institute (RUSI) for Defence and Security Studies occasional paper. Retrieved from https://www.sfcg.org/wp-content/uploads/2018/04/RUSI-report_Central-Asia-Radicalisation_ENG_24042018.pdf.

Eurojust. (January 15, 2019). *Criminal gang recruiting women into sham marriages dismantled.* Joint Eurojust/Europol Press Release. Retrieved from http://eurojust.europa.eu/press/PressReleases/Pages/2019/2019-01-15.aspx.

Europol. (2017). *European union serious and organised crime threat assessment (SOCTA) 2017: Crime in the age of technology.* Retrieved from https://www.europol.europa.eu/activities-services/main-reports/european-union-serious-and-organised-crime-threat-assessment-2017.

Europol. (2018). *Criminal networks involved in the trafficking and exploitation of underage victims in the European Union.* Retrieved from https://www.europol.europa.eu/publications-documents/criminal-networks-involved-in-trafficking-and-exploitation-of-underage-victims-in-eu.

Frontex. (2019). *Common core curriculum for border and Coast guard basic training in the EU: Revised edition 2017. A guide to the modifications from the CCC 2012 to the CCC 2017.* Luxembourg: Publications Office of the European Union. Retrieved from https://publications.europa.eu/en/publication-detail/-/publication/ccaed831-3978-11e9-8d04-01aa75ed71a1/language-en/format-PDF/source-87833245.

Ganor, B. (2004). Terrorism as a strategy of psychological warfare. *Journal of Aggression, Maltreatment & Trauma, 9*, 33–43. https://doi.org/10.1300/J146v09n01_03.

IOM. (2017). *World migration report 2018.* Geneva: International Organization for Migration. Retrieved from https://www.iom.int/wmr/world-migration-report-2018.

IOM SEECA. (2018). *Migration health division Annual newsletter 2018. IOM Regional office for South-Eastern Europe, Eastern Europe and Central Asia.* Retrieved from https://rovienna.iom.int/sites/default/files/publications/MHD%20Newsletter_SEEECA_2018_Final.pdf.

Jupe, L., Leal, S., Vrij, A., & Nahari, G. (2017). Applying the verifiability approach in an international airport setting. *Psychology, Crime and Law, 23*(8), 812–825. https://doi.org/10.1080/1068316X.2017.1327584.

Lilienfeld, S. O., & Landfield, K. (2008). Science and pseudoscience in law enforcement: A user-friendly primer. *Criminal Justice and Behavior, 35*(10), 1215–1230. https://doi.org/10.1177/0093854808321526.

OSCE. (2014). *Preventing terrorism and countering violent extremism and radicalization that lead to terrorism: A community-policing approach.* Vienna: Organization for Security and Co-operation in Europe. Retrieved from https://www.osce.org/secretariat/111438?download=true.

O' Shea, J., Crockett, K., Khan, W., Kindynis, P., Antoniades, A., & Boultadakis, G. (2018, June 8). Intelligent deception detection through machine based interviewing. In *Paper presented at IEEE world congress on computational intelligence, special session: The role of computational intelligence technologies in controlling borders, Rio de Janeiro, Brazil.* https://doi.org/10.1109/IJCNN.2018.8489392.

Parliamentary Assembly. (2018). *Counter-narratives to terrorism (resolution 2221).* Retrieved from http://assembly.coe.int/nw/xml/XRef/Xref-DocDetails-en.asp?FileID=24810&lang=en.

Reuters. (June 4, 2019). *Portuguese police halt human trafficking network, 20 women freed.* Retrieved from https://www.reuters.com/article/us-portugal-crime-trafficking/portuguese-police-halt-human-trafficking-network-20-women-freed-idUSKCN1T526N.

Schmid, A. (2005). Terrorism as psychological warfare. *Democracy and Security, 1,* 137–146. https://doi.org/10.1080/17419160500322467.

SEF. (2019a). *SEF detains four foreign nationals associated to illegal immigration networks.* Retrieved from https://www.sef.pt/en/pages/noticia-sef.aspx?nID=122.

SEF. (2019b). *SEF detains a "facilitator" of minors at Lisboa Airport.* Retrieved from https://www.sef.pt/en/pages/noticia-sef.aspx?nID=179.

Stephens, W., Sieckelinck, S., & Boutellier, H. (2019). Preventing violent extremism: A review of the literature. *Studies in Conflict and Terrorism,* 1–16. https://doi.org/10.1080/1057610X.2018.154314.

Tyler, T. R., Goff, P. A., & MacCoun, R. J. (2015). The impact of psychological science on policing in the United States: Procedural justice, legitimacy, and effective law enforcement. *Psychological Science in the Public Interest, 16*(3), 75–109. https://doi.org/10.1177/1529100615617791.

United Nations General Assembly. (November 15, 2000). *United Nations Convention against transnational organized crime and the Protocols thereto (resolution 55/25).* Retrieved from https://www.unodc.org/unodc/en/organized-crime/intro/UNTOC.html.

UNODC. (2018a). *Global report on trafficking in persons 2018.* Vienna: United Nations Office on Drugs and Crime. Retrieved from https://www.unodc.org/documents/data-and-analysis/glotip/2018/GLOTiP_2018_BOOK_web_small.pdf.

UNODC. (2018b). *Global study on smuggling of migrants 2018.* Vienna: United Nations Office on Drugs and Crime. Retrieved from https://www.unodc.org/documents/data-and-analysis/glosom/GLOSOM_2018_web_small.pdf.

U.S. Department of State. (June 2019). *Trafficking in persons report*. Retrieved from https://www.state.gov/wp-content/uploads/2019/06/2019-Trafficking-in-Persons-Report.pdf.

U.S. Government Accountability Office. (2013). *Aviation security: TSA should limit future funding for behavior detection activities*. Retrieved from https://www.gao.gov/products/GAO-14-159.

van Veldhuizen, T. S., Horselenberg, R., Landström, S., Granhag, P. A., & van Koppen, P. J. (2017). Interviewing asylum seekers: A vignette study on the questions asked to assess credibility of claims about origin and persecution. *Journal of Investigative Psychology and Offender Profiling, 14*, 3–12. https://doi.org/10.1002/jip.1472.

World Economic Forum. (2019). *The global risks report 2019*. Retrieved from https://www.weforum.org/reports/the-global-risks-report-2019.

World Health Organization. (2019a). *The thirteenth general programme of work, 2019–2023*. Retrieved from https://www.who.int/about/what-we-do/thirteenth-general-programme-of-work-2019-2023.

World Health Organization. (2019b). *Ten threats to global health in 2019*. Retrieved from https://www.who.int/emergencies/ten-threats-to-global-health-in-2019.

Afterword
Contributions of
psychology to policing

Psychology is often defined as the scientific study of the behavior of individuals and their mental processes (see, e.g., Gross, 2015). Most psychologists are committed to the scientific method, and the key question is: What is the evidence? (on which any statement is based). There is an emphasis on quantitative data, on reliability and validity of measurement, on systematic observation, on experimentation, on falsifiable theories, on evaluation, on replication of results, and on testing causal hypotheses, especially those specifying that changes in an explanatory variable are followed by changes in an outcome variable. The main contributions of psychology to policing are based on the use of scientific methods to advance knowledge about human behavior. Psychologists are very concerned to apply fundamental knowledge to try to solve real life applied social problems. For example, it is important to determine to what extent differences in crime rates reflect differences in criminal behavior or differences in police practices (Farrington & Dowds, 1985).

It is a pleasure for me to welcome this up-to-date and encyclopedic book, which demonstrates very well the recent great advances in the applications of psychology to policing. It contains a great deal of information that will be very useful for the practice of law enforcement. It clearly demonstrates the enormous benefits of collaboration between psychologists and police personnel, and the need for more psychologists to be employed in law enforcement agencies. In this final chapter, I can only discuss a few of the many contributions of psychology to policing that are extensively documented in this book.

As shown in this book, psychologists have a great deal to contribute to the selection of police officers and to decisions about promotion (see e.g. Bartol & Bartol, 2015, Chapter 2). There has been quite a lot of research on "the police personality" (see, e.g. Harmening & Gamez, 2016, Chapter 2), but some personalities probably need to be screened out of policing! Psychologists can also contribute a great deal to police training, especially skills training for interacting with members of the public. Police officers need to be trained in understanding human behavior, in dealing with aggressive incidents, in crisis intervention, in conflict resolution, and in hostage negotiation (see, e.g. Harmening & Gomez, 2016, Chapters 4 and 5). Psychologists can also help the police by counseling officers who have been exposed to traumatic experiences, in suicide prevention, and in helping officers to deal with their relationship problems. Psychologists can also help to train officers in dealing with large-scale public order incidents, mentally disturbed persons, radical extremists, domestic violence and sexual assault incidents. All these important topics are extensively reviewed in this book.

It is important that police agencies should be informed about knowledge gained in high-quality scientific research. For example, a landmark experiment in Minneapolis showed that, in cases of misdemeanor domestic violence where both the victim and the offender were present when the police arrived, arresting the offender and jailing him overnight was more effective in preventing future violence against the same victim than counseling or separating the two parties. Importantly, six replications of this experiment were carried out in the United States, but the results were apparently not consistent. Sherman (1992) resolved these apparent inconsistencies by concluding that offenders with a lower stake in conformity (those who were unemployed, unmarried, or African-American) tended to get worse after arrest, whereas those with a greater stake in conformity tended to get better. Sherman (1992, p. 187) recommended that "jurisdictions with large populations living in concentrated ghetto poverty areas should strongly consider repealing a mandatory arrest policy," since arrest for domestic violence did more harm than good in these cases. Furthermore, a 23-year follow-up showed that arrested offenders in Milwaukee were more likely to be killed later (Sherman & Harris, 2013), and that African-American victims in Milwaukee were twice as likely to have died of all causes if their partners had been arrested and jailed than if they had been warned and allowed to remain at home (Sherman & Harris, 2015). This series of classic experiments has advanced knowledge about how police officers might deal with domestic violence incidents, and it shows the great value of carrying out experiments and longitudinal studies. Other landmark experiments (for example, those on "hot spots policing"; see Weisburd, 2018) have also been extremely important and informative for police agencies.

This book shows that psychologists have made great contributions to criminal investigation, especially in methods of interviewing suspects (see, e.g., Davies & Beech, 2018, Chapters 7 and 8; Farrington, 1981). Other important topics that have been studied by psychologists include detecting deception, false confessions, eyewitness testimony, and identification parades (see, e.g., Kapardis, 2014, Chapters 2–4 and 8). Forensic hypnosis has also been used to try to improve the recall of suspects and witnesses (see, e.g., Bartol & Bartol, 2015, Chapter 3), but there is a problem of suggestibility. Unfortunately, techniques that encourage guilty people to confess correctly may also encourage innocent people to confess incorrectly! CCTV evidence is potentially important in police investigation, detection, prosecution, and conviction (Farrington, Jolliffe, Bowles, & Barnard, 2010). However, CCTV seems less useful in preventing crimes, except for those committed in car parks (Piza, Welsh, Farrington, & Thomas, 2018).

Evidence-based offender profiling can be very useful to police agencies, especially if it is based on empirical evidence about statistical regularities between types of offenses, types of victims, and types of offenders (Fox & Farrington, 2018). I studied these regularities in Nottinghamshire in England in the 1990s (with Sandra Lambert) for burglary and violence offenders (see Farrington & Lambert, 1997, 2000, 2007). For example, for violence, we compared the location-site-time-day profile of the offense with the sex-age-ethnicity-address profile of the offender. We found that, when the offense occurred in the city in the street during nighttime on a weekday, the offender tended to be an older white city male. However, when the offense occurred in the city in other places during daytime on a weekend, the offender was more likely to be a younger non-white city female. We recommended that these statistical regularities between features of offenses, victims, and offenders should be used by the police, in trying to solve undetected crimes, in order to narrow down the range of possible offenders; 90% of burglars and 80% of violent offenders were already stored in police records for a previous crime.

Bryanna Hahn Fox then developed and greatly extended these ideas in research on burglars in Florida (see Fox & Farrington, 2012, 2015; Fox, Farrington, & Chitwood, 2014). She found that there were four types of burglaries (opportunistic, organized, disorganized, and interpersonal) that were committed by four types of burglars (younger non-whites, older white males, younger whites, and older black males, respectively). She then trained detectives in one police department to use this information in trying to solve burglaries and compared the results with three control police departments. Remarkably, she found that the burglary arrest rate increased significantly from 11% before to 30% after in the experimental police department, while it decreased nonsignificantly from 16% before to 11% after in the three control departments. The probability of a conviction following an arrest did not change between the before and after time periods. This experiment shows the potential benefits of evidence-based offender profiling in detecting offenders (see also Fox, Farrington, Kapardis, & Hambly, 2020). As the authors pointed out, "police will spend their time first investigating the offenders who are statistically most likely to have committed a certain burglary style and will not waste precious time looking into offenders who are statistically unlikely to have committed the offense" (Fox & Farrington, 2015, p. 165).

As this book shows, psychologists have also advanced knowledge about the important topic of violence risk assessment. The accuracy of risk assessment is usually measured using the area under the ROC curve or AUC (Singh, 2013, p. 19). The AUC has a simple meaning; it is equal to the probability that a randomly chosen future offender is given a higher risk rating than a randomly chosen future nonoffender. If the prediction was perfect, the AUC would be 1.00, while its chance expectation is .50. Farrington, Jolliffe, and Johnstone (2008) carried out a meta-analysis of the accuracy of various risk assessment instruments in predicting violence and found that the most commonly used instruments (HCR-20, PCL-R, and VRAG) all had a weighted mean AUC of about .69—70. The challenge for psychologists in the future is how to improve this predictive accuracy.

Finally, I believe that there is great scope for psychologists and police officers to collaborate in the early developmental prevention of offending (see, e.g., Farrington, Ttofi, &Lösel, 2016). A good example of this is the SNAP (Stop Now and Plan) program in Toronto. In Canada, the Young Offenders Act 1984 raised the minimum age of criminal responsibility from 7 to 12. This led to concerns that apprehended young offenders under age 12 might not receive any services. Therefore, in 1985 in Toronto, the SNAP program started to be offered by the Child Development Institute in conjunction with the Metropolitan Toronto Police, for children aged 6—11 years who were in conflict with the law or engaged in antisocial behavior (see Augimeri, Walsh, Kivlenieks & Pepler, 2017). Initially, 75% of referrals were from the police, but later centralized service referral mechanisms widened the number of referring agencies.

The SNAP program for children is based on skills training, cognitive problem-solving, self-control, and anger management, aiming to teach children to identify triggers that make them angry or upset and then to develop coping strategies to minimize anger and avoid impulsive behavior. Groups of about 7 children stratified by age (6–7, 8–9, or 10–11) meet for 12 weeks with a facilitator, and there are parallel meetings for their parents at the same time. Several evaluations (e.g., Burke & Loeber, 2015; Koegl, Farrington, Augimeri, & Day, 2008; Lipman et al., 2008) have shown that the SNAP program is successful in reducing later offending and antisocial behavior. Furthermore, Farrington and Koegl (2015) carried out a cost–benefit analysis and concluded that, based on the reduced number of convictions, between $2.05 and $3.75 was saved for every $1 spent on the program.

I hope that this chapter, and this excellent book, will encourage more collaboration between police services and psychologists. That would be in everyone's interests!

David P. Farrington

References

Augimeri, L. K., Walsh, M., Kivenieks, M., & Pepler, D. (2017). Addressing children's disruptive behaviour problems: A thirty-year journey with SNAP (Stop Now and Plan). In P. Sturmey (Ed.), *Assessment, prevention, and treatment of individuals: Vol. 2. The Wiley handbook of violence and aggression* (pp. 355–367). Hoboken, NJ: Wiley.

Bartol, C. R., & Bartol, A. M. (2015). *Introduction to forensic psychology* (4th ed.). Los Angeles, CA: Sage.

Burke, J. D., & Loeber, R. (2015). The effectiveness of the Stop Now and Plan (SNAP) program for boys at risk for violence and delinquency. *Prevention Science, 16*, 242–253.

Davies, G. M., & Beech, A. R. (Eds.). (2018). *Forensic psychology: Crime, justice, law, interventions* (3rd ed.). Chichester, UK: Wiley/British Psychological Society.

Farrington, D. P. (1981). Psychology and police interrogation. *British Journal of Law and Society, 8*, 97–107.

Farrington, D. P., & Dowds, E. A. (1985). Disentangling criminal behaviour and police reaction. In D. P. Farrington, & J. Gunn (Eds.), *Reactions to crime: The public, the police, courts and prisons* (pp. 41–72). Chichester, UK: Wiley.

Farrington, D. P., Jolliffe, D., Bowles, R., & Barnard, M. (2010). *Feasibility study on the impact of CCTV on criminal justice outcomes.* Report to National Policing Improvement Agency, London.

Farrington, D. P., Jolliffe, D., & Johnstone, L. (2008). *Assessing violence risk: A framework for practice.* Edinburgh: Risk Management Authority Scotland.

Farrington, D. P., & Koegl, C. J. (2015). Monetary benefits and costs of the Stop Now and Plan program for boys aged 6–11, based on the prevention of later offending. *Journal of Quantitative Criminology, 31*, 263–287.

Farrington, D. P., & Lambert, S. (1997). Predicting offender profiles from victim and witness descriptions. In J. L. Jackson, & D. A. Bekerian (Eds.), *Offender profiling: Theory, research and practice* (pp. 133–158). Chichester, UK: Wiley.

Farrington, D. P., & Lambert, S. (2000). Statistical approaches to offender profiling. In D. Canter, & L. J. Alison (Eds.), *Profiling property crimes* (pp. 235–273). Abingdon, UK: Ashgate.

Farrington, D. P., & Lambert, S. (2007). Predicting offender profiles from offense and victim characteristics. In R. N. Kocsis (Ed.), *Criminal profiling: International theory, research and practice* (pp. 135–167). Totowa, NJ: Humana Press.

Farrington, D. P., Ttofi, M. M., & Lösel, F. A. (2016). Developmental and social prevention. In D. Weisburd, P. Farrington, & C. Gill (Eds.), *What works in crime prevention and rehabilitation: Lessons from systematic reviews* (pp. 15–75). New York: Springer.

Fox, B. H., & Farrington, D. P. (2012). Creating burglary profiles using latent class analysis: A new approach to offender profiling. *Criminal Justice and Behavior, 39*, 1582–1611.

Fox, B. H., & Farrington, D. P. (2015). An experimental evaluation on the utility of burglary profiles applied in active police investigations. *Criminal Justice and Behavior, 42*, 156–175.

Fox, B. H., & Farrington, D. P. (2018). What have we learned from offender profiling? A systematic review and meta-analysis of 40 years of research. *Psychological Bulletin, 144*, 1247–1274.

Fox, B. H., Farrington, D. P., & Chitwood, M. (2014). An evidence-based offender profile for burglary. *The Police Chief, 81*(2), 14–15.

Fox, B. H., Farrington, D. P., Kapardis, A., & Hambly, O. C. (2020). *Evidence-based offender profiling*. Routledge: Abingdon, UK.

Gross, R. D. (2015). *Psychology: The science of mind and behaviour* (7th ed.). Banbury, UK: Hodder Education.

Harmening, W., & Gamez, A. (2016). *Forensic psychology*. Boston, MA: Pearson.

Kapardis, A. (2014). *Psychology and law: A critical introduction* (4th ed.). New York: Cambridge University Press.

Koegl, C. J., Farrington, D. P., Augimeri, L. K., & Day, D. M. (2008). Evaluation of a targeted cognitive-behavioral program for children with conduct problems — the SNAP Under 12 Outreach Project: Service intensity, age and gender effects on short and long term outcomes. *Clinical Child Psychology and Psychiatry, 13*, 419–434.

Lipman, E. L., Kenny, M., Sniderman, C., O'Grady, S., Augimeri, L., Khayutin, S., & Boyle, M. H. (2008). Evaluation of a community-based program for young boys at-risk of antisocial behaviour: Results and issues. *Journal of the Canadian Academy of Child and Adolescent Psychiatry, 17*, 12–19.

Piza, E. L., Welsh, B. C., Farrington, D. P., & Thomas, A. L. (2018). *CCTV and crime prevention: A new systematic review and meta-analysis*. Stockholm: National Council for Crime Prevention.

Sherman, L. W. (1992). *Policing domestic violence: Experiments and dilemmas*. New York: Free Press.

Sherman, L. W., & Harris, H. M. (2013). Increased homicide victimization of suspects arrested for domestic assault: A 23-year follow-up of the Milwaukee Domestic Violence Experiment (MilDVE). *Journal of Experimental Criminology, 9*, 491–514.

Sherman, L. W., & Harris, H. M. (2015). Increased death rates of domestic violence victims from arresting vs. warning suspects in the Milwaukee Domestic Violence Experiment (MilDVE). *Journal of Experimental Criminology, 11*, 1–20.

Singh, J. P. (2013). Predictive validity performance indicators in violence risk assessment: A methodological primer. *Behavioral Sciences and the Law, 31*, 8–22.

Weisburd, D. (2018). Hot spots of crime and place-based prevention. *Criminology and Public Policy, 17*, 5–25.

Index